MEDIEVAL PANORAMA

CONTENTS

ILLUSTRATIONS

PLATES

Between pages 408 and 409

TEXT-FIGURES

Full descriptions are given here of the subjects and
sources of these illustrations

Dinkelsbühl, from Merian's *Topographia Bavariae*. (Frankfurt a/m. 1644.)

Dinkelsbühl had in 1500 a population of between 5000 and 6000; perhaps nearer to the latter. Cambridge at that time had perhaps 4000, and Lynn nearly as many.

From Richard Lyne's map of 1574.

Note that "Gunwell" (i.e. Gonville Hall) is named separately from Caius College, and St Sepulchre's (the Round Church) is called "St Pulcheur".

From a map of that date in the Bodleian Library.

This whole map of England, Wales and Scotland is procurable at 1s. 6d. from the office of H.M. Ordnance Survey, by whose permission this portion is here reproduced.

From a fourteenth-century MS. of the Chronicle of Abbot Gilles li Muisis, figured in De Smet, *Corpus Chronicorum Flandriae*, vol. I, p. 348.

From H. E. Salter, *Map of Medieval Oxford* (1934), plate 3.

The shaded portions mark the present sites of two colleges and a church. Underneath these may be seen the multiplicity of medieval tenements and shops, worked out by Dr Salter's marvellous industry.

From Bellenden's translation of Boece's *History of Scotland*, printed about 1536.

It is thus headed; and, below, five lines of Latin poetry are added, to the following effect:

"Behold, I, the type and figure of Justice, ascend thus mine own tribunal. With right-hand uplifted I support those who maintain truth, and this my lily is their reward. But if any man be otherwise minded, my downward left-hand sends him down to the waters of Styx, and to the edge of the Sword."

Traced from the scratch in Ashwell Church, Herts., hand of fourteenth or fifteenth century.

It will be seen that the right- and left-hand branches represent not only individuals, but whole classes, who cannot lawfully intermarry. This is expressed by the editor in a Latin hexameter:

"Non tangunt dextros qui stant in parte sinistra."

"Those who stand on the left side touch not those on the right."

The text runs: "This fourth figure telleth of the great and grievous pains which the devils inflict upon damned and lost souls."

PREFACE

He that contemneth small things shall fall by little and little
(Ecclesiasticus, xix. 1)

ALMOST three generations ago, Carlyle complained that
historians seldom tell us how our forefathers actually lived
and thought: "What all want to know is the condition of
our fellow-men; and, strange to say, it is the thing of all least
understood, or to be understood as matters go." Even in those
days, no doubt, the public had Macaulay's classical Third Chapter;
and J. R. Green's more recent work is priceless; but much more
remains to do. Too rarely does any great archivist, like Siméon
Luce, condescend (or, as some might say, rise) to pregnant
exercises of imagination. The popularization of the linen shirt in
the fourteenth century (argues Luce) marks not only an obvious
advance in personal hygiene, but also an impetus presently given
to the manufacture of rag-paper, and thus to literature; so that
this century of social refinement became "the worthy precursor,
or rather the indispensable preparative, of the age of printing".*
Right or wrong, a suggestion like this is certainly stimulating, and
deserves our gratitude.

It may be natural and right that universities should spend more
time and labour upon the collection and minute criticism of
evidence than upon weaving the threads into historical tapestry.
But the fact is so; although to-day's public thirsts more than ever,
probably, for history that shall be picturesque, yet reasonably
accurate. The intelligent reader—professional or business man
or artisan, who has some leisure for quiet thoughtful browsing—
is too often puzzled to see what it is all about, or is even driven to
wonder whether the writer himself sees quite clearly. The Cinema
has indeed stepped in to supply the demand, but only in its own
garish fashion. The most successful film can present little more
than superficialities; moreover, even among these, there is an
almost irresistible temptation to falsify the proportions for the
sake of spectacular effect. For many years past I felt this very
strongly. Then circumstances seemed practically to command
"Now, or never": and this volume marks the reaction to that

* *La Jeunesse de Bertrand du Guesclin* (1882), p. 64.

challenge. There is little here which I have not said already before widely different audiences, during the past thirty years. Much, I need hardly say, has been learned from pupils and critics. The book makes no pretence either to exhaustiveness or to finality. It tries to bring some sort of order into a mass of details, each interesting in itself, but resting necessarily, in most cases, upon other men's researches and judgments. It looks forward to correction and amplification by others; but it hopes to supply, for the time being, the sort of scaffolding which the author would have been very glad to find before him fifty years ago.

It is difficult, even at the present day, to find one's way through the medieval jungle without a good deal of direct axe-work; but those controversial matters are relegated as far as possible to the notes. References are given only for points on which the reader might wish to verify the statement for himself from the original record; or, again, where the subject is interesting enough to tempt him farther than I have found possible to go within my limited space.

My debts are too many to acknowledge here in full; but I must specially thank Professor G. R. Potter, Professor R. W. Chambers, Mr H. S. Bennett and Mr J. E. A. Jolliffe, who have read my proofs critically. The officials of the University Press have given me the most ungrudging help and invaluable advice: and I owe warm gratitude to my fellow-townsman, Mr Walter Dexter, R.B.A., for his admirable miniatures of Lynn Town Hall and St Margaret's Church.

G. G. COULTON

August 1938

INTRODUCTION

"The true field of Historic Study is the history of those nations and institutions in which the real growth of humanity is to be traced: in which we can follow the developments, the retardations and perturbations, the ebb and flow of human progress, the education of the world, the leading on by the divine light from the simplicity of early forms and ideas where good and evil are distinctly marked, to the complications of modern life, in which light and darkness are mingled so intimately, and truth and falsehood are so hard to distinguish, but in which we believe and trust that the victory of light and truth is drawing nearer every day."

W. STUBBS, *Lectures on Medieval and Modern History* (1886), p. 83.

To many of us, and perhaps especially to those whose daily task is most modern and monotonous, the medieval scene brings all the charm of foreign travel. In both cases we find a change of sights and sounds, buildings and fashions of dress, work and play and gestures and accent, things commonplace to them, but holiday things for us. Thus the merest trivialities bewitch us away from the daily routine of home, revealing our own human nature in a fresh, and therefore refreshing, light.

To borrow an almost inevitable simile, the reader may thus stand upon Malvern Hills, in the heart of England, and look down with the medieval dreamer William Langland upon the Field Full of Folk. Looking eastward and westward by turns, he may get a clear and balanced vision of the whole, and mark how the level and populous east shades off into the mountains of the scattered Western folk. Not, of course, that the Westward view is entirely mountainous, or the Eastward unbrokenly flat. Bredon rises almost in the Eastern foreground, and Malvern can listen to those Sunday bells which Housman has immortalized. Next come the Cotswolds, with Edgehill in the far distance; and then, beyond our bodily vision, those Eastern counties which, with their Fenland, were once the wealthiest and most populous of the Kingdom. Westward, again, we know that Snowdonia rises in the background, far overtopping these Black Mountains which close our view. Thus, however East and West may shade off into each other, yet as we stand here facing the rising sun there is a real gulf between the forward and the hindward landscape; a wide difference, in the mass, between Eastern or Western land, Eastern or

Western folk. We must not exaggerate this; but we shall go still further astray if we ignore it. Geographically and historically, the division is real.

Again, though in the mass East differs thus from West, and Past from Present, yet each has its own interior differences which cannot be ignored. While insisting that there was once a distinctively medieval civilization, and therefore a medieval mind, a medieval character, we must not forget that this medievalism had its own variations from time to time and from place to place. Especially must we bear in mind that in this far-off world nothing *is* for more than a moment; everything is in process of *becoming*. The England of Edward III differed much from that of William I; and Henry VIII's England differed widely from both. This needs special emphasis in a volume like the present, where the necessary division into subjects rather than into periods renders it almost impossible to remind the reader of change at every turn. It is to be hoped that the constant supply of dates may enable him to trace for himself, if only roughly, both the extent to which medieval society was not static but organic, and also the actual trend of its evolution from 1066 to 1536.* Yet the matter is so important that it may be best to start here explicitly upon this note, and to sum up, in a few pages, the action of that long drama which will occupy my fifty-two formal chapters. What were the Seven Ages of this Medieval Man?

Roughly speaking, the Conquest made William into the Universal Landlord of England; the Battle of Hastings gave him the right of transferring confiscated Saxon lands to his Norman followers. But the Anglo-Saxon law, on the whole, suffered no violent interruption; though it was necessarily patched and amended and added to as time went on, yet it is still the foundation of English Common Law, upon which, again, the United States of America founded their own. Thus, when Abraham Lincoln saw that, to win the war, he must needs follow the example of the South and conscript all able-bodied men for his armies, this was done in virtue of the obligation which had been part of English Common Law from time immemorial, before the Conquest and afterwards.

With such important basis of law in common, the conquering

* Where dates are definite, they will be found in round brackets ( ); where they are only approximate, in square [ ].

minority and the conquered majority had practically coalesced within three generations. They were now strong and united enough to resist further invasion, and to work out their own political salvation undisturbed by forcible interference from interested outsiders. King and barons, here as on the Continent, struggled for supremacy: but the balance was nice enough in England to make both parties appeal for popular support; and thus the generally beneficent despotism of the earlier kings—altogether beneficent as compared with the anarchy which was then the only alternative—was gradually modified by those constitutional checks which are at the foundations of modern democracy.

In process of time, the Commons were summoned regularly to the King's council. They came at first merely to approve of what he decreed for them, on the old legal principle that "what concerns all should have the consent of all". Then, from at least 1314 onwards, they permit themselves a certain boldness of initiative, laying their petitions before the King. Presently we find that such petitions are fruitful; that they result in new royal Statutes. Then, we find the Commons bargaining with the Crown; taxes are voted in return for redress of grievances; and this is the thin end of that almost irresistible modern wedge, the Power of the Purse. The growing strength of the Commons is emphasized by the fact that, under a Common Law which made every man his own soldier and his own policeman, the King could never control the whole armed forces of the country with that directness with which they were controlled under hireling professional armies elsewhere. The depositions of Edward II and Richard II were done not only in legal form but with legal reason at their back. Even when medieval society began to disintegrate at the end of the fourteenth century, and a generation of civil wars set in, foreign observers admired the comparatively clean and decent prosecution of those quarrels in England; there was no *tertius gaudens* from the Continent to foment English civil wars for his own profit. When, again, a strong monarchy emerged under Henry VII and his descendants, this was far less despotic, far more considerate of popular opinion, than in any parallel case on the Continent.

Meanwhile the material progress, though slow and sometimes fitful, kept pace with the slow and fitful constitutional development; men felt the growing-pains; theory outran practice, and eager spirits experienced the sickness of hope deferred. But, gradually, forest and fen and fell were subdued to the plough; buildings increased in scale and in elaboration; even where the high-water-mark of taste was past in art, the wealth of ornament still increased. By 1500, the inventories of furniture and plate in our parish churches show double the value of those in 1300; for this, again, was part of the forward movement of the common folk. If one of William's Norman knights or his Saxon tenant could have seen Tudor England, the change in outward aspect would have bewildered him. So was it, again, with the inward organization, quite apart from Parliament and the Court. The growth of the Jury system was a great step: so, again, was the fourteenth-century development of Justices of the Peace, intermediary between the royal judges and the minor magistrates: "an extraordinary experiment in justice which was at once anti-feudal and a reversal of the hitherto universal trend towards centralization."*

So, again, with the rapidly increasing franchises of the towns, and their experiences in local self-government which bore rich fruit in the national councils of later generations. Then, as now, men were everywhere struggling to combine personal freedom with collective action and efficiency; and the sum-total was progress, if only that of a man who is pursuing a rainbow. There is a deep pathos for all generations in Dr Salter's quiet remark about the Oxford citizens of 1199: the city obtained royal licence to elect a mayor, "and there seems to have been a general impression that to have a mayor would bring the millennium".† English trade had expanded by 1500 to a point which would have amazed the Conqueror. Modern capitalism had begun, and society had long since abandoned the original absolute prohibition of taking interest for moneys lent. Edward I had expelled the Jews; but the Christian usurer had not proved more merciful; soon, therefore, the State ceased to interest itself in the lender's soul, and set itself only to limit his rate of interest. As the citizen grew richer, and was proud to enrich his parish church with paintings or carvings or plate, so he became dress-proud for himself. Our later medieval satirists echo in substance, though in other words, Dante's yearning retrospect to the palmy days when great citizens were not ashamed to go girt with leather belts and clasps of bone. More

* J. E. A. Joliffe, *Constitutional History of Medieval England* (1937), p. 413.
† *Medieval Oxford* (1937), p. 49.

simple and graceful forms of mantle and tunic, which had reigned even in the highest classes down to the latter half of the fourteenth century, gave way to a vulgar extravagance of form and colour; eccentricity often killed good taste. It seems fair to trace here a symptom of greater changes on the horizon: even where the old things were perfect in their own simpler fashion, men must needs have something newer for sheer novelty's sake. Archdeacons, on their visitations, would condemn a church as "too small and too dark": in other words, they would have had the little Norman or Early English building replaced by one in the new-fashioned Perpendicular style.

So much for the building: and the great institution itself, the Roman Church, had gone through a similar evolution. Throughout the period covered by this volume, Eastern and Western Christianity were eager rivals, and sometimes even bitter enemies; but this must not make us forget how much they always had in common. Though the break between pagan antiquity and medieval Christianity was neither so sudden nor so complete as is often imagined, yet the Middle Age was definitely a Christian era in a sense which cannot be predicated of preceding or of succeeding generations. The belief in one body of Scriptures and (though less uniformly) in one common tradition of Heaven and Hell, one ethical code, one common core of liturgical worship in spite of local variations, had leavened the whole of European thought and practice more deeply and widely than anything else. By William's time, the Western branch of this Church, the *Ecclesia Romana* as it constantly called itself both colloquially and officially, had become one of the completest examples of a Totalitarian State that history records. It claimed to swallow up and standardize all important variations, so that there should be only one Party, that of the State. For this end almost all means were justified; almost all were employed; and, for many generations at least, they were employed with success.

Yet before 1500, for all her greatness, this Church was in many ways out of touch with the "modern" world, to use an adjective which was in men's mouths from the twelfth century at least. In England, however, as compared with the Continent, the Church might claim to have run something of the orderly course which we have traced in our political institutions. Each, of course, acted and reacted on the other. The Conquest brought us strong prelates, some of them equally conspicuous for piety, and therefore a stricter discipline. The impulse for founding monasteries was almost stronger here, for five generations or more, than anywhere else. Even when the abbeys had become overloaded with riches, the English political and social atmosphere tempted less to that unabashed worldliness which disgraced so many Continental prince-bishops, prince-abbots, and monasteries into which none were admitted but scions of noble stock. Our prelates were among the most prominent lawyers, especially under Henry II and Edward I; thus the State reaped the great benefit of their help, in those days when learned laymen were almost non-existent. But the Church herself lost those men's individual services almost altogether; and the system of clerical lawyers, reprobated at first by Popes themselves, brought its final Nemesis. Great Churchmen were among the most prominent statesmen in the earlier fight for liberties, even when they, like the barons, were mainly and most directly concerned with the liberties of their own order. But, as time went on and the richer Church endowments went more and more systematically by royal appointment (apart from papal nominees who were often non-resident aliens), then prelates and archdeacons and rich rectors were increasingly degraded to the position of courtly tools or pettifoggers or clerical drudges. If the Churchman had not become so much of an ordinary politician, that division between clergy and laity would have been avoided of which our ancestors complained with increasing bitterness; and the Church herself, under Henry VIII, would have been far less vulnerable to the slings and arrows of baser political conflict.

Meanwhile, the Church's own beneficent work had raised up rivals against her. Such schools as existed had always been clerical, and the population had slowly begun to grow out of its primitive illiteracy. Before the end of the twelfth century, writing was entirely superseding oral tradition among the lawyers. By the thirteenth, manorial accounts were written everywhere, and manorial customs were frequently committed to parchment. The growing numbers of "copyholders" were peasants whose position at law depended primarily on a written "copy". Then, in the fourteenth century, while some of the countryfolk could see nothing better than to burn all the manorial records in revenge, others of their class, and still more among the citizens, were listening to the subversive doctrines of Wyclif and clamouring for an Open Bible. At the same time there was intensive multiplication of orthodox religious treatises and pious manuals for the people. This movement was enormously hastened on both sides by the invention of printing. Thus, before our period ends, the serious and resolute peasant or artisan is often in a position to form some religious judgment for himself; while the bishop or the University scholar has at his disposal, if he chooses to taste of it, the vast and epoch-making work of Erasmus.

Everything, therefore, is ripe for revolution in English thought by the time we come to 1536; and on the verge of that revolution we stop. The defeat of Roman Catholicism in this country, and the follies or crimes with which the revolutionaries sullied their victory, and the subsequent alternations of success or failure in a war of ideals which is not yet fought out, would belong to quite another story. In this volume, it is enough to attempt a picture of the social drama as it was acted between two crucial events in our early annals—the Norman Conquest and the Reformation.

I. THE CAULDRON OF GOD'S WRATH

WE cannot deal with the civilization even of a single country at a definite period without a preliminary glance at the world-culture upon which it was grafted. Thus the Middle Ages can be rightly understood only as a period of convalescence—slow at best, and with continual relapses—from the worst catastrophe recorded in the whole history of the Western World.

The Roman Empire had begun with benevolent despotism, an active and fairly healthy body: it ended as an unwieldy machine. "Augustus, with his genius, succeeded in restoring not only the State but also the prosperity of the people; Diocletian and Constantine, on the other hand, doubtless against their own will, sacrificed the interests of the people to the salvation and security of the State"; such is the summary of the greatest modern authority on this subject.[1] The Empire was defended no longer by its old citizen armies, but by hirelings recruited mainly from the less settled frontier districts. Finances were disorganized; taxation pressed intolerably upon the middle class, and especially the yeoman-farmers, while multitudes lived upon the dole—*Panem et Circenses*. Literature and art showed less and less originality. A period of peace, unexampled in world-history for depth and duration, had not in this case made for higher civilization, by whichever of the current standards we may judge. Crude experience had belied the philosophic ideal. The Higher Pacifism, an active virtue, was too heavily alloyed with that passively defensive mood which claims the same title: War had still her victories, but Peace had not. What wrecked the Empire, as I shall presently try to show, was not such peace as Christ had preached, but, in part at least, the dilettantist patriotism which puts words before deeds. Men followed the line of least resistance, and called it peace. On the other hand, what carried the invading barbarians forward was not their brutality, but the energy and courage which are so often bound up with that vice. We may say of the Roman Empire that, as so often occurs in history, it was more concerned for peace than for justice.

Be that as it may, one thing is certain: the break-up of this vast

Empire was followed by scenes of disorder, not only far more intense than what we have seen in the most unhappy districts of modern times, but prolonged for a period exceeding the worst that we can reasonably fear as a result of the present international rivalries and class-conflicts. Even in the comparatively fortunate East, and before the great barbarian invasions, Origen had struck a painfully modern note in his commentary on Matthew xxiv. 7–8. The earth, like the human body, must naturally decay before its final dissolution; and thence "it follows that, through lack of food, men should be stirred to greed and wars against those who suffer no want; and that, through comparison with others who abound in things needful, some men should rise against their fellows, and nation should fight against nation, and kingdom against kingdom. For it is not possible that, together with the lack of other things, there should also be a lack of men who have good sense, so that there should be no quiet and peaceful life among many folk; yet insurrections and quarrels and perturbations come to pass, sometimes through greed, sometimes again through covetousness of leadership, sometimes by reason of mad longing for vainglory, sometimes also through vainglorious greed of princes, who are not content with their own kingdoms but desire to extend their principalities and subdue many nations to themselves." Generations later, when the barbarians had burst in and Alaric the Goth had even taken Rome, men felt as though the sky had fallen. Jerome, who had played so great a part in the civilization of the Eternal City, wrote from his retreat at Bethlehem, in his Preface to Ezekiel: "No doubt all things born are doomed to die....But who would have believed that Rome, victorious so oft over the universe, would at length crumble to pieces?...She who made slaves of the East has herself become a slave; and nobles once laden with riches come to little Bethlehem to beg. In vain I try to distract myself from the sight by turning to my books; I cannot fix my thoughts on them." The oppression and the tumult grew worse and worse; and we find St Gregory the Great, five generations later, writing in even deeper despair:[2] "What is there now, I ask, to please us in this world? Everywhere we see mourning and hear groans. Cities are destroyed, strong places are cast down, the fields are depopulated, and the land is become desert. No inhabitants remain on the land, and scarce any in the towns; yet even these scanty relics of humanity are beaten with daily and incessant stripes. Moreover, the scourge of God's justice resteth not, because men's guilty deeds have not been corrected even under this scourge. We see some led into bondage, others mutilated, others slain...nay, what is left of that Rome which once seemed mistress of the world? She is ground down with manifold and immeasurable pains by the desolation of her citizens, the pressure of her enemies, and the frequency of ruin; so that we see that fulfilled in her which Ezekiel saith against the city of Samaria: *Set on a pot, set it on, I say, and put water into it; heap together into it the pieces thereof*: and a little further: *The seething thereof is boiling hot, and the bones thereof are thoroughly sodden in the midst thereof*: and again: *Heap together the bones, which I will burn with fire; the flesh shall be consumed and the whole composition shall be sodden and the bones shall be consumed; then set it empty upon burning coals, that it may be hot and the brass thereof may be melted*.... For where is now the Senate, and where is the people? The bones have been dissolved and the flesh consumed; all pride of worldly dignity hath been extinguished in her. The whole composition of her is sodden, nevertheless even we, the few who are left, are yet daily oppressed with the sword and with innumerable tribulations. Let us say, therefore: *Set it empty upon burning coals*, for, seeing that the Senate is gone, the people have perished, and yet, among the few that are left, pain and groans are daily multiplied; now Rome stands empty upon the fire. Yet why do we speak thus of the men, when ruins multiply so sore that we see even the buildings destroyed? Wherefore it is aptly added concerning the now deserted city: *Let it be hot and let the brass thereof be melted*: for now the pot itself is being consumed wherein aforetime the flesh and bones were consumed; for since the men have failed the very walls are falling. But where are they who once rejoiced in her glory?...Boys and young men of the world and the sons of worldly folk flocked hither from every hand when they wished to profit in this world. No man now hasteneth hither for worldly profit; no mighty and violent man is now left to snatch his prey by oppression.... Moreover, whatsoever we say concerning this grinding of Rome to pieces we know to be repeated in all the cities of the world. For some cities are desolated by ruin, others consumed by the sword, others tormented with famine, others swallowed up by earthquakes. Let us, therefore, despise with all our heart this world, present or destroyed.

Let us at least end our worldly longings with the end of the world."

Though Jerome's first cry had been one of despair, yet he laboured on as before for ten years longer; and his contemporary Augustine was nerved only to greater efforts by the fall of Rome. Augustine's greatest work, which dominated the whole Middle Ages, expressed the most vehement reaction against what so many others regarded as an irremediable disaster. Paganism was now raising its head again; men cried that this collapse had been due to Christianity, and that the one cure was to recant this modern heresy and go back to a Golden Age. In face of this, Augustine insisted that the true lesson was one of hope in the deepest sense. Rome, after all, had not lasted longer, and was not greater, than other empires which had perished before her; nor had she been so pure that we must look upon her fall as an irremediable loss. The city itself had been founded in fratricide. Its history had been stained by an endless succession of bloody wars, both foreign and civil; and when she had ruled supreme her hands had reeked with the blood of Christian martyrs. The first half of Augustine's *City of God* is thus devoted to destructive criticism; he exposes the Roman Pantheon in all its absurdity and immorality. On the other hand he fully admits all the true greatness that was to be found in her past, and claims Rome as the παιδαγωγός—half-nurse, half-tutor—providentially appointed to prepare the world for Christianity. Thence he passes to his main theme, the indestructibility of spiritual life. Rome had perished, as all earthly things are destined to perish; but the spirit is immortal. All the evils of this life fit together into a divinely-appointed scheme of trial; gradually the evil dies and the good survives. "There remaineth therefore a rest for the people of God"; upon that note, from the Epistle to the Hebrews, he concludes.

The immense and enduring influence of this book was due not only to its great literary merit, but also to the special needs of St Augustine's and many succeeding centuries. In coldest blood we may claim that this *City of God* expounds a true philosophy of history in the main. The dualism of its theme is, at bottom, true for all ages. There always has been this contrast between spirit and matter; between the visible existing institutions which we obey as a matter of present duty, and the future world which we hope for, to be built some day upon the ruins of what now exists. The problem is equally insistent at all periods of the world, though different ages state it in different terms. Augustine commended it with the eloquence of a deep and passionate soul, which had probed every corner of human nature, and with the uncompromising courage of a man ready to die for his opinions, in days when death was the too frequent fate of men who proclaimed the truth as they saw it. And, at that particular time, it is difficult to see how the world could have done better than to follow his lead. For we must try to visualize the void which Augustine strove to fill. In the earlier days of Graeco-Roman civilization, a man's duties were confined, in the main, within the four walls of his own little city. Righteousness meant to be in a right relation towards one's πόλις and its tutelary deities. Then, as city after city was swallowed up by Rome, the outlook widened: the righteous man was he who stood right with the Empire. Here, then, in that Empire, was a society which had often thrust aside all abstract considerations of morality or theology in its reliance upon its own greatness, and upon the comparative peace which that half-divine institution assured to all its citizens. But now Rome was sacked: the Empire was breaking up: sixty years later, it would cease to exist even in name. For the Western World, drifting now without rudder or compass, it was necessary to find some system of thought which not only accepted far wider responsibilities than the old (except, of course, the higher philosophies, which were held only by a few), but which should also be far more independent of outward and visible support from the State. In this, Augustine succeeded. Apart from his extraordinary knowledge of human nature, and his contagious earnestness and eloquence, his philosophy rested in the main upon an impregnable foundation; upon the assertion of the reality of the spiritual life, and of its indestructibility. To cling to a Crucified Leader, to insist upon the truth of spiritual brotherhood among all mankind—a brotherhood which could not be broken by all the changes or revolutions of states or cities—to insist upon these truths was to steel the soul against all outward enemies; for everything was thus based upon the fundamental fact that outward failures may be turned to inward success; he that loseth his life shall find it. We cannot escape the fact that all real life is a great adventure; we are all either adventurers or sluggards.

Gibbon casts ridicule on Tertullian's boast, early in the third century, that a Christian mechanic will now give a ready answer to questions which have puzzled the wisest heads of antiquity. From one point of view the criticism is justified; such dogmatism often springs from the valour of ignorance. Yet century after century discovers for itself that truth is not a matter of naked intellect; that character is sometimes even more important for the conduct of life than scientific observation or rigid logic; that the world is ruled, and rightly ruled, almost more by the imponderables than by the ponderables. Gibbon's sneer, therefore, ignores a factor as important as that on which he himself rests; the factor admirably expressed in Robert Browning's *Christmas Eve and Easter Day*, where he gives an imaginary epitaph from a martyr's tomb in the Catacombs:

> I was born sickly, poor and mean,
> A slave: no misery could screen
> The holders of the pearl of price
> From Cæsar's envy; therefore twice
> I fought with beasts, and three times saw
> My children suffer by his law.
> At last my own release was earned:
> I was some time in being burned,
> But at the close a Hand came through
> The fire above my head, and drew
> My soul to Christ, whom now I see.
> Sergius, a brother, writes for me
> This testimony on the wall—
> For me, I have forgot it all.

Thus it was that the faith in a crucified carpenter revolutionized European civilization. It took more men out of themselves, and took them farther out of themselves, than any other recorded event in Western history, and, as most of us would think, in the history of the whole world. By whatever process, it fused into one single wire the main strands of pre-existing thought: Roman State Religion, Philosophy, Judaism, and the Oriental Cults. From the first it took its impressive ceremonial and system of government; from the second, higher speculation; from the Jews their monotheism, and from the Cults their mystic exaltation. Not, doubtless, without some of their weaker qualities also; not without State formalism and philosophic word-splitting and Jewish intolerance, and something of that temperamental licence which, in the Cults, put enthusiasm above morality. Yet these weaknesses came out mainly in the course of time, and with the dilution of the original impulse. Primitive Christianity was democratic, however autocratic the hierarchy may have finally become; it was spiritual at first, however rigid in its later institutionalism. Gibbon's and Tertullian's artisan had in many ways the valour of ignorance; but courage at least he had, and that is always one of the rarest of human virtues. He had a fire of mind and soul which took him out of those decadent dilettante surroundings; which compelled him to regard deeds rather than words, and brought him face to face with the problems of to-day and to-morrow. The first step in all learning is that of interest. Descartes, in that brief *Discours de la Méthode* which is often taken as the primer of modern philosophy, insists that the first and foremost requisite for the discovery of truth is not to be born with a great brain, nor to live in the happiest circumstances, but to have the determination of arriving, by hook or by crook, at such measure of truth as our own capacities can contain. From Socrates onwards, philosophy herself proclaims the superiority of character over what is called pure intellect.

So, at least, it would seem to have been in those days in which the fermentation of good and evil in Europe can be studied on so great a scale. Next to St Augustine's *City of God*, no book is more illuminating here than his *Confessions*. In this, he invented a new literary type: it is the first of formal autobiographies. But its historical value surpasses even the psychological: the story of this man's conversion shows us, incidentally, how Europe was converted. In the 8th book (chs. 2–6) he recounts the story of Victorinus, and that of the two young officers at Trier. The latter is perhaps the more striking tale; but the former teaches the deeper lesson. Here was a man, among the oldest and most learned professors at Rome, who had taught so many noble senators that he had even earned, in his lifetime, the honour of a statue in the Forum. His insatiable love of reading brought him at last to the Christian Scriptures; and he felt their force. He began to say privately to his friends, but quite plainly: "I am now at heart a Christian." But he still shrank from public conformity, and from the breach that this must make with his past. "Why need I do this? Does God ask us for more than our hearts?" Why, indeed, should he leave the marble temples, the accumulated statues and paintings of all the centuries, the stately ceremonial, the white-robed priest and the incense, the grave honourable well-born men and women, thronging the sanctuary? Why leave these people, whose mere conformity with the ancient ritual, however superficial or careless, grouped them round the daily sacrifice into a picture more impressive than any on the walls of the temple itself? for, though modern writers may claim that the Roman Mass-ritual is "art at full tide", yet Pagan worship, under that Southern sun, must have been even more picturesque. How could he leave all this, to go and worship, after the fashion of the Christians of those early days, in a little room bare of statues or pictures, bare even of all the rudest ornaments, where his own tailor's or shoemaker's son might be the celebrant of the new-fangled uncouth mysteries? Could he not accept all that was best of the new, without making so cruel a breach with the old? But Augustine tells us how the working of Victorinus's own thoughts gradually drove him out of all these excuses; how justly he feared to be denied in heaven by a Christ whom he had shrunk from confessing on earth. We read how he left his colleagues, his friends, his equals—left them to go on in their stately way which to them seemed the only part in life's pageant that could possibly be played by scholars and gentlemen—and, himself, made the most public possible profession of faith in the Christian conventicle. He accepted meekly what Clough's fastidious Oxford scholar calls "the horrible pleasure of pleasing inferior people", and suffered the crowd of cobblers and weavers to hail him as a brother in triumphant chorus—Victorinus! Victorinus!—while he made his public profession of faith and bowed his head to the baptizing priest.

Against this new spirit the Pagan reactionaries fought in vain. With all its faults, this Christian enthusiasm roused men from a past which, however dignified at its best, had often been scarcely more than a state of respectable stagnation. The economic historian Rostovzef, who will not be suspected of bias in this direction, writes most emphatically here:[3] "The watchwords of the State were oppression, coercion, and persecution; the maxims of the Church were love, compassion, and consolation. The Church, and she alone among the different religious communities, offered not only spiritual comfort but also practical assistance amidst the miseries of present life, while the State oppressed and persecuted the comforters."

In this Ezekiel-cauldron, seething over the fire of God's indignation, there was no practical contact between the Higher Paganism and the masses. Stoicism and Neoplatonism had lofty thoughts; but here was now a world in which exalted idealisms must stoop to conquer. We see this at its crudest in King Bogoris of Bulgaria [910], converted by the missionary Methodius whose artistic skill enabled him to paint the walls of the royal palace with realistic scenes of hell-fire and the eternal torments of unbelievers. Again it comes out, under a far more sympathetic form, in Bede's story of the conversion of King Edwin of Northumbria. After bishop Paulinus had pleaded Christianity before him, the Pagan high-priest, Coifi, assented approvingly, on the selfish grounds that these gods of his had never fitly rewarded his own merit. Then an old noble took up the word: "O king, I see the present life of man upon earth, in comparison with all that time which is dark to us, as when thou art sitting at supper in wintertide with thy warrior-chieftains and thy ministers, while the fire burns bright in the midst of the hall and spreads its warmth all around, and everywhere outside the furious gusts rage with sleet or snow; then comes a sparrow and flutters hastily through the hall, entering at one door and departing forthwith by another. For that brief space that he passes here within, he is sheltered from the wintry tempest; but that little respite of calm is quickly past; from the winter he came and to winter he returns forthwith, and is lost to thine eyes. Thus doth man's life pass for a while before our eyes; but that which shall come after, or which did come before, is to us altogether unknown. Therefore, if this new doctrine brings us more light upon this matter, it would seem right and just that we should follow it."[4]

In these two cases we see both the strength and the weakness of Christianity. It compelled men to face the future; and prevision is one of the matters in which man differs most from the lower animals, and the civilized man most from the uncivilized. But that picture of the future was distorted, in the Middle Ages and beyond, to an extent which brings its own retribution in modern times. Its strong point was that it gave greater faith in the future; the faith of St Paul and of the Epistle to the Hebrews. Life is a struggle, but that struggle is a trial under just conditions, and "there remaineth a rest for the people of God". The weak point was that this faith was also bound up with the past, and a past which tended more and more to gain the upper hand. Man's chance of this Saints' Everlasting Rest was now made to depend upon his attitude towards past events and traditions; and the main deciding factor, according to this present creed, was his belief in the past at the moment when his soul quitted his body. This naturally threw an overwhelming weight upon the Church's Sacraments, and especially upon Extreme Unction. Thus sudden death was regarded, in spite of Christ's express words, as a special judgment of God; and burial in consecrated ground was sometimes denied to those who had died intestate. From this naturally followed two extremes of thought: two exaggerations in opposite directions. The thoughtless man, as priests complained, would plead, in defence of his irregular life, "Three words at the last will save me!" Disciplinarians, on the other hand, shocked at this prevailing levity, were driven into the conviction that the large majority of mankind must go to hell; we shall see that there was more unanimity on that point throughout the Middle Ages, and even beyond, than on a large number of the present-day questions at issue between the Roman and other Churches.

Christianity, interpenetrating Paganism, was much modified by Pagan influences, and in no matter more strongly than in this of heaven and hell. The few words of Christ on this subject were now interpreted in a fiercely literal sense in which the Jews of His own day would not have understood them. The infernal pains of Graeco-Roman poetry, which Lucretius so freely satirized, pale before those often-quoted words in which Tertullian, maddened by the savage persecutions of his time, hurls back at the persecutors the prospect of an eternity filled with still more intolerable torments. Yet even those words, which form one of the crudest pages in Lecky's *History of Rationalism*, were outdone by the descriptions of medieval mission-preachers. More significant still, the Schoolmen themselves adopted all this; so that, as we shall see, the measured and conscientious logic of St Thomas Aquinas speaks here with a voice weightier than the most passionate rhetoric.

These matters will occupy us in greater detail as our survey proceeds; but, at this point, it is opportune to emphasize the three considerations which, more than any other, differentiate medieval from modern thought. First, faith became more and more a matter of loyalty to tradition, and that tradition changed imperceptibly but steadily into something very different, in certain important respects, from primitive Christianity. Secondly, faith became more and more definitely bound up with such beliefs about the next world as are no longer held by any religious body in their medieval crudity. Thirdly, the anarchy and distress of the invasions bred in almost all men's minds a passionate longing for unity; unity even at the cost (if so it must be) of tyranny. These will explain many things which are too often ignored or minimized in polite history, but which are perfectly natural if we forget modern British or American ideas and consider the actual circumstances of these distant times. England, from the Conquest to the Reformation, was peopled by men and women who, born at that earlier age of the world, had less political and social and even religious experience than the average reader of to-day. In the sight of God they were doubtless very much as we are. That, however, is a mystery which no man can attempt to penetrate: in every age, to the question: "Lord, what shall this man do?" Christ's answer comes: "What is that to thee? follow thou me!" But, in the things which man is able to judge, and in judging which he shows his superiority over the lower animals—in those things after which ordinary good folk have striven from generation to generation, and are striving still—in those manners and attainments which are the outward and visible signs of civilization—it will be natural to find our ancestors, at the distance of so many centuries, living at a somewhat rudimentary stage. There need be no guilty censoriousness in noting these things narrowly, nor is there any solid virtue in ignoring them as a matter of deference to polite conventions. We should rather hope that succeeding generations may tell equally plain truth about ourselves. Moreover, the recognition of plain truth about the past is an integral part of our own culture. Only thus can we measure the gulf which society has crossed, through the brave efforts of good folk from age to age; only thus can we find solid reasons, as apart from easy and superficial hopes, for future progress. Some of the worst among human errors are rooted in ignorance of the past, whether accidental or slothful or wilfully perverse. European society, during all that welter of invasion, and even while it was struggling out of disorder into a civilization of its own, was as unlike to the world in which we live as trench-life in war is unlike to the normal life of peace. Therefore we cannot understand the Middle Ages unless we are willing to bear constantly in mind two complementary truths: first, the essential similarity of human nature in all ages: and, secondly, the dissimilarity of men's environment—we may sometimes say, the almost incredible dissimilarities—at that distance of time. These will explain on the one hand the remarkable self-devotion and self-discipline of the best characters and, on the other, the carelessness of the multitude, into whom the current theological teaching seldom penetrated beneath the surface.

II. BISHOPS OF ROME

WHILE this Christian Church, little by little, was emerging from the general dissolution of the Roman Empire, there also emerged gradually at its head a new figure, the Pope.

We must face this fully; for it is at the very foundation of our subject. Beyond all questions of our agreement or disagreement with the Papacy lies the fact that this is one of the most remarkable phenomena in social history. The Papacy, even to-day, is one of the strongest forces in European society; it illustrates the value of a positive and definite programme, however imperfect, as against any programme of mere negation. This is a point which needs to be emphasized most strongly by those of us who feel bound most uncompromisingly to combat whatever we judge to be hollow or excessive in the claims of the Roman Church. Whatever may be said of the line of Japanese Emperors, at least in this West of ours there is no succession of sovereigns comparable in length to that of the Popes; and that is all the more remarkable because, even at the most worldly times of the Papacy, the armies which any Pope could directly command have been so insignificant in number. Lamentably as Roman Catholicism (like many other Churches) has often employed physical coercion, it has never relied preponderantly upon brute force. The Pope's dominion has always been, in the main, what it has professed to be—a power exercised rather over men's minds than over their bodies. With this reservation, we can echo the celebrated epigram of Hobbes in the seventeenth century: "If any man will consider the original of that great ecclesiastical dominion, he will easily perceive that the Papacy is none other than the ghost of the deceased Roman Empire, sitting crowned upon the grave thereof." So far as that word "ghost" might imply contempt, it is mainly false; the Roman Church was far more than a mere pallid shade, a mere reflection, of the Roman Empire. If, however, we might take it as laying stress on the comparatively abstract and intangible nature of the papal dominion, then we should need to make no reservations.

The Pope was something very different from anything known to Graeco-Roman civilization. Perhaps the nearest parallel, strange as it may seem at first sight, was the Roman Emperor, who, in his later development, claimed a dominion over religion as complete as that which the later medieval Popes claimed over the sovereigns of Europe. In both cases the mainspring of power was men's passionate desire after unity; after any escape from mere anarchy. The Roman Republic, weary of a civil strife which was followed regularly by proscription and murder of the beaten party, had been finally content to let Augustus assemble all the key-offices in his single person, and thus to rule despotically under time-honoured traditional forms. So the Church, in its turn, became the one constructive thing which emerged from the welter of anarchy; and it gradually commanded the same loyalty to a central idea. The totalitarian State in one form or another, Soviet or Fascist, is a natural, if not inevitable, reaction from excessive social decomposition. Christianity, democratic in its origin, had split during its first hundred years into almost a hundred sects. Thus these centrifugal forces became intolerable, and the large majority of Christians gravitated definitely to that body which, from one point of view, was only the greatest of such sects, owing its unquestionable majority to its combination of tradition with such modifications as appealed to the average man. Representing thus a nucleus of enthusiastic inspiration tempered by natural human instincts, good and indifferent, it made so strong an appeal that in cases of direct conflict it could almost always claim an over-whelming majority over its rival of the moment. Thus, through a series of victories in separate conflicts, it made its own prepon-derance still more conspicuous; and therefore, in those times of intolerance, more overwhelming both physically and spiritually. Hence it is natural that, almost from the earliest of the Christian records, we should find this dominant majority claiming the title of *Catholic*, i.e. *Universal*; a name which rests upon no more obvious exaggeration than other flattering epithets which other institutions or peoples have arrogated to themselves. When, there-fore, we say that the Pope was a unique person in many ways, it would be more correct to say that he was representative of a unique institution. He had grown as the Church grew.

Among the many bishoprics of Christendom, Rome had gradually forged far ahead. This was neither the earliest bishopric, nor the most learned; but many causes had contributed to bring her as definitely to the front as Birmingham now is in the midlands or London in the whole kingdom. She relied mainly upon the literal interpretation of Matthew xvi. 18: "Thou art Peter, and upon this rock I will build my church." True, the majority of the Early Fathers interpreted this text more or less metaphorically; but the letter always appeals to the multitude, and it would be difficult to name any single written sentence in world-history, except perhaps the parallel *Hoc est corpus meum*, which has been more desperately fought over than this. Not only have thousands been ready to die for one or the other interpretation, but thousands have died for it.

Yet, in these days, it is possible to look at it without too much prejudice either way; and the questionable basis of this Petrine claim has been brought out even by the most distinguished among modern Roman Catholic Church historians of our generation, Monsignor Duchesne. Although the Early Fathers had mostly interpreted this text metaphorically, and St Paul had been put side by side with St Peter even at Rome, yet gradually in that city men began to insist that the one Apostle, Peter, had a God-given primacy over all other Christians. Thence they jumped to the conclusion that the primacy thus promised to Peter necessarily descended to his successors. This, again, rested upon the further hypothesis that Peter had been first bishop of Rome. Yet in fact, though historical documents do indeed point to the high probability (we might almost say the practical certainty) that Peter ended his life at Rome, they do not prove, and rather tend to disprove, that he was ever bishop there. His name is absent from the earliest list, and St Paul has a better historical claim to the actual foundership of the Christian community in Rome. The very base, therefore, is uncertain, and every joint of the superstructure is loose. To the majority of historians it seems one of the most confused theories that ever took real hold of the imagination of so large a proportion of the civilized world: some, indeed, would compare it with that "Nordic" theory on which the present-day German Reich takes its stand. Yet the real cause of power, in both cases, is not the theory itself, but the facts upon which it is based. Not on past historical facts, which they vainly claim in their favour, but on present political facts; upon what men could then see, and can see now, under their eyes. The striking fact of Mahomet's magnetic personality and generally beneficent influence made it possible for whole tribes to believe in his revelations while his own wife disbelieved them. Similarly, it was the fact of the Church's enormous and generally beneficent power which enabled men to believe that Christ had formally conferred the divine sovereignty of the world upon those bishops of Rome who had inherited some of the prestige of the old Empire, who could have relied more and more definitely, as time went on, upon a plebiscite in their own favour, and who possessed hitherto unprecedented opportunity for, and organization of, propaganda. In those days when history in the modern sense was impossible, and when the comparison of conflicting records and their impartial valuation was practically beyond the reach even of the most learned, a movement of this kind was irresistible. Nearly all men whose voices could be heard were echoing identical doctrines, and the few exceptions whispered dissent at their own risk. Then, as in all ages, men mostly believed what they found it convenient to believe; and the system worked, century after century, with sufficient success to bring the Popes at last to a point at which they might truly have anticipated Louis XIV's claim: "L'Église, c'est moi."

In his person itself, the Pope had many striking points reminiscent of antiquity, quite apart from the costume, the ceremonies, and the bureaucratic framework which he inherited quite naturally from Pagan Rome. At a very early date, we find bishops from different parts of the world appealing to him as arbiter; he occupied here an interior angle. These appellants very naturally addressed him in language of high-pitched praise, not to say adulation. True, this never quite rose to that level of flattery to which the Emperors were accustomed; and even those modern writers who claim a quasi-imperial position for the Roman pontiffs have never produced anything approaching the *Maximus pius felix invictus augustus sempiternus* of Constantine I, to omit whole pages which might be quoted of later and more bombastic imperial titles.[1]

Yet, within less than 500 years from the Crucifixion, this Leader of the Christians had reached a point at which his Church began so far to overlap the State that a concordat became necessary. This may be read in a famous letter from Gelasius I to the Emperor Anastasius.[2] In secular matters, it is for the Emperor to make laws, and for the Churchman to obey them. In matters of religious faith, and in the administration of the sacraments, it is the Pope's duty to decide, and to tell the Emperor without reserve what he thinks. And it is the Emperor's duty, not as a sovereign, but as a Christian, to accept the doctrine taught by the Church, and the sacraments as administered by her priests. But hundreds of cases must necessarily occur in which the limits between religious and secular authority are highly disputable; and it is all-important to note here the attitude of one of the greatest and boldest of early Popes; of that St Gregory I who was the second converter of England, just a century after this Gelasian Concordat. Writing to the Emperor Maurice,[3] he confessed himself "sorely affrighted" by an imperial decree which "closed for many men the way to heaven", since it prescribed that no man, once sworn in as a soldier, might enter a monastery until he had served out his time in the army. Here was a question which touched religion very nearly: yet Gregory, even while remonstrating with the Emperor, writes: "What am I but dust and a worm?...Being subject to [your] command, I have caused this law to be promulgated throughout all parts of the earth." He showed that same Christian moderation in refusing the title of "Universal Bishop"; and again in his instructions to his missionaries in England. Let them shock no prejudices without necessity: while yielding nothing in essentials, let them do all in their power to ignore minor differences. Let them adapt the existing heathen temples to Christian worship; let them suffer men to keep the old feasts, only slaying their oxen no longer as a sacrifice to devils, but in thanksgiving to God.

It is well to dwell a little more on this Gregory, to whom England owes so much. Not only that his reign marks a definite step in the development of the modern Papacy, but that it comes at a period when the Western Church and its Ruler were still incontestably among the greatest, and probably the very greatest, of civilizing forces in Europe. Gregory, like his contemporaries and predecessors and successors, was haunted by the imminence of Antichrist and Armageddon and the shrivelling of this world like a parched scroll. His overpowering other-worldliness led him into injustice towards the great classical past. He had spent a long time as ambassador in Constantinople, yet had never learned the Greek language. He valued Roman habits of business in politics and in social life, just as he valued the great Roman palace which he had inherited from his ancestors, and which he made into a monastery. But he had no value for Roman literature as such. In one well-known preface he repudiated care for mere moods and tenses; the Oracles of God must not be enslaved to the rules of the grammarian. In another often-quoted letter, he rebuked the bishop of Vienne: "We hear that thou expoundest grammar [that is, classical literature].... Our former good opinion of thee is turned to mourning and sorrow. The same mouth singeth not the praises of Jove and the praises of Christ.... [Cast away] the idle vanities of worldly learning." Those who read this too literally do not realize how much religious reason underlies it all; for it was common to give boys Virgil's *Eclogues* to begin upon for their next step after the rudiments, and here they found: "We begin with Jove, O ye Muses; all things are full of Jove." Yet John of Salisbury records the tradition that Gregory burned the great Palatine Library as a hindrance to Bible studies; and, though there is no real evidence for this, the very legend is significant. But the greatest of all his own books is that on *Pastoral Care*, of which our Alfred gave a translation to his people; a book which starts from the maxim that the art of arts is the rule of souls. He had lived this book before he wrote it; his contemporaries called him *Argus luminosissimus*; his eyes were everywhere: even in remote England. He is the first Pope of whom we know that he kept a thoroughly businesslike register of all his important letters. There were other imperfect registers before him, but this of Gregory's marks an epoch. He supervised the vast papal estates (many as far off as Sicily) as carefully as the hardest business-man could have done, grudging the waste of every farthing that might have been collected and given to the poor. He kept his hand tightly over every bishop in the West. As a ruler, he held his own in diplomacy against the Emperor on the one side, and the half-barbarous Lombards, Visigoths and Franks on the other: and the term *Gregorian Chant* reminds us of his love of sacred music, though it may be doubtful how far he was in fact its active reformer.

In those days, there still remained much of the original democratic spirit—or, at least, egalitarian—in Christianity. At first all Church offices had been elective, just as the State offices had been for centuries before Christianity was born. Priests and bishops were chosen by their flocks, and for many centuries men saw no reason whatever why the bishop of Rome should be chosen differently from any other. They did not even trouble to keep exact record of the names of the first few. St Cornelius (251) was elected Pope (writes St Cyprian) "by the testimony of nearly all the clergy, by the college of aged bishops, and of good men". But, when the Church grew more worldly, this became more and more inconvenient, especially as there was no formal delimitation of the parts to be played by clergy, bishops and "good men" respectively. In 366, the papal election ended in wholesale blood-shed. The adherents of Damasus held the Liberian basilica; those of Ursinus stormed it, and 137 corpses were counted there at the end of the day. The Pagan historian Ammianus Marcellinus remarks that the temptation was overwhelming, since the bishop of Rome, through the munificence of pious ladies, was able to enjoy comfort and pomp, and to give some of the best dinner parties in the metropolis. Thus popular election became increasingly unreal; and Professor C. H. Turner gives the succeeding steps very clearly in the first volume of *The Cambridge Medieval History*. In the sixth and seventh centuries, Popes were often practically appointed by the Emperors. In the eighth century, the part of the laity was reduced to mere acclamation. In 824 Louis the Pious exacted an oath from the Romans that none should be consecrated Pope without the permission and presence of his ambassadors; and in 898, in consequence of very serious election-riots, John IX gave papal sanction to this imperial control. The Emperor Otto I (963) compelled the Romans to swear that they would never elect or ordain a Pope without his or his son's consent: and it was the Emperors who, at one point, rescued the Papacy from the control of unscrupulous local barons, and from the lowest degradation in all its history. Even such bold and organizing Popes as Gregory the Great and Nicholas I had never grasped this nettle; and when, in 1059, Nicholas II attempted so to regularize those elections as to dispense with imperial control and to obviate disputes, he built upon the foundation of a gross and fatal ambiguity. This matter is so important not only in its direct bearing upon religious and social history, but also in its side-lights on medieval mentality, that I must treat it here at some length, following mainly the great legal historian Esmein, in his essay on *l'Unanimité et la Majorité (Mélanges H. Fitting* (1917), vol. I).

The Church "accepted the law of simple and absolute majority only with difficulty, and at a late date, when canonical election had lost its most important applications". After the distant and obscure years of early Christianity, we find that the bishop is elected by the clergy and the community; *a clero et populo*. But, already at that date, the clergy play the principal part; they choose, and the people are called in to accept and confirm the choice. St Ambrose's election by mere popular acclamation at Milan in 374, before he had even been baptized, was a relic of the earlier Christian practice. In principle, the whole population—the males at least— might take part in the election. But, strange as it may seem, their choice was, theoretically, unanimous. We find this in England even as late as Lucius III (1181–4), whose decree, enshrined in Canon Law, bids the clergy "procure the king's assent, and agree unanimously upon an honest, literate and proper person, and elect him consentaneously as pastor and bishop"—*unanimiter conveniatis, eligatis concorditer*.

Here, at least on the face of it, we have the old Germanic principle, common to rudimentary civilizations, of compulsory unanimity. Agreement to differ is one of the latest steps in social evolution. Tacitus describes these Germanic people, still far removed from such political organization as the Roman Empire could boast, where the magistrates had little executive power, and the operative factor was the assembly of the whole tribe or clan, and yet the decisions were unanimous. The hearers showed disapproval by a hollow murmur, or approval by the clashing of shields and spears, and the result was something like the unanimity which reigns in certain countries of to-day. In twelfth-century London the chronicler gives us something like the same picture of a folk-moot, the populace securing decision by their shouts of "Ya, ya!" or "Nay, nay!"[4] This same principle of unanimity survives in our modern jury, not always entirely free from all elements of intimidation or coercion. Yet this principle may be traced in many councils, civil or ecclesiastical, in East and West. At Nicaea, for instance, the minority of twenty out-and-out Arian bishops was gradually reduced to two by imperial and other pressure; and those two, obstinately refusing to sign, were sent into exile. Therefore we need not choose between the great authority of Gierke, who traces the unanimity principle to Germany, and Esmein, who would stamp it as a Christian idea. "In itself", writes Esmein, "the choice [of the populace] for the election of the bishop, God's minister *par excellence*, is not a natural and comprehensible thing.... But, so long as this electoral system persisted, the idea crept in that such elections took place in peculiar conditions, under the inspiration of the Holy Ghost, whose invocation was always the first of electoral acts....The election must needs be unanimous, but God provided for that." Yet "this unanimous election was at the same time informal. Votes were not collected and counted. It is possible that, in the earliest ages, there had been a show of hands; but [in the early Middle Ages] the popular voice was expressed by clamours, by acclamations or by hooting. That was one of the reasons which facilitated unanimity: it was enough that the choice should appear unanimous. It sufficed that there should be no manifest opposition; or, if any such appeared, that it should be silenced. This latter result might be obtained by the exhortations of the [presiding] bishops: it might also be due to other methods, such as the fear of one's opponents." Those were the practical facts underlying this very rudimentary procedure in one of the matters most important for the well-being of Christendom; for the Pope was a bishop, and all that is said here applied to him also. It took many centuries to bring Europe to the idea of majority-election, whether in the barest sense or in any clear and business-like form. Meanwhile the Church, so meticulously prudent and business-like in some ways, neglected human nature in some of its most obvious impulses, and left things to arrange themselves in one of the most vital fields, the election of "Christ upon Earth". She deified Chance under the name of Holy Ghost. Stephen VI (886–9) decreed: "The election pertaineth to the priests, and the consent of the faithful populace must be obtained; for the people must be taught, not followed." Very similar, at this period, was the election of civil magistrates: on the Continent the count proposed the candidate and the people acclaimed him, and things seem to have followed much the same course under the sheriff (*viscount*) in early England.[5]

St Leo the Great (440–61) had ruled that, where the election was not unanimous, the archbishop should choose the fitter of the two candidates. The fact that this decretal was enshrined in Canon Law and became the foundation of future legislation shows how embryonic the whole system was. Even when the great Lateran Council of 1215 had fixed new and preciser methods for ecclesiastical elections, it still left room for the old idea of unanimous acclamation; the electors need not follow the new forms "if the election had been made by all in common, without fault, as if by inspiration".

Then, as the greater precision of the numerical voting system became evident, the principle of majority decision crept in little by little. At first it was hedged in by a very serious qualification; a bare majority would not suffice; it must be a majority not merely of numbers but of quality; one of the two sides must be able to show not only more, but "sounder", electors: *major et sanior pars*. That principle appears already in St Benedict's Rule (ch. 64); it was taken into Gratian's *Decretum* as a supplementary note, and consecrated by Innocent III at his Ecumenical Council of 1215. Here it is decreed that the candidate is to be counted as bishop elect "upon whom all, or the *major et sanior pars* of the chapter, have agreed".

But here is a gross ambiguity. A child can count the *majority* among fifty votes, but who is to distinguish the *saniority*? No Pope or council, through all the medieval centuries, ever attempted this. Innocent himself can scarcely have been ignorant of the fact that, some eighty years earlier, Europe had been plunged into conflict and bloodshed by a disputed papal election. There, the numerical minority of electors claimed superior *sanioritas* for Innocent II because they had on their side more cardinal bishops; and the numerical majority, because they had more who had been raised to the cardinalate earlier than their opponents. To one side, "soundness" meant rank, and to the other, seniority: hence civil war. When the canon lawyers were confronted with this crucial phrase, and mere evasion under vague generalities was no longer possible, it may almost be said that their professional definition was even more vague than that which they set out to define: *ignotum per ignotius*. This is so important for the estimate of medieval mentality that I must here add another paragraph for the sake of all readers who are interested in the progress of human thought; other readers may prefer to take it as read.

Esmein (p. 375) quotes the definition of one of the greatest medieval canonists, Panormitanus, who died in 1453 and had the collective wisdom of two centuries of predecessors to work upon. It runs thus: "*Sanioritas* consists in *authority*, *zeal*, and *merit*. *Authority* may be seen in the dignity of the electors, their greater age, their more ancient appointment, and their higher [ecclesiastical] orders. Those who are superior in these different claims have weighty voices [*ponderosas*]. *Zeal* consists in feeling: that is, in the motives actuating the electors, whether it be kindred or friendship or bribery; whether they have accepted payment or have voted by reason of the elect's merit. And, since zeal consists in feeling, it must be proved by presumption, since feeling admits of no other proof. It is said also that this sort of *sanioritas* consists not only in zeal but in facts and the operation itself. But operation concerns merit; for the party which elects a better candidate appears the sounder party; and that refers to the persons elected, considered from the point of view of morals, life, etc. It may also refer to the electors, if we consider that, being more honest, they have more *merit*, and that this renders their votes all the fatter [*pinguiores*]." What pettifogger could wish for a richer job than a lawsuit in which the crucial question was that of greater age, earlier appointment, and higher orders, in a community in which it might happen that one-third were older and one-third senior by appointment (or, again, one-third bishops, one-third priests, one-third deacons); with no criterion whatever to decide whether age, seniority or rank was to be taken as the weightier consideration in case of conflict? Or, again, consider this system in which comparative morality was supposed to be crucial, and in which lawyers might claim the morality of the elector as reflecting decisive light upon the fitness of the person elected or (to make confusion worse confounded) *vice versa*. Moreover, Panormitanus reveals to us these difficulties not merely in theory but in practice. He writes: "The gloss here...concludes that the sounder part, even though numerically less, ought to prevail. But [five of the greatest authorities] hold the contrary opinion here, saying that, since the two qualifications are copulatively required [major *et* sanior], therefore either, taken by itself, is insufficient." As Esmein points out, although Innocent III prescribed a comparison of extreme delicacy (morals, etc.) yet "singularly, he had not prescribed who was to make this comparison, or the authority whose duty it was to proclaim the result of the voting": and the exposition of Hostiensis, one of the earliest and greatest commentators on this decree of 1215, amounts to "mere anarchy". St Bernard, whose piety and zeal and intellect and personal fearlessness and nobility of birth made him for a while the arbiter of Christendom, did indeed solve admirably that election disputed between Innocent II and Anacletus on the dubious point of *sanior*; but he cut the knot with the sword of the Spirit, and in the teeth of statute-law. How many equals had St Bernard, in that combination of qualities, during the whole Middle Ages?

Therefore so little can we wonder at the papal schisms which sometimes rent the Latin Church, or even at the shattering magnitude of that Great Schism in the fourteenth century, that it might rather have been counted a miracle if no such convulsions had occurred. This, to the medieval mind, would of course present far less difficulty than to us; the presumption in those days was as strongly in favour of miraculous intervention as it is against it to-day. St Francis, in the matter of the Portiuncula Indulgence, is said to have refused the proffered papal bull, saying: "The Blessed Virgin Mary shall be the charter and Christ the notary, and the angels shall be the witnesses." The result was that, as soon as the story of this Indulgence was really spread abroad, it was violently contested by the Dominicans, and there have been the gravest historical doubts down to the present day. So was it also with papal elections, as with those of meaner importance; the hierarchy might take refuge in their reliance upon miracles, yet none came in answer to their cries. It is natural therefore to ask whether these disastrous failures might not reasonably have suggested to the ecclesiastical legislator that, by his hugger-mugger treatment of plain business issues, so vital to the health of Christendom, he might be tempting the Lord his God. For it is now admitted on all hands that the Great Schism was one of the prime causes of the Reformation.

Slowly, then, the modern idea crept in of counting by percentages, which do at least give a clear verdict. As early as 1203, Innocent III had decided a disputed election in a monastery on the ground that one candidate had received nearly two-thirds of the votes (24 out of 38), and must therefore be presumed to have been elected "by good zeal", unless he could be proved unfit in other ways.[6] And then, in 1215, Innocent III brought in the percentage rule "in order to avoid discord in the election of the Roman Pontiff", because, in spite of former regulations, the Church hath suffered grievous schism through the audacity of wicked ambition." If two-thirds of the cardinals are on one side, that majority shall be decisive: only in case of lesser majorities shall the question of *sanioritas* come in.[7] And, finally, this rule was extended to all ecclesiastical elections by Gregory X in the second

Council of Lyons (1274). Thus, though the old uncertainties of *sanioritas* persisted throughout the Middle Ages in normal cases, yet, when a two-thirds majority could be secured, it was superseded. The Council of Trent, by instituting the secret ballot, finally consecrated the majoritarian principle; for, obviously, where no voter could be identified, no superior *sanioritas* could be pleaded.

Condemnation of Honorius I.

The doctrinal history of the Papacy had been almost equally haphazard; a process of gradual consolidation far less through definite foresight than through a series of opportunisms. When the Church was rent with disputes as to the validity of heretical baptism, the salvation of thousands or millions was at stake, since both orthodox and heretics looked upon baptism as the necessary gate to heaven. St Cyprian and his fellow-bishop Firmilian here defied the Pope, who contented himself with condemning them by letter, and made no attempt to beat them down by his authority in open fight. It was no Pope, but St Augustine, after many generations, who settled that question, once for all, against Cyprian. Honorius I, again, was condemned for heresy; that condemnation stood for priests to read yearly in the Breviary until the seventeenth century, when it was silently expunged. Whatever may be thought of fine-drawn modern arguments in defence of this Pope, the fact still remains that, all through our period, his heresy was regarded as notorious and undisputed. Again, Charles the Great has been described by the great Roman Catholic scholar Edmund Bishop as "his own Minister of Public Worship". Once even, with his clergy in full synod, he contradicted a Pope on the crucial question of image-worship, and called upon him by implication to reverse his solemn judgment. By an extraordinary perversion of the facts, it is often asserted that, from 597 onward, all our archbishops had to receive their pallium from Rome, and to take a special oath of obedience. That claim, for the generations down to the eighth century, was exploded by Professor J. P. Whitney in *The Cambridge Historical Journal* for 1932. It does not become fully true until the eleventh century. Moreover, between A.D. 688 and 1050 there were consecrated 376 bishops in England by the action of the Chapters, the King and Witan, but without a trace of papal interference. I have verified", adds Professor Whitney, "this calculation." These things, and many more for which there is no place here, must be borne in mind when we try to visualize the light in which Popes appeared to far-off England from the Norman Conquest onwards. William had landed at Pevensey with a Papally-blessed banner: Gregory VII reminded him, later, that he himself had incurred no little obloquy from his fellow-cardinals for his own encouragement of this bloodshed. Yet, though William was quite willing to follow the Pope's bidding in the matter of married clergy, he was not equally ready to renounce his traditional right of appointing bishops; and, when Gregory claimed homage from him, he answered bluntly: "I neither would nor will do homage; for I never promised it, nor can I find that my predecessors ever did homage to yours."

Yet, as we shall see, papal power was very great here in our islands, in spite of its basis in custom rather than in law, and the fitful incidence of its claims. We can best see this if we go back here, for a while, to earlier times.

The original British Church was comparatively independent of Rome. Its origins are lost in the mists of antiquity: but, when it first comes into the light of history, it differs strongly from the Roman upon two points which to us seem trifling, but to which contemporaries attached so much importance that, sometimes, quite good Christians of the opposing parties refused to sit down to table together or to use each other's dishes. One was, the precise shape of the clerical tonsure, and the other, the date of Easter. On this latter point Rome herself had been as inconsistent as in the matter of papal elections. In the earliest times, there were considerable differences in calculation between the Roman and the Eastern Church; the latter calculating Easter on the same principles on which the Jews had calculated for their Passover, while Rome reckoned differently. In 460, however, Rome adopted one of the Eastern principles, though without thus obtaining complete uniformity. In about 530 she made another concession; and this was the state of things when Augustine came to England as missionary from Gregory I. He thus found himself, naturally enough, at variance with the English, Irish and Scottish Churches, which were still calculating by the earlier Roman cycle, and had also introduced a change of their own. The great Celtic missionaries, St Columba, St Columban, St Aidan, and their whole school of Iona, were thus at variance with the Roman use; and Bede notes how, when St Chad was consecrated bishop, "there was but one canonically ordained bishop in the whole of Britain": only one, that is, whose ordination came from those who followed the orthodox Roman use. Thus, at the court of King Oswy, the bishop was of the Celtic Church, while the queen had brought "a priest of Catholic observance" from her native Kent; "whence it is said to have befallen sometimes that Easter was twice celebrated in one year; for, while the king had dissolved his [Lenten] fast and was celebrating Christ's Paschal feast, the queen and her followers persisted in fast and were keeping Palm Sunday." This had been tolerated in Aidan's time, in consideration of his saintly character and the fact that both Celts and Romans, at heart, were celebrating the same essential mysteries. But then came St Wilfrid, tutor to Oswy's son, who had made the pilgrimage to Rome and come back to fight for Unity with all his inborn passionate zeal. The king, therefore, held a synod at Whitby at which Wilfrid confronted Colman, the bishop who now held St Aidan's see. It was Oswy's set purpose now to secure Unity; and therefore he was resolved to decide once for all between these hitherto irreconcilable parties. Colman pleaded that his method was what had been handed down by his predecessors, going back ultimately to St John, the Beloved who had lain at the Last Supper upon the Lord's breast: in other words, his was the Eastern tradition, as opposed to the Roman. Wilfrid confessed the discrepancy, but pleaded that St John was, in the nature of the case, a Judaizing Christian who, like other Apostles, was unable to make a crude breach with Jewish customs. He then pointed out that the Celts did not, in fact, follow St John's observance exactly: thus "ye are in conformity with neither John nor Peter, neither the [Mosaic] Law nor the Gospel". Colman fell back upon the immemorial tradition of his own Church, consecrated by Columba and other saints, through whom so many signs and miracles had been wrought. The reply was crushing: "I might answer that there are many who will plead with the Lord that they have prophesied in His name, and cast out devils and wrought many miracles, yet to whom He will reply that He has never known them. But far be it from me to speak thus of your Fathers." For, behind this, he had the usual appeal to St Matthew. "If that Columba of yours (and, I may say, ours also, if he was Christ's servant) was a holy man and powerful in miracles, yet could he be preferred before the most blessed prince of the Apostles? to whom our Lord said, *Thou art Peter, and upon this Rock I will build my Church, and the gates of hell shall not prevail against it, and to thee I will give the keys of the kingdom of heaven.*" "When Wilfrid had spoken thus, the king said, 'Is it true, Colman, that these words were spoken to Peter by our Lord?' He answered, 'It is true, O king!' Then said he, 'Can you produce any such power given to your Columba?' Colman answered, 'None.' Then added the king, 'Do you both agree, without dispute, that these words were principally directed to Peter, and that the keys of heaven were given to him by our Lord?' They both answered, 'We do.' Then the king concluded, 'And I also say unto you, that this is the door-keeper, whom I will not contradict, but will, as far as I know and am able, in all things obey his decrees; lest perchance, when I come to the gates of the kingdom of heaven, there should be none to open them, he being my adversary who is proved to have the keys.' The king having said this, all present, both great and small, gave their assent."[1]

The victory here was complete, and Wilfrid did much in other ways to strengthen the bond between Rome and England. He brought in books and learning, and especially artists, to whom, as will be seen later on, we may attribute with great probability those magnificent Northumbrian crosses which, at first sight, seem so impossible for England at that early date. Yet in one respect neither he, nor those others who were naturally attracted by the culture of that great capital, ever dreamed of Romanizing to the extent which has sometimes been claimed for them.[2]

Soon after this fateful Synod of Whitby, Roman discipline gained even greater victories on the Continent through the direct agency of another Englishman, St Boniface. Here, as often, it is the most turbulent and difficult stock which produces the most fiery and energetic converts. Gaul and portions of Germany had already been evangelized to a great part by Celtic missionaries, not very ready to render strict obedience to Rome. Now, this distant Anglo-Saxon outsider came forward to do more for Roman Unity than had been done, for some time, by any churchmen of Latin race or of closer geographical proximity to the capital of the West.

Boniface (in Old English, Winfroth) was certainly a Wessex man; and the tradition is very probable which makes him born at Crediton and educated at Exeter. At that time (about 680) Exeter was a city of two tongues, and thus, to a certain extent, of two creeds. The most conspicuous church in the north of the city was dedicated to the British saint Petroc, while in the south there was the Saxon church of St Sidwell. British Christianity had its own customs differing from those which were afterwards brought in by St Augustine and his Roman fellow-missionaries: and, as is common between close neighbours, these minor differences caused quite disproportionate friction; in some cases the clergy of one observance would refuse even to eat with the other. This boy Winfroth cannot but have been impressed by the fact that the two churches differed about the computation of the most important among Christian feasts, so that, every seven years, while the people of St Sidwell were fasting and mourning for the Passion, those of St Petroc were in full rejoicing for the festival of Easter. Such scenes of disunion, so crude and so distressing to any impressionable youth, would go far to account for the later activities of this Devonshire monk who did more than any Italian of his age to bring not only the Germanic tribes, but even Frankish Gaul, under the direct discipline of Rome. He had apparently become an "oblate" monk (i.e. offered at the altar by his parents) before his seventh year; his piety and learning gradually earned him distinction; and, at the age of thirty-eight, he felt the missionary call. Our Saxon kinsmen of Friesland were among the hardiest of European populations, and among the most obstinate pagans. Their king, Ratbod, was reported by later tradition to have refused baptism on the ground that, since his ancestors were in hell, it would be disloyal to desert them. Boniface, refusing an abbacy in England, left for Rome in order to obtain the blessing of Gregory II. This was in 714; two years later he began his preaching in Frisia, where Ratbod had destroyed the Christian Churches erected by the Anglo-Saxon Willibrod, and had reinstated the idols. Ratbod died in 719; Charles Martel had imposed Christianity upon the Frisians by force of arms, and the mission prospered. In 722, the Pope consecrated Boniface as missionary bishop, compelling him to swear absolute obedience to the Roman Church, and sent him with a commendatory letter to Charles Martel. Henceforward he became the special apostle of Germany, beginning with Hesse and Thuringia. Thence to Bavaria, where, as in England, there were remnants of Celtic Christianity which Boniface subordinated to Rome. Thence, again, to Franconia, and then back westwards to Frankish Gaul, where he held a council in 745 which definitely imposed the Roman organization and discipline. Even this summary and imperfect list of his activities may show how justly Berthelot can write:[3] "The régime of pontifical authority, established already in England and Germany, was thenceforward accepted by the ancient Church of Gaul. It was purified, disciplined, and commanded; and we know very well how great was the place which it held in Gaul."

All this had cost Boniface not only much faith and energy, but also much of difficult—we may even say, of bitter—compromise. The clergy at the court of Charles Martel disgusted him; yet (as he wrote to his former bishop in England, Daniel) he cannot break with them entirely: for "without the patronage of the Frankish King I can neither govern the people nor defend priests or deacons, monks or nuns, nor even forbid the pagan rites and idolatrous sacrileges in Germany without the commands and the fear of that man [Charles]."[4] Among those pagan rites were actual human sacrifices. The story told by Boniface's letters to the Holy See and to English bishops is gloomy indeed. The one all-important point is that religious and cultural progress is being made, yet with a slowness disappointing to those who were giving their lives to the work. Anarchy or tyranny in the State reacted upon the Church.[5] The layfolk had invaded ecclesiastical offices and revenues; Charles Martel, recently dead, had been the worst offender here; it was with Church plunder that he had maintained the army which saved Europe from the Saracens. Moreover, the Church herself was struggling but slowly from that quagmire of ignorance which had inevitably followed the barbarian invasions. We see this most plainly, perhaps, in her hesitation about marriage, not yet formally claimed as a Sacrament in those days. In 742, Boniface appealed to Pope Zacharias concerning a great difficulty which had arisen in the person of a layman of great authority who "asserted that he had received licence from Pope Gregory of holy memory to take in marriage the widow of his own uncle, who herself also was the wife of his cousin, and she, during his lifetime, departed from him...moreover she vowed to God the vow of chastity, and took the veil, and then cast it away and was married for the second time. For the man aforesaid asserts that the Holy See hath permitted him such a marriage." Zacharias, who was a saint and a strong Pope, naturally supported Boniface in so glaring a case as this; yet Boniface's question was not so superfluous as it might seem, since he had received from the preceding Pope, Gregory II, a matrimonial decision most embarrassing to many theologians of to-day.[6] It ran: "As to the point you propose, what if a woman, who has been seized by an infirmity, is incapable, what shall her husband do? It would be good if he would so remain, and give himself to abstinence. But, since this is for great souls, he who cannot observe continence should rather marry; but he should not cease to support the woman who is prevented by illness, not cast out by loathsome sin." As to the "priests or bishops, involved in many vices, whose life defileth the priesthood in their persons",[7] Boniface should not refuse to eat or speak with them; by kindly intercourse he might possibly gain some of them over.[8] Some years later, Boniface complains that the synod he held has brought upon him "many injuries and persecutions, especially from false priests and adulterine deacons and fornicating clergy". There is a good deal of social significance, also, in the smaller matters which troubled Boniface and his Popes, behind the great questions of religion and morality. Zacharias is so troubled by pagan customs that he forbids the consumption of "jackdaws [or jays] and rooks and storks, which Christians must by all means avoid eating: moreover beavers and hares and wild horses should be much more strictly avoided". Patients with jaundice are to be segregated, lest others catch the contagion.[9] Most interesting of all is the Pope's attitude towards the Antipodes. A certain Virgilius or Ferghil, probably the same man of that name who was Bishop of Salzburg, had come into conflict with Boniface, whom he scandalized also by his geographical theory. The Pope's decision ran: "concerning this man's perverse and iniquitous doctrine, which he hath spoken against God and his own soul, if it be clearly proved that he professeth that another world and other men are beneath the earth, or a sun and moon, then do thou take counsel [or, hold a council] and expel him from the Church, depriving him of the honour of priesthood."[10]

If Boniface had remained at home in England he would have been confronted with much the same problems, as we may see from his letter to his fellow-archbishop, Cuthbert of Canterbury. Among the Anglo-Saxons there was more than one bishop who cared less to feed his flock than to shear it: "Who doth not tremble at these things, save only those who have no belief in the world to come?" He exhorts Cuthbert: "Let us die, if so God will, for the holy laws of our forefathers, that we may earn with them an everlasting inheritance." "Moreover I do not conceal from you, loving brother, that all God's servants here [in Germany] who seem most approved in Scripture or in the fear of God, are displeased that the good and honour and modesty of your Church are mocked; and it would be some relief from our shame if your synod and your princes would forbid to women and to veiled nuns

that frequency of pilgrimages that they make, going to the city of Rome and back; for the greater part of them come to ruin, few remaining intact. For there are very few cities in Lombardy or Franconia or France wherein is no adulteress or harlot of English race; and this is a scandal and a foul blot upon your Church."*
He goes on to speak of the extent to which earls or great men, "manslayers of the poor", seized upon the abbeys and appropriated the wealth "which had been bought with the blood of Christ". Finally, he reprobates the extravagant worldly dress of clergy and monks, harbingers of Antichrist, whose cunning it was "to introduce, through his ministers, fornication and lechery into the monastic cloisters".[11] This was written probably in 745; and, just ten years earlier, the Venerable Bede had drawn a still gloomier picture in his appeal for reform to Archbishop Egbert of Canterbury. Egbert, he hopes, will not act like so many of his fellow-bishops, and surround himself with men not of religion or continence, but rather buffoons and belly-gods. Every nerve must be strained to teach the so-called Christian folk at least the Apostles' Creed and the Lord's Prayer in their own tongue; it is significant that there is no mention here of the Hail Mary, which in the parallel episcopal injunctions of five centuries later had become a third item inseparable from those two. This teaching is necessary "not only for the layfolk, who are yet living the life of the people, but even for clerics or monks who are ignorant of the Latin tongue...wherefore I myself have oftentimes given both these, the Creed and the Prayer, translated into the English tongue, to many unlearned priests". There are many remote villages and hamlets in which a bishop has never been seen for many years past; and thus the folk are never confirmed; for this rite, all through the Middle Ages, was performed normally only by bishops on their travels of visitation. Greed of money is here at fault: bishops grasp, for money's sake, at a greater extent of territory than they can truly administer. Bede complains how, in this "modern" Church of the eighth century A.D., by contrast with that of the first age, too many Churchmen not only do not sell the possessions they have, but even grasp at such as they have not. The whole of England [together with Southern Scotland] is divided into only twelve bishoprics. The abbeys are rich, and this wealth should be employed in part for the foundation of new sees;

* See below here, Chapter LI.

for "there are innumerable so-called monasteries, as we all know, who have nothing whatever of monastic conversation: I would that some of these might be transferred, by synodical authority, from lechery to chastity, from vanity to temperance, from intemperance of the belly and gluttony to continence and piety; and they might be taken in aid of an episcopal see which should lately have been founded." On this subject of monastic decay he harps again and again: there are only too many who spread a moral plague around them; and, by a still graver abuse, powerful layfolk "give the king's money, and buy for themselves, under pretext of founding monasteries, estates wherein they may more freely exercise their lusts", and procure foundation-charters and privileges signed not only by kings but also by bishops, abbots and worldly potentates. "It is thine office to see to it that the Devil should not usurp his reign in places consecrated to God." As to general piety, even "those [of the population] who seem among the most religious do not presume to take the Holy Communion except at Christmas and Epiphany and Easter, although there are innumerable boys and girls, young men and maidens, old men and women, innocent and of chastest conversation, who, without any controversial scruple, are fit to communicate every Sunday, or even on the days of holy apostles or martyrs, as thou thyself hast seen done in the Holy Roman and Apostolic Church." Here, again, we may compare this with the thirteenth century, by which time the laity, all over the Latin Church, very seldom communicated more than once a year, at Easter. But to return to Bede. It may too often be said now as Christ said to the Pharisees: "Wherefore do ye transgress the commandments of God through your tradition?" Men think to redeem their sins by "the alms which, amid their daily concupiscence and delights, they seem to give to the poor", but alms, to weigh in God's balance, must be brought by clean hands. "Let these things be said briefly against the poisonous love of money. But if I would treat in the same way concerning drunkenness and surfeiting and lechery and other such contagions, the length of my letter would extend to immensity."

Even if those words stood alone, and were not supported by evidence from other angles, they would suffice to warn us against over-estimating the power of the Church during the so-called Dark Ages, while we freely admit that she was the greatest existing power for good in those half-civilized societies. For Bede is the last man to be dismissed as a mere rhetorician or purblind carping critic. True, he had the monastic mentality; he had fled from Vanity Fair to save his soul; but, among all those who looked down from that cloister-refuge upon the follies and crimes of the world, there was none more understanding and temperate and reasonable than he.

To return to Boniface. His letter of 745 may very reasonably be connected with the fact that, two years later, a synod was held at Cloveshoe which stands out as a landmark in English Church legislation. The assembled Fathers grappled there with many of the abuses he describes and (*inter alia*) made the first attempt, not very effective, as we shall see, to set up something like a school system throughout the land. Boniface's work cannot be summarized better than it has been by a Devonshire educationalist, Mr F. H. Colson, before a Devonshire audience. "He stands, in fact, for efficiency, for hard work, for firmness of principle, tempered, however, with that opportunism which springs from good sense and reasonableness; for organization, for discipline. And, indeed, we may regard him not only as the father of English missionary work, but as the first-fruits of the colonial and imperial instinct of Englishmen, as the spiritual father of Raleigh and Drake, of the Pilgrims, who sailed from Plymouth in the *Mayflower*....Except, of course, in one matter. That Boniface was a loyal adherent of the Pope is obvious, and it may well be argued that he did more than any one in history to make the Papacy what it was during the next few centuries. Personally, I hold that he was right, and this I think is an opinion in which both halves of Western Christendom may well acquiesce. Those who feel most thankful that the North of Europe threw off in the sixteenth century the authority of the Bishop of Rome, may still quite logically believe that that authority was necessary for the world's development in the earlier centuries."

Thus, though the wild men who had conquered Rome were being gradually Romanized again, the extent of this victory was limited. St Vitus (for instance) christianized the island of Rügen in the Baltic; but, a few generations after his death, the inhabitants were found to be worshipping a great idol which they named Santovit, and to which, by preference, they offered sacrifice of Christian blood. The Monk of St Gall tells how the Danish ambassador would seek baptism at each of his yearly visits, for the sake of the new clothes and accoutrements that were given when he rose from the purifying waters. Charles the Great converted the Northern Saxons by fire and sword and banishment; with the result that these exiles cast in their lot with the sea-rovers, and he lived to see them sailing up his own rivers. The monasteries founded by Boniface and his fellows became a sort of papal blockhouses. In North Italy, for example, though Columban's Celtic foundations were originally very independent in their attitude towards the Pope, the essential similarity of aim soon produced close alliance, and it was precisely these Celtic Continental abbeys whose influence was decisive in favour of Rome when the Lombard princes leaned rather eastwards, and seemed likely to found a rival Patriarchate at Milan. But this mixture of politics with religion, however natural and inevitable, had its weaker side. The converted Germans or Slavs received their commands in terms which distinguished imperfectly between the moral and the legal sanctions. "Thou shalt pay thy tithes to the priests" was decreed in the same tones as "Thou shalt do no murder"; and in each case transgression was punished both by Church and by State. This, however convenient in many ways for the Church, did in later days render her far more vulnerable on the spiritual side; for she thus gave heavy hostages to fortune.

Such, then, was the Papacy at the beginning of our period: incomparably the strongest spiritual power in Europe, and rapidly extending that power by encroachment upon the civil sphere. There was as yet no theory of Papal Infallibility in the modern sense; and, when the question definitely emerges in the fifteenth century, it will be decided almost unanimously against the Pope. Yet already in the eleventh century there is a general agreement that what Rome thinks to-day is pretty nearly that which the Western World will think to-morrow. On the strength of this, it has become comparatively easy for the Pope to condemn a sovereign so definitely in the religious or moral sphere that there can be but one consequence in the civil sphere: this man is unfit to reign. The story of Gregory VII and Canossa is known everywhere; but there is perhaps even greater significance in Gregory's letter to Sweyn, King of Denmark, offering to his son, to conquer and take for himself, "a certain most opulent province hard by us, which is held by vile and grovelling heretics"—*quam viles et ignavi tenent haeretici*.[12] Here is the assertion of a principle big with consequences for the future. For by this, and by their utilization of those False Decretals which had been forged neither by themselves nor for this immediate purpose, the Popes constructed a bridge which enabled them now to trespass upon the sphere reserved for the civil powers by the Gelasian concordat; but a bridge which lent itself, when the world had developed still further, to devastating counter-attacks. We shall see later on how this Gregorian doctrine of the Omnicompetence of the Church gave occasion, by reaction and by a reversal of weapons, to a harshly contradictory doctrine, that of the Omnicompetence of the State.

IV. FEUDALISM EMERGES

WE have seen how the Church emerged from this welter of barbarism. Let us now trace the emergence of feudalism. This system is proverbially difficult to define; and many writers escape from the difficulty by denying that there is any system at all. Yet at least feudalism is a collection of customs which, however much they may differ from time to time and from place to place, have certain main characteristics in common; and to that extent we may certainly speak of it as a system. We must therefore consider it fully, detail by detail. First, let us glance briefly at its growth from a mingling of Roman and Germanic ideas. Then we can come to a rough definition; and thence we can pass to a fuller view of its development step by step.

As a general description of its growth we may say that it sprang from composite Romano-Germanic society: let us therefore look at these two elements separately. We cannot say that it is only necessary to take Germanism and Romanism and shake them together, and that the mixture will produce feudalism; but at least feudalism did grow naturally out of those two separate roots.

The *German*, as described by Tacitus, was an individualist. He was a peasant, herdsman or agriculturist or hunter, and inclined to say, as the Mongols said: "We are all kings in our own country." He was dimly conscious of duties to his village: more vaguely of certain duties to his tribe. The idea of a nation he grasped, in so far as he ever grasped it at all, only in such great crises as those of war; very much as it needed the Great War of 1914 to make Europe think seriously of a League of Nations.

The *Roman* of the Empire at its full development was, on the contrary, brought up in strict collectivism: he was forced to feel that the State was infinitely more than the individual. He lived under a most complicated bureaucratic machinery, in which he knew himself to be only one of a hundred million cogwheels, and he knew that the Emperor was the mainspring of it all. He passed his life, therefore, under the most perfect and comprehensive system of laws devised up to that time by the genius of man. He was met at every step by "the State commands this", "the State forbids that"; and at every step he found a State official to enforce these commands and these prohibitions, until he scarcely felt that he had a will of his own.

Such, it may be said almost without exaggeration, was the civilized Roman mentality, although we must remember that there was much evasion or violation of the laws whenever the subject thought he could find a chance. Feudalism, then, is a step forward in collectivism for the German, a step backward for the Roman. Yet the germs of it are clearly traceable in both systems. Roman society, in its decay, tended to feudalism; German society, in its forward growth, tended the same way. We associate it mainly with the most Romanized Germans—the Franks—among whom it had its fullest development. Yet in England also a real rudimentary feudal system existed already before the Norman Conquest, among that mixed population of Celts, Anglo-Saxons and Scandinavians who had practically forgotten the Roman element that in earlier times had worked in British civilization. We may consider this Romano-Germanic development under two heads; first from the social and next from the political point of view.

Socially, feudalism grew up through the loss of the ordinary man's independence; or, shall we say, of such small measure of independence as he could enjoy under the imperial bureaucracy. When the barbarian invasion came, there was a more or less sudden dissolution of those laws which, while they restrained him in a hundred little details of life, did nevertheless protect him within the network of those details. Life became so definitely a struggle for survival that the smaller man had no chance, either financially or physically, without the protection of some bigger man. Thus many little peasant-proprietorships gravitated together into a single great estate, resembling what in medieval times would be called the *manor*: here alone was a financial unit strong enough to survive, the only change being that the lord was now one of these military conquerors instead of the old hereditary possessor. Thus the yeomen proprietors became vassals to the lord of the manor; and this gave them not only some sort of protection from physical violence, but might also supply the financial support which enabled the small man to outlive a bad harvest.

Politically, the change may be traced mainly to financial causes. Civilization was now almost altogether agricultural. On the one hand the great arts and commerce of the Roman Empire had almost entirely perished; on the other, those arts which were destined to raise our Gothic cathedrals, and that trade which carried Marco Polo all over Asia, will not come for many centuries yet. Thus the main, and almost the only, financial reality is land and the produce of land. Even money is extremely scarce. This we can see very plainly in the ordinances of Charles the Great. That great Emperor had no means of spending a considerable part of his income but by eating and drinking it, he and his servants, straight from the farm. We see him, as we see sovereigns and great nobles all through the Middle Ages, travelling from one estate to another with his ministers and his train: eating up the year's produce in a week or a few days, and then passing on to eat up a fresh estate. Under those primitive conditions tenants naturally paid their rent in kind or in service, more especially in the latter. The peasant held his little plot on condition of three days' work for his lord and three for himself; and, since fighting was a very prominent part of the world's work, therefore the peasant must march under his lord's banner. Again, since the royal law-courts are distant and probably weak, perhaps in some cases almost non-existent, therefore the lord naturally asserts jurisdiction over the tenant; especially since medieval jurisdiction is a very profitable job, resting mainly upon a tariff of fines for each offence. Hence the medieval maxim, *magnum est emolumentum iustitia*. Not only was it thus the landlord's interest to judge, but the tenant would rather be judged by the petty tyrant of his own fields than have no judgment at all. Therefore he accepted the system of manorial courts which grew up, with such rights of appeal to royal courts as good luck might enable him to preserve.

Thus then we have already a rudimentary political system, in so far as we can give the name of *system* to that which grew up mainly through custom, and which differed so widely in details at different places and times, and which never arrived at so high a point of definition but that it left great room for disputes. It is difficult to make a modern reader realize how far custom and verbal agreement took the place of written law, not only in the Dark Ages, but even to the end of the Middle Ages; yet, on the other hand we must beware of a tendency to exaggeration on this point which has shown itself, especially in the last thirty years or so. The men of those times were themselves under no illusions as to the inferior preciseness of tradition when compared with the written word. In the eleventh and twelfth centuries, when written charters become frequent, it is almost common form for the contracting parties to explain that they commit this to writing for the sake of the superior durability of parchment, or (to quote the exact words of one monastic charter): "Man is a forgetful animal." In the later Middle Ages, therefore, we find the earlier customs constantly committed to writing. Thus, at least in the modified sense here indicated, feudalism was not only a system, but a political system. Groups of peasants were bound to a lord in three senses alike—financial, legal and military. The lord himself, with many of his fellows, was probably similarly bound to a greater noble; the greater noble again to his count or his duke; and the count or duke still owed service and obedience, if only nominal, to the sovereign.

In this way, apart from those who depended directly upon the sovereign as immediate tenants (*tenants-in-chief*, as they were called), the shadow, at least, of central authority was kept up by this network of responsibilities all converging upon the prince. The legal theory which accounted for both aspects of the system, social and political, crystallized finally into this: that the whole land of the State belonged in fact to the prince; that he was the one Universal Landlord; that he let out large districts to the counts and dukes under certain conditions of service; they in their turn to smaller lords; and so on down to the peasant. In other words, you could measure a man's status in the Middle Ages by his land, possession always implying a corresponding proportion of service. Moreover, although under this fully developed feudalism tenure had become hereditary, the lands passing by immemorial custom from father to son, yet the theory which distinguished such mere occupation from ownership in the strictest sense was maintained, among other ways, by the system of wardship and marriage. When a man died leaving children under age, the over-lord took over his lands and administered them until the heir came to his majority. If it was a girl-heiress, the overlord had similar rights. In France, indeed, he had only a veto on the girl's marriage: he could prevent her taking a hostile, or in any way inconvenient, husband. But in England the guardian might himself dispose of her in marriage; and our nobles may be found openly making large sums in this way; trading in marriages—to use the brutal word—practically as men trade in shares and investments to-day.

Thus (to take a last look at the system from this point of view of development from Romano-Germanic origins), in theory it kept up collectivism. It was highly centralized; it was an elaborate network leading inevitably upwards towards the sovereign. In practice, however, it was Germanic individualism in larger groups. The unit was no longer the family, but the manor or group of manors; and these larger groups had become practically independent of the sovereign. In its most developed form—that is in eleventh-century France—the national system had become obliterated. The central authority was nominal; nearly all the sovereign's power had passed into the hands of his greater tenants, each of whom was a petty sovereign on his own lands, enjoying practically every one of those rights which the sovereign enjoyed only in theory throughout the whole State.

There, then, is a rough-and-ready description of the development of feudalism, as a practical necessity under the circumstances of that time. The German conqueror knew too much now to go on living that primitive life of forest-clearings as described by Tacitus. But he did not yet know enough to organize a great bureaucratic state such as Constantine's Empire had been. Some dim resemblance to Constantine's state was possible for a moment under Charles the Great; but under his successors the centrifugal forces became too great for the rudimentary coherence of this vast mass. The Empire, therefore, from being one great planet rolling in the heavens, split up into a planetary system, a multitude of stars revolving more or less regularly round the Emperor or some other sovereign.

From this rough sketch of the stages of development we can now proceed to a definition. Feudum, or fee, or fief, is land (or office, or revenue) held in dependence upon any person. In its most definitely crystallized form, all landholders thus depend upon the sovereign. All are his dependents, either directly *in capite* or indirectly through some other lord. Then, as a complement to this, every man owes homage and service, especially military service, to the man from whom he holds land. Thus, he stands to that man not only as tenant to landlord, but as vassal to over-lord. So that, as Maitland says,[1] "Feudalism" is an unfortunate word; it expresses only half the thing; the full word should be "feudo-vassalism"; for under real feudalism the two ideas were inseparable—the ideas of financial dependence and personal dependence. We must therefore bear in mind Maitland's further warning that "the difficulty is not one that could be solved by any merely verbal devices. The impossible task that has been set before the word *feudalism* is that of making a single idea represent a very large piece of the world's history, represent the France, Italy, Germany, England, of every century from the eighth or ninth to the fourteenth or fifteenth."

Having followed the growth of feudalism just sufficiently to make that brief definition comprehensible, let us now try to form a clearer conception of it by tracing its growth in closer detail. We will trace it first in the Roman State; secondly, in the Germanic; and thirdly in the medieval State, developed from those composite Romano-Germanic origins. Moreover, we will take notice of its double character, personal and financial.

(1) ROMAN.

(*a*) The personal relation is here the oldest; that relation of the client to his patron which we find from almost the earliest times in Roman civilization. In later times, under the Empire, this system by which the small man formally placed himself in dependence upon a great man is called *patrocinium*.

(*b*) The financial relation of dependence grew up under the Empire, and was called *precarium*. This originally signified a tenancy by friendship or favour, from *precare*; X prays Y, as a favour, to let him have the use of a plot of land. "It is a flea-bite to you," he says, "but it would be a godsend to me"; and the other answers: "Yes, you shall have it on a precarial tenancy, giving you no legal claim upon it. I may alter the terms at will, or resume the whole grant at will; and at my death my heir is not in any way bound to continue this agreement." Hence, at Roman law, a *precarial* tenant has no rights as against his landlord, though he has such against other people. When, in times of trouble, a poor man besought a great man to protect his farm, the great man would naturally reply: "I can protect my own property, but not yours; make the land mine, and you shall have it back as a *precarium*." Thus the bargain would be struck. After the tenant's death, his children would make the best terms they could. The great man's interest was not to be too harsh, and custom consecrated increasingly the idea that these precarial tenancies should be allowed to continue so long as the tenant did his duty.

There can be little doubt that the enormous financial burdens of the later Roman Empire, which laid all the stress of taxation on the middle-class proprietors, ended by reducing thousands of those men to absolute poverty. They thus found themselves compelled to abandon all, responsibilities and ownership alike, to some other landholder who was ready to bear them. Therefore, just as some of these bankrupts would protect themselves personally by *patrocinium*, others would protect themselves financially by *precarium*, and many would take advantage of both customs. Thus we have already a rudimentary feudo-vassalage system.

(2) GERMAN.

(*a*) Personal. Here again the "client" system meets us from the earliest times. Tacitus describes how distinguished warriors would gather around them a whole following of satellites, in proportion to their own reputation and influence; he calls this companionship *comitatus*. He describes this fellowship-tie as stronger than that which bound the man to his State. It was a lifelong dishonour for the companion to come back alive from a battle in which his lord had fallen.

(*b*) Financial. There was no early German analogy here. They had nothing resembling a *precarium*; probably because early German society was as yet too undeveloped to admit of such financial relations.

(3) THE ROMANO-GERMAN.

(*a*) When invasions and conquests came, then these barbarian conquerors found themselves face to face with Roman institutions, to which they had frequently the wisdom to adapt themselves. Their *comitatus* and the Roman *patrocinium* shook hands at once; it is difficult to say that either needed to undergo much modification; except perhaps a numerical increase. The times were more turbulent, the poor man stood in greater need of protection; *patrocinium* therefore was more frequent and systematic than under the Roman Empire.

(*b*) For the same reasons the *precarium*, though new to the conquerors, was rapidly adopted by them. With the Germans, as with the Romans, the great man was glad to add to his estate; the poor man needed help even more; and therefore the *precarium* developed as rapidly among the Franks as the *patrocinium*, only changing its name to *beneficium*. Moreover, under the Merovingian kings two steps were taken which were most important for the development of feudalism. First, even great men adopted the *precarium* tenure: and, secondly, *precarium* and *patrocinium* were fused into one single system.

Here, as so often in the Middle Ages, the Church led the way even in matters of worldly business. Her estates soon became very great, tempting the spoiler; therefore the obvious policy was: "Let us enlist the spoiler on our side." Moreover, the bishop or abbot had official public functions as a great landowner; and it was convenient to shift those upon the shoulders of fighting men. Therefore they often let considerable estates on *precarium* tenure to great men, who were glad to get them on such terms. Gradually, therefore, precarial tenure increased in dignity; in the first place it was founded on written contract; secondly, the tenant held it for life; and thirdly, the landlord, for his part, received some sort of rent, though not the full value.

While the Church was protecting herself by thus enlisting great lords on her side through precarial tenures, small cultivators were using the same device to secure this powerful spiritual protection. Vinogradoff points out that "the monastery of Fulda, the famous foundation of St Boniface, gathered 15,000 *mansi* in a short time from pious donors.*...A considerable part of this property came from small people, who tried in this way not only to propitiate God, but also to win protectors in the persons of powerful lords." That is these peasants granted to the monastery the *lordship* of the land, and received it back as a *precarium*.[2]

Then, under the Mayors of the Palace, *precarium* and *patrocinium* coalesced, and became full-fledged feudo-vassalism.

(c) Merovingian kings had secured fighting men by grants of royal land; indeed, one reason of the impotence into which they lapsed was that they had thus squandered their lands so recklessly as nearly to exhaust their own power. But their successors, the Mayors of the Palace, lacking a legitimate hereditary title, were under still stronger necessity of buying the support of fighting men. To this we must add the fact that the average warrior, by this time, had become a much more expensive person. The

* *Mansus* is very nearly equal to the *caput* of Constantine's taxation—i.e. enough land for one man to till in a year.

formidable Arab invasions from Spain had shown the value of the mounted man. The long warfare in Southern Gaul, by which the Franks held these Arabs in check, necessitated a large body of cavalry; and this broke down the prehistoric principle that the soldier is not only recruited by compulsion, but must serve at his own expense. Hitherto it had only been necessary to pay the greater men who led the armies; the rank and file, in so far as they were paid at all, were rewarded from the booty. But the ordinary peasant cannot buy and keep horses at his own expense. On both sides, therefore, the question of payment for military service became vital and highly perplexing. The obvious temptation was to fall back here upon the Church, which by this time had become immensely rich; it is often estimated that her lands amounted to one-third of the whole soil of Gaul. The problem was solved in this sense by the conqueror of the Arabs, Charles Martel, who argued: "the army lacks money, the Church abounds; let us therefore pay the army out of Church lands, and by the methods which the Church has already invented." Thus these Church lands were granted on precarial tenure, the rent being paid in military service. In this way *precarium* (*feudum, beneficium*) coalesced with *patrocinium* (vassalage), and we have a real system of feudo-vassalism. This is why Charles Martel, in spite of the fact that he had saved Christendom by his battle at Poitiers and by other successes against the Arabs, was seen after his death by a pious visionary writhing in the lowest depths of hell.

Charles the Great seems to have seen clearly the centrifugal tendency of this system, and for a time he combated it; though at last the necessities of his vast Empire reduced him to compliance. The first necessity was this, that he had organized his dominions on the county system; this meant that the count had exceptional advantages for increasing his own body of vassals. He could take care, at least, that all who did not thus seek his protection should get rather more than less than their full share of military and other public duties; and in many cases he applied the screw more tightly still. We therefore find Charles legislating firmly against this, and trying to make it easier for the poor man to fulfil his military duties directly to the State. But the task was too great; Charles had to give it up, and we find him finally facing the facts. Then he simply compels the count or great lord to appear in the field with so many men, and leaves it to him to raise them, thus lightening the central government of a great burden, but sowing the seeds of future troubles. The great vassals, being thus allowed to surround themselves with an army of smaller vassals, became more and more independent. They reverted more and more to the old Germanic custom noted by Tacitus, where the *comitatus*, the personal tie between a great fighting man and his dependents, was far stronger than the ordinary citizen's loyalty to the State. He was no longer the Emperor's man, so much as the count's (or other lord's) man. Feudal loyalty overshadowed State loyalty. This, which seems so strange to us, that even formal legislation should treat loyalty to the immediate lord as a matter of such supreme importance, comes out very strongly in the Laws of Alfred. The testimony is all the more important, because it is not that of an extremist; England at this time was not more feudalized, but distinctly less, than most European countries. Yet, under Alfred, murder may be compounded for by a fine, a fine will atone for almost any other offence; but not treason against the lord—whether king or minor lord. And this is put on Christian grounds: the traitor's crime is the crime of Judas. When the law treated disloyalty to small and great lords alike as capital crimes, the subject naturally obeyed not that distant abstraction, the king, but rather the near and tangible authority, the immediate over-lord.*

It will be seen, then, that we can call this a "system", and speak of it as "logical", only in the sense that it had the logic of natural growth. Indeed, the comparatively homogeneous character of Anglo-Norman feudalism is one of the most exceptional phenomena in this whole sphere. In other words, here, even more than elsewhere in the Middle Ages, to be regular is itself an irregularity. In A.D. 800 Charles the Great was still casting all his weight against it: yet, scarcely more than a century later, it reigned everywhere as the alternative to anarchy. The small Latin kingdom of Jerusalem did indeed draw up deliberately a feudal constitution, though it is very doubtful how far this ever worked. But, among great States, feudalism was most regular and logical in England after the Conquest, for the simple reason that it was introduced as a fairly well-grown plant from Normandy, by a sovereign who intended, and was able, to keep his new kingdom in a firm grasp. The extent to which pre-Conquest England had already become feudalized by a natural process of growth is still disputed; but it is

---

* Compare similar evidence from the Laws of Edmund Ironside and Henry I in Pollock and Maitland, I, 300. In the former, the vassal's loyalty to the smaller lord is actually taken as the model of his loyalty to the king: "He shall swear fealty to King Edmund as a man ought to be faithful to his lord."

generally admitted that, until that date, we and the Scandinavians were the least feudalized of nations. William, by his Oath of Salisbury, initiated the policy of assuming that all his vassals should swear allegiance to the Crown, whatever other allegiance they might owe to each other. Thus, and by Edward I's statute *quia Emptores* (1290), England never suffered from anything approaching to the complexity of feudal relations which developed in France (for instance) through changes and divisions of ownership. The Count of Champagne was one of the greatest lords in France, yet for only a small fraction of his princely territories did he own the king as over-lord. The rest he held from a foreign sovereign (the Holy Roman Emperor); from the Duke of Burgundy, who owned small allegiance to France; from two archbishops, four bishops and an abbot. Seignobos quotes a case where he has found one man holding "the third part of the half of two-thirds of the tithe" of such-and-such an estate:

$$\tfrac{1}{3} \times \tfrac{1}{2} \times \tfrac{2}{3} \times \tfrac{1}{10} = \tfrac{1}{90}.$$

Cases could be quoted of nine different men holding the same piece of land, in gradation, above the tenant who tilled it.[3] Pollock and Maitland quote instances for England; but far less complicated than this. Even here, however, a man might hold his lands from a dozen lords, and in those cases personal service necessarily broke down; whether *military* service, which was the commonest form of tenure, or *socage*, as most forms of non-military service were called. This is admirably exemplified in the case of copyholds, which by the conservatism of English law survived until a few years ago. In the later Middle Ages, even great men thought it no degradation to hold lands in socage tenure from others far below themselves in the social scale; and sometimes they even held copyholds, which rendered them liable to the pecuniary burdens of villein tenants. I have heard that, in the later nineteenth century, Lord Rothschild bought an estate of which part was copyhold under New College, Oxford. The Warden and Fellows, therefore, were in that respect his lords, and he had to redeem the freehold in all haste lest, at his death, these over-lords should claim as a heriot his "best beast" which, in the case of so distinguished a racing man, might have been worth £20,000 or more. Whether the facts were exactly thus or not, the case was certainly quite possible. Therefore, already in the twelfth century, lawyers had begun to distinguish between "liege-homage", which was unlimited, and simple "homage". In the latter case, the tenant swore: "I do you homage, saving the fealty that I owe to my liege lord." Thus, finally, by far the greatest number of tenures became practically confined to financial and judicial relations. First came the tenant's rent, either in produce, labour, or money. Then, for all cases of dispute resting upon his tenure, he was bound to plead in the lord's court.

In England, therefore, with our comparatively regular feudal arrangements from the Conquest onwards, we may look upon it as normal (amid many exceptions) that all land belongs in theory to the sovereign; others are his tenants, whether directly or indirectly. All tenancies involve homage and service. The tenant must sue in his own lord's court for all cases except murder or "mayhem" (maiming), for which even the bondman may go for redress to the king's courts. Finally, these conditions are hereditary; the lord has no option but to admit the heir to his predecessor's tenancy, so long as he is ready to do homage and render the attendant services.

It will be seen how all this consecrated the division of classes; in eleventh-century Christendom it was almost as in Islam; we had a fighting caste supported by a working caste. Liberty was but half-developed: as Lord Acton says, it depended upon property; or, as Maitland puts it, *libertas* in legal language meant freedom to oppress others. Even in the towns with their gilds, "democracy, as they understood it, was nothing but the democracy of the privileged".[4] The Church did indeed help a little; yet, as we shall see, no orthodox Churchman protested against the principle of serfdom; that was left to the heretic Wyclif. As we shall see again, even the democratic author of *Piers Plowman* felt it perverse that a bondman's son should be made a bishop, rare as such an occurrence might be. Outside the clergy, barriers were far more severe. It was difficult, within our period, for a man to break through these class distinctions even by the greatest services in war. There was then no parallel to that which might happen under the Pagan Empire, when (for instance) the Asiatic peasant Justin fought his way up from a common soldier's pay to the imperial throne. Du Guesclin himself, the ablest commander on either side in the Hundred Years' War, was long kept in the background by the disadvantage of birth: he was noble, indeed, but only of the lesser nobility.

V. LAND AND FOLK

HAVING now taken a brief constitutional survey of the rulers, both civil and ecclesiastical, we may cease for a while to consider them in their daily action, and look at the land and the people upon whom they were to act. English Common Law is in its foundation a collection of folk customs; and, again, it might perhaps be as true to say that the folk made medieval religion, as that the religion made the folk. The story of development here will help to illustrate a truth too often neglected in our present natural reaction against the Great War: that nationalism is a necessary and healthy step towards internationalism.

Anglo-Saxon England clearly showed a want of national coherence. It needed the Conquest to bring the people to that point of civilization at which they should be conscious of nationality all over the country. For instance, a year after Hastings, the South-West was still unsubdued, openly defying William; so again was the North—Yorkshire and Northumberland. Yet there was no attempt at concerted action. The two risings were not even timed to be simultaneous; so that William was easily able to beat each in detail. He had the immense military advantage of a more despotic government. This Saxon incoherence was remedied by the Conquest. Here was a strong man, able to hold the country when once he had taken it, and supported by companions in arms whose interests coincided with his own; so that the Norman rule, continuing unbroken for nearly a century, welded England together by its heavy irresistible pressure. It was well for us that the victory at Hastings lay with such a race as the Normans, men whose coming into France marks an epoch in the history of that nation, and even more definitely of our own. The Norman was certainly a very remarkable social element, which asserted itself wherever it went; an element so important that we must consider it in closer detail. Let us first regard the Norman characteristics in themselves, and thence proceed to enquire how far they were strictly racial, or how far they were due to other than hereditary causes.

The Norman characteristics have never been better described

than by the eleventh-century Italian chronicler, Geoffrey Malaterra, who had observed these people closely during their conquest of Sicily and Southern Italy. He writes: "They are a most cunning and revengeful race. They leave their native fields for the hope of richer booty; greedy of gain, greedy of dominion; prone to imitate whatsoever they see; evenly balanced between lavishness and greediness [i.e. you never know whether you will find them spendthrifts or robbers]. Their princes are most generous where they hope to earn fame by their generosity. These Normans can flatter when they choose, and are so eager to become accomplished speakers that even the boys argue like trained rhetoricians. They are headstrong to excess unless they be curbed by the stern hand of justice. They are patient of cold if need be, patient of hunger, patient of hard work; they are passionately fond of hawking, of riding, of warlike armour, and of splendid garments." Freeman (whose article in the 11th edition of *The Encyclopaedia Britannica* is most valuable and illuminating) notes this curious combination of the masterfulness of the man of action with the pettifogging lawyer's mind. He points out how this comes out not only in William the Conqueror, but in several of his descendants, down to Edward I at least; and he adds: "If the Norman was a born soldier, he was also a born lawyer." Very remarkable also was the similar combination of strength with pliancy. No people have ever shown themselves more adaptable to changing circumstances. When they settled in North-Western France, Neustria, they became rapidly more French than the French: in twelfth-century Ireland it was noted of these Norman invaders that when once they had settled down they became *Hibernis ipsis Hiberniores*. These Normans—or Northmen, as at first they had been called —were the last and most terrible of the heathen invaders who broke into the Roman Empire. Yet they soon took their place among the most loyal sons of the Christian Church. They were, as Freeman says: "The most lavish in gifts to holy places at home, and the most unwearied in pilgrimages to holy places abroad.... The Norman was a crusader before the crusades." Their restless energy is emphasized by two early English historians, William of Malmesbury and Henry of Huntingdon; and these characteristics were doubtless to a great extent racial, shared by the modern Norwegian, Swede and Dane. The country of Nansen, Ibsen, and so many fruitful democratic experiments in our own day, still keeps much of the rough energy, yet ready adaptability, which a race naturally acquires in a long struggle against a rigorous climate and a dangerous sea. But we must not imagine complete racial homogeneity among those Northmen of the Dark Ages, who, when they settled down, came to be called Normans. Hastings, one of the most celebrated "Northmen" pirates of the ninth century, is said by the chronicler Ralph Glaber to have been a French peasant from the district of Troyes. It is most probable, indeed, that many of the so-called Normans who began pillaging the Empire during the last years of Charles the Great were really heathen Saxons who had been driven out by his conquests, refusing to reconcile themselves on any terms with Christianity. We may take it as practically certain that, though the large majority would come from one northern land or another, yet the bond of union was community rather of circumstances than of race. Something had turned them all into sea-robbers: they were a horde of pirates which welcomed recruits from all quarters indiscriminately. And the circumstances may be roughly enumerated as follows.

First, the struggle for life, naturally fierce in those simple times under so inclement a sky and over so niggardly a soil as are usual in the North. In Jutland, for instance, there was a formal law that, every five years, the population should be reduced by sending younger sons into exile; and even without such a regular law the fight for existence would naturally reduce many either to slavery at home, or to exile. In those circumstances the bolder spirits would unquestionably choose exile. Then again, a man might flee or be banished for some crime; the thief, the manslayer, would naturally take refuge with these outlaws. Thirdly, we must reckon with the sheer love of adventure, such as that which drove so many before the Great War to turn their back on the deadly dullness of village existence and "see life" in the army. In all these cases the Northman who left his native land would be a rougher, more resourceful man than the average of those who stayed at home. And, as they were thus picked men to begin with, so also their mode of life would sift them into a sort of uniformity. Seafaring is a rough job at best. Dr Johnson was accustomed to wonder how any man went to sea who had the alternative of going to prison; and in the tiny open boats of those days the hardships must have been incomparably worse. These sea-rovers lived in continual conflict, in which the weakest would go to the wall. They suffered terrible hardships of storm and hunger and thirst: and, what perhaps would be still more trying to nature, the wild excesses at moments when they had successfully plundered a ship or a town. All these conditions would give the Northern pirate a particular stamp, quite as marked as any racial character. The only men who could survive this kind of life would be precisely of the kind which Malaterra describes—uniting violence with cunning; restless energy with the most pliant adaptability. The Anglo-Saxons, of course, had once been a people of this kind. But they were a numerical minority in England; these conquering races have always been minorities. By long intermarriage with the conquered, by long devotion to agriculture and forgetfulness of his past seafaring habits, the Anglo-Saxon of 1066 had become a very different person from his ancestors who first came over. The people of England, and English civilization, needed a fresh stimulus and a strain of new blood.

Before the Conquest, then, these original Northmen had settled in Italy, and had adapted themselves to that Southern civilization; in France, again, they had picked up all they could learn from their more cultured neighbours. The insular Saxons, on the other hand, in their comparative backwater, were at a distinctly lower stage of civilization. Ordericus Vitalis, who was of mixed parentage and knew both nations well, writes: "The Normans found the English a rustic and almost illiterate folk." William of Malmesbury, who again was of mixed blood, tells us how in process of time the desire after literature and religion had decayed, for several years before the arrival of the Normans.[1] "The clergy, contented with a very slight degree of learning, could scarcely stammer out the words of the sacraments; and a person who understood grammar was an object of wonder and astonishment. The monks mocked the rule of their Order by fine vestments, and the use of every kind of food. The nobility, given up to luxury and wantonness, went not to church in the morning after the manner of Christians, but merely, in a careless manner, heard Matins and Mass from a hurrying priest in their chambers, amid the blandishments of their wives. The commonalty, left unprotected, became a prey to the most powerful, who amassed fortunes, either by seizing on their property, or by selling their persons into foreign countries; although it be an innate quality of this people, to be more inclined to revelling than to the accumulation of wealth. There was one custom, repugnant to nature, which they adopted; namely, to sell their female servants, when pregnant by them and after they had satisfied their lust, either to public prostitution, or to foreign slavery. Drinking in parties was a universal practice, in which occupation they passed entire nights as well as days. They consumed their whole substance in mean and despicable houses; unlike the Normans and French, who, in noble and splendid mansions, lived with frugality. The vices attendant on drunkenness, which enervate the human mind, followed." We must make that allowance for these picturesque descriptions which is nearly always necessary when we use medieval literary sources for social life. Authors wrote then with more impulse and less restraint; and these two quotations must be discounted by the studies of Professor Chambers (for instance) in pre-Conquest social history.

There, then, are the two different races. Now let us consider their interaction after the Conquest. The political change was the most obvious. To describe it roughly, something like 20,000 foreigners replaced 20,000 Englishmen, and naturally took the highest places. The king was a Norman; so were the earls, the bishops, the abbots, and nearly all the owners of great estates. Again, the greatest among the townsfolk were generally displaced by these conquerors. In a few cases the invader married the widow or daughter of the man he displaced, but such cases were naturally exceptional. The men who thus took the pick of the country to themselves were better educated, better managers, hardier and thriftier, and in far closer touch with Continental civilization. The spirit of adventure was fresher in them than in those Anglo-Saxons who were so many generations removed from the old conquering days. Again, these adventurers had not yet settled down into the content natural to a saturated population. They were quicker to seize upon new ideas, and had the unscrupulousness which is the natural effect of such qualities. They introduced far better organization into the country; and their adaptability and sense of reality saved them from any attempt to suppress the native language. The bulk of the conquered nation retained this as obstinately as Alsace kept German under the French Governments from Louis XIV to Napoleon III. It has often been remarked that, whereas our flesh foods are all French in name, christened as they came to the Norman table, yet this "beef" and "pork" and "mutton" were still called "ox" and "swine" and "sheep" by the Saxons who tended them.

Giraldus Cambrensis, whose descent from Welsh kings gave added force to his natural scorn of a rival nationality, rejoices to think that "the English are servants to the Normans—and basest of servants". Yet within an extraordinarily short space these two nations were practically fused. The Danish conqueror had soon become almost indistinguishable from those whom he had conquered; and, if something like the same result took place with the Normans, it was to a great extent because they also came originally from a northern stock or civilization. To begin with, William showed a sense of justice (or, if you will, of enlightened prudence) such as was shown by few medieval conquerors. He retained the old English laws as much as possible; fortunately for us, the Norman laws had not been committed to writing, so that it was only a case of conflict between the unwritten custom of a small minority and the partly written customs of a great majority; the concordat was therefore comparatively easy. We are told also that he even tried to learn English for the sake of dealing justice himself. Again, the two great Norman archbishops, Lanfranc and Anselm, did very much to soften the rigours of conquest; and, in spite of natural exceptions, it may truly be said that the Church in general contributed much to this process of fusion. The cases of St Elphege and St Wulstan of Worcester will explain this. Elphege, the Saxon, would have been expunged by Lanfranc from the calendar but for St Anselm's defence; and Wulstan's story is so picturesque that it may well find a place here in the racy English of Caxton's *Golden Legend*. Whether the details given by the biographer be historically true or false, they are none the less significant for the spirit of Norman and Saxon at that moment. "When William Conqueror had gotten all England, and had it under his power, then he began to meddle with the Church, and by the advice of Lanfranc, the holy bishop S. Wulstan was challenged that he was not able of letters, ne of conning for to occupy the realm and office of a bishop, and was called tofore Lanfranc, and willed him to resign by the consent of the king to the said Lanfranc, archbishop, that a man of greater conning might occupy the dignity. To whom Wulstan said: 'Forsooth father, I know well that I am not worthy to have this dignity, ne am not sufficient to occupy so great a charge, for I knew well mine unconning at such time when I was elect thereto, but I was compelled by our holy father the pope, and by good king Edward, and sith it pleaseth the council that I shall resign, I shall gladly resign, but not to you, but to him that compelled me to take it.' And he departed incontinent from the archbishop Lanfranc, and went straight to the tomb of S. Edward [the Confessor] with his cross in his hand, and he said to S. Edward, as he had then been alive: 'O thou holy and blessed king, thou knowest well that I took this charge on me against my will, but by constraint of the pope and thee I obeyed to take it, and it now so is that we have a new king, new laws, and giveth new sentences, in reproving thee of thine error for so much as thou gavest it to me, simple and unconning man, and me, for the presumption that I would consent to take it. That time thou mightest well have been beguiled, for thou wert a frail man, but now thou art joined to God, whereas thou mayst not be deceived. Thou gavest to me the charge, and to thee I here resign it again.' And with that he fixed his staff into the hard stone of his tomb, saying: 'Take this and give it to whom it pleaseth thee.' And the hard stone that lay upon his tomb resolved by miracle, and received his cross or pastoral staff, and held it so fast that it might not be taken out by man's hand. And anon he did off the habit of a bishop, and did on a cowl, and stood among the monks in such degree as he did tofore ere he was bishop. And when word came, and was reported to them that had consented to his resignation, they marvelled greatly and were all abashed, and some of them went to the tomb and would have pulled out the staff, but they could not move it. And when the archbishop Lanfranc heard thereof he commanded to Gundulf, bishop of Rochester, to go and fetch to him the pastoral staff, but when he came he set hand on it and pulled at it, but the stone held it so fast that he might not move it, wherefore he was sore abashed, and came to Lanfranc, and told to him of this miracle. Then the king and Lanfranc were abashed and came both in their persons to see this thing, and there made their prayers. And after, with great reverence, Lanfranc assayed and set hand on the staff for to have pulled it out, but it would not move. Then the king and the archbishop were sore afraid, and repented them, and sent for to seek Wulstan, whom they found among the monks and brought him tofore the king and the archbishop, who anon kneeled down and asked forgiveness. And Wulstan meekly kneeled down and prayed them not so to do to him, and humbly and meekly pardoned them and prayed the archbishop humbly to bless him." Yet, although the influence of the clergy here and always was internationalistic to a certain degree, that was far from sufficient to bridge the gulf completely. Becket was the first English-born Archbishop of Canterbury, and even he was not English by race: his father was a Norman who had become an English citizen. Some of our sees, again, had no English bishop until even later dates.

Another cause which made for fusion between the two nations was Anselm's resistance for conscience sake to William Rufus, and afterwards to Henry I. This tended to bring together all who were inspired by the spirit of freedom in their resistance to royal despotism. Another step was marked by that Charter of Henry I which definitely fixed the "Laws of King Edward" as English Common Law, and by his marriage to the Saxon Princess Matilda. These were definite statesmanlike concessions in favour of the English. Moreover, for several generations common sufferings and common dangers bound the two races together. When the barons revolted under Rufus, he used the Saxon term in appealing to all his subjects; he would brand as *nithing* every man who refused to march with him against these undisciplined depredators. So, again, the feudal anarchy under Stephen created in all orderly people a common interest to support the Crown; and, lastly, when the Scots invaded England, the two races vied with each other in bravery at Northallerton (1138). But perhaps the most important cause of all was one which has run throughout our post-Conquest history like a consecutive thread. Since 1066 we have had no real invasion. No foreigner has ever succeeded in interfering in our politics, and hindering us from working out our own salvation. Thus the problem of English politics has always been essentially simple: just the eternal difference between the conservative and the progressive mind. We have never had, in England proper, those other national factors which complicate the problem indefinitely, since each fresh party in a contest increases the difficulty not in arithmetical but in geometrical progression. Nor, again, have we had that foreign invading element which would find its natural interest in fomenting the quarrel between the other two. We have only to think how Ireland has suffered in that way, and how the worst difficulties of the French and the Russian Revolutions came from the interest which power-ful neighbours found in fomenting discord. Thus faced only with the simple problem, England acquired a feeling of real nationality within a surprisingly short time after the Conquest. Henry of Huntingdon, writing before 1150, coined that phrase which has become proverbial—"Merry England"—*Anglia plena jocis*. In the face of the random use of this phrase in our own day, it is necessary to point out that the England of which Henry was writing was the England mainly of his own upper class, from whose standpoint he writes. We shall see presently how little the words were strictly applicable to the vast majority of the popula-tion. But the phrase was borrowed, a century later, by the ency-clopaedist Friar Bartholomew, whose description is worth quoting in its fourteenth-century translation: "England is a strong land and a sturdy, and the plenteousest corner of the world; so rich a land that unneth [*scarcely*] it needeth help of any land, and every other land needeth help of England. England is full of mirth and of game, and men oft-times able to mirth and game; free men of heart and with tongue, but the hand is more better and more free than the tongue." Moreover, Henry incorporates in his Latin Chronicle a great deal of Old English literature: the *Battle of Brunanburh* and a number of other poetical fragments. So also does his contemporary, William of Malmesbury, himself of mixed Norman and Saxon race. But the plainest of all testimonies to the mingling of the races comes to us from a law-book of about 1180, the so-called *Dialogue of the Exchequer*. By the Conqueror's disposition, whenever a Norman was found dead, and the slayer could not be discovered, it was presumed that he must have been slain by a Saxon; the utility of this provision is obvious for the protection of a small foreign garrison. In virtue of that presump-tion, a heavy fine was imposed upon the Hundred; i.e. that section of the community in which the corpse was discovered, unless indeed they could clear themselves by producing the murderer and giving him up to vengeance. "Then", asks the pupil in this Dialogue, "why is there no such disposition when an Englishman is found slain?" To which the master replies: "There was no such disposition at the first institution of this law, as thou hast heard; but now that English and Normans have lived so long together, and have intermarried, the nations have become so intermingled (I speak of freemen only) that we can scarce distinguish in these days betwixt Englishman and Norman; excepting of course those serfs bound to the land whom we call *villeins*, and who cannot quit their condition without leave of their masters. Wherefore, in these days, almost every secret manslaughter is punished as *murdrum*, except those of whom (as I have said) it is certain that they are of servile condition."[2] Yet, although that law had practically fallen into desuetude by 1180, it was not formally abolished until 1399.

Moreover, we must remember that, though this fusion may be spoken of as practically complete, there would be a good many exceptions: numerous survivals, for many centuries, of the ancient divisions. In the first place nearly all the serfs, as we have seen, were of Saxon origin. Then, again, "Norman" on the one side, and "English" on the other, become fairly common surnames. It is true also that the French tongue long remained that of the upper classes. We find allusions to this, as late as the end of the fourteenth century, in *Piers Plowman*; and again, in episcopal visitations to nunneries at the same time, when Latin was not used the language was French. Moreover, the diversity of English dialects did a good deal to maintain Norman-French in this superior position. Yet the sense of practical fusion between race and race was so strong that Higden, at the beginning of the fourteenth century, describes this mingled people in very much the same terms as those which Malaterra had used for the Normans alone. He writes:[3] "The Englishmen that were in England, that have been mingled with other peoples...are so uneasy, also unpatient of peace, enemy of business and loving of sloth.... These men be speedful both on horse and on foot, able and ready to all manner deeds of arms...and curious, and can well enough tell deeds and wonders that they have seen. Also they go to divers lands....They can better win and get new than keep their own heritage. Therefore it is that they be y-spread so wide, and consider that every other land is their own heritage." He adds: "The men be able to all manner sleight and wit, but before the deed blundering and hasty, and more wise after the deed; and they leave often lightly what they have begun....These men despise their own and praise other men's, and be scarcely pleased with their own estate." At the same time he is strongly conscious of the distinction between North and South. "Scots be light of heart, strong and wild enough, but by mixing with Englishmen they be much amended. They be cruel upon their enemies, and hate bondage most of anything, and they hold it a foul sloth if any man dieth in his bed, and great worship if he die in the field. They be little of meat and may fast long, and eateth well seldom while the sun is up, and eateth flesh, fish, milk and fruit more than bread, and though they be fair of shape they be defouled and made unseemly enough with their own clothing. They praise fast the usage of their own fathers, and despise other men's doing." It is a thousand pities that no contemporary Scottish chronicler has left us his own judgment on these and similar points.

Now that we are in a position to deal with ordinary life in greater detail, there can be little doubt as to the class with which we must begin. In the England of our period, at least 90 per cent. of the population were villagers; and the main features differentiating life in those days from life in ours were the ordinary differences between urban and rural civilization. Moreover, it is precisely these village communities to which modern reactionaries look back most fondly, and, on the whole, with most justice; since it must be the concern of all men that we should not lose anything that was of permanent value in that simple and patriarchal state of society. It would be well to take the evidence here mainly from about 1280 to 1380, as the century in which the manorial system is fully developed and for which trustworthy written business documents are abundant to check the literary evidence.

The general population at that time was probably about three and a half to four or four and a half millions, that is little more than one-tenth of what we have to-day. The villages were very small; the average for Western Europe would run from two hundred to 400 or 450 souls: that is, from forty to eighty adult males. Let us travel from Cambridge to Trumpington one day in mid-August. Sir Giles de Trumpington, the lord of the manor, who is now about thirty-three, if we had an introduction to him, might show us with some pride what is still one of the sights of the district; the monumental brass, under its sculptured canopy, which commemorates his lately deceased father. He might also offer us wine from the Trumpington vineyard, for which documentary evidence has survived. We should not drink lavishly of this. After that courtesy, he might well charge his steward to show us round the village. The cottages are small; here for instance is the specification of one which a new tenant is bound to build in order to house a predecessor. "He is to build her a competent dwelling for her to inhabit, containing thirty feet in length within the walls, and fourteen feet in breadth, with corner-posts and three new and competent doors and two windows."* Another specification of

* Most of the details in this and the next two chapters have been printed, with full references, in my *Medieval Village*.

1325 describes a cottage 24 ft. by 11, built "to the use of Geoffrey Whitring and Mabel his wife and John their son." The dilapidation of an ordinary village is described, perhaps with some rhetoric, on p. 69 of the *Magna Vita S. Hugonis*: "decrepit hovels, with rotten beams and half-ruined walls." The same source, among many others, shows how easily the ordinary cottage could be dismantled and removed. We have similar evidence from Halesowen and from Kirkstall Abbey farms; even more vivid, again, from Italy at about the same time. For the Friar Salimbene, describing the civil wars of 1287, names six villages in his neighbourhood where "the men carried away their houses and rebuilt them" on hill-tops, for security against marauders. Again, speaking of the bonfires lighted that year by exultant victors, he says, "even as the country-folk do at carnival-times, when they burn down their cottages and hovels". Here, again, is an extract from a manorial record: "Richard, son of Thos. Sibil, granted to Thomas his elder brother a parcel of land; and, if it so befall that the said Richard wishes to move his house, the said parcel of land where it now stands shall remain in possession of the said Thomas, and he shall pay 2*d.* rent per annum." Even at the end of the fifteenth century, when St Catharine's College was founded at Cambridge, the three original Fellows seem to have lived, for a time at least, in a timber house set up first at the neighbouring village of Coton, bought and transported later some six miles across the river to Horningsey, and brought back in the third instance to Cambridge.[2] Nearly all of these Trumpington cottages and farms we shall find clustered together in the village, each with its little garden or toft. A few may possibly be scattered outside; but in most cases it was too dangerous to live far from the hue and cry of one's neighbours. As for the peasants' tools, here is a chance inventory. The man had a hoe, a spade, an axe, a bill-hook, two yokes for buckets, and a barrel. The total value was estimated at 10*d.*; about 30*s.* in modern values. As we pass through the village into the open field, we see the peasants and their wives reaping, with an overseer holding a long stick over them. This is "Walter son of Alger, who holds three hundred acres for which he doth homage to Sir Giles; and he will come personally to all the extra workdays, holding his rod over the workers; and on those days he shall have his dinner in Sir Giles's kitchen." If we ourselves were Cambridge University men of that day, we might very well recognize several undergraduates among the harvesters; the Long Vacation, such as it was, would include both hay and corn harvest, and some students, like their brethren of America to-day, must have been able to do manual work in part payment of their expenses. It is similarly significant that university account and audit days were in early October. Even so solemn an assembly as the Convocation of the Clergy, if the session were unduly prolonged, might adjourn for harvest. The arable land is divided into three distinct "fields", entirely without hedges, but often separated into strips by narrow "balks" of unploughed turf. This "three-field system" is on the whole the commonest, though there is sometimes a "two-field system", and sometimes again there is scarcely any general system at all. Where the fields are three, the crops are alternately wheat and barley, with a third year of fallow. In 1300, for instance, we will suppose that all plough and sow wheat in October and reap it in the following autumn, 1301. In 1302, ploughing will be done in March and barley will be sown. After the autumn harvest of 1302 the land is untouched until June 1303, when it is ploughed twice and left to rest until October; then it is sown with wheat, and the round begins again. By the "two-field system" the treatment seems to have been alternately wheat or barley one year and fallow the next. Under both systems the crop was necessarily prescribed by the lord; only under such compulsory uniformity could the tillage work. There must also have been—and of this we have occasional documentary proof—a good deal of communal tillage, as there is still communal cheese-making in the Alps. Where the strips were much intermingled, it was obviously advantageous for all parties to treat the most intricate parts as one block, the different owners ploughing in common, sowing in common, reaping together and dividing the proceeds in proportion to the area that each held. At Martham in Norfolk, where the details have been worked out by the late W. Hudson, an extraordinarily laborious and accurate antiquary, we may see that many tenants had more ploughs than land, while others had more land than ploughs. He concludes: "The whole was sown with one crop and reaped in common."[2] This explains why (in the Durham Halmote Rolls, for instance) it is a punishable offence for the peasant to sell his crops separately. After harvest, the cattle and fowls were allowed to wander free over this wide unhedged communal field: hence the gastronomic reputation of a stubble-goose, or Michaelmas-goose, that is, a bird killed at the exact point when there was no more left to gather from the grains scattered by the harvesters or buried at the roots of the stubble.

For the question of subdivision of holdings we may take this same manor of Martham as typical. The peasant's original holding was somewhere about ten or twelve acres; in other districts something like thirty seems to have been typical. At Martham, the pre-Conquest population had been mainly Danish and, by Danish custom, freemen. But when, in 1101, its lord the Bishop of Norwich granted the village to the monks of his cathedral priory, the thirty-six freemen were gradually turned into villeinage tenants, and the twenty-seven socmen into customary tenants. Mr Hudson succeeded in ascertaining, with mathematical exactness, the subdivisions in 1292 of two tofts—i.e. a block of six acres—which had once been held by Ivor Blackman, and was now divided among ten different tenants. Only one tenant now bears the original name; this is William Blackman, and he holds only three perches. It seems plain that this was just a garden round his cottage; that he was by this time superannuated, and that the main arable land had gone to the younger generation. Clement Rediere, again, is in an exactly similar position. A third, Thomas Elsey, has likewise his cottage and three perches, while around him are other Elseys, probably his children, and also some Longs, between whom and the Elseys Mr Hudson traces a connection by marriage. Of the remaining seven tenants, four hold from an acre and a half to just short of an acre, and three about a quarter of an acre each. And, although this Blackmanstoft is the only holding which the documents have allowed Mr Hudson to map out with absolute certainty, yet all are similarly broken up. Between Domesday and 1292, the Martham tenants had naturally increased in numbers; from 63 to 107. But the subdivision had gone on at an enormously greater rate of increase; there were now 935 holdings, in more than 2000 separate strips. Each tenant, that is, had on an average nearly twenty separate strips, and these might be scattered about anywhere on the manor: in some cases, perhaps, no two were actually contiguous. We possess no contemporary map of any manor until after the Reformation, when the process of consolidation of holdings had already been powerfully at work; yet even those Elizabethan and Jacobean maps always show a bewildering maze of tenements.

The self-sufficiency of the medieval village has often been exaggerated; but it was still very great. The number of adults, even in the larger villages, was no greater than could be contained in two London omnibuses; and of these at least one-tenth might never have strayed outside in their lives. On the busier roads there would be coming and going; but these were comparatively rare; and, outside, the ways or tracks were not designed for continuous travel; they made only for the nearest village, without any more distant horizon in thought. The nearest market might well be too distant to be worth while: *à fortiori* the nearest annual fair. One or two of the most prominent villagers would be called away occasionally on business, to the Hundred or Shire Moot, or as bailiff from manor to manor, or as sidesman to an archidiaconal or ruridecanal visitation. The pedlar would bring a little news: better still, the wandering friar. If the church were to be built or rebuilt, that would bring a whole group of wandering masons, with the ideas of travelled men. But, when every allowance has been made, the average medieval villager was more cut off from the world than can easily be imagined in our own day. There must have been very many who, like the Veronese peasant of Claudian's poem, had spent childhood to old age in one and the same cottage:

> Felix, qui propriis aevum transegit in arvis.
> Ipsa domus puerum quem videt, ipsa senem.

Normally, the village supplied everything: home-grown food, clothes of home-spun and home-woven wool or linen, home-made tools shod with iron at the village smithy, cottages and carts built by the village carpenter or wheelwright. The satiric theme of the rustic staring wildly about him in the town had something of the same actuality in those days as it has in ours.

Domesday Book is a record of unique value for English village life. We have seen already how William of Malmesbury stigmatizes the prevalence of slavery in Anglo-Saxon times; and this is borne out by a Statute of the Council of Eynsham in 1005:[3] "The Wise Men decree that innocent Christians be not sold beyond the bounds of this land, or at least not unto heathen folk; but let men beware diligently lest that soul be lost which Christ bought with His own life." Domesday records a good many slaves, in this strictest sense of the word. The real freemen form a definite minority of the whole population. For the unfree, apart from those actual slaves, there is more than one medieval name: *serf*, *villein*, *bondman*; terms between which it is impossible to distinguish with exactitude, even when they were not interchanged at random. For these unfree there was one general rule, as definite as anything could be in those ages of unwritten custom, so variable at different times and places as to preclude absolutely correct generalizations at any point. That principle was, that the serf possessed nothing of his own; yet he might enjoy his land so long as he rendered three days' work in the week to his lord in lieu of rent. Before those days of the later thirteenth century, when the multiplication of records enables us to get a far clearer view of the details, it is evident that a so-called "day's work" had often been reduced to a half-day of real honest labour. At Great Chesterford, in 1270, each villein owed 714 week-works, each of which occupied a quarter of his day. In addition, at ploughing time he had to plough 16¼ acres. This totals at nearly three days a week. Some of these customary burdens are very complicated; here, for instance, are the requirements on a Glastonbury manor. Between Michaelmas and November 11th the serf had to plough one acre; another half-acre later when called upon. He must harrow every Monday in the year; three times a year he must carry a load for my lord; he must mow three days, and go to the vineyard. All this he must do anyhow; then comes a rather more complicated list of works for which he may compound, if he chooses, by a payment of 3s. 4d. a year. Beyond this also he must pay certain parish contributions in money to the Church.

It is obviously advantageous both for lord and for tenant to simplify such a tangle; therefore, even before 1300, the tide was setting definitely towards commutation of these services for money payments. At Chesterford the week-work was valued at ½d.; this would mean that, if the lord allowed the bargain, the tenant could redeem that whole burden for £1. 9s. 9d. a year, a figure which might represent about £59 nowadays. Moreover, it is obvious that the old complicated customs left far more room for quarrel than modern money transactions. Walter Algerson with his stick, for instance, has disappeared from our English harvest field. He is four whole centuries out of date; whatever friction there may be in a modern lock-out, that is less than under any system of corporal chastisement. But the medieval lord, personally or through his officials, had always the legal right of chastising his serf, provided that neither death nor mutilation ensued. In those two extreme cases the king's court would intervene; otherwise nearly all disputes between the lord and his unfree tenants were heard in the manor court, presided over by the lord's bailiff or steward. It is true that another village official, the reeve, was elected by the peasants, nominally at least, to act as their representative in the court; and, again, the judgments, the "dooms", were pronounced by the peasants themselves, with reference to ancient custom, oral or written. But, as a matter of fact, we constantly find the reeve appointed from above and not from below; and, though the manor court probably achieved about the same proportion of abstract justice as the other courts of those days, yet it must be obvious that the lord was able to load the dice even more than any plutocrat can load them to-day. We shall see this more fully in Chapter xxx. In *Piers Plowman*, there is bitter complaint against the perjured jurors; and, as we shall see later, contemporary medieval descriptions of justice stigmatize, almost without exception, the venality even of the king's and the Pope's judges. It was one of St Thomas More's most definite claims to sanctity that he never took "gifts" on the bench.

The single matter of measures may give us some idea of these medieval difficulties. In my *Medieval Village* I have devoted a chapter to the subject (no. v); and a few examples may suffice here. On one manor of the Abbot of Ramsey, the serf had, among other labours, to do one day's work in the abbot's wood, collecting "one hose of reasonable size, full of nuts well cleaned of their husks". Hosen, by this time, commonly came up well above the knee, and were on their way to that further growth which, with junction at the hips, has created the modern trousers. It must be evident how much compromise was needed in the interpretation of that simple phrase "of reasonable size"; how much tyranny the steward might exercise, or how dishonestly the man might shirk. Again, after reaping, the serf sometimes had permission to carry off as much as he could bear on the handle of his scythe; if in his greed he overloaded it to the breaking-point, then he lost all that he had tried to carry off, and must compound with the abbot as best he could for a fine. Again, a reeve, after his year of office, may take for his perquisite as much of the bottom of a haystack as he can pierce with one stroke of his pitchfork. In Germany, where the manorial customs are more detailed and have survived in greater numbers, such "natural measures" are even more frequent and peculiar. A new settler in the village may take for his fowl-run as far as his wife, sitting on the roof ridge, can throw an egg wrapped in her scarf. One of the most regular dues was one or more "Easter hens". The tenant obviously would not offer his best; what then is to be the test of fitness in face of his lord? The hen is placed in front of a fence or a gate; if, when frightened, she has strength enough to fly or scramble over, the bailiff must accept her; she is fit. A gosling, again, must be accepted if it is mature enough to pluck grass without losing its balance and sitting down ignominiously. The tenant, again, has sometimes the right of carrying as much wood from the forest as he can manage without getting caught. Even in England, and in cases where measures were more definite and more or less protected by royal or provincial or urban proclamations, they often differed considerably. Many lords were obliged to suffer half a dozen different measures on their different manors, each having grown up separately by local custom. The almost incredible variations of measures in France, where these medieval conditions lasted until the Revolution, are notorious.

Another great difficulty was that of accidental interruption to labour. If for any cause a day is lost, is the lord to accept the loss, or shall he cast it upon his tenant? At some of the Ramsey manors, "if any holy-day come upon the day when the serfs should work [for the abbot] it shall not be allowed to them, but they shall work on another day instead". On others, again, the division is equitable. "Of all the holy-days which come on work days, one shall be accounted to the lord abbot, and the next to the workers." If bad weather stops the work, the peasant must do it some other day. If the serf be too ill to leave his house, he may be excused from all work except the ploughing and half the harvest (the other half, no doubt, he must pay for in some way) until a year and a day. After this respite, he must begin to satisfy the lord again; the only alternative, no doubt, would be to give up his holding. Some customs gave him only a fortnight or three weeks. At Barton, under the Abbot of Ramsey, "if he be so ill as to take the Holy Communion, then he shall be quit of all work for the next fortnight following".

Again, where so many payments on either side were rendered in kind, there was far more chance of disagreement than with money. A labourer may have a right at harvest time to three herrings and a loaf; much will here depend upon the age and condition of the herrings. No doubt all these little bickerings would affect our medieval peasant far less than ourselves; we must always bear in mind that, for good or for evil, his mind was in many ways simpler and less sensitive. In Southern Italy, to the present day, bickering over trifles in the market is not only part of the housewife's daily work but often one of her daily interests in life. This, however, has its limits; and therefore, as we have already seen, money compositions had become fairly common even before 1300. The Black Death naturally hastened this evolution; although, as modern researchers have proved, it had far less influence here than students assumed thirty years ago.

There was always a proportion of peasants who had never been unfree; moreover, modern research is tending to show that the free labourer, living as best he could by casual work, was much commoner in our period than historians have often assumed. At Borley, in 1301, little more than half the work on the lord's demesne was done by villein labour; the rest was performed by free labourers, partly paid by the money contributions of villeins who had compounded for their services. The compounding villein was called a "copyholder"; since the conditions of his composition had been written upon a slip of parchment of which he had one copy and the lord another. This copy secured both sides from quarrel on almost all questions of mere rent; but rent was far from exhausting the hold which the lord had over him. Originally all the serf's earnings belonged to his lord; so that, even in the thirteenth century, when the Abbot of Burton quarrelled with those on his manor, we find him boasting against them that in law they possessed "nothing but their own bellies". In practice, that was long out of date, yet it was still the strict legal theory: and that is only one of many similarly significant touches. Again, in England the serf had no right of migration. In France and elsewhere he could often abjure the whole contract and go out into the world, on condition of leaving not only the land but all his possessions behind him. In England, however, he was bound to the land, with the only counterbalancing advantage that the land, little as it might be, was bound in turn to him, so long as he succeeded in fulfilling the customary dues. As he was riveted to the land, so he and his children could be sold with it.

His progeny were not called *familia* in legal documents, but *sequela*—"brood" or "litter". Again, since this little holding was not legally his own, and he was only a life tenant, therefore the lord took a fine to himself at every change of tenancy. At the serf's death (or at that of the copyholder, who lived under many servile disabilities) the lord could claim his best beast under the name of "heriot"; and in many cases the priest took the second best as a "mortuary". If he died with less than three beasts, the best domestic possession could be claimed; a brass pot, for instance, or a cloak. Thus, when the man left only three beasts, the death duty would amount to at least 50 per cent., i.e. the proportion of super-tax paid nowadays as death duty on an estate of £2,000,000. Again, just as the serf was not permitted to leave the land, so neither was his offspring. If a girl married without leave, the father was fined; and in some cases a fine was taken even for marriage by permission. Still more odious and unpopular than the heriot was the "merchet", or fine taken for a girl's marriage off the manor. By such marriages the lord lost the hope of her brood, and must therefore be indemnified in money. Originally such marriages had been treated as null and void in manorial law; the Church, however, defended their legality, and the only question became one of pecuniary compensation. Sometimes, especially on the Continent, the matter was settled by a division of the brood among the two competing manors, without regard for the serf's family feelings. For the bondman's whole position was such as to put economic questions in the foreground; therefore widows, like unmarried girls, were often treated as chattels. They were fined for marrying without the lord's leave; or, again, they might be compelled to marry at his will, when he felt that the holding was being neglected for the lack of a strong labourer's arm. It may be that this did not happen very often; but certainly it was frequent enough everywhere to mark a strong distinction between medieval and modern society. Here are examples from the monastery of Halesowen in 1274. "John of Romsley and Nicholas Serval are given until next court meeting to decide as to the widows offered to them." Three weeks later, "Nicholas Serval is given until next Sunday [we are now at Tuesday] to decide as to the widow offered to him in the Cellarer's presence." [The abbey Cellarer, in this case, represents the abbot and brethren, lords of the manor.] Then (December 11th, 1279), "Thomas Robins of

Oldbury came on summons, and was commanded to take Agatha
Halesowen to wife; he said he would rather be fined; and, because
he could find no guarantees, it was ordered that he should be
distrained. Thomas Bird of Ridgacre and Richard of Ridgacre
were summoned also because they would neither pay the fine nor
take the wife, and were distrained." Then (January 7th, 1280) only
Robins and Richard of Ridgacre are "distrained to take the wives
as ordered in last court". On January 22nd Robins at last paid
his fine, three shillings; Richard was still under distraint. On
February 12th Richard is still holding out under distraint; his
heroic resistance was apparently rewarded, for there is no record
in the rolls of his fine or of his further molestation. On the manor
of Liestal, near Basel, in 1411, it was prescribed that "every year
before Shrove Tuesday, when folk are wont to think of holy
matrimony, the bailiff shall bethink him what boys and girls are
of such age that they may reasonably take wife or husband, so
that he may then allot to each his mate, as husband or wife". That
would doubtless be exceptional at so late a date; but as late as the
tenth century such forced marriages were general among the
German peasantry. In the thirteenth century, when Richard of
Cornwall, King of the Romans, gave a charter to the inhabitants of
Wetzlar, one clause ran: "we grant as a special indulgence that
we will never force any citizen to give his daughter, niece, or
cousin in marriage to any man without the full consent of the man
[or of the lady?]."

In our English court-rolls, the commonest presentments are for
very ordinary and natural things: trespasses of cattle, disrepair of
hedges, shirking of common works, neglect of land or of buildings,
defiling the common springs, or digging clay pits (after the
medieval fashion) in the public highway. Cognizance was very
justly taken of tenants who harboured undesirable lodgers.
"Common thieves of poultry" are presented; and quite a number
of tenants who made a practice of stealing firewood from the
hedges. Others moved boundary-stones, or appropriated such
waifs and strays as a stranded porpoise, a find of wild honey, etc.,
etc. The cucking-stools for scolds were indispensable village
institutions; villages are repeatedly fined, or threatened, for
neglecting to provide them.

Among the peasant's minor disabilities came the compulsory
common mill or common oven. The former especially had begun

as an advantage to the village, since nobody but the lord was rich enough to build a mill and this on the whole was beneficial. Even then, however, there were some who preferred to grind more cheaply at home in their own hand-mills and who resented the lord's monopoly; this was one of the main causes of the bondmen's revolt under St Albans Abbey in the fourteenth century. The common oven had much the same origin. It was comparatively exceptional in England, but regular in France, where it was called *four banal*, community-oven. The bread there baked was naturally inferior to the best that could be made in other ways; hence the French adjective "banal" subsists to our own day in the signification of "commonplace", and has found its way into modern journalism. The lord, again, had the right of keeping a dove-cote, and his pigeons preyed terribly upon the crops; we have a similar complaint from the Bishop of Chichester's tenants against the waste committed by his lordship's rabbits. Lastly, the peasant paid a fine for getting his son promoted to clerical orders or even sending him to a grammar school or university; for there the scholars were tonsured, and enjoyed clerical privileges, and thus, by such promotion, the manor lost a labourer and the landlord must be compensated.

IT may be asked: How did the peasant bear all this? We must not forget that, under the simpler and rougher conditions then prevailing everywhere, men did not feel the contrasts as they would be felt in our own day. Again, the medieval labourer did in some ways grapple more directly with nature, and at his actual work (as apart from his leisure) was less tempted to look upon himself as a mere cogwheel than the modern operative. This, however, is often exaggerated beyond all reason by modern writers; and, even so far as it is true, we must counterbalance it by the consideration that the modern wage-earner, when not at work, has the run of a far wider world, both physically and intellectually, that was closed to his forefathers. The sociologist Durkheim has pointed out that, in spite of many things which still remain to be remedied in the modern worker's lot, he has more originality of mind than the noble savage. If we take a hundred of these latter at random, we shall find great uniformity of taste; what one likes, all like, what one dislikes, all dislike. A hundred operatives, on the other hand, liberated from their eight hours of mechanical drudgery in the workshop, scatter to a multitude of various occupations until the work hours come again. At any rate, we have the plainest evidence that the medieval peasant was not content with his lot, quite apart from the bare fact of those bloody revolts which are recorded in almost all countries. In Germany the earliest written laws, the *Sachsenspiegel* and *Schwabenspiegel*, show a clear yearning for earlier conditions of comparative freedom. In England, chroniclers describe the bitter resentment of men who felt themselves formed in Christ's image and treated like beasts. The great Froissart, for all his aristocratic tastes and his personal dependence upon the rich of this world, is never more eloquent than when he reports the preaching of John Ball, the socialist priest of Chaucer's day. "Ah, ye good people, the matters goeth not well to pass in England, nor shall not do till everything be common, and that there be no villeins nor gentlemen, but that we may be all united together, and that the lords be no greater masters than we be. What have we deserved, or why should we be kept thus in servage? We be all come from one father and

mother, Adam and Eve: whereby can they say or shew that they
be greater lords than we be? saving by that they cause us to win
and labour for that they dispend....Let us go to the king, he is
young, and shew him in what servage we be in, and shew him how
we will have it otherwise, or else we will provide us of some
remedy; and, if we go together, all manner of people that be now
in any bondage will follow us to the intent to be made free; and
when the king seeth us we shall have some remedy either by fairness or otherwise." "Thus", continues Froissart, "John Ball
said on Sundays when the people issued out of the churches in the
villages; wherefore many of the mean people loved him and such
as intended to no goodness said how he said truth."[1] A century
later, when the peasant's lot was already bettered, and he was
probably in greater material comfort than ever again until quite
modern times, we find a bondman under the Abbot of Malmesbury, who had been able to amass a little competence, writing:
"If I might bring [my freedom] about, it would be more joyful to
me than any worldly good."

These things are too much neglected by those who stress the
comparative material comfort of the labourer in the fifteenth
century, when his position was at its best, and who exaggerate the
monotony of the modern workshop as compared with the daily
struggle against earth and the elements. The dead-weight of
modern capitalism must not be ignored; we must not forget that
there is less freedom in the contract between employer and employed than appears on the surface, and that a man free before the
law may yet be a slave to circumstances. But this has been true, to
a great extent, in all ages and must remain true so long as nature
works for inequality. The weaker in mind or in body must always
stand towards the stronger in a position which, in their discontent,
they may feel and describe as slavery. Even where, in the modern
factory, the worker is merely a "hand", at least the overseer bears
no rod, and the "hand's" offspring are no longer just "litter".
Circumstances may still make it impossible for a man to rise from
class to class—though such facilities have multiplied enormously
within the memory of many folk still living—but at least the law
no longer consecrates and reinforces the division of classes, or (it
may almost be said) of castes. In 1388, a royal statute ran: "Item.
It is ordained & assented, That he or she which used to labour at
the Plough and Cart, or other Labour or Service of Husbandry

till they be of the Age of Twelve Years, that from thenceforth
they shall abide at the same Labour, without being put to any
Mystery or Handicraft; and if any Covenant or Bond of Apprentice be from henceforth made to the Contrary, the same shall be
holden for none."[2] The House of Commons even petitioned
against the sending of villeins' sons to school; but that was too
odious to be accepted; the man might still give the boy education,
so long as he could find or pay a teacher, and afford the fine
claimed by his lord.

The extent to which the medieval peasant might look to the
Church for help will be dealt with later on. But here is the place
to confute the too-frequent misstatement that Poor Laws came in
with the Reformation. True, the Dissolution was, for a time, one
cause of a serious economic crisis in the sixteenth century. But
England before that event had long been in trouble with her poor:
and, afterwards, those of our heretical country had no cause to
envy their orthodox brethren on the Continent, until the French
Revolution brought in a new spirit everywhere. We may see this
clearly enough by turning back from William Cobbett to Arthur
Young's *Travels in France*, and onwards again to J. P. Cobbett's
Ride through France (1826), where we see clearly the immense
improvements in the peasant's condition since the Revolution.

The statutes passed by Parliament after the Black Death aimed
at preventing any rise either in wages or in prices of commodities.
That of 1349 not only fixed a maximum wage, but strictly forbade
the migration of labourers in search of a better livelihood. Beggars
strong enough to work were to be imprisoned; and strictly
speaking, it was punishable to give them alms. The statute of 1360
enacted that "labourers and artificers that absent themselves out
of their services, in another township or another county", might
be recovered by their employers as runaways and, at the discretion
of the justices, branded on the forehead. In 1376 the Commons
petitioned that vagrant beggars should be imprisoned till they
promised to return home to work, and that it should be forbidden
to give alms to persons able to labour. It was proclaimed in 1388
that artificers employed in crafts whereof "a man hath no great
need in harvest time" (e.g. the village weaver or carpenter)
"shall be compelled to serve in harvest, to cut, gather, and bring
in corn". Beggars able to work were to be treated like wandering
labourers, and put in the stocks. "But in this act of 1388 we find

the recognition of an additional element in the problem. What was
to be done with 'impotent beggars', beggars really unable to work?
The legislators fell back on the idea of local responsibility: impotent beggars were to remain where they were at the passing of
the act, and if the inhabitants of those places were neither willing
nor able to maintain them they were to be taken to other towns
within the hundred, or to the place of their birth, and there they
were to abide for the rest of their lives. The provision was vaguely
stated, and no machinery was provided for carrying it out; but it
may fairly be looked upon as expressing the hope of the legislators
that the charity of the parish clergy, of the monasteries, the
hospitals, and private persons would provide in their own neighbourhood for the destitute who were really unable to labour....
The law as it had thus grown up in the years following the Black
Death remained unchanged for a century and a half."[3]

We get very significant glimpses of village manners from
records of manor courts such as the Halmote Rolls of Durham. In
disputes between the lord and his tenants we have seen that the
dice were loaded somewhat in the former's favour. But in matters
of village discipline the lord's authority was mainly beneficent.
In 1366 it was enjoined to all the householders that they should
"chastise their servants who had been accustomed to play at
dice", even as the householders themselves did. Football, too,
was strictly forbidden; and this was not altogether undeserved.
The fact is that at those mass-matches between village and village,
in which the whole male population took part, bloodshed and
vendettas were frequent. Extraordinarily interesting, here, is the
attitude of the monastic chronicler of King Henry VI's miracles.
In one case the witness tells "how William Bartram, being struck
in his most sensitive parts by the foot of one who played with him,
sustained long and intolerable pains; but, having seen in a dream
the glorious King Henry, suddenly received the benefit of health".[4]
This was at Caunton in Nottinghamshire, and the monk adds his
own reflections: "The game at which they had met for common
recreation is called by some the foot-ball-game. It is one in which
young men, in country sport, propel a huge ball not by throwing
it into the air but by striking and rolling it along the ground and
that not with their hands but with their feet. A game, I say,
abominable enough, and, in my judgment at least, more common,
undignified, and worthless than any other kind of game, rarely

ending but with some loss, accident, or disadvantage to the
players themselves. What then? The boundaries had been marked
and the game had started; and, when they were striving manfully,
kicking in opposite directions, and our hero had thrown himself
into the midst of the fray, one of his fellows, whose name I know
not, came up against him from in front and kicked him by misadventure, missing his aim at the ball."

Moreover, as the sports might lead to a general affray, so also
might the women's tongues. The Durham roll records: "From
Agnes of Ingleby—for transgression against William Sparrow
and Gillian his wife, calling the said Gillian a harlot, to the
damage of £2 whence they will take at their will 13s. 4d.; as was
found by the jury—by way of penalty and fine 3s. 4d.; reduced
in mercy to 6d. It is ordained by common assent that all the
women of the township control their tongues without any sort of
defamation." Sometimes, again, we find such general proclamations as this: "It is enjoined upon all tenants of the township of
Wolveston that they should procure the arrest of all such as revile
their neighbours, or who draw knives or swords against the peace;
and if these will not be arrested, let hue and cry be raised, and let
every man come to aid." Nor are these complaints mere fancies
in the air. There are frequent items such as: "John Smith, for
drawing a knife to smite the curate, fined 3s. 4d."; "Thomas
Milner, for shooting arrows by night, and Lawrence Hunter,
3s. 4d.", probably a poaching affray. Again we may see how one
single act of violence could lead to a general tragedy. In the
village of Rowsley, in 1271: "on the feast of the exaltation of the
Holy Cross, towards vespertide, Hawise came home from the
alehouse—de cervisia—with her two daughters, and shut her door,
shutting out her eldest daughter, who was followed by her
husband. He, wishing to enter as usual, was unable; and therefore
he entered through a certain window, breaking into the house and
smiting Hawise his wife's mother; whence the hue and cry was
raised and the neighbours ran thither. Walter came and assaulted
Nicholas and Henry Hall with drawn knife, and the said Walter
was wounded, but it is not known by which of the two aforesaid;
but it is thought that Nicholas smote him."

Yet these Halmote Rolls are far from presenting a mere catalogue of crimes and petty offences; and for any reader who loves
village life and regrets the frequent careless and unjustifiable

inroads of modern civilization there is an old-world charm in the very names: John Jentilman, Ralph Jolibody, William Littlefair, John Cherryman, John Merriman, Gilbert Uncouth, Roger Mouse, Roger Litilannotson, John Stoutlook; and most medieval of all, Robert Benedicite. Then, among the ladies, Agnes Redhead, Cicely Wikinsdoughter, Maud Malkynsmaydin, Diote Jaksdoughter, Evote Wheelspinner, Agnes Gibbesdoughter, Alice Robinsdoughter, Emma Androwsmayden, Margaret Merry; and Watsdoughter, so homely to the manor that the steward feels she needs no second name.

It will be noted that the majority of facts quoted in this present chapter are from monastic estates; this is because so many more records have survived for these than for lay manors. In the Dark Ages these ecclesiastical estates were unquestionably better managed than those of the average baron or knight or squire. In the period with which we are mostly concerned, I think the balance was still in favour of the ecclesiastic, though not by very much; the natural kindliness of his profession and the altruistic aims of his institution were often counterbalanced by his conservatism (both personal and collective) and by the fact that the average monk was naturally tempted to put his own well-being as the first charge upon the abbey's revenues. Peter the Venerable [1120] might justly claim that his own model abbey of Cluny contrasted sharply with the outside world in its kindly treatment of the serf. But, a century and a half later, the Dominican Cardinal Hugh of St-Cher stigmatized his fellow Religious as more unfeeling in this respect than the ordinary layman. Again on the very verge of the Reformation, Bishop Longland of Lincoln, who was a stern enemy of the Lollards, wrote a plain-spoken letter to the Abbot of Oseney. In this he wrote of avarice as having attacked "the foundations and columns of the Church, viz. abbots and priors". He continued: "They are intent only upon money and not upon the increase of religious life; and, outside [their monasteries], they flay their tenants worse than the secular clergy or the laity do"—*plus quam seculares aut laici suos firmarios excoriant.*[5] We must not take these indignant words too literally; even in the highest medieval society there was more licence of speech and less cool reflection than we expect from similar classes in our own day. But there are masses of undeniable facts in the background which go far to support these criticisms. To begin with, the Church

never fought against the *principle* of serfdom, any more than she
had done against the principle of slavery under the Roman Empire. Again, Church laws actually forbade the churchman to free
his serf, in all cases where such liberation meant loss of ecclesiastical
funds. We find the Bishops of Ely and Norwich, for instance,
seeking papal dispensation to free even a single serf; and the
Bishop of Exeter, in a deed of manumission, excuses himself on
the plea that the man has served long and well and is now past
work. Otherwise, the "giving away" of this "chattel" would
have been a violation of the oath imposed upon prelates-elect, to
alienate none of the possessions of their Church. Hence, although
the clergy did good work in recommending manumission to lay
lords as an act of charity, yet they themselves liberated very few in
comparison; and, wherever we have detailed evidence, it nearly
always proves that they sold, not gave, this freedom: sold it for
cash, and at market-price. It was on Church estates in England
that serfdom lingered longest; and in France the great Abbey of
St-Claude, for instance, clung to the system until the Revolution
swept it away by force. No passage of Barbour's *Bruce* is so well
known as that which begins:

> Ah, Freedom is a noble thing!
> Who freedom hath, hath great liking.

Yet Barbour himself, as Archdeacon of Aberdeen, was in part
a serf-owner and a dealer in serfs. He and his fellow-canons
farmed out one of their estates; the lease, which is still extant,
runs to the effect that they let the land "with its hawkings,
huntings and fishings; with its serfs and their brood". The conservatism of the Bury monks, in this matter, as recorded by
Jocelin of Brakelond, has often been noted; and, though the serf's
condition did steadily improve on the whole during the later
medieval centuries, yet, even then we sometimes find clerical
reaction and the recrudescence of the earlier brutal disabilities. It
was an Abbot of Burton, as we have seen, who told his serfs that
they possessed nothing but their bellies; and the Cistercians of
Vale Royal are to be found adopting something of the same
attitude. One of the cruellest and bloodiest revolts of our whole
period was the Bauernkrieg, the Peasants' War in Germany. This
was partly brought about by the policy of the great Abbey of
Kempten, which had deliberately set itself to force its serfs back

into the cruel conditions of the Dark Ages. Thus the Peasants' Revolt of 1381 in England was marked by great bitterness against the higher clergy, and the monasteries in particular. On the other hand it is on monastic estates that we sometimes find definitely charitable manor customs, such as permission in cases of childbirth for a man to poach on the abbey fish-ponds or to take extra wood from the forests. In Scotland, again, an enquiry into the estates of the Abbey of Dunfermline [1320] suggests that the monks acted upon the principle of a sort of clan-solidarity with their tenants. I quote the document in full on p. 185 of my *Medieval Village*.

But, when we weigh both sides, we shall easily understand why the medieval peasant would have found it hard to understand the halo of glory which regretful modern writers sometimes see round his head. Chaucer's and Langland's Ploughman are indeed noble figures; but in each case the emphasis is on its exceptional character. Langland paints his opposite more than once.[6] One of his liveliest pictures is where Piers Plowman has set himself to mend society with his gospel of hard work; but the enthusiasm rapidly wanes; and those who were busy in the morning prefer to sit and sing in the afternoon, so that Piers can only warn them how idleness must lead to want. In another passage, the Dreamer sees a typical labourer of the looser sort, careless of real work, and driving through the long day with a light song in his mouth: *Deu vous save, Dam Emme!* At harvest time, idlers flock in who hope "no deed to do but drink and to sleep"; and the ale-house causes great waste of time.

After all, the man is naturally shaped by society's treatment of him; and, quite apart from the purely business questions, the serf was inevitably humiliated by many of the Ghetto-regulations which fenced him in. On the manors of the monks of Durham fines were decreed against those who taunted their fellow-villagers with the despised name of Serf. Everywhere we find similar evidence; and two of the most striking examples may be taken from France. A chronicler writes concerning Queen Blanche, the mother of St Louis: "Since she had pity on the folk who were serfs, she ordained in many places that they should be freed and pay some other due. And this she did partly for the pity she had on girls of that condition, for that men would not take them to marriage, and many of them were deflowered."

Again: "In 1472, a poor servant-girl of Champagne, convicted of child murder, excused her misconduct by pleading that she had not been able to marry after her own heart; her father had refused to unite her to 'the man she would gladly have taken' because he was a serf."

It was natural, therefore, that Wat Tyler and his fellow-rebels in 1381 should demand the complete abolition of serfdom, with leases of all lands at a flat yearly rate of 4d. an acre. The flatness of rent was doubtless unworkable; but the rate, as an average, was certainly reasonable; for in practice we commonly find land let on those terms after the revolt. In spite of its immediate failure, this movement cannot have failed to affect the landlords in the long run. After a few generations we find servile conditions steadily giving place to more modern arrangements. First came the stock-and-land lease; and then, little by little, the ordinary plain money rent of to-day which made room for the growth of a yeoman class. Latimer's description of his father is not so hackneyed but that it may be repeated here. "My father was a yoman, and had no landes of hys owne; onely he had a farme of iij or iiij pound by yeare at the uttermost, and hereupon he tilled so muche as kept halfe a dosson men. He had walke for an hundred sheepe, and my mother milked xxx kyne. He was able, and did finde the king a harnesse [soldier's arms], with him selfe and his horse, while he came to the place that he should receyve the kinges wages. I can remember, that I buckled his harnesse, when he went unto Blacke heath fielde. He kept me to schole, or els I had not bene able to have preached before the kinges majestie now. He maryed my sisters with five pound, or xx nobles apiece, so that he brought them up in godlinesse, and feare of God. He kept hospitality for his poore neighboures. And some almes he gave to the poore, and all thys did he of the sayde farme."[7] That class, Latimer feared, was dying out; yet when we settled down under Elizabeth a whole mass of yeomen-farmers grew up from the unthrifty dispersion of many estates that had fallen into the hands of the robbers of Church property.[8] The old system had been too wasteful to hold its own against the necessities of change. In Flanders, for instance, much of the land had been reclaimed by pioneers who received each a solid block, and had therefore an independence in methods of cultivation which contrasted with our own mechanical uniformity under the scattered strip-system. There, consequently, there was progress; the modern rotation of crops, by alternating roots with corn, was common in Flanders as early as the beginning of the fourteenth century; with us it became general only four hundred years later.

As to the comparison in prosperity between the pre-Reformation and post-Reformation peasant, we have one indication, fairly precise within its limits, from the increase of population. There is pretty general agreement that England and Wales had about 2½ millions at the Conquest and about 5 under Henry VIII; in other words, that the average increase, in those 450 years, was at most about 0·147 per cent. per annum. Thus, taking a village of average size, with 300 souls or 60 families, it would take nearly seven years before this could rise to 301 souls; and a man of 60 could boast no more than that it had grown to 308 in his lifetime. Such was the increase during those 4½ medieval centuries. But when we look onwards from 1536, we find that the then population more than doubled itself in 275 years: it was 10,160,000 at the census of 1811. Thus the post-Reformation rate of increase was, from the first, far more rapid than the earlier, even before we come to the enormous rise in recent standards of living. If, again, we count the whole period, down to the present day, then we find the population multiplied eightfold in the last 300 years, as against only twofold in the preceding 450. When all allowances are made for the predominantly urban character of modern times, and for the fact that longevity is not, by itself, a conclusive proof of prosperity or happiness, these figures must yet retain a significance which demands serious and scientific answer.

Pirenne, whose exceptional learning and moderation are everywhere recognized, writes of the fourteenth century: "The lord had ceased to consider himself the protector of the men on his estate. His position in relation to his tenants was no longer that of a hereditary chieftain whose authority was accepted by reason of its patriarchal character, it had become that of a landlord and recipient of dues.... The large farms established [by the monks] on the demesne lands were a crushing weight upon the villagers." We need no more than this to explain Wat Tyler's revolt in 1381. But why was not that rising more successful, and why was there even less result from similar peasant revolts on the Continent? A great Franciscan mission preacher, Berthold of Regensburg, had already given his explanation of this problem in mid-thirteenth century. In one of his sermons, comparing different social classes with animals, he says:9 "The fish is a very poor and naked beast; it is ever cold, and liveth ever in the water, and is naked and cold and bare of all graces. So also are poor folk; they, too, are help-less....Because the fishes are poor and naked, therefore they devour one another in the water; so also do the poor folk; because they are helpless, therefore they have divers wiles and invent many deceits....None are so false as the country-folk among each other; for these are so untrue that for envy and hatred they can scarce look upon one another. One will drive another's cattle to his harm and damage, and another will buy his fellow-peasant out of his farm; all from untruth." Then, as now, side by side with the endless little charities that we may find in the dealings of poor with poor, we find no less multitude of petty jealousies and thwartings. If the mills of God grind slowly here, it is because the poor can become politically and socially effective only in so far as they have learned things which cannot be got except through a certain reasonable modicum of physical well-being distributed among the whole population, with freedom for social and political experi-ments. Here is a vicious circle which meets us constantly in human life; and it would be strange if any single and simple device could get us out of it. Yet here, as in so many other fields, the naked facts of social history should go far to render us, if not optimists, at any rate meliorists. For, when we have faced the worst that can be truly said against our modern world, and made all due allowance for the rhetoric of two great preachers in far-off times, we may congratulate ourselves that the modern villager can no longer be described in the words which St Bernardino of Siena applied to the fifteenth-century peasant in Tuscany, one of the most civilized districts of Europe, and nearest to the fountain-head at Rome.

Yet nobody will doubt that, in all lands, there were many village heroes, and even some village saints, though Berthold of Regensburg feels bound to remark how few were the villagers who had ever been canonized by his Church. Rural life has never lent itself to glaring colours; the true glory of our countryside has always been its meadow-green and its ripening corn and the deep shade of its woods; the thatched roof and the quiet stream; all in harmony with William Morris's picture of the harvesters' meal in the noonday shade; bread and cheese and strong onions, with a jug of corny ale. Within that framework, we may well look back upon the old English village with full appreciation of Virgil's

Felices nimium, sua si bona norint. The bare facts of our forefathers' village life lend themselves neither to easy optimism nor to cheap pessimism.

It is difficult to express identical thoughts in two sets of words; and I can only sum up here in a briefer repetition of what I wrote ten years ago in my *Medieval Village* (p. 392).

The medieval peasant was, essentially, the kind of man who still meets us by the thousand in outlying districts of the Continent, and by handfuls even in Great Britain. He lacked some very important things which his descendants now enjoy even in the remotest corners of Europe; yet, in the main, his existence was what may still be found here and there. Looking closely at him and his village, we see the rough life of labouring folk hardened by their constant fight against land and weather; we see task-masters whose interests necessarily conflicted with the needs of those elementary breadwinners; yet who, to their credit be it said, did not always enforce every advantage that the strict law might have given them. Our general impression will be that of a society very engaging in its old-world simplicity, but with much to learn before it can struggle through into modern civilization. The old-world villagers show us mankind in the making; human nature in its elementary aspects. If we try to reckon up the things which they most truly enjoyed, we shall find that all, or nearly all, are common to every country and age. That the life of the medieval village had a true dignity at its best, and even a true glory in the highest sense of that word, no man can doubt who reads Chaucer's brief description of the Ploughman. The land is eternally healthy, and we suffer when we feel the least divorce or estrangement from it. But, so long as urban life and village life exist, the peasant will always be a child compared with the city dweller. We should find even Chaucer's Ploughman a child in his serene unconscious conservatism and dead-weight of inattention, concentrated on his own things in his own little corner, while we vainly dangle a crown of more complicated civilization over his head—yet childlike, again, in his divine receptivity at sudden moments, and in his resolve to take the kingdom of glory by force. We should find in him the child's April moods of sunshine and shower; a nature sometimes hidebound and selfish and narrow to the last degree, and sometimes generously impulsive; with the child's pathetic trust at one moment, and unreasonable distrust at another; and, above all, with a child's fear of the dark.

VIII. VILLAGE DANCE AND SONG

THE depopulation emphasized in my preceding chapter was, of course, often due to infectious diseases; but war and famine were possibly even more operative on the whole, when we reckon not only national conflicts, but civil war between province and province, town and town, village and village. Famine was not only a frequent concomitant of plague, but sometimes, apparently, its actual begetter by reducing the frame to defenceless exhaustion: "*Fames* and *mortalitas*, for the medieval annalist, are almost inseparable conceptions."[1] And, happy as the more well-to-do medieval peasant might be in the possession of his own little holding, the majority lived always on the edge of an abyss into which a single bad harvest might, and a succession must, precipitate them. Even in England, where frosts are never so terrible as on the Continent, the primitive plough never scratched deep enough to protect the grain from any very exceptional winter. Nothing in our own annals equals the Belgian winters recorded in the twelfth century, twelve years of bad weather in one case and thirteen in another: but there was a terrible succession of crop failures with us in the early fourteenth century. The Liége chronicler notes minutely the weather from 1195 to 1198: it is a heart-rending story. More than once, at different times, corn went up to ten times its normal price. In England, apart from the frequent formal records of famine in the annals, we sometimes get sidelights which are still more significant. The barons complained to Henry III in 1258 "that many men come from divers parts of the realm by reason of times of famine; and, passing through divers provinces, they die of hunger and starvation", and then the coroners treat this as a case of murder, in order to get a fine from the township because it has not raised the hue and cry. Here, in famine, was something worse than any pestilence; for this meant death by slow torture: stark foodlessness from day to day, until death came as a friend. "Men ate all kinds of herbs, and even the bark of trees", says one chronicler; and another: "they devoured meadow-grass uncooked, like oxen." A twelfth-century Bishop of Trier, beset on his journey by a famishing crowd, would have given them money: but that was useless to them then and there; they demanded his fat palfrey, which they tore in pieces and devoured under his eyes. Occasionally the chroniclers even tell of cannibalism: the folk-story of Hansel and Gretel is founded, if not on facts, certainly on possibilities. In those days of difficult communication, there was hope of finding a little more in some other province; here, therefore, we find the story of Joseph and his brethren: every famine drove thousands of peasants away from their land, while others were glad to give it up and work for a bare subsistence as hinds. The great Bavarian Abbey of Benediktbeuren, in the famine of 1005, records some 150 tenants who thus deserted in the hope of bettering themselves. And, side by side with the charity, sometimes heroic, shown by clergy and laity, we find contrary records of men who usuriously exploited the misery of their weaker brethren. "The chronicler of the Abbey of Andres records, with a certain naïve pride, how Abbot Iterius, during his whole reign in the great famine-years at the turn of the twelfth century, never sold a bushel of corn for less than 10 *solidi*, and often much higher, even to 40: and thus [in his own words] the penury of his neighbours brought him abundance"—*sicque vicinorum penuria ei habundantiam ministravit.*

All these things may truly be said of the medieval peasant; as truly as Ruskin presses upon us similar reflections, and darker still, in his chapter on *The Mountain Gloom* (*Modern Painters*, vol. IV, ch. XIX). But those peasants of the Valais, of whom Ruskin writes, suffered more than the average share of work and anxiety; and we miss the true balance if we leave the medieval serf at this point. We have had our temperate English skies and our fertile plains and undulating uplands ever since the beginning of historical time; and, though man's heart is, strictly speaking, insatiable, yet a very little will often satisfy him:

> I said it in the meadow-path,
>   I said it on the mountain stairs—
> The best things any mortal hath
>   Are those which every mortal shares.

"Hope springs eternal in the human breast"; and, while the best of these men had the steady confidence, even the majority of them had some flickering hope, of a happy world beyond the grave. The preacher, as we shall presently see, often did his best to inculcate what is now called puritanism, and to warn them of the predominant chances of eternal torment; yet it was with the peasant as with Dr Johnson and his old friend Edwards. Though the parishioner, at moments, might "try to be a philosopher", yet "I don't know how, cheerfulness was always breaking in".

For we must bear in mind the elasticity of human nature, as displayed for instance, within living memory, among the peasants of unreformed Tsarist Russia. Nature, the homely nurse, does all she can; she has her own ways of comforting those who hang directly at her bosom. We need not doubt that medieval famine, like plague, was borne with a stoicism unfamiliar to us of this happier century. With many folk, this was doubtless a sort of fatalism; not merely that reasoned and philosophic determinism against which orthodox medieval writers and preachers had to contend as with one of their greatest spiritual enemies, but the half-dumb fatalism of a suffering animal. The land labourer is so nearly the same in all ages that it may be allowable to quote here from the authentic experience of a modern Norfolk parson. "One of [the new vicar's] earliest pastoral visits was to a small farmer who had lost his wife and been left desolate and alone. The good vicar spoke such comfort as he could, and more than once insisted on the obvious truth that the ordering of 'Divine Providence' must not be murmured at, and that 'Providence' must needs be submitted to with resignation. The sorrowing farmer listened patiently and silently for a few minutes. At last he could refrain no longer, but opened his mouth and spoke, saying 'That's right enef, that es! There ain't no use a gainsayin on it; but somehow that there *Old Providence* hev been agin me all along, he hev! Whoi! last year he mos' spailt my taters, and the year afore that he kinder did for my tunnips, and now he's been and got hold o' my missus! But', he added with a burst of heroic faith and devout assurance, 'I reckon there's *One abev* as'll put a stopper on ha if 'a go too fur!'" Though the food and the general household conditions of the lower peasantry and artisans were such as would arouse strong and just protest from the modern unemployed, and though we find constant signs of dissatisfaction, yet it may well be doubted whether the benumbed souls of those days felt the injustice so clearly and so bitterly. It was only on rare occasions that the pent-up fury burst fully forth. That, again, is another characteristic of those centuries which, as compared with ours, were marked by their own violent contrasts.

Thus the poor man who was not yet far advanced upon the road of "large and liberal discontent", and who had so little of our own social and religious and political freedom, created minor liberties for himself in those corners where Church and State either left him alone or were unable completely to control him. Here again comes in the parallel with Russia; and, for the matter of that, with the old North American slave-states. When time and opportunity came for merriment, it was loud and boisterous; medieval disciplinarians are never tired of preaching against the paradox that Sundays and holy-days were marked by more drunkenness and crime than all the rest of the week. The most orthodox theologians had begun to plead for restriction, or even abolition, of some of those holy-days long before Henry VIII's parliament put such suggestions into actual practice. But, little as this orthodox puritanism, inherited from the earliest ages of the Church, allowed for mirth and dance and song, we may be glad that the people took it for themselves and let the preacher go his own way. To that extent—and to very little more—we may claim for our country that advantage which, in the form of "Merrie England", has become a cliché dear to the journalist, though historical students appeal in vain for any but the rarest use of the phrase in pre-Reformation times. This chapter of Dance and Song is so pertinent to the whole true picture of medieval peasant and artisan life, that it deserves a few more pages here. Chaucer's contemporaries, as compared with us their more sophisticated descendants, had much of that picturesqueness which the wild animal in wood or field shows as compared with his cousin in the farmyard.

We shall come later on in the poem of *Piers Plowman* to a great literary work which had a beggar for its father; of the medieval ballad we may almost say that it knew not its own father or mother. We must not accept in its literal exaggeration Jacob Grimm's epigram "The Folk is the Poet" [*das Volk dichtet*]. He himself did not so intend it; but the majority of modern scholars do tend, on the whole, in that particular direction. G. L. Kittredge, in his essay on "The Ballad", points out how in the Faroë Islands, a few generations ago, the whole crowd would stand round an unlucky fisherman and satirize him in verse, each extemporizing a stanza in turn.[1] The same kind of thing was done also in the Russian cigarette-factories; and I myself, in the Wales of fifty years ago, have driven twenty miles home from a football match in a drag full of men who chanted nearly all the way at the traditional satirical song of "Crawshay Bailey", with its perpetually recurring refrain, and stanzas supplied by each in turn, mainly from memory but sometimes topical and extempore. There we have one of the strands in the complex of causes which produced the medieval ballad. The very name betrays its intimate connection with dance, for which the Italian verb was, and still is, *ballare*, surviving with us in *ballet* and *ball*. Another name for this in Middle English was *carole*. It was a round dance, the performers joining hand to hand in a ring. The thirteenth-century poem on St Hugh of Lincoln uses that word *carole* to describe the polished marble columns which still may be seen grouped round the great stone pillars of the cathedral; "those slender columns which stand round the great piers, even as a bevy of maidens stand marshalled for a dance."[2]

The medieval dance was in its origin pre-historic and therefore pagan. Among churchmen it met with almost universal reprobation. Scholastic philosophers, like Albert the Great and St Thomas Aquinas, could not rule it out altogether, since they found it mentioned without reprobation in Scripture, as in the cases of Miriam and Deborah and David; they therefore allow the dance on very exceptional occasions, such as one's country's victory over the enemy, or the homecoming of a friend from a distant land or even sometimes at weddings. St Thomas, again, points out that such bodily exercises were in themselves, quite apart from moral considerations, healthy. Moreover, one popular writer at least, the author of *Dives and Pauper*, who was probably a Franciscan of about Chaucer's time, takes the same comparatively liberal view. Men (he says) may lawfully make mirth on holy-days, "God forbid else". True, St Augustine seems definitely to forbid the dance; but that was "when Christian people was much mingled with heathen people". Dances (except where they lead to fleshly transgressions and to idleness "and to other vices, as it is right likely they do now in our days") are lawful even on holy-days.[3] This, however, is very exceptional liberalism. Among the rest of the numerous moralists and preachers who touch upon the subject, not only is the village dance reprobated in language as strong as that of any later puritan, but one French preacher of about 1500, Pepin, actually stigmatizes the Sunday dance as a

mortal sin. For such intolerance as this there was a certain amount
of justification in fact. The medieval dance was not only pre-
Christian in origin but often un-Christian in practice. Preachers
reminded their people that the first biblical account of it comes in
the story of the Golden Calf; and how, when Aaron had made
that idol in the absence of Moses, "the people sat down to eat and
to drink, and rose up to play". Not only history but fact often

Mummers and Minstrels.

compelled the priest to regard this riotous and unbridled sport
much as the modern missionary regards many native African
customs. Canon Law explicitly forbade the participation of any
cleric under any excuse soever; yet the priest himself would sometimes "go fanti" with his parishioners.[4] Cardinal Jacques de
Vitry [1210] expresses the general clerical disapproval most
picturesquely. There was always one leader of the dance (generally
a woman, and the same in each village) who marked the time with
a little bell. Vitry writes, in one of his anecdotes for preachers:
"When a man wishes not to lose his cow, he binds a bell to her
neck, that he may hear the sound and be sure that she is still there.

Even as the cow that leadeth the rest hath a bell to her neck, so may the woman who leadeth the dance be said to have the devil's bell on hers. For the Devil, hearing the sound, is easy in his mind and saith 'I have not lost my cow; [she is safely mine]'."[5] His younger contemporary Étienne de Bourbon tells us how the country folk often danced on the eves of saints' days in the churchyards or even in the churches, as their forefathers had done with their heathen temples. In one French village "certain young folk were wont to come and ride upon a wooden horse and to dance masked and disguised in the church and through the churchyard on the eve of the dedication-day". A missionary persuaded the majority to desist; but one youth harnessed himself, with curses upon all who should obey this crabbed shaveling. "When, therefore, the aforesaid youth pranced upon his wooden horse into the church, while the congregation were keeping their vigils in peace and prayer, then on the very threshold of the sanctuary, a fire caught him by the feet and utterly consumed him, horse and man...from whose body rose so fierce a flame that it seemed to issue forth from the windows of the spire."[6] But the stock example is quoted first from Colbigk in a German chronicle under the year 1013, and thence by the English chronicler William of Malmesbury and by the moralist Robert of Bourne. It tells how, "Upon a Christmas night, Twelvë fools a carole dight". Their refrain was in the shape of an incitement to renew the dance whenever it flagged: "Why standë we, why go we not?" He thus proceeds:

> The priestë's daughter they tempted out
> With them to carole the church about...
> The priest put on his robes for Mass
> They kept their carolling nevertheless...
> From the altar down he bent
> And to the churchë porch he went
> And said "on God's half I forbid
> That ye no longer do such deed,
> But come ye in in fair mannere
> Godes service for to hear."
> For all his bidding left they not,
> But dancëd forth, even as they thought.
> The priest therefore was sore agrieved,
> He prayed God, that he on believed,...
> That they might ever right so wend,
> Until that time twelve moneth end.

The curse was effective; their hands became inseparably inter-

locked. The priest's son rushed forward to bear his sister away:
her arm broke off in his hands like a dry bough.

> Then he unto his father went
> And broughte him a sorry present...
> "Look, father," he said, "and have it here
> The armë of thy daughter dear...
> Fell was thy curse, and over-soon
> Thou askedst vengeance; thou hast thy boon."
> These folk that went so carolland
> All that yearë, hand in hand...
> Night nor day, they wist of none,
> When it was come, when it was gone;
> Frost nor snow, hailë nor rain
> Of cold nor heat felt they no pain...
> Thunder nor lightning had none effect,
> So did God's mercy them protect,
> But ever sang they the song they wrought
> "Why standë we, why go we not?..."
> Their time of grace came, by God's might
> At the year's end, on Yulë night.
> That same hour that the priest them banned
> In that same hour God loosed their hand,
> And, in the twinkling of an eye
> Into the churchë gan they fly,
> And on the pavement fell they down,
> As they were dead or fallen in swoon.

For such dances, then, verses were composed, and nearly always
in lines of four beats, convenient to mark the time. There was
commonly, as in this Colbigk story, a refrain which had the
advantage of lengthening the poem and the dance. As to the
authorship of these poems, no doubt in the main they had as
personal a composer as any other; but there are several senses in
which we must modify this in accordance with Grimm's dictum
"the people poetizes". In one sense the community may be said
to have found the subject; for in most cases this is either some
well-known legend, or a notorious local tragedy or comedy, such
as *The Two Sisters of Binnorie*. Again, the people would not only
take up the refrain but sometimes dictate some traditional burden.
Many phrases, again, or even whole verses were common property;
traditional literary clichés. Moreover, all the earliest ballads were
circulated orally. The earliest English that has survived in writing
is of the thirteenth century: then come a few in the middle of the
fifteenth, but, when we have counted all, only eleven are existent

in MSS. older than the seventeenth. Therefore not only did the author compose under communal influence, but he committed it to the communal keeping; and many parallel versions survive to show how the people remodelled it, whether consciously or unconsciously, for better or for worse. Lastly, these ballads show us, even though we had no other indication, the strong survival of pre-Christian traditions among the people. There are, it is true, a few ballads of definite Christian religious character; the finest of these is "The Falcon hath stolen my Make away". But, in most of them, the supernatural is pure magic and witchcraft, with fairies and elves and metamorphoses into wild beasts. If, again, heaven is mentioned, the tone is mainly pagan. The Wife of Usher's Well is able to conjure her sons back again by laying a curse on the winds and the sea until their return. When they have come for that brief moment to comfort her, they must needs return before the dawn:

> The cock doth crow, the day doth daw,
> The channerin' worm doth chide;
> Gin we be miss'd out o' our place,
> A sair pain we maun bide.

Again, in the paradise from which they have come, there grows the birk, the familiar tree of their own native valley, the earliest to come out in real splendour of spring green and therefore a tree mystical in its significance. Lastly, even to paradise they cannot return without regrets for the old home comforts:

> Fare ye weel, my mother dear!
> Fareweel to barn and byre!
> And fare ye weel, the bonny lass
> That kindles my mother's fire!

In "Clerk Saunders", again, the murdered man comes from heaven to see his love and regrets the things of earth; even celestial psalmody is envisaged as his task to which he must return:

> O cocks are crowing on merry middlerd,
> I wot the wild fowl boded day,
> The psalms of heaven will be sung
> And ere now I'll be missed away.

A very large proportion of the best ballads tell of love and death together; yet there the most impressive theme is that of union not in heaven, but in the grave. In the story of Tristram and Yseult, it is a vine and a rose that sprout in token of that past love; so, also, in "The Douglas Tragedy":

> Lord William was buried in Mary's Kirk,
> Lady Margaret in Mary's quire,
> And out of her grave grew a bonny red rose,
> And out of the knight's a briar.

Pre-Christian also are these survivals of simple uncivilized conceptions, as of gold and silver and ivory and silk used for the commonest objects; for instance the "web of silken cloth" with which the leak is to be staunched in *Sir Patrick Spens*. Many, again, make the birds and beasts talk, according to the rooted belief among savages. And, finally, their extreme antiquity is suggested by their remarkably wide distribution. W. P. Ker instances the theme of the boy playing roughly at ball and told in taunt to inquire how his father was killed; a theme which appears as wide apart as Scandinavia, Arabia and New Guinea.

Thus far, then, we may maintain that "das Volk dichtet". We may truly call these "folk-songs", so long as we bear in mind that "folk" means the whole population, not only the masses. As the Scottish Bishop Lesley wrote in the late sixteenth century: "Our border men delight in their own music and in the songs that they themselves compose concerning the deeds of their ancestors or their cunning tricks in border frays." The knight would sometimes sing of his own deeds; the lady, some plaintive ballad of "old forgotten far-off things and battles long ago"; the peasant of his own love and labour!

> O I'm wat, wat,
> Aye wat and wearie!
> Fain would I get up and rin
> If I could be with my dearie.

Upon which verse a Scottish critic has noted the expressive force of the native dialect: *wat* is as much wetter than *wet* as a Scotch mist is wetter than the English one.

The priest indeed might proclaim not only his personal prohibition but the curse of the Church; we have abundant evidence that he warned them beforehand in his sermons, and those stories tell us how naturally he might come out to defend his own church and yard. But, despite such tales of heavenly vengeance, little impression was made; there might be a few minutes' pause and hesitation, but tradition and impulse were too strong: one dancer, at least, would strike up the well-known refrain "Why standë we, why go we not?" and all protests would be swept away:

> On with the dance; let joy be unconfined!
> No rest till morn, when youth and pleasure meet
> To chase the glowing hours with flying feet.

Ballads, then, were composed by all sorts, even by professional minstrels or by wandering scholars of the Langland type. Alphonse Daudet tells us how his first great editor worked with complete success upon the theory that every man had *dans le ventre* one good article for his paper. We are told that there is enough latent force in a bronze penny to carry a liner to New York and back, if only it can be rightly liberated; and there is more latent poetry in a stockbroker or a soap-boiler than all that is expressed in Shakespeare's plays. Ballads were composed by all sorts, for all sorts; and that is why the best of them live so wonderfully to-day. This was a People's Literature, answering to the People's Art of the Middle Ages; limited, but never falling below a certain standard because the ballads had been sifted through the sieve of memory, generation after generation, before they came down to us. "Oral transmission and its concomitants are not the accidents of the ballad, they are essential to it.... Without them the ballad would not be the ballad."[7] Many of the best are those which have been most recently discovered and printed. That is, such as have passed through the longest selective trial; such as had enough life in them to survive centuries of transmission from mouth to mouth. They illustrate, in short, Goethe's dictum that the unsophisticated man is more the master of direct, effective expression in a few words than he who has received a regular literary education.

IX. NATURE AND SUPERSTITION

NEARLY all superstitions—perhaps we may briefly say, all —are different forms of nature worship. When the Hebrew teacher warned his people not to look up at the stars and worship them he was dealing with a strong temptation of his age; for indeed, of all inanimate creatures, none could be more worthy of man's worship, and none, in fact, did attract it more. Let us look upon Old England now from this point of view—man and nature. The surface of the country, as we have seen, was far wilder than it is now. There was far more forest and fen; and, although a great deal had been done by pioneers in the past, plenty of clearing still remained to be done. We see this, for instance, in some of the enormous parishes in the North or in the Fenland. On the Yorkshire moors, at first, there were villages only at the very edge. Then, as in the cases of Blackburn and Whalley, the hinterland of moor was gradually exploited, and the priest found himself parson no longer of a handful of parishioners, but of several hamlets also, with their attendant chapels. So again at Doddington, on the edge of the Cambridgeshire Fens. That parish, by gradual draining, became so large and so rich that within the last century the tithes of the rectory were worth £10,000 a year. Everywhere, then, the population was thinly scattered in the Middle Ages, and yet in one way less scattered than it is now. There were next to no outlying farms. Nearly all the habitations were grouped in villages, as we see now on the Rhine plain or in many parts of Normandy and Northern France. The village and the town, again, were each mostly self-supporting. One of the best descriptions of this is to be found in Ruskin's *Praeterita*, where he writes on Abbeville as he first remembered it (ch. IX).

There is a great social lesson in that picture from *Punch* of the London suburban boy who was boarded out for a fortnight in the country, and reported well of it when he came home, with one exception. "Here, we get our milk from clean brass cans; and there they get it from a nasty dirty cow." Four-fifths, at least, of the medieval population had grown their food in their own fields; had spun and woven wool from their own sheep or linen from their toft; and very often it was they themselves who made it into

clothes. Nature, therefore, was their immediate friend and benefactor. She fulfilled Wordsworth's lines:

> The homely Nurse doth all she can
> To make her Foster-child, her Inmate man,
> Forget the glories he hath known,
> And that imperial palace whence he came.

Nature, then, was man's immediate friend; but she was his enemy
also; his God, but his Devil. The wild and picturesque is romantic
to us, but it was repugnant to the average man of the Middle Ages.
Even nowadays a farmer in North Wales, who goes down to
Shrewsbury or Oswestry Fair for the first time, will come back and
say that England is a beautiful land, "as flat as a penny". In Dante
himself we find little enjoyment of mountain or forest as such; nor
again in sunset or moonlight. Chaucer's Dorigen walks by the
sea as a natural place for gentle exercise; but the rocks shock her
with a wifely shudder of danger. Again, in the Man of Law's Tale,
Ruskin notes his indifference to the poetry of the ocean. Constance
voyages for five years long: "yet all this while Chaucer does not
let fall a single word descriptive of the sea, or express any emotion
whatever about it or about the ship.... Neither he nor his
audience appear to be capable of receiving any sensation, but one
of simple aversion, from waves, ships, or sands." When St Bernard
said that he himself had learned most from the trees, this was not
in Wordsworth's sense:

> The clouds that gather round the setting sun
> Do take a sober colouring from an eye
> That hath kept watch o'er man's mortality.

St Bernard spoke only of the solitude, the remoteness from human
interference. He was capable, another time, of journeying a whole
day long beside the Lake of Geneva, without even realizing its
existence. As in literature, so in art: there is no medieval painting
in which landscape is treated for its own sake. The exhibition at
Burlington House in 1936 showed us Chinese artists of Chaucer's
age dealing as earnestly and successfully with landscape art, in the
modern sense, as no Englishman did until the eighteenth century.
In the medieval miniature, and even as late as Giotto, nature comes
in only as a background to man; and, we may almost say, studiously
and deliberately unnatural even then: carefully bent to something
different from its direct purpose. Professor Herford has noted

truly the extent to which Chaucer's landscapes are conventional, in spite of that deep sensibility for such simple everyday things as come out in his Nun's Priest's Tale. "Everyone now recognizes that we owe his multitude of May mornings and daisied lawns to no such spontaneous, untaught delight in these things as gave us Wordsworth's celandines or daffodils. But we need not ignore his delight in Nature because it is enriched and directed by his evident delight in the far-off reflection of Nature caught in the verse of Lorris or Boccaccio.... There is in any case no doubt of Chaucer's general preference, as an artist, for the trim and ordered landscape. But we should say that in this, as in other respects, the genial freedom of Nature won a securer hold upon his sympathies as his mind and taste matured; and that the man who sent forth his pilgrims in admirable disarray to tell their tales, not in symmetrical decades, or in a closed garden, as in the *Decameron*, but as 'aventure, or cas', or the whim of Harry Bailey might decree, along the Kentish highway, was also by this time no longer quite the poet who had described that severely uniform 'grove' of the *Boke of the Duchesse*, where 'every tree stood by hymselve, Fro other wel ten foot or twelve'. The Athenian forest where Theseus breaks in upon Palamon and Arcite is no such magnified quincunx as this. But, when all is said, it is clear that Chaucer was no fanatical lover of the green wood, like the singers of Robin Hood and of Gawain."[1] For that poem of *Sir Gawayne and the Green Knight*, with its companion *Pearl*, are in this respect exceptional in English literature. The Scottish poets do indeed show something approaching to the modern sense of the picturesqueness of wild country or bad weather, but we find this very seldom elsewhere in the Middle Ages. It is true that the monks chose "romantic" sites; but that was because part of their business was to fight with the fiend. Forest and wilderness were haunted by devils: and the monks had come to molest their ancient solitary reign. At Novalese, under Mont Cenis, the monastic chronicler tells us how he himself had often seen devils in the woods, in the form of serpents or toads. Again, when St Guthlac came to Croyland in the Fens, he constantly heard devils booming like bitterns in the dark, as well he might. Moreover, he heard them sometimes speaking in the Celtic tongue, which he himself had known when he lived in the West. Devils rode in the storm that unroofed the monks' cloister, or in the fire that fell from heaven upon their steeple and burned the church. When St Edmund Rich was a young man he saw at sunset a flight of black crows: these he recognized at once as a swarm of devils come to fetch the soul of a local usurer at Abingdon; and sure enough, when he came to Abingdon, the man was dead. In order to look upon nature as purely beneficent we need to be town-dwellers, taking our milk from brass milk-cans; or, by the latest refinement, from bottles.

This dualism, this constant fight between God and the Devil, was frequently manifested in the grossest forms. In the ninth century St Agobard, Archbishop of Lyons, wrote: "The wretched world lies now under the tyranny of foolishness: things are believed by Christians of such absurdity as no one ever could aforetime induce the heathen to believe, who knew not the Creator of all." He had to contend against weather-wizards who took toll of the peasants' credulity: "We have seen and heard many who are overwhelmed by such madness, carried away by such folly, that they believe and assert that there is a certain region called Magonia [the Magic Land], whence ships come in the clouds: the which bear away the fruits of the earth, felled by hail and destroyed by storms, to that same country; and these sailors of the air, forsooth, give rewards to the weather-wizards, and receive in return the crops or other fruits. Certain folk have we seen, blinded by so dark a folly, who brought into an assembly of men four persons, three men and a woman, as having fallen from the said ships; whom they held in bonds for certain days and then presented before an assembled body of men, in our presence, as aforesaid, in order that they should be stoned. Howbeit the truth prevailed, after much reasoning, and they who brought them forward were confounded."[2] Elsewhere he complains of the image worship which, under official encouragement, was flourishing among these newly converted pagan tribes. "Perchance a man will say that he does not imagine anything divine inherent in the image which he worships [adorat], but that he pays it such veneration only in honour of him whose image it is. Such a man can easily be answered; for, if the image which he worships is not God, it ought by no means to be venerated, as though it were for the honour of the saints, who are far from arrogating to themselves divine honours. . . . If those who had left the worship [cultum] of devils were bidden to venerate the images of saints, methinks they would seem to themselves not so much to have quitted their idols

as to have changed the outward form thereof." So also his contemporary Claudius, Bishop of Turin: many folk "worship
images of saints after the fashion of devils...they have not left
idols, but changed their names. For if thou dost draw or paint on
the wall the images of Peter and Paul, of Jove and Saturn or
Mercury, the former are no more truly apostles than the latter are
gods; again, neither the former nor the latter are men; and thus it
is a [mere] change of name [ac per hoc nomen mutatur]. Yet, in
both cases, then and now, the error itself remains the same." He
continues in almost the same words as St Agobard. Dr R. L.
Poole comments upon both: "It was an age of materialism; and
there was no possibility that the images should remain in churches
without the people worshipping them, or that if they worshipped
them they would understand the nice distinction between this
worship and that of God laid down by the second Nicene Council."3 The cult of images and relics, it may almost be said, was
implicit in the religious spirit of the Middle Ages: it often comes
out strongest in the light of religious revivals. The Cluniac
chronicler Glaber tells us much of struggles for reform in his own
age, and of the "white robe of churches", and of the heresies
which grew with this growing movement of Catholic revival, and
therefore of the beginnings of bloody repression on a great scale:
but he complains also of the false relics and false saints which were
coming to veneration in those times. He gives concrete examples,
and adds: "We, however, have recorded these things in order that
men may beware of the manifold errors of demons or of men
which abound everywhere in the world; more especially in the
matter of springs or of trees incautiously venerated by sick folk."4
Three centuries later, the chronicler Gervase of Tilbury [ch. XIII]
tells of folk who came out of Mass one morning and saw an anchor
let down from such a cloud-ship and grappled to a tomb. They
heard the cries of the embarrassed cloud-sailors in the fog, until
one came down the rope hand by hand and released the anchor.
"When, however, he had torn the anchor from the tomb, he was
caught by those that stood around, in whose arms he gave up the
ghost, stifled by the breath of our gross air even as a shipwrecked
mariner is stifled in the sea. Moreover his fellows above, judging
him to be wrecked, after an hour's delay, cut the cable, left their
anchor, and sailed away." Again he tells us: "It befel upon a time
that a native of Bristol sailed to Ireland, leaving his wife and

children at home. Then, after a long sea-voyage, as he sailed on a far-off ocean, he chanced to sit banqueting with the mariners about the hour of tierce; and, after eating, as he washed his knife over the ship's side, it slipped suddenly from his hands. At that same hour, at Bristol, the knife fell in through that same citizen's roof-window (which men in the English tongue call *dormer*) and stuck in the table that was set before his wife. The woman, marvelling at so strange a thing, was dumb-founded; and, laying aside this well-known knife, she learned long afterwards, on her husband's return, that his misfortune had befallen on the very day whereon she had found it. Who, then, will now doubt, after the publication of this testimony, that a sea lieth over this earth of ours, whether in the air or above the air?"

This dualism, again, was encouraged by very many Roman Catholic ceremonies. The priest came out and rang church bells to drive off an approaching storm, or sprinkled holy water to exorcize it. Holy water was in constant use in church and in the house. One of the earliest prayers in the Mass is one for exorcism of the house, borrowed from a Frankish liturgy. In this matter, one of the most curious chapters is that of the Excommunication of Animals, which I treat more fully in *The Medieval Village*. Concrete instances of this are numerous; and the practice was formally defended in 1531 by Chassenée, a celebrated legist, in his book *De Excommunicatione Animalium Insectorum*. All beasts (he argues) are subject to man (Genesis i. 26); therefore all are subject to Church Law. We know (he continues) that such excommunications are in fact effective. We know that they can destroy eels in a lake, or the sparrows that infest a church; it is well known how a priest at Toulouse turned a white loaf black by excommunication, and white again by absolution, and how the miracle was repeated by a bishop at Troyes. Since, therefore, caterpillars and other rural pests would simply laugh at a condemnatory sentence from the ordinary civil courts, let us use the weapon of Canon Law; let us strike them "with the pain of anathema, for which they have greater fear, as creatures obedient to the God who made them". A solemn monastic formulary of 1526–31 proclaims that "cater-pillars, palmer-worms, or by whatsoever name they be called" are banished from the diocese of Troyes, and all the faithful are summoned, as a requisite preliminary, "to join together in good works and pious prayers, and to pay their tithes without fraud and according to the custom of the district". This due payment of tithes is emphasized as a *sine quâ non*: at these times of common danger, tithe-payer and tithe-taker, parson and peasant, were united against the pests. It was natural, therefore, that the practice should long survive. In the three years 1831–3 the grasshoppers were regularly combated in parts of Champagne by the weapon of ecclesiastical processions and exorcisms.* On this point, Abbé Bergier's religious encyclopaedia of a century ago is most instructive. In defence of those parish priests of his own day who still "exorcise and adjure storms, rural pests, etc." he writes: "Priests have several times got into trouble for refusing to give way to their parishioners' requests.... It would be excellent to teach the people natural science, if they were capable of understanding it and incapable of misusing it; but they are neither one nor the other. When people learn that all natural phenomena are the natural effect of physical laws, they will draw the unbeliever's conclusion, that the world made itself and governs itself. Will the people gain much by this? If those who criticize the priests knew the people better, they would be less ready to condemn the priests."

Thus, in most minds, Satan bulked almost as large as God: in some, even larger. The regions of cold and bad weather were his especially; the Devil lived in the north, as we see from Chaucer's Friar's Tale (*Canterbury Tales*, D, 1413). This superstition was doubtless reinforced by such Bible texts as Jeremiah i. 14 and iv. 6: "Out of the north an evil shall break forth", "I will bring evil from the north, and a great destruction". We may thus almost say that the Devil was the God of winter and Jehovah God only of summer and spring. For we must remember the privations men suffered in those ill-built and draughty houses—their food of salt meat killed and preserved in the autumn, since there was no fodder to keep the cattle through the winter; scarcely any vegetables available in the cold months. Even in castles, accommodation was very scanty: the ladies sat all day long over their embroidery or gossip or parlour games, longing for the summer to come again. At last spring comes, and that is the outburst that greets us everywhere in medieval poetry. The Minnesinger records the thrill of

---

* We may compare with this the medieval custom of condemning and executing criminal beasts—the sow which has devoured a child, or the ox which has gored a man.

delight when the linden shows its emerald green in the castle court:

> Ich bin worden gewahr
> Neues Laubes an der Linde!

Already among the Anglo-Saxons the gods were mainly nature-gods; their worship was connected with the holy well, the holy glade in the forest, the great holy tree. St Augustine of Canterbury, by the advice of Pope Gregory who sent him, took care not to shock this belief too much. Bede has recorded St Gregory's message to the first missionaries in England (Book 1, ch. 30). This ran that the pagan temples in that country should not be pulled down; it being sufficient that the idols in them be destroyed. "Therefore let these places of heathen worship be sprinkled with holy water: let altars be built and relics placed under them: for if these temples are well built, it is fit the property of them should be altered; that the worship of devils be abolished, and the solemnity changed to the service of the true God: that when the natives perceive those religious structures remain standing, they may keep to the place without retaining the error; and be less shocked at their first entrance upon Christianity, by frequenting the temples they have been used to esteem. And since it has been their custom to sacrifice oxen to the devils they adored, this usage ought to be refined on, and altered to an innocent practice." He advises, therefore, that "upon the anniversary of the saints, whose relics are lodged there, or upon the return of the day the Church was consecrated, the people should make them booths about those churches lately rescued from idolatry, provide an entertainment, and keep a Christian holy-day; not sacrificing their cattle to the devil, but killing them for their own refreshment, and praising God for the blessing; that thus, by allowing them some satisfactions of sense, they may relish Christianity the better, and be raised by degrees to the more noble pleasures of the mind: for unpolished ignorant people are not to be cured all at once. He that intends to reach the top of an eminence must rise by gradual advances, and not think to mount at a single leap: thus God, when he discovered himself to the Israelites in Egypt, did not forbid them the customary rites of sacrificing, but transferred their worship from the devil to himself."

This accounts for the so-called "Church Houses", of which a good many remain in western England: a house generally recognizable by its age and its proximity to the church; evidently something more important than the ordinary cottage. It was in such buildings that the "Church Ales" were celebrated; a custom directly continuous from these early pagan rejoicings. On stated occasions food and ale were collected by voluntary contributions; and all who would might come and pay their scot and eat and drink their fill for the benefit of the church funds. It was found convenient in later times to build small houses for this and similar church functions, and records show us that these were sometimes let also to strolling players.

The village dance also was, as we have seen, a direct inheritance from pre-Christian times. It is absolutely necessary to realize that nobody whatever doubted the actual existence of these old pagan gods. They existed as truly as the great God; but, whereas the pagans had taken them for gods, the Christians knew them to be devils. Such gods can be driven out only by the power of a greater God; and, though worsted for a moment, they still linger in the background, ready to snap up everything that the greater God does not definitely protect. Hence, since the Church took a very one-sided view of human life in many ways, whatsoever the ecclesiastic in his narrowness or intolerance cast out, that became the natural domain of the Devil. We must not be pharisaical here. Nowadays not only very good Churchfolk, but very excellent agnostics, may be found fidgety about the spilling of salt, the walking under ladders, or the omission of touching wood. Superstition is, after all, only faith based on ignorance, and we are all very ignorant: ignorance is only a relative matter. But, relatively with our own day, superstition was certainly then enormously prominent. Many of the medieval devils have been driven out more effectually by Pasteur and his fellow-scientists than they were by the ringing of bells or the sprinkling of water. We must remember the unavoidable ignorance of natural phenomena in those days. St Thomas Aquinas, for instance, argues that "to the ignorant it seemeth miraculous that the magnet draweth iron, or that a little fish holdeth back a ship". The first part of this statement is as definitely accepted to-day as in the thirteenth century, but the second part rests upon the ancient superstition of the *remora*, an imaginary fish scarcely a foot long, through which the sailors explained to themselves otherwise unaccountable hindrances or disturbances of their navigation. Take again, for mixture of fact and fancy, the description of the crocodile by Bartholomew the Englishman, one of the stock encyclopaedists of the thirteenth century: "His teeth ben horyble and strongly shape, as a comb or a sawe and as a bores tuske...and is a beaste nouryshed in greate glotenye, and eateth ryghte moche: And soo whan he is ful, he lyeth by the brynke or by the clyffe and bloweth for fulnes. If the cocodril findeth a man by the brim of the water or by the cliffe, he sleeth hym if he may, and then he wepeth upon hym and swoloweth hym at the laste."

Not only was scientific observation enormously difficult in those days, but it was not even sufficiently esteemed in itself. In very many cases not only men could not observe patiently, but they did not care to do so. We cannot accept the plea that this fantastic zoology of the medieval mind was due not to lack of intelligence but only to lack of observation; for the unobservant habit is one of the unintelligent habits. We must remember, again, that the Church deliberately inculcated further ignorance of great portions of human life: for instance, we shall see that anatomy was forbidden. Moreover, in those ages when nearly every educated man was a cleric, in Minor if not in Major Orders, the clergy were strictly forbidden to shed blood with their own hands, even in a beneficent cause; so that a priest attempting to relieve a sufferer and inadvertently causing a breach of the skin or bloodshed was suspended from his sacerdotal functions until he had confessed and been absolved by a bishop or some other high ecclesiastic entitled to deal with "reserved" cases.

The Church often suspected nature. We have seen how St Edmund interpreted the flock of crows. St Dominic, again, when his studies were disturbed by a sparrow fluttering about his lamp, recognized at once the Devil, caught the bird, and, plucking it alive, triumphed in its screams and his own victory over the powers of darkness.[5] It is true that we find love of nature recorded in a small minority of medieval saints' lives. St Francis, St Hugh of Lincoln, St Anselm, and perhaps a dozen others, were notable for their love of, and control over, animals. These, however, are exceptional; and a recent French writer, compiling a book on *The Church and Pity for Animals*, has not been able to swell the medieval testimony beyond about a hundred pages.[6]

The child, nature's work, is impure, tainted with original sin— *massa perditionis*. Nothing but baptism can redeem it from hell, even though St Thomas might persuade himself, and try to persuade his readers, that hell without actual physical torture might be a place of relative happiness. The Church cast nature away, and the Devil took nature for his own. So again with laughter and the dance. Of St Francis and St Bernard their intimate biographers assure us that, though they spent their lives in holy joy, they seldom or never allowed themselves actual laughter. They acted on what had been a tradition in orthodox Christianity, from the time of St John Chrysostom: "Christ is crucified, and dost thou laugh?" Yet laughter, as we all know, is an essential function of human nature. Here we have the testimony of the Franciscan Salimbene. To him, as to Dante, the Emperor Frederick was a man of heroic proportions in his very sins: he made linguistic experiments on the vile bodies of hapless infants, "bidding foster-mothers and nurses to suckle and bathe and wash the children, but in no wise to prattle or speak with them; for he would fain have learnt whether they would speak the Hebrew language (which had been the first), or Greek, or Latin, or Arabic, or perchance the tongue of their parents of whom they had been born. But he laboured in vain; for the children could not live without clappings of the hands; and gestures, and gladness of countenance, and blandishments." As for the dance, we have seen its almost universal discouragement or prohibition by the Church. So, again, in the matter of clerical celibacy, with these thousands of priests and deacons and sub-deacons and monks and friars and nuns. To each of those, half humanity was in many senses professionally non-existent. The practical result we have already seen; a great many very honest and self-denying ascetics, whose religious enthusiasm was, however, sometimes very Utopian and unpractical. Against these we may set many law-breakers and a certain number of downright rascals; and, in between, a middle mass who, on the whole, would have been rather better for leading more natural lives. The practical upshot was that, in spite of attempts to avoid this Manichaean conclusion, family life was put on a lower plane; it was not the choicest offering to God, and therefore it was comparatively favourable to the Devil. It is of the earth, earthy; St Jerome's words were famous: "marriage fills the earth, virginity fills heaven"—*Matrimonium replet terram, virginitas coelum.* Too often, again, the Church suspected human reason. In a sense, no doubt, all her philosophers rested mainly upon it; from their own premises they reasoned with rigorous logic, and Newman could contend in that sense that the scholastic age was pre-eminently an age of reason. But their premises, as we shall see, were commonly derived from tradition, and popular tradition at that; yet traditions of which the Church forbade denial, or even serious doubt, at the risk of death, thus taking away with one hand the rational processes which she had encouraged with the other. There, again, the Devil was too often able to claim reason for his own province.

Moreover, the Church not only left room for many superstitions, but too often deliberately encouraged them. The sceptic on the one side, and the superstitious man on the other, took strength to themselves from the reckless way in which the clergy introduced the miraculous into ordinary life. Not only did they sometimes teach that sovereign virtues were inherent in mere attendance at their services, attentively or unattentively, and in the mere sight of such images as that of St Christopher, but they endowed relics and pious gestures and exclamations with the same miraculous powers. We have a tale first told by a thirteenth-century Cistercian and copied again and again into handbooks of anecdotes for preachers: here it is in fifteenth-century English. "Som tyme ther was a burd that was lernyd to speke. So on a tyme she flow away in the feldis, and the Goshalk [pur]sweid after hur and wold hafe kyllid hur. And whan she saw hym com, as she was lernyd at home, she began to cry, and sayd: '*Sancte Thoma! adiuua me!*' A! Saynt Thomas, helpe me!' And onone this goshalk fell down dead, and this burd esskapid and had none harm. Lo, surs, what vertue it is to call on Saynt Thomas, martir of Cantyrbery, in any tribulacion!"[7] Nor were the clergy always above practising deliberate fraud and boasting of it. From that same Book of Tales for preachers comes the story of the rustic who, having received a bad penny in the course of the year, kept it to offer at Easter as his compulsory Mass-penny. The priest, noting the fraud, slipped that same penny into his mouth instead of the consecrated wafer, to the amazement and repentance of the sinning peasant, who in his simplicity accepted this legerdemain as a miracle from on high. The Mass was naturally the main centre of popular superstitions. One of the most often-repeated stories from all ages and centuries is that of the worshipper who could not believe in Transubstantiation, until one day he saw a wafer turn into a living child in the priest's hand as he blessed it. Again, almost equally frequent is the story of the consecrated wafer, which, if broken or pricked with a dagger, sheds blood. That story was found particularly convenient for anti-Semitic propaganda, as an excuse for massacre and plunder.[8]

The natural result was that such popular superstitions were utilized for the purposes of definite witchcraft, as in the case of the old woman who crumbled the consecrated Hosts over her cabbages to destroy the caterpillars, and of the priest who used one as a love-philtre.[9] The water in the font, having once been consecrated, tempted folk to superstitious uses. In the same way, the people kept up (and the Church often contended against) pagan ceremonies at Christmas and at Eastertide, and especially the mid-summer bonfire. Pagan holy wells, again, the Church often baptized to her own purpose; it is admitted by historians of all religious creeds that the majority of medieval saints' wells were inheritors of a worship from the time of the older gods. We may take, for instance, Tarter's or Tawder's Well, which existed at Grantchester, near Cambridge, until coprolite-digging in the Great War destroyed the flow of water. That well was rebaptized in the Middle Ages to the greatest of local saints—St Etheldreda of Ely. The name Etheldreda was gradually corrupted to Audrey; the great annual fair at Ely was St Audrey's Fair, and the attractive little articles which formed its speciality were first called *St Audrey* articles, then *tawdry*, and have thus given their name to an uncomplimentary modern adjective. Thus St Etheldreda's Well became Tawder's and then Tarter's. It was natural that, whether for love or for fear, the medieval population should still haunt the ancient fountain or glade or tree. At St Joan's trial she admitted that she and her fellows had danced round a particular sacred tree. The mission preacher Herolt, and the medieval witch-finder Sprenger, both agreed that more women will be found in hell than men; because, although the women lead in other respects more regular lives, it is they who are specially given to witchcraft. Berthold of Regensburg [1250] says in one of his sermons: "Many of the village folk would come to heaven, were it not for their witchcrafts.... The woman has spells for getting a husband, spells for her marriage; spells on this side and on that; spells before the child is born, before the christening, after the christening; and all she gains with her spells is that her child fares the worse all its life long.... Ye men, it is much marvel that ye lose not your wits for the monstrous witchcrafts that women practise on you!" The Camden Society volume of proceedings against Dame Alice Kyteler is most instructive on this subject. Michelet was probably right; women's minds are more conservative and compassionate; therefore many of them could never tear from their hearts the deep pity for these last survivals from the Twilight of the Gods. Constantly we catch, in the Middle Ages, hints of an undercurrent, of a yearning after the pagan past which was in many ways as temperamental as the regret expressed by a modern Huysmans or De Gourmont for the vanished thirteenth century; or, if it comes to that, by the utterly unconverted Heine:

> Das Herz ist mir beklemmt, und sehnlich
> Gedenke ich der alten Zeit:
> Die Welt war damals noch so wöhnlich,
> Und ruhig lebten hin die Leut':
> Und jetzt ist Alles wie verschoben,
> Es gibt ein Drängen, eine Not;
> Gestorben ist der Herrgott oben,
> Und unten ist der Teufel tot.

Or by Victor Hugo in *Notre-Dame de Paris*; and again his cry in the poem of much later years:

> O! reprends ton néant
> Gouffre, et rends-nous Satan!

The superstition of the Evil Eye was specially prevalent and strong. Old women, once suspected of this or of other occult powers, would naturally sometimes encourage the suspicion, for the sake of money or influence. Among the Records of Depositions in the Durham Court, witchcraft plays a prominent part in parochial visitations; and, no less naturally, it is the love-charm that comes to the fore.[10] In 1435 three men accuse Margaret Lyndysay of having cast a spell which renders them impotent; she purges herself with the oath of five women neighbours, and is restored to her good fame, and the three are forbidden to repeat the slander under pain of excommunication. In 1446, two women were accused of "using the art of witchcraft, and saying to spinsters desirous of marriage that they would make them to have the men whom they affect and desire to have". One or two others are accused of witchcraft in general, and are usually submitted to compurgation by the oaths of five or six neighbours. A report was spread that another had so bewitched the curate of the parish to sin and to spend money on her, that he had found his way to prison. At Bromyard "the parishioners say that Alison Brown holdeth such doings that, when she hath cursed any body, in virtue of her curse God shall take vengeance upon him without delay; and this she hath oftentimes done by her [power], which is against the Catholic faith and would tempt God". We find this treated seriously even in the highest places: there are four cases in vol. 1 of the *Calendar of Chancery Petitions*. At the end of the fifteenth century, for instance, John Dunn of York complained to the Lord Chancellor of England how "Thomas Mell of the County of York, husbandman, through divers erroneous acts, and contrary to the Catholic faith, to wit through sorcery, and in evil example to all folk in the aforesaid county, as is openly known to many folk, hath withdrawn the water from a certain pond" on the complainant's land. Another suit is against "Richard Kirkeby, late a Scholar of Cambridge, and said to use necromancies to make himself go invisible".[11] Such a reputation, however, was not without serious dangers. We may see this in a Northumberland Assize Roll for the thirteenth century, where a man is accused of having run an old woman through with a pitchfork, and excuses himself on the ground that she had cast a spell over him. The jury decided that he had killed her in self-defence against the Devil— *quasi se defendendo contra diabolum.*[12] Witch-hunting, however, although it grew in the later Middle Ages, never attained the same proportions in medieval England as in Scotland and on the Continent, among both Protestants and Roman Catholics, in the sixteenth and early seventeenth centuries. The conflict between Sorcery and the Church is told in detail by H. C. Lea in the third volume of his *History of the Inquisition in the Middle Ages*.[13] In the tenth century the Church almost tolerated it; partly no doubt because it was too strong for her to venture upon a life-and-death struggle, but partly also because a few great Churchmen, as we have seen, were enlightened enough to believe that these pagan survivals were groundless superstitions. The real conflict came after the founding of the Inquisition; and, even then, not at first. It is in the first half of the fourteenth century that inquisitors begin to treat witchcraft no less seriously than heresy. But the beliefs were too deep and widespread; and doubtless persecution also gave them the stimulus of advertisement. Thus, in 1398, the University of Paris adopted a series of twenty-eight articles against demonology, declaring at the same time that it is a theological error to doubt the reality of sorcery and its effects. Any denial of this pronouncement was thenceforward sufficient to justify vehement suspicion of heresy. "The Church lent its overpowering authority to enforce belief on the souls of men. The malignant powers of the witch were repeatedly set forth in the bulls of successive popes for the implicit credence of the faithful; and the University of Cologne, in 1487, when expressing its approval of the *Malleus Maleficarum* of Sprenger, warned every one that to argue against the reality of witchcraft was to incur the guilt of impeding the Inquisition." Here, then, war to the knife is declared. But the worst was that, though Holy Water and the Sign of the Cross and other ecclesiastical safeguards might ward off the danger, yet, when once the spell had been cast, nothing could counteract it but counter-spells. It may be doubted whether Lea is altogether right in his belief that the practice of witchcraft actually grew in volume from the fourteenth century onward. On the contrary, there seems evidence that the difference resided not in any greater prevalence of sorcery, but in the more desperate resolve of the Church to adopt remedies against so inveterate a foe. It was only then, when the general public was becoming more educated, and the Inquisition had armed the Church with such enormous fighting power, that she determined at last to drive her adversary to extremities. The Dominicans Nider and Sprenger in the fifteenth century devoted their main writings and activities to witch-hunting; and it was this spirit which was largely responsible for the condemnation of Joan of Arc. At the end of the fifteenth century Sprenger and his colleague boasted that they had burned forty-eight sorcerers in five years. In the sixteenth century "Protestant and Catholic rivalled each other in the madness of the hour. Witches were burned no longer in ones and twos, but in scores and hundreds. A bishop of Geneva is said to have burned five hundred within three months; a bishop of Bamberg six hundred, a bishop of Würzburg nine hundred. Eight hundred were condemned, apparently in one body, by the Senate of Savoy.... Paramo [in his history of the Inquisition] boasts that in a century and a half from the commencement of the sect, in 1404, the Holy Office had burned at least thirty thousand witches who, if they had been left unpunished, would easily have brought the whole world to destruction."

X. POPES AND PRELATES

CONVENTIONAL historiography duly emphasizes the Church's work in shaping medieval Society; but we must not stop there. It is equally important—some might say, even more important—to mark how Society shaped the Church. Roughly speaking, theirs was a peasant world, with peasant mentality. The village was one of its greatest formative forces, operative even in its passivity. Social conditions were the outcome not only of what the peasant actively desired, but also of that which his conservatism could not suffer to be removed or altered. It is only a half-truth to point out that medieval theologians were able to impose a long-disputed dogma upon the official Church. The complement of this is, that the populace could do much the same, almost without enlisting the theologians' services. Image worship, a question so contentious that it led to actual civil war, was finally decided not as the great early Fathers had thought, but as the populace required. In the long catalogue of recognized saints, those who have been canonized by popular acclamation will be found far more numerous than those who have received their credentials directly from Rome, after such examination as the present generation has seen in the cases of Fisher and More. The strength of the winning cause in the Transubstantiation dispute was in its direct and commanding appeal to the people, while scientific theologians could justify it only by the invention of logical devices hitherto unknown to any philosophy. Even the Feast of Corpus Christi, which consecrated that victory, was forced at first upon unwilling theologians by a village girl and a young village priest. The doctrine of the Immaculate Conception, which for centuries no Pope dared to decide, was one which had been rejected by St Bernard and by the whole of the Dominican order, that is, by the most learned theologians; but the people demanded it, and so also did the Franciscans, as representatives of the people, and their guides in the sense of "I am your leader; therefore I follow you". Thus, to understand medieval society, we must follow closely not only Church history proper, but also this interaction of village and Church. The upper hierarchy had, of course, great importance; but that consideration is more obvious and needs less emphasis here. We may glance at those great folk; and, at certain moments, we must mark the special influence of one prelate or another. But we must look with far closer attention, and in more minute detail, at this obscure multitude, lay and clerical, out of whose thoughts and wishes the prelate's action normally grew. It is natural, therefore, that from the village flock we should pass on to the spiritual shepherd.

We must begin by getting rid of modern ideas. There is much truth (though we shall have to qualify this later on) in the contention that the Western Church was only one form of the State; that State and Church were different sides of the same institution. The Church included nearly the whole of civilized Europe; all baptized folk were its subjects, and it was punishable to neglect baptism for one's children. Therefore the whole population might be reckoned as Churchfolk. This was the legal basis of the treatment of heresy throughout the Middle Ages as a form of treason. The Jew and the Pagan were under heavy disabilities, but in normal times they were not punished for disbelief. The heretic, on the other hand, was reckoned as a traitor and must therefore be treated as such.

Let us look at this from the point of view first of the clergy themselves, and secondly of the congregations. From that first point of view it will appear that nearly all men of culture were clerics—students, authors, journalists, lecturers, even lower university officials, parish clerks, bedesmen, anchorites and pilgrims. From the other point of view, the congregation was the whole population. It included potentially all elements of present denominations. It included the potential sacerdotalist and the potential Puritan—extremes of superstition, of free thought, and even of infidelity. In short, the strength and the weakness of the medieval Church were not only those of an institution, but those of human nature itself. We must never forget how it had come to dominate the Western World; nor again the extent to which religion gave depth and seriousness to ancient Latin and Greek thought. The Church services, again, kept up to a considerable extent the study of the Latin language; and the Church in its organization was an object lesson in social solidarity. Even under papal despotism there remained more remnants of free discussion and election, on the whole, than could generally be found in civil life.

The Papacy, then, was a great bureaucracy, a network of

officials from top to bottom. From at least the time of Hildebrand, that Pope Gregory VII whose relations with William the Conqueror we have already seen, it was a despotism. Though William refused homage to Gregory, John was compelled to pay it to Innocent III, and this was not repudiated until 1374. We may, therefore, divide our period into three portions. First, two centuries of growing papal influence; then one century of waning influence, ending with the Statutes of Provisors and Praemunire, and the repudiation of John's tribute; and, thirdly, two more centuries during which the Great Breach was preparing.

At the head of this bureaucracy was the Pope, ruling from Rome, except for the seventy years of "captivity" at Avignon. He commanded an army disciplined not, it is true, in the strictest modern sense, but very strictly disciplined in comparison with medieval society in general; moreover, most ubiquitous. Under him were the Cardinals, who by this time had become a college of electors for the Papacy, and were constantly used by the Pope as legates to override the local prelates in any country in which he chose to interfere. Under these came the Archbishops and Bishops, the Archbishop's jurisdiction covering roughly the Roman imperial province and the Bishop's that of the Roman *civitas*. The *civitas* under the Roman Empire had been about the size of a modern English county or of a French *département*; thus an ecclesiastical map of France before the Revolution would show divisions answering pretty exactly to the Roman *civitates*. For several centuries, after the rule of popular election had died out, these prelates were appointed mainly by kings, and we may say of England as Imbart de la Tour does of France: "We do not find in fact in documents of the ninth century any texts which allow us to suppose that such bishops had to swear fidelity to the Pope."[1] The contrast between medieval and modern discipline, in this particular respect, is enormous. England had many less bishops than old imperial districts like Italy, France and Spain. At the Conquest we had only 14, increased by two under Henry I; and the want was felt so severely that Wolsey, shortly before the Reformation, proposed to create 20 new bishoprics. Our 16 were divided into two provinces—Canterbury and York. The bishops periodically met their clergy and passed by-laws in synods. Less frequently, the clergy of the whole province met for the same purposes in council.

England had thus, like all other countries, a Canon Law of its own; but only as a code of by-laws subordinate to the Pope's Canon Law, which was binding on the whole of Western Christendom. That law was administered in ecclesiastical courts, by the Archbishops, the Bishops and the Archdeacons. In archdeacons also we were comparatively poor at the Conquest; there was only one for each diocese. Soon, however, multiplication was found necessary, and we presently find about one archdeacon to each county. This official was often called "the bishop's eye". It was his function to exercise, as deputy, the bishop's supervision over the morals of his diocese, as every reader of Chaucer must remember. In this, the archdeacon did very much to supersede our next official in the hierarchy—the Rural Dean. This was a parish priest elected from among the rest of the clergy and unsalaried, answering very nearly to our unsalaried Justices of the Peace of the present day. On the other hand, since medieval justice reposed so greatly on the system of fines, these rural deaneries were to some extent lucrative. They were generally roughly conterminous with the minor divisions of the county, the "hundreds". In Norwich diocese, for instance, there were 45 rural deaneries to 58 hundreds, but in only two cases was the boundary of the rural deanery different from some hundred boundary. As assistants to the bishop in discipline, these rural deans were concerned with matrimonial and testamentary and moral questions; but the first of these matters became more and more complicated; thoroughly trained lawyers were obviously required; and therefore presently we find the archdeacon practically swallowing all these duties and privileges. Rural deans are not even mentioned in Chaucer, though they do occur once in *Piers Plowman* under the title of "sub-deans". John of Ayton, commenting on English Canon Law [1340], mentions the system as nearly dead; but it has been revived in modern times.

We next come to the ordinary Parish Priest. When Augustine first converted England there was no attempt to divide it into parishes. Each bishop was a missionary, having a staff of missionary clergy living with him, grouped round his cathedral and scouring the surrounding districts. Then, with the complete conversion of the different kingdoms, the pagan ecclesiastical system was naturally merged in that of the conquering religion. Under the heathen Anglo-Saxons, landowners had erected temples on their own estates; and the priests had been paid by tithes or contributions from the peasants. That system in England, as elsewhere, passed naturally into a parochial organization. The land-owner still appointed the priest; and the priest claimed his tithes and other offerings in virtue of universal Canon Law. Thus the rural parish was, as a rule, simply the village in its ecclesiastical aspect. The main endowments of the parish clergy came from tithes. In Norwich diocese, for instance, tithes were two-thirds, offerings one-fifth, and glebe one-eighth of the average total income of the incumbent. This average total endowment in that diocese was roughly about £11. But this was a rich district; and the average of some other counties would be distinctly lower. That £11 represents roughly £400 a year in present currency, in addition to which the priest had his house and garden. This income was nominally earmarked into three portions—one for the priest himself; one for the upkeep of the church buildings and services; and one for the poor. That theory, however, as we shall see later, represented only a pious ideal; nobody has ever attempted to produce documentary evidence from any time or country in which it regularly worked.

England had during our period a little less than 9000 parishes, for a population which probably ranged from about two and a half millions at the Conquest to, at most, four and a half or five millions under Henry VII. Thus the average number of souls per parish was at most about 450—that is, about 180 adults. The town parishes were on an average considerably smaller than those of the villages. Although, then, there were less than 9000 parishes, yet before the Black Death there were probably some 20,000 priests; Cardinal Gasquet has calculated 50,000, but it is very difficult to follow the reasoning by which he arrives at so high a number. It may be worth while to point out that at the present day we have some 21,000 Anglican priests to nearly ten times the medieval population; the reason for this large medieval proportion will be seen later on. Beneath the priest came the clergy in lower orders. There are seven Orders in the Roman Church—four "Minor", and three "Major" or "holy". These minor clerics were extremely numerous; even grammar-school boys were often tonsured as clerics, so were all students of the university. These lower clerics frequently worked as attendants on noblemen, as accountants (hence the modern term "clerical work" for writing and similar occupations), or again for performing minor services in the church—the *Dirige* and *Placebo* of *Piers Plowman*. The most important of these minor clerics, to whom we shall come in detail later on, were the Parish Clerks. Taking them all together, and including the "regular" (i.e. cloistered) clergy, there was probably at least one cleric per hundred of population—that is, about one among every thirty adult males.

All these, then, were organized into a system more elaborate than anything analogous in the State. Here was, in theory, a vast disciplined army at the Pope's beck and call; and, theoretically, the fullest and most elaborate provisions on the one hand for the spiritual needs of the population through teaching and public worship, and on the other for the relief of the poor, whether in their own cottages or as destitute travellers; and, thirdly, even to some extent an educational system.

That is the skeleton of the organization. Let us now trace in greater detail its working in England from the Conquest to the Reformation. In Popes we began well; for 1073 saw the advent of Gregory VII, one of the greatest in the whole series; and the two centuries which followed him were distinctly above the average. We have seen how William I definitely repudiated his claim of homage; yet in most matters the two worked harmoniously: this is very clearly brought out by Dr Z. N. Brooke in his recent *English Church and the Papacy*. William was, on the whole, heartily in favour of Gregory's reforming energies: but he "was determined to be master of all his subjects, a dual authority in the kingdom was to him unthinkable". Like all contemporary kings, he appointed the bishops and ensured their obedience to himself. He allowed Lanfranc to go to Rome for his pallium; by this time, that had become customary: but later, when Gregory again demanded Lanfranc's presence, William refused to permit it, and Lanfranc obeyed the king. In other respects also, the great archbishop behaved rather as the king's than as the Pope's man. We may not go quite so far as Dr Brooke, who seems to imply that, if it had come to an open trial of strength between the two, Lanfranc would have sided with William on these issues, and flatly disobeyed the Pope. In the face of the Forged Decretals, which Lanfranc knew and believed in like everybody else of his day, such definite defiance of a Pope's clear commands would seem impossible. But in fact there never came any such demand for a clear-cut

decision between Pope and king; and Gregory, for all his conviction
of authority and his masterful spirit, was prudent enough to let
sleeping dogs lie. This, in fact, was one of the earliest of those
compromises in which English history has been so rich. But papal
policy was so consistent, in comparison with that of the lay rulers,
that the balance of power tended more and more in favour of the
Church as time went on. William I had stoutly maintained his
right of recognizing, in disputed elections, the Pope of his own

Gratian's Inspiration.

choice. William II, under pressure from Anselm at a moment
when he was taken at disadvantage, gave up that right. Henry I,
again, under pressure of political difficulties at home, finally gave
way to Anselm's insistence and admitted the claims of Paschal II
in the Investiture quarrel. Henceforward "not merely the old
[Canon] Law, but the new decrees passed at Rome were enforced
in England. It was the first breach made in the royal barrier, and
it was never during the Middle Ages completely closed again".
The next step came with the disputed claim of Stephen to the

crown. The barons, in Henry's lifetime, had solemnly sworn to recognize Matilda; Stephen appealed to Rome for a general absolution from that oath. John of Salisbury, who hints broadly that Stephen's money won him the victory here, probably voices the general opinion of his day; but Dr Brooke inclines to the milder judgment that the Pope had made up his mind beforehand, "influenced rather by ecclesiastical than by judicial considerations". In any case, here was the papal wedge driven in a great deal further; and, throughout Stephen's reign, his political weakness compelled him to submit to the dictation of the Church. That fatal blunder in Becket's case which brought Henry II to surrender, and John's grovelling at the feet of Innocent III, are too well known to need repetition here. England was thenceforward, politically as well as theologically, vassal to Rome, until Edward III repudiated the homage and tribute, and restricted ecclesiastical encroachments in his Statutes of Provisors. Yet, even then, the only supreme Church Law in England was Roman Canon Law: and this is a point so often falsified or obscured by interested special pleading, that it needs emphasis here. It was first brought out briefly by Rashdall; and then by F. W. Maitland so conclusively as to leave no further excuse for Bishop Stubbs's theory of a separate English Canon Law, independent in any real sense of Rome. The Statutes of Provisors logically prove this; for they carefully erected a barrier against the chances that the clergy, even when lay resistance to Rome gave them the most solid support, would capitulate and surrender to the Pope their own rights of presentation, often very lucrative. The omnipotence of Canon Law is most explicitly asserted in Archbishop Arundel's notorious decree of 1407/8, in which (*inter alia*) he condemns as heresy, and therefore as a burning matter, any misinterpretation or repudiation of any papal decretal. So far had papal pretensions grown, in spite of growing lay opposition, within our period.

In the memoirs of Schaunard, dealing with Bohemian life at Paris, there is an anecdote which may be used as a parable to illustrate the subtle growth and pressure of papal power. A sculptor had a model so perfect in manly symmetry and strength that he resolved to immortalize him with a plaster cast. He constructed a great box in which the man stood, while the liquid plaster was poured in up to the neck. In half a minute the model was gasping for breath; a few seconds more, and he was purple in the face: only by the utmost promptitude with hammer and chisel was the sculptor able to break his prison and save his life. It was perfectly simple; the liquid plaster had been "wax to receive, and marble to retain". At each breath that the man gave, his chest contracted a little; and the quiet insinuating cream crept in thus far. Then he would have expanded his chest to draw air, but found not the slightest concession: the more he gasped and struggled, the more inexorably was he crushed in this velvet-gloved vice. That is why the violence of Henry VIII, in its results though not in its methods, was welcomed by so many men in his own generation, and is approved by so great a majority of later historians. This, however, is a matter which will engage our attention in my last chapter.

But a few words must be added here with regard to the Popes as politicians; a brief sketch, that is, of their dominance, and of lay opposition, in affairs of State. Innocent III worked so preponderantly for ecclesiastical righteousness that his claims over princes were the less resented. But he died in 1216; and a generation later, under Innocent IV, the moral decline is evident. This Pope was learned, and we need not deny him piety; but he was by nature a politician. He gave a distinctly greater impetus to the political strivings which had always been a temptation concomitant with papal power; and under him we already find murmurings of European revolt. The ominous suggestion of appeal to a General Council of Christendom against this centralized despotism began to be heard. Half a century later, however, Boniface VIII raised papal claims to the highest possible point. The Emperor was to be subject to the Pope not only in the religious, but even in the civil, sphere; and this was proclaimed in a bull, *Unam Sanctam*, which is universally admitted to have been *ex cathedra* in its last paragraph, although attempts are made to explain away those earlier and more plainspoken paragraphs which are discordant with present-day ideas. In another bull, *Clericis Laicos*, he attempted to exclude the clergy from taxation, with the result that he was met with direct resistance not only in France but from our Edward I, who practically told him that if the clergy would not pay taxes, neither should they have the use of the king's courts, but must be prepared to find themselves treated as outlaws. Thenceforward, although English sovereigns were always loyal in their professions and obedient in the majority of their actions, the feeling steadily grew in this country that the Pope, however theologically necessary, was politically a foreign potentate, mainly noticeable through his habit of fleecing this distant flock.

As our period begins favourably with a great Pope, Gregory VII, so also with our Archbishops Lanfranc and Anselm. These men, both born on ancient Italian soil, and imported through Normandy, were among the greatest European Churchmen of their age. For a long time prelates were thus introduced to us as civilizing foreigners. Becket was our first English-born archbishop; and in some of our sees there was no English-born bishop until later. The bishops, like the archbishops, were barons in the State by reason of their rich possessions; and one (Durham) had a palace and council of his own, as a necessary bulwark against invasions from the North. But even in Durham the bishop did not approach in power or in secular temptations to the prince-bishops of the Continent; and all through our period English bishops were distinctly above the foreign standard, though not generally equal in brilliancy to the very pick of the Continent. Their temptations were not so great, nor their fall so spectacular. Thus, in England, there are very few traces of that feeling so strong during the thirteenth century in France, Germany, and Italy, that a bishopric involved serious risk to the soul, and that any thoroughly religious man was bound to avoid this distinguished, but dangerous, office, since it would necessarily not only implicate him in worldly cares, but also imperil his spiritual life. Often as they preferred the royal court to residence in their own dioceses, perhaps no other bishop could have been described as the Benedictine chronicler Greystanes paints his own diocesan in 1318. "Louis, Bishop of Durham, was an illiterate person, not understanding Latin, and pronouncing it with difficulty. Wherefore, having to make his public profession at his consecration (although he had taken instruction in the matter for many days beforehand), he was unable to read it; and having at last stumbled on, with the help of kindly prompting, as far as the word *metropolitanus*; and, after many gasps, having found himself unable to pronounce it, he said in the French tongue, 'Let us take that word as read.' Similarly also, when he was ordaining candidates for Holy Orders, and found himself unable to read the words *in aenigmate* ['*through a glass darkly*', I Cor. xiii. 12] he said to those who stood by: 'By St Louis, that was no courteous man who wrote this word!'"[2]

This bishop, naturally enough, has left no register; and scanty indeed are the business records of our three canonized bishops of English blood: St Edmund Rich of Canterbury, St Richard Wych of Chichester, and St Thomas Cantelupe of Hereford. From Grosseteste of Lincoln, whom many would count as greater still than these before man and God, we have no really full register, but (apart from his scientific writings) letters and sermons testifying to his struggles against unruly subjects under him in his own diocese, and an increasingly worldly Roman court set above him. For St Anselm, on the other hand, we have a loving and intimate biography from the pen of a true historian, his fellow-monk Eadmer. This great philosopher was also a great administrator, because he brought to each of those tasks the single eye of perfect inward truth. The medieval bishop was also a medieval baron, whose vast estates involved him in heavy political responsibilities and, often, in the most perilous and difficult litigation. It excited little comment when his manner of life, and his bearing towards his inferiors, were frankly baronial, so long as they kept within the bounds of baronial decency. His origin had sometimes been of the humblest; but he was expected to enrich his kinsfolk. Giraldus Cambrensis quotes Alexander III's saying: "When God deprived bishops of sons, the devil gave them nephews." But of Anselm Eadmer tells us how he made good his power not by self-assertion but by honesty and common sense.[3] He would never suffer any of his people to take advantage of legal quibbles, "making a conscience not to do to others what he would not have done to himself....So it happened that, sitting among the contending pleaders while his opponents were taking counsel by what skill or by what trick they might help their own cause or damage his, he, not minding it, was conversing with any one who wished to address him, either about the Gospel or some other divine Scripture, or some point of right conduct. And often, when he had no one to listen of this kind, quietly at peace in the purity of his heart, he would close his eyes and sleep; and often it came to pass that the cunning devices against him, when they came to his hearing, were at once exposed and torn to pieces, not as if he had been asleep all the while, but as if he had been fully awake and keenly watching. For charity, which envieth not, vaunteth not itself, seeketh not her own, was strong in him, whereby he saw at a glance the things that he ought to see; for the truth was his guide." [4] Thus we see in him the indomitable strength of the true ascetic, upon whom worldly authority can get no hold, because there is nothing worldly about him to hold him by; and, in addition to all this, the persuasive and magnetic strength of human love, when the great man is found as gentle to others as he is strict with himself. Therefore he was the one man who had some power over Rufus. "To all others so harsh and terrible, in Anselm's presence he seemed, to the wonder of the bystanders, another man, so gracious and easy of speech. Years after, when King William was on his forlorn death-bed, Anselm was the man whom he most wished to see." [5]

There, of course, was a man in ten millions, a whole horizon removed from poor Louis of Durham; we should be fortunate if, in those days, such English bishops had kept a formal register of the later pattern. But several such registers have come down from those who were betwixt and between those commanding saints and the ignorant or idle prelates. The bulkiest of these, and perhaps most valuable in every way to the historian, is that of John de Grandisson of Exeter. His three stout volumes, running to 1610 pages, give perhaps the fullest extant picture of any medieval bishop in his diocese, except that of Odo Rigaldi for the diocese of Rouen. The record is so precious that I must beg the reader to forgive here, even at the cost of weariness, sufficient details to make him realize that the picture is not mine, but that of the bishop himself. The real difficulty, in fact, is to avoid quoting at far greater length than this from Grandisson's own text.

His register is all the more precious because the Black Death came nearly in the middle of his long reign. His predecessor had been Stapeldon, a royal minister almost always absent from the diocese, whom the London populace had murdered in the streets at the fall of his master Edward II. To this crime, the editor of the register attributes some of the difficulties encountered by Grandisson; but in fact there is scarcely any incident in this episcopate which cannot be paralleled from elsewhere.

In theory, bishops were still elected by their cathedral chapters; but in fact the king and Pope, instead of merely confirming such elections, habitually overrode them. Ayermine, though duly elected to Norwich, had to take sanctuary in his own cathedral (1325); Tottinton (1406) was imprisoned by the king for daring to accept the monks' choice of him. On the other hand, in 1333, though Graystanes was not only elected to Durham but actually consecrated by the Archbishop of York, this was set aside by the Pope. Out of 25 English bishops in 10 years, 17 may be counted who held high ministerial offices under the Crown. Every contested choice, whichever way the verdict might finally go, entailed heavy additional law expenses at Rome. Grandisson's appointment, on the other hand, was by papal favour, and this was a worthy choice. He was of a noble Burgundian family, whose castle still stands beside the Lake of Neuchâtel, a stately monument for visitors. Our John was cousin to the poet who was Chaucer's friend, and brother to the beautiful Countess of Salisbury who is the heroine of Froissart's story of the Garter. The Papal Court claimed 12,000 florins in fees for his appointment, and, though this was afterwards reduced to 5000, it compelled him to borrow at heavy interest from the Florentine banking-house of Bardi, and to beg humbly from all his friends and his superior clergy. A little earlier than this, Archbishop Pecham of Canterbury had been plunged into such hopeless debt by the sums due to Rome for his appointment, and therefore necessarily borrowed from the Pope's Italian usurers, that for a while he was under excommunication as a defaulter, and dared not show his face in his own diocese.

Grandisson, from the first, met with very serious difficulties in his own cathedral. His primary visitation, in 1328, disclosed the following facts. Some canons, as hirelings or even robbers of the Church, keep up only the merest pretence of residence, caring more for their hawks and hounds than for the Church. They seldom come to service, and then they come in late and often go out before the end. Some, again, both of the canons and subordinate ministers, "spend their time not in offering to God due sacrifice of praise, but rather in gabbling through the service, with frequent interruptions of vain and unprofitable discourse, and unlawful murmurs to each other". They neglect to give alms to the poor according to the conditions of their office; the service books are defective, and not duly repaired; some canons are not in priest's orders; the vicars choral (minor canons) are given to tavern hunting and other "insolencies"; the service is unduly hurried through; hence decay of divine service, a falling off of devotion on the people's part, and general scandal of all. Though the editor here pleads exceptional disorder after Stapeldon's murder, yet the visitations of Southwell, Ripon, Beverley and

Wells are quite worthy to be put beside this. In several Continental cathedrals, one of the statutes prohibited canons from talking to each other, during divine service, "beyond the 4th [or, in some cases, 5th] stall". Moreover, after two years of this strong bishop's rule, we find him again reprimanding the clergy of his cathedral for their "laughing, giggling, and other insolencies during divine service itself"; for the sorry practical joke of casting candle-snuffings from the upper stalls upon the shaven pates of the clergy in the lower; for their custom of exclaiming aloud, in the vulgar tongue, when a bad blunder had been made in singing or reading, "Cursed be the fellow who told that last lie!" and for the haste with which they gabble through the service, or "cry aloud to their officiating brother, bidding and enjoining him to make haste".[6] Three years later, again (1333), there are the old "damnable and irreverent jests, laughters, gigglings and other insolencies" during divine service, under excuse of the Feast of Fools. And in 1360, after thirty-two years of strenuous work, the bishop finds this same abuse flourishing not only in his cathedral but also in the three great collegiate churches of Ottery, Crediton and Glasney.

Grandisson's further difficulties, to the very end, were such as we find in other episcopal records. The precentor of the cathedral was persistently non-resident; so also the chancellor. This latter, in 1337, had been absent for ten years: Grandisson remonstrated and threatened with ever-increasing vigour; yet in 1339 he was still away, and seems to have retained his dignity and revenues till his death in 1345. In 1344 the canons in general were mostly non-resident, in defiance of their statutes confirmed by a papal legate, and of Grandisson's repeated injunctions and warnings: moreover they embezzled the stipends of the vicars choral and compelled these to hire themselves out for duty elsewhere, thus defrauding the cathedral services. At the monastery of St James, Exeter, Grandisson can produce no effect upon the shockingly dissolute prior; so also at Tavistock, with two abbots in succession; so again at Barnstaple, where again two disreputable priors came in succession. To the rebellion of an archdeacon we shall come presently; and there was trouble with false miracles, with pardoners, with a pre-Wycliffite heretic parson, and with Exeter citizens.

But perhaps the most significant of all these contests, and certainly the most piquant, was with a fellow-prelate, the Bishop of Damascus.7 Readers may well wonder how that apparently distant dignitary can have crossed the Bishop of Exeter's path, except that there is a D in Damascus and a D in Devonshire. This man was a bishop *in partibus*. The recapture of the Holy Land by the infidels had naturally involved the exile of a whole hierarchy: equally naturally, Rome was unwilling to accept this loss as final. Thus there had grown up a whole hierarchy *in partibus infidelium*; prelates who had never seen, nor would ever see, their diocese, but who were utilized as suffragans, or to whom the Pope gave roving commissions. These were nearly always friars; for the ubiquitous organization of those four orders, and the natural conformity of their interests with those of the Roman see, singled them out for this kind of work as naturally as the Jesuit order in post-Reformation times. Such emissaries did not always command respect; Langland is quaintly contemptuous of these bishops "of Bedleem and Babiloigne", "of Neptalym, of Nynue and of Damaske";8 and certainly our present subject might richly have earned his scorn. In 1347, just before the Black Death, the Austin friars had been building a chapel at Dartmouth, and thus encroaching upon the spiritual and temporal preserves of the Abbot of Torre: Grandisson had forbidden this. The friars appealed to Rome: judgment was given against them. But they got hold of one of their fellow-friars, Hugh, titular Bishop of Damascus, who came treacherously to Dartmouth disguised as a layman "in a short tight buttoned jacket, with a long sword and buckler by his side". At the Austin convent he doffed his lay attire, put on a friar's frock, and then, crozier in hand and mitre on head, he assembled the people of Dartmouth and told them he was the Bishop of Damascus, sent by the Lord Pope and the Lord Cardinals to consecrate this chapel; which he duly did, and gave an indulgence of 100 days to all the congregation present. After that he confirmed children, and absolved certain persons, in virtue of his papal commission, from the excommunication which they had incurred by laying violent hands on clergy. "Thence he went to many taverns in the said town and drank therein, and showed both to men and women his hand with a ring on it, which he said the Lord Pope had given him with his own hand." Asked why he did all this without leave of the bishop of the diocese, "he answered and said that he cared naught for the aforesaid Lord Bishop, and did and said other abusive things, to the scandal and disgrace of our Lord the Pope and the Lord Cardinals and the Apostolic See and the Cathedral church of Exeter; which things, for the honour of religion, I leave untold for the present". So wrote Grandisson, appealing to Canterbury. This brought from the intruder partly a denial, partly a very humble apology. He pleaded that he could not have passed over the lands of the Abbot of Torre without grievous bodily peril, unless he had thus gone in disguise; as for the absolution given for laying violent hands on clergy, a certain mariner beat him, the Bishop of Damascus, on the arm with his bow, thinking he was the Abbot of Torre; and then, finding that he had incurred the greater excommunication by this blow, "the aforesaid mariner, with many other aiders and abettors, followed him with grisly threats that, if he [the bishop] did not give him absolution, he should never leave the town of Dartmouth alive; and the bishop, overcome by fear, which may fall at times even upon the stoutest hearts,* granted the mariner the required letter of absolution". Upon which humble confession the Archbishop of Canterbury absolved the Bishop of Damascus from the excommunication laid upon him by the Bishop of Exeter.

Worse still was Grandisson's trouble in the matter of archdeacons. We may read it in his formal letter to a brother prelate, making allowance for the probably exaggerated language of a legal indictment.[9] In 1344, a certain John Peris claimed the archdeaconry of Totnes. On St Luke's day, Grandisson was celebrating a Mass in thanksgiving for the sixteenth anniversary of his promotion to the see. While he was preaching, "certain sons of perdition, viz. William de Clavile (alias Wyteprest, alias Hamond), John Attewater nephew, and John de Bodevile cousin of John Peris, with many accomplices, armed both with bows and arrows and with divers other sorts of weapons, having (as is asserted and credibly believed) conspired against my life, broke into the aforesaid church without respect for the place, or the holy-day, or my person or sacred office, and interrupted my devotions and those of the people, like infidels, blasphemers, and barbarians. And whereas I thrice solemnly warned them in vain to depart from the sacred edifice, at length I excommunicated them with all due formalities, as the enormity of their offence required. Therefore, most reverend Father in God, lest the aforesaid children of Satan

---

* This is the common legal formula in the Middle Ages for pleading violent compulsion.

infect your flock also, may it please you to let it be proclaimed publicly throughout your diocese that the aforesaid evildoers have been and are excommunicate."

In this matter of archdeacons, we English can scarcely plead any superiority over Western Christendom in general. They were, in fact, under almost irresistible temptations. They were mostly either of distinguished birth, or men who had risen by their abilities at the courts of great men; and they needed a professional education far more exacting than that of the bishop or archbishop. It was far easier for a comparatively illiterate prelate to do his work decently, than for an uneducated archdeacon. The difficulties which must always attend marriage law were multiplied tenfold by the labyrinthine perplexities of medieval matrimonial jurisdiction. Testamentary cases, again, are always extremely difficult; and therefore the archdeacon needed to be a first-rate trained lawyer if he was to be at all efficient. That meant that the aspirant needed an expensive education; he must study, probably, at a foreign university, of which Bologna was the greatest in this subject, under the ordinary university temptations and with the necessity of making money when he came back to England, in order to recoup himself for this outlay. The Archdeacon of Ely in the fourteenth century, though far from one of the richest, had two benefices amounting to nearly £95 yearly, with £27 in legal fees from the clergy of the diocese; the equivalent of nearly £4000 to-day. To this we must add the fines which, through his summoner, he took for immoralities; thus he was under the greatest temptations to accept bribes. His financial position in fact resembled that of the *Publicanus* in Christ's day; and this explains all that underlies the unvarying satire of his contemporaries. Even those opening fifty lines of Chaucer's Friar's Tale are less plainspoken than what his friend the Moral Gower has to tell us about archdeacons. Long before Chaucer or Gower, again, Giraldus Cambrensis had accused archdeacons of actually fomenting litigation, and preventing amicable arrangements "unless their hand be greased"—*nisi peruncta manu*. "For this office is so wholly given over to rapacity nowadays, beyond all others in the Church, that the name of *archdeacon* rings in some men's ears with a sound as horrible as that of arch-devil; for the devil steals men's souls, but the archdeacon steals their money."[10] St Thomas Becket did, in fact, call Archdeacon Geoffrey Ridel "archidiabolus noster."[11] If these writers are ruled out as satirists, let us take John of Salisbury, perhaps our greatest publicist of the Middle Ages. He alludes to a question debated in his time: Can an archdeacon come to Heaven? and here is his own serious characterization of them, for which we need no further discount than for ordinary medieval exaggeration of speech. "They love bribes; they are revengeful and prone to injury. They rejoice in calumny, eat and drink the sins of the people, and live on robbery.... Their high office makes it their duty to keep God's Law, yet they keep it not."[12] Henry II, though he again must be heavily discounted, complained that the "archdeacons and rural deans of this realm" extort a greater yearly sum than royalty itself receives. Thus, as Professor Hamilton Thompson writes, "the more valuable English archdeaconries, especially in the latter thirteenth and early fourteenth centuries, were frequently perquisites of cardinals and well-born satellites of the papal court; and at all times it was not uncommon for an archdeacon, especially if he were occupied, as was often the case, in the royal chancery or other office at Westminster, to perform his duties exclusively through an official and the official's clerks".

Hitherto, we have dealt only with the "secular" clergy: those that lived in "The World" (*in saeculo*). The "Regulars", those who lived by Rule, and were cloistered, are almost equally important, but must be described later on.

XI. RECTOR AND VICAR

THERE is, however, one important region common to both Seculars and Regulars, which must be treated here.[1] The distinction between *rector* and *vicar* is so little clear, even to many well-informed readers of to-day, that it must be explained before we go farther. The rector is what his name implies, the spiritual "ruler" of the parish. His "benefice" is a freehold; he retains it for life, in default of the gravest causes for deprivation. He is the "parson", the person *par excellence*, in his little domain. Originally, the man who did the spiritual work of the parish was always a rector. But in process of time, partly because the lay patrons so often abused their position to rob the presentees of a great portion of their tithes, and reduced them generally to such servile dependence, it was felt to be a pious act for the layman to give "his church" to some monastery. This was an improvement, so long as the monks either did the parish work themselves or chose their assistant priests with conscientious care. But Popes were soon compelled to forbid that first course, as prejudicial to the discipline of the monastery itself; and, under the second alternative, monks yielded increasingly to the temptation of taking just such toll from their presentees as the lay patrons had been wont to take. Soon, in fact, even the theory which had made them into mere trustees of these parochial endowments broke down altogether; then, with increasing frequency, Popes and bishops permitted the monks (or the cathedral canons) to "appropriate" the "church" which the lay patron had "given" to them: to convert it (as the legal phrase went) "to their own uses"—*ad proprios usus*. From that time forward the monastery was the "rector" of the parish, and the work was done by a hired underling under the title of "vicar": *vicarius* being the regular word for a substitute of any kind. At first such vicars were "curates" in the lowest modern sense of the word; that is, hirelings with no security of tenure beyond the will of their employer. This position, however, led to such obvious abuses that energetic bishops stepped in and compelled the appropriators to consent to a definite legal "ordination" which should give the vicar a living wage and security of tenure. The wage aimed at was, in general, one-third of the total parish revenues, the appropriators taking two-thirds. Sometimes the vicar got more than this, when the parish was large and he in turn was compelled to hire one or more assistant priests. More often than this, however, the vicar who did the work received even less than his one-third of the revenues. But at least he now held his office, such as it was, for life; his vicarage was as truly a "benefice" as the rector's. For that was the distinguishing legal mark of *beneficium*, that it should be a freehold; the *vicarius* of earlier days, the man dismissible at will, had held only an *officium*. We must pursue this question farther when we come to the "regular", or cloistered, clergy; meanwhile the reader will already see the significance of this "appropriation" system for parish life. Before the Reformation came, about one-third of all our rectories had thus been reduced to vicarages, and two-thirds of their revenues had been diverted from parochial purposes to other quite different—indeed, often distant and almost unknown —beneficiaries. Moreover, in the nature of the case, it was generally the richer livings which fell a prey to these appropriators.

This distinction being clearly grasped, we may now look into the method of presentation to English benefices. Our evidence is sufficiently multitudinous and varied to place beyond a doubt that, as we might expect, the richer livings went to kinsfolk or friends of the patrons, while the numerous peasant-born priests had to content themselves with vicarages or such stipendiary work as assistants in the parish, chaplains to great folk, or Mass-priests on some chantry foundation.

Here, our episcopal registers yield the most curious and startling results. It is a testimony to the comparative orderliness of social, political, and religious life in England, that we possess incomparably more of these records than any other country; but it is not to our credit that so little use has yet been made of them for statistical purposes in history. All past attempts to write our ecclesiastical history without these witnesses are comparable to the fashion, perhaps scarcely dead even now, of writing Old Testament history mainly from Bible records, with comparative neglect of the thousand illustrative documents and monuments. These our episcopal registers, which afford evidence of unique value as to clerical mortality during the Black Death, give us also the most lively picture of the effect which that plague had upon the personnel of our parish clergy.

Exeter diocese was ruled from 1308 to 1324 by that Stapeldon who, like so many other bishops, was a royal minister and frequently away from his flock. During those years, he instituted 376 incumbents to livings in lay presentation; and the examination of those men's status gives surprising results. We must confine ourselves to lay presentations; since, where the "patron" was also "rector" (that is, a religious corporation which left the actual parish work to be done by a man who was practically a perpetual curate), it would have been most scandalous to put in anyone who could not even say Mass. We do, indeed, find the thing sometimes done, and the wretched parishioners thus deprived even of the most necessary spiritual aid; but such flagrant abuses were rare enough for us to ignore them here in this calculation. Under lay presentation, the incumbent was normally rector, and received all the parish revenues, and could afford, if he was ordinarily conscientious, to keep an assistant priest who would do such work as the rector could not perform himself. Those lay advowsons, therefore, are the instances which alone left the patron any real freedom of choice as to the status of the presentee. A mere vicar must needs be a priest, since the salary was scarcely ever such as to enable him to pay an assistant priest, and there must be somebody in the parish for daily Mass and deathbed absolution and unction, with other functions reserved for priests alone. How, then, did the lay patrons exercise their choice, and what were the sort of men whom the bishop instituted at the presentation of these layfolk, finding it probably almost impossible to refuse them even though he should wish? Out of those 376 rectors instituted by Stapeldon, only 135 were in priest's orders: scarcely more than one-third! Three years after Stapeldon's death came Grandisson (1327–69), one of the most energetic and conscientious prelates of our whole period. Taking his first 5 years, we find that he instituted 31 priests, as against 40 non-priests. Again, in the last 5 years before the Black Death, the proportion was similar: 26 to 35. Thus Grandisson's record is far more respectable than his predecessor's; the minority of 28 per cent. on the priestly side has become a minority of only about 14 per cent. But, if we now pass on to take the 5 years which included and followed the Black Death, we find the balance suddenly reversed: 115 priests stand here against 63 non-priests: the earlier steady deficit has now swung round to a favourable balance of 29 per cent. Moreover, when we pass again to Grandisson's last 5 years, the balance is still on the right side: 25 to 13; i.e. 31·6 per cent. more priests than non-priests. The evidence is similar from other dioceses. To the evidence of those 16 years under Stapeldon, and the 20 years taken from Grandisson, we may add full statistics from Brantyngham at Exeter, Rigaud de Asserio and Wykeham at Winchester, Drokensford and Ralph of Shrewsbury at Bath and Wells. From those registers we get a total of 675 lay presentations before the pestilence, and 472 after it. In the earlier period the priestly presentees number 249, or nearly 37 per cent.; in the later 342, or 72·5 per cent. No two students, perhaps, would exactly agree to a unit in the calculation of these figures; but I do not think that any two could differ by more than 10 per cent. at most. The sudden change which the statistics mark, and, what is more, the abiding change, are almost unexampled in Church history. It will be seen later how exactly this statistical evidence fits in with the observations of the chroniclers.

What, then, was the previous history of these rectors and vicars? A multitude of small indications enable us to form a fair general idea. The rectories, numbering about 5500 in all, went mostly to men of middle-class or higher extraction; or at least to those who had some sort of social influence. The bishops disposed of valuable preferments; Winchester, one of the richest, had the patronage of 80 parishes, with an average income of £31. 10s. [say, £1260 modern];[2] but, as the prelates themselves were often statesmen, so the episcopal presentees were often distinguished rather for business than for strictly ecclesiastical qualifications. Among such presentations, the most honourable were those which enabled prominent university scholars to continue their study or teaching; for there was no regular endowment for any professorship until the last pre-Reformation years; so that Wyclif the reformer was himself for many years an absentee rector. On the other hand, most of the 3000 vicars, with cantarists and chaplains—that is, some 14,000 priests—would come in overwhelming majority from the peasant, artisan, or, at most, lower-middle classes; the villager's spiritual father was very often, as in Chaucer, his blood-brother. It has in all ages been partly the strength, partly the weakness, of the Roman Church that so large a proportion of her priests are drawn from the least leisured classes. In the Middle Ages, as now, it was a source of legitimate pride to parents, and often of considerable advantage, that they saw their son at the altar. At the same time, this gave point to the very frequent complaint that the moral and intellectual difference between spiritual father and son was regrettably narrow. Great churchmen, from quite early days, and thence again through St Bernard, who gave further currency to the words, were accustomed to quote from Isaiah (xxiv. 2): "As with the people, so with the priest", and to add, with the rhetorical exaggeration of despondent idealists, "nay, but our priests are worse than the people".

Let us follow one of these men from the plough-tail to the altar. The question of medieval education in general must come in a later chapter; but here we may anticipate for a moment and consider the narrower question of clerical training.

XII. THE MAKING OF A PRIEST

IT is impossible nowadays to accept the optimistic estimate of Bishop Stubbs in his *Constitutional History* (ed. 1878, III, 370). He writes: "The existence of a clerical element in every class of society, and in so large proportion, must in some respects have been a great social benefit. Every one admitted even to minor orders must have been able to read and write; and for the sub-diaconate and higher grades a knowledge of the New Testament, or, at the very least, of the Gospels and Epistles in the Missal was requisite. This was tested by careful examination in grammar and ritual at every step; even a bishop might be rejected by the arch-bishop for literary deficiency; and the bishop who willingly ordained an ignorant person was deemed guilty of deadly sin." The fact that so great a man as Stubbs could write thus is, in itself, one of the most painful testimonies to the neglect of our immense stores of ecclesiastical records. Stubbs, no doubt, knew the cases quoted by Giraldus Cambrensis, but felt justified in ignoring them as the mere exaggerations of a satirist. The study of the registers had not advanced far enough to make him realize that even Giraldus's testimony is outdone by the most cold-blooded ecclesiastical documents.

Dr Rashdall, with the advantage of a whole later generation of study, wrote very differently in answer to Newman's rosy and regretful picture. His words run: "So much party capital has at times been made out of the supposed 'religious' character of the medieval Universities that it is necessary to assert emphatically that the 'religious education' of a 'bygone Oxford', in so far as it ever had any existence, was an inheritance not from the Middle Ages but from the Reformation. In Catholic Europe it was the product of the counter-reformation." Elsewhere Rashdall writes of "the very small proportion of students who ever attained even the B.A. degree, in spite of the mildness of medieval examiners"; and he adds: "There is considerable reason to believe that in the Middle Ages a larger proportion than at the present day of the nominal students derived exceedingly little benefit from their University education."[1] If the register of Bishop Stapeldon of Exeter, in the earlier fourteenth century, can be taken as typical (and certainly it ought not to be far below the average), there were only 25 Masters among the whole cathedral and parish clergy of the diocese; only 25 clergy, that is, who had gone through the full university course, let alone proceeded afterwards to a degree in theology. Again, in the specially important Convocation of 1433, which had to decide whether the English clergy should side with the Council of Basel or with Eugenius IV, there was a proviso in the proclamation of summons that the proctors of the clergy should all be *graduati*; all, that is, at least Masters of Arts.* Nor was this paucity of university graduates atoned for in other ways. The Middle Ages knew nothing answering to the modern seminary system. There were indeed episcopal schools, teaching grammar and a certain modicum of divinity and philosophy: but these were small at the best, and probably often dormant; they come very little into our records. They may sometimes have been among the *studia* to which bishops occasionally sent young rectors to qualify for ordination; but such documents refer far more often to universities. It seems evident that the great majority of medieval parish clergy attained to priesthood very much as a gild apprentice obtained his mastership, by practice and rule of thumb. At the present stage of historical research, far more study is required for any scientific and exhaustive account of clerical training; yet a brief sketch must be attempted here.

We may start from a specially interesting concrete example: the author of *Piers Plowman*. The evidence, after all that has been written on both sides, seems definitely in favour of the old tradition that this man was William Langland, and that the apparently autobiographical touches in his poem are as truly autobiographical as they profess to be. All that, however, is irrelevant to the present argument, since the most sceptical critics admit, if only tacitly, that those professedly autobiographical touches are coherent and consistent; in other words, that, even if the portrait they compose is not *vero*, at least it is *ben trovato*; if our poem does not record the actual career of this particular author, yet at least it describes the sort of career that was natural for such an independent clerical author as he professes to be. Moreover, the

* I do not think we can interpret the term *graduatus* less strictly than this. The B.A. was not then a degree, but only a step towards one; it would be difficult to find it quoted anywhere in the official way in which "master" is prefixed to a man's name after complete graduation.

question is all the more topical at this present moment, when attempts are being made to present Langland to us as a full-blown priest, in contradiction to what seem his own explicit assertions. Starting from the fact, noted long ago, that he sometimes quotes Biblical texts not from the Vulgate version but from the Breviary, it is argued that this proves his priestly status. But, quite apart from the gross logical fallacy of arguing "priests, by Canon Law, must read the Breviary, therefore the man who knows the Breviary must be a priest", the theory does violence to notorious medieval conditions, and rests upon a misunderstanding of Canon Law itself.

There was never in England, until the lifetime of many now living, a real general educational system for all, down to the lowest; nor did such exist anywhere else in the Western Church. Charles the Great might strive after something of the kind; so again might Pope Eugenius II shortly afterwards, but no attempt can be found on the part of Pope or prelate to enforce this as a disciplinary matter: nothing (for instance) comparable for one moment to the systematic campaign against clerical marriage. It remained, therefore, only a pious ideal that the priest or his parish clerk should teach gratis any child who wished to learn. We do find, very sporadically, priests who taught gratis; and, more commonly, clerks who taught for small fees. So far I must here anticipate a later chapter dealing with education in general. From some such priest or clerk, then, a peasant's son might receive the rudiments of education; a better born boy might learn from a private tutor or at a grammar school; but these at the Conquest were extremely few, and, even under Henry VIII, offered far less opportunity than to-day. If the boy's father were a serf he would need to pay a fine for sending his son to school or when the boy took orders. Langland seems clearly to imply, in one passage, that he was bondman-born, but freed by his scholarly tonsure.

The youth, then, learns enough, partly at school and partly perhaps by serving the priest at the altar, to receive one or all of the four Minor Orders, which were commonly given in a lump.* Thenceforward he is qualified to act as parish clerk: a person too much neglected in English history and yet second, perhaps, in

---

* These were Door-Keeper, Reader, Exorcist, and Acolyte, generally summed up in the single term *Clericus* or *Acolitus*. The Major Orders were Subdeacon, Deacon, and Priest.

sociological importance only to the priest. From very early times it had been decreed in Canon Law that the priest should have a deacon or clerk or "scholar" to help him at his daily services. The ordinary function of this assistant was to render the responses; but, in the absence of the priest, law enjoined upon him to read the Matins and Evensong himself. It is evident that this would form a natural stage of apprenticeship towards the priesthood. A man who, year after year, had followed the service enough to read the responses, and was capable at a pinch of reading the whole service himself, had already gone four-fifths of the way; and it is natural, therefore, that at last we should find this officially recognized. Archbishop Boniface, of Canterbury, decreed in 1260: "We have often heard from our elders that the Benefices of Holy Water were originally instituted from a motive of charity, in order that from their revenues poor clerks might be kept in the schools, and so advance in learning that they might be fit for higher preferment." Therefore (he continues), in churches not more than ten miles distant from cities and towns in Canterbury province, the rectors and vicars must all endeavour to find such clerks and appoint them to this "benefice". In 1280 we find Archbishop Pecham ordaining for a parish and its dependent chapels that the two parish clerks there should also keep school. Thus the system provided for a continuity of ecclesiastical education, after a simple fashion. The canonist Lyndwood, commenting in the fifteenth century on this and on one other similar passage, explains that the clerk in lower orders was *beneficiatus* only if he had a *titulus*. He points out that some of these lower clergy performed simply menial offices (bell-ringing, church-sweeping, etc.); and that it was indifferent whether such a man were married or not; he did indeed count as a *clericus* outside the church, but not inside; his place at service was not in the choir but among the layfolk in the nave. If, however, he were parish clerk in the full sense, then his position would be different. As we have seen, he had there a *titulus*, he had been formally appointed by the incumbent or the parishioners; thus he had in the full sense an *ecclesiasticum beneficium*; and therefore his place must be in the choir, "since the cleric had to serve with the priest at the altar, to sing with him and read the epistle". Therefore he must not, as a general rule, be married; and in fact we find concrete cases of bishops who object to a married parish clerk. But, at a pinch, "in defect of unmarried clerics" a "married cleric" may act as full parish clerk, and therefore (by implication) take his place in the choir. Here again, therefore, was a possibility for Langland even after his marriage. But we, who still believe in him as an autobiographer, must note that he gives no such hint: he describes himself as living in a far more hand-to-mouth fashion than if he had the *beneficium* of a parish clerk. There seems, however, to exist no real reason why he should not, long before he ever met his wife Kitte or begat his daughter Kalote, have picked up all that knowledge which he shows of the Breviary and the Bible and other patristic or moral scraps. For it must not be forgotten how many scrap-books and common-place books of that kind have survived, first made by one man for his own use, then perhaps sold or left to another, and added to from generation to generation. To treat it as a marvel that Langland was able to quote all the Latin we find in *Piers Plowman* is as perverse as the belief that Shakespeare could not have written as he did unless he had really been Francis Bacon.

In the light of this, it will be easier to understand the jolly clerk Absolon of Chaucer's Miller's Tale. To cense the congregation in church was part of his daily duty at Matins, Mass, and Evensong; on other solemn occasions he sprinkled holy water (in his capacity of "exorcist") from house to house, and received a small fee from each, as also at other times. If Matthew Paris does not exaggerate, such "casualties" might come to 20s. a year: i.e. at least £40 in modern terms. He was qualified to sing on his own responsibility (and here again for small fees) such services as the funeral Matins and Evensong for departed relatives, which were called *Dirige* and *Placebo* respectively from the opening words of their anthems: hence our "dirge" for any melancholy song. He could earn small fees for teaching; and, if careful and ambitious, get at least some little training at the university, or at the nearest episcopal school, on the strength of these savings; and thence proceed to the three Major Orders.

But at that point came definite crossways, and a call for final choice. The clerk in Minor Orders was not cut off from marriage. Even if he lost his "benefice" of parish clerk thereby, which was no matter of necessity, there were still certain kinds of "clerical" work open to him, as for instance the keeping and enrolment of accounts. Thorold Rogers assumed too hastily that the dog-Latin of manorial rolls showed unexpected education on the part of the bailiffs; a closer study often reveals the actual sum paid to the "clericus" for doing that job. Even in great monasteries, we often find this item at the end of an account-roll: *item, clerico scribenti hunc compotum*, and so on; and the major monastic officials sometimes had each his own clerk in his office. In very large towns the clerks sometimes formed a gild; "Clerkenwell", just outside the ancient walls of London, is where the clerks of that city were accustomed to hold religious theatrical performances; so they did also at another extra-mural spot, "Skinner's Well". Absolon, it will be remembered, could not only "make a charter of land and a quittance", but, on occasion, he "playëd Herod on a scaffold high".

Such, then, were Langland's chances even after his marriage. A hand-to-mouth existence, unless he were able to retain his benefice as parish clerk; yet with no more chance of actual starvation than that which confronted all casual labourers. The life suited him better, he tells us, than the field-work with which he was familiar enough, but for which he was too long in body (and, we must suppose, too frail) to stoop. Then, as now, the attractions of brain-work had begotten a "learned proletariat". A fortunate few, like the poet Hoccleve, Chaucer's pupil, found permanent employment under the king: a few others, again, under great nobles or prelates, or at abbeys. Professor Tout has published an interesting monograph on the Civil Servants of those days. But, as we shall see in Chapter XLIII, even Hoccleve, in the royal office of the Privy Seal at Westminster, looked upon himself as an ill-paid drudge, and remained long unmarried for fear of cutting himself off from what was the great hope of every "clerk", whether at or outside the universities, namely, a fat rectory. When a rise came for him, it was in the shape of a pension of twenty marks, to be paid until he could secure some benefice, without cure of souls, of £20 a year. That benefice, however, was so slow in coming, that the expectant burned his boats at last, and took a wife. Reading the rest of his frank autobiographical confessions, we shall see that he was well out of that priesthood and that expected benefice of £20 a year, except in so far as he might have put in a better man to do the parish work for small pay, and enjoyed the remainder here in London and Westminster. For if, with no professional education whatever, he had joined that priestly class and worked his own parish, he would have found himself in a village where those who could read anything whatever could probably be counted on the fingers of one hand, and where none even of those had ever read half a dozen volumes from beginning to end. We must not lay too much stress on mere book-learning; but, on the other hand, it is impossible to ignore the social significance of this comparative illiteracy.

The scattered evidence of episcopal examinations tends to show that, though conscientious prelates took this duty seriously, they had seldom time to deal strictly and searchingly with the large number of candidates. In a few cases, we have record of the actual answers of rejected candidates; these imply that the questions were, in the main, upon elementary points of Latin grammar, or upon ability to sing by note. On one other point, however, the references are rather less scanty, and give more opportunity for testing the success of the examiners. This was the question of "title", which, as an integral part of the system, needs a few words of explanation here.

The law prescribed that the ordaining bishop should assure himself, by personal enquiry, of the candidate's fitness in education and in morals. Besides this, he had to ascertain that the man was insured against becoming a burden upon the Church; for the bishop himself, in the last resort, was bound by law to keep from starvation any man whom he or his predecessors had ordained. Therefore a "title" was always demanded. If the candidate could not show, or swear, that he had a sufficient patrimony, then some other responsible person must go surety for him, and accept the responsibility of his maintenance in case of necessity. A large number of these "titles" were given by monasteries. The reason has never been proved by documentary evidence, but it is possibly connected with the undoubted fact that monks became so overburdened with statutory Masses for departed benefactors that they had no alternative but repudiation of contract or the hiring of priests from outside. Be that as it may, the records show clearly that this question of "title" seriously affected the examination system. Mr H. S. Bennett allows me to quote here from an unprinted study, based upon wide reading in the Episcopal Registers and the Calendars of Papal Petitions and Letters. He writes: "The examiners were often extremely pressed for time; for, besides the more spiritual side of their task, they were entrusted with the very important office of ascertaining the candidates' worldly standing and prospects. This enquiry was very important, and no doubt frequently absorbed much ill-spared time. In short, the examiner's judgments must frequently have been hasty and based on a few minutes' observation and enquiry." Thus, although bishops are often found taking their duty of examination seriously, the results were not always satisfactory. Giraldus Cambrensis, writing as an archdeacon of long experience, one of whose main duties was the supervision of clerical education, speaks twice of episcopal examinations as a farce.[2] The Exeter Synod of 1297 complained that "criminous clerics, or clerics of illegitimate birth, or otherwise unfit for Orders" often flee into other dioceses to get ordained by alien bishops, "from whom they not only conceal their defects but, what is more detestable, often lyingly assert that they have already [Minor] Orders, or that they have higher Orders than in fact they possess": therefore for Exeter diocese strangers must produce their letters dimissory, or at least show testimonials and undergo examination before they are allowed to settle in any incumbency.[3] Mr Bennett's evidence corroborates this. He writes: "Examples might be quoted of cases in which one or another of all the essentials enquired into by the examiners was falsely represented. The *Papal Registers* give us a wealth of information on this subject. Thus, dispensations are gained by men who acknowledge receiving Orders (and therefore of withholding essential information from the examiners) although they were under age, or had not received the necessary inferior orders, or were illegitimate.[4] Serfs were able to pass as free men, while many candidates asserted they had a 'title', which was in truth only a fictitious one. St Thomas More, discussing the weaknesses of the clergy, emphasizes this. 'For it is by the laws of the Church provided to the entent that no priest should, unto the slander of priesthood, be driven to live in such lewd manner or worse, there should be none admitted to priesthood, until he had a title of a sufficient yearly living, either of his own patrimony or otherwise. Nor at this day there be any otherwise accepted.' 'Why', quod he [More's interlocutor], 'therefore go there then so many of them begging?' 'Marry,' quod I, 'for they delude the law and themselves also. For they never have grant of a living that may serve them in sight for that purpose, but they secretly discharge it ere they have it, or else they could not get it. And thus is the Bishop blinded by the sight of the writing, and the priest goeth a-begging.'"[5]

Side by side with this, let us take the evidence of More's intimate friend Erasmus. He tells us how David, Bishop of Utrecht, "had heard that, among so many who took Holy Orders, there were very few who were educated—*paucissimos esse qui literas scirent*". *Literae* doubtless means here, as nearly always in the Middle Ages, Latin as distinguished from the vernacular. Therefore he conducted his own ordination examination himself, and found only 3 candidates out of 300 who were sufficient for their profession. He was at length compelled to pass the rest, because he found that no better could be found at the starvation wages of a sixteenth-century curate.[6] In the bishop's court, there was the same gulf between legal theory and actual practice which we shall trace later on in other courts. Elsewhere, in his Ἰχθυοφαγία (a colloquy between the Butcher and the Fishmonger), the former complains bitterly of the morals and ignorance of too many clergy. He goes on to speak of perjury, which ruins a business man's reputation, and adds: "Yet no perjury is laid to the account of the priest who lives in public lewdness, though he has publicly sworn himself to chastity." To this the Fishmonger replies: "Sing that song to the bishops' vicars-general, who take an oath at the altar that they have found all the candidates whom they bring up for ordination to be of fit age, learning, and morals; whereas sometimes there are scarce two or three tolerable persons in the whole batch, and many are scarce fit for the plough-tail."

"But" (continues Mr Bennett), "after the examination, the candidates returned to their villages and parishes and pursued their everyday lives; and it is there that we see them in their true colours. Hence the real value of the examiner's work is better tested now, as it was then, not by the records of a brief interview in the examination hall, but by the records we have of the behaviour and learning of the clergy from year to year, and even from century to century. It is sufficiently evident from the reiterated exhortations of the Archbishops and Bishops that they were painfully aware that all was not well with the clergy. Throughout these centuries immediately preceding the Reformation, there was a growing feeling that the condition of the Church would never be improved until the quality of her clergy was improved."

To follow the line of evidence thus suggested, we cannot do better than turn to Chaucer and his two famous contemporaries,

Gower and Langland, for a picture of clerical life as seen by educated English folk of that day. These literary sources must be read, of course, with our usual allowance for medieval rhetoric. But a series of other testimonies, many of them from the coldest and most unexceptionable documents, will enable us to judge whether these poets have stepped beyond legitimate satire into caricature.

Gower is by far the most voluminous of the three. In his *Vox Clamantis* and his *Mirour de l'Omme* he devotes nearly 7000 lines to the Church; and the burden of it all is the decay of religion in his own day. True, a very large part of this is "conveyed" whole-sale from Anglo-Norman satirists of the twelfth century, especially Neckham and Wireker; but, though this literary theft is of the frankest medieval type, Gower explicitly makes the stolen matter his own. He claims to speak for the man in the street: twice in the *Vox Clamantis* he writes: "It is the voice of the people which dictates these words of mine"; and in the *Mirour*, complaining of the Pope and his Church, he tells us he is writing not his own ideas but those of "all Christian folk".[7] Moreover, he had not the slightest sympathy with Lollardy: his dogmatic orthodoxy was irreproachable. Little as he sympathized with the doctrinal innovations, we could select from him an indictment almost as formidable in substance, though less bitter in language, as from Wyclif himself.

In the *Mirour* he deals specifically with the *Pope*.[8] This great pontiff loves to be called *Your Holiness*; but that is all the holiness about him. Not Christ but Antichrist rules at the papal court. The Cardinals wear red hats, "like a crimson rose opening to the sun; but that red is the colour of guilty pride". The Bishop is often luxurious, and adds to his great income by taking bribes from rich adulterers: so also does the Archdeacon: they actually find their profit in the sins of the people. The Universities are too often given to idleness and riot; in the parishes the priest is frequently absent; often again he sets a bad moral example to his flock; or is so ignorant that he scarcely knows what he is saying when he mumbles his Latin prayers.[9] Worst of all, the clergy always support each other; even the better priests shield their peccant brethren from justice.[10] This accusation was to some extent admitted by St Thomas More in his own day. The Monks, again, were originally men of self-denial and penance: but, "nowadays they have everywhere abandoned this observance; for gluttony guards every gate of the monastery, lest hunger and thirst should enter in and bring leanness into their fat paunches".[11] The old sort of monks have been ousted from the abbeys by a new sort; Dan Charity has been slain by Dan Envy; Dan Hatred has expelled Dan Unity. Dan Patience has lost his temper; Dan Obedience has departed; it is Dan Pride, Dan Murmur, and Dan Backbiter who reign nowadays; and, what is worse, Dan Unchaste and Dan Incontinent.[12] Thence, turning to the Canons Regular and the Friars, he is equally plain-spoken and uncomplimentary. And, though here in the *Mirour* he says nothing either way about the Nuns, in the parallel passage of *Vox Clamantis* he gives them no better character than the Monks.[13]

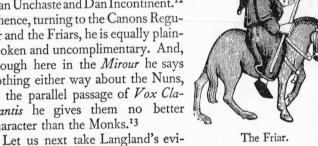

The Friar.

Let us next take Langland's evidence. Here, politically, we have a radical, in contrast to the conservative Gower; and, in religion, a stirring broad-Churchman in contrast to something of a conventionalist. Moreover, Langland's main interest is in the moral betterment of the whole world, and he refers to the clergy, as a rule, only in incidental connection with that betterment. Yet his testimony, on the whole, supports Gower's. We have first Sloth, the careless parson, who can scarcely read his own Mass-book, and cares only for his tithes and his hunting. Then the negligent bishops, who ordain men unable to read the Mass or the Psalms, and proportionally neglectful of their other duties, with the result that few clergy will come to heaven in comparison with simple layfolk. The root of all this evil is at the very foundation of the Church—in the Pope himself.

> God amend the pope, that robbeth holy church
> And claimeth before the king to be keeper over Christians,
> And counteth not though Christians be killed and robbed
> But hire folk to fight, and Christian blood to spill.

Next to the Pope, the greatest power in the Church is wielded by the friars; and these are as bad or worse than he; for it is well known that, when a man cannot get absolved by his parish priest from his sins, he can bribe a friar to whitewash him.[14]

In Chaucer we have a very different poet from either of these. In his wit there is always the flavour of reticence; and our clearest clue to his attitude is the fact that, of all the clergy who went with him to Canterbury, there are only two for whom we can feel real respect. The Poor Parson is admirable: but, as we have seen, the very praise of this particular man is a criticism of his class in general: *he* did *not* do (Chaucer tells us) what was commonly done around him. The Prioress, again, is a dignified figure; and the respect which she commanded from the whole company is obvious. Yet, in Chaucer's detailed description of her dress and her manners, satire lurks under his very praise. Apart from that French of Stratford-atte-Bowe, her seemly-pinched wimple, her conspicuous forehead, her pet dogs, and her brooch with *amor vincit omnia* were all things which a strict bishop, at his visitation, would have been bound to disapprove. Thus Chaucer himself, like our ecclesiastical satirists of the twelfth and thirteenth centuries, and the Oxford Chancellor Gascoigne in the fifteenth, is no exception to what has been confessed by a most orthodox French historian: that, "whether rightly or wrongly, medieval literature does censure monastic morals in crude terms and without distinction".[15]

"Whether rightly or wrongly"; there, of course, is the real question. It is certainly dangerous to rely too much upon literary sources, and historians have often fallen into that trap in the past: for it is the line of least resistance. Yet it is still easier and more dangerous to dismiss such sources with a shrug of the shoulders, and a facile "nous avons changé tout cela". The literary evidence must be tested by side-lights from cold-blooded documents: we may then have to make very heavy discount, or even sometimes to reject our author's conclusions altogether. But when we find, wherever we can test him, that the cross-lights show his substantial veracity, then we may place upon him the same reasonable reliance as we do, in practical affairs, upon our banker or our lawyer or our doctor. At this stage, then, we may now pass on to weigh and test from official sources, point by point, that picture of the clergy which Gower and Langland and Chaucer have given us.

XIII. CHURCH STATISTICS

THIS chapter deals with a number of subjects important for the comprehension of English social life. Amid this multiplicity, logical sequence seems preferable to chronological. Sufficient dates are given to guide the reader, who can thus judge roughly for himself how far conditions improved or deteriorated during our period. He will probably conclude that time wrought here its usual effects. Men were struggling onwards to something better, but fitfully and sometimes blindly, as in other ages before or since. Wherever the betterment was only piecemeal or superficial, the old abuses went on wearing deeper and deeper ruts; so that Hildebrand's reforming efforts cannot be fully understood without reference to the state of things in More's age; nor is More's age fully comprehensible except in the light of Hildebrand's struggles.

We have seen how often the better livings either went to influential young men or were absorbed by monasteries and cathedrals who put in vicars, generally at starveling wages. But an even greater abuse was that of pluralism, with its natural consequence of non-residence. It was not only that the fattest benefices were often distributed for unspiritual reasons; this has been the case to some extent in all ages, although the last two or three generations of our own time have made an enormous difference, and the Anglican Church has at last the theory, and to some real extent the practice, that a curate, by efficient work and steady merit, shall within a reasonable time find his way into a benefice. That was not so in Trollope's time, nor was it so in medieval England: and, far worse, the less spiritual candidate might hold not only one rectory as rich as four or five vicarages put together, but a multiplicity of such benefices: it might almost be said, an infinity. Alexander III, one of the strongest of medieval Popes, rebuked the Archbishop of Genoa for introducing into his diocese this custom of pluralism, which (he writes) is a vice of the French Church, "contrary to Canon Law, and disapproved by Us, although the multitude of offenders renders it impossible to amend it". Some clerics, he says, are reported to have six benefices or even more.[1] In his great Lateran Council of 1179 he legislated expressly against it, as "involving the certain peril of souls". At the next Ecumenical Council (1215) Innocent III repeated this with greater emphasis and the addition of fresh sanctions. Yet twenty-two years later, when the papal legate Otho held a reforming council at St Paul's, London, he needed a strong armed guard of nobles and soldiers to protect him against the vengeance of the pluralist clergy to whom he proposed to apply these sanctions.[2] The later years of that century saw the worst abuses of English pluralism. Bishop Cantelupe of Worcester, uncle to St Thomas Cantelupe of Hereford, protested quite frankly: "Many like ourselves, of noble blood, hold a plurality of benefices: if we are to be deprived of one, we will resign them all in a body." John Mansel, a royal minister, is said (though doubtless in unfriendly exaggeration) to have held 300 benefices. His younger contemporary, Bogo de Clare, who had not even Mansel's excuse of great learning and ability, but was simply a younger son of an Earl of Gloucester, can be traced step by step in Professor A. Hamilton Thompson's *Pluralism in the Mediaeval Church* (*Ass. Archit. Soc. Reports*, vol. XXXIII). Professor Thompson writes: "This [man's] astonishing list [of pluralities] includes two canonries and prebends, which were sinecures, three dignities in cathedral and collegiate churches, and twenty-four parish churches or portions of such churches with cure of souls. London, Bath and Wells, Carlisle and Worcester were the only four English dioceses which did not reckon Bogo among their clergy. That he personally served any of his churches is most unlikely: it is to be hoped, at any rate, that he paid chaplains to officiate in them in his absence." It is certain that he was not yet a priest in 1283, when he had amassed the twentieth of these endowments: probably he never was. He died in 1294. Walter Langton, who was a contemporary of Bogo, though not quite his equal, is fit to be mentioned by his side. Perhaps there has never been any prohibitionist law which has lent itself to such open and systematic bootlegging as this of ecclesiastical pluralities. The more illegal endowments a man succeeded in amassing, the more dispensations he could buy from Rome. One of Bogo's dispensations gave him leave to hold pluralities not exceeding 400 marks (about £10,000 modern); he took advantage of this inch to take an ell. Here is a fairly ordinary specimen from papal letters to the Archbishop of York in 1289. "Transumpt of a dispensation from Pope

Nicholas IV under the seal of the Bishop of Exeter, to Boniface, a clerk, son of Thomas, Marquess of Saluzzo, in the diocese of Turin, to hold [in England] two benefices with cure of souls, without being obliged to be ordained or to reside, notwithstanding any defects in orders or age."[3] A large proportion of the richest English endowments went to such papal protégés who never set foot in this country. The significance of this clause "without being obliged to reside" will be obvious. Our universities were staffed mainly by absentee rectors; that was a natural and comparatively pardonable form of endowment for research; we have seen how Wyclif profited by a system which, however indefensible in strict theory, had been a matter of course for more than a century before his day. But elsewhere the wholesale growth of pluralism spelt equally wholesale absenteeism. The episcopal visitation of the county of Oxford in 1520, covering 193 parishes, reports 58 absentees, i.e. 30 per cent.

Nor, as we have already seen, was that common-sense papal and conciliar decree strictly kept, that the rector of a parish should be in priest's orders, and therefore competent to celebrate Mass and perform the other necessary parochial duties. In 1282, eight years after this decree, even a strong prelate like Giffard of Worcester, backed up by the Archbishop of Canterbury, had great difficulty in applying the specified sanctions, and depriving a noble presentee who held the valuable living of Chipping Campden, yet refused to take priest's orders. The already quoted statistics from the registers show how, before the Black Death, this decree had become almost a dead letter; and, even in the improvement which followed upon that plague, there was still a proportion of non-priestly incumbents which could not be remotely paralleled in any civilized country of to-day. In the later generations of the Middle Ages, there grew up in England a class of brokers called "chop-churches", who dealt in benefices and arranged exchanges. In about 1470, for instance, there came before the Chancery Court the case of Sir John Thomas, parson of Flamstead, against William Lincoln, parson of Great Hallingbury and William Wever, "chopchyrch", of Markyate, "for false representation of the value of Great Hallingbury Church, on a proposed exchange". Later on, the records give us "John Polyng, clerk, alias Chopchirch, of Exeter".[4]

The ordinary priest was not what would be called, in any

country of to-day, an educated man. Even in the exceptional case of his having completed his course of study at a university, he would have found there no faculty of classics or mathematics or history or science. The *Gesta Romanorum*, stories from Roman and other history compiled for the use of preachers, was a classic in its way; yet it informs us at the outset that "Pompey was a great and noble *king*", and goes on to confuse Marcus Aurelius with the legendary Mettus Curtius who closed an earthquake-gulf in the Forum by leaping, horsed and armed, into the chasm! Even of Latin, the priest needed to know scarcely more than what would enable him to read aloud correctly, without construing, the services of the Church. Yet, incredible as it might seem, we have definite evidence that a small minority could not even go so far as this. At the great Lateran Council of 1215, Innocent III had made a determined effort to raise the level of clerical education. In 1222, the Council of Oxford stigmatized some of the clergy as "dumb dogs", and doubted whether they could read even the Canon of the Mass; that is, the essential portion of the Eucharist, not so bulky as a page of this present book. Archbishop Pecham, in 1287, issued a statute in council which begins: "The ignorance of priests casteth the people into the ditch of error; and the folly or unlearning of the clergy, who are bidden to instruct the faithful in the Catholic Faith, doth sometimes tend rather to error than to sound doctrine." Similar complaints meet us again and again in the records of later Synods; and, as late as 1518, Wolsey found himself compelled solemnly to reissue Pecham's statute, *Ignorantia Sacerdotum*, in the very same words.[5]

Let us try to fathom this ignorance, bearing in mind that the whole services of the Church, from beginning to end, were in Latin; that the only Bible authorized by Rome was in Latin; so also was every accessible commentary, and, until the last few generations of our period, nearly every religious book. The Venerable Bede [730] speaks of "clerics or monks who are ignorant of the Latin tongue...on which account I myself have often given to many unlearned priests these two things, the Apostles' Creed and the Lord's Prayer, translated into English".[6] This may be compared with that which Tyndale asserted and St Thomas More, I believe, never denied: "I dare say that there be twenty thousand priests, curates, this day in England, and not so few, that cannot give you the right English unto this text in the

Paternoster, *Fiat voluntas tua, sicut in coelo et in terra*, and answer thereto." Bishop Hooper's visitation of 1552 shows that there were scores of clergy who could not tell who was the author of the Lord's Prayer, or where it was to be found.[7]

But to return to our earlier times. St Boniface [750] referred to Pope Zacharias the question whether a child had been effectually baptized by "a priest who was utterly ignorant of the Latin tongue, and who, in his baptism, not knowing the Latin speech, broke that language and said 'Baptizo te in nomine Patria et Filia et Spiritu sancta'" [for *Patris et Filii et Spiritus Sancti*]. The Pope replied that, since the priest had introduced no theological error or heresy, but "had simply broken the language in his ignorance of Roman Speech", therefore the sacrament was valid. King Alfred, in his complaints of English ignorance, includes the priests. Giraldus Cambrensis [1200] quotes startling concrete instances: two may here suffice.[8] One priest, reading in his Breviary *In die* (and then, on a fresh line) *bus illis* (Luke ii. 1) thought this must mean "in Busillis's day", and asked who Busillis was. Another explained to the congregation that the *piscis assus* (broiled fish) of Luke xxiv. 42 was an "ass fish", according to the medieval notion that the ocean-world is in every way a counterpart of our own. Yet all this pales before the cold-blooded documentary record of that priest who, examined by the Bishop of Sarum's commissaries in 1222, could not construe the first sentence of the first prayer in the Canon of the Mass, or reach even lower-form standard in parsing. The words run: *Te igitur, clementissime Pater...rogamus*, "we beseech thee therefore, most merciful Father...." Let us hear the examiners' exact report. Simon, curate of Sonning-on-Thames, asserted that he had been ordained subdeacon "at Oxford, by a certain Irish bishop named Albin, then suffragan to the Bishop of Lincoln. *Item*, from him he received the Order of deacon. *Item* the Order of priest from Hugh [of Wells], now Bishop of Lincoln, four years ago." In all this he may possibly have lied; but the certainty is that "he was tried in the Canon of the Mass, *Te igitur, clementissime Pater*, etc. He knew not what case *Te* was, nor by what it was governed: and when he was told to look more diligently and see what part could most properly govern *Te*, he said *Pater*, for He governeth all things. Asked what *clementissime* was, or what case, or how it was declined, he knew not. Asked what *clemens* meant, he knew not....Moreover, he said that it seemed indecent to him that he should be tried before the dean, seeing that he had already been ordained. Examined as to where he had been when he received the Order of priesthood, he said that he did not remember. He is sufficiently illiterate"—*sufficienter illiteratus est.* In the seventeen parishes visited on that occasion, all of which were in the gift of the dean and chapter of Salisbury, four others beside Simon were found unable to construe that familiar and crucial Latin sentence. "After [the second of those priests who had been found utterly wanting] had left the church after the examination and had come to the others, all with one accord agreed that they would not answer; yet some separately answered afterwards under great urgency on the dean's part." 9 A generation later, the Archbishop of Rouen notes several similar examinations in his register; these tell much the same tale; yet Normandy was one of the most civilized corners of Europe in that day.

Instances of this kind were ubiquitous and notorious. "There are", wrote St Bonaventura [1260], "so many inexperienced clerics that, even if they be well taught in grammar and other knowledge, yet where 100 or more rectors and vicars are gathered together, there are scarce any who have in fact enough knowledge of the Scriptures to manage either the souls committed to their care, or other things necessary for salvation." He speaks here specially of Italy, and says that things were better in France and England. But St Thomas Aquinas, writing at Paris, complains of "the inexperience of many priests, who in some parts are found to be so ignorant that they cannot even speak Latin, and among whom very few are found who have learnt Holy Scripture". Roger Bacon, writing about the same time in England, and wishing to give an instance of mere parrot-learning, says "just as boys gabble through the Psalter which they have learnt, and as clerks and country priests recite the Church services, of which they know little or nothing, like brute beasts". Gerson, at the beginning of the fifteenth century, speaks equally strongly and far more frequently on this subject. He contrasts what he calls the restless and ill-digested Scripture studies of the heretics with the supineness of even "great prelates", who neglect "the wine of sacred wisdom", and cry, "What is this ye say to us of faith? It is enough that we are Christians, in good simplicity: that is enough; for he who pries into majesty shall be oppressed by its glory; and there is no need to seek things so lofty for us." Again he asks: "Are all ecclesiastics bound to study God's Law? It would seem so...yet on the other side it may be argued that to assert this is to place by far the greater part of ecclesiastics outside the way of salvation, and to assert that they are doomed to damnation." He speaks of the lamentable lack of religious books of any kind among the parish clergy, and complains that there is no organized attempt to multiply good writings against the rising tide of infidelity: to this supineness, and to the ignorance of the beneficed clergy, he attributes a great deal of what he calls the notorious decay of the Catholic Church. To omit much intermediate evidence, we have evidence of the same kind from the verge of the Reformation. When Dean Colet, in 1509, complained that all applicants were admitted indiscriminately to Holy Orders, so that the Church swarmed with "a multitude of unlearned and evil priests", he was only repeating, almost in so many words, what the Bishop of Mende had said to the Pope at the Council of Vienne in 1311. Moreover, both Colet and the bishop lay stress on the fact that laws had been frequently enacted against these abuses, and that the Church needed no new legislation, but simply sufficient courage to enforce those time-honoured and repeatedly enacted laws. More, even in the heat of his controversy against Tyndale, quoted the case of "him that, because he read in his Mass-book *Te igitur clementissime Pater*, preached unto the parish that Te Igitur was St Clement's father".[10]

I have heard a distinguished Roman Catholic layman maintain that his Church does not want a learned clergy: that the Faith is enough. He, like William Morris, was fascinated by Gothic art, and the picturesque side of medieval life. There is much in this plea; for the claims of the medieval Church were strong in imponderables, though far weaker on those sides which she tried to buttress with considerations vulnerable to scrutiny and to reason. The man who daily "made God's Body" found in that a claim far above all others. Just about the time of the Norman Conquest the righteous and courageous Gregory VII submitted the clergy, practically, to the moral judgment of their congregations, by forbidding the laity to attend the Masses of concubinary priests. But it soon became evident that this would eliminate from the Church not so much the offenders as their congregations. Therefore this Pope, who dared to bring the Emperor to public penance, shrank from pushing these sanctions to their full limit; and, in later generations, it became a definite note of heresy to maintain that a priest's morals affected the efficacy of his Mass. Here, therefore, in the superhuman character of the Mass, was a superiority unassailable because it was so intangible; and Quivil, Bishop of Exeter in 1287, used no more than the ordinary clerical language of his time when he issued a decree complaining against those layfolk who, *modernis temporibus*, are mad enough to outrage clerical immunities. "Alas! unhappy wretches, walking in darkness! Is not God our Father who created us? and is not the Church our Mother in whom we were born again by baptism? and is it not written in Canon Law: 'He that stealeth anything from his father or his mother and saith: This is no sin, is the partner of a murderer'? Is it not evident and marvellous madness that the son should attempt to lord it over his father, the disciple over his master? and that a man should strive to subject by unjust obligations those whom he believes to have the power of binding and loosing him not only on earth but in heaven also?"

For the Mass, according to Church teaching in our period, was an *opus operatum*; a ceremony which affected the congregation quite apart from their attention to the service or their state of mind. In Myrc's *Instructions*, the parish priest is bidden to explain to his people the virtue of attendance at the making of the Consecrated Host:[11]

> For glad may that man be
> That once in the day may Him see;
> For so mickle good doth that sight,
> (As Saint Austin teacheth aright,)
> That day that thou seest God's Body,
> These benefices shalt thou have securely;
> Meat and drink at thy need,
> None shall thee that day begrede;   [reproach, accuse
> Idle oaths and words also
> God forgiveth thee both;
> Sudden death that ilk day,
> Thee dare not dread, without nay;
> Also that day, I thee plight,
> Thou shalt not lose thyn eyë-sight.

It need hardly be said that St Augustine had never taught anything of this kind. But the superstition was ineradicable as many others which falsely claimed that great doctor's name; and, in the next century, we find Gerson, the great Chancellor of Paris, writing bitterly of the priests who still taught it. Here (he said) is a false-hood which, often enough, men find plainly contradicted by experience, and which can only help to weaken their faith. Yet the great scholar's protests had little effect; the priest could always promise such miracles that he was thereby raised to an untouchable height.

Yet medieval society oscillated between this childish credulity and childish indifference or petulance. Our earliest records show the priest, despite his lofty spiritual claims, greatly depressed on the material side. For Merovingian and Carolingian France, Imbart de la Tour emphasizes the menial or even servile relation of the village priest to the lord who "owned" the church.[12] Charles the Great had to legislate against the tendency towards drawing clerical recruits mainly from the servile class. For Norway, L. M. Larson quotes from the eleventh-century civil code: "As often as the priests give us wrong directions, or disobey the orders which the bishop puts forth...they shall atone to the bishop with a money fine; *for we have abolished the custom of punishing them with blows*, since we have entered into marriage relations with them and allow them to give our sons instruction."[13] William of Malmesbury describes their menial position in the houses of the Saxon nobles; and St Thomas More, on the verge of the Reformation, deplored the number of grovelling chaplains and hedge-priests in his own day.

The question of the priest's fees and dues is very important; the power of the purse was almost as weighty a factor in the Reformation as in the Rebellion of 1642. The "great tithes" (on crops and cattle) formed the greater part of the priest's income; and, except in cases where custom softened the strictness of the law, it imposed upon every parishioner an income-tax of 10 per cent. on his *gross* revenue, making no allowance for working expenses. It is sometimes asserted that this was cheerfully paid;[14] but this is contradicted by multiple and notorious documentary evidence. It is irreconcilable with the fact that one of the priest's most definite duties—far older and more insistent than that of preaching at Mass—was that of excommunicating periodically and publicly all who had defrauded the Church of this tax. It was one of Chaucer's Good Parson's conspicuous virtues that he was "full loth to cursen for his tithes"; yet curse he must, and in the grisliest earnest. Chaucer's contemporary, the Canon Myrc, gives the text in his *Instructions for Parish Priests*. It runs, "we curse them by the authority of the Court of Rome, within and without, sleeping or walking, going and sitting, standing and riding, lying above earth and under earth, speaking and crying and drinking; in wood, in water, in field, in town. Curse them Father and Son and Holy Ghost! curse them angels and archangels and all the nine orders of heaven! curse them patriarchs, prophets and apostles and all God's disciples and all holy Innocents, martyrs, confessors and virgins, monks, canons, hermits, priests and clerks, that they have no part of Mass nor Matins nor of none other good prayers that be done in Holy Church nor in none other places; but that the pains of hell be their meed with Judas that betrayed our Lord Jesu Christ, and the life of them be put out of the Book of Life till they come to amendment and satisfaction made. *Fiat, fiat! Amen.*"[15]

The "lesser tithes" were on everything except crops and beasts; here is a fair specimen. The monks of Sawley granted to the vicar of Tadcaster, in 1290, that he should have, as part of his stipend, "the tithes of wool, flax, pot-herbs, leeks, apples, cheese, butter, milk, eggs, calves, chickens, geese, hens, sucking-pigs, bees and honey, together with the tithes of servants in Lent, to wit, of hirelings, hawkers, bakers, carpenters, quarrymen, masons, *caprarum* [coopers?] and limeburners, while for a time such exist in the parish; *Item*, of carters and brewsters..." together with half a dozen other small dues from his parishioners.[16] This, though characteristic enough of England, would in one sense have been exceptional elsewhere; for Continental customs seldom recognized these "personal" tithes imposed on men's wages, even on those of all menial servants except the poorest. This formed the subject of serious complaints early in the sixteenth century, when the lay spirit was beginning to assert itself. The discontent was so serious that, in 1518, Wolsey decreed for his province of York that a labourer receiving no more than 6s. 8d. a year (he would also have board and lodging, let us say 1s. a week) must not be compelled to pay personal tithes.

To put this in modern terms, a labourer at £2. 10s. a week would be excused; but one whose wages were £2. 11s. would have to pay a yearly tithe of more than a week's wages to his rector. That this was felt as a real burden by the poor can be proved from one of the fragmentary Yorkshire visitations published by Canon

Raine. The parishioners of Masham are found enquiring of the visitors in 1510: "Also we desire to know what a servant should pay to tithe for his hire, for as much as draws ten shillings, for poor servants that hath but a small wage to find them, it is sore for them to take so mickle." The neighbouring parish of Kirby Malsherd put a similar question in a briefer and more grammatical form: "We desire to know what a servant should pay to tithe for ten shillings wage."[17] But, for many centuries before this, the tithe system had been a fertile source of quarrels and bad blood; it was responsible for more litigation, we may safely assert, than any other subject. There is a decree from Bishop Quivil of Exeter (1287) which, though specially piquant, tells us nothing more than we could prove in the main from other sources. "Seeing that certain persons for their tithe which hath hitherto been given in cheese (according to the custom hitherto approved in our diocese), maliciously bring the milk itself to Church and—what is more wicked still—finding there no man to receive it, pour it out before the altar in contumely to God and his Church." The bishop continues with a long list of similar frauds and subterfuges on the part of tithe-payers.[18] In 1419, Convocation dealt solemnly and very heatedly with the Franciscan Russell, who, with certain fellow-friars, had so heretically championed the people's cause as to teach the non-payment of tithes. Moreover, the whole system of "mortuary", or "corpse-present", which had become strictly compulsory long before the end of our period, reposed upon the assumption—one may say, the almost certainty—that the dead man must at some time have withheld some of his tithes, so that the mortuary, by redeeming this fault, would save him from hell or shorten his purgatory.

There were many other dues which became either strictly or practically compulsory upon all but paupers, even when the priest did not break Church law by exacting money for the Sacraments, an offence which disciplinarians stigmatized as only too frequent. And, finally, the priest had a strong hold upon the man's deathbed. He who had not made a written will (and only an infinitesimal fraction could do this) was expected to make one by word of mouth to the priest or to two unexceptionable witnesses. It was the Church, again, which had exclusive jurisdiction over the probate of wills. Thus "There arose a feeling that intestacy, except in the case of sudden death, was disgraceful. We have seen that there were traces of this feeling as early as the reign of Cnut. It was intensified after the Conquest."[19] Let us put ourselves for a moment in the dying man's place. Whatever else the poor wretch may believe or disbelieve, of hell and purgatory he has never been allowed to doubt. Whenever he entered his parish church, there stood the great ghastly picture of the Last Judgment staring down on him from the walls—blood and fire and devils in such pitiless realism that, when they come to light nowadays, even sympathetic restorers are often fain to cover them again under decent whitewash. A picture of that kind, seen once or twice a week for fifty years, is indelibly branded into the soul of the dying man; and, however little he may have allowed these things to influence the conduct of his life, however deliberately he may have overreached and cheated and robbed in his generation to scrape this little hoard together, here on his deathbed he has at least the faith of a devil—he believes and trembles. He knows that gifts to the Church are universally held to be one of the surest preservatives against the pains of purgatory; he has perhaps even seen men burned at the stake for denying a truth so essential to the Roman creed. What wonder, then, that deathbed legacies to the clergy and to the churches became so customary that the absence of such pious gifts was sometimes taken for proof presumptive of heresy, and that the intestate was in consequence buried in unconsecrated ground.

The priests' incomes varied even more than now. In parishes where much land had been gradually reclaimed—moorland, as in Blackburn, or fenland, as in Doddington, the tithes sometimes ran into four figures in modern values. William Hudson worked out the average value of an incumbency in Norwich diocese (more wealthy than most) at nearly £11 towards the end of the thirteenth century. We may compare this with those of a knight and a peasant farmer. In 1353, all holders of land to the value of £15 and over were decreed worthy of knighthood, and were fined if, in order to avoid the duties and burdens of that order, they neglected to seek that honour. On the other hand, Thorold Rogers calculates that a peasant farming 20 acres of ploughland would spend about £3 a year upon himself, wife, and children.[20] The incumbent, if rector (and sometimes even as vicar), had the upkeep of chancel and service books to face, with traditions of almsgiving and hospitality: we shall see later what this meant. On the other hand, he had not, or ought not to have, a wife and family. The vicarages were, of course, definitely poorer than the rectories: orthodox writers constantly complained that the appropriation system was starving the parish clergy. The bishops, therefore, often stepped in to do what they could against this sweating system. The earliest statistics we have for such "ordinations" of vicarages are for Lincoln diocese in 1209 and following years. Out of the 134 thus "ordained", 113 amounted to less than £4; that is, scarcely more than the peasant farmer's income. The amounts required for a "title" help us also here. In Durham diocese, 1334–44, 96 per cent. of the ordinands assessed their title at 5 marks (£3. 6s. 8d.), which was evidently the regular requirement. In Carlisle diocese, 1292–1324, 75 per cent. claimed 5 marks, but 25 per cent. only 3. In Worcester, 1302–13, only 3 marks were required: one candidate alone was able to boast 5. Vicars' wages rose slowly even to the end of our period, but not more than the cost of living. Mr H. G. Richardson sums up judicially: "If we suppose the average [stipendiary] Chaplain to have had from all sources before the Black Death an income of from six to seven marks, and accept forty-eight shillings as a moderate estimate of the income of a first-class agricultural labourer, such as a plough-man or carter of the same period, we have some indication of whereabouts in the social scale to place the great mass of poorly-paid parish clergy."[21]

The facility with which the clergy accepted first Henry VIII's revolutionary measures and then the final change of faith under Elizabeth cannot be wholly dissociated from the natural discontent of a numerous and underpaid class. Professor E. F. Jacob has noted the contrast between the attitude of Convocation towards taxation in the thirteenth and the fifteenth century. When the legate Otho demanded heavy contributions (1237), there was apparently no discussion; the levy was forced upon the clergy without delay. In 1424/5, however, the proctors of the lower clergy pleaded that their constituents would not permit such a levy; they complained that fraudulent pardon-mongers were unusually active—*plus solito*—and demanded closer restrictions. The discussions lasted from October 18th to November 20th, when Convocation adjourned till after Christmas. Thence they sat till February 8th, when the lower clergy still refused assent, and Convocation was dissolved. Earlier, in 1401, special exemption had been made for "scanty" livings: the limit was set at 8 marks.

In these circumstances, the time-honoured theory of clerical almsgiving could not be strictly practised by any vicar; and, even if there were a few rectors who attempted it, as St Gilbert of Sempringham seems to have done, these are cited as marvels. The theory, in the earliest times, had demanded a fourfold division of the parish revenues, between the bishop, the poor, the upkeep of church and services, and the serving priest. The bishop dropped out at an early date; later canonists speak only of the other three. But a vicar who, by the settled custom of the time, scarcely ever got more than a bare third of the revenues, and more often got less, was obviously incapable of giving that third to the poor. Nor did the appropriating monastery fill up this gulf. After all the emphasis with which Archbishop Stephen Langton had decreed in 1222, and Archbishop Pecham in 1279, that the poor parishioners should not be defrauded of their share of the tithes, it was still necessary for Archbishop Stratford to repeat their decrees even more emphatically in 1342. In spite (he complains) of theories to the contrary, "yet monks and nuns of our province, procuring appropriations of churches, strive so greedily to apply to their own uses the fruits, revenues, and profits of the same, that. . . they neglect to exercise any works of charity whatsoever among the parishioners. Wherefore, by this their exceeding avarice, they not only provoke to indevotion those who owe them tithes and ecclesiastical dues, but also teach them sometimes to become perverse trespassers on, and consumers of, the said tithes, and abominable disturbers of the peace, to the grievous peril of both monks' and parishioners' souls, and to the scandal of very many."[22] The system, it is true, was not quite so bad as some of the malpractices which had preceded it. When the tithes were thus appropriated to a monastery, the church and the priest and the poor might get a little more than in those cases where, by a frequent abuse, the lay patron of the benefice had robbed the church which it was his duty to protect. But in England these lay robberies had been far less frequent than on the Continent; nor, again, did the lay abuse of paying royal ministers with Church livings affect one-tenth as many as were absorbed by the monastic appropriation system. The undeniable result of this was to render the poor man's portion ludicrously small in comparison with the time-honoured theory. The English parliament, a little before and after 1400, dealt over and over again with this scandal; but to no effect, since Popes and bishops had a pecuniary interest in it. At last parliament, losing patience, prescribed that the bishops should definitely earmark a reasonable proportion for the poor. But this prescription, again, was constantly neglected; and, in the few cases where the documents permit us to trace the actual sums, these come on an average not to the statutory one-third of the parochial income, but to about one-sixteenth at most.[23] The monasteries which thus drew two-thirds of the income from nearly one-third of the English parishes were, it is true, the main distributors of such charities as could be counted upon by the medieval poor: but we have irrefragable evidence that they thus gave back far less than they took. The monks' own account-rolls, where they survive, have never yet been found to record charities even to the extent of one-tenth of the abbey's gross income. Moreover, the documents show the monks sometimes even embezzling moneys which had never been their own, but had simply been left to them as charity trustees. At Finchale, a cell to Durham, they were able to claim income-tax reduction on 26s. 8d. which they held in trust for distribution to the poor every Maundy Thursday: yet their private accounts show them distributing only 10s. of this sum. At Dover Priory, they had endowments in trust for the poor to a total amount of £13. 19s. 2d.; their account-roll for the year 1530 still exists, and shows that they distributed only 8s., that is, one-fortieth.[24] Peter of Blois, at the end of the twelfth century, drew a harrowing picture of monastic luxury and neglect of the poor. This description was felt to be so true that the Franciscan Gilbert of Tournai, when the Pope consulted him for the General Council of Lyons (1274) repeated the same accusations, often in Peter's own words; and again, about 1450, Dionysius the Carthusian utilized the passage in his description of the monasticism of his own day. Christ crucified (these three writers said) lies at the gate, in the shape of His poor; and the dogs do not lick his sores but bite him; meanwhile the abbot, like Dives, is feasting within. At that same time the great Oxford Chancellor Gascoigne described the Seven Rivers of Babylon, the seven floods of iniquity; one of these was this absorption of parochial funds by the monasteries. In the north of England, where parishes were fewer, the loss of monastic doles at the Dissolution was more severely felt than elsewhere;

but, during the centuries succeeding that event, the English poor have suffered less, on the whole, than those of France and Austria and Italy and Spain. The ecclesiastical visitation of Oxfordshire in 1520 deals with 193 parishes; in 35 it is complained that alms-giving is neglected.[25] Ten of these are monastic vicarages. The rich Abbey of Oseney had appropriated six Oxfordshire churches; five of the vicars do not give alms, and one of them has even embezzled from moneys that he had in trust for the poor: so, again, did one vicar under the rich Abbey of Eynsham. That friar, contemporary with Chaucer, who wrote the moral dialogue called *Dives and Pauper*, says no more than others said who were equally orthodox. He writes:[26] "Thys poynte of manslaughter toucheth moche men of holy churche; for, as the lawe saythe, The tythes of holy churche be tributes of them that be in nede, to releve theim in ther nede; and alle that men of holy churche have, it is the pore mennys goodys, and ther housys shulde be comon to alle men at nede....But they be not bounde to fede the rych folke, but goostly, and them that have noo nede wythe holy churchys goodys. And of the pore folke yeve they no tale, but to pylle [pillage] them and have of them and get of them what they may by hypocrisy, by fraud, by dread and violence; and therefore God undermynethe [warneth] them by the prophet Ezechiel and saith thus to them: 'woo be to the shipherdis of israel, that is to saye to the prelatys and curatis of holi churche, which shuld be shepherdys of goddys shepe, and of the soulis that criste bought so dere, woo be to the shepeherdys, for they fede theimsylfe and of the pore people yeve they no tale.' And therefore God accepthethe not the praier of such men of holy churche, for they be wythoute charite and ful of crueltye in pyllinge of the pore people."

An excellent conspectus of medieval poor relief may be found in Sir W. Ashley's *Economic History* (vol. I, pt. ii, p. 338). He writes: "No attempt was made by the State as a whole, or by any secular public authority to relieve distress. The work was left entirely to the Church, and to the action of religious motives upon the minds of individuals. If it had ever been attempted to organize charity in a systematic way, making the parish priest the 'relieving-officer' for his parish, and the tithes the fund whence aid was to be furnished, that attempt had altogether broken down. Well-nigh all the assistance that was given to the poor was in the form of almsgiving; almsgiving by magnates, ecclesiastical and lay, by monasteries, by hospitals, by gilds, by private persons; and almsgiving that was in the vast majority of cases practically indiscriminate, whatever it may have been in theory. No attempt was made by any public authority, secular or ecclesiastical, to take a comprehensive view of the situation, and to co-ordinate the various agencies. The reckless distribution of doles cannot have failed to exercise a pauperizing influence in many localities, by rendering it easy for those who did not care to work to live without. But it has been well observed that if the poor relief of the Middle Ages in some directions did too much, in others it did too little. Voluntary charity always has the defect of being more abundant in districts which need it least, and least abundant where there is most want. The towns get more than their share; the fertile and prosperous districts have their richly endowed foundations; while the unhealthy or barren regions are left unprovided for. Thus, in Italy, where medieval conditions have been retained more completely than in any other country, owing to the power of the Church, districts containing scarcely a fourth of the population received until lately three-fourths of the revenue of charitable endowments; while, to give a further illustration, the healthier districts have most of the hospitals (in the modern sense of the term), and those constantly troubled by malaria and pellagra scarcely any. No doubt the same condition of things existed in England. Shameless beggars who were ready to wander from place to place in search of alms had an easy life: the honest hardworking poor, who were visited by misfortune and unable or afraid to leave their homes, would often find no relief at hand."

XIV. THE SHEPHERD

At this point, we may try to picture the priest in his parish as revealed by surviving official visitation records. Such records must, of course, be discounted by the consideration that the visitor's direct duty was that of noting faults for future amendment. Yet, with this discount constantly in mind, we shall be able to observe the extent to which our literary testimonies are borne out by the cold-blooded evidence of commissaries and clerks who were thinking of nothing less than of possible readers four or five centuries after their death.

The routine was always pretty much the same. The bishop's commissary, or the archdeacon, went round the district, and heard evidence either in each village or, more often, at certain accessible points. The clergy were supposed to attend in person; and from each parish came four "synodsmen" (*sidesmen*, by modern corruption) to answer a regular questionnaire, the points of which were nearly the same in every case.

One of the first and most important questions touched the cleric's morals; and on that point we must begin with a brief explanation. Though priestly celibacy had been decreed from very early times in the Roman Church, the law was very generally neglected both in Saxon England and in Normandy. The story was told fully and accurately by the late Dr H. C. Lea of Philadelphia, whose essential fairness and whose laborious scholarship, in spite of occasional lapses, have on the whole survived even the most hostile criticism from those who are interested to contest his conclusions.[1]

Lea begins by tracing the vain attempts to enforce the celibacy rule from 1049 to 1063. In 1074, the great and resolute Hildebrand (Gregory VII) took the extreme step of forbidding attendance at the Masses of concubinary priests, thus making the laity judges of their pastor to an extent which even he dared not push to its conclusion, and which gave excuse for later heresies. In 1076 the Council of Winchester set itself to enforce celibacy: yet William gave no help here, although in Normandy he had sided with the prohibitionists. In 1102 St Anselm faced the problem with his usual straightforward determination. The decrees of his council contained no sanctions; but Anselm for his own part threatened the offenders with deprivation of their benefices. Yet the Pope himself, Paschal II, though a strong man, definitely gave way here, and frankly abandoned the Hildebrandine attitude; it was better, he said, to suffer an unchaste priest than to die without the rites of the Church. And, though Henry I approved Anselm's policy, yet Eadmer, the saint's biographer, confesses its failure. Many priests went on strike, and locked up their churches. Even in Anselm's own diocese of Canterbury, many more flatly defied his excommunication and went on their usual way. In 1107, Paschal II again yielded, and gave dispensations to priests' sons: "in England, the larger and better portion of the clergy fall within the scope of the prohibition" of marriage. It is significant that, by this time, the mere unchastity of a priest was far less offensive to the authorities than his formal marriage. In 1108, Henry I held a council which supported Anselm's contentions; but next year the saint died, and Eadmer admits the increase of secret and scandalous unchastity: "There were few indeed who continued to preserve the purity with which Anselm had laboured so strenuously to adorn his clergy." The papal legate himself, sent in 1126 to lead the orthodox campaign, was caught by night with a harlot after celebrating Mass that day; and, though Henry I professed to enforce the law, Matthew Paris suggests with much probability that he used prohibition as a lever for blackmail. In Wales and Ireland, clerical concubinage was even more widespread. This story of councils repeating prohibition, and by that very repetition tacitly confessing the past failures, need be continued no farther here. It must be added, however, that the Papal Court was notoriously the most immoral in Europe relatively, and perhaps even absolutely. When Durand, Bishop of Mende, was asked what reforms were most needed to be carried out by the Ecumenical Council of Vienne (1311), he began by insisting that all amendment must begin at the fountain-head, and specified, among other things, that brothels were kept at the doors of the Pope's palace, and that his marshals made an income by their upkeep. Thus, in process of time the great cities of Europe, London included, learned to defy those papal laws which protected clerical sinners from condign punishment. Priests caught in open unchastity were dealt with like other folk, and the Londoners kept a separate prison for them.

Without this preamble, it would not have been possible to

realize the exact significance of these episcopal visitations: for clerical marriage was a primary question, not only moral but economic. Peccant priests had not only a partner and children to support, but might also be paying blackmail to the archdeacon, though this was not quite so general a practice in England as in Wales and Ireland. Even though there were no such secret boot-legging, there was the specified legal fine, the significance of which was brought out by the late Master of Balliol in his Ford Lectures. He wrote: "There is in existence a set of canons for Coventry diocese; they are dated 1237, but are evidently prior to those of Otto, and curiously timid in their attitude to clerical sinners. For incontinency a priest on the first two convictions is to be fined only. 'We fine in money because men fear money penalties most, and because it is wealth that is the cause of wantonness. . . . But for all our threats of excommunication we fear they will not return to the Lord, for the spirit of uncleanness is among them.'"[2] This, with masses of corroborative evidence which might be quoted, is even more significant than the bare statistics which are to be gleaned from the reports. Such cases as are reported on those visitations might easily be abused by an historian, consciously or unconsciously, to give an exaggerated picture, yet there is one point which tells its own incontrovertible tale. Whenever, beside the actual fact of the transgression, we note its comparative tolerance by the community and even by the authorities, there we are on safe ground. A law broken not only frequently but with comparative impunity, is scarcely a law at all. Although systematic breach of chastity was legally punishable by deprivation, yet it is extremely rare to find the very strongest bishops, even once in a way, applying that final sanction among the multitude of lawbreakers. Wherever the official records give us a glimpse behind the scenes, there we find the same story. The Chapter Acts of Ripon and Southwell, for instance, record many cases which, by law, should have resulted in deprivation, but in which a money fine sheltered the sinner even from public penance. "At Ripon, for instance, the full sentence on erring priests is recorded in 5 cases; in only one was it actually performed. In one case the culprit redeemed it for a private penance and a fine of 3s.; in the other three, it was redeemed for similar fines without even the private penance."[3]

In the 281 parishes of the Hereford visitation (A.D. 1397) 72 clerics, nearly all priests, were presented by the parishioners for incontinence: this gives more than 25 per cent. Even if we omit the 9 cases where the accused "purged himself", by a process of ecclesiastical swearing which the Oxford Chancellor Gascoigne branded as "an occasion of intolerable iniquity", the fraction is still more than 22 per cent. Moreover, in these same records we find the usual sidelights upon the actual working of this "compurgation" system, by which a man was acquitted if he would swear innocence, and procure a specified number of "compurgators" to swear that they believed him. At Dodynzob [*sic*] the report runs: "Sir William Westhope is incontinent with one Jane Stale, whom he keepeth always in his house." A later hand adds: "The man appeared, denied, and is given a day to purge himself with five compurgators: he was also admonished to remove her from cohabitation within six days." Here we have practically the verdict of "Not guilty: but you must not do it again!" Next, at Colwall, the probable birthplace of William Langland: "Richard of Reye complained publicly in the presence of me, the Registrar, and of the parishioners, that Sir John Comyn, curate of Colwall, hath held his [Richard's] lawful wife Jane by night and day, against his will, wherefore he holdeth them grievously suspect of sin committed. Moreover, that the said Jane absenteth herself from the society and cohabitation of the said complainant her husband, and hath absented herself these six years past, because the said Sir John enticeth her to absent herself." [Added in another hand: "the man purged himself."]

The priest's position being such as it was, his social and moral relations with his parishioners form one of the most important chapters in the history of medieval civilization. It would overburden this volume to give any reports in full beyond that which I have relegated to my notes; readers who wish to pursue the matter into all its details may find the whole original documents in *The English Historical Review* for 1929 (p. 279) to 1930 (p. 444),[4] and Canon Bannister's article upon them in *The Nineteenth Century* for 1927 (vol. CII, p. 399). There are ten parishes among which it is difficult to assign the palm of bad pre-eminence; Goodrich, Westbury, Monmouth, Kempley, Coddington, Taddington, New Radnor, Ullingwick, Wentnor and Clunbury. The last will be found fully translated in my Appendix[5]; it will remind some readers of the rhyme quoted in *A Shropshire Lad:*

Clunton and Clunbury,
Clungunford and Clun
Are the quietest places
Under the sun.

Goodrich and Westbury show how prejudicial an ill-governed monastery might be to village morality. Three parish priests were presented for incontinence by the sidesmen at these two places, and thirteen laymen, one of whom was an abbey servant. The incontinent monks were nine, including the Prior of Flanford and the Abbot of Flaxley. The latter was "defamatus" with three separate women; so was another of his monks, and another with two. These are by far the two worst parishes in this particular respect; yet others show even more neglect and indiscipline under other heads, and few parishes show anything like a clean bill. In 45 cases the church fabric is presented as more or less ruinous; frequently, the roof is not watertight; as the Herefordshire author of *Piers Plowman* puts it, the clergy "care not, though the rain fall upon their altar". In 22 cases Mass is neglected. In 13 the priest, for the sake of extra fees, sings two Masses daily for different places, in flat defiance of Church law. In 14 churches there is not even a Breviary, the book indispensable for Matins and Vespers; in 7 other cases service books are missing, and in 2 others "insufficient". In 21 parishes the churchyard was not properly enclosed and protected from beasts. Nine of the priests were presented for usury, 2 for forgery of wills, and 1 for sorcery. In 3 cases even the statutory alms were not given, and in 9 cases the font was not locked, though this was a statutory precaution lest folk should practise witchcraft with that "sanctified" water. This point, upon which medieval visitors always laid great stress, can be verified by any tourist in any church: it is an infallible test of a medieval font. Unless the remains of iron hinge and hasp be found opposite each other on the rim of the font, or at least the scars which betray their removal, then the font is certainly post-Reformation.

But to return to personal reports of these Herefordshire parishioners upon their clergy. We find priests tavern-haunting "and chattering indecently there", celebrating clandestine marriages for small bribes, trading, embezzling, neglecting Mass and other church ceremonies, selling the Sacraments, and in one case even revealing confessions made under the Sacrament of Penance.

At Curshope (p. 448) half a dozen lines reveal the state of the parish: "The chancel is defective in roof, walls and windows, by default of the rector. *Item*, they have no Masses or other divine services except only Mass on Sundays, and that at their own expense [by hiring a priest], by default of the rector. *Item*, children are not baptized there, by default of the rector.....*Item*, Sir Owen, curate, is incontinent with a certain Gladys, Jokkyn's daughter."

Hereford diocese was, of course, considerably influenced by "wild Wales"; and this report is the worst I know except the almost contemporary visitation of the diocese of Lausanne (i.e. the most civilized part of those districts which are now called Switzerland) which I have analysed in my *Medieval Village*. But we have other evidence as to the extent to which Hereford may be taken as typical. The Oxford Archaeological Society's *Report* of 1925 reproduces in full an episcopal visitation of Oxfordshire in 1520, dealing with 193 parishes. Of these, 37 have a clean bill (19 per cent.). In 58 cases (30 per cent.) the parson was an absentee: in 15 more the services were defective. In 109 cases (62 per cent.) there was serious disrepair. In 47 waste or embezzlement was reported, and in 35 (10 of which were monastic vicarages) almsgiving was defective.

Nor can we here bring in the Black Death. Our records for the pre-plague period, though much scantier, tell essentially the same tale. A visitation of Norwich city in 1333 is preserved in the Bodleian Library (Norfolk Rolls, no. 18). It shows 10 parish clergy accused of incontinence. Three of these "purged" themselves, for what that record may be worth; the remaining 7, even when they "purged" themselves of the crime in the present tense, admitted it in the past. The last few paragraphs may be given here. "Robert, nephew to the vicar of Costessey [and apparently himself chaplain or incumbent of St George at the Gates] keeps incontinently, and has kept for 3 years, Beatrice of Brok. He denies this from all time; let him be admitted to purge himself with 4 compurgators. Roger, rector of Drayton, is ill-famed [*notatur*] with the same woman; he confesses the sin and abjured it (Jan. 31st) under penalty of 5*s*. Master Robert of Knapton, chaplain of St Magdalen, is ill-famed with the same woman, and with Margaret of Hampton; this he denies from all time; to purge with 6 compurgators; also with Jane of Whitlingham, this he denies since he was corrected [*word illegible*]; to purge himself with four;

purged himself on Jan. 31st. Ralph Pecke, vice-dean of Rockland, is ill-famed with the same Beatrice and with Juliana Methelound of Shropham; he confesses the sin and abjures it Jan. 31st under penalty of 5s." These are the worst cases, on the whole; but the cumulative effect of such details can be imagined. In this same visitation, the parishioners present only 19 layfolk for incontinence, as against these 10 clerics; yet Norwich, even with her many churches, cannot possibly have had more than one cleric to every 50 adult layfolk: more probably one to 100. Therefore, though it is likely that many lay sinners escaped presentment through their comparative obscurity, yet the fact that the defamed clerics should have been so incomparably more numerous, in proportion, cannot fail to have produced its effect. The Bodleian Library possesses also a visitation of a Norfolk archdeaconry in 1499 (MS. Tanner, 100, fol. 56 ff.). There, among the 73 accusations of incontinence, 15 were against the clergy. In the Ripon Chapter Acts, to take the most favourable estimate, the numbers run 126–24. A visitation of 1498 (Lambeth, *Reg. Morton*, fol. 75 ff.) gives 48–9. On the aggregate of these four records, therefore, we have 58 clergy to 251 laity, or 23·5 per cent. Yet the clergy cannot have formed more than 2 per cent. of the total population of these districts: probably a good deal less.

Here, again, are one or two Devonshire cases. At Clyst Honiton, in 1301, the parishioners reported their "capellanus" as honest and pious; but he is now past work. "The chancel is so ruinous that Mass cannot be said at the high altar; the service books are imperfect; there is no chalice, and all other appurtenances of the church may be said to be insufficient." In 1330, King Log has been replaced at Clyst Honiton by King Stork. The present chaplain is defamed with three different women, one of whom "he keepeth and hath long kept, as it is said", while another is the wife of one of the sidesmen. A long list of church appurtenances, including the Missal, are reported as "insufficient". At Dawlish (1301) one of the two chaplains "hath kept his concubine for ten years and more, or longer still; and, though often corrected on that account, he incorrigibly persists". At St Marychurch (1301) there is no pyx for the Eucharist, and no chalice for bearing it to the sick. The vicar is suspected of embezzling part of a legacy for the building-fund. "The sidesmen say that the said vicar puts all sorts of beasts into the churchyard, whereby it is evilly trodden down and foully defiled. Item, he appropriates the trees in the churchyard that are blown down, and uses them for his own buildings. *Item,* he causes his malt [*or,* his brewing] to be prepared in the church, and stores his corn and other things therein; whereby his servants, in their exits and their entrances, open the door, and at time of tempest the wind comes in and is wont to uncover the church [*discooperire*—loosen the tiles or shingles?]. He preacheth well and exercises his office laudably in all things when he is present; but he often absents himself and stays at Moreton-Hampstead, sometimes for 15 days, sometimes for 8, so that they have no chaplain, except when Sir Walter the archdeacon's chaplain is present, or when they beseech another to come from elsewhere." Though these full reports deal only with comparatively few Devonshire churches (those appropriated to the dean and chapter), yet they are eloquent of neglect and disrepair. Of the service books, 29 volumes are condemned as indifferent, 54 more as positively bad, and 19 as missing. The pyx itself, in 13 cases, had no lock; in two others it was otherwise deficient, and in 3 cases it was altogether missing (in one of these, stolen). Roofs out of repair were 13, often very badly: 12 chancels were condemned for the same reason, and in 4 cases the whole church. The statutory image or reredos over the high altar was bad in 5 cases, and altogether wanting in 12. The reports on vestments and other church furniture were in proportion.[6] The same tale is told in a visitation of Totnes archdeaconry (1346) which I edited textually in vol. XXVI (1911) of *The English Historical Review.*

In face of these records, who can reject Langland's picture of the clergy as mere slander, or see nothing but sectarian malice when Wyclif writes indignantly: "[The clergy] haunten tauernes out of all mesure and stiren lewid men to dronkenesse, ydelnesse and cursed swerynge and chydynge and fighttynge.... Thei fallen to nyse pleies [foolish games], at tables, chess and hasard, and beten the stretis, and sitten at the tauerne til thei han lost here witt, and than chiden and stryuen and fighten sumtyme, and sumtyme neither have eighe ne tonge ne hond ne foot to helpe hem self for dronkenesse."

Sicut populus, sic sacerdos—"As the priest is, so are the people". Those words of Isaiah were echoed from mouth to mouth, throughout our period, by men who were seriously concerned for the religion and morals of their own day, and who often saw no hope but in the Second Coming of Christ. Certainly we must not lend ourselves to the injustice of blaming our fore-fathers wherever they aimed high, and attempted to take the Kingdom of God with violence. But we should have had all the best of those men upon one side in the effort to see the past exactly as it was, and thus to estimate its true relations to the present.

St Thomas More, in reply to the outspoken criticisms of the lawyer St Germain, pointed out with some real truth that these, by implication, struck at the laity also, since it is from the laity that clerics are recruited, and a stream cannot rise above its source. If medieval society had been more advanced in civilization, it would have demanded, and would have got, a better clergy. It is good for us of to-day to remember this, and not to ignore the fact that our criticism of Christianity and its professional exponents is necessarily to some extent a criticism of our own time and our own selves. Let us bear this in mind with regard to the village parson, present and past in all ages. Until those who reject his creed as no longer credible, and who take no stock of his advice on morals or politics, can find similar points of crystallization in town and country, around which beneficent impulses and societies will naturally group themselves, and in communion with which, at frequent meetings, all classes can assemble naturally and habitually to confess their brotherhood and to mingle their ideal aspirations—until Secularism can construct something of this kind, the Church will remain, what with all its shortcomings it always has been, the chief school of moral co-operation. We may emphasize this consideration the more unhesitatingly, because it raises us from mere negative criticism to positive effort, from destructive rivalry to St Paul's "covet ye the best gifts". The faith of the Christian, and the Agnostic's resolve to follow Truth alone, so far as he can apprehend it, are alike satisfied in the mutual promise: "Show me something better, and I will embrace that."

In that spirit, then, let us pass on from the priests to the people. Here, again, we may take those parochial visitations for our main text, and illustrate them by parallel evidence.

The priest, with the hierarchy at his back, was in theory almost everything to his people. It is still imperfectly realized that the extreme domination over men's morals, and sometimes over their smallest actions, which we think of as the main characteristic of Puritanism in the sixteenth and seventeenth centuries, was a direct inheritance from the Middle Ages. The medieval theory of usury may be taken as an instance. This (as apart from men's practice) was so impossibly strict, even when modified by the later school-men, that the Papacy of the nineteenth century finally forbade confessors to trouble their penitents with questions about so difficult a matter. The greatest saints often proclaimed an in-difference to painting and sculpture and music, or even a dislike and suspicion, from which many of the later "Puritans" were quite free. As we shall see presently, that which is popularly called "Calvinism" has its roots in the medieval Scholastics. Again, it was practically taken for granted that the majority of mankind would go to hell; upon that point there was greater unanimity among orthodox theologians than on any of those which divide the Roman Church of to-day from other Christian bodies.* Laughter and dancing and play, as we have already seen, were often reprobated: against dancing, the orthodox were almost as unanimous as they were in favour of hell-chances. The best minds often discouraged elaborate Church ritual: St Francis's biographer tells how an otherwise excellent friar was damned everlastingly for his share in the construction of that splendid basilica which still stands in honour of the saint's bones at Assisi.[1] The constant medieval wars resulted in frequent destruction or mutilation of sacred buildings: and even deliberate vandalism was not unknown. The Puritans of our English Reformation owe their unsavoury reputation less to their actual tenets than to their honest, but

---

* One of the heretical propositions for which Raymund Lull was condemned in the fourteenth century runs thus: "God hath such love for His people that almost all folk in the world shall be saved; for, if more were damned than saved, Christ's mercy would be without great charity" (Eymericus, *Directorium Inquisitorum*, pars II, quaest. ix). Long after the Reformation, Malebranche takes it as an admitted fact. One of his characters argues: "But if you are so charmed with the idea that God acts solely in pure kindness to men, how comes it that there will be twenty times, or a hundred times more damned than saved?" (*Entretiens sur la métaphysique*, 1688, ent. 9, q. iii; *Œuvres*, ed. Simon, 1846, vol. I, p. 194.)

mistaken and blundering, attempt to enforce those ideals. The Covenant for which they fought was essentially the Covenant drawn up by medieval orthodoxy; but they blundered over the Sanctions. All this I have argued at such length in my *Ten Medieval Studies* and the first volume of *Five Centuries of Religion* (Appendix 23) that I may be excused from repeating it here. That journalistic parrot-cry of our own day, "Merrie England" is (it must be repeated here) a phrase almost unknown to the Middle Ages. As misused at present, it belongs to the mentality which mocks our countryside with *Ye Olde Inne* and *Ye Olde Shoppe*.

The Goodrich, Westbury, Clunbury cases have shown us how the bishop or archdeacon reckoned with the flock—and, directly or by implication, with their pastor—in matters of parish finance. In these 281 parishes, no less than 109 cases of misapplication or embezzlement of funds were reported. The other main subjects of inquisition were unchastity, usury, witchcraft, quarrelsomeness, churchgoing and Sabbatarianism. *Non venit ad ecclesiam*—he cometh not to church—is reported in 46 cases. In 31 more, a parishioner is denounced for Sabbath-breaking: he is *communis operator* on Sundays or Holy-Days, and must therefore be punished unless he redeems himself by repentance and promise of amendment.

Here is an important subject ordinarily ignored or distorted by social historians. So far is Sabbatarianism from being a later English and Puritan invention, that it is part of a very early and widespread Christian tradition, Catholic in a far truer sense than many other observances which claim that title.[2] Tertullian [220] alludes to a Sunday rest; and Constantine I decreed it for all his subjects. Two councils, at least, prescribed that the faithful should spend all day in prayer, except, of course, for meals. In about A.D. 590, a sabbatarian letter appears, claiming to have been written by Christ and to have fallen from heaven: this reappears at intervals; at Cologne it was reprinted even as late as 1648. Theodore of Tarsus, who became Archbishop of Canterbury in 669, "assures us that his fellow-Greeks would neither sail nor ride (except to church) or bake or bathe or write any unnecessary letters on Sunday". A Spanish council, in 1050, forbade all travelling except in cases of necessity: so did a version of the Christ-Letter written in Germany about the same time. And, though England was the scene of a great sabbatarian revival about the year 1200, the impetus for this came from Rome.[3] Roger of

Hoveden, followed by Matthew Paris and Walter of Coventry, tells the old story of this miraculous letter; how it fell from heaven upon the altar at Jerusalem, straight from Christ Himself, with terrible threats against Sabbath-breakers.* A brief excerpt from its commands and its causes may suffice. "It is My will that, from noon [or, perhaps, 3 p.m.] on Saturday to sunrise on Monday no man do any work, unless it be good, and that whosoever doeth work shall make amends by penance." In case of continued disobedience: "I will send upon you beasts with heads like lions and hair like women and tails like camels; beasts so hungry that they shall devour your flesh and ye shall desire to flee to the tombs of the dead and hide yourselves there for fear of them.... Ye shall perish like Sodom and Gomorrah.... I will send upon you worse beasts, which shall devour the breasts of your women." This letter, say the chroniclers, so impressed Innocent III that "he forthwith ordained preachers who went to divers parts of the world and preached everywhere according to the tenour of this letter, the Lord working with them and confirming the word with signs following". The missionary to England was Eustache, Abbot of St-Germer-de-Fly or Flai, among whose many miracles was one in exact accordance with the Heavenly Letter. A Norfolk woman, despising the warnings of the man of God, set out to wash linen one Saturday afternoon. A man of imposing figure warned her: but she persisted, "pleading her poverty, saying that she had hitherto earned a miserable livelihood by this kind of work and that, if she ceased from her accustomed labour, she would be in peril of starvation". The heavenly monitor disappeared; but the perverse female "hastened more busily than before to wash her linen and hang it to dry in the sun. But God's vengeance was not withheld; for straightway a beast like a sucking-pig, of coal-black hue, fixed upon the woman's left breast and could not be torn away; nay, sucking assiduously and drawing her blood, it had soon consumed almost her whole body." With the aid of such miracles, Eustache reaped a rich harvest of conversions. "He so strictly forbade Sunday fairs and markets that nearly all those which had customarily been held on Sundays throughout England were now fixed for some week-day; and thus the people spent their

* We may use this word *Sabbath* safely; for the later Middle Ages habitually summarized the 4th Commandment in two words *Sabbata sanctifices.* Abailard, in his famous hymn, speaks of the blessed in heaven as "sabbatizing" to eternity: *perpes laetitia sabbatizantium.*

Sundays on divine service alone, and altogether abdicated all servile labour. Yet, in process of time, many returned like dogs to their vomit."* True, Church Councils went on to forbid Sunday markets: but it is characteristic of the medieval gulf between law and practice that the Prior of Walsingham habitually held market on Saturday and Sunday, finding this a very lucrative arrangement.4

The fifteenth-century canonist Lyndwood writes: "Canon Law tells us that we must do nothing on the Lord's Day except to spend our time on God. No work is done on that holy day, but it is spent exclusively in hymns and psalms and spiritual songs." We must abstain from all *opera servilia*; i.e. works which primarily benefit the body, as distinguished from *opera liberalia*, pious and intellectual work. Thus field-work is explicitly forbidden, and markets, and pleas in court, except in cases of necessity. In Lyndwood's judgment: "The man who doth such work sinneth mortally, if by reason of such work he knowingly omits that which pertaineth to God's worship, and whereunto he is bound."5 Charitable works, on the other hand, though wrought with our hands, are lawful, as when Christ permitted men to carry the sick man on his couch for healing.

Naturally, therefore, in the Durham records, we find a series of sabbatarian punishments.6 In 1435, seven men and one woman of Hesilden are presented for "working on Sundays and holy-days". In 1441, "John Huchonson of South Shirburn worked with three carts on the day of the Decollation of St John Baptist. [The judgment is] suspen[ded]." In 1443 two women "are accused of having mown on the feast of dedication of St Oswald's Church; and they have to purge themselves with the 6th hand of honourable women, their neighbours".† In 1448 John Robinson, "walker" (i.e. fuller) is accused "that he violated the Sabbath [*diem Sabbati*] in that he laboured at the fuller's art on the day of the Lord's Epiphany. He confesseth, and hath submitted himself to correction; and it is enjoined upon him that he do not so in future under pain of 6s. 8d." In 1450 it is alleged against James Dennant "that he was at the mill, with his cloths to be fulled, on the day of the Lord's Ascension. He confesseth, and for this he

---

* Another of his missionary themes was to "admonish rectors and priests, with their parishioners, to keep a light always burning before the Eucharist"; a custom which was not made general in Switzerland until two centuries later.

† That is, they must each find five women to swear belief in her innocence. Her own hand made the sixth.

hath to go before the procession on three Sundays in his shirt and
drawers, after the fashion of a penitent, and that he abstain henceforth under pain of 10s., to be applied to the Lord Prior's almoner."
In 1450, a woman is condemned for a similar offence "to go before
the procession for two Sundays after the fashion of a penitent".
Next year, two women confessed to washing linen on St Mary
Magdalene's day: "they are to have two fustigations with a hank
of linen yarn." In that same year, at Billigham: "William Dalby
practiseth servile work almost habitually, and keepeth shop outside the churchyard on holy-days and on Holy Cross Day. He
had two women winnowing corn at the time of Matins." Four
others commonly fish for salmon on Sundays and holy-days. Two
tailors and a mower are presented, and five in an adjacent hamlet
"leave their parish church to frequent markets on Sundays in
Lent". The sentences on that batch are not recorded; but two
others, who confessed to mowing a meadow on St Oswald's Day,
"have to go before the procession, with four fustigations around,
and each having in his hands a bundle of hay [*botell feni*], and that
they do no such work henceforth under pain of 10s." A woman
"violated St Mark's day by washing her garments. She confesseth,
and hath for her sin two days before the procession, bearing her
shift in her hand, under pain of 6s. 8d. [for repetition of the
offence]." In 1455, a man is accused of absence from church on
Sundays and holy-days: another, for not having received Holy
Communion since he has been in the parish. In 1436 Adam Gray
of Acle "cometh not to his parish church on holy-days, as was
enjoined upon him at the last visitation under pain of 4d. for every
time, in default of impediment or lawful excuse. He confesseth;
therefore he is at the judge's mercy; and again he was warned to
come to church on Sundays under the same penalty, to wit, 4d.,
and on other holy-days on pain of 2d., every time, to be applied
to the fabric-fund of Durham Cathedral." So, again, a great
Archbishop of Rouen twice records in his diary [1250] how,
finding peasants working on Sunday, he punished them. Erasmus
(as we shall see in Chapter LI) exposed the folly of ecclesiastics
who made it a crime for a cobbler to do a little work on the holy-
days, yet who shut their eyes to far more serious infractions of
divine and moral law. In his *Praise of Folly* he pillories those who
dispute "whether it is a smaller crime to kill a thousand men than
to mend a beggar's shoe on Sunday". Though sensible priests
made sensible allowance (this is well brought out by Fr Thurston,

with a little natural exaggeration), and though the multitude very commonly went their own way without too strict attention to the priests, it was always possible to suffer in the Middle Ages from rigid Sabbatarians.

Let us now pass on to the question of medieval religious education.

Of the Bible, the ordinary man knew only a few stories like that of Adam and Eve, and a little of the Gospels. It has been claimed that the church walls were his Bible; but wall-paintings, statues, and stained glass told far more of the saints' legends than of Bible history. I have dealt fully with this subject in *Art and the Reformation*. The Knight of La Tour-Landry's book, written for the education of his daughters, became a classic: there are two medieval translations of it into English. He tells us that he composed it with the help of two priests, and two clerks of his household. For the girls' edification, he tells the story of Ruth at length: it is a pretty story, but has no contact whatever with the actual Bible narrative except in the heroine's name and the fact that she was a widow. Many such instances might be quoted. Chaucer's Clerk Nicolas knows that the Carpenter will recognize the most un-Biblical of all the stories that had gathered around Noah. *Gesta Romanorum* was one of the most approved among the many manuals for preachers. Its fifteenth-century English translator quotes, as from the Gospels, texts from Revelation, Ezekiel, and Canticles. He attributes to St Paul a text from Job. Genesis is confused with the Psalms, Isaiah with St James, and scraps of the Fathers are palmed off as Bible texts. St Thomas More tells how a lady of his time was shocked to discover that Mary was a Jewess: she confessed that, thenceforward, she would love her the less all her life long. The Dominican Étienne de Bourbon, one of the most prominent of thirteenth-century heresy hunters, confesses frankly that one of the main characteristics of these men was their Bible knowledge, even among their poor, in contrast (he says) to the shameful ignorance of the orthodox. The result was that, gradually, Bible knowledge on the part of any but a cleric or a great person aroused almost as definite suspicions of heresy as was aroused by the objection to profane oaths: Chaucer's Shipman is one of our many witnesses on that point. If any complete translation of the Bible into English was ever made before Chaucer's day (which is more than doubtful) it never became public in any real sense: the task was left to Wyclif or his followers.

A few earnest clerics, like the author of *Dives and Pauper*, were shocked at this policy. The author, complaining that "now men say that there should no lewd folk entermit them of God's law nor of the gospel nor of holy writ, neither to conne it nor to teach it", continues: "This is a foul error and full perilous to man's soul."7 Archbishop Arundel's notorious decree of 1407, by which the making or the use of translations unlicensed by the hierarchy was forbidden under the ultimate penalty of burning alive, amounted practically to a heretication of Bible knowledge. For, as St Thomas More confessed even in his defence of the Church, it was most regrettable that, while unlicensed translations were thus forbidden, no licensed versions were made. No Roman Catholic version of the New Testament in English was printed until 1562; and 27 years elapsed before this was followed by the Old Testament. In 1870, Lord Acton wrote from Rome: "Here you may find a lottery-book in almost every house, but never a New Testament, and extremely seldom any religious book at all."8 Facts of this kind must necessarily be emphasized in the face of persistent modern falsifications which have no excuse but the slender plea of ignorance. Cardinal Gasquet is still quoted as an authority for the admirable religious education of the past; and *The Catholic Times* refers his readers to this "age when there would have been no difficulties over an Education Bill; a time when the Church had it all its own way, and yet the Bible was taught...when such immense portions of Scripture were committed to memory, and that by Catholics".

We find no trace in the Middle Ages of anything resembling the modern Sunday-school system. No doubt individual priests sometimes taught individual children, and one in a thousand like St Gilbert of Sempringham, might be a most zealous missionary in his own village. But many indications go to support Étienne de Bourbon's complaint that the average orthodox parent did not even teach the Lord's Prayer to his family or servants. Haymo of Hythe, Bishop of Rochester in the fourteenth century, founded an almshouse not for the very poor, but expressly for middle-class folk of decayed fortunes. He made it a primary condition that the candidate should know the Lord's Prayer, the Ave, and the Apostles' Creed. We have seen how, at the Reformation, some priests were found who could not repeat the Lord's Prayer, nor name its author.

CHURCH behaviour was childlike in both directions: it had the child's happy familiarity and, sometimes, the child's embarrassing lack of restraint. Even unwilling Protestants have often admired, in Continental churches, not only the figures constantly flitting to and fro for private prayer, but the engaging bonhomie with which the women, in especial, make themselves at home in the Father's House; one sitting at the sermon with her basket full of cabbages from the market on the floor at her feet: another with the company of her pet dog. The earliest mention of a private pew is Italian, of about 1200. In England, not later than 1320, the Lady de Dalton had her private pew, and "of her humility" did not allow her servants to eject the stranger who was found kneeling in prayer there. In some of our thirteenth-century churches a stone bench runs all round the walls; but the Friar Salimbene, in 1248, found Louis IX of France, with his retinue, sitting on the ground in a wayside village church to which they had repaired for prayer. Hence the nave lent itself to that abusive use which we have seen at St Marychurch in Devon, and which meets us in many other records; the storing of corn, barrels, and similar unecclesiastical furniture. Many indications show that talk at divine service was rather normal than exceptional. The sermons of Berthold v. Regensburg and St Bernardino of Siena testify to this; cathedral canons, as we have seen, had statutory permission to converse during service, as far as to the third or fourth stall away. Chaucer's Host describes his wife's fury if any rival lady competed with her in priority for the Kiss of Peace at Mass: hence arose vendettas which, he intimates, might even end some day in bloodshed. Such bloodshed, official documents assure us, did not infrequently result from quarrels between parishes in the solemn cathedral processions, the struggle for precedence ending in a fight with banner-poles. Bishop Quivil of Exeter solemnly warned his diocese against the "grave scandal in the churches, and frequent hindrances to divine service" generated by the scrambling of parishioners for seats at Mass. The Knight of La Tour-Landry warns his daughters: "Some clerks maintain that none should speak no manner thing whiles they be at Mass, and in especial [while the priest readeth] the Gospel." He tells us of a case when there was such "chattering, laughing, jangling and jesting aloud", that the priest "smote his hand on the book to make them hold their peace; but there were some that did not".[1] At King's College, Cambridge, a special home of orthodoxy in the fifteenth century, the royal founder prescribed by statute that, in chapel, the students should not "in any wise make murmurs, babblings, scoffing, laughter, confabulations or indiscreet noises, lest, through their inordinate tumult and the various sounds of voices and other talk among themselves, the devotion and exercise of those singing psalms in the choir be in any wise impeded". The writer of *Dives and Pauper*, in Chaucer's day, thinks that the glories of architecture and church furniture are signs less of devotion than of "pomp and pride of this world, to have a name and worship thereby in the country...or else by sly covetise of men of Holy Church". "For" (he argues) "the people nowadays is full undevout to God and to Holy Church, and they love but little men of Holy Church, and they ben loth to come in Holy Church when they be bound to come thither, and full loth to hear God's service. Late they come and soon they go away. If they be there a little while, them thinketh full long. They have liever go to the tavern than to Holy Church. Liever to hear a song of Robin Hood or of some ribaldry, than for to hear Mass or Matins or any other of God's service or any word of God. And since the people hath so little devotion to God and to Holy Church, I cannot see that they do such cost in Holy Church for devotion nor for the love of God. For they despise God day and night with their evil and wicked living and their wicked thewys [manners]."[2] St Bernardino of Siena [1440] puts it more pithily still: folk come in late to Mass, and hasten out the moment after the Elevation of the Host, "as though they had seen not Christ, but the Devil". Kings and magistrates, as we shall see, might turn the hour and place of Mass into a regular business office; and even exceptionally pious bishops might do this on occasion. Ordinary folk had only a vague inkling of the service itself, for the Mass was an *opus operatum*, independently of the hearer. Berthold of Regensburg, that Franciscan whom Roger Bacon extols as the greatest mission preacher of his time, says in one of his sermons: "It irks some to stand decently for a short hour in church, while God is being served with singing or reading; they laugh and chatter as if they were at a fair....And ye women, ye never give your tongues rest from useless talk! One tells the other how glad the maidservant is to sleep, and how loth to work; another tells of her husband; a third complains that her children are troublesome and sickly!" At this a cry of expostulation rises from the audience: "Yea, Brother Berthold, but we understand not the Mass, and therefore can we not pray as we had need, nor may we feel such devotion as if we understood the Mass. The sermon indeed we can follow word by word, but not the Mass; we know not what is being sung or read, we cannot comprehend it." St Thomas More also tells us how little the congregation understood the Mass. The *Lay Folk's Mass-book* was composed by Dan Jeremy, a cleric, Norman or English, who wrote in French about 1150, for readers of the upper class. It was translated into English about 1300, and repeated in other versions down to the fifteenth century. In this book, as in those commonly used at Mass on the Continent nowadays, "the devotions are not a translation from the Missal", except in four places. "There is a version of the Apostles' Creed instead of the Nicene Creed." Moreover, that version itself is falsified at one point in favour of the doctrine of Transubstantiation. The last section begins:

> Well I trow in the Holigoste
>   And Holi Kirk that is so good;
> And so I trow that Housel is   [the consecrated Host
>   Both flesh and blood.[3]

Again, bishops and disciplinarians struggled, with indifferent success, to put down the irreverences of dancing, theatrical performances, and markets (with their attendant quarrels and occasional bloodshed) in churches and churchyards. The late Cardinal Gasquet, in his attempt to minimize the treatment of churchyards, speaks of these customs as only "growing" in the latter part of the fourteenth century, and as first mentioned in a constitution of 1367. This statement is made in favour of his theory that the later medieval Church was an innocent victim of the Black Death. But, in fact, that constitution of 1367, in which Archbishop Thoresby fulminates against holding markets on Sundays in churchyards *or in churches* (these italics mark another of the Cardinal's suppressions), is not the first but nearly the last of its kind. Between 1229 and 1367 there are eleven such episcopal injunctions recorded; while from that date to the Reformation

there seems to be only one. Bishop after bishop had thundered
in vain, long before the Black Death, against those who "turned
the house of prayer into a den of thieves"; and, if such anathemas
grow rarer in the century before the Reformation, it is probably
only because a large number of prelates were then non-resident,
and the bonds of discipline were notoriously relaxed. Gasquet's
picture is further falsified by the omission from his quotation,
without the least warning, of Quivil's complaints of the scandal
caused by Mass-scrambling. Moreover, he silently ignores 16
other clauses of that bishop's decrees which reveal parochial
scandals scarcely less grave: for instance, the gross superstitions
which in Exeter diocese, as in some others, led ignorant folk to
"abhor" one of the pillars of medieval theology, the Sacrament
of Extreme Unction. Again, the rite of Confirmation was disgracefully neglected by the bishops: it was performed only
sporadically as they journeyed (when indeed they did so) through
their dioceses. Archbishop Pecham [1280] complains of the
"numberless people, grown old in evil days, who had not yet
received the grace of Confirmation"; and we have similar evidence
for Continental countries. Sacchetti, whom Chaucer might have
met in Italy, speaks of "a good many" who did not even feel
certain that they had been baptized, and consoles them with the
assurance that God would take their faith as equivalent to the
deed. Gascoigne says that many children died unbaptized through
the fault of the monastic clergy.

Preaching was another weak point of the medieval Church.
Such preaching as was done in all these thousands of English
parishes, after the middle of the thirteenth century, was mainly
performed by a few scores of itinerant friars.[4] Originally, it was
only bishops who normally preached; others did so, very occasionally: sometimes never. Confessions, again, could not be
effectually heard and dealt with but by some physician of souls far
better technically instructed than the ordinary parochial clergy, as
described by their orthodox contemporaries. It is almost common
form for disciplinarians to complain that the average rector or
vicar was quite unable (in Biblical language) "to discern leprosy
from leprosy": i.e. to deal with really difficult cases. This defect,
with that of preaching, was to some extent remedied by the
friars in the thirteenth century: but, when these in their turn lost
their savour, England possessed two sets of soul-physicians

lending themselves almost equally to criticism. Chaucer's infallible eye caught both sides of this truth. His friar boasts his own
preaching against that of the parish priest, and claims quite truly
to have received from the Papacy powers of confession and
absolution far beyond those of his rival. On the other hand, we all
know how far Chaucer felt that this particular man of God had the
true God behind him.

What Chaucer felt was echoed more plainly and fully in *Piers
Plowman*, and was expressed to some extent even by a broad-
minded friar of that age, the author of *Dives and Pauper*. For the
friar of this day was already turned to conservatism; he was even
readier than his older rivals to persecute all innovators.[5] The
author writes: "Also men of Holy Church slay men and women
ghostly of God's word and of good teaching....Since that God's
word is life and salvation of man's soul, all those that let God's
word, and let them that have authority of God and by order take
to preach and teach, that they may not preach and teach God's
word and God's law, they be manslayers ghostly, and guilty of
as many souls as perish and die ghostly by such lettyng of God's
word; and namely these proud covetous prelates and curates that
neither can teach nor will teach, nor suffer others that can and
will....As Saint Austen saith, God's word ought to be worshipped as much as Christ's Body....There the Gloss sheweth,
that it is more profitable to hear God's word in preaching, than
to hear any Mass; and rather a man should forbear his Mass than
his sermon. For by preaching folk be stirred to contrition and to
forsake sin and the fiend, and to love God and goodness and be
illumined to know their God and virtues from vices, truth from
falsehood, and to forsake errors and heresies. By the Mass be they
not so; but if they come to Mass in sin, they go away in sin; and
shrews they come, and shrews they wend." It will be noted how
boldly this thinker rejects the cruder forms of the *opus operatum*
doctrine, and how he appeals to the [pseudo]-Augustinian text,
enshrined in Canon Law, against the excessive importance
attached to mere attendance at Mass. A far greater friar, St
Bernardino of Siena himself, is even more emphatic in the same
sense.[6]

So, again, we learn from the Dominican Minister-General,
Humbert de Romans. In his *Book on the Preparation of Sermons*
he reminds the young preacher "that men of exalted position are

rarely wont to hear sermons....Note also that poor folk come
seldom to church, seldom to sermons."[7] Important as this subject
is, it need not be laboured further in face of the evidence now
accessible in Dr Owst's two learned and attractive volumes. It
will suffice here to give two characteristic extracts from these.[8]
Dr Owst is describing the sermon: "How, then, will our audience
behave? Whether within the sacred precincts or upon the public
square, in its motley character, it will probably reflect most of the
great feudal class distinctions and class prejudices which seem to
run deeper in medieval flesh and blood than even differences of
nationality. Some of the portraits sketched in our manuscripts are
wonderfully realistic and amusing. The lord and lady of the manor
with their circle will probably be present. They have a bad habit
of sleeping late in those too cosy new-fangled bedrooms of theirs.
By the time my lady has completed her extravagant toilet, and sets
out churchwards with her spouse, the parson and all the people of
the parish are weary and exasperated with waiting for them."[*]
Again: "Bishop Brunton makes it clear that then, even as now,
men were in a minority, and the churches were attended mainly
by the womenfolk. The sexes are probably separated,[†] the latter
'sitten all a rewe', as we have seen, and with good reason. For
strange things are done in churches and strange folk go there.
Gower's lover, like Dante, is amongst those 'in chirches and in
minstres eke, That gon the women for to seke'; harmless enough,
in his case, it is true. But the 'lechour' may go, too, as the
preacher describes."[‡]

One word must be added concerning the Sacrament of Penance.
The evidence is not in favour of its beneficent effect, on the whole.
Dr H. C. Lea's exhaustive study in his *History of Confession and
Indulgences* is almost as conclusive as his other volumes. The
testimony of the Hereford visitation, and others of the kind, is
definitely unfavourable to the laity. But we must bear in mind
that the medieval parishioner usually confessed only once a year,
before his or her Easter Communion. And the complaints of the
clergy themselves, supported by the testimony of neighbours at

---

* The Knight of La Tour-Landry also shows how the common folk were
sometimes kept waiting at Mass for the squirearchy. It was the great folk alone,
also, who might sit with the clergy in the chancel. (G.G.C.)

† The Hereford visitations show this plainly in one church. (G.G.C.)

‡ Italian tales, especially, show us amorous young men frequenting church in
order to ogle the ladies, as in the Introduction to the *Decameron*. (G.G.C.)

the parochial visitations, and even to some extent by medical evidence, give us no reason to suppose that the pre-Reformation village or town was more moral than that of to-day. St Antonino, Archbishop of Florence, was reputed to have heard more confessions than any other of his day, a generation after Chaucer. His was perhaps the most civilized corner of Europe, almost under the shadow of the Seat of the Apostles. In reading him, we have only to discount the bitterness of a disciplinarian and mission preacher who saw disappointingly little fruit from his labours, and who, like all missioners from Elijah and John Baptist to Wesley, found average humanity no very malleable stuff. He writes concerning the Tuscan peasants of the fifteenth century: "In the churches themselves they sometimes dance and leap and sing with women. On holy-days they spend little time on divine service or hearing of the whole Mass, but in games, or in taverns and in contentions at the church doors. They blaspheme God and His saints on slender provocation. They are filled with lies and perjuries: of fornication, and of worse sins still, they make no conscience. Very many of them do not confess once a year, and far fewer are those who take the Communion, under the false belief that they need not communicate except when they grow old or are sick unto death. They do little to instruct their families in the manner of faithful folk. They use enchantments for themselves and for their beasts. Of God, or their own soul's health, they think not at all. And, being commonly ignorant, and caring little for their own souls or for keeping God's commandments, which they know not, this it is which helps to bring them along the broad way leading to destruction, to wit, their ignorance of their own vices and the carelessness and evil conscience of their parish-priests, who, caring not for the flock committed unto them, but only for their wool and their milk, do not instruct them through preaching and the confessional, or by private admonitions, but walk in the same errors as their flocks, following their corrupt ways and not correcting them for their faults; whereby it cometh to pass that, living like beasts, they sometimes die the death of a beast."[9] His contemporary, St Bernardino of Siena, writes in equal fire of indignation: men often "believe in nothing higher than the roof of their own house"; and this is directly traceable to "the evil lives of the Religious [i.e. monks, friars, and nuns] and of the priests".[10]

We shall see later how, under Henry VIII, the Spanish envoy could report from London to his master: "Nearly all the people here hate the priests." For nearly a thousand years before this, the maxim had been current in Church Law that "the laity are thoroughly inimical to the clergy"; Boniface VIII took that sentence as the text for his famous bull *Clericis Laicos*. The priest was too often then such as Lina Duff-Gordon describes in her *Home Life in Italy*; the man in black who takes toll of the parish, and who is seldom seen in the house until he brings with him the Last Unction, and the shadow of death. *Dives and Pauper* alludes to the medieval superstition that it was ill-omened to meet a priest by the way. "Some man hadde levyr to mete with a [toad] or a frogge in the way than with a knight or a squier or with any man of Religion or of Holy Church; for than they say and believe that they shal have gold." Again, it is unlucky to hunt with a priest; or, again, if men meet "a man of Holy Churche or of Religion, and namely with a frere" in the road, "they will leave him on their left hand".[11] Two centuries earlier, Cardinal Jacques de Vitry had testified to a similar superstition. "I have seen how, in certain parts, when men met a priest, they crossed themselves at once, saying that it is an evil omen to meet with a priest. Nay, I have learned for certain that in a French village, seeing that many died on all hands, they said one to another 'This plague and mortality can never cease unless, before burying any corpse, we cast our priest into the same grave.' So it came to pass that, when the priest came to the grave to bury a dead parishioner, then the peasants and women, with one accord, seized upon him in his holy vestments and cast him into the pit. These are devilish inventions and illusions of demons."[12]

It must be added that Church life was still more irregular in Wales, Scotland, and Ireland than in England. I have given some detailed evidence for this in my *Scottish Abbeys*; but readers may easily verify it for themselves by taking, at random, any volume of the Calendar of Papal Letters.

There was a dualism in our ancestors' ordinary religion which comes out well in Froissart, a witness almost as valuable for England as for France, and all the more trustworthy when his evidence is merely incidental; merely an "aside" from a speaker mainly intent upon something else. He shows us a curious mixture of reverence and disrespect. "In our faith", he writes, "there ought to be no variation; for, as there is one God in heaven, so also there ought to be but one God on earth." Again, he disapproved the anticlerical policy of Gian Galeazzo Visconti: "He held the error and opinion of his father that was, how one should neither honour nor worship God. He took from abbeys and priories much of their revenues and took them to himself.... These lords in their days lived like popes: they did great despites in their time to men of Holy Church: they set nothing by the pope's curse, and specially after the Schism began and that there was two popes; that the one cursed, the other assoiled." Yet when we look carefully into some of Froissart's other pages, we may find certain significant tales and side-remarks for which he evidently counted on sympathy from his aristocratic audience. The tragedy of the unpopular minister Bétisac shows how easily the Inquisition could be used by a political party in a purely political quarrel; it throws much light on the story of Joan of Arc. Again, Froissart is perfectly aware that, though much could be pleaded in his day, as in our own time, in favour of an established and endowed Church, yet establishment and endowment can never be quite compatible with religious freedom in the strictest sense. In 1399, the most Christian King of Aragon "saw well the Pope's letters, but he made no force of them, and said to his council that were about him... 'Let the clergy alone; for, if they purpose to live, the prelates must obey the great lords under whom their rents and revenues are.'" Again, he shows us how little the King of England cared for the excommunication even of an undoubted Pope. The Great Schism he traces to the personal fears of the cardinals, intimidated by the Roman populace, "for they had rather 'a died confessors than martyrs". He sees clearly enough the seamy side of the Indulgence system. When the disbanded soldiers, the "Companies", were wasting France, "even as the Vandals had done in times of old", then Innocent VI offered the Plenary Indulgence of a crusader—complete "pardon from penalty and guilt" up to date—to "all those that would take on them his croisey, and that would abandon their bodies willingly to destroy these evil people and their companions". The Cardinal Bishop of Ostia "retained all manner of soldiers, such as would save their souls in attaining to these said pardons, but they should have none other wages; wherefore that journey [expedition] brake, for every man departed, some into Lombardy, some to their own countries, and some went to the said evil Company, so that daily they increased". One day he found himself talking with "a squire of England, called Henry Christead, an honest man and wise", who had been much in Ireland and who explained that Richard II had now subdued that country "by treaty and by the grace of God". To which our good Canon Froissart replied: "Indeed the grace of God is good; who-so can have it, it is much worth; but it is seen nowadays that earthly princes getteth little without it be by puissance."[13]

LET us turn now to the other side of the ledger. With all these undeniable failings, I cannot doubt that the Church was, on the whole, a power working for good, and that she would have been far the greatest of then existent powers for good, if only she had been able to work in harmony with other religious, moral, and intellectual movements, instead of threatening and even employing fire and sword against them.

Even the priest's unpopularity had its other side, illogical perhaps but most natural psychologically. The man who hated his parson most might well be he who most deeply felt, and shrank from, his supernatural powers. A modern French-Canadian, in a penetrating study of the Church there, quotes the words of a peasant farmer from whom the priest had turned haughtily away in the course of a heated dispute about tithes. "I longed to plant him a hearty kick on the part which he exposed to me; but then I thought my leg might shrivel up!" For many centuries the feudal lord had been tolerated, and even in a sense welcomed, as a protection against worse evils; and the priest, even at his worst, wielded the most effectual weapons against the Devil. He might damn his own soul every day that he touched the Lord's Body with sinful hands; but his Mass was none the less an *opus operatum*. One of the *Gesta Romanorum* tales was composed expressly to illustrate this doctrine. It tells how men drank from a stream of perfect clearness and purity; yet, traced to its well-spring it was found to gush forth from the very jaws of a dead dog! The scientific practical possibility of this was no more doubted by the faithful than its theological and allegorical truth.

But we may truly go a great deal farther than this. Though the brighter touches are not always so explicit and emphatic as the darker, yet, amid that multitude of clergy, there were doubtless many in every time and country who were the salt of the earth. We must think here not only of the saints whom Rome has canonized; though but a small proportion of those were indeed parish priests, as a still smaller proportion were peasants or artisans. Behind those striking, and often theatrical, figures, we must think also of the hundred and forty-four thousand who, if all could be seen, would be worthy of the same crown and palm. Chaucer's Poor Parson was the forerunner of men who have lived serener lives in less troubled times, such as George Herbert's Country Parson, or convinced and unquestioning clerics of the Clapham School and of the Oxford Movement. Side by side with those others whom our documents brand as a dishonour to their profession, we must not forget those who lived and laboured unknown, though they daily faced their duty in the spirit which Keble holds out as a modern model:

> Think not of rest: though dreams be sweet,
> Start up, and ply your heavenward feet.
> Is not God's oath upon your head,
> Ne'er to sink back on slothful bed,
> Never again your loins untie,
> Nor let your torches waste and die,
> Till, when the shadows thickest fall,
> Ye hear your Master's midnight call?

The life as parish priest of St Gilbert of Sempringham (d. 1189) is told us in detail 300 years later by Capgrave, the Austin Friar of Lynn. He was of noble birth; his mother was English, his father a Norman knight who had come over with William the Conqueror. When he was promoted to the order of priesthood he was a model to his parish. He taught wisely in his preaching and his good example. In his parish there were no insolent drinkings, no wrestlings, bear-baitings or other unthrifty occupations to interfere with divine service. His parishioners prayed devoutly in the church, paid truly their tithes, visited the poor and spent their wealth in ways pleasing to God; in church they might be distinguished from others, since he had taught them to bow their knees to God and so devoutly to "bid their beads". In process of time, he founded the only purely English monastic order, for monks and for nuns. Even this man, with his social advantages, seems to have begun as a parish clerk; he certainly acted also as parish schoolmaster. Again, in those earlier generations when, apparently, a larger proportion of priests were ordained on their own title, and certainly there was less appropriation of the wealthier livings by monastic and other bodies comparatively disinterested in the parish, then we not infrequently find a handsome chancel, or a whole church, built by the rector himself. At Great Shelford, near Cambridge, the monumental brass of such a priest still exists, within the altar rails. Gascoigne, again, tells us: "I knew a Rector who had but one living, yet from the profits of that single church he sent twenty youths, [one after the other], to school and to the University and made priests of them."

Again, Professor Chambers has taught us to see the great literary and cultural value of those English religious pieces, in prose and in verse, which run on from Anglo-Saxon times in a stream never quite dried up, growing fast in the fourteenth century, and flowing most abundantly in the fifteenth. From that source, with the rich tributary stream of studied talk in court and council, flowed quite naturally the prose of Malory, of More, and (when Renaissance and Reformation had enriched it) of Bacon and Hooker and the Authorized Version. It is true that even the most orthodox of these religious pieces are sometimes directly traceable rather to the village prophet than to the village priest, or to one who combined both capacities; and certainly neither the literary nor the theological student can ignore the parallel influence of semi-orthodox and frankly Lollard writers. Yet, from one source or another, all this mass of writings must be taken fully into account in any survey of parish life. It is to the later Middle Ages that we owe the charming prayer which, to-day, is so often sung as a finale in Anglican services:

> God be in my head,
>   And in my understanding;
> God be in mine eyes,
>   And in my looking;
> God be in my mouth,
>   And in my speaking;
> God be in my heart,
>   And in my thinking;
> God be at my end,
>   And at my departing.

Here, again, is the metrical prayer which Myrc [1400] gives for the parish priest to teach his people, that they may say it to themselves while he goes on with his Latin after the Elevation of the Host:

> Jesu, lord, welcome Thou be,
> In form of bread as I Thee see!
> Jesu! for Thy holy name
> Shield me to-day from sin and shame;
> Shrift and housel, Lord, Thou grant me bo[th]
> Ere that I shalle hencĕ go,

And very contrition of my sin,
That I, Lord, never die therein;
And as Thou wert of a maid y-bore
Suffer me never to be for-lore,
But when that I shall hencë wend
Grant me Thy bliss withouten end.

Most frequent of all, perhaps, are the rhymes that remind worshippers of the bleeding Crucifix and of their own latter end. In
several cases, the poet gives a traditional computation of the actual
wounds: these differ in different versions, but one may be taken as
typical:

Five hundred wounds and five thousand,
And thereto sixty
And fifteen
Was told and seen
On My body.[1]

Sometimes, but far less frequently, these treatises contain episodes
taken directly from Christ's parables, and treated with charming
freshness and spontaneity. Perhaps the best of these is the parable
of Matthew xx, as told in the poem of *Pearl*, where however the
difficult English demands some modernization for unspecialized
modern readers.[2] The poet sees the soul of his infant daughter in
heaven, clad in the white robes of the Apocalypse, and jewelled
with transcendent pearls. She bids him cease to mourn for one
who is now, by God's courtesy, a queen in heaven. At this, he
expostulates:

That courtesy is too free in deed,
If it be sooth that thou dost say;
Not two brief years with us didst lead,
Too young to please thy God or pray,
Nor never knew'st thou Pater or Creed
And yet made queen on thy first day!
I may not trow it, so God me speed,
That He would deal so wrong a way.
Of countess, damozel, *par ma fay*,
'Twere fair in heaven to hold the state;
Or e'en to be lady of less array;
But a queen! That is too dear a date.*

She answers him with the Gospel parable, concluding with the
dialogue between the lord and his labourers.

* End, goal, aim.

At the date of day, at evensong,
One hour before the sun went down,
He saw there idle men full strong
And said to them with sober sound:
'Why stand ye so idle this whole day long?"
"Our hire", said they, "is nowhere bound."
"Go into my vine, ye yeomen young,
And work as ye may ere the sun go down."
   Soon the world became right brown,
    The great sun sank and the hour waxed late;
    To take their hire he made summoun;
    The weary day was past its date.

The date of day the Lord did know
And called to the Reeve: "Let pay my meinie:
Give them the hire that I them owe;
And further, that none may me repreny,
Set them all upon a row
And give to each alike one penny.
Begin at the last that standeth low
Till to the foremost thou atteny."
   And then the first began to pleyny,
    And said that they had travailed sore;
    "These but one hour did strive and streyny;
    Us think us ought to take ful more.

More have we served, us thinketh so,
That suffered all the long day's heat,
Than these that wrought not hourës two;
Yet to us thou dost them counterfeit!"
Said the lord to one that answered so:
"Friend, no wrong dost thou here get,
Take that is thine own and go:
Our bargain was at a penny set.
   Why beginnest thou now to fret?
    Was not a penny thy hire of yore?
    No man may claim beyond his debt,
    Why then should'st thou thus ask for more?"

Thus it is (says the daughter) with your own child:

   More have I of joy and bliss herein,
   Of ladyship great and life's full bloom,
   Than all the wives in the world might win,
   Seeking their own by righteous doom.
   Though night was nigh ere I could begin,
   (So late was I to the vineyard come,)
   First of them all my hire did I win,
   And was paid outright the whole full sum.

> Yet others had labour more burdensome,
> Toiling and sweating from hour to hour,
> Whose time of reward is not yet come—
> Nor shall be, perchance, for a whole year more.

How the poet's theology diverges here from Dante's, we shall see in the next chapter.

There are certain imponderables which no true historian can afford to neglect; least of all, those who deal in any way with the Middle Ages. The intuition of survival after death, apparently absent from some minds, faint in others, overmastering with a few, cannot be destroyed by any formal logic. Those who feel it have the same right to that conviction as to other ultimates: a right as legitimate as any doubter or contradictor can have. This belief, reasonably regulated like other beliefs, does unquestionably give greater significance to life. A Persian envoy in England, some eighty years ago, wrote home to a friend that there were people here who worried themselves with the fear lest, fifty years hence, the coal-mines should be exhausted: "Who is there, in Persia, that would care twopence for what happens fifty years after them?" Anything must be a gain which suggests to the multitude, even fitfully, that our present actions may be of abiding significance for good or for evil; and the world will not gain much by swinging back from medieval eschatology to a scramble for mere momentary advantages. Those who feel most deeply the liberation from a tyrant-god of past imagination—"our soul is escaped even as a bird out of the snare of the fowler"—are most strictly bound to face whatever flaws may exist in these modern ideals which take his place. No doubt it is a gross anachronism to take for granted that this or that pious man of the past, if confronted with all the alternatives which face the modern world, would have thought and written and acted as he did then. But, on the other hand, we must not exaggerate in the contrary direction. A modern Aquinas, familiar with Einstein and wielding the motor car with consummate skill, might still conceivably think essentially as the old Aquinas did. Renan, in his *Souvenirs d'Enfance et de Jeunesse* (p. 258), points out how a modern philosopher may still adapt himself to those words of Antonius in the fourth century:

> Discussi fateor sectas attentius omnes,
> Plurima quaesivi, per singula quaeque cucurri,
> Nec quidquam inveni melius quam credere Christo.

We cannot fairly expect from the Church more than there is in human nature. Both the strength and the weakness of medieval Latin Christianity lay in this, that there were normally no parties, but one single State to which every man must conform, on peril of his life. The liberal Bishop Thirlwall, when first the question of relaxing statutory attendance at college chapels was seriously discussed, found himself confronted with an opponent who argued: "It comes to this plain question: Are we to have compulsory religion, or none at all?" The bishop replied: "My powers of logical analysis do not enable me to grasp that subtle distinction." Yet, to the enormous majority of English folk in our period, the question never presented itself at all: like the majority of all times, they did not think deeply enough. The parishioner's attitude, in most cases, was at worst that of Tennyson's *Northern Farmer*. He heard the parson dutifully every Sunday:

> An' I niver know'd whot a meän'd, but I thowt a'ad summut to saäy,
> An' I thowt a said whot a owt to a said an' I coom'd awaäy.

There was much of the herd-instinct in all that; but the exaggerated modern scorn of this herd-instinct is warranted neither by history nor by common everyday experience. Humanity is not predominantly evil; and men are the better for acting and thinking normally in masses; thus they keep their ideals warm; and there is, on the whole, more good than evil in every ideal which appeals to the multitudes, be the Intelligentsia never so impatient. "The inner life of Christianity, its very essence, resides in the social character of religion itself, what it has of most spiritual."[3] The words "Our Father", and the insistence on the brotherhood of man, represent ideas which humanity will never let go, whatever may be the language in which men will clothe them. And there is nothing in our medieval documents to weaken the probability that, to very many, the Lord's Prayer was a religious reality, whether taught by the parents or by the priest. "Thy kingdom come" is a call to effort, and "Thy will be done" is a call to brave endurance, in every mind that realizes prayer not only as an asking for favours, but also as a loyal surrender to demands for action and patience. A modern French scientist, not without malice, analysed the liquid in the holy-water stoup that happened to be nearest to his laboratory, and found in it a great diversity of bacilli. If he could have analysed with equal patience and accuracy the feelings of the multitudinous worshippers, then also he might have been surprised by the variety of spiritual bacilli that hang about a parish church. The best religion any man learns, with ordinary good fortune, is at his mother's knee. One of the most moving passages in St Joan's answers to her inquisitors runs: "I learned my Pater and Ave and Creed from my mother; nor did I learn any belief from any other than from my mother."[4] But behind that mother was the Village Church.

Moreover, the existence of the one great Church, with its stable traditional framework, had considerable influence upon that agricultural life which, after all, formed some 90 per cent. of the whole national life. Its ritual, of which it had inherited part from Roman or Germanic paganism, and created still more for itself, gave consistency to village routine even in some of its most important factors: this is well brought out in a recent essay by Mr G. C. Homans.[5] The farmer's calendar was pinned to the Church calendar: there were "a set of acts, to be carried out in a particular way, on particular occasions. . . . One of the functions of a religious calendar is to help people get things done at the proper times. . . . Arrangements like this accomplish two things. They make it perfectly plain to a man and to his neighbors when he is late with his work, and give the neighbors an excuse for laughing at him for it. They also allow a man to get through the routines of the year to some extent without taking thought, simply by doing the customary things at the customary times. . . . A religion of ritual, then, like that of the Catholic Church, gives rise to well-regulated conduct in at least two ways. It helps insure that the routines of life are carried on in the usual manner, since these routines are tied to the religious calendar. And it gives men's feelings of helplessness and those linked with the changing seasons adequate and orderly social expression." And Mr Homans clinches this by a quotation from a study of the modern Polish peasant: "The fact is that when the peasant has been working steadily, and has fulfilled the religious and magical ceremonies which tradition requires, he 'leaves the rest to God', and waits for the ultimate results to come; the question of more or less skill and efficiency of work has very little importance."

Thus, in the Middle Ages as in our own day, the parson and his church afforded a natural centre of good thought and good works; a point of brotherly crystallization. The hope of heaven may not be the highest of human motives; but, just as Dr Johnson's robust common sense drove him to point out that a man is, in point of fact, seldom more innocently employed than in making money, so he would have suggested that few people live in a mood so lofty that they can justly look down upon the Christian in his hope of heaven. Even when we have reduced all religions to the category of Enlightened Selfishness, and assigned a slightly higher pigeon-hole in that same cupboard to all other forms of humanitarian-ism and altruism, such ideals will still remain superior, if only by a few degrees, to Selfishness Unenlight-ened; and human society, up to the

The Poor Parson.

present, has been painfully unsuccessful in working out any third alternative. A prominent and deservedly beloved Agnostic of our own day has been heard to confess sadly that the religious folk seem, hitherto, to excel in getting things done. Nor, again, need the religious man share that fear of finding himself duped at the last, which seems sometimes so strongly to sway his opponents. Lord Acton quoted once from Fénelon that the most habitually incredulous persons are sometimes the most grossly duped. But let us face the idea just as crudely as it is suggested. If any soul, at the Last Day, having believed on the strength of no base or merely careless impulse, found itself face to face with some grinning, all-powerful deceiver, then, by any civilized ethical standard, that trusting soul represents something divine in contrast with diabolism. The mere belief of humanity in a law of order, and that instinct of order which, traceable even in the lowest man, rises in the chosen few to an overmastering passion, would seem in themselves a cogent argument for a fundamentally Orderly Universe, if not in being, at least in becoming. To that belief in Order, everything bore witness in the theory of the medieval Church: and, even in its practice, there was more order than in the rest of society; sometimes incomparably more. Her very disorders were those of the rudimentary civilization around her, magnified sometimes by the greatness of the stage on which they were played. Her insistence upon a higher and rational ordinance throughout the world ought, as Professor Whitehead has pointed out, to enlist the sympathy of all truly scientific enquirers of to-day. Whatever the science of the future may be able to bring us in the way of coherent explanation, this will be in a true sense continued not only from the Greek philosophers, but also from Judaism with its insistence on the Divine Ruler, and on Christianity its successor.

The Order of the Universe finds its highest expression in Dante; and, though there is so little direct connection between him and any medieval Englishman except Chaucer, yet the whole scheme of his *Commedia* is so exact an epitome of religious-philosophic thought at the crown of the Middle Ages, that he may well be used here in illustration of that thought, rather than any of the distinguished English Schoolmen. For in fact there was no very distinctively English Scholasticism. The use of one common Latin language, together with the constant drift of scholars from one university to another, and, especially, the unquestioned supremacy of Paris as a focus of theological thought, forbade the formation of definite national schools in our period.

W E come here to the first really learned layman of the Middle Ages in Western Europe, and the first great vernacular poet of the later medieval centuries. The Troubadours, the Trouvères and the Minnesänger were now definitely on the downward slope. Moreover, Dante is the greatest poet of the whole Middle Ages, more unrivalled there in his superiority than Homer in antiquity, or Shakespeare in modern times. And finally, even though he had written nothing, his life itself is full of dramatic interest.

He was born in 1265, the year of the battle of Evesham, epoch-making for England. Then, in 1266, came the battle of Benevento, equally fateful for Italy. The mid-point of his life, reckoning by the Psalmist's computation of three score and ten years, was the equally epoch-making Jubilee year 1300. His home was in Florence, the most civilized town in the Western World, at a moment when Italian city life was perhaps at its highest ferment. Individual effort was still strong, and Florence was one of the city republics still unsubdued by the rising tide of despotism.

This later thirteenth century was the climax of several movements, especially in Italy. In religion, Europe had seen the fermentation of the year 1000. A century and a half later came St Bernard; and, a century and a half further on, in 1300, the Franciscans and Dominicans had come and had already passed their meridian. On the other hand, there was great activity of heresies and freethought. Gerardo Segharelli, one of the most remarkable of these heretics, was burned in 1300; and then, in 1307, Fra Dolcino, whose heresy was of extreme political, as well as religious, significance. In learning and philosophy, again, we trace the revival from about the year 1000. Europe saw teachers like Lanfranc and Anselm and Abailard, and the classical school of Chartres; and by 1200 universities existed already at Paris and Bologna. When Dante was born, Oxford and Cambridge were already formed, and many more. Aquinas was already writing his great *Summa*, and Roger Bacon was thinking out more modern philosophy. Dante must have known the *Summa* well, and had studied also Aquinas's brother-saint and philosopher, Bonaventura. In politics, Italy had seen the growth of civic liberties, the

Lombard League with its victory over the Empire at Legnano (1176), and its position secured by the Peace of Constance in 1183. From that time forward the civic autonomy of Italy was practically safe from serious imperial encroachments; and the cities were left each to work out its own salvation, except so far as each relied upon alliances with others, after the fashion of the modern nationalistic balance of power. Thence came intense political life, with kaleidoscopic changes and incessant war; as Dante himself confessed in later years, Italy was "a hostelry of pain". In art the French had been far ahead at the beginning of the century; and in 1265 they were still ahead in sculpture, despite the work of Niccolo Pisano. The French might then have been called the equals of Cimabue and his contemporaries in painting; but, by 1300, Giotto was in full work. Italy thenceforward led the Western World in painting, and was soon to be foremost in sculpture also. In poetry France, again, had held the first lead; then the Sicilians and Germans imitated the Troubadours, and Dante himself praises the poetry of Frederick II and his son Manfred. The great German lyric poet, Walther von der Vogelweide, had died shortly before Dante's birth. Then, in the second half of the century, the poetic laurels passed to the communes of Lombardy and Tuscany. If Dante had been born a century earlier, there would scarcely have been a language for him to write in. But now, in his youth, he found himself in a society where the interchange of sonnets and *canzoni* was a fashionable recreation. To this early education and healthy competition he added himself the *bel stilo* of Virgil, to whose mastership over him he bore such emphatic tribute. Most of all, however, he owed to his varied personal experiences. Sacchetti, Chaucer's contemporary, recording an anecdote of Dante's life, speaks of his eyes which nothing escaped: "Dante, che tutto vedea." Dante, that is, who had been everything—lover, painter, scholar, ambassador, councillor of the Republic, and finally exile. That last was the hardest school of all; one which gave force to all the rest. He tells us of that stern discipline. He had learned (he says) "how bitter is the taste of another man's bread, and how weary a path it is to climb and descend another man's stairs"; and again he describes the *Commedia* as "this book over which I have grown thin all these years". It may have been begun just before his exile, but it was emphatically the work of that period, from 1302–21.

His life should be read in his own poetic autobiography, the *Vita Nuova*, which is now so easily accessible in D. G. Rossetti's translation. He first saw Beatrice when each was nine years old, and, steeped as he was in medieval symbolism, this for him had the utmost significance. Three is the perfect number, the number of the Trinity. Nine is the square of three; three raised to a still higher power. It was natural, therefore, that Beatrice should have been what she was, a lady of superhuman perfection. He first heard her voice speaking to him nine years later at a feast. Yet we do not know for certain who she was, or even her name, or whether she died unmarried or had a husband and a large family. Of two things, however, there can be no legitimate doubt. First, that she was a real woman; attempts to prove her a purely ideal and imaginary figure, though supported by enthusiasts like D. G. Rossetti's father, may be relegated to the limbo of Baconian theories. On the other hand, there can be no doubt that she was intensely adored, sainted after death in his memory; and that, penetrated as he was with the study of Augustine and his *City of God*, in this woman who had so deeply influenced his life he grew to see a type of Holy Church herself. After her death he confesses to having fallen into an irregular life, from which he was partly saved by the study of philosophy. That, however, was in itself not enough, until religion came midway in his life, in that year 1300, as mystic in its world-significance as in its particular significance to him. He makes this the central point of his *Divina Commedia*. It was the year of the first Papal Jubilee that was ever held, and of the first bloodshed of Blacks and Whites among Guelfs in Florence; bloodshed which was fateful not only for Dante, but to a certain extent for all Europe. We in modern England can scarcely realize the significance of the fact that, since 1066, so little blood has been shed in our political quarrels. When, shortly after the Great War and during a great coal-strike, one of the Labour Leaders went so far as to predict that there would be "bloodshed" if the men did not get their way, that word betrayed his ignorance of Continental politics. Great Britain is the only great country of Europe in which there is no deep stain of blood on the hands of politicians; in which neither party can say to the other: "You are they who put our fathers up against the wall and shot them, when the political pendulum had swung in your favour." Therefore our less instructed politicians are tempted to take this for granted as a piece of good fortune, without realizing the significance of cause and effect; they are too narrow-minded to understand what a strict and solemn account will have to be paid by any party which first starts a reign of bloodshed within this island. In that fatal year 1300, Dante was one of the six elected priors. Next year the French prince, Charles de Valois, and the Pope intervened, nominally as mediators, but really as betrayers of the Whites. Dante himself was exiled; and when, in 1302, the sentence was confirmed, it was added that he should be burned alive if he were ever caught on his native territory.

Already before this, however, Dante had produced two of the most remarkable books of the Middle Ages. The *Vita Nuova* is "the most ideal book of love ever written", and certainly the most remarkable autobiography between St Augustine's *Confessions* and those of the Renaissance artist, Benvenuto Cellini. His *De Monarchia*, again, is "the most ideal of political works ever written", at any rate since the *De Civitate Dei*. When he crowned these with his *Divina Commedia*, he put himself side by side with Homer and Shakespeare; and, if we take the general verdict of cultured classes throughout the world, he stands perhaps not lowest of the three; certainly he is not least read of the three at the present moment. The poem was christened "Divina" in the seventeenth century; "Commedia" Dante himself calls it in his letter to his patron Can Grande, the Prince of Verona. A tragedy, he explains in that letter, is a poem that treats of the transition from bliss to evil: but this poem travels from evil to bliss, and therefore he calls it by the antithetical name of "Commedia".

He plunges straight into his subject from the very first, disregarding the tradition of cautious advance recommended by the genial Horace, as definitely as Daniel does in his story of Belshazzar's feast—

> In the midway of this our mortal life
> I found myself in a dark wood, astray—

So wild and desolate was this forest, that he felt it as the bitterness of death even to think himself back there. How had he found his way thither? He scarce knew: a sleepy dullness had benumbed his senses and he had strayed from the path. But, as he climbs, the trees begin to thin off at the top of the ravine, and he emerges on a mountain-side just touched by the first rays of dawn. Here is hope, and he breathes again, looking back upon the dark forest of his wanderings as a spent swimmer lying upon the shore pants and looks back upon the waves that had so nearly beaten the life out of him.

Already in these few lines we see Dante's main characteristics as a poet. In the first place his consummate art; the opening line arrests our attention, and each fresh verse beats the image in. We see this again in his selection of metre, the *terzina*; a metre regular enough, like Milton's blank verse, to carry him steadily to the end of a long epic, yet varied enough, with its constant change of rhyme, to escape monotony. Again, we see how firmly he takes his stand on the solid facts of this world. Even in his wildest flights, as Macaulay noted long ago, his imagination was always based on things seen, and especially on his own dear Italy; the mountains (not only Apennines, but even Alps), the blue Mediterranean, the farmers and herdsmen, down to their very gestures and every movement of the cattle and wild beasts and birds. Equally microscopically he shows us the outdoor and indoor life in the crowded streets of his native Florence; the butcher at his stall, the tailor on his bench. His poem is, on the one hand, such a repertory of daily life as we ourselves may enjoy by looking through the back pages of *Punch*; and, far beyond this, all those similes are heightened by his powerful use of metaphor. It has been suggested by a modern critic that his preference for simile over metaphor was a piece of instinctive art; that, since his whole poem might be considered as one vast metaphor, therefore he might spare the metaphor in detail. Yet in one of the very passages selected by the critic for this thesis we find, side by side with an obvious simile, a metaphor which he has failed to recognize. One of the shades, surprised to see in this fresh wanderer something so nearly resembling a man whom he had known in Florence, "sharpened his eyebrows at me" as a tailor eyes the needle which he tries to thread in scanty light. That metaphor of the sharpening of the eyebrows is characteristic of Dante's intense poetic force; and, with regard to the similes, if we take at random two or three pages of the *Commedia* and the *Aeneid*, we shall find in the latter an even greater preponderance. This use of similes, in fact, lay in the classical tradition in which Dante was steeped. All this art, however, is bent in Dante to serve the purposes of the mystic meaning. He is possessed with that conviction expressed in

Goethe's *Faust*, that the visible things of earth are an adumbration of the invisible things of God: that Nature may say,

> Here at the roaring loom of time I ply
> And weave God's garment that you see Him by.

The poem, then, may very truly have been called a great allegory, centred round a day and a year of the deepest mystical significance. The story begins on Good Friday in this year of Jubilee, which was the thirty-fifth of the poet's own life. Dante himself may very likely have believed in the pseudo-historical excuse given for that great celebration. According to a story written by Cardinal Stefaneschi, an intimate friend of Boniface VIII, a man had come to that Pope saying that he was 107 years old and that his father, in childhood, had told him, "If you live a hundred years longer you will see the great Jubilee which marks the beginning of each fresh century in Rome." All historical evidence is against the truth of this, and in fact the Jubilee of 1300, so far from being long foreseen, was so hastily announced, even in the fateful year itself, that it scarcely gave time for distant pilgrims to take advantage of it at all. Multitudes, however, did come. It is calculated that two hundred thousand pilgrims came to reverence especially the *Vernicle*, the napkin with which St Veronica had wiped our Lord's face, and which bore the lineaments of it thenceforth to all eternity. The crowds were so great that they motived, for the narrow bridges of Rome, what is perhaps the first Rule of the Road recorded in history; and the whole event stimulated Giovanni Villani, the Florentine citizen-historian, to write his great work; much as the Franciscan friars, chanting their vespers in the erstwhile Temple of Jupiter, suggested to Gibbon his story of the Decline and Fall of the Roman Empire.

To Dante this year brought new spiritual life. This was the moment of his issue from the gloomy wood. He had felt himself unworthy after Beatrice's death; how unworthy, we do not know. Philosophy had only partially cured him. He had woken up to find half his life already spent; but here at last was a dawn of promise. On the other hand, the World, the Flesh and the Devil still haunted him. He needed grace directly from God. This grace came to him through his purified human love, which undergoes a final apotheosis in his mind, and elevates Beatrice to a type of the Church. But all must be in order; artistic gradation is here the gradation of truth. First, in the *Inferno* he must look back upon sin and realize all its loathsomeness; then trace, step by step, the Purgation of Souls; and finally catch a vision of Eternal Bliss as an incentive to perseverance. No other poem ever undertook to give so complete a picture of life as this, and no other of equal length has been so carefully planned. It consists of a hundred cantos, in three groups of 33 each, with one introductory in the first group. Each of these cantos is so exactly balanced, that between the longest of all and the shortest there is only a margin of 38 lines. To keep up the sacred number of three, *Inferno*, *Purgatorio* and *Paradiso* are divided each into nine sections.

On these mountain slopes, then, at sunrise, Dante is confronted by three wild beasts, the panther, the lion, and the she-wolf: Uncleanness, Pride and Greed. A figure appears as his guide; this is Virgil, the godlike poet of his study, who will conduct him through Hell and Purgatory, but may not cross the threshold of Heaven; there he must be left behind, and thenceforward Beatrice alone can lead the poet. For the present, however, Virgil is all-powerful. He drives off the beasts; and the two wayfarers climb this mountain by an arduous and savage way which brings them by nightfall to the gates of Hell. Here they find that inscription which has since become a byword in literature:

> Through me you pass into the city of Woe,
> Through me you pass into eternal pain:
> All hope abandon, ye who enter here.

They come first to an Ante-Hell, the place of the cowards and irresolute, peopled first by those angels who were neutral in the conflict between God and Satan, and whom therefore Heaven had spewed forth, while Hell itself disdained to receive them to its full hospitality. There it is that Dante finds the shade of "him who made the great refusal"—Pope Celestine V, sainted by the Church, but odious to many as having despaired of that worldly machine which it was his task to control as pope, and as having, by his resignation of that divine office, made way for Boniface VIII, the despot who had wronged not only Dante and his Florence, but, in Dante's opinion, the whole Christian world. Hence the poet and his guide pass the river Acheron in Charon's boat (for he owes much to Virgil's story of Aeneas' descent to Hades), and they enter the first circle of Hell proper.

Here is the Limbo of the Unbaptized. The air is thick with the sighs of these souls, though they suffer no physical pain. The multitude consists first of heathens, concerning whom Virgil explains: "for defect [of baptism] and no other fault, are we lost; and only in so far afflicted, that without hope we live in desire." Here (he says) am I myself with Homer and Horace and Lucan and Ovid, Hector and Aeneas and Caesar; nay, even the semi-divine Aristotle, the Master of all Science, with his fellow-philosophers of Greece and Rome. With these heathens are the unbaptized children of Christian parents: for no orthodox Latin theologian of that day admitted the salvation of the unbaptized since Christ's coming, apart from a few miraculous or semi-miraculous instances, some of which legend might have consecrated. St Augustine even laid such weight upon the doctrine of original sin that he assigned eternal physical torture to the unbaptized children of Christian parents; and medieval writers speak with horror of those priests or midwives who, in their negligence or ignorance, failed to baptize truly and effectually. St Thomas, it is true, assigns to them no punishment but the deprival of the Beatific Vision; but, seeing that this deprival was also reckoned by philosophers as the bitterest of all the woes suffered by the damned, the subtle logic by which he convinces himself that this Limbo of the Unbaptized is compatible with a certain degree of natural happiness can scarcely have comforted any but a small minority of bereaved mothers. Dante, as we have seen, does not follow his master quite so far; and Boccaccio, in his Commentary, speaks plainly of physical pain.

We have here the keynote of the *Inferno*, and the rest may be told more briefly. If Original Sin, the taint we all inherit from Adam and Eve, must be paid so dearly, how much heavier is the debt of wilful transgression! The travellers climb down from circle to circle, which are like mountain precipices. The second is peopled with those who suffer for crimes of passion overbalancing reason; and here comes the famous episode of Paolo and Francesca. He finds in this circle a hurricane whirling the souls for ever through the air. They are driven round like flocks of starlings in the winter blast, without hope either of rest or of lesser pain for all eternity. Here are Cleopatra, Helen, Dido, Tristram—heroes and heroines of the greatest romance—and here is a couple who move Dante immediately to cry: "Poet, I would willingly speak

with those two that go together and seem so light upon the wind."
Virgil here gives Dante an unfailing spell; and Dante, obedient to
his teaching, cries: "In the name of that love that leads you, come
and speak!" At those compelling words the two left the flying
multitude, "gliding as swiftly as a dove glides on steady pinions
to her nest", and Dante recognizes clearly now that he has spoken
to Francesca, aunt to Guido da Polenta, who was his own great
patron in his last refuge at Ravenna. She answers his challenge
in those words of Boethius: "There is no greater pain than to
remember one's happy days in times of misery." But his appeal
was irresistible, and she must tell her story:

> Amor, che al cor gentil ratto s' apprende,
> Prese costui della bella persona
> Che mi fu tolta, e il modo ancor m' offende.
>
> Amor, che a nullo amato amar perdona,
> Mi prese del costui piacer sì forte,
> Che, come vedi, ancor non m' abbandona.
>
> Amor condusse noi ad una morte;
> Caina attende chi vita ci spense.
>
> Love, that in gentle heart is quickly learnt,
> Entangled him by that fair body, which I
> Lost in such cruel sort, as grieves me still.
> Love, that denial takes from none belov'd,
> Caught me with pleasing him so passing well,
> That, as thou seest, he yet deserts me not.
> Love brought us to one death. Deep Hell awaits
> The soul, who spilt our life.

The force of this triple repetition may be compared with one of
the most wonderful passages in the Bible, where David receives
the news of his rebel son's death: "And the king was much moved,
and went up to the chamber over the gate, and wept; and as he
went, thus he said, 'O my son Absalom, my son, my son Absalom!
Would God I had died for thee, O Absalom my son, my son!'" In
both cases we have primarily not art, but passion; the words that
strike the hearer with this almost intolerable repetition of pathos
are the very words that must burst from a heart that could bear no
more. So it was with Dante; if the syllables come back again and
again to the same point, it is because the heart beats again and
again upon the same theme. The throb of the verse echoes the
actual pulsation; here we have primarily the reality of passion; all
that art had to do was to fix this in an abiding form. We are told

of Michael Angelo that his chisel, even in old age, stripped and flaked the marble with such direct vigour that it seemed as though he were not hewing from an inert block, but removing foreign accretions from a pre-existent statue. So with Dante; we feel not so much that he is relating, nor that he is creating, as that he stands by, removes a veil, and shows us a truth pre-existent from all eternity and living to all eternity; a picture that impresses itself as irresistibly upon the mind as (to use his own simile) the seal impresses itself upon the wax.

The *Inferno* is the most scathing satire in all literature—devastating because it is so inevitable in its justice, which, after all, is the true touchstone even in satire. He finds the angry and sullen together in one circle; the first tearing each other through endless ages as they sought to tear each other in life, and the second sunk in a filthy marsh in which their very existence was seldom revealed except by the bubbles that rose to the surface from their sighs:

> Fixed in the slime they said: "Sad once were we
> In God's sweet air made gladsome by the sun,
> Carrying a foul and lazy fume within us;
> Now in this dismal sediment are we sad."

Here and everywhere, we have a punishment that fits the crime; and thus we pass on from circle to circle, as through terrace after terrace of a great Alp; not up into the clouds here, but down into the deepest pit. No earthly rank or profession saves them from Dante's judgment. Even with Popes and cardinals and proud prelates, we must say of the *Inferno*, as the Psalmist says of the proud sinners of his own world, "they lie in hell like sheep". Here are five Popes and one Emperor; Anastasius among the heretics, side by side with the godless Emperor Frederick II; but Dante here was probably mistaken: he apparently confused Pope Anastasius with the Emperor of that name. In the circle of the fraudulent, again, Dante places three Popes of his own lifetime—plunged head foremost into circular cavities of white-hot rock, with tongues of flame flickering up from their protruding feet. It is one of these who utters that sentiment familiar to moralists of the Middle Ages:

> Ah Constantine, to how great ill gave birth
> Not thy conversion, but that plenteous dower
> Which the first wealthy pope received of thee!

In the lowest pit of all are the traitors; Brutus and Cassius, who, by murdering Caesar, betrayed the Empire; and Judas, who betrayed his Lord. Last of all comes Lucifer, cast down head-foremost from Heaven to mid-earth, a gigantic figure, past which they climb through the chasm made by his fall, and at last, emerging, find themselves beneath the stars of the Southern Hemisphere; for Dante knows of the Southern Cross.

Here, then, they find Purgatory; a mountain rising in terraces that correspond to the falling terraces of Hell. We have here that most natural idea of purgation by pain before the soul can be pure enough to endure the presence of God: a doctrine naturally evolved as a spiritual counterpart of the public and visible penances required by the early Church before the faithful would restore a sinner to communion with the rest. But between those days and Dante's it had gone through a treble current of debasement. First, spiritually, through even so great a Pope as Gregory I, who did much to systematize the idea, and may be said practically to have originated it as a dogma of the Church; and secondly, in practice, through the custom of commutation. Originally these public penances necessary for restoration to communion had sometimes been commuted, by an equitable compromise, for something equally difficult in itself, yet bearing less hardly on this particular case. Then, by a natural transition, the commutation was softened to something not equal, but easier. Augustine had shown this in the case of Victorinus, where it was suggested that, in deference to his specially dignified position in the intellectual and social and political world, he might be allowed to make his baptism and profession of faith in private. Then, thirdly, came the worst debasement of all, a money commutation. This led naturally, and it may be almost said inevitably, to such doings as Chaucer satirizes when he depicts the friar as pleading on behalf of those sinners who are too hard-hearted to weep or sorrow for their sins, and must therefore atone for them by giving money to the professional Religious, who will do the mourning for them. This, again, bred that whole system of Indulgences, in which remission of sins was almost invariably bound up with more or less of money payments. It is true that, in theory, the Indulgence was valid only in cases where the sinner was already repentant and confessed; but in fact the great Franciscan preacher Berthold of Ratisbon, contemporary with Dante's father, speaks of "penny-preachers" who promise so much Indulgence, as from the Pope himself, for a penny or a halfpenny, that many thousand Christians imagine they have got rid of their sins for the money, and go to hell. Two centuries later, on the verge of the Reformation, we shall find Gascoigne, the Chancellor of Oxford University, writing in even stronger terms. But of such abusive views there is no trace in Dante; and many feel the *Purgatorio* to be, on the whole, his greatest poetical achievement, though the general opinion will place the *Inferno* as the most powerful and the *Paradiso* as the most beautiful. He had entered Hell on Good Friday. He emerged at the foot of the mountain of Purgatory on Easter morning before daybreak. He and Virgil climbed thus, terrace after terrace, up this island mountain; for Dante, like the most enlightened geographers of his time, believed the Southern Hemisphere to be purely oceanic, apart from this rock on whose summit was the Paradise from which Adam and Eve had been expelled. The Pit of Hell, according to his cosmography, was exactly below Jerusalem, and the Earthly Paradise exactly opposite. The place of Adam's sin was thus, not only spiritually but geographically, the Antipodes to that of Christ's redemption. There is here an Ante-Purgatory, as there was an Ante-Hell. Then come seven terraces, one for the purgation of each of the Seven Deadly Sins; and these, together with the Ante-Purgatory and the Earthly Paradise, form nine divisions, as Hell was in nine circles. Here from terrace to terrace they climb, by stairs steep and narrow and rough, but easier in gradation as they ascend. At each stair stands an angel chanting one of the seven Beatitudes to comfort the toiler as he reaches the next. Some of the punishments here are almost as painful as in the *Inferno*; but there is this essential difference, that here we have no abiding sense of pain; and not only is there this alleviation in time, but (and herein we feel Dante's greatness) the toiler's will is felt to be in unison with his fate. Even great theologians in the Middle Ages speak of haste through Purgatory as a mercy. It is the constant theme of preachers that money must be given for Masses and prayers which will shorten this passage; and even nowadays, in the wayside shrines of Italy and Roman Catholic Switzerland, we see souls writhing in the flames and the money-box by their side for charitable alleviation. In Dante, the spirit of these souls is "we would not abbreviate one moment of the process, any more than we would quarrel in any other way with our final good". Moreover, Dante exercises the same independence of judgment here as in his *Inferno*. The first soul he met in Hell was a Pope canonized by the Church; and the first with whom he spoke in Purgatory was that Manfred, arch-enemy of the Popes, who died excommunicate in battle against them. "Horrible were my sins", he confesses, "but God's mercy is even greater. True, I died with the full curse of the Church upon me, yet the trunk is not so blasted but that one green shoot can sprout and the whole tree be some day restored."

The most beautiful cantos, except the Earthly Paradise, are perhaps the 2nd [Casella] and the 7th with the 8th—the Valley of the Princes. Here, Dante found the most conspicuous figures of an age almost unrivalled in its wealth of such men—the Emperor Rudolf, Charles of Anjou, with his mortal enemy, Peter of Aragon, Henry III of England, and many more, resting at eventide in the Valley of Flowers: a flock of majestic souls nestling humbly under the guard of two angels assigned to watch over them through the night. Finally, at the top of the mountain, they come to the wall of fire that rings the Earthly Paradise; and here Dante's flesh shrinks naturally, while the disembodied Virgil and his fellow-poet Statius were at their ease.

> I still, though conscience urg'd, no step advanced.
> When still he saw me fix'd and obstinate,
> Somewhat disturb'd he cried: "Mark now, my son,
> From Beatrice thou art by this wall
> Divided." As at Thisbe's name the eye
> Of Pyramus was open'd (when life ebb'd
> Fast from his veins), and took one parting glance,
> While vermeil dyed the mulberry; thus I turn'd
> To my sage guide, relenting, when I heard
> The name, that springs for ever in my breast.
>
> He shook his forehead; and, "How long", he said,
> "Linger we now?" then smil'd, as one would smile
> Upon a child, that eyes the fruit and yields.
> Into the fire before me then he walk'd;
> And Statius, who erewhile no little space
> Had parted us, he pray'd to come behind.
>
> I would have cast me into molten glass
> To cool me, when I enter'd, so intense
> Rag'd the conflagrant mass. The sire belov'd,
> To comfort me, as he proceeded, still

Of Beatrice talk'd. "Her eyes", saith he,
"E'en now I seem to view." From th'other side
A voice, that sang, did guide us; and, the voice
Following, with heedful ear, we issued forth
There where the path led upward. "Come", we heard,
"Come, blessed of my Father." Such the sounds,
That hail'd us from within a light, which shone
So radiant, I could not endure the view.

Then comes the culmination of all—the Earthly Paradise.

From this Earthly Paradise we pass now to that of the Heavens, with Beatrice as guide. To Dante, as to his contemporaries, the earth was the centre of the universe, surrounded by concentric hollow crystal spheres in each of which a planet was set like a gem in a ring. Each planet, as it circled farther from the earth, offered a higher stage of beatitude. Here again Dante follows the ordinary scholastic teaching of his time, that there shall be different degrees of perfection in the bliss of souls in Heaven. The only great philosopher, perhaps, who gave equality to all, was our English Archbishop Bradwardine; and, among remarkable poets, only the author of *Pearl*, who here follows literally Christ's teaching in his parable of the Vineyard and the Labourers. With Dante, as with Aquinas and Bonaventura, the difference of gradations is no obstacle whatever to the perfect and supreme content of each soul, which has no will outside the sovereign will of God: *E la sua voluntate è nostra pace.*

Those words are what our poet hears in the first and lowest Heaven—that of the moon, a planet which Dante conceives as one vast eternal pearl wherein move souls yet whiter than itself— just so much whiter, just so delicately visible, as a pearl itself is on the forehead of a beautiful girl. Thus they passed on from sphere to sphere, from Heaven to Heaven, speaking with saints that will always live in history—Bernard, Bonaventura, Aquinas, and with other folk of whom we should never have heard but for Dante— men and women that had lived with him, at the sight of whose faces and the sound of whose voices his pulse had beaten—souls to whom he wished immortality because he loved them in the flesh, and to whom his poem has given immortality. Such was Cunizza, the tender-hearted and high-born, multi-adulteress; so also had Dante done already in his Purgatory, immortalizing Pia, the obscure victim of a husband's murder in a desolate Italian "moated grange", and his friend Casella, the musician, whom he makes to sing, among those suffering souls, as he had sung on earth; a song, moreover, of Dante's own. At last they reach the Empyrean, that Heaven of Flame above all other Heavens, in which dwells the Godhead Itself. Here he sees the Mystic Rose, formed of the palpitating souls of all the saints. Here St Bernard intercedes for him to the Virgin Mary, and the Virgin grants him grace to see for one brief division of a moment that Beatific Vision of the Divine Essence to which it is the whole aim of his life to attain one day for all eternity. And here we must remember what the man was—how rich were the faculties and the experience which in this moment were to receive their intensest possible satisfaction. Let us remember Dante's love of visible things—*Dante, che tutto vedea*—and the ignominous Hell he created for those who were sad even while they trod God's good brown earth, and were bathed in His genial sunshine. Let us remember his love of abstract thought and dialectics; the extreme—the pedantic—minuteness with which he comments on his own poems in his *Vita Nuova*. And then, reading the last few lines of the *Paradiso*, we see how these and all his other faculties were for once swallowed up in one supreme moment of direct intuition. All visible things, all think-able things, were seen suddenly as existing only in God, narrowed down, at that indivisible point of space and time, to a single ray of light, into which the rapt soul plunged its gaze—plunged dizzily on ("I had been lost, had mine eyes turned away from it")—plunged on and on, and saw "ingathered within its depths, bound by [Almighty] love into one volume, all that which is scattered in single [Sibylline] leaves throughout the whole universe". Dante, thus seeing, felt himself for the moment in fact, and to some extent for ever afterwards in recollection of that fact, in absolute harmony, through every fibre of his being, with the infinite invisible forces of this vast universe: "My will and desire were rolled, with the even motion of a wheel, by that Love which moveth the sun and the infinitude of the stars." Here, again, the feeling is no less truly Dante's own, although the words are an echo from Boethius.

St Augustine had given, as his briefest and best definition of Virtue: "it is the setting-in-order of Love"—*Ordo est Amoris*. The Franciscan poet-mystic Jacopone had cried: "Set this love of mine in order, O Thou who lovest me"—*Ordina quest' amore, o*

Tu che m' ami! Dante sums up all this, in a poem not only inspired by the characteristic medieval passion for order, but displaying its completest artistic exemplification. No other epic can rival this steady and effortless passage from the tumult of Hell, through the gradual pacification of Purgatory, to the perfect peace of Paradise.

XIX. THE ROYAL COURT

WITH Dante, we are on the Mount of Transfiguration. It is good for us to be here; it is good to repair hither again and again; but at the foot of this mountain the world is going very much its own way: that motley world, that Vanity Fair, from out of which so many struggling souls cry: "Lord, I believe, help Thou mine unbelief!" We have taken stock of the true foundation of lay society, the Village; let us look now at its apex, the Court.

The Conquest made England the home of a more powerful monarchy than any other state of equal size. Not that the general population was worse off; quite the contrary; but the barons were more restricted. From William the Conqueror to Henry II, the power of the English king was far greater than that of his contemporary in France—let alone Germany. King and barons alike were foreigners, and were compelled to hold together in face of a hostile population. Again, the king had made himself, and had made the barons. The Duke of Normandy had become King of England; and the adventurers, distinguished or undistinguished, who shared his fortunes, thus became great nobles. Hence, William being a character strong enough to take advantage of this position, the feudal nobility was curbed here as nowhere else on the Continent. Michelet says truly: "The Anglo-Norman State and Church were organized with a firmness which was a model to the rest of the world. Continental kings envied the omnipotence of their English brethren; continental peoples envied the despotic but orderly discipline which reigned in Great Britain." Much importance must be given to the predominantly northern character of our constitutional development. Upon Anglo-Saxon civilization was grafted that of these Norman customs. On both sides, we find little or no trace of direct Roman influences, in spite of modern attempts to extol these as a primary factor. Thus this baronage, disciplined at first to stand by the king, became gradually a class disciplined to resist him in turn. For the Norman kings, by restricting the powers of the barons, made them gradually drift into alliance with the people. In France some barons became, while others might hope to become, petty sovereigns, almost absolute on their own lands; these were able to defy the king, sometimes even singly, and at any rate by twos or threes. In England there was no such possibility: barons could not thus assert themselves except in large numbers; and, since a strong minority would always stand by the king, they could not even do that without the help of towns and the lower gentry.

Again, our French possessions were disadvantageous to royalty, and advantageous to the opposition. Kings were constantly involved in Continental affairs to which they attached equal or greater importance than to home affairs. Therefore this created a baronial-popular opposition such as we find in the famous case of Edward I in 1297, when Roger Bigod refused to go on one of Edward's oversea expeditions, and the king insisted: "By God, you shall either go or hang!" only to provoke the retort: "By God, my Lord King, I will neither go nor hang!" It took long, however, to produce the beginnings of such reasoned resistance. Constitutional monarchy began under John. It is true that Magna Carta was at bottom an opportunist document, voicing mainly the class grievances of the baronage, with which popular grievances were bound up in virtue of the popular-baronial alliance; yet it gained in fact far wider significance, at least in the form in which it was later republished and repeated from reign to reign. Although its provisions about taxation were in themselves temporary, they formed the basis of that pressure on the king through the power of the purse, which has been so remarkable a factor in the English struggle for liberty. So again with other clauses; practical and opportunist in themselves, they "gave a solemn sanction and a definite statement, to which appeal could ever after be made, to certain fundamental principles of liberty, much wider in their application than their framers knew"; so that nearly every insurrection against absolutism in England has been able to appeal to Magna Carta. Its value is best expressed by Maitland in Traill's *Social England* (ch. IV, § 4, p. 409); and, as Maitland insists, its main significance lies in the fact that it is "a grand compromise, and a fit prologue for all those thousands of compromises in which the practical wisdom of the English will always be expressing itself.... And then in its detailed clauses it must do something for all those sorts and conditions of men who have united to resist John's tyranny—for the bishop, the clerk, the baron, the knight, the burgess, the merchant—and there must be some give and take between these classes, for not all their interests are harmonious.[1]

The next great step came under Henry III, with government by a committee of barons. This broke down; fortunately, for it would have meant an oligarchy. Then, with Edward I, we get what may be called a parliament; and, within a generation of this, England is politically in the forefront of Europe and destined to outpace the rest more and more. This, again, had a definite effect upon our literature. Mr V. H. Galbraith, in his valuable paper on *The Literacy of the medieval English Kings*, read before the British Academy in 1935, has shown how early-ripe our vernacular prose was before the Conquest. Alfred had consciously stimulated what had already begun through natural causes, "the precocious development of English as an educational, even literary language and as the language of government.... In so far as [this] affected law, government and business, lay society must have been more developed in England than abroad, where the force of tradition and a higher standard of clerical Latin retarded the development of the vernaculars, and thus kept the layman a stranger to the written word." The immediate effect of the Conquest was to strangle this vernacular prose through the importation of Continental clerics, well versed in Latin, by whose help our kings did their business; our Anglo-Saxon Chronicle flickered out in the next generation but one. But the literary student cannot ignore the fact that our later writers grew up among a people rapidly outdistancing other European peoples (except in corners: e.g. Aragon, and Sicily during certain periods) in the assertion of liberty and the practice of liberty. This gave us very early a spirit of independence even in literature; not in the narrow sense of that word, for we borrowed enormously from other nations, more perhaps than any other people; but true independence in our use of this material. Chaucer's works and *Piers Plowman*, with the Pearl-cycle, are more truly national, more original in the modern sense, than anything in French literature of the time.

Yet, for some time, the only post-Conquest vernacular encouraged by our kings was the French. Mr Galbraith points out very truly that the Middle Ages divided society into three classes, "those who fought, those who worked, and those who prayed", and that "the social prejudices of the military class discouraged learned tastes in its members; and the occasional exception, as we learn from Ordericus Vitalis, was nicknamed 'the Clerk'", i.e. Henry I. Mr Galbraith dismisses as "pure journalism" the story that Henry I as a youth was given to quoting, even in his father's hearing, the proverb "Rex illiteratus, asinus coronatus". But he points out that this *cliché* must yet be taken into account, and that the ordinary opinion of the later twelfth century was "that kings needed to be 'educated'": i.e. that, if they could not themselves read Latin, at least they should take real interest in what might be heard from men who could. He sums up briefly: "From 597 to 1100 it is exceptional for a king to be able to write at all, or to read Latin; in the twelfth and thirteenth centuries kings learn to read Latin but do not (even if they can) write it; in the fourteenth and fifteenth centuries they are taught in youth both to read and write Latin, but in fact are far more occupied with French and English."

But "literacy" in the ordinary medieval sense, i.e. the knowledge of Latin, was not necessarily "education" as understood nowadays; and Mr Galbraith argues very truly "that the medieval potentate did not read and write (if indeed he could not) because he had neither the need nor the wish, having others [i.e. the clergy] to do these things for him; that social prejudice rendered reading and writing *infra dig.* for the noble class; and that in any case they are no necessary index to the level of education". In those days men were wont to read aloud even when they read only for their own enjoyment; therefore it would be natural to find, quite apart from the class of professional reciters, an amateur here and there who advanced as far in knowledge of the available literature of his day as the non-performing musical amateur does in modern music. We see this in Froissart's noble patron, Gaston de Foix, for whose entertainment our chronicler read during so many weary midnight hours. Thus, throughout the pre-Chaucerian period and for a good while later, royal and baronial life exercised a very direct influence on literature. Except for religious writings, the author's best hope of patronage was either in a royal or noble household; or at least by attracting royal or noble attention; Chaucer and Froissart are stock examples here. It was in such courts that the English language was formed as a literary tongue, quite apart from written literary work. Courts and castles were regular schools of manners; and we must here include the households of the spiritual barons also—bishops and abbots. The influence of Theobald of Canterbury in this way, and of his successor Becket, are well brought out by Miss Norgate. All our kings, down to Henry IV, spoke French; even of Edward I we only know that he was master of just enough English to make that simple and irreverent pun upon *Bigod*. His grandson, Edward III, is sometimes credited with something more by modern writers; but there is no clear evidence that he could talk English with any fluency. Yet the barons and prelates were becoming more and more English; and it seems probable (though I know no explicit text) that a good deal of English was spoken at their courts even during the first half of our period. The result was a gradual formation, on the tongues of able and cultured men, of a real literary taste. Choice and elaborate speech, as we shall see, was counted as an accomplishment of the perfect knight.

Let us come, therefore, to a more detailed and intimate glance at a royal court, contenting ourselves with a single specimen. Let us take as typical that of Henry II. In the first place we have here many first-rate literary witnesses; again, this was specially a resort of literary men; and, thirdly, it stands roughly midway in our period, both in time and in evolution. Henry II's court was far more civilized and national than William's, less civilized and national than that of Henry VIII. This king's crowning marked, "scarcely less than that of William the Conqueror, the beginning of a new era...and it was distinctly recognized as such by the men of the period". We have his portrait from different contemporaries. We cannot trust that which is on his sculptured monument at Fontevraud; not only because this was made whole generations after his death, but also because monumental sculpture did not aim at exact portraits till a much later date. The earliest, probably, is that of Philippe-le-Hardi of France [1298], whose mouth is slightly distorted at one corner, evidently in reproduction of what the sculptor found on the death-mask. Henry II was of middle stature, thick-set, with broad shoulders and brawny arms; his hands were coarse and neglected, and his legs of iron. He was naturally given to corpulence, but he kept it down by temperance at the table and hard work. He had a large round head, short neck, reddish hair, and freckled skin. He was great in war and in the council chamber; always ready with his facts and with his words; a ruler who never forgot a face he had once seen, or a fact that had once interested him. Above all, his contemporaries describe his energy; when not at war, he was always hunting in his spare time; his legs and feet were chronically black and blue. If not on horse-back, then he was on his feet; scarcely ever sitting. Thus he tired out his whole court: "Whensoever he can breathe freely from cares and anxieties, he busies himself with private reading, or labours to unravel some knotty question amid a throng of clerks." His sons all took after him, if only at a distance; all had more than average intellectual vigour and interests.

Here, then, will be a picturesque court; let us look at it mainly, though not exclusively, from the point of view of literary students. What were the court manners of that time? We may understand them best from a few concrete examples. We shall here again be reminded that there was far more room for impulse then than in our own drab age; in that respect our ancestors of 800 years ago were children in comparison with modern times. On the one hand was royal dignity, on the other, liberties all the greater because there was so little fear lest familiarity should breed con-tempt. Mr Galbraith here quotes very appositely from that half-unwilling tribute to William I in the Anglo-Saxon Chronicle: "He was very dignified: thrice every year he bare his crown, as often as he was in England. At Easter he bare it in Winchester; at Pentecost in Westminster; at Mid-winter in Gloucester. And there were with him all the great men over all England, arch-bishops and suffragan bishops, abbots and earls, thanes and knights." Solemn scenes of that kind impressed a very living conception of sovereignty not only upon beholders but upon thousands who would only hear the story told, with bated breath, at second or third or fiftieth hand. At other times, in contrast to this, the king might be a mere grown-up schoolboy in his passions or in his play. Many instances of this are well enough known; John, for example, after his disaster at Runnymede, rolling on the floor and gnawing the straws and rushes that littered it; or, again, Henry II pulling off Becket's costly cloak to give to the beggar: the whole street crowding round to see what the king and chancellor were fighting about. But far less known is that which Fitzstephen tells us in the same place—how the king would ride on horseback into the chancellor's hall, bow in hand, on the way to or from hunting; how he would dismount and leap over the table and sit by Becket's side and drink with him: "They played together like two boys of the same age." Less known, again, is what several chroniclers tell of Henry II's last year of life, when he burst out in fury against God, as he rode away for the last time from Le Mans and saw the town burst into flames: "For that Thou, O God, hast taken from me this day the city that I most loved in this world, [wherein I was born and bred and my father lieth buried, therefore] I shall requite Thee. For, from this time forward, I shall take from Thee the thing that should please Thee most in me, and that is mine heart." Salimbene, again, gives us a characteristic instance from the court of Henry III. A jester cried aloud in his presence: "Hear ye, hear ye, my masters! Our king is like unto the Lord Jesus Christ." "How so?" asked the king, hugely flattered. "Because our Lord was as wise at the moment of His conception as when He was 30 years old: so likewise our King is as wise now as when he was a little child." This Henry, like other weak men, had his fits of sudden fury; he ordered the untimely jester to be strung up out of hand. His servants, however, only went through an empty form of execution, and bade the unlucky fool keep carefully out of the way until royalty should have forgotten or forgiven.

As for Henry II, we may learn much from what is in every way an admirable book, the *Magna Vita S. Hugonis*, an intimate biography of St Hugh of Lincoln by his chaplain, which may be found excellently summarized in C. Marson's *Life* of St Hugh. This pious and bold Bishop of Lincoln had excommunicated the king's chief forester for infringing the liberties of the Church; again, he had refused the king's request for a Lincoln canonry in favour of one of his courtiers who was not ecclesiastically suitable. The king summoned him to Woodstock. Hugh found Henry sitting on the turf in his park, his courtiers in a ring round him. Not a soul rose to greet the bishop, and he realized that this was at the king's bidding. Therefore he "quietly laid his hands on the shoulders of a great councillor who sat next the King, and made a place for himself at the royal side". Still there was dead silence. Henry, to show his unconcern, told a courtier to give him a needle and thread, and began to stitch at a bandage on his wounded left finger. At this the bishop remarked: "How like you are now to your ancestors of Falaise!" an allusion to the fact that William the Conqueror's mother was daughter to a tanner of Falaise, and in those days leather-dressers were commonly leather-sellers and leather-workers, so that "the cobbler" may well have become a proverbial nickname. The king, "struck to the heart by this smooth yet razor-like stroke, clenched his fingers and burst into uncontrollable laughter, rolling over on the ground with his head in the grass and his face in the air; in which posture he long gave way to his laughter without control". The courtiers, even the most shocked, could not repress a smile. Henry explained the jest: then he turned to Hugh and argued both cases reasonably with him. He found himself wrong on both points, and was frankly reconciled. The chief forester and his accomplices were first publicly flogged and then ecclesiastically absolved; afterwards they became Hugh's firm friends. We must remember that Hugh the man is exceptional here; there is abundant evidence that his character gave him immense power not only over men, but over animals; yet his and Henry's manners are typical of the time, except possibly for the comparative politeness of Hugh's retort, the stroke "so keen yet so polished".

We may now pass on to see the same saint in contact with Richard I. Hugh had refused to render Richard military aid *outside* the kingdom; therefore Richard had ordered the confiscation of the Lincoln episcopal possessions [1198]. "St Hugh crossed the Channel", writes his biographer, "and went confidently to seek Richard. He found him in the chapel of his new castle of Château-Gaillard, hearing Mass on St Augustine's day; St Hugh immediately approached and saluted him. Now the King was hard by the chapel door, on his royal throne, and at his feet were the Bishops of Durham and Ely. To Hugh's greeting Richard answered no word; but, scanning him awhile with a frown, he turned his face away. Then Hugh, unmoved by his wrath, said: 'Kiss me, my lord King': whereat the King averted his face all the more, turning his whole head away. Then the saintly bishop, grasping the two lappets of the King's mantle firmly at the breast, shook it with some force, saying again, 'Thou owest me a kiss, for I am come from afar to see thee.' 'Not so', replied the King; 'For thou hast merited no kiss from me.' Then the bishop shook him more strongly by the mantle, which he still held tight in his grasp, and made answer boldly, 'nay, but I *have* merited it; kiss me, I say!' Then the King, marvelling at his constancy, smiled faintly and kissed him. The two archbishops and five bishops [who sat betwixt the King and the altar, would then have made room for

St Hugh]; but he went straight past them to the side of the altar, where he stood with his eyes resolutely fixed on the ground, attending now to naught else but the divine service."

If the saintliest of bishops conversed thus at Mass in certain circumstances, we may imagine how kings and nobles behaved habitually. This *Magna Vita* gives us a vivid picture of John at Lincoln minster, on Easter Day, 1213. The king was then humbled by adversity. A day or two before, when Hugh was preaching to him of the pains of hell, John had led him to the other wall of the minster (where the Blessed were represented rising at the Last Day, with good kings resplendent in eternal crowns) and had said to Hugh: "Those are the men I aspire to imitate." Yet on Easter Day, approaching the altar to offer at Mass, he took the twelve gold pieces from his chamberlain and began tossing them about in play instead of offering them. The bishop asked him what he was doing. "I was thinking", he replied, "that, a few days ago, I would never have offered these; but take them now!" The bishop withdrew his arm on hearing this, and would neither touch the gold nor allow John to kiss his hand: "Cast them into the basin here", he said, "and depart." Then he addressed himself to his sermon, and dwelt long upon the punishment of evil princes, with the reward of the good. John, liking neither the theme nor the delay, sent thrice to the bishop to suggest that he might wind up, since the king was fasting and wanted his dinner. But the bishop continued preaching to the people, till all acclaimed him and some wept tears of devotion; then he summoned them to the altar for the Eucharist. John, "caring neither for the food of God's word nor for that of the Holy Sacrament, but hastening to saturate his flesh with the flesh of beasts, hurried from the Cathedral".

This was all very well in John, who would not communicate even on his Coronation Day, and was said never to have taken the Eucharist since he had come to years of discretion. But of Henry II, who was quite an average God-fearing man as medieval kings went, Giraldus tells us that, "either forgetting his own sacramental unction as King, or putting it out of his mind, he would scarce lend to God's worship the time of the Mass; and even during that time (perchance by reason of his royal cares and the heavy business of the State) he was more busy with his council and talk, than with devotion to the Sacrament". "When he went into his chapel", says another contemporary, "he would spend the time in whispering and scribbling pictures."[1] Numerous illustrations of these last words may still be seen in many of our English and Continental churches. Wherever the stone is soft, and not smothered in whitewash and paint, nor, again, too conscientiously scraped by the restorer, we may often find names and sketches and tags, moral, religious or satirical, scratched on the pillars and walls. At Sion in the Valais, on the pulpitum of the old cathedral church, there is an unusually rich collection of these graffiti, several of which represent just such knights and squires and castles and combats as Henry might have drawn. A still more significant story is told in the Chronicle of Battle Abbey. The Abbot of Westminster, a few days after Henry II's coronation, was so anxious to get confirmation of a charter of privileges for his abbey, that he came to the king during Mass and persuaded him to read and approve it; the king then sent for the chancellor and got it sealed: then, up came the Bishop of Chichester and protested against it; all this certainly went on during Mass, and apparently almost at the foot of the altar.

We have said that Henry II's was a specially literary court. He and his wife both patronized not only scholars, but poets. It was here that the troubadours of the south and the trouvères of the north met together; and literary historians date roughly from this marriage the beginning of written French vernacular poetry. Yet it was an unrestful court for the literary man, and we find those who frequented it complaining in terms which prove that the primitive conditions of twelfth-century life were sometimes very painful, not only to our own modern imagination, but also to the actual feelings of sensitive and cultured contemporaries. Giraldus Cambrensis, Walter Map and Peter of Blois, three of the greatest scholars then living in Europe, were all attached to Henry's court, and knew it only too well. Their verdict, from the point of view of comfort and personal respect, is unanimously unfavourable. Map institutes a formal comparison between the king's court and hell. "It is true", he points out, "that from the former we escape by death, though not from the latter. Otherwise (he concludes) "there is about as much difference between the two as between a horse-shoe and a mare's shoe." The discomforts were doubtless aggravated by Henry II's physical strength and restless energy; but to a far greater extent they were inherent in the circumstances of the time. We have already seen how kings and nobles were obliged to flit from manor to manor to consume their supplies; and then to pass on elsewhere, where they could be fed. Thus that *Northumberland Household Book*, which tells us incidentally so much about upper-class manners at the end of the Middle Ages, shows us how the chaplains were treated in a great baronial household. The baronial order of removal, in that record, specifies minutely how many horses or vehicles there should be, and calculates "for six priests three beds, at two to a bed...and to have no more carriages [i.e. baggage] allowed them"; the narrowest possible allowance is made for these six men's luggage. Unquestionably, therefore, whether at court or at castle, the literary man must be prepared to rough it. It was the natural policy of the officials and upper servants to send the king out hunting all day, and meanwhile to work their own will at home. Our most eloquent witness here is Peter of Blois, one of those archdeacons whose weaknesses from the strictly religious and moral point of view are so plainly indicated by his contemporary John of Salisbury, Bishop of Chartres. Peter's whole letter is far too long for reproduction here; I have printed elsewhere all the relevant portions of it; but a few brief extracts may serve as samples of the whole.[2] The court's constant peregrinations (says Peter) condemn the scholar, with his love of sedentary life, to a continual purgatory. He finds himself served with the rough-and-ready meals of the traveller; "bread hastily made, without leaven, from the dregs of the ale-tub; leaden bread, bread of tares, bread unbaken. The wine is turned sour or mouldy; thick, greasy, stale, flat and smacking of pitch [from the cask]. I have sometimes seen even great lords served with wine so muddy that a man must needs close his eyes, and clench his teeth, wry-mouthed and shuddering, and filtering the stuff rather than drinking. The ale which men drink in that place is horrid to the taste and abominable to the sight. There, also, such is the concourse of people that sick and whole beasts are sold at random, with fishes even four days old; yet shall not all this corruption and stench abate one penny of the price; for the servants reck not whether an unhappy guest fall sick and die, so that their lords' tables be served with a multitude of dishes; thus we who sit at meat must needs fill our bellies with carrion, and become graves (as it were) for sundry corpses." Moreover, just when the unfortunate retinue hopes to dine or sleep, then the king suddenly takes it into his head to break up camp and start for a fresh stage. "Then may ye see men rush forth like madmen, sumpter-mules jostling sumpter-mules and chariots clashing against chariots in frantic confusion, a very Pandemonium made visible." "The abyss seems to have been opened, and hell to vomit forth his legions." "We therefore, wandering for three or four miles through unknown forests, and oftentimes in the black darkness, esteemed ourselves fortunate if perchance we fell upon some vile and sordid hovel. Oftentimes the courtiers would fight bitterly and obstinately for mere huts, and contend with drawn sword for a lair which had been unworthy of contention among swine." When we read the further complaint that the chaplain or the man of letters must endure all this in company with the court jesters, sycophants, pampered menials who accept the proffered guerdon with scornful ingratitude, washer-women, and worse, we then realize that even the Maître de Philosophie felt himself less out of place in Monsieur Jourdain's household, than Peter and Map and Giraldus in that of Henry II.

XX. CHIVALRY

HERE we come to an institution more closely bound up with most men's ideas of the Middle Ages, perhaps, than any other. And, like most things distinctively medieval, here is one which has provoked the most opposite judgments. For Walter Scott, it came next in value to Christianity itself. To Arnold of Rugby it was the spirit of Antichrist; to J. R. Green "a picturesque mimicry of high sentiment"; and even the conservative Bishop Stubbs writes: "What is the meaning of Chivalry? Is it not the gloss put by fine manners on vice and selfishness and contempt for the rights of man?" All this, and much more, may be read in Professor F. J. C. Hearnshaw's essay on *Chivalry and its Place in History,* the thirty-three pages of which provide a useful collection of accurate facts, tempered with sympathetic and judicious reflections.[1] His last two pages are especially valuable; and few who have read the whole essay will dissent from its concluding reflection, that, taking it all in all, chivalry marked a distinct social advance. "Above all, it inculcated an ideal of social service; service without remuneration; service, however humble its nature, free from degradation or disparagement; service of the weak by the strong; service of the poor by the wealthy; service of the lowly by the high." Again, his earlier verdict deserves careful consideration: "In England, particularly, it set that tone which has been perpetuated in the great Public School tradition."

The Knight.

The fact is, that no other institution displays more clearly that contrast between theory and practice which was so characteristic of medieval society. The contrast is always with us, of course, but never so crudely as then. In the cathedral, the saint stood side by side with the demon or grinning buffoon; God's Body hung over the altar, but the king might be drawing and scribbling on the walls, or talking, or doing business; indeed, the Burgomaster of Strassburg's pew was one of his regular working offices at Mass time. In chivalry we have that same contrast of splendour and squalor; dresses of brocade and cloth of gold, of which the sleeves might dip into a sauce on the table, or the train drag in the filth of the streets or of the floor; and beneath the table dogs fighting for the bones and leaving whatever they had not consumed. Partly due to this, and partly a symptom of it, was the disproportionate stress (from the purely modern point of view) laid upon impulsive virtues, and the preference given to intuition over logic. In chivalry the stress lay always on the generosity of the moment rather than on plodding business-like justice; and, if the world in general gave special admiration to the impulsive virtues, still more did the minstrel. It was his life's business to give fame to the men who could give him gold. Henry II's eldest son— Henry III as he was sometimes called, Il Re Giovane of Dante's great poem—was held up after his early death as a pattern to all chivalry. Giraldus Cambrensis emphasizes that in his book on the *Instruction of Princes*.[2] "He had made it a fixed rule of conduct that he would never deny to any man any gift worthy of him, thinking it unworthy of his dignity that any man should depart from him either sad or lacking his heart's desire. In short, he counted every day as wasted whereon he had not drawn many men to himself by his manifold largesses, buying both their hearts and their bodies by his profuse liberality.... [When, as a rebel against his father, he fell into misfortune] it seemed miraculous that almost all men clung to this man who had utterly lost his lands and his treasure." Richard, again, with his energy and fiery spirit and unbounded generosity in largesse, "was second to his eldest brother only in age, not in virtue". Salimbene tells us how on one occasion, when all were resting by the side of a spring after a hard hunt, and it turned out that the servants had brought only one flask of wine for the whole party, the Young King refused to take it for himself, and poured all into the spring that it might be shared by all. The *Novellino*, which may still be bought for a few pence in Italy, and which gives such a vivid picture of court life under Frederick II, has also much to say in honour of this Henry's impulsive generosity. Take, again, the romance of *Fulk Fitzwarine*. Here we have a man who, after a long and adventurous life, had many sins to repent of; but he balanced his account by founding a great abbey; and "he was very hospitable and liberal, and he caused the highway to be turned [aside so that it ran] through the hall of his manor of Alleston, to the intent that no stranger might pass that way without meat or lodging or other reward or goods from him". The prisoner-king of Edward III, Jean le Bon, earned that complimentary title not from any wisdom as a ruler, for there he was sadly to seek, but from those chivalrous qualities which, blundering him into defeat as general at Poitiers, still sustained him in his hand-to-hand fight to the end; and which, when he was a prisoner in London, made him pay generously to the poor milkmaid whose pails the king's riotous greyhounds had spilled. John of Gaunt was typical of the great nobles here: "his almoner distributed twelve pence daily; John of Gaunt was accustomed to distribute twelve shillings and sixpence ever Friday, and ten shillings every Saturday, amongst needy persons. He helped the poor also in other ways from time to time; in 1372, he sent the poor lazars of Leicester three cartloads of wood for fuel in winter, and the same year he gave the prisoners at Newgate a tun of Gascony wine."[3]

The same stress upon impulse is indicated by those unrestrained expressions of feeling which are even more significant, perhaps, than hastiness of action. The modern world may be excessive in its conventions for the repression of emotion; but to us the medieval man must seem to exceed in the other direction. Weeping and crying aloud were evidently rather encouraged. It is not only that we find this constantly in romance, as when Launcelot "wept as it were a child that had been beaten". It comes out frequently in the chronicles also. Joinville describes the tears and lamentations of fighting men confronted with what seems certain defeat and death; and again, when the barbers were called in to cut away those scorbutic growths from the soldiers' gums, he shows us the whole camp echoing as with the cries of women in travail. So again Froissart, when Sir John Chandos lay dying at the bridge of Lussac: "They wept piteously that were about him.... They wrung their hands and tore their hairs and made pitiful complaint, and specially such as were of his own house."[4]

As a rule, the young English noble had little literary training, or even none at all. Mr Galbraith appositely quotes Walter Map's words to Henry II's great justiciar, Ranulf Glanville: "The high-born of our country disdain letters, or delay to apply their children to them." They left that to the lower classes; to those whose ambitions might be served through book-learning. It was only in Italy, the least feudalized of all countries, that the nobles kept up some of the literate traditions of their Roman predecessors. On this side of the Alps "there was clearly no normal provision for the education of boys and girls of the noble class in the feudal age; and the 'palace schools' [of Charlemagne] are a myth". The young aspirant to knighthood, the squire, learnt his future job, like the apprentice to any other trade, mainly by rule of thumb. He is drawn by Chaucer not only in his personal attractions but in the helpfulness of his social service: "Curteis he was, lowely and servysable, And carf biforn his fader at the table." So also in the romance of *Blonde of Oxford*, where the hero, Jehan, is Blonde's special squire.[5] "He waited not on his lady alone, but up and down throughout the hall; knight and lady, squire and

The Squire.

page, groom and messenger, all he served according to their desire, and thus from all he earned good will. He knew well to seize the moment for serving and honouring each guest; so that Blonde, the fair and shapely, found her needs none the worse supplied. After the dinner they washed their hands, and went to play, each as he would, up in the forest or down by the river or in some other sort of pastime. Jehan went with whom he would; and, on his return, oftentimes would he go to play in the countess's bower.... Well he knew all chamber-games—chess and tables and dice—wherewith he diverted the lady Blonde; often said he *check!* and *mate!* to her."

Knighthood itself we must trace briefly from its first origins. It was a prehistoric institution, much modified by the growth of medieval society, and especially by its connection with the Church, from which in its most flourishing times it derived a definite religious sanction. On the other hand, it was also influenced to a very real extent by the Muslim civilization of Spain. Tacitus shows the germ of it in his description of the Germans. "They transact no business, whether public or private, except in arms; but it is not their custom that any man should receive his arms [arma sumere] until the State has proved him and found him worthy. Then, in full council, the youth is equipped with shield and spear by one of their chiefs, or by his own father or kinsman. This is to them like our assumption of the toga virilis; this is the first honour of early manhood. Until now, the youth was part of his home; henceforward, he is part of the State." This national custom developed under growing civilization, and especially under the wing of the Church. As early as the ninth century we have scattered allusions to the formal arming of a young prince or noble. These multiplied as time went on. When we come to the twelfth century, we are at what many writers reckon to be the high-water mark of chivalry; this, however, is very likely an optical illusion, because it is certainly the time of the first great epics and romances. By this time we find knighthood established as a military gild; voluntary, but very much moulded by outward forces. It rested on the principle of co-optation; however nobly born a man might be (except, later, in the case of princes of blood) knighthood added something to his dignity. St Louis, again, steadily refused, at the risk of his life, to bestow knighthood on the Muslim chiefs who had captured him. Being co-optative, therefore it was a freemasonry. All knights in theory were brothers everywhere. Froissart indeed complains that the Germans and Spaniards were often too rude to realize this; but it was clearly recognized between the English and French. The hundreds of French prisoners after Crécy and Poitiers were guests to the English nobles of Chaucer's day, sharing in their feasts and their sports: and the chronicler Walsingham gives us an admirable instance from the campaign of 1389, in which John of Gaunt and the King of Portugal fought the Spaniards and French. Famine and dysentery broke out in the Anglo-Portuguese camp, and the surviving English knights got a safe-conduct to go and convalesce among the French. The King of Portugal was scandalized: "They are deserting!" But John denied this; and in fact, after a brief period of convalescence, they came back to exchange blows with the French. "For", adds the chronicler, "both nations, French and English, though they be bitter foes in their own countries, yet abroad they often help each other like brethren, and keep inviolable faith one with the other." Thus chivalry was partly a check on feudalism, although it owed so much to that institution. In the first place, as we have seen, though the feudal fiefs soon became hereditary, knighthood was never hereditary except for blood-princes. Again, a fief was not necessary for knighthood. There were *knights bachelor*, who were not yet *bannerets*, but a sort of apprentice-knight. These, then, are sometimes treated in the romances as the stuff for the forlorn hope; if a deadly breach has to be stormed, then "The bachelors to the front!" Moreover, in its earlier stages even serfs were sometimes admitted; but this was forbidden by the later codes. Yet this freemasonry, like that of the gild, had its exclusive side. Froissart shows us plainly enough how, after the bloody capture of a town or castle, the gentles were spared, but the common soldiers were massacred without protest from their more exalted companions in arms. Sir E. K. Chambers pointed out in his paper on Malory how "in *Morte d'Arthur* itself, the distinction between noble and churl is fundamental. If there are sparks of nobility in a cowherd's son, like Tor, or a kitchen knave, like Gareth, you may be sure he will turn out to be a king's son in disguise."[6] And Miss A. Abram writes, from her studies in legal documents as well as in romance: "Class distinctions were far more real and important in the Middle Ages than they are to-day, and the distance between the upper and lower classes was much greater."[7] We may say, therefore, that chivalry was the blossom of a caste system, and that to some extent it rested, like the blossom of Periclean civilization, upon slave labour. Ruskin, with all his love for the Middle Ages, noted the weakness of chivalry in its contempt for the manual worker. He points out the gulf between *Aucassin and Nicolette*, with its Caliban-peasant, and that great literature of antiquity where noble and peasant were nearer to each other: Homer's Laertes working in his own vines with stout gloves to protect him from the thorns; or Virgil's pastoral heroes and his elegy for the dead ox. There was something of the parvenu, something of the Philistine, in the medieval descendants of these barbarian conquerors, except when religion brought them into the cloister at those times and places where the monk actually followed St Benedict's prescription of manual labour and study. Even their literary interests were small, apart from those who, like Lanfranc and Abailard and St Thomas Aquinas, gave up as boys the paternal inheritance and went out into the world as learners and teachers. It was only at the end of the twelfth century in France, and two centuries later in England, that great nobles like the Lord of Berkeley employed chaplains to translate for them from the Latin; and, even at the Renaissance, our authors found few patrons comparable to those of Italy or France.

In one respect, however, more important than is often recognized, chivalry did promote literature. Tacitus had noticed among the Germans that elaborate and effective speech was much esteemed by those fighting men, as it has been among the Arabs of the desert from time immemorial. It was the same in our own baronial courts. In *Sir Gawayne and the Green Knight*, when the hero came to the Enchanted Castle, and the lord, having first given him his fill of meat and drink, asked his name and discovered that the guest was of Arthur's Round Table, then:

> Loud laughed he thereat,
> And uch segge ful softly sayde to his fere,   [person, companion
> "Now schal we semlich se sleghtes of thewes [curious arguments
> And the teccheles termes of talking noble!"[8]   [flawless

In those days when literature was so preponderantly oral, much of it was fashioned at the tables of the great, as a sculptor fashions his work first in clay. It has been argued that, while Colonel Newcome is the natural nineteenth-century counterpart of Chaucer's knight, he is in one way markedly inferior: "Colonel Newcome would have been ill at ease in the company of a housemaid." Such truth as there is in that contention tends, under analysis, in the direction indicated above. It is often the absence of essential and universally recognized differences which makes free social intercourse more difficult. King Edward VII was godfather to one of his gamekeeper's sons; both parties here knew that there was a gulf over which the gamekeeper had not the slightest temptation to trespass.

On its moral side, knighthood was based on two eternal principles. The first was that of *noblesse oblige*—privileges implying responsibilities—and the second, that indefinable something connoted by the word "gentleman" in its best sense; a person not only "gentle" as we say that a nurse is gentle with a patient, but also in the more literal sense of the word, a person of *gens*, of race; a pedigree-person, a thoroughbred, so long as his actions do justice to his breeding. The author of *Piers Plowman* speaks of the knight first on his political side:

> Then came there a King, Knighthood him led;
> Might of the Commons made him to reign.

Then, later on, when the knight promises to help this ploughman to set the world right:

> By St Peter, quoth Piers, for thou profferest thee so low,
> I shall swinken and sweaten, and sowen for us both
> And eke labour for thy love all my lifetime,
> In covenant that thou keep Holychurch and myself
> From wastours and from wicked men that would us destroy.
> And go thou hunt hardily to hares and to foxes
> To boars and to roebucks that break men's hedges:
> And fetch thee home falcons, the wildfowl to kill
> For they comen into my croft and croppen my wheat.

Chaucer's definition is too well known to repeat. We need only note that his model knight was "worthy", that is dignified, as became an inheritor of a great name and wealth, who was conscious of the duty to use these profitably. On the other hand, he was meek and plainly dressed. Without forgetting his own rights, he had no wish to override those of others. We have here, therefore, a sort of social contract. The division of classes is frankly accepted —even a hereditary division of classes—but the higher class must live up to its higher fortunes. Knighthood is no mere soft option. So again it is in the philosopher John of Salisbury, from whom the words in *Piers Plowman* are very likely a dimly remembered echo. John writes: "What is the function of orderly knighthood? To protect the Church, to fight against treachery, to reverence the priesthood, to fend off injustice from the poor, to make peace in your own province, to shed your blood for your brethren, and, if needs must, to lay down your life." So, again, does Malory define the ideal to which "were all the knights sworn of the Table Round, both old and young". They were solemnly bound "never to do outrageousity, nor murder, and always to flee treason. Also, by no mean to be cruel, but to give mercy unto him that asketh mercy...; and always to do ladies, damsels, and gentlewomen succour upon pain of death. Also, that no man take no battles in a wrongful quarrel for no law, ne for no world's goods." Yet, as Sir E. K. Chambers points out, Malory was here contrasting the Arthurian theory with the too-frequent practice of his own day:[9] and similarly, from a distinguished contemporary of John of Salisbury, we have practice contrasted with that philosopher's ideal. We must discount the words as those of a rhetorician, but we cannot altogether ignore them. Peter of Blois, Archdeacon of Bath, writes to a friend: "I cannot bear the vaunting and vainglory of the knights your nephews.... The Order of Knighthood, in these days of ours, is mere disorder. For he whose mouth is defiled with the foulest words, whose oaths are most detestable, who least fears God, who vilifies God's ministers, who feareth not the Church—that man nowadays is reputed bravest and most renowned of the knightly band....Even nowadays, aspirants receive their swords from the altar in order that they may profess themselves sons of the Church, acknowledging themselves to have received their weapons for the honour of the priesthood, the defence of the poor, the avenging of wrongs and the freedom of their country. Yet in practice they do the contrary....If these knights of ours are sometimes constrained to take the field, then their sumpter-beasts are laden not with steel but with wine, not with spears but with cheeses, not with swords but with wine-skins, not with javelins but with spits. You would think they were on their way to feast, and not to fight."[10]

There was never any official written code of chivalry, but several unauthorized codes have come down to us. We must lay stress on the influence of the Church in moulding it; this may best be traced by showing the development of the ritual. There were three manners of conferring knighthood. In the first and commonest there was little or no religious ceremony, the king or great noble dubbing the worthy recipient on the field of battle or in his own hall. The knighting of an eldest son always entailed an expensive feast: this, therefore, was one of the occasions on which a king might tax his subjects. In the second method, although the consecrator was a layman and his language was the vernacular, yet there was a good deal of definitely religious ritual. The candidate kept vigil all through the preceding night in face of the altar on which his arms were laid. This, however, was not universal: there is no trace of it in Germany. Next morning he took formally a purifying bath; the Order of the Bath still bears testimony to this part of the ritual. Then he heard Mass, after which his spurs were put on; he was dubbed with the sword and exhorted in a formal sermon. A third and much rarer ceremony was purely clerical, performed by a bishop according to a service sometimes found in the liturgy, *Benedictio Novi Militis.*

So far the Church; but modern research seems to point more and more strongly towards emphasizing the influence of Mohammedan civilization, as imported from the south of Spain. We find Alvares of Cordova [950] complaining to his fellow-Christians that nowadays everything Mohammedan is fashionable among the upper classes. Again, Provençal poetry was confessedly influenced by the earlier romantic poetry of the Arabs. Chivalry, therefore (so runs the theory), spread first from Spain into Provence, and then northwards, eastwards and westwards through France. Certainly, there are considerable coincidences. This Arab civilization did place women on a high pedestal; that is, at least, the warrior's own woman. A great boot manufacturer once told me that when, in his early struggling days, he toured all Europe again and again to sell his own boots, the two districts where he could scarcely produce anything fine or expensive enough for men to buy for their women were Turkey and Asia Minor. Moreover, in Southern Spain military societies apparently crystallized into definitely religious form earlier than elsewhere; and, again, the Mohammedans unquestionably preceded the Christian countries of their day in refinement of social manners. The Arab chronicler Ousâma, in the twelfth century, expresses plainly his disgust at seeing the Christian knights amusing themselves by setting old women to run after a greased pig, and at other social manners which to him were equally barbarous.

Yet no doubt the code of chivalry did something in the long run to raise women's status. It brought greater politeness into a society in which, when a woman was left with a fief, she was naturally given to someone who could defend it and her. It was probably connected in some degree, both by action and by reaction, with that worship of the Virgin Mary which received such definite impetus from the Normans of the eleventh century. But the progress was slow; and, as we shall see in Chapter XLV, it did not prevent wife-beating. Even England, though it had no Salic law, could not quite do with Matilda as queen; and Fortescue in the fifteenth century rules out feminine sovereignty. It was not until Tudor times that this was possible; but unquestionably a good deal was done by the knight's theoretical duty to serve God and the ladies.

By Chaucer's time chivalry was in decay. Froissart, whose chronicles tell us perhaps more of its brilliance than any other source, cannot disguise its decadence from any searching eye. Yet we may here speak of decay not in the sense that Chaucer's knight and his fellows were in any way inferior to those of the twelfth century; that "golden age of knighthood" owes doubtless much to the effect of distance and mirage. Decay was only comparative, not positive; the real operating cause was the gradual rise and improvement of the middle and lower classes. The knight of Chaucer's day had as much courtesy and honour as in the days of Henry II and his son the Young King; perhaps even more. But at this later time he competed less advantageously with those outside his own class. Land cannot be multiplied: and nearly all the medieval clearing efforts or draining of swamps that was done with us had been completed before 1350. Therefore, since estates could not grow in size, and they were liable to constant subdivision for the sake of younger sons, the knight was at an increasing disadvantage as compared with the rapidly growing towns and the wealth of their merchants. This movement, inevitable in any case, was immensely hastened by the Crusades; nearly all monastic chartularies show us nobles selling their lands cheap to the monasteries in order to defray the expense of these expeditions. Thus they got into the hands of the usurers, a trade by no means confined to the Jews but very commonly exercised, as we shall see later on, by merchants, and sometimes even by ecclesiastics. Therefore, not only was the knight obliged to be something of a trader, but the trader might become a knight, as for instance Walworth and others of Chaucer's friends. His contemporary, in *Piers Plowman*, puts this into one bitter epigrammatic line:

Soap-sellers and their sons for silver are made knights.

Doubtless the Black Death had some effect here, as it had upon all institutions. Chivalry was already losing something of its vitality, but by far the strongest operative cause was the Hundred Years' War, to which we shall come in Chapter XXXIX.

Without minimizing the beneficent working of the chivalric ideal, we must recognize that barons and knights were often, under the pressure of their circumstances, very hard business men. On every side, we may find scattered evidence for that state of things which is implicit in that manual for the great Percy castles and manors, *The Northumberland Household Book*. In England, especially, the increasing security of the kingdom tended to obliterate the distinction between the rich landowner and the rich trader. Castles, which in earlier times were shockingly uncomfortable, military considerations being paramount, were already far more habitable under Henry III; it is remarkable how often that king granted licences to great men to "crenellate" their houses; in other words, to supply some great comfortable mansion with such moderate fortifications as would secure it under any other conditions than that of a formal siege by an army. Moreover, there was often the strictest business in their social relations. When a father died leaving children under age, these became wards of the overlord. Such tutelage was not, as nowadays, an honorary and burdensome duty, but a matter of considerable profit, since the guardian handled most of the endowment until the child's coming of age, and was able to dispose of him or her in marriage almost as he chose. Thus we find great nobles, lay or ecclesiastical, dealing in wardships as we deal nowadays in commercial investments. Again, when the eldest son married, he very commonly continued life with his wife in his father's castle. The heir of that Earl of Northumberland for whom the Household Book was compiled did in fact live many years in utter dependence, and on a miserable pittance, under his father. Marriage itself, again, was commonly a matter of business bargaining, as we see in the *Paston Letters*. Lastly, the laws for Distraint of Knighthood clearly emphasize the business side of that institution. The law of Edward I prevented rich men from shirking the duties attendant upon rank, by compelling everybody to be knighted who had a landed income of £20 a year or over: that is, no more than twice the income of an average incumbent of a parish in the diocese of Norwich. The account-rolls of the Lords of Berkeley, who were among the greatest of baronial families, show the lady superintending the dairy herself, and the lords selling the fruit from their orchards or the wine from their vineyards, just as nowadays we may approach a side-window at a count's palazzo in Florence and buy a bottle or two of the noble's own vintage. Miss Abram points out how in 1345 "the gardeners of the earls, barons, bishops and citizens of [London]...had been in the habit of standing at the side of the gate of St Paul's Churchyard to sell the garden produce of their master, 'pulse, cherries, vegetables and other wares to their trade pertaining', and they were allowed to continue the practice, but were ordered to stand in a different place."[11] In 1372, we find the Bishop of Ely selling vegetables from his garden in Holborn, where his beautiful palace-chapel still stands in Ely Place. And, as they followed mercantile methods, so also they often knew the merchant's burden of debt. The surviving fifteenth-century letters of the Plumptons, great landed gentry in Yorkshire, show them in perpetual difficulties. Mrs Green, in her *Town Life in the fifteenth Century*, tells how "during an unwonted visit to Westminster in 1449, the poor Lady of Berkeley wrote anxiously to her husband, one of the greatest landowners in England, 'At the reverence of God, send me money, or else I must lay my horse to pledge and come home on my feet'; and he raised £15 to meet her needs by pawning the Mass-book, chalices and chasubles of his chapel."[12] As the great men dealt in wardships and marriages, so also in prisoners' ransoms. Froissart is astoundingly cold-blooded on this subject: he estimates battles in terms of money with a frequency which must delight the Marxist historian.[13] At Aljubarrota, for instance, when a false alarm impelled the victorious English and Portuguese to kill their Franco-Spanish prisoners out of hand, he adds: "Lo, behold the great evil adventure that fell that Saturday! for they slew as many good prisoners as would well have been worth, one with another, four hundred thousand francs." There is no worse anachronism than to suppose that, because money in the Middle Ages was not plentiful enough to breed multi-millionaires, therefore the reign of the Almighty Dollar is a modern evil. In proportion to population, there are as many money-quarrels and money-murders among the thrifty French peasant-proprietors of to-day as in districts of Big Business.

LET us take a final survey of chivalry as portrayed in two of the greatest achievements of English literature, Chaucer's *Troilus and Criseyde* and Malory's *Morte d'Arthur*. It need not embarrass us that the one is in great part translated from Boccaccio, and the other from "the French Book" which Malory had to his hand. For each has made the stuff his own not only by deliberate choice here and rejection there, but by additions and changes which, in Chaucer's case at least, have greater literary and human value than anything in the original.

If Chaucer's *Troilus*, which a good many readers have ranked even above the *Canterbury Tales*, is so little read in comparison, this is partly because it is so long. That is a very common defect in medieval literature, especially among the non-Latin nations: higher civilization means greater concentration. If every reader of *Troilus* would frankly mark off the parts that seem obviously redundant, these would probably amount to 1000 lines at least, and the different readers would be roughly agreed. And, on analysing these redundant passages, they would be found to fall under three heads, all of which are characteristic of Chaucer's time, and of the aristocratic society in which he moved as royal page and squire and member of parliament.

First, the speeches are often too long. As we have seen, speech was studied among great folk as a fine art: a knight of Arthur's Round Table might be counted upon to display "the flawless terms of talking noble", and it was for the new Round Table founded by Edward III that he had built the great Round Tower at Windsor. Here was a matter in which not brevity but verbosity was a note of highest culture; it survived long in England, and the Venetian Envoy of Henry VII's time was much struck by our elaborate ceremoniousness in this respect. The fact that Chaucer makes game of this in his Squire's Tale does not save him from falling into it at unguarded moments.

Secondly, we should eliminate most of the discussion on Free-will and Predestination. But, here again, this problem, especially in its crudest form of fatalism, was popular among the upper classes. Chroniclers tell us of it; Caesarius of Heisterbach cites a

Markgraf who justified his moral lapses by pleading that, however he might behave, God knew already whether he would be damned or not. His physician, however, when urgently summoned in face of serious illness, cured him of this mental aberration by suggesting that, whatever he himself might prescribe or administer, God already knew the final result. In short, Predestination was still a comparatively new and living subject of discussion among the educated in Chaucer's day. We have abundant evidence that it was an exciting topic, not only among high-brows, but also in political and anti-clerical circles. It has lost its freshness now; but it was then quite as burning a question as the League of Nations. And, thirdly, Wertherism in love was a literary convention which had very real roots in the social conditions of that age. If we are to understand either Chaucer's society or Malory's, we must face what Sir E. K. Chambers calls "the queer spiritual tangle of the twelfth century *amour courtois*"; the spirit which inspired, or is said to have inspired, a solemn verdict of the Provençal Court of Love to the effect that real love is impossible between husband and wife. Professor Hearnshaw can write without injustice: "Marriage was, and always remained, to the troubadours, not the sacrament and consummation of love, but its most formidable obstacle and dangerous enemy. They deepened, indeed, the schism which feudalism had created between the two." Therefore we must compare and contrast medieval and modern love-making. Not, of course, that this contrast is absolute. Even sex-distinctions are not absolute; in a solemn public debate some years ago on the question of women's status in Cambridge, it was aptly pointed out that old women are not always of the female sex. We have plenty of medieval lovers among us to-day, and there were modern lovers long before Chaucer's birth; but, on the whole, there is a very real contrast in this matter between Chaucer's court environment and the ordinary modern public, even as it has been since the War. In Chaucer's society, woman-hunting was, it may be said, a normal sport. The Knight of La Tour-Landry speaks very emphatically here; St Bernardino of Siena more emphatically still. Chaucer himself, in his Doctor of Physic's Tale, lifts the veil for a moment; his contemporary, the Dominican Bromyard, tells enough to assure us that we are not misinterpreting Chaucer's hints. In such a society, where the men were commonly out for prey and all the women more or less on the defensive, and where the *mariage de convenance* was the rule, romantic love was nearly always illicit, difficult and dangerous. First, the woman's natural instinct of self-defence was here at its strongest. Next, the rival might very likely be murderous. Last, but not least, there was always a *tertium quid*, the "spier" of romance, or perhaps a multitude of "spiers", all agog with mean curiosity or jealousy or sheer love of mischief. The jealous husband, or the intrusive "spier", are almost as essential to the medieval love-drama as the hero and heroine themselves. It is difficult to exaggerate the want of privacy in the Middle Ages, or the influence of this overcrowding upon social intercourse, and therefore upon literature. Even in a great and roomy castle there was no more privacy than on a modern Atlantic liner; and, in those crag-castles that are so picturesque on French and German rivers, there can have been scarcely more solitude than on a tramp-steamer. Therefore it was almost a conventional necessity that the love-story of medieval romance should rest upon a basis of difficulty and pain, even where there was no nobler tragedy to account for this, as (for instance) in the story of Tristram. Chaucer begins the poem by announcing it as his own business to relate the "double pain" of Troilus. It was the first pain of Troilus to fall in love at all; Troilus's "Sorrows of Werther", which to us often seem tedious and artificial, were as much a court fashion as any cut of dress or hair was; so also was the secrecy of the lovers' final enjoyment. Chaucer took his society as he found it, spiced Boccaccio's story with a Pandarus who is practically a new creation in literature (though the poet probably took him to a great extent from life), and displayed in those first three books of the poem a psychology and a power of artistic development which have often been compared with Richardson's.

This brings us to a far more complicated question, and one which more deeply affects the question of Chaucer's art. It seems to me that Professor Jack is very right in indicating how Chaucer grows weary, whether consciously or unconsciously, of the more sordid elements in his story. He takes the plot as he finds it; he rules out mere common-sense solutions of the Antenor difficulty, but, it would seem, without genuine conviction. Again, the Diomede incident, which he might easily have treated in such prominent or cynical detail, and which his audience would probably have enjoyed in such detail, he dismisses with artistic brevity.

And finally the epilogue, one of his greatest achievements in the matter of style, amounts almost to a retractation of all that he has taken such pains to narrate in the five preceding books: it is like his epilogue to the *Canterbury Tales*. Is it too fanciful to suggest that we have here something of an analogy to Thackeray's *Shabby-Genteel Story*? Chaucer had drunk deeply of Boccaccio; but he was not an "Italianate Englishman" in Ascham's sense. He remained, to the end of his life, too great a poet not to be something of a moralist; and he must have known more and more, as he worked through *Troilus*, that this subject was not compatible with the highest poetry of all. Here and there, indeed, Chaucer does rise as high as his subject permits, for instance, in Troilus's waitings at the town gate, and in his faith that remains steadfast against all but the last ocular demonstration of Criseyde's fickleness, and in Criseyde's self-contempt at her own weakness. Moreover, in that epilogue, he turns upon himself and his public with no merely conventional criticism; he seriously asks himself and them: "Is this game worth the candle?" Surely the Chaucer of that moment meant this as sincerely as the Chaucer of other moments meant to ask that other very different question: What do we know, after all is said and done, about life beyond the grave?

If this, or anything like it, be the true interpretation, then we may read *Troilus* with even greater appreciation of its extraordinary beauty and interest. We may skip whole stanzas, and blocks of stanzas, as the mere conventional Wertherism of that day. We may skip a great deal more, as mere exercises in polite conversation; or, again, as attempts to talk the current philosophical talk of the day in language not too intellectual for the man in the street. We may skip here, in fact, just as all readers probably do skip when they read, for the second time at least, another love-story equally remarkable and still more popular, but which is debarred, like *Troilus*, by the nature of its plot from the very highest success of all; I mean *Manon Lescaut*. Both are very great books; both are growing rather than dwindling as time goes on; yet neither is in the very first rank of world-stories, and for much the same reasons. Both are either too immoral or not immoral enough. Their plot would give free scope to a frankly barbarian writer—free scope of a certain kind—but a man with some remnant of real decency left in him, like Chaucer or Abbé Prévost, was pulled up every now and then by breaking his shins over the stones of offence with which the whole ground is littered. Manon Lescaut knows her own weakness—knows and deplores it, as Criseyde knows hers—but she cannot mend it. She ruins a man's life; but the story forces us to ask ourselves what was the real worth of the life that she ruined. Both Manon and Criseyde fall very low; the Chevalier Desgrieux and Troilus are dragged down in the fall; but in neither case can we get the highest effects of tragedy, for in neither case was the fall from any such outstanding height; we cannot pity Troilus as we pity Hamlet, nor Criseyde as we pity Desdemona. The tragedy is that of Murger's stories in his *Vie de Bohême*—the tragedy that we sometimes think we demand so little from life—imagine that we ask no more than this, that love should endure—yet bitter experience disabuses us. But, on reflection, we must answer Chaucer and Prévost here as we answer Murger. Few indeed are those who do truly ask so little as this from life. Not all men, far from it, even ask for this first of all, that love should endure; and are we sure that those few who do ask for love first, or who ask for love only, do not in fact get abiding love? The tragedy of bitter disappointment is very real; but must we not always ask ourselves, consciously or unconsciously: How far did the victims deserve success?

An able modern critic has argued that *Troilus* is difficult to understand because of the poet's religious attitude: "He was an English Catholic long before the Reformation—superficially more remote from us in religious sensibility than either Dante or Shakespeare.... Chaucer does not pass a moral judgment either upon Criseyde or upon Troilus or upon Pandarus; only a high and dispassionate view of the place of these persons in a fixed and firm moral order."[1] The whole article seems inspired by the belief, common enough, that it is not only very difficult for outsiders to grasp certain *nuances* of medieval Catholicism—a suggestion which is true of all dissenters from all *-isms*—but almost impossible to comprehend its *essence*. Yet, to begin with, we are faced with the fact that Chaucer does condemn, and that very plainly. For Troilus, from that "eighth sphere"

> as he lookëd down,
> He damned all our work that followeth so
> The blindë lust, the which that may not last.

What is this but an explicit "moral judgment", and one independent of sectarian difficulties among Christians? There was no orthodox writer of Chaucer's time who would not have condemned that "blindë lust", which fills so much of the poem, as definitely as any modern Evangelical or Nonconformist does. Perhaps the greatest Churchman of the whole fifteenth century was Jean Gerson, Chancellor of Paris, who found it worth while to write a whole treatise in condemnation of the *Roman de la Rose*. If he had dealt in the same spirit with *Troilus*, might he not have condemned it as soundly as Roger Ascham condemned the *Morte d'Arthur*? This critic, if it be not rash to suggest this, has failed to realize how characteristic it was of medieval mentality to be, even more than the modern man, moral at one moment and immoral at another, without any great effort to paper over the cracks.

This is illustrated even more clearly by Malory, to whom we may now pass on. Here we have a book equally wonderful in its contrasts and in its harmony. It has all the violent antitheses which are so characteristic of medieval life, but, withal, the harmony of a single mind which has absorbed a mass of ancient legend and reproduced it not mechanically but organically, making it into flesh and blood of its own. Though medieval society was less simple than is often imagined, yet it was naturally far less complex than ours. The factors were simpler; men's fashions and manners were more elementary and more frankly displayed. We can even illustrate these factors, alike in their simplicity and in their contrasts, by putting the problem into the form of a colour-scheme, so long as we bear in mind that this is a mere illustration; no tangible argument, but only a parable. We may think then of that colour-scheme, dear to the medieval artist and especially to the simplest craftsmen, which illustrates two of the most striking lines in all medieval poetry. Walther von der Vogelweide writes:

> die werlt ist ûzen schoene, wîz grüen unde rôt
> und innân swarzer varwe, vinster sam der tôt.

> The world is fair to look on, white and green and red,
> But inly it is black of hue, and dismal as the dead.

We find the same picture again in Chaucer's Squire,

> Embrouded was he, as it were a meede
> Al ful of fresshë flourës whyte and reede;

a description which is equally to the point even though the actual cloak he describes may have been of any colour, powdered with those flowers; for that "mead" brings the green at once to our minds. The same, again, is implied no less distinctly, though not so briefly expressed, by Dante when he suddenly reveals to us the Earthly Paradise (*Purg.* XXIX). There he shows us the green boughs and the eternal verdure of the meadows, with flames of ruddy fire moving in the air and leaving rainbows behind them as they moved; and, finally, the whole place peopled with "a folk clad all in white, of a whiteness that was never seen among us". There, then, is the colour-scheme; green and red, the two most striking contrasts among strong colours that are common in ordinary nature, complemented by white, which stands out in equal contrast from both. We see it in young corn with poppies and marguerites and white campion, or in white houses and heavy trees massed against a crimson sunset. The other natural contrast, between orange and blue, is far less common in England; but we may see it, for instance, in the Black Forest wherever the foreground rises in ripe corn to the brow of the hill and then, without any softening middle-distance, we get the deep indigo of a pine-clad mountain twenty miles away. But to the ordinary country folk, under the blue sky, mother earth at her best and richest was clad in green and white and red. And that was the rustic painter's colour-scheme, still visible in much of its freshness on all the great Norfolk rood-screens such as Ranworth and Barton Turf. There then we have it on the art side; the simplest possible scheme of colour-contrast, getting its harmony not by the blending of the tints into one other, but by the balance and disposition of these three frankly contrasted factors. So also it was in medieval life. Men often held conflicting ideals; they did homage, as men must in every age, to things which in strict logic seem ultimately almost irreconcilable; but their conception of harmony between those opposites differed greatly from ours. We ourselves generally aim, as Aristotle taught, at the Golden Mean, striving by all sorts of concessions and compromises to temper one ideal with the other. They, on the other hand, strove far less to be all things at all times; to be, for instance, at every given moment just as warlike as we should be, and yet just as pacific and merciful as beseems a man dealing with his fellow-man. The medieval man aimed much less at this than at being frankly and unmixedly combative at one moment and counterbalancing this at a later moment with an equally unqualified generosity. We have seen how, when Geoffrey Malaterra described the Normans as "evenly balanced between greed and lavishness", he did not mean that they avoided both extremes, but that they oscillated with rough impartiality between one and the other. Medieval harmony, therefore, was reached not by the blending but by the balance of opposite factors. Here our own Black Prince is typical; at one moment he serves his captive enemy, the King of France, on bended knee; and then, another day, when he had recaptured the revolted city of Limoges, he was borne in his litter to watch an indiscriminate massacre that spared neither age nor sex. "There was not so hard a heart" (writes Froissart) "within the city of Limoges, an if he had any remembrance of God, but that wept piteously for the great mischief that they saw before their eyen; for more than three thousand men, women and children, were slain and beheaded that day. God have mercy on their souls, for I trow they were martyrs!"[2]

Thus, then, we may even venture to interpret this colour-scheme in terms of those elementary factors in human life which stand out most clearly in medieval society. Or, to put it more accurately, we can use this white-green-red picture as a sort of *memoria technica*, helping us to visualize the main elements of medieval romance. Blue we must not forget; blue the favourite colour of the missal-painter, blue of the all-pervading sky, just as the Church's teaching was almost universally accepted, in theory at least, and thus was taken in a measure for granted. But with that we are not here concerned; only with the colours of earth; green and white and red. Green, the colour of spring and summer; standing for the restfulness of earth, the fruitfulness of earth, the quiet content in earthly things. Red, the colour of passion and of conflict; red roses and red blood; the battles of this life, its victories and its defeats. White, in one sense the sum of all possible colours; so complete a blend of all that it has none of its own; the colourlessness of eternity, and of a peace beyond even the quiet green of the meadows, beyond even the blue of the Church and of all visible religion. As Shelley writes:

> Life, like a dome of many-coloured glass,
> Stains the white radiance of Eternity.

Or Henry Vaughan:

> I saw eternity the other night,
> Like a great ring of pure and endless light
> All calm, as it was bright;
> And round beneath it Time in hours, days, years
> Driven by the spheres,
> Like a vast shadow moved, in which the world
> And all her train were hurled.

This imagery comes out even plainer in more definitely theological literature. Take that sermon of Newman's which fascinated Matthew Arnold. "After the fever of life; after wearinesses and sicknesses; fightings and despondings; languor and fretfulness; struggling and failing; struggling and succeeding; after all the changes and chances of this troubled unhealthy state, at length comes death, at length the white Throne of God, at length the Beatific Vision."[3] Or, to go back farther and higher, Isaiah i. 18: "Though your sins be as scarlet, they shall be as white as snow"; or Revelation vii. 9–14: "And lo! a great multitude which no man could number...clothed with white robes, and palms in their hands.... These are they which came out of great tribulation, and have washed their robes, and made them white in the blood of the Lamb." Those are the main notes of medieval life; the delights of the world and the battles of the world in brilliant contrast; and, apart from both, the pure white of unworldliness, the charm of deep and simple religion, not only of the official Church, but also that still more primeval religion; the unselfish love of friend for friend, of man for woman and of woman for man, with the conviction that this love is, in some most real sense, eternal. All these in startling contrast; yet always, in virtue of the purity and simplicity with which each colour is laid on, and of the just balance between contrast and contrast, the three colours grouped into one harmonious whole:

> A meede—Al ful of fresshë flourës whyte and reede.

All these are admirably represented in Malory. Green, by the Queen's Maying, at the beginning of book 19: Red, by the fights on every page; White, by the Graal, from its very first pages, with Galahad nurtured in that Nunnery of Nuns, down to the very last, where the Sacred Quest is finally achieved. Nor is the sense of religion in that episode alone: it pervades the book, and comes out in the minutest touches. "Then heard they Mass and rode forth"; "There they came to a ruined chapel"; "Then to an hermitage", "Then to a great abbey of black [or white] monks", and so forth. Here is a whole paradise of romance; the idealized picture of an heroic past.

We must emphasize that last point; for the days of knight-errantry, in so far as they ever existed, lay far behind when Malory wrote. Whether the late twelfth century was or was not the golden age of chivalry, certainly it was that of knightly romance. Not only had the Hundred Years' War come between, with its emphasis on the practical business side of warfare and its breach of many older class conventions, but the whole world had changed greatly between 1150 and 1450. A real knight-errant would have been as hard to find in that fifteenth-century society, and would have been quite as much out of place, as Charles Gordon and T. E. Lawrence were in ours. We cannot imagine the first John Paston in the rôle of knight-errant, nor either of the two Sir Johns, his sons! Yet all the mere body of chivalry was still there in Malory's time; heraldry, and feast in hall, and song and dance in bower, and the great abbey for hospitality, and the ruined chapel and the hermit. Men were familiar with these things as part of their daily life; these were the colours, so to speak, fresh to any painter's hand who wished to revive the ancient ideal before men's eyes. And, if that ideal was in one sense dead already, yet in another and deeper sense it has never died, from that day to this. André Maurois, in his *Silences du Colonel Bramble*, shows us something of this, inarticulate but none the less real. But to Malory's contemporaries, it must be repeated, the Arthur story must already have had much of the same archaic charm which it has for us. Even where men could still see the outward things he described, the soul of those things needed imagination for its comprehension then as now. And the author's own life, as we now know, was very far from that of a hero of Arthurian legend.[4]

XXII. THE MONASTERY

ALL civilization proceeds by alternate emphasis on individualism and collectivism. In one age, men lay most stress on the unhampered development of the individual, in spite of the claims of his surroundings. In another, they most emphasize the fact that individuals must be disciplined to act in masses, or the world cannot advance. Man (they feel) shows his superiority to the brute in nothing more than in this power of forming groups, and then groups of groups, and still wider, still more complicated groups of groups of groups; so that, for such formations, self-control is even more necessary for the multitude than energy and self-assertion. It would be no gain to civilization that the exaggeration of "My country, right or wrong!" should give place to a counter-exaggeration: "My own personality, right or wrong!" Monasticism, Chivalry, and the Gild were perhaps the greatest collectivist movements of the Middle Ages. All of them are unduly depreciated by many people nowadays, while they are loaded with exaggerated praise by others; the difficulty is to reach a fair balance. We have to reconcile two widely different facts which seem equally indisputable in the light of historical documents. First, that monasticism grew up by what seemed an overmastering impulse, and became one of the chief social forces of the Middle Ages; at one time, even perhaps *the* chief. Secondly, that (apart from those boys who form the vast majority of converts under the Roman and the Greek Church) so few even of the chosen, even of the most religious men, adopt nowadays that life which, before the Reformation, was called *the* religious life *par excellence*. For it may safely be asserted that, at least from the twelfth century onwards, in nine cases out of ten, the word *Religion* is used by medieval writers in the technical sense of a monastic order, and the word "*conversion*" means entering Religion, i.e. joining some monastic order. Those facts will perhaps be best explained and reconciled if we deal with the development of monasticism under three heads. First, the spontaneous and natural genesis of the ideal. Then, this ideal materialized in a formal and world-wide institution. Finally, the decay of that formal institution, and its loss of all special legal privileges; although, even nowadays, the fire of the ideal still glows to some extent amidst the embers.

Monasticism, then, represents a natural (perhaps even necessary) stage in the development of the Christian Church. In every generation a few earnest men have suddenly rediscovered for themselves, with overpowering force, that Christ may have meant literally what he said in those words "many are called and few are chosen". Such men realize with intense force that the majority of the baptized, in their own generation, are Christians scarcely more than skin-deep; that they cannot in the strictest sense be said to be Christians at heart; that we cannot strictly call our fatherland a Christian country; nay, more, that no steamship or airship can bear us away to any land which is thoroughly Christian. Therefore those individuals who in their own hearts say with St Paul "to me, to live is Christ and to die is gain" must almost of necessity be in some sense strangers to their own kith and kin. This has been true of every generation in every country, for the last 1900 years. Figgis, a true historian and devoted monk, emphasized this fact that, in the deepest sense, the Western World never has been Christian. However our further deductions may differ, the fact itself must be fully faced in its actual historical perspective. It is not that Christianity has been tried, and failed, but that it has never been strictly tried. St Augustine, in whose father's lifetime Christianity had won its world-wide political victory under Constantine, recognized as clearly as we can that many are called and few are chosen. Indeed, we can go back much farther than that; the conviction was already overmastering in many minds two hundred years before Augustine.[1] As early as about A.D. 170 arose the Montanists, Puritans for whom the official Church was already too worldly, and who were joined by the great Church writer Tertullian. Indeed, the movement may be traced still farther back; and we find the germ of it even in the earliest days of Christianity, bringing with it a definite divergence of opinion as to how far the Christian should separate himself from the world. And, if the earnest Christian's attitude towards the world around him was not always quite simple, it grew more complicated in process of time, in proportion as the world changed, and, above all, as the Church herself changed. Men sometimes ask: "Was Christ a socialist?" At least He wished His more immediate disciples to be unencumbered with earthly possessions and family ties. Moreover, only thus could they have done their missionary work; and we must remember that they were in daily expectation of the second Advent. But, as years passed on, and generation succeeded generation, this exclusively missionary element naturally fell more and more into the background. Many men had their family, their business, their office; they were bound by ties of all sorts. Should they leave these, or could they not do better by using them for Christian purposes? Already in apostolic times, St Paul puts this problem in the form of marriage to an unbeliever: "For what knowest thou, O wife, whether thou shalt save thy husband, or how knowest thou, O man, whether thou shalt save thy wife?" Moreover, the problem naturally became more insistent as the end of the world seemed more and more remote. This, then, was the individual's problem; and that of the Church, the Christian society, was similar. Should the Church (or, as we may say at first, the Churches) remain as obscure, as detached as possible, or should it enter into civic life, imperial life, form an *imperium in imperio*, and so pursue its missionary work by ordinary business methods? The Quakers of our own day, faced with these alternatives, have definitely chosen the latter. So, for the Church, it is difficult to find an answer different from that which history gives; and yet that meant relegating some very plain gospel precepts to the limbo of counsels of perfection. Property, family ties, office in the city or in the State, all meant either a silent abandonment of, or a difficult and perpetual struggle of adaptation to, certain distinctive Christian tenets of the first generation. Hence the growing worldliness of the Church was acutely felt for at least a century before Constantine made it a State Institution.

The history of Tertullian and the Montanists shows us two most important developments. First, in morals; the Church is losing her disciplinary hold over the congregations; she no longer exacts more than the minimum penance for sin as a condition of communion in the Christian rites; she is glad to retain all she can, and afraid of frightening any away. On the other hand, she is drawing tighter the reins of dogmatic discipline in proportion as she loosens the moral reins. These Montanists, for instance, in reward for their inconvenient zeal and their peculiar tenets, found themselves cast out from the pale of the orthodox Church. From that time forth, if not before, we may say that Christian society is no longer bound together mainly by the bonds of fraternal love, but by the framework of an official hierarchy. And the hierarchy, in order to keep its power over the mass of the baptized, has to make constant concessions to ordinary social customs; in other words, to the worldly spirit. When, therefore, a century after this Montanist expulsion (or secession, for, like Wesleyanism, it was half-and-half), Constantine made Christianity into a privileged Church, then the incompatibility of the two ideals became more evident. Some aimed at apostolic simplicity; others aimed at a great organization on the lines of the imperial bureaucracy; few indeed were able to reconcile both ideals. Therefore we find now an increasing stream of Christians going out to live the hermit life in the wilds of Egypt and Syria. "They fled from the world, and therefore from the Church which had admitted the world into her bosom." This separation was not in a controversial spirit, but in self-defence. The impulse came partly from Alexandria, which was then the centre of Christian thought; partly, again, it was in imitation of pagan ascetics who had long lived in the Egyptian desert. Concerning the earliest Christian hermits, Paul and Anthony, there is much uncertainty in detail: they lived about A.D. 250. But certainly, by about A.D. 350, Egypt contained thousands of such. And their manner of life was necessarily unsacerdotal, without being anti-sacerdotal: unsacramental, though not anti-sacramental; that was also a distinguishing mark of nearly all the monastic reforms of later ages. For the monk's ideal of the religious life, in the earliest times, differed widely from that of the official Church. To him, the essence of Christianity lay in asceticism. Personal self-denial and constant prayer were, in his mind, prior to Christian brotherhood, public worship with its common liturgy, and the bishop's teaching. It is difficult (as Monsignor Duchesne points out) to see how St Anthony ever received the Holy Communion during his twenty years of seclusion in the desert.[2] St Thomas More speaks of monasteries in the distant past which had only four priests to five hundred monks. Here he probably spoke without book; but the ancient *Historia Lausiaca*, a trustworthy source, shows only eight priests to the five thousand monks of the Nitrian desert; and one alone of these performed all the ordinary celebrations of the Holy Communion.[3] These recluses needed no more than Elijah did; the desert for quiet, the oasis for food, and the sustaining belief in God's final government. Yet there was as a rule no antagonism, or, at any rate, no conscious antagonism, to the secular Church, the World-Church. The difference was simply one of emphasis and division of labour. The monks, for their part, were devoted to prayer, contemplation, and mortification of the body; but the World-Church recognized all these things as very holy, and was very glad that others should do them. It said in effect to the monks: "Mortify yourselves, and pray for us." On the other hand, this World-Church had its imposing traditions, its organization, and its worship. But, here again, the hermits were glad that the hierarchy should impress and even control the laity. Thus each party comforted the other against heresy and paganism; and the divergence of ideal was settled in a sense acceptable to both. There need now be no general reform of the whole Church; each took one part, and each exaggerated it. The monastic ideal became more and more ascetic, while the World-Church became more and more worldly; so that, by A.D. 350, the contrast was enormous and there were thousands of such hermits. Then, gradually, these developed an organization of their own; and consequently, in process of time, the ritual and sacramental system of the Church became as necessary to the monk as to the rest: indeed, for the last five centuries of the Middle Ages, the abbey churches were in the front rank for size and splendour. The monks thus received an organization quite as rigid as that of the hierarchy; and their collective enthusiasm was often enlisted in Church politics. Hypatia [410] and, later, the Iconoclasts were routed by physical violence on the part of the monks; more than one Church council was overawed by their turbulent enthusiasm. The Emperor Theodosius, pious as he was, found it necessary to take measures against them; he wrote to St Ambrose: "The monks commit many crimes."⁴ Their intrusion into secular life was constantly forbidden by State edicts: the cry of the public was: "Return to your own deserts!" Indeed, this it was which prompted the final recognition of the indelibility of monastic vows by Justinian in 532. For at first there were no vows at all; and, even after their introduction, for a long time they were merely conditional and revocable, if not from the strict ecclesiastical point of view, at least from that of the State. The modern indelibility of the vow has its origin far less in grounds of religion than of civic expediency.

We have thus reached the stage of organized monasticism; let us briefly trace its fortunes. In the Eastern Church, its main features have remained unchanged to the present day. The monk, withdrawing from the World, leaves the World-Church mainly to shift for itself. The monasteries are increasingly drawn upon to supply bishops; but the bishop is mainly a conservative and mechanical State officer; for such work, the best man is a monk trained under a conservative and mechanical system, which has stood almost unaltered for ages. Thus we get a curious contrast; the Eastern parish priests are regularly married, generally to daughters of priests, while the bishops are always celibate monks. We may contrast this with the West, where the Benedictines alone, beginning two centuries later, claimed to have produced, by the middle of the fourteenth century, twenty-four Popes, two hundred cardinals, seven thousand archbishops and fifteen thousand bishops; the list was probably exaggerated, but nearer to the facts than large figures usually are in the Middle Ages.

This brings us to the central fact of Western monastic history. St Benedict's Rule, having been composed about A.D. 529, was thus contemporary with Justinian's work on Roman Law, and his closing of the Schools of Athens. There were already many monasteries in the West, and even monastic lawgivers. There existed a whole system of Celtic monasticism in early times, bound up with tribal organization. Again, Cassiodorus, Theodoric's great minister, and two other Western churchmen, Cassian and Caesarius of Arles, composed monastic rules after the types already classical in the East; Caesarius only a few years before St Benedict. But all these soon became obsolete, while St Benedict's survived. Partly, no doubt, because this came at a time of crying need for codification. For instance, the first chapter of the Rule complains bitterly of monks who were a law to themselves, sometimes mere pseudo-religious tramps. Again, it is significant that, in 532, Justinian began publishing that series of laws which made monastic vows irrevocable, and which allowed secular magistrates to clap apostate monks into prison. The circumstances, therefore, called for a legislator: but here also was the man, for Benedict was certainly a man of genius. His Rule shows a splendid combination of the ideal and the practical. It was possible for the great architect and medievalist Viollet-le-Duc to call it, without intolerable exaggeration, "the most important document of the Middle Ages". Reading it carefully, and interpreting it in the light of early practice, we find much in Benedict's own Rule different from the average medieval, let alone modern, monastic practice. In the first place there was still much of the *monos* principle. It insisted on strict claustration. Again, each house was an independent unit, except that the monks, originally, were under the authority of the diocesan bishop; their frequent later escape from this control was an abuse. Secondly, St Benedict insisted upon the necessity and moral value of manual labour; reading and writing were only by-occupations in his mind. Thirdly, there was still a good deal of unsacerdotalism long after St Benedict's death; we find monasteries which did not possess a single priest, and all early lists show us a decided majority of non-priests. It was only the Council of Vienne (1311) which at last compelled monks to proceed to priestly orders. "For the increase of divine worship", it directed every monk to take priest's orders if bidden by his abbot: the reason being that, by this time, the abbeys were saddled with multitudes of statutory Masses undertaken for the souls of past benefactors. From the first, therefore, there was in monasticism a strong temptation towards the "holy boorishness" which "profiteth itself alone"; *sancta rusticitas solum sibi prodest*, wrote St Jerome. But healthy monasticism was too strongly bent towards the real service of God to remain strictly obedient to that "boorish" side of the Rule. At first, Benedictinism seems to have been confined to the dozen houses founded by St Benedict himself. But the burning of its headquarters at Monte Cassino by the Lombards brought the monks to Rome, where Gregory I established them in his own palace, and probably became a monk himself [580]. Thence it was carried by St Augustine of Canterbury to England; thus Canterbury was probably the first Benedictine monastery founded outside Italy. The significance of these two facts is enormous: they strike the two keynotes of the world-history of Western monasticism. First, its close alliance with the Papacy and, secondly, the missionary spirit which inspired it wherever it was really fresh and living. It is no accident that Gregory the Great, who was in one sense the founder of the medieval Papacy, was the first monk (or, at least, monastically living person) to sit in the chair of St Peter. Nor, again, that Gregory's letters in answer to the difficulties propounded by his monastic missionaries constantly harp upon one theme: If you would win souls, you must conform yourself to others' points of view; be all things to all men, in so far as you can do so without sacrifice of principle.[1] In other words, to become a true missionary, the monk must break through many of the narrower prescriptions of his Rule. Here is the radical difference between Western and Eastern monasticism. If in the Western political world there was more disorder, at least there was more life, more abundant energy. And, again, this Northern climate is unfavourable to Fakirism: it "turns earth's smoothness rough, and bids nor stand nor sit, but go". One cannot, even in Italy, exist as in the Egyptian deserts, lying in the sand and the sun, and eating a couple of dates a day. Therefore, in the West, the best monks were seldom able to school themselves into mere passive receptacles of the Holy Ghost. They were called to the world's work, and obeyed the call. Men like Anselm and Bernard were most unwilling to leave the quiet of their cloister; but, recognizing God's voice in the summons, they went out whensoever and whithersoever they were needed to do the world's work. Moreover, this spread of monasticism in the West coincided very closely with the decay of the Roman Empire. Thus, during the period when barbarian forces were everywhere working most busily for disruption, this institution was interpenetrating barbarism in the contrary direction, and making everywhere for consolidation. We cannot find a better example of this than the life and work of St Boniface the Englishman, with which I have dealt already.

The Western monks, then, at their best, became not only ecclesiastical statesmen, but often secular politicians also; historians, poets, even artists and schoolmasters, though far less than is generally supposed. But all these activities are in no wise contemplated in St Benedict's Rule; so that Benedictine disciplinarians frequently insisted that a monk can seldom mingle with the world, even in order to do good in the world, without contracting himself something of the worldly taint. The ideal monk should be, according to the twelfth-century *Speculum Monachorum*, "like Melchizedek, without father or mother or kinsfolk". It is this conflict of ideals within monasticism which partly justifies Professor Grant's somewhat agnostic sentence: "The social influence of monasticism was very great, though it is difficult exactly to analyse it." Its social influence was indeed enormous, if only because the institution itself grew to such enormous proportions. Monks, friars, and nuns numbered about 8000 in Tudor England with its $4\frac{1}{2}$ millions; about 2 millions of these would be adult, and that proportion would make 80,000 Religious in modern Britain. Again, their income, though it can only be roughly guessed, was in all probability at least one-tenth of the whole national income, and very likely considerably more.[5] In 1200, both numbers and incomes were probably at least half as great again, in proportion to national population and income, as in 1500. Their numerical and territorial influence therefore, even apart from the influence of their ideal, was enormous.

And what, then, was the influence of their ideal? We may divide the monks roughly into three classes. First, those who kept strictly to the original principle of complete separation from their fellow-men. Of these the Carthusians are the type; always very few in numbers, scarcely more than one-hundredth of the general monastic population, but strictly secluded, and therefore able to boast with approximate truth: "We have never been reformed, because never deformed"—*nunquam reformati, quia nunquam deformati*. Secondly, there were those who relaxed this principle of retirement in favour of the stronger principle of charity, and made their monasteries centres of beneficent practical work, living a life not very ascetic, but as dignified and regular as in any other such institution known to history. Thirdly, those who relaxed the principle of claustration for their own comfort, and lived a worldly life under the religious habit. On the whole, the second and most beneficent type certainly preponderated during the best ages of monachism. An admirable example of this kind of average monastic life, or somewhat above the average, at Bury St Edmunds, may be read in Jocelin of Brakelond's Chronicle. Undoubtedly, again, there was no age at which the standard of cloistered practice was not on the whole higher than that of the average layman outside; and, in certain times and places, the monks were the very salt of the earth.

Their contributions to civilization (apart from their direct influence on Church life) may be briefly summed up as follows. Their *charity*, though it is often much exaggerated by authors who quote exceptional instances as normal, was yet considerable. We have seen above that they took more out of the parishes than they gave back: but the alternative to the monk was often a layman who would have taken still more; and the monastic dole was certainly missed at the Dissolution, especially in the comparatively backward Northern counties of England. *Manual work* was an integral part of both Benedictine and Augustinian Rules, from which every monastic order of the later Middle Ages more or less directly derived except the Friars. But the actual amount of work done by monks is often ludicrously exaggerated. This Benedictine precept was soon neglected; and, often as monastic reformers recalled it, real manual work was short-lived in practically all those revivals. What the monks did for agriculture was far more as landlords than as labourers. Even such work as copying or binding books was scarcely ever practised by the majority in a monastery, and often for whole generations by nobody at all: this can be proved by their own records. Comparison of successive catalogues, even in flourishing monasteries, suggests that the actual rate of increase was no greater than would be accounted for by one monk out of every fifty spending all his spare time as a copyist. Moreover, in spite of frequent assertions to the contrary, the monks very seldom taught outside pupils; St Jerome's words, repeated by St Bernard, were often echoed afterwards: "The monk's business is not to teach but to mourn" —*monachus non docentis sed plangentis habet officium.* The nunnery schools, of which there were a few in the later Middle Ages, were generally of the most unpretentious description, and had grown up mainly from financial causes. For the nuns were often miserably poor; and, in spite of discouragement or even prohibitions from their ecclesiastical superiors, they received children to board or teach as one way of making both ends meet. But, although it was only in exceptional cases or times that the monks set a really brilliant example of labour, unquestionably the institution as a whole did a good deal to counteract that scorn of manual work which marked all the barbarian invaders. Monastic contributions to *Art*, *Literature* and *Science* will be considered under those heads in later chapters. Meanwhile, it must be noted that the monastery was to some extent an object-lesson in *democracy*. Here, again, however, we must beware of exaggeration. Much natural favour was shown to the rich and high-born; moreover, monks did not usually come from a stratum of society below the citizen class, and nuns were still less often of really humble extraction. Savine, using the word "democratic" in its strict modern sense, is right in saying that "the monasteries could not be democratic institutions:...the majority [of the monks] could not but sympathize with the upper and middle classes".[6] But they were democratic in the sense in which the English parliament of the eighteenth century was democratic, oligarchical as it may seem to us in a more advanced age. Not only might the very poorest be admitted sometimes to a rich abbey, but he might be elected abbot, and, theoretically, have absolute sway. Popular election had been the strength of the early Church; bishops and priests were really elected by flocks at a time when municipal elections had become a farce in the Empire; and much of this system remained a reality down to the ninth century at least. Within the monasteries, in spite of illegal encroachments from popes, kings, and nobles, election remained the general rule in England down to the Reformation, thus keeping up some reminder of that republican maxim which Napoleon cherished: *la carrière ouverte aux talents.* On the Continent, election in the abbeys had given way almost everywhere to appointments by king or pope, or by both in collusion; scarcely one great house in France was free from what Montalembert called "this leprosy of monasticism"; that is, a "commendatory" abbot, who consumed nearly all the revenues, yet was commonly not a monk, and often not even a priest. From this plague England was saved by steady resistance from kings and layfolk against papal pressure; the "leprosy" was only beginning to take root with us when Henry VIII dissolved the monasteries. Thus, in their most living days, the monks had set an example of election and representative government to society around them; the elaborate representative systems of the Cluniacs and Cistercians, and the organization of Dominicans after them, could scarcely fail to exert some influence upon the parliamentary movements; especially in England, where monastic life was on the whole more regular than in any other great country.

XXIII. CLOISTER LIFE

IT remains to enquire rather more closely how the Rule worked out in practice. We must take the Benedictine, which was followed by far the most and the greatest houses, as type; the Augustinian, which comes next in importance, resembled it strongly, but was a little less strict.

Disciplinarians insisted that their Rule contained three essential principles—*tria substantialia*—viz. Obedience, Poverty, and Celibacy. From these not even the Pope could dispense the sworn Religious. He could, indeed, relieve him of the whole vow— could, as it were, annul his marriage to that ideal—but, short of this step, of which there are very few historical examples, those *substantialia* were as inviolable as matrimony itself. In reinforcement of them the authorities insisted on four main pillars of discipline laid down in the Rule: Propertylessness, Labour, Claustration, and Diet. But, even before the Black Death, those four pillars had been cut away in practice; the Canonist John of Ayton [1340] tells us this in so many words, and monastic records themselves bear him out. Between then and the Dissolution, they were not only neglected in practice but even whittled away in theory. The monk not only had pocket-money, from which he might amass a private hoard and lend it out at usury (we have definite evidence of this), but he would complain to the official visitor if that pocket-money were not regularly paid. Chapter 66 of the Rule prescribes, most emphatically, that he must not go outside the precincts, and early disciplinarians interpreted this in the strictest sense; yet in the fifteenth century such strict claustration was not the rule, but a rare exception. The English General Chapter of 1444 published a statute to the effect that a monk who called his brother "liar" should be restricted to the interior monastic buildings for three weeks; if he struck him with fist or knife, for a year. Diet, again, was by Rule quasi-vegetarian; butcher's meat was strictly forbidden except to the sick. Yet first the habit grew up of resorting to the infirmary in order to enjoy those forbidden flesh-pots; then, when this was prohibited by papal statute, of creating a sort of half-way chamber, in which meat was eaten without polluting (so the canonists argued) either refectory or infirmary. At Peterborough this was called "seyny house", at Durham, "loft" (it is now the Chapter Library); but its ordinary name was "misericorde"—the Chamber of Mercy. This, again, was definitely forbidden by papal statute (Gregory IX); but a century later (1339) Benedict XII recognized the concession as inevitable, and contented himself with permitting the misericorde to only half the congregation at a time; so that the alternate half would be maintaining their vegetarian rule in the refectory. Yet, only a few years later, the English Chapter General complained of that restriction as difficult to keep; and visitatorial injunctions bear this out. Finally, labour was abandoned earlier and more completely than the other three pillars. Field-work was first dropped, as superfluous for houses that were so richly endowed, and as scarcely compatible with monastic dignity: writers even pleaded here the example of St Maur, who had been St Benedict's own pupil. Then kitchen and house work went by the board; so that, during the last two or three monastic centuries in England, we find even shaving, gardening, washing, the mowing of the cloister-garth, done by paid servants, who, in the wealthier houses, outnumbered the brethren, sometimes by 50 per cent. Moreover the monk's own special labour, that on which he fell back in excuse and by which he gained his endowments, was the *Opus Dei*, his psalmody and Masses. Yet, long before the Dissolution, even statutory Masses were being neglected in great numbers, to the defrauding of benefactors' souls. The other liturgical services, again, were so irregularly maintained even at such great and wealthy abbeys as Peterborough, Ramsey and Norwich Cathedral, that the visitors found less than half of the community in choir, and recorded the scandal which this caused among the laity. As to the rule of celibacy, though it is seldom that we find a house so ill-reported as we have seen of Flaxley, yet the episcopal visitations leave no doubt that there were sufficient scandals to affect monastic reputation very seriously. Not only satirists, but the most unexceptionable witnesses, are practically unanimous upon this point. Most convincing of all is the comparative silence of anti-Lollard apologists. These men fill one folio page after another in defence of the monks on other points, yet they show striking diffidence and hesitations upon this, the most serious point of Lollard attack. St Thomas More, in his controversial discussions with the innovators, where he says the worst that could be said against them with any semblance of truth by an honest and indignant champion of orthodoxy, yet goes out of his way to relate three anti-monastic anecdotes which, from the pen of a modern Protestant, would be cried down as mere bigotry.

That, after all, is the most important question: What did the laity think of these Religious, for many generations before the Reformation? We have already glanced briefly at the evidence of Gower and *Piers Plowman*; let us here take Chaucer, the most Shakespearian among all medieval writers in his pictures and his estimates of all sorts of men. Let us consider, in the light of cold-blooded ecclesiastical documents, his Friar, his Monk, and his Nun.

With the Friar he had plainly least sympathy: the man is, as Professor Trevelyan pithily remarks, a medieval Stiggins. St Francis and St Dominic, almost at the same moment, had set themselves to inaugurate a new era in monasticism. The older orders had become rich: the monks' own friends were confessing that this child Wealth was destroying its parent Religion, and therefore the Friars adopted the principle of poverty, not only individual, but corporate also. The Friar must possess nothing, and his house must possess nothing: all life must be lived from hand to mouth. Moreover, the good monk's Rule had confined him for life within his own precincts; and the relaxed monk, when he broke that rule of claustration, had brought disorder rather than order into the society round him; for Chaucer's Shipman's Tale might be paralleled from visitatorial reports. The Friar, on the other hand, abandoned the whole principle of strict claustration; he used his monastery only as a base of operations: his main work was to be done outside, as evangelist and physician of souls. It was a golden ideal; but this gold had rapidly become encumbered with dross. Long before Chaucer's birth, those Friars who fought for their Rule in its primitive strictness had become a persecuted minority: in the lifetime of Chaucer's father (1318) four Franciscans at Marseilles had been burnt alive for disobedience when their General had commanded them to do things incompatible with St Francis's own Rule and Testament. Piers Plowman cites such "poor fools" as rare exceptions among the general Franciscan decay.[1] Therefore, much as the Franciscans and Dominicans, with their brother-orders of Carmelites and Austin Friars, had done at one time to rejuvenate Church life, yet Chaucer and his contemporaries already visualized them as men who professed to do the parish priest's work but were in fact his rivals, and too often mere stumbling-blocks in the way of true religion and morality. In so far as Chaucer is capable of flaming indignation, he spends that upon the Friar.

To the Monk his satire is far more genial; it is rather that of Thackeray, who has a good deal of good-humoured fellow-feeling with the human failings of the cleric, so that we cannot resist a sneaking sympathy with the Rev. Jedidiah Ramshorn, whom the

Spirit has commissioned to go and convert the Pope of Rome; or, again, with that Bishop of Bullocksmithy of whom the club steward can quote, as a testimonial to the meat there served, that he has just eaten three chops from this same loin; or even with Charles Honeyman. Let us look at Chaucer's Monk, then, in this spirit and through the microscope of ecclesiastical records.

We see at first sight the humour of his hunting Monk; but what is that "text" at which he snapped his fingers, "that seith that hunters beth nat hooly men"? The Vulgate Bible, at the passage where our Authorized

The Hunting Monk.

Version makes Nimrod "a mighty hunter *before* the Lord", has "*against* the Lord". He thus became a type of the godless despot, and finds his fitting place in Dante's *Inferno*. His case, equally naturally, was quoted in Gratian's *Decretum*, the first volume of Canon Law, in support of the strict prohibition of hunting for all clergy, and, *à fortiori*, for the nominally cloistered clergy. There, Canon Law comes in again; one of its best known texts was that which smote monastic wanderers with the words of St Jerome: "A monk out of his cloister dies spiritually, like a fish out of water." Chaucer knew well, and most of his readers knew roughly, how many papal and conciliar injunctions might have been quoted against this hunter-monk, and how often he was the target for moral preachers who loved the habitation of God's house, and were not inclined to make their lives a portion for foxes. We hear his bridle jingle gaily in the whistling wind, as clear and loud as the bell of his own chapel: we see how his admirably supple boots are in exact character for this huntsman. Here are obvious unclerical touches; but few modern readers realize their full force. Few know how often and how earnestly such worldliness and expense had been forbidden to these men whose whole life was vowed to poverty; men who claimed to be *par excellence* "Christ's Poor"—*pauperes Christi*—and therefore to be even more worthy of alms than the non-Religious poor. Let us see how the contemporary *Dives and Pauper* treats this subject. "To them that have the benefices and the goods of Holy Church, it longeth principally to give almesse and to have cure of the poor people.... Therefore these men of Holy Church that boocle their shone with boocles of silver, and use great silver harneys in their girdles and knyves, and men of Religion, monks and chanones, and such other, that...ride on high horses with saddles harnessed with gold and silver more pompously than lords, be stronge thieves and do great sacrilege, so spending the goods of Holy Church in vanity and pride [and] in lust of the flesh, by which goods the poor folk should live. A lady of a thousand mark by year can pin her hood against the wind with a small pin of laton [brass]; xii for a penny. But a monk that is bounden to poverty by his profession will have an ouche [locket] or a broche of gold and silver, in value of a noble or much more."[2] Here again Chaucer's Monk fits in most exactly:

> For to festne his hood under his chyn
> He hadde of gold y-wroght a ful curious pyn,
> A love-knotte in the gretter end there was.

This Monk's scorn of study and manual work is in obvious keeping with his repudiation of his own Rule as "old and some-deal strait". St Augustine, it is true, laid even more emphasis than St Benedict upon manual labour; but "let Austin have his swink [work] to him reserved!" "Greyhoundes he hadde", while episcopal visitors were recording, over and over again, in words which this generation of ours can now at last read in print after centuries of historical neglect, that it was scandalous to nourish hunting dogs in monasteries, and to "give the children's bread unto dogs". Again:

> I seigh his sleves y-purfiled at the hond
> With grys, and that the fynest of a lond.

Gris was the fur of the grey squirrel, finest and most expensive of all except ermine and vair. It was expressly forbidden to monks, as also was *burnet* (fine black cloth of the quality that we now call "broadcloth") as a luxury which belied their profession. Yet, in Chaucer's day, it was already common—the papal registers prove it—for individual cloisterers to buy from Rome private indulgences for this forbidden gris; bribing, as the boldest and most successful always do in every age and place, at the very fountainhead. Moreover, with regard to burnet, we find an Archbishop of Canterbury, Simon Langham, leaving by will to every monk of his great house a measure of this cloth for his frock or, if he preferred, its equivalent in the no less sinful money. Yet this man who thus drove his coach through two solemn monastic statutes, in order to earn the prayers of the brethren for his own soul, was himself monk and abbot, and had been Bishop of Ely before his translation to Canterbury.

Finally, our Hunting Monk has a good appetite, and is something of a *bon vivant*. On this point we need not rely upon Giraldus Cambrensis's account of the feasting that he found at Canterbury, for we possess the "consuetudinaries", the household-books, both of that cathedral priory and of its rival, the Abbey of Westminster. In these books and in many similar documents, we find the minutest and most stringent prescriptions as to the quantity and quality of meat and drink. Of bread and ale there are different qualities, and the brethren in each case are to have the finest. Here, as in all other cases where similar records have survived, the lowest allowance of ale is a gallon each *per diem*. At Westminster, the fish must be sought from the best in the market, and each monk's portion is six, whether of bream or mullet or "salted Cambridge eels" or flounders or herring.* Much of this may be accounted for by the superior wealth of Westminster, and its neighbourhood to the royal court. But at Spalding, a house definitely of the second or third rank, a

---

* It is possible (though the context makes it improbable) that these specifications are not for each *separate* monk, but for each *pair*, eating from one dish. In that case, each monk would have only three fish for that course.

contemporary abbot left money by will in order that, whereas in the past each monk had had four eggs or flounders or herrings, the future allowance should be six each. Not all of this, of course, was actually eaten; this may be proved, if in no other way, by the fact that, in all such specifications, the prior has always a double allowance. Nominally, all that was left was gathered up by the almoner and given to the poor. But in fact visitatorial injunctions very frequently turn upon the abuse of feeding the servants or dependents or friends with this food which the statutes had ear-marked for charity; and the monk himself often employed his superfluity for hob-nobbing with his cronies in the town. There, again, Chaucer gives us an illustration of this custom in his Ship-man's Tale with its monk of St-Denis. The Middle Ages, like ancient Greece, recognized the custom of reciprocal dinners or suppers, each guest bringing his own contribution to the common feast (ἔρανος). The Monk of Chaucer's tale, who could bring from a wealthy abbey his "jubbe of Malvoisie"—his great pitcher of rich wine—was a welcome guest in any company.

Let us turn now to the best known and most sympathetic of all Chaucer's Religious. There is perhaps no single phrase of his that is so often quoted as that *French of Stratford attë Bowe*; and his dear Prioress is perhaps the character whom we have most clearly visualized from the first, and with whom we have lived most familiarly ever since. From our schooldays onwards, if asked to name the most conspicuous instances of Chaucer's sly humour, we should probably have turned to her. Yet I will venture to say that some of his most delicate touches here, and not his least humorous, are missed by those who do not know some-

The Prioress.

thing (if only indirectly and at second hand) concerning the most formal ecclesiastical records. Even her French of Stratford-attë-Bowe gains something from a glance at those visitatorial injunctions in Norman-French which bishops often addressed to the nuns, at a time when similar injunctions to monks were still drawn up in Latin. And even the Prioress's favourites and ours, those *smalë houndës*, gain something in effect for those readers who have realized how stubbornly the orthodox visitors tried to eliminate such pets from the convents, and with what small success. At Romsey, in 1387, the bishop found two nuns bringing into church birds, rabbits, and hounds; at Queen Matilda's *Abbaye aux Dames*, they brought their squirrels. Then our Prioress's dress: "full semëly hyr wympul y-pynched was". What a charming picture of this demure lady in her cleanest of black and white, as dainty as the daintiest worldling, yet with all the added charm of pure religion! Chaucer meant all this, no doubt; nothing is more significant than Harry Bailey's natural and unfeigned respect for the Prioress. But (and here is the point) Chaucer meant something more, which contemporaries saw at a glance, but which we can only see when some historical Dryasdust serves us by focusing his microscope upon it. This seemly pinched wimple was, ecclesiastically, most unseemly; disciplinarians warred against such fashions even more persistently than against pets, and with more unquestionable support from the law, both in letter and in spirit. A wimple so pleated as to earn Chaucer's commendation was technically as irregular as a guardsman's moustache would be on the quarter-deck of a man-of-war. Those who miss this fact are almost as far from the full comprehension of this particular verse as the old lady who is said to have loved Gibbon's *Decline and Fall* for the inexhaustible mine of pious reflections which she always found in his footnotes. Let us read on for the next three lines. The Prioress's nose and eyes and lips are as attractive as those of our favourite partner at the dance. This she could not help, of course; God may have made her to dance, and the world may have made her into a prioress. The large majority of nuns were of the upper or upper middle class—younger daughters lacking the necessary dowry for marriage—and, in the cloister, promotion naturally went very often by good birth and good connections; it may well have been that Madam Eglantyne was of nobler lineage than the Knight himself. "But sikerly she hadde a fair forheed"; there comes the crowning glory of her features, and it lifts us to a higher plane; she has charmed us as a woman, and now she impresses us with her intellect. Here again we need not doubt Chaucer's good intentions; yet to his original hearers this very praise must have suggested something beyond his plain words, and something very different. The nun's wimple was officially supposed to be not only puritanically plain, but also of Mohammedan amplitude and efficiency; let it hide as much of the face as possible (so ran episcopal injunctions); let it come down to the very eyebrows. This was distressing; for the forehead was one of the great points of medieval comeliness, and those girls who had the misfortune to be formed by nature for the Rossetti type of beauty would painfully standardize themselves by plucking out the superfluous hairs. Those, however, were mere worldlings. In the world, if you had not a forehead, you might make yourself one; but this nun had no business to possess any forehead at all, so far as Chaucer was concerned. She had no more right to a forehead than the young lady in Richardson's novel had to possess ankles or toes.

Let me not be taken to suggest that either Chaucer or his hearers sympathized with all this official puritanism; I only mean that they cannot possibly have ignored it. Chaucer meant to show the Prioress as she really was; an individual portrait, yet true to type; a caged creature charming even to worldlings, and scarcely less dignified because hers was not merely the angelic and incorporeal dignity of Tennyson's nun, breathing out her soul in the winter moonlight. Chaucer knew the artistic value of contrasts as well as that of harmonies; especially of subtle contrasts; of those gleams of summer-lightning which quicken our general appreciation without disturbing it, making us laugh inwardly and read on with heightened expectation. And in this we are not disappointed, for now comes the climax in a touch of sly humour which must have set even Gibbon's old lady a-thinking. The Prioress wore "a brooch of gold ful sheenë, On which ther was first writ a crowned A, And after, *Amor vincit omnia*". Here Chaucer plainly wishes us to ponder over this equivoque. And later on, while the Miller and the Reeve tell their tales, he knows we cannot help glancing sideways at the Prioress and her two nuns, and wondering *que diable faisaient-elles dans cette galère?* For, at the very beginning of Chaucer's century, one of the boldest and most masterful Popes of the whole Middle Ages had undertaken to grapple with this perilous abuse (so the bull *Periculoso* phrases it) of the nun wandering outside her cloister. Strict claustration was commanded thenceforward by Boniface VIII for all, except at the rarest moments of extreme necessity; and disciplinarians were so far from admitting pilgrimages among the pious and justifiable exceptions here, that they thundered against this practice on the part of nuns with an emphasis which we can scarcely find outdone by the Lollards themselves.

Such, then, are the historical facts which supply a key to the poet's real meaning. This, the least tedious of our poets, is supported by the most tedious records of ecclesiastical legislation; records which have been among the most neglected down to our present day. Legislation may not be a poetical subject in itself; but in many different countries, and at many different times, poets have found their material either in legal humours or in legal tragedies. Thus, if we dream that we can ignore medieval law without missing something of the poet's mind, we deceive ourselves. We may, of course, understand a great deal of Chaucer at first sight; but we shall never comprehend the full Chaucer but by studying those minutiae which are matters of history to us, but which were present everyday commonplaces to the people for whom he wrote. Nobody who reads Professor Eileen Power's *Medieval English Nunneries* can fail to rise from that book with a deeper sense of the humour that lurks in those fifty lines of Chaucer.

Let us now leave our gentle satirist, and go backwards a century and a half to hear Hugh, that canon of the model Augustinian monastery of St Victor at Paris to whom Dante assigns a high place in heaven. Hugh, side by side with his mystical writings, composed a manual of behaviour for novices, which became classical not only in his own order but in others also. The evidence contained in this book is all the more important, because Hugh is writing for men drawn from one of the most cultured districts in Europe.[3] Naturally enough, he is much concerned with "deportment". "We should keep discretion of action in our limbs, so that each limb should do that for which it was made. Let not the hand speak, nor the mouth listen, nor the eye usurp the office of the tongue. For there are some who cannot listen but with gaping mouth, and who open their palate to the speaker's words as though the sense thereof could trickle through the mouth into the heart. Others, worse still, when they act or listen, thrust forth their tongue like thirsty dogs. Others swim along with their arms, and, by a double monstrosity, at one and the same moment they walk with their feet on earth and fly with their arms in the air.... But, lest I should seem perchance to utter rather satire than teaching (though there are still many things which might be set forth) here also I must not forget moderation." Then he turns specifically to table-manners. "Taciturnity is necessary at our feasts [*epulas*] because the tongue, which at all times is prone to sin, is more perilously loosened to speech when it has been inflamed with liberal food and drink [*per crapulam*]; it was for that reason that the rich man who had given way to loquacity at his feasting, felt the more vehement fire in his tongue as he lay in hell....Let nothing be done [at table] with tumult or noise....Not as some do, who, when they sit down to eat, show their intemperance of mind in a certain restless agitation and confusion of their limbs.... They pant and groan in anguish, so that you might think they are seeking another wider orifice for their roaring maw, as though their narrow throat could not minister sufficient abundance to their hungry stomach. Though they sit in one place, their eyes and their hands roam around everywhere, far and near; at the same moment they crumble the bread, pour the wine into cups and goblets, draw the dishes round, and mount to the assault like kings against a beleaguered city, doubting at what point to attack first, since they hunger to take all at once by storm. It may be that we, writing thus, have too far forgotten our modesty; but sometimes impudence cannot be brought to blush unless it be plainly confounded." Thence Hugh goes on to speak not only of manners but of appetites. He depicts the cloisterer who finds that ordinary fare gives him indigestion or headache; and, again, the ascetic who tries to feed more plainly than his fellows. Some "seek after new and unwonted sorts of food, so that oftentimes, for the sake of one man's belly, a host of servants scour all the villages around, and, after all, can scarce quench the petulance of this single appetite either by tearing up roots from wild and distant mountains, or by profound investigation, dragging a few little fishes from the deepest whirlpools, or by collecting untimely berries from the withering bushes....Others pay too fastidious attention to the preparation of food, excogitating infinite sorts of stewings and fryings and seasonings; now soft, now hard; now hot, now cold; now sodden, now roast; seasoned now with pepper, now with garlic, now with cummin, now with salt, after the fashion of women in their pregnancy." Above all, novices must shun one of the great temptations of the cloisterer, to whom, in his less inspired moments, dinner or supper are happy oases in a sea of monotony. "Some, at meals, in their anxiety to empty the dishes, wrap in their napkins, or cast upon them, the foursquare gobbets of the mess, dripping with the fat or the grease that has been poured upon them, until, having again scooped them out, they restore the remains to their former place. Others, while they drink, dip their fingers half-way down the cup. Others wipe their greasy hands upon their garments, and come back again to handle the food. Others fish with bare fingers, instead of spoons, for their pot-herbs; so that they seem to seek, in that same bowl of soup, both the washing of hands and the refection of their belly. Others dip repeatedly into the dish their half-gnawed crusts and the sippets which they have bitten, and plunge the leavings of their own teeth, in the guise of sops, into the gobbets. These things, as I have said above, would have been shameful in those who relate them if they had not been presumptuously acted in deed; let that man now suffer discipline in hearing who would not keep discipline in his acts." Four generations later, the Franciscan David of Augsburg wrote more briefly, but in a similar vein: "Fall not upon thy meat with tooth and claw like a famished dog." Bernard of Besse, secretary to St Bonaventura, writes in greatest detail of all, quoting from Hugh but outdoing him in plainness of speech; I have translated his evidence in my *From St Francis to Dante* (2nd ed. p. 65). Humbert de Romans, the great contemporary Minister General of the Dominicans, makes similar complaints against his fellow-friars' table-manners.

With regard to behaviour in church, the Franciscan disciplinarians warn their novices against sleep, laughter, perambulation, late coming or premature departure, and talk during Mass: "for Canon Law forbiddeth this at such times even to the secular clergy". In brief, it is evident that the authorities were confronted at times with something of the same difficulties which beset Bishop Grandisson in his Cathedral of Exeter.

Yet this chapter must not end upon that note. Chaucer, like Thackeray, had at bottom a true reverence for religious goodness, and he would very likely have agreed less with the Lollards than with the apologists of his own day. The attitude of those apologists has been too little studied from this point of view, beginning with the Carmelite Netter of Walden and ending with the St Thomas More the Martyr. Each of these men, in his natural attempts to minimize, practically confesses a great deal of the accusation. Yet each pleads that we should not only look at the failings, but recognize also the better side; and, above all, that with one eye on the ideal we must keep the other on human nature; first of all, indeed, upon our own conscience. Netter, Pecock, More all ask in effect *Can you cast the first stone?* We have the League of Nations, at the present moment, as a parallel only too obvious and painful. An institution may aim at an ideal which all men confess to be lofty, and to which they will subscribe by the million; yet its history in practice may be one long record of disillusionment. There may be no alternative left but reform or extinction; and yet there will remain something of the generous impulses that prompted it and of the good work done by a devoted few: mankind will never be ashamed of it. These monastic ruins of ours, which attract more attention in these days of easy locomotion and cheap advertisement than in any other generation of the last four hundred years, were peopled by men and women who resembled mostly our ordinary selves, and who lived, if not strictly according to the Rule, at least with more regularity than the average of their fellow men and women outside. More can tell us Rabelaisian tales from the monasteries even while he is defending the institution as a whole; but there is real, though not conclusive, force in his reminder that, among all the loudest lay critics, there were not many who would face the ordinary requirements of monastic discipline.

THE modern distinction between municipal and village life had comparatively little force in the Middle Ages. The town was often scarcely more than an overgrown village, and indeed there were few whose population would raise them above village rank in Yorkshire or Lancashire of to-day. In this field, as in many others, many significant indications come from that record which Carlyle has made famous in his *Past and Present*—the chronicle of Jocelin of Brakelond. We see there how the townsfolk of Bury St Edmunds, at the end of the twelfth century, were still not only under village, but even to a great extent under servile, conditions. They paid yearly "reap-silver" as a commutation for the harvest work to which they had formerly been bound. They paid a "sor-penny" for free pasture. There were dunghills in the streets, as in any farmyard. They had ploughing to do for the abbot, a remnant of their past condition as bondmen. Their sheep had to be folded in the abbot's field, in order that he might profit by the dung; and they were still subject to forced labour in the matter of fishing, or of carting eels. "The men of the town were wont, at the cellarer's bidding, to go to Lakenheath and bring a convoy of eels from Southery, and oftentimes to return empty and thus to be vexed without any gain to the cellarer; wherefore they agreed that, in future, each thirty acres should pay one penny yearly, and the men should stay at home. But, in these days of ours, those lands have been divided into so many parts that it is scarce known who owes that due; so that I have seen the cellarer one year take 27 pence, yet now he can scarce get $10\frac{1}{2}d$."

Take, again, the case of Leicester. There were, to begin with, the great fields in the suburbs in which the citizens pastured their cattle, and which by a fortunate concurrence of circumstances have become, since the nineteenth century, a series of public parks such as perhaps no other great town in England can boast. Then, about 1200, we find the citizens buying themselves free of the yearly payments which they owed to the earl in lieu of field service; and, thirdly, the borough financial year begins when the harvest was well gathered in, generally the first week in October.

Again, we have definite traces of rural conditions in the presentment of a Leicester jury. The jurors say on their oath "that in the time of the same Earl Robert [d. 1118], the forest of Leicester was so great, thick and full, that it was scarcely possible to go by the paths of that forest, on account of the quantity of dead wood and of boughs blown down by the wind; and then, by the will and consent of the Lord Earl and of his Council, it was allowed to those who wished to look for dead wood, to have six cartloads for 1*d.* and a horse-load a week for ½*d.* and a man's load a week for ¼*d.*" Even in the case of London, Becket's biographer, Fitzstephen, says "the arable fields of the town of London are fertile"; not merely "fertile arable fields can be found in the neighbourhood of the town of London"; moreover, throughout the whole of the Middle Ages, the citizens enjoyed hunting rights throughout Epping Forest, and southwards "to the waters of Cray": i.e. far down into Kent. At Lynn, the small public park eastward from the town is still called "The Chase".[1]

How, then, did these agricultural communities become urban? How did the "township", in which land alone counted, become the modern "town", in which trade is the predominant factor? How did so many urban communities grow up and take place beside the comparatively rare survivals of Roman cities, so that Southampton rivalled Winchester, and Norwich probably displaced Caister altogether?

The process was perfectly natural, by a sequence which has created our political liberties. On the Continent, Professor Pirenne would find the normal origin of the municipality in the suburb of some city or fortress: in the outer enclosure (forisburgus = *faubourg*) of some *bourg*. Such settlements would be created by the great revival of commerce shortly before the year 1000. Enough men would specialize in trade to outgrow the mainly agricultural interests of the old community. Nestling at first under the protection of the city or fortress walls, they would soon become rich enough to entrench themselves in turn; and thus we get that very common Continental phenomenon of two or more fortified enclosures, one the nucleus of the rest. "There were no unfortified towns in the Middle Ages", writes Pirenne (p. 54).

This, however, will not do for England, as we shall see presently; for there are many English towns of note which never had even such rudimentary defences as the earthen bank which surrounded Wallingford. Cambridge would seem far more typical for England than the more artificially created cities from which Pirenne drew his evidence; and here we are on pretty firm ground, thanks to Miss H. M. Cam's excellent summary of all that previous historians and antiquaries have collected. At Cambridge both fortress and town sprang from the same cause—a bridge (or, earlier, a ford) where an important road crossed an otherwise impassable river. It was natural, again, that this same point of the river, should become less easily navigable; so that Cambridge was counted as a sea-port even at the end of the thirteenth century. Thus, almost inevitably, traders gradually settled here; there is definite evidence of trade with foreign merchants as early as the tenth century, and presumptive evidence for a still earlier date. The Romans had already fortified the bridge-head; a Norman castle was built there afterwards; thus castle and town derived importance from each other. But there was no sudden and artificial creation, and no clear differentiation between merchant and agriculturalist, such as Pirenne has traced in so many Continental cities. Agricultural Cambridge became urban Cambridge by exactly the same slow and irresistible development which has gradually transformed England from a country of villages to a country of towns. Almost everywhere we can trace the same causes at work. The original village would find itself in a particularly fortunate position—a natural halting place on a great road hard by the bridge or the ford of a river, or a point commanding a pass through the forest or between the hills, or at the gate of a castle or monastery. This would cause a natural influx of inhabitants. They themselves would no less naturally evolve communal ambitions as they grew more numerous; and a wise lord would find it convenient not to discourage them too much. Otherwise he would always find himself with a miserable hamlet, instead of a multitude of subjects prosperous themselves and able to pay him heavy dues. Moreover, in many cases the lord granted these urban privileges mainly at other people's expense, in so far as he could do so without getting into trouble with the suffering parties. Here, for instance, is the first charter of the town of Cambridge, granted by Henry I about 1125: "Henry King of the English to Hervey Bishop of Ely and all his barons of Cambridgeshire greeting. I forbid that any boat shall ply at any hithe in Cambridgeshire, save at the hithe of my borough of Cambridge; nor shall barges be laden save in the borough of Cambridge; nor shall any take toll elsewhere, but only there." The natural result of that would be a large influx from the country around. Mr W. Hudson, whose studies on Martham we have already seen, has worked out similar results for the city of Norwich. He shows how, before the end of the thirteenth century, the city had attracted natives of at least 400 Norfolk and perhaps 60 Suffolk towns or villages or manors. Moreover, Henry I was doubtless heavily paid by the citizens in a lump sum for this monopoly. In the case of London we have an exact record; it paid King John £2000, at least equivalent to £80,000 in modern terms, for its charter. Therefore it is natural that we find the great grantors of charters in England to have been kings who were desperately in want of money, like John, or who had great and costly schemes. In any case, however, the charter was not only to some extent the result of past prosperity, but an earnest of prosperity to come. Cambridge, which had only about 325 habitable houses at Domesday, had 534 in 1279. At ordinary village rate of increase for the Middle Ages, there would have been only about 450 houses at that later date. We may get a rough estimate of the population in each case if we multiply the houses by five.

All this was done, then, on a definite money foundation. Abbot Samson, of Bury, was very wise in commuting reap-silver and other such dues, and putting them on a firmer business basis. Jocelin, it is true, tells us how the more conservative monks grumbled at this sale of past privileges and dignities; yet even the most impenetrable must have seen the advantage of commuting that hollow farce of fetching eels from Southery. The townsfolk had now increasingly more profitable occupations than servile labour. They could afford to pay richly, and were glad to pay, for every new liberty that they could purchase. So all wise lords saw; but all were not wise; and in town evolution circumstances perhaps played a greater part than wisdom; at any rate on the lord's side. We must distinguish here very clearly, however, between the spiritual lords—bishops and abbots and so forth— and the temporal. Not only were the spiritual more naturally conservative in their disposition, but in many cases they were bound by laws which made any transfer or sale of rights difficult. The bishop at his consecration took an oath not to diminish the revenues of his see. The abbot, even without any such definite oath, was under equally definite legal pledge. Moreover, the Churchman had nearly always a more powerful and consistent policy than the lay baron. Thus, "almost to a man they [the great prelates] offered resistance to the municipal movement, which at times developed into an open struggle" (Pirenne, p. 55). The whole medieval history of Lynn centres round its attempt to escape from the power of its lord, the Bishop of Norwich. In the Middle Ages the town was always known as Bishop's Lynn; it was only Henry VIII who, by a forced exchange of properties, turned it into King's Lynn. In the same way at St Albans, Reading, Dunstable, Burton and Bury St Edmunds, we find the citizens struggling from generation to generation to escape from the lordship of their abbot, or at least to gain more favourable terms by purchase or encroachment. At Bury the struggle led to bloodshed in 1381; but the reprisals for that bloodshed were so stern that this final revolt left the citizens as helpless as the men of St Albans. Those last two stories are told in most picturesque detail by Mrs J. R. Green in the first volume of her *Town Life in the Fifteenth Century*, and by J. A. Froude in his *Short Studies*.

To turn now to the secular barons. These were constantly running into debt, especially from the Crusades onwards. Therefore we find towns on their estates steadily buying fresh liberties. The lords thus profited doubly. Each got a handsome sum in hand for granting his charter, and he profited steadily by the increasing prosperity of his townsfolk, which enabled them to bid high for fresh liberties, piece by piece. The most fortunate municipalities, however, were those which grew up on royal estates. The king's lordship made the freëst towns: from the very first these enjoyed the rights and privileges of "ancient demesne". The king's liberties thus protected his immediate tenants. Another consideration is that kings were comparatively unmeddling. They were remote; they were too busy and too great to worry so much about details as the baron or knight under whose nose the villagers might be living. Thirdly, the king's protection was far more efficient than any other for curtailing the often abusive power of neighbouring barons or county sheriffs; and, lastly, the king was habitually more deeply in debt than the average baron, and therefore more willing to sell liberties for cash.

An admirable concrete instance of such payments comes from Leicester, whose earl was one of the greatest barons in England, about 1110. He, like other Norman earls, had introduced the custom, much resented by the conquered Saxons, of trial by battle, even in a large number of civil cases. At Leicester two kinsmen had disputed a piece of land. There was no alternative (unless either was willing to yield altogether what he believed to be a just claim), but to fight it out. They fought (says the report) from prime (6 o'clock) "to noon, and longer"; until at last one, pressing upon his opponent, drove him to the edge of a ditch. Then, at that point, with a sportsmanlike impulse, he warned his enemy of his danger; at which "such a clamour and a tumult" arose from the bystanders that the lord heard it in his castle and enquired its meaning. The result was that the burgesses, "moved with pity", agreed to give a yearly tribute of 3d. from each house which was assessed as a tenement, in order to purchase reversal to the old English custom of clearing such cases before a jury of 24 sworn men.

Here, again, we may turn for similar evidence from Cambridge, which has been so admirably studied in detail by F. W. Maitland in his *Township and Borough*. In 1186 it bought from the king its *Firma Burgi*; this "borough farm" was one of the first liberties to be bought by nearly every town. It meant that, instead of a variety of urban dues which the lord's bailiff would have the right of collecting from house to house, the citizens should henceforth pay by agreement a yearly lump sum, and be left to their own devices for the collection of it. Thus one of the most vexatious and dangerous forms of lordly interference was removed. Then came a series of liberties under John's charter of 1201; Cambridge bought itself free of "New Year's gifts" and "Scot-ales", exactions by the sheriff. The latter supplies an admirable instance of official oppression. "Scot-ales" were originally in civil life what "Church-ales" were in ecclesiastical. But under the sheriff's management they changed from a friendly and beneficent feast into a burdensome tax; he insisted upon collecting contributions, and there was nobody sufficiently strong to control his management of them; thus the system forms a subject of grave complaint, until it eventually dies out. Next, the town got its "Gild Merchant"—that is its trade union of all who bought and sold on a sufficiently important scale. Probably at Cambridge, as often elsewhere, this Gild included all the burgesses. None had citizen rights but those who belonged to the Merchant Gild; and a fresh step in liberty was freedom of toll for this Gild on all royal lands. Then came the town's own rights of justice; no longer trial by battle, but by compurgation. Next came the grants from King Henry III, including the right of reprisals; which, however, was reciprocal and valid only in relation to other boroughs. The king, herein, "did not grant an absolute exemption to the townsfolk of Cambridge. The man of Cambridge and his goods are to be free from arrest for the debt owed by another unless that other is solvent and the Cambridge burgesses in their court have made default in justice: so, if the Cambridge court has 'denied right' to a man of Huntingdon, it will still be imprudent for any man of Cambridge to visit the neighbouring town. Not until 1275 was an end put to this system of intermunicipal reprisals, and long after that the old principle was still enforced against foreigners." By 1256 the town had obtained the right to elect its own coroners; and, by a coincidence, that same year gave the city of Norwich independence of the sheriffs, and freedom of managing its own taxation and its own borough courts for everything but felony. Cambridge and Norwich, then, are now practically free from all interference from the shire officers. In 1313 the Cambridge burgesses obtained the right of bequeathing lands or tenements within the borough as though they were chattels; a right most important in those ages when land could not be transferred except through complicated legal fictions, with proportionate want of security. At the Peasants' Revolt, the townsfolk joined hands with the rioters and avenged the many ancient grudges they had nursed against the scholars; among other outrages, they burned most of the university documents. Naturally, the reaction in 1382 was highly unfavourable. The *Firma Burgi* was increased by the king, and the profitable "assizes"—that is, rights of controlling the market and taking fines for violation of regulations concerning bread, wine, beer, weights and measures—were transferred from the townsfolk to the university. Thenceforward there was practically no change until Elizabeth in 1589 granted the citizens a secure title to Sturbridge Fair, over which they had exercised practical rights of ownership for 300 years. This last is a very interesting case, as showing how often towns earned their liberties by gradual and natural encroachment. Here again I may quote textually from Maitland. This of Sturbridge was "'by far the largest and most famous fair in all England', which was held in the fields of Cambridge. Seemingly their title was of this sort: A fair had been granted by John to the Lepers' Hospital, which stood in the remotest corner of the territory of Cambridge, where its chapel may be seen to this day. But that hospital had been founded and endowed by the community of the town; and the community claimed to be its patron. Then we may suppose that, as leprosy became much rarer than it had been in the twelfth century, and the hospital was not required, the burgesses began to regard themselves as entitled to the profits of the fair. From Elizabeth they obtained the statement that the fair had been theirs from time immemorial and a grant which would set the question at rest for all time to come."

At this stage we may profitably change our point of view. Hitherto we have regarded urban development almost exclusively from the side of the citizens. We see in these towns the force of the future, the small seed destined to grow and grow until the townsman has become the strongest political power in the State; a little collective nucleus struggling to its own proper development against feudal disorder and individualism, against ecclesiastical conservatism and against royal despotism. There is, however, another side to this. Though much of this town development was unselfish, an instinctive expression of man's social impulses, yet much also betrays man's anti-social impulses; the instinct of rivalry and exclusiveness, and therefore of pugnacity, which we all inherit side by side with our higher social qualities. Cambridge had been born, we may say, in monopoly, in the invidious possibilities forbidding men to trade at any landing place but this. That Cambridge right of reprisals, again, was an anti-social manifestation; and here, finally, we see Cambridge gain one of its most profitable rights by downright encroachment upon the Lepers' Hospital. Moreover, the Merchant Gild, here as in all other towns, like the Craft Gilds which followed by later development, though for their own members they were highly social and beneficent institutions, were often anything but socially inclined towards outsiders.

The Gild is a prehistoric institution; one might even say prehuman, for we see it among all more or less sociable animals.

Sheep in a thunderstorm instinctively congregate together under the same tree. Bird-watchers know very well how often rooks or swallows may be seen banded together to drive a hawk out of their purlieus. But, side by side with this natural instinct for protection through unity, the medieval Gild was moulded also by outside forces. The first movement may well have come from pure inward impulse, but certainly that impulse was controlled by lordship from without. True, it was to the citizens' interest to form a trade union; but it was also to the lord's interest that they should do so, and thus give him a definite body to bargain with; security in collective bargaining is one of the main factors of civilization, as we see around us every day of our lives. Therefore, side by side with the citizens' "We will combine" worked the lord's "You shall combine; for otherwise I don't know how to deal securely with you."

In the fourteenth century there were three distinct types of Gild. First the social-religious, answering to the modern benefit societies. The members paid certain fees; they worshipped together at a certain church, or a certain altar of that church. The officers were elected yearly, and the audit of accounts was accompanied by ale-drinking. In such Gilds the money was spent partly on Masses and wax tapers for the services; partly on help for the sick and poor of the Gild; again, for the ale at the yearly audit; and, lastly, sometimes they had sufficient balance to help churches or bridges or the building of town walls. The rules demanded good behaviour—for instance, no member might turn up barelegged at the meeting—and obedience to the officers. Breach of the rules was punished by fines, or sometimes even with the rod. They were naturally concerned also with the reconciliation of members who might be at variance. For instance: "Hugh of the Solar having struck Roger Alditch in the market of Boston, and the latter having struck the former, both were fined a barrel of beer by the Community of the [Merchant] Gild [of Leicester]."

The next, and perhaps historically earliest, form was the Gild Merchant, for the mutual protection of members, and for the regulation of trade. Such Gilds always rested on a monopoly; no "foreigner" might buy or sell wholesale except from or to its members. At Derby, for instance, a jury convened by royal commission in 1330 reports: "by reason of this Gild the custom has prevailed among them that, if anyone bring neats' leather,

wool, or wool-fells into the said town to sell, and one of the said
Gilds places his foot upon the thing brought, and sets a price
for which he would like to buy it, no one but a member of the
said society will dare buy it, nor will he to whom it belongs dare
sell it to anyone save a member of the said society, nor for a higher
price than that which the member of the said society offers.
And they [the jurors] say that the profit arising therefrom does
not accrue to the advantage of the community of the borough,
but only to the advantage of those who are of the said society."
The corollary of this was, that only Gildsmen had shops: the
rest could sell or buy only in the market; and outsiders paid
heavy tolls when they brought goods to market. But within its
own limitations the Gild system aimed at absolute fairness. It
ruled that everything should go to market, and be offered to all
buyers, until the ringing of a bell closed business for the day.
Only then might the remainder be bought up for retail trade;
and, even at that point, none but "honest profit" was to be made.
At Würzburg (and by a similar London regulation) when a boat
brought a cargo of coal, this could be sold in retail only during
the first 8 days, each family being entitled to no more than 50
basketfuls. The remaining cargo might be sold wholesale, but
the retailer was allowed to raise a "decent" profit only, the
"indecent" or dishonest profit being strictly forbidden. Hence
the guilt of "forestalling" and of "regrating" (otherwise "en-
grossing"). To forestall was to buy the goods up before they
had been offered in open market. To regrate or engross was to
buy wholesale in order to create a "corner" and gain retail profits.
Thus, we have such regulations as the Statute of Kilkenny made
for all Irish ports (1367). "It ordered that the mayor, sovereign,
or other chief officer of the town should call before him two of
the most discreet men of the place, as well as the merchant to
whom the said wares belonged, and the sailors of his ship. The
merchant and the sailors were to state, on oath, the first cost of
the goods, and the expenses of transportation. Then the mayor
or chief officer of the town, and the two discreet men, were to
name a price at which the wares must be sold." The next natural
step was towards municipal trading, the so-called "common town
bargains". These were cargoes purchased by certain civic officials
in the name of the town, and then distributed in shares among
the merchant burgesses, no one being allowed to buy wares landed

in the port, unless the municipal authorities refused to purchase them. This seems to have been quite a common practice in England, Ireland, Wales and Scotland. That was an obvious way of meeting oppressive trusts: it may be compared with the present-day proposal to nationalize coal, banks, and all key industries. There is much to be learned from the medieval gild by social students who can avoid the extremes of indiscriminate admiration and indiscriminate blame.

Thirdly come the Craft Gilds, which began to grow up in the thirteenth century, often having the same members as the Gild Merchant. In their way they had also the same objects, to maintain trade interests and to keep up the standard of work. They only differed, first in that they admitted only the special trades—the tailors, saddlers, etc., each forming one gild—and, secondly, that they were therefore to a certain extent more democratic, although this quality has often been exaggerated. We often find them including all the members of the Gild Merchant, and thus in time superseding it. Then, after this decentralization, there often came a process of centralized action, and the heads of the respective Craft Gilds became the Common Council of the town.

The advantages of these Gilds were obvious. First, they protected trade in a rude society; secondly, they settled the qualities of workmanship; and, thirdly, they had great social qualities. But at the best of times they did not work without considerable friction. That report from the Derby jury to the commission of 1330 complains that the usages of the Gild Merchant "redound to the injury, oppression and pauperization of the people". Moreover, at later times, when the system had become conservative, it caused unspeakable stagnation, especially in its absolute forms in France before the Revolution. And, finally, though its principle was based on sociability, that was a sociability strictly limited; the Gildman loved his friend, but fought his enemy. A Derby charter of 1204, ratified in 1330, provided *inter alia* "that no one should dye cloth within ten leagues of Derby, except in Derby and in the liberty of the Borough of Nottingham". When, about 1550, Bishop Voysey of Exeter tried to transplant the manufacture of kerseys from thence to his own native town of Sutton Coldfield, Bishop Godwin denounced this as a "horrible sacrilege", which God could not bless.

Thus the study of English town life, like that of early Roman history, shows the people learning self-government through a series of petty quarrels. It was a great advance to have a system of representation, yet that was rudimentary; offices were often forced upon unwilling recipients. Even membership of Parliament was frequently avoided wherever possible. Hence, though medieval town life was a step forward in freedom, in England it never got beyond the oligarchic stage; and on the Continent, whenever it became truly democratic, as for a short time in North Italy and the Low Countries, there was a rapid "fascist" reaction. The town burgesses in England always formed an oligarchy. As Maitland puts it, *liberty* and *franchise* in the Middle Ages meant too often liberty to oppress someone else. Lord Acton, again, draws this distinction between medieval liberty and modern, that the former depends upon property. Thus, even at the end of our period, we must beware of supposing that the town is as definite and vertebrate, so to speak, as a modern borough. Maitland puts this clearly in his account of the Sturbridge incident: "The Fair was their [the townsmen's] Fair, and they (each for himself) meant to make profit thereout. The Town in its modern sense—the Town which has rights and duties, the Town which owes and is owed money, the Town which can make a contract even with one of the townsmen, the Town which can be landlord or tenant, the Town with which the treasurer can keep an account, slowly struggles into life."

Such is the growth of a fairly ordinary country town, exceptional only in the slowly growing reputation and power of its university. Let us pass on now to consider London, incontestably the capital already in those days, yet with scarcely more inhabitants, even at the end of our period, than modern Cambridge has. How did the city of Chaucer and Gower and *Piers Plowman* differ from other great cities of that time or of our own age?

London was one of the few English towns in which there was a really considerable foreign element. England as a rule was insular: London could be called cosmopolitan; not, it is true, in the sense that Venice and Bruges and Florence were, but still enough to give a great stimulus to English life. Especially conspicuous here were the merchant vintners of Gascony, from whom Chaucer sprang. The London records are full of foreign names until the middle of the fourteenth century; but when we put our own metropolis side by side with that of many cities on the

Continent it shrinks in comparison. Certainly its population was far inferior to that of the greatest, such as Milan or Bruges or Paris. Again, we were far behind some of those other cities in the organization of trade. At Zwin, for instance, the port of Bruges, there was a regular packet service to Genoa and back as early as the fourteenth century. London never had anything of the kind. In buildings, again, with the exception of the Tower and St Paul's Cathedral, and Holy Trinity Priory, and Westminster Abbey and Palace, it could scarcely compare with any great Continental city: certainly not with the semi-oriental splendour of Venice, or with a royal palace like the Ste-Chapelle, or with Cloth Halls such as those of Ypres and Bruges. Its few stone houses were not comparable to those of the Cologne merchants which still survive; nor again had it that republican spirit which distinguished some of its Continental rivals: cities which could make war upon kings themselves. Even in its width of seafaring life London was only in the second rank. Chaucer's model Shipman knew only the coasts from Gothland (Jutland) to Finisterre. We did generally command the narrow seas, but Henry VII was the first who gave real breadth to our maritime energies.

In pre-Conquest days a man who had been thrice oversea in his own ship acquired thereby the status of a thane. Our merchants, therefore, could not compare with the greatest of the Baltic ports or Genoa or Venice: Marco Polo, the Venetian traveller, was only one representative of a very large class. The Florentine merchants published guides for their agents which have handed down for us to the present day the rate of exchange in London, together with lists of monasteries where wool was to be had. Again, when we turn from trade to the mind, we must confess that London was not a very intellectual capital. When Fitzstephen wrote [1190] there were only three regular schools— St Paul's, St Martin's le Grand, and St Mary's le Bow—though occasionally the Church allowed other masters to teach when they were distinguished enough. In 1446 this was found insufficient, and two new schools were authorized, at St Dunstan's in the East and St Anthony's Hospital. Yet at the same time strict measures were taken against unauthorized teachers. Evidently the demand far exceeded the supply. Next year four London rectors of other churches petitioned Henry VI for leave to set up schools in their parishes. Permission was granted, and one set up a school; of the others no trace can be found. It is probable that they were nipped in the bud by monopolists. There was no London University until just a hundred years ago. Even Oxford, which was among the most distinguished in Europe, invented nothing really comparable to that book market, minutely regularized, which had grown up at Bologna and Paris, and which Oxford imitated in their wake. Again, in a city like Florence the literary and artistic activity permeated the whole population: wealthy young citizens and nobles vied with each other in poetry and song. Cologne and Mainz and Bruges, the earliest homes of printing, with Ghent, the great weaving centre, far surpassed us in mechanical activity. Except for the distinction of our chroniclers, some of whom were among the greatest—and Matthew Paris may probably be counted greatest of all in Europe—book-learning was low among us compared with Italy and France. When Boccaccio comes to mention us in his Latin poem, he writes: "Hispanus et Gallus studiis tardusque Britannus." Certainly those private letters which have survived in English, written by nobles and squires and merchants and clergy, contrast most unfavourably with French and Italian and German contemporaries, not only in literary style but in uniformity of grammar and spelling. Medieval London, like modern, was greater as a practical than as an intellectual school.

Moreover, it needs to be repeated that the immediate political influence of our cities, even including the metropolis, was not comparable to that of some on the Continent. The Lombard cities and those of the Low Countries were at times almost independent states, showing all the bitter nationalism and internecine wars against each other which are sometimes imagined to be peculiar to post-Reformation society; war, moreover, not only with each other, but sometimes with emperor, king or pope. Ghent, when blockaded by her own count in alliance with the King of France, was strong enough to take the city gates defiantly off their hinges for two years: let those come in who dared! Paris University, again—not merely the city but this mere trade union of masters—became in the later Middle Ages one of the Great Powers of Europe in politics. She was the mainspring of that Conciliar Movement of the fifteenth century which for a short time introduced a sort of Whig constitutionalism into the despotic papal State. Yet though London on all these points was manifestly inferior to the greatest of the Continental cities, the very inferiority of our towns was in one respect a political advantage. Our cities were not abnormally developed to the detriment of central authority. They grew only by slow evolution, under efficient discipline from the royal executive. Thus, while in detail they worked out their own liberties surely and solidly, so also by expansion they worked to promote the national liberties. A tyrant could not neutralize the English towns by appealing to their jealousies and their ingrained hatred of each other; London did not hate Bristol or Norwich or York as Florence hated Pisa. The English towns were just moderate-sized areas of local government, and therefore moderate schools of political capacity. Their general interest was in favour of good government for the whole country; while at home, within their own walls, the citizens learned daily the habits of self-control, of give-and-take, which make good government possible. Thus, in England, where the cities were governed with the least bloodshed, least quarrels and fewest revolutions, they played politically the least brilliant part. Yet they played perhaps a more solid and enduring part than even in Italy. Wherever a great cause was to be fought for, the towns in general were on the side that had the future before it: under Henry III they backed De Montfort; in the Wars of the Roses they backed the Yorkist party. For any cause of good government their support was perhaps all the more effective in the aggregate, because their individual pretensions were so much smaller than those of the Italian cities. And these qualities they brought into the councils of the nation, all the more certainly because the whole movement was so gradual and so impersonal. Freeman justly remarks that, if the town of Exeter had had a brilliant political history, then the political history of the English nation would have been less brilliant than it has been.

Here, however, some exception must be made for London. Its political importance came out perhaps more conspicuously in revulsion from Richard II's attack on it. At first, we see the king making and unmaking mayors as he chooses, supporting one city faction against another; then comes the reaction, and we see the Merciless Parliament beheading Nicholas Brembre, Richard's appointed mayor, for illegalities committed during his office. Even the monk Walsingham, who had no sympathy with the Londoners bears testimony to their formidable character. He writes: "They were of all people almost the most proud, arrogant, and greedy, disbelieving in God, disbelieving in ancient customs": and he goes on to say how, to break their spirit, Richard II had to get together a considerable army of professional soldiers. Froissart, again, who knew the great cities of the Low Countries very well, wrote: "Where the men of London are at accord and fully agreed, no man dares gainsay them. They are of more weight than all the rest of England; nor dares any man drive them to bay; for they are most mighty in wealth and in men."

The effect of this was that no king prospered in English history who had made enemies of the Londoners. Richard II's fall may be said to have begun with that quarrel; and from quite early days the Londoners had claimed to speak for the whole kingdom. For instance, in Magna Carta London is the only town mentioned or provided for. The citizens there claim from the king certain liberties, just as the barons do. They are a sort of Fourth Estate, as the Trade Unions are in modern English politics; and, from much earlier times still, they had taken a very prominent part in royal elections. They had the boldness to choose Edmund Ironside when the Witan chose Cnut. There they had absolutely no constitutional right; London was simply a city like the rest; but they asserted their practical right. Later, again, they elected Stephen before the barons had met at Winchester to choose him; and J. R. Green brings out rightly the significance of this gesture: for we must remember that those were days before formally constituted parliaments, and before England was largely populated; so that this assembly which could be gathered in a few minutes at the western end of the London market-place, within the walls, would probably far exceed in number and intelligence, as well as in wealth and military power, any assembly likely to be gathered elsewhere in England at the time.

But, though London stood above the other cities of England almost as incontestably as in the present day, yet it was still in full touch with country life. The Middle Ages produced no revolted cockney like Keats, Blake, Turner and Ruskin; country and town joined each other naturally and harmoniously. Here, as at Cambridge and elsewhere, the citizen was often an agriculturalist. Chaucer, dwelling in the great tower of Aldgate, had literally only a step from his own door to the fields and the daisies.

Little as we may wish to go back into anything like the totality of medieval life, this will always stand in history as a reproach to many of our modern failures. There is a world of social significance in the fact that, when a rich modern suburban house invites a bevy of London slum girls to a day in its own meadow and paddock, the strangers imagine the daisies and buttercups to have been planted there. Medieval London, even at the full of its development, had that picturesqueness and freshness and simplicity, those relics of the self-sufficing theory of the village with all its necessities made and consumed on the spot, which Ruskin shows us in that magical description of old Abbeville in his *Praeterita* (ch. IX).

XXV. HOME LIFE

Hitherto, we have regarded the town mainly on its constitutional side. Let us now look at its daily life; and here again Cambridge will give us a fairly typical country borough before we come to London.

We must take care to enter before dark, or we shall find the Trumpington and the Barnwell Gates closed in our faces. Cambridge, it is true, never had town walls, but only a ditch and palisade which may still be traced in the lay-out of its streets, and which was crossed by two gated bridges. Here is an admirable example of the superior orderliness of English life, both civil and religious, as compared with any district of equal extent on the Continent of Europe. I have already suggested that this comparative order is due to the effective though slow fusion between Normans and Saxons, and to the fact that we have never been seriously invaded since those days. But, whatever the cause, the fortunate superiority is in itself unquestionable. In a letter received from the late Dom Ursmer Berlière not long before his death, he alluded casually to the greater orderliness of English Church life as a thing that needed no proof. In the civil domain it suffices to consider that Lynn was scarcely better defended than Cambridge, though it was perhaps the richest town in England per head of population in the Middle Ages, somewhat analogous to Frankfurt a/M. in modern Germany, or Hartford in America. Lynn was originally defended only by its great river on one side and a ditch with two gates on the other. It is true that, at the end of the thirteenth century, the citizens began building a wall, which within the next two generations grew to cover perhaps one-third of the circuit; but there the building stopped and was never resumed. On the other hand, in Rhineland, or on the Neckar and Main, elaborate fortifications still survive round villages which could scarcely, or never, have attained to urban rank even in medieval England; walls at least as high and strong as those of York and Chester. For in Germany, where feudalism remained a political force down to the Reformation and beyond, as Götz von Berlichingen's autobiography shows us, any mere "free knight" of the Empire needed only to send a letter

of defiance in order to justify his making war against another
noble or city; hence the elaborate defensive precautions which
were needed to protect the peaceful trader. With us, except during
the wars of Stephen's anarchy, nothing of the kind was needed,
not even during the Wars of the Roses.

We come in, then, by the Trumpington Gate, and may put
up at the signs of inns which still exist, The Black Bull, or The
Blue Boar, or The Red Lion. Two explanations have been given
for these inn signs, apart of course from the fact that there was no

Medieval Fortifications.

law, nor apparently even custom, to prevent a host from choosing
after his own fancy. In some cases the lord and his retinue would
frequent one inn rather than another, and his shield might be
seen hanging out at the door or on the balcony; or, again, the
lord might actually allow his steward during his absence to enter-
tain for payment at his town house. When we say "lord", it
must be remembered that each town had originally been as
definitely the property of some landlord, lay or ecclesiastical, as
the man's own park was; so that he retained rights and influence
over it, if only moral, even when it had come to so much fullness
of municipal liberty as towns ever did reach in the Middle Ages.

We go to our inn, then, and retire to bed soon after curfew,
unless we prefer to sit awhile drinking with others over the
embers of the fire in the hall. There is little temptation to go out
after dark; and indeed, on the other hand, there may be considerable danger. Eavesdroppers and night-walkers, men who
prowled on the chance of robbery or manslaughter, are constant
objects of medieval town legislation. At Oxford, for instance,

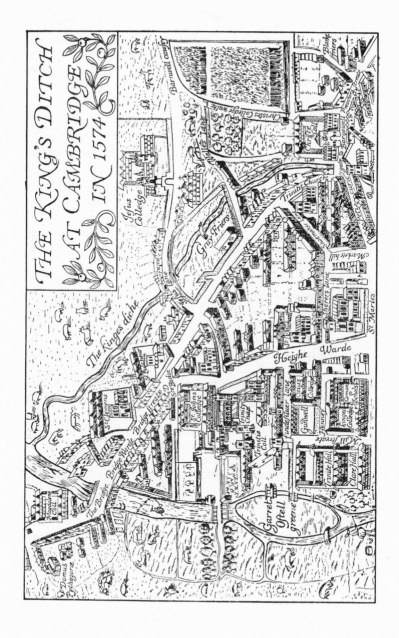

The King's Ditch at Cambridge in 1574

the penalty for habitual night-walking was twice that of shooting an arrow at the proctor with intent to wound him. If we are rich enough, we shall have brought our bedding with us on our sumpter-beasts; otherwise, we may commend ourselves to sleep as Gascoigne did, with pious reflections on our Last Rest:

The hungry fleas which friske so freshe, to wormes I can compare,
Which greedily shall gnaw my fleshe, and leave the bones ful bare.[1]

We shall wake up to a ringing of bells, bells of all kinds. This is the "Île Sonnante" of Rabelais. Of our thirteen parish churches at Cambridge three or four will doubtless have "morrow-Mass" at dawn, for travellers or early working folk. Then there is the service of prime at all the conventual establishments: Dominicans, Franciscans, Augustinians and Carmelites, with more distant bells from St Rhadegund's Nunnery, and more distant still over Mid-summer Common from Barnwell Priory; and possibly a morrow-Mass at Chesterton just beyond. John Major, the Scottish historian, who studied for a while at Cambridge, recalls in a memorable passage the sweet sound of her bells over the water; and the numerous London churches fostered bell-ringers who were proud of their art. Moreover, in great towns like Coventry there was also a special town bell for the opening of the market, or for early work: "the bell called *daybell*". In most cases, however, the church bell was a sufficient guide.

To market nearly everybody would go for a few minutes at least, as they do in the smaller towns of Italy to the present day. This was the main commercial focus of the town. Shops were neither large nor numerous. An enquiry of 1301 gives us an exact list from Colchester, a considerably larger town than Cambridge. There were 31 shoemakers, tanners, and leather-sellers, a fact which may remind us that Colchester is not far from the edge of the great Essex forest, part of which still survives round Epping. Smiths were 10, weavers 8, butchers 8, bakers 7, carpenters 5, mercers 13. The enquiry gives in each case an inventory of the contents of the mercers' shops. They were nearly always the same—gloves, belts, leather-purses, needle-cases and other small ware. One, however, a considerable capitalist, possessed a good deal of cloth and silk. Another had a stock of verdigris and quicksilver, articles which entered into very many medieval ointments or lotions.[2] In the early part of our period there would be nothing to distinguish a shop from an ordinary dwelling house, the goods being sold either in the street or in the dwelling room. Later shops, however, were of a type that still survives here and there, built of wood with shutters outside, which could be let down into the street so as to form a table for the exhibition of wares, and a little penthouse roof to shelter this table. By this time the whole lower storey was often occupied by the shop, the upper storey containing the hall and bower, or sometimes several bedrooms. At that stage of development the shop itself (as again in modern Italy) would often be let by the owner, whose family would occupy nothing but the upper storey, the "solar", as Chaucer calls it. Men of the same trade or craft commonly congregated together; we still see this at York in the Shambles, and nearly every town had its Mercers' Row. In London, the "cooks" (i.e. restaurant-keepers) were mostly on Thames-side; at Cambridge they gave their name to Petty Cury (i.e. "Little Cookery"). Most of the scenes that would interest us in the town would be commercial or quasi-commercial. This is so even with the churches. Wool might be found stacked in the nave of a church at Southampton, and we have seen how a Devon parson even brewed in the church. Again, at Cambridge as elsewhere, booths were often erected in the churchyards, and fairs might be held there. These entailed frequent quarrels, and both there and at Bury St Edmunds we find churchyards polluted by bloodshed. Gallows, the stocks, the pillory, the cucking-stool and the penal tumbril, which form conspicuous objects in streets or the market-place, are kept there as sanctions for the municipal and commercial laws. The gallows are mainly for theft, the others for breach of market rules, unfair trading or downright fraud. This may be illustrated by a few London scenes. A man is guilty of selling corrupt wine, and the City court decides "that the said John Penrose shall drink a draught of the same wine which he sold to the common people; and the remainder of such wine shall then be poured on the head of the same John; and that he shall forswear the calling of a vintner in the city of London for ever, unless he can obtain the favour of our Lord the King as to the same". Next year, John Russell, at Billingsgate, "exposed 37 pigeons for sale, putrid, rotten, stinking, and abominable to the human race, to the scandal, contempt and disgrace of all the City. And the said John Russell says that the same pigeons are good and proper for sale to mankind, and he offers to prove the same, etc. And hereupon, two pie-bakers, being sworn to inspect and examine whether the said pigeons are good and proper or not, say upon their oath that the said pigeons are not good or wholesome for mankind, but rather to the corruption of man. Therefore he is to have judgment of the pillory, and the said pigeons are to be burnt beneath the pillory, and the cause of his punishment is to be there proclaimed."[3]

At Cambridge, to take a few scenes almost at random, we find criminals running for sanctuary to the church, sometimes as the final goal of a wild hue and cry and a breathless chase down the street. Then, the burning of heretical books, and sometimes even of heretical persons; and in 1441 we might see duly exposed one quarter of the body of a priest who had been accused of necromantic attempts on the king's life. Very common presentments are those which testify to terrible disorder and filth in the streets—dung heaps are as ubiquitous here as at Bury St Edmunds, though a great advance was made in 1401 by the enactment that such heaps should be cleared every week. Again, trunks and stocks of trees lying about, signs projecting to the danger of men's heads as they walked, neglect to pave one's own part of the road; and, worst of all, "certain noxious open gutters made by the Masters of Michaelhouse and Gonville Hall, which ran from those colleges to the High Street, through which many masters and scholars had access to the schools of the University", gutters which "gave out an abominable stench, and so corrupted the air that many masters and scholars passing fell sick thereof"; quite apart, we may suppose, from their noxious effects on the actual inmates of Michaelhouse and Gonville Hall. This was a glaring case which brought down royal interference; and it is not insignificant that the first Urban Sanitary Act in English history, that of 1388, was passed by a parliament held at Cambridge, and preceded by active measures to make the town presentable for this august assembly. Swine ran about the streets and rooted amid its garbage: only in a few model cities like London was this forbidden: "he who will nourish a pig, let him nourish it in his own house"; swine that run wild in London may be slain. Fevers, consequently, were almost endemic; St John Fisher, in his sermon before Henry VII, described how they had decimated Cambridge University. Less than a generation after this, in 1524, Erasmus wrote that letter to Wolsey's physician, his friend, which is too briefly summarized in the *Letters and Papers of Henry VIII*. "I often wonder and grieve to think why Britain has now been afflicted so many years with chronic pestilence, especially the Sweating Sickness, a disease which seems almost peculiar to that land. We read that a city was once freed from long-standing pestilence by changing the buildings at the advice of a philosopher. Unless I am mistaken, England might be freed in the same way. First, they never consider towards which quarter of the heaven their windows or doors look. Next, their halls are almost always so constructed that no air can be carried through them, as Galen earnestly warns us. Again, a great part of their walls is transparent with panes of glass, which so admit light as to exclude wind, and yet through their crevices they admit that thin-drawn air, sometimes somewhat pestilent, which is long stagnant there. Again, almost all the floors are of clay and rushes from the marshes, so carelessly renewed that the foundation sometimes remains for twenty years, harbouring there below spittle and vomit and urine of dogs and men, beer that hath been cast forth and remnants of fishes and other filth unnamable. Hence, with the changes of weather, a vapour exhales which in my judgment is far from wholesome for the human body. Add that England is not only completely surrounded by sea, but is also marshy in some parts and intersected by salt rivers, to say nothing meanwhile of the salt fish* in which the multitude take wonderful pleasure. I feel certain that the island would be far more healthy if they gave up the use of rushes; again, if their bedrooms were to be built so as to be open to the air on two or three sides, with all glass windows so constructed as to be fully opened or fully shut, and so shut as not to admit the entrance of noxious draughts through the gaping crevices: for, even as it is sometimes wholesome to admit God's air, so it is sometimes wholesome to exclude it. The common herd scoffs at any one who is offended by the cloudy heavens. I myself, thirty years ago, if I had entered a bedroom which no man had occupied for some months, began immediately to suffer from fever.† It would help also if the multitude could be persuaded to a sparer diet and more moderate use of salt meat; and, again, if public opinion required of the officials that the streets should

---

* *Salsamentis*: see Erasmus's *Ichthyophagia, passim*.

  † I.e. rise of temperature: Martial uses this word *febricitare* of the common "cold".

be less defiled with filth and urine, and that the roads in the neighbourhood should be cared for. You will laugh, I know, at my idleness which allows me to trouble myself about such things. I feel favourably towards the land which gave me hospitality for so long time, and in which I would gladly end the rest of my life, if that be possible. I do not doubt that you, in your prudence, are better informed; yet I wished to advise that, if my judgment be consonant to your own, you should persuade the great folk of these things: for, in past time, Kings were wont to care for such."[4]

The very tone of this letter shows us that we listen here not to the mere satirist, gloating over his prey, but to the observant scholar and traveller, writing from painful experience. Wolsey's biographer describes his master's custom, when going to Westminster Hall, of "holding in his hand a very fair orange, whereof the meat or substance within was taken out, and filled up again with the part of a sponge, wherein was vinegar, and other confections against the pestilent airs; the which he most commonly smelt unto, passing among the press, or else when he was pestered with many suitors". His royal master, in 1526, ordained "for the better avoydyng of corruption and all uncleannesse out of the King's house, which doth ingender of infection, and is very noisome and displeasant unto all the noblemen and others repaireing unto the same" "that the three master cookes of the kitchen shall have everie of them by way of reward yearly twenty marks, to the intent they shall provide and sufficiently furnish the said kitchens of such scolyons as shall not goe naked or in garments of such vilenesse as they now doe, and have been accustomed to doe, nor lie in the nights and dayes in the kitchens or ground by the fireside; but that they of the said money may be found with honest and whole course garments, without such uncleannesse as may be the annoyance of those by whom they shall passe".[5] Almost equally significant is the ordinance for the royal barber: "This barbour shall have, every Satyrday at nyght, if it please the Kinge to cleanse his head, legges, or feet, and for his shaving, two loves, one picher wine. And the ussher of chambre ought to testyfye if this is necessaryly dispended or not."[6] It must also be borne in mind that, even at this date, the pocket-handkerchief was almost unknown, and the sneezing noble might shift as even the peasant is learning not to shift nowadays.

Erasmus, as we see by the apologetic tone of his letter to a physician, was before his age in the importance which he attributed to health of body. We find it natural that St Bernard should scout the fear of fever: "The holy fathers our ancestors sought for damp and narrow valleys in which to found their monasteries, in order that monks, being often ill and having death before their eyes, might not feel themselves to be in possession of any certain lease of life." But it is startling to find that his great opponent, the comparatively rationalistic Abailard, took much the same view; and it is a tribute to the sturdy common sense of Bishop Grosseteste that he dissented from them both, believing in the maxim *mens sana in corpore sano.*

This question, however, has brought us away from the country town, Cambridge, to a London which was then as definitely our capital as now, though with no more than about 50,000 inhabitants. It is true that the Venetian ambassador in Henry VII's reign gave, as a rough estimate, that London had about the same population as the Florence of that day, but this must be one of his many exaggerations, unless Florence was far less populous than we have every reason to believe. To see medieval London we must imagine a clear-flowing river; an undulating site; a ring of walls; and, at the very gates, gardens and fields and moors. The name of Moorgate tells its own tale. Northward rose the hills of Hampstead and Highgate, mostly clad in bare heath; on the south the wooded slopes of Sydenham and Norwood; and beyond all this a more thickly wooded country, especially in the direction of Epping and Harrow; Epping Forest was continuous almost as far as Bishop's Stortford. All this was almost visible from London streets; those streets which William Morris, judging merely as an artist, has celebrated as "London small and white and clean". Very clean, at least to the outward eye, was London then in comparison with the modern city. Medieval builders knew very well that one of the best preservatives of stone or timber is lime-wash. Therefore, not only were the houses whitewashed or painted, but often the greatest buildings. In Henry III's Account Rolls we find the expense of prolonging the gutters of the White Tower of London, in order that the rain might not drip down the walls and disfigure them. A London clean, then, yet in its way almost as busy-looking as at present. Narrow streets, open shops with projecting walls and penthouses, and hanging signs, and noises as multitudinous to the ear as those picturesque irregularities to the eye—the sawing and scraping of the carpenter, the tick-tack of the weaver's shuttle, the tap of the coppersmith, and the blacksmith's ringing anvil. There will be much singing of folk at work. Chaucer's younger contemporary, Hoccleve, complains of the ordinary artisan's freedom in this respect, in comparison with his own sedentary and silent labour as a scribe in the royal office of the Privy Seal at Westminster. Above all, in the busiest parts, such as the market of Cheapside, we should hear the stentorian, brazen voices of masters, mistresses or apprentices inviting us to buy their wares. We see this plainly in *Piers Plowman*:

> Cooks to their knaves cried "Hot pies, hot!
> Good griskin and geese—go dine, go!"   [pork
> Taverners unto them told the same tale—
> White wine of Oseye, and red wine of Gascoyne,
> Of the Rhine, and of Rochelle, the roast meat to digest.

And if we look into one of these taverns, especially one of the side-street taverns for the poor, there we have Langland's unforgettable picture of the miscellaneous company—mostly handi-workers and women of the lowest classes, but with an unclerical priest among them, and a hermit—sitting and soaking their ale in an atmosphere that you could cut with a knife. That was one side of medieval London—the side that the author of *Piers Plowman* knew, perhaps, best, but which was not unknown to Chaucer also.

In the streets, we should see many picturesque Gild liveries, such as Chaucer mentions in his Prologue; and, even apart from these, we should be interested in the trade uniforms, one of which (the butcher's slop) still survives among us. Then, again, the liveries worn by barons' or knights' retainers, and the costume of the clergy, would add a note of colour. In the Middle Ages there were only two definite requirements for clerical costume. In the first place the outer garment must be long—almost to the ankles—and buttoned or fastened the whole way down: in other words, here was the ancestor of the modern cassock. The colour, however, was at the wearer's choice, except that the three most expensive and fashionable were forbidden—red, green and striped or parti-coloured.

The town meetings were mainly held in the open air. In one London record we have a very vivid picture of the folkmoot at St Paul's Cross, with its voting by cries of "ya, ya" or "nay, nay, nay".[7] Here, again, is another scene from 1388. "William Wottone, Alderman...went to the Shambles of St Nicholas in London, and seeing divers pieces of meat lying for sale at the shambles there of Richard Bole, butcher, asked the said Richard at what price he sold the same; to which he made answer, that four shillings was the price. Whereupon, the Alderman said that the meat was too dear; to which the said Richard made reply;— 'I do verily believe that the meat is too dear for thee; who, I suppose, never bought as much meat as that for thine own use.' And thereupon, the said Richard immediately observing that William aforesaid was wearing a hood of the Aldermen's pattern, and so knowing thereby that he was an Alderman, he further said to him,—'Art thou an Alderman?' to which the other answered— 'Yea; why askest thou?' whereupon he said,—'It is a good thing for thee and thy fellows, the Aldermen, to be so wise and wary, who make but light of riding on the pavement, as some among ye have been doing.' For which words so uttered,...after due consideration had upon the matter, because that the same words were expressly uttered in disparagement of our Lord the King, as well as to the scandal and dishonour of the said Mayor, Sheriffs, and Aldermen, and all other the officers of the city aforesaid, it was adjudged that the said Richard should be imprisoned in Neugate for the next half year; and that, on his leaving prison, with his head uncovered, and bare legs and feet, he should carry in his hand a wax torch, weighing one pound, and lighted, from Neugate through the Shambles aforesaid, and so straight through Chepe as far as St Laurence Lane, and through that lane to the Chapel of the Guildhall, and there make offering of the same; unless he should meet with increased favour in the meantime. Afterwards however, on the same day, as well at the instance of the Archbishop of Armagh, Primate of Ireland, who entreated the Mayor and Aldermen in behalf of the same Richard, as at the entreaty of the reputable men of the said trade of butchers, the imprisonment for half a year was remitted unto him; on the understanding that on the same day he was to be taken back to Neugate aforesaid, etc., and there make offering of the same; which done, he was to be released."[8]

Then, as now, political life was not always a clean job. Men
not infrequently needed compulsion to sit in parliament; and it
was common to prescribe pecuniary sanctions for refusal of civic
office. In the fifteenth-century poem *How the Wise Man taught
his Son*, the father says:

> And sonne, also I warne thee,
> Desire noon office for to beere,
> For than it wole noon other fee,
> Thou muste thi neighboris displese and dere,
> Or ellis thou muste thi silf forswere,
> And do not as thin office wolde.[9]

If we look into one of the better houses, we shall find the type
which still survives at Alfriston Vicarage and in a few others of
fourteenth-century date. In nearly every case it is the carpenter
who builds it; stone is too expensive for anyone but aristocrats
or great ecclesiastics or Jews; sometimes a house in a small town
is described as "The Stone House". Even brick is unusual until
quite the end of our period. Miss Abram quotes a typical example.
"In 1483, a man at Gloucester agreed to build a house forty-seven
feet by fifteen, and eighteen feet high, of 'standard werke', and
'all the timber of oak', for £14." Hence frequent fires. In London
a city regulation insisted on stone party-walls between house and
house, in order to limit these; and in towns each parish had great
poles with hooks for pulling down the blazing house before it
could kindle its neighbours; such a hook survives in St Benet's
Church in Cambridge.

The furniture we shall find to be very scanty. Here is an inventory
of one of the wealthiest at Colchester, at the end of the thirteenth
century. The citizen had a trestle-table; this was the ordinary
arrangement, so that the boards could be put away in a corner
except at meal-times; it was a distinctive note of Chaucer's
Franklin's great hospitality that he had a "table dormant" in his
hall. Nothing in the way of chairs; some sort of settles or stools
was doubtless taken for granted, and not inventoried. Two silver
spoons, a cup, a table-cloth and two towels, a brass cauldron,
a brass dish, washing-basin and ewer, trivet, and iron candlestick,
two beds, two gowns, a mantle, one piece of russet cloth (for
making up into clothes some day); three pounds of wool, two
barrels. So much for the household furniture.[10] The man was
a butcher, and thus he possessed pickling tubs, meat, fat, corn,

hay, and a cart. The purely household furniture is priced at £2. 5s. 5d., his stock-in-trade at nearly £3. This we must multiply by 40 or a little more. If this seems almost incredibly meagre, we must remember that the inventory was for taxation purposes, and no doubt all was not confessed, while that which was confessed was considerably underestimated. The general impression of scantiness, however, is entirely borne out by contemporary wills and inventories, which survive in considerable numbers.* The richer folk had hangings for their rooms, which might run to considerable expense, and feather-beds with valuable quilts. Even kings and popes had no easy chairs, but would often sit on their beds to receive ambassadors. Still, when all has been reckoned, these things were not only primitive according to our modern ideas, but comfortless and insanitary. The fork was not yet invented for meals; handkerchiefs were almost unknown; folk ordinarily slept either naked or in their day-clothes, and the rushes on the hall floor were changed quarterly or yearly. Even in highly civilized Florence, and at the middle of the fourteenth century, when the artist Cennino Cennini gives a recipe for particularly fine plaster to be made from calcined chicken-bones, he advises us to seek the oldest and driest chicken-bones we can find lying about the floor.[11] Add to this that dogs and animals were freely admitted, and that the servants would often sleep in the hall unencumbered by any table dormant.

As Cutts points out, many of the Colchester citizens had only one living room which served all purposes. Fever was as great an enemy as fire. One of the things, however, which would pinch us most immediately would be the cold; in rooms with ill-fitting doors and windows, which in the majority of cases were unglazed, so that there was no alternative between darkness and open air. The fire burned commonly in a brazier in the middle of the hall, the smoke escaping as best it could through the roof; but here again, in a great town like London, there was provision for stone chimneys. In Montaigne's *Voyages*, when he goes to Switzerland, he notes with a special emphasis how the rooms are so well warmed with porcelain stoves that one actually takes off one's hat and one's furs when sitting indoors![12] In mid-sixteenth-century France, as in England, warm clothes were needed even

* See, for instance, wills of wealthy clergy in E. L. Cutts's *Parish Priests and People*, pp. 174 ff.

more indoors than in walking abroad. Molière's plays and Thomas Ellwood's autobiography show how regular it was to wear one's hat indoors, even in the seventeenth century. To quote again from Miss Abram (fifteenth century, p. 178): "In some towns windows, doors, lattices and locks were regarded as tenants' fixtures." "Carpets are seldom mentioned in wills and inventories until the close of the fifteenth century. Henry VII had one in his bedchamber, but some of his rooms were strewn with rushes, or straw" (p. 182). "It is probable that, as civilization advanced, reception-rooms were used more frequently, and bedrooms less frequently, for the purposes of hospitality. Nevertheless, we have come across two cases of men of good social standing (a canon of Wells, 1492, and a Sergeant at Law, 1500) who had beds in their parlours....In one of Hoccleve's poems, *Jereslaus's Wife*, an earl and countess, their daughter and her governess, all slept in the same room" (p. 175). Again (p. 185): "A point which has struck us very forcibly in reading descriptions of medieval houses, and at which we have already hinted, is the small number of bedrooms possessed even by people who were not too poor to pay a fairly high rent."

Artificial light, again, was extremely expensive. In its cheapest form it was a dim cresset of oil or a rushlight of mutton-fat; and, winter fodder being so rare, the result was that a pound of fat cost four times as much as a pound of lean meat. There was thus a great temptation to sit up by the embers of the fire and drink into the night. Fitzherbert attacks this from the business point of view. "One thinge I wyl advise the to remembre, and specially in wynter-tyme, whan thou sytteste by the fyre, and hast supped, to consyder in thy mynde, whether the warkes, that thou, thy wyfe, and they servantes shall do, be more avauntage to the than the fyre, and candell-lyghte, meate and drynke that they shall spende, and if it be more avantage, than syt styll: and if it be not, than go to thy bedde and slepe, and be uppe betyme, and breake thy faste before day, that thou mayste be all the shorte wynters day about thy busynes."[13]

Thus, to the very end, there were glaring contrasts between the cloths of gold and brocade of the greatest folk, the elaborate art lavished on all their buildings, their furniture and even the commonest domestic articles, their extraordinarily ceremonious manners (duly noted by the Venetian envoy in Henry VII's reign), and those other things in the background which strike us as strangely uncultivated, even when we have made fullest allowance for the true gentility which may underlie a rough exterior. The meals, again, showed the same contrasts. Here, for instance, is an extract from the famous *Northumberland Household Book*, regulating the castles of perhaps the greatest baron in England at the beginning of the sixteenth century:[14]

"Braikfastis for my lorde and my lady. Furst a Loof of Brede in Trenchors* ij Manchetts [small loaves] j Quart of Bere a Quart of Wyne half a Chyne of Muton or ells a Chyne of Beif Boilid.

"Braikfastis for my Lorde Percy [aged 10] and Mr Thomas Percy. Item Half a Loif of household Breide. A Manchett j Potell [4 pints] of Bere a Chekynge or ellse iij Mutton Bonys boyled.

"Braikfastis for the Nurcy for my Lady Margaret and Mr Yngram Percy. Item a Manchet j Quarte of Bere and iij Muton Bonys boiled.

"Braikfasts for my Ladys Gentylwomen. Item a loif of Household Breid a Pottell of Beire and iiij Muton Bonys boyled or ells a Pece of Beif Boilid.

"Braikfasts for my Lords Breder his Hede Officers of Household and Counsaill. Item ij. Loofs of Houshold Briede a Manchet a Gallon of Bere ij Muton Bonys and ij Peces of Beif Boilid."

The Percy meals were the same in Lent, except that (1) it was only the children who then breakfasted daily; the rest, only four times a week; (2) fish was substituted for flesh; e.g. the nurse and the babies had a piece of salt fish, a dish of sprats, or three white herring. This was extremely cheap—the nurse's and children's breakfasts together cost only about 1s. 6d. of modern money. If the amount of beer seems startling, we must remember in the first place that our ancestors were under no temptation to drink water. It was only in a few towns of the later Middle Ages, and then almost entirely through the monasteries or friaries, that aqueducts were brought in. Again, practically no hot drinks were known, except alcoholic or medicinal. Thus ale and beer not only supplied very considerable calories from the strictly

* Trenchers were slices of bread which our ancestors used as plates, eating their meal upon them and leaving them as remnants for the poor or for their dogs.

dietetic point of view, but comforted the stomach after the fashion of modern tea and coffee. The monastic allowance, where we find it specified, is seldom less than a gallon of ale a day. A priceless record from Coventry in 1520, which gives both the population of the city and its consumption of malt and wheat, points to a consumption of a quart of ale per diem per soul, man, woman and child. Thus, the men's average would run at least to two quarts. Side by side with this rough Gargantuan plenty we find at exceptional times the greatest extravagances, especially in so-called "subtleties", many specimens of which, at the Bishop of Ely's installation feast in 1478, I have printed in *Life in the Middle Ages* (III, 150). The records of the Percies and the Pastons show how it was quite common for young married couples to live, often for many years, in the house of one of the parents. A Chancery petition of about 1475 shows an action brought by Thomas Alexander, Gentleman, against the executors of John Jeny "for breach of agreement to provide complainant with meat, drink, and lodging if he married Agnes, daughter of the said deceased [John Jeny]".[15] Marriages were generally, in the main, business contracts, the French *mariage de convenance*; which, however, as P. G. Hamerton shows us from his experience in modern France, results very often in a healthy and pleasant *camaraderie* between husband and wife. The Church law of prohibited degrees, though less inconvenient in town than in village, where perhaps half the population stood in prohibited kinship to each other, did nevertheless bring a good deal of uncertainty into married life. Miss Abram points out how "on one occasion, in May 1357, no less than fifty men and as many women received dispensations to remain in marriages so contracted, because they had acted in ignorance. It was apparently not very difficult to obtain dispensations: in 1413 the Pope granted his nuncio a faculty to permit any men or women related in the third degree only, or in the third and fourth, or in the fourth and fifth, to marry; and to allow a hundred persons so related to remain in marriages already contracted, and to declare their children legitimate."[16] In the matter of wardship, by which the marriage of wealthy young heirs was often sold, townsfolk had a great advantage on the feudal nobility. In many towns, unless the parents had appointed definite guardians by will, the mayor and aldermen took charge of boys and girls during their minority, and were allowed a good percentage of the profits received from the estate which they administered, but rendered business accounts when the time of majority came. One case recorded in Riley's *Memorials of London* shows that a ward, left with £300, found himself, after 13 years' minority, possessed of £580. 1s. 4d., even after all expenses of food and maintenance had been paid, through the good management of his guardian, who had traded with the money at an interest of 4s. in the pound, half of which he had kept for himself. "Some boroughs also provided legal aid for widows and orphans: at Hereford, the bailiff and steward were ordered to help them at all times, both in court and out of it, if any wrong or injustice were done to them."[17]

After all these prosaic details, necessary enough in themselves, we cannot leave medieval London without recalling two poetic testimonies. The Scottish poet Dunbar, writing at a time of bitter warfare between the two countries, was such a true Chaucerian that he could not but admire Chaucer's city.

> Above all rivers, thy river hath renown;
>   Whose beryl streamës, pleasant and preclare,
> Under thy lusty wallës runneth down;
>   Where many a swan doth swim with wingës fair!
>   Where many a barge doth sail and row with oar!
>   Where many a ship doth rest with top-royal!
>   O town of towns, pattern and not compare!
>   London! Thou art the flower of cities all!
>
> Upon thy lusty Bridge of pillars white
>   Beën merchants full royal to behold!
> Upon thy streets goeth many a seemly knight,
>   In velvet gownës and in chains of gold!
>   By *Julius Caesar*, thy Tower founded of old,
>   May be the House of *Mars* victorial;
>   Whose artillery with tongue may not be told!
>   London! Thou art the flower of cities all!
>
> Strong be thy wallë that about thee stands!
>   Wise be the people that within thee dwells!
> Fresh is thy river, with his lusty strands!
>   Blithe be thy kirks, well-sounding be thy bells!
>   Rich be thy merchants, in substance that excels!
>   Fair be their wives, right lovesome, white and small!
>   Clear be thy virgins lusty under kells!   [caps
>   London! Thou art the flower of cities all!

Side by side with this, we have William Morris's picture, where he bids us dream of

> London, small and white and clean,
> The clear Thames bordered by its gardens green;
> Think that, below bridge, the green lapping waves
> Smite some few keels that bear Levantine staves
> Cut from the yew wood on the burnt-up hill,
> And pointed jars that Greek hands toiled to fill,
> And treasured scanty spice from some far sea,
> Florence gold cloth, and Ypres napery,
> And cloth of Bruges, and hogsheads of Guienne,
> While nigh the thronged wharf Geoffrey Chaucer's pen
> Moves over bills of lading....

XXVI. TRADE AND TRAVEL

ENGLAND during nearly all our period was quite in the second class as a trading country. The fullest trade in Europe was carried on by the cities of North Italy, the Rhineland and the Baltic and the Low Countries. So far as England is concerned, the early beginnings of travel and trade are best illustrated by the lives of Saewulf and St Godric of Finchale. Both of these sea-adventurers plunged finally into the great spiritual adventure of their time, the strict monastic life.

Saewulf was a merchant who chose for his confessor the saintly Bishop of Worcester, Wulfstan. The bishop tried to "convert" him; Saewulf shrank from taking the vow, but Wulfstan prophesied that he would do so before he died. Six years after Wulfstan's death, Saewulf undertook a penitent pilgrimage to Jerusalem, deliberately choosing the most adventurous route, as one "conscious of his own unworthiness". He was wrecked near Bari; when he started again, it took him thirteen weeks to reach Jaffa. Here he landed at once; next day a hurricane destroyed, before his eyes, 23 of the 30 great ships in the harbour. He saw and worshipped at all the holy places; then, through many dangers from Mohammedan fleets and pirates, he reached Constantinople safely after a voyage of four months from Jaffa. Some years later we find him a monk at Malmesbury.

At Finchale, near Durham, there died in 1170 a hermit named Godric, who had lived very many years, perhaps as many as forty, in fasting, cold, and prayer. One of the Durham monks took every opportunity of haunting his company, and jotted down many of his words and many particulars of his life on the evenings (as he assures us) of the very days on which he had heard them.[1] He writes: "This holy man's father was named Ailward, and his mother Edwenna; both of slender rank and wealth, but abundant in righteousness and virtue. They were born in Norfolk, and had long lived in the township called Walpole.... When the boy had passed his childish years quietly at home, then, as he began to grow to manhood, he began to follow more prudent ways of life, and to learn carefully and persistently the teachings of worldly forethought. Wherefore he chose not to follow the life of a husbandman, but rather to study, learn, and exercise the rudiments of more subtle conceptions. For this reason, aspiring to the merchant's trade, he began to follow the chapman's way of life, first learning how to gain in small bargains and things of insignificant price; and thence, while yet a youth, his mind advanced little by little to buy and sell and gain from things of greater expense. For, in his beginnings, he was wont to wander with small wares around the villages and farmsteads of his own neighbourhood; but, in process of time, he gradually associated himself by compact with city merchants. Hence, within a brief space of time, the youth who had trudged for many weary hours from village to village, from farm to farm, did so profit by his increase of age and wisdom as to travel with associates of his own age through towns and boroughs, fortresses and cities, to fairs and to all the various booths of the market-place, in pursuit of his public chaffer. He went along the highway, neither puffed up by the good testimony of his conscience nor downcast in the nobler part of his soul by the reproach of poverty....At first, he lived as a chapman for four years in Lincolnshire, going on foot and carrying the smallest wares; next he travelled abroad, first to St Andrews in Scotland and then for the first time to Rome. On his return, having formed a familiar friendship with certain other young men who were eager for merchandise, he began to launch upon bolder courses, and to coast frequently by sea to the foreign lands that lay around him. Thus, sailing often to and fro between Scotland and Britain [Brittany?], he traded in many divers wares and, amid these occupations, learned much worldly wisdom....He fell into many perils of the sea, yet by God's mercy he was never wrecked; for He who had upheld St Peter as he walked upon the waves, by that same strong right arm kept this His chosen vessel from all misfortune amid these perils. Thus, having learned by frequent experience his wretchedness amid such dangers, he began to worship certain of the saints with more ardent zeal, venerating and calling upon their shrines, and giving himself up by whole-hearted service to those holy names. In such invocations his prayers were oftentimes answered by prompt consolation; some of which prayers he learned from his fellows with whom he shared these frequent perils; others he collected from faithful hearsay; others again from the custom of the place, for he saw and visited such holy places with frequent assiduity. Thus as he aspired ever higher and higher, and yearned upward with his whole heart, at length his great labours and cares bore much fruit of worldly gain. For he laboured not only as a merchant but also as a shipman...to Denmark and Flanders and Scotland; in all which lands he found certain rare, and therefore more precious, wares, which he carried to other parts wherein he knew them to be least familiar, and therefore coveted by the inhabitants beyond the price of gold itself; wherefore he exchanged these wares for others coveted by men of other lands; and thus he chaffered most freely and assiduously. Hence he made great profit in all his bargains, and gathered much wealth in the sweat of his brow; for he sold dear in one place the wares which he had bought elsewhere at a small price. Then he purchased the half of a merchant ship with certain of his partners in the trade; and again by his prudence he bought the fourth part of another ship. At length, by his skill in navigation, wherein he excelled all his fellows, he earned promotion to the post of steersman.... For he was vigorous and strenuous in mind, whole of limb and strong in body. He was of middle stature, broad-shouldered and deep-chested, with a long face, grey eyes most clear and piercing, bushy brows, a broad forehead, long and open nostrils, a nose of comely curve, and a pointed chin. His beard was thick, and longer than the ordinary, his mouth well shaped, with lips of moderate thickness; in youth his hair was black, in age as white as snow; his neck was short and thick, knotted with veins and sinews; his legs were somewhat slender, his instep high, his knees hardened and horny with frequent kneeling; his whole skin rough beyond the ordinary, until all this roughness was softened by old age.... In labour he was strenuous and assiduous above all men; and, when by chance his bodily strength proved insufficient, he compassed his ends with great ease by the skill which his daily labours had given, and by a prudence born of long experience....He knew, from the aspect of sea and stars, how to foretell fair or foul weather. In his various voyages he visited many saints' shrines, to whose protection he was wont most devoutly to commend himself; more especially the church of St Andrew in Scotland, where he most frequently made and paid his vows. On the way thither, he oftentimes touched at the island of Lindisfarne, wherein St Cuthbert had been bishop, and at the island of Farne, where that saint had lived as an anchorite, and where St Godric (as he himself would tell afterwards) would meditate on the saint's life with abundant tears. Thence he began to yearn for solitude, and to hold his merchandise in less esteem than heretofore.... And now he had lived sixteen years as a merchant, and began to think of spending on charity, to God's honour and service, the goods which he had so laboriously acquired. He therefore took the cross as a pilgrim to Jerusalem; and, having visited the Holy Sepulchre, he came back to England by way of St James [of Compostella]."

Here, then, is an English merchant-adventurer, splendidly endowed by nature for his job, but restricted by the smallness of his ship and the simple navigation of those days. His limits were "Denmark and Flanders and Scotland"; to Rome and Jerusalem and Compostela he went by the ordinary pilgrims' ways, like any other man. Even Chaucer's Shipman of two centuries later, that weather-beaten master of his trade, knew only from Jutland to Cape Finisterre in Portugal; or, possibly, even the less distant Finistère in France. For the great adventurers of the Middle Ages we must go to Italy and Flanders, where commerce and manufactures were incomparably more developed than in Britain. It was through travellers from those countries, whether for religion or for gain, that the Far East became better known between 1250 and 1350 than at any other period until after the Reformation. And the pioneers of this movement were Franciscan friars; the missionary showed the way to the trader.

Similarly, before that date the Crusades had increased enormously the importance of the Mediterranean merchants and sailors, who carried troops and munitions oversea, built siege machines for the Crusaders, and often fought as well or better than the soldiers. Moreover, they were better organized and disciplined. Making all allowance for the enormous gulf between theory and practice in the Middle Ages, there is great significance in the sea-laws, which were decreed by our Richard I for that fleet which sailed from Gascony in 1190. These ran: "Know ye that we, by common counsel of men of worth, have made the rules of justice written here below. He who on shipboard shall kill a man, let him be bound to the corpse and cast into the sea; if he kill him on land, let him be bound to the corpse and buried in the earth. If any be convicted by lawful witnesses of having drawn his knife to smite another, or if he have wounded him to the blood, let

him lose his hand. If, however, he have only smitten him with his hand, without effusion of blood, let him be thrice plunged into the sea. If any man speak opprobrious or despiteful words, or invoke God's hatred, against another, let him give an ounce of silver for every such offence. If a thief be convicted of theft, let his head be shaven as though for the ordeal by battle, and let boiling pitch be poured on his head, and the feathers of a feather-bed be shaken over his head, that he be known for what he is; and, at the first place at which the ship may touch, let him be cast forth." This, being a war-code, was of special stringency; doubt-less it was seldom enforced with literal strictness; but it expressed the king's determination to maintain far sterner discipline on board ship than any land forces ever reached in those days.*
And we have sea-codes, some perhaps earlier than this, which testify to the efficiency aimed at, and to some extent obtained, by the best sea-traders. The Laws of Oléron, which date at least from 1266, were accepted by Western France, Flanders and Holland, England, Castile, and most of the Baltic cities. Very similar were the Laws of Wisby, of Jutland, and the code of "the Consulate of the Sea" in the Mediterranean, with other derivative codes which were carefully recorded, for the use of medieval English law-courts, in the *Black Book of the Admiralty*. These laws prescribe severe, but only reasonably severe, punishments for indiscipline or crime on the sailors' part; they protect the men, on the other hand, from unfair treatment; and they regulate the conflicting interests of the captain and the merchants, whose cargoes or whose persons he is carrying, in almost modern detail; they are evidently the fruit of centuries of experience.

Another definite step forward in civilization may be found in the institution of "consuls" at different ports, and the consequent agreements, verbal at first but afterwards written, for the guidance of such consuls and the fellow-countrymen whose interests it was their duty to guard. The earliest of these written agreements dates from 1184; and, as time went on, we find these commercial relations between Christian and Mussulman often regulated on higher principles than were yet recognized by feudal law at home. In 1270, for instance, the principle of reprisals was repudiated;

* Joinville (§ 644) gives us a glimpse of Crusaders' naval discipline; thieves and similar offenders were banished to the cock-boat, which was towed behind the ship.

again, the right of wreckage was abolished here centuries before it was abolished in Europe. Moreover, freedom of worship was allowed to these Christian traders in Mohammedan ports. Numerous documents testify to the commercial peace which often reigned between these political enemies, even in the thick of the Crusades. Indeed, this was one great difficulty both in Church and in State. We find popes and princes legislating against the supply of war material from Mediterranean ports to Saracen enemies; but Venice and Genoa and the Spanish ports drove a busy clandestine trade in these articles. After Saladin's victories, commerce became still busier between West and East. Not even a Pope like Innocent III could seriously check it; while the rulers of Aragon and Venice and Genoa were not always serious in their professed steps against this "blasphemous trade". After all, if the Italians had really cut off commercial intercourse with the infidel, either in ordinary articles or in war materials, their places would probably have been taken by Flemings or Baltic smugglers. Thus, in spite of the plainer and plainer proof that such commerce prolonged Mohammedan resistance and thwarted Crusading energies, the hope of gain steadily counteracted national or religious emnities.[2] In 1250 there was a "street of the English" at Acre; and most of the great maritime cities of the Mediterranean had their "street" in the main Syrian ports. Chronic piracies and frequent international wars had to be reckoned with; but so great was the pilgrim's spiritual and the trader's worldly gain that intercourse grew in proportion with general prosperity. Indeed, war itself provided one lucrative article of commerce; Narbonne, for instance, had a slave-market at a regular tariff: two slaves there cost as much as a mule, two mules as much as a horse. Two prelates in England, Lanfranc of Canterbury and Wulfstan of Worcester, share the credit of having put a stop to the selling of native slaves to the Irish. But in Southern France and Italy the slave-trade continued all through the Middle Ages, and the milder servitude of villenage was justified on moral and economic grounds by orthodox medieval philosophers; Wyclif alone has been marked as an exception to this general rule. No Pope or Church Council fulminated against slavery; the Archbishop of Narbonne, in 1149, left his Saracen slaves by will to the Bishop of Béziers; and, in 1251, another Archbishop of Narbonne complained that the viscount had withheld from him his rightful profits on two slave-markets, to the amount of 2500 sols, or about £15,000 in modern purchasing power.

In the later Middle Ages, Flanders and the North German Hansa were of most importance for English trade. This great corporation had its depots, with extra-territorial privileges, in many great towns: the Steelyard in London; smaller factories, under the control of the captain of this London Steelyard, in Lynn, Boston, York, Bristol, Ipswich, Norwich, Yarmouth, and Hull. In the later fifteenth century, English and Hansa interests conflicted very definitely; there was much rivalry, friction, and complicated negotiations, in the course of which we find the Germans writing: "The English, after their fashion, gave us many soft words": that chapter of history is admirably told by Mr Postan.[3] The *Libelle of English Policye*, and Henry VII's business-like efforts to strengthen our fleet, are familiar to all readers of history. For the present purpose, it is more important to bring out the adventurous side of this subject. St Godric's life shows admirably on the one hand the physical qualities required by the medieval merchants, and on the other, their daring and resourcefulness not only in speculation, but in the carrying out of plans. Whenever a merchant worked thus for himself, he was not the equivalent of the modern bald man sitting in a counting-house, but essentially a merchant-adventurer, ready in many cases not only to meet the buccaneer or pirate in self-defence, but even to do a little buccaneering on his own account.

From trade now we may pass to travel. Though the difficulties may very easily be exaggerated, they were unquestionably very great. Commonly the roads were only tracks, though in great cities abroad the towns were paved. Consequently, except along the main roads, wagons were seldom used except from the field to the barn. Otherwise transportation was by lighter carts or on the backs of the beasts. Moreover, such as they were, these tracks were ill kept. The city streets might be encumbered with blocks or trunks or branches, and in the road itself there were often pits. One of the fifteenth-century statutes of the city of Coventry runs: "Also that no man from henceforth dig clay upon Cheyles-more Green, nor in the highway betwixt Summerleaze Butts and Spon market, upon pain of 40*d*."[4] Similar references may be found elsewhere; and Mrs Green, in her *Town Life* (II, 31) tells a tragic story to this effect. "In 1499 a glover from Leighton

Buzzard travelled with his wares to Aylesbury for the market before Christmas Day. It happened that an Aylesbury miller, Richard Boose, finding that his mill needed repairs, sent a couple of servants to dig clay 'called Ramming clay' for him on the highway, and was in no way dismayed because the digging of this clay made a great pit in the middle of the road ten feet wide, eight feet broad, and eight feet deep, which was quickly filled with water by the winter rains. But the unhappy glover, making his way from the town in the dusk, with his horse laden with paniers full of gloves, straightway fell into the pit, and man and horse were drowned. The miller was charged with his death, but was acquitted by the court on the ground that he had had no malicious intent, and had only dug the pit to repair his mill, and because he really did not know of any other place to get the kind of clay he wanted save the highroad."

An average day's journey was from 20 to 25 miles, though sometimes we find surprising feats of travel. The ordinary rate may be seen in a Fellow of Merton, Oxford, who visited the Pope on business at Avignon in 1331. He and his servant, carrying their bedding with them on the third horse, took 34 days on the journey. But this included a good many stops; and the return journey from Avignon to Wissant took only 14 days. There were evidently regular and traditional stages, as in more modern posting days: this man made 18 stages from London to Lyons, and Sir Richard Guildeforde in 1504 made 17. Each time they made an offering after their safe-crossing of the Channel; at Canterbury, homewards, "four pence sterling"; but at Calais, outwards, only 1d. to the Church of St Nicholas, so dear to Ruskin in our own day.* One of their horses "died through the tempest"—a loss of 9s.—and the passage from Wissant to Dover cost 3s. 6d.[5] A century and a half later, the *Northumberland Household Book* prescribes: "Whensoever any of his Lordeship Servauntes be comaunded to ride on message in Winter...that every of theym be allowed for the tyme for his being furth in his jornay...ij^d for every meall and *ob* [$\frac{1}{2}$^{d}] for every his baiting; and for his Hors every day and night of his saide jornay iiij^d,

---

* "In some sort, it is the epitome of all that makes the Continent of Europe interesting, as opposed to new countries....That Calais tower has an infinite of symbolism in it, all the more striking because usually seen in contrast with English scenes expressive of feelings exactly the reverse of these." (*Modern Painters*, IV, Pt. v, ch. i, § 2.)

viz. a penny for his baiting ande iij ᵈ at night for his provounder. The whiche is in all for a Man and his Hors in the Daie in Winter viij ᵈ if it be Etting-Daye; and, if it be Fasting-Daie, than ij ᵈ to be abated; the which is vj ᵈ on a Fasting-Day."[6] In summer, the man's expenses are the same, but the horse's only 1½*d*.: total 5½*d*. per eating-day and 3½*d*. per fast-day. The halfpenny for the man's "baiting" is mysterious; we must probably read it as "lodging", but it is not counted in the addition either of the winter or of the summer total. The Lestrange accounts of half a century earlier give much the same prices (*Archaeologia*, xxv, 411 ff.).

By sea, things went naturally less smoothly. When Eustache Deschamps, Chaucer's friend and fellow-poet, crossed the Channel, he described the little ship as "a perilous horse to ride"; and dangerous or fatal passages were matters of common history. Froissart tells us how Sir Hervé de Léon "took the sea [at Southampton] to the intent to arrive at Harfleur; but a storm took him on the sea which endured fifteen days, and lost his horse, which were cast into the sea, and Sir Hervé of Léon was so sore troubled that he had never health after."[7] King John of France, a few years later, took eleven days to cross the Channel; and Edward III had one passage so painful that he was reduced to explain it by the arts of foreign "necromancers and wizards". This gives emphasis to a case registered by Blount in his *Antient Tenures* (pp. 61, 63). There he recounts how, under Edward I: "Solomon Attefeld holds land at Keperland and Atterton in the county of Kent on serjeanty, to wit that, whensoever the Lord King may wish to cross the sea, the said Solomon and his heirs are bound to cross with him to hold his head on the sea, if need be." On another roll the usual ports of crossing are specified: Dover and Whitsond—i.e. Wissant by Calais. Here, again, are extracts from a fifteenth-century poem on the pilgrimage to St James of Compostela:

> Men may leve alle gamys,
> That saylen to seynt Jamys!
> Ffor many a man hit gramys,   [grieves
>   When they begyn to sayle.
> Ffor when they have take the see
> At Sandwyche, or at Wynchylsee.
> At Brystow, or where that hit bee.
>   Theyr hertes begyn to fayle.
>
>   ·   ·   ·   ·   ·   ·

A boy or tweyn anone up styen,   [climb
And overthwart the sayle-yerde lyen;—
"Y how! taylia!" the remenaunt cryen,
    And pulle with alle theyr myght.
"Bestowe the boote, Bote-swayne, anon,   [stow
That our pylgryms may pley theron;
For som ar lyke to cowgh and grone
    Or hit be full mydnyght."

"Hale the bowelyne! now, vere the shete!—
Cooke, make redy anoon our mete,
Our pylgryms have no lust to ete,
    I pray god yeve hem rest!"
"Go to the helm! what, howe! no nere?   [nearer
Steward, felow! A pot of bere!"
"Ye shalle have, sir, with good chere,
    Anon alle of the best."

"Y howe! trussa! hale in the brayles!   [ropes
Thow halyst nat, be god, thow fayles!   [slackest
O se howe welle owre good shyp sayles!"
    And thus they say among.
"Hale in the wartake!" "hit shal be done."   [rope
"Steward! cover the boorde anone,
And set bred and salt therone,
    And tary nat to long."

Then cometh oone and seyth, "be mery;
Ye shall have a storme or a pery."   [squall
"Holde thow thy pese! thow canst no whery,   [curse?
    Thow medlyst wondyr sore."
Thys mene whyle the pylgryms ly,
And have theyr bowlys fast theym by,
And cry aftyr hote maluesy,   [Malmsey
    Their helthe for to restore.

And some wold have a saltyd tost,
Ffor they myght ete neyther sode ne rost;   [boiled nor roast
A man myght sone pay for theyr cost,
    As for oo day or twayne.
Some layde theyr bookys on theyr kne,
And rad so long they myght nat se;—
"Allas! myne hede wolle cleve on thre!"
    Thus seyth another certayne.[8]

From about the same date, we have evidence from a Travellers'
Guide. A little work of *Dialogues in French and English* was
printed by Caxton about 1483. He took the French portion from
a French-Flemish phrase-book compiled at Bruges, probably in
the first half of the fourteenth century: this he printed side by side

with an English translation of his own for the use of travellers: we may take this as a sample.

"Yf ye owe ony pylgremages, so paye them hastely. Whan ye be mevyd* for to goo your viage, and ye knowe not the waye, so axe it thus, in comending the peple to god: 'To god, goode pepel; I goo to Saynt James, ([or], to our lady of boloyne). At whiche gate shall I goo out, and at whiche hande shall I take my way?' 'On the right hande, whan ye come to a brigge, so goo ther over; ye shall fynde a lytill waye on the lyfte honde, whiche shall brynge you in a contre there shall ye see upon a chirche two hye steples; fro thens shall [y]e have but four myle unto your loggyng. There shall ye be well easyd for your money, and ye shall have a good Jornet.'

"'Dame, god be here!' 'Felaw, ye be welcome.' 'May I have a bedde here withinne?—May I here be logged?' 'Ye, well and clenly, alle‡ were ye twelve, alle on horsback.' 'Nay, but we thre. Is there to ete here within?' 'Ye§, ynough, god be thanked.' 'Brynge it to us. Gyve heye to the hors, and strawe them well; but that they be watred.'

"'Dame what owe we? We have ben well easyd. We shall rekene to morrow, and shall paye also, that ye shall hold you plesid. Brynge us to slepe; we ben wery.' 'Well, I goo, ye shall reste. Jenette, lyghte the candell; and lede them ther above in the solere‖ tofore; and bere them hoot watre for to wasshe their feet; and covere them with quysshons¶, se that the stable be well sherte**.'

"'Dame, may men goo by ship from hens to boloyne?' 'Ye, now ther is a shippe redy ful of peple. God wel them conduyte††! God brynge them in savete!'"

Of travel in the modern aesthetic sense there was little in the English Middle Ages. Men went abroad to fight, as Chaucer's model knight did, or on business, like Chaucer himself, or on pilgrimages, in virtue whereof (as *Piers Plowman* cynically assures us) "they had leave to lie all their life after". The greatest of these liars (as we shall see later) was Sir John Maundeville. Although this man does really seem to have had some connection with St Albans (his name is scratched in a contemporary or sub-contemporary hand on that pillar of the abbey church which has

| * moved. | † journey. | ‡ even though. | § yea. |
| ‖ upper room. | ¶ cushions; i.e. quilts. | ** shut. | †† conduct. |

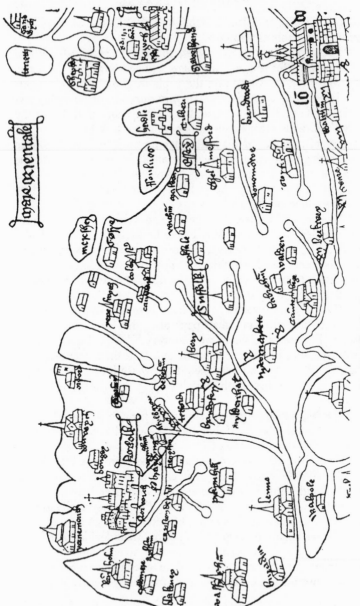

East Anglia about 1350

also a painted inscription concerning him), yet he cannot be trusted in any one of his assertions: modern students have left scarcely one shred of his *Travels* which is not demonstrably stolen from earlier and more veracious travellers. Those others do show, however, the extent to which a few friars or knights interested themselves in the natural or social peculiarities of foreign countries; and, even among those whose main interest was business, Marco Polo shows a lively and scientific curiosity which may bear comparison with Darwin's *Voyage of the Beagle*. Chaucer, too, though his work in Italy was that of ambassador and commercial negotiator, made such use of his opportunities that we may fairly dwell a little on his travels there as a matter not merely of personal but of deeper social interest. It marks the first definite and visible stage of Italian influence over English thought. Little as Chaucer's successors imitated him on that particular point, it is from this time that we must begin the English Renaissance, in its first glimmerings of dawn.

Italy was to Chaucer both what Europe is to a modern American, and what America is to a modern European. On the one hand, he found in Lombardy and Tuscany, even more than at Bruges, newer methods in trade and industry, and incomparably vaster business buildings, than even in his native London. On the other, he found in Italy what so delighted Ruskin at his first landing under Calais tower: here "the links are unbroken between the past and present; and, in such use as they can serve for, the grey-headed wrecks are suffered to stay with men". Crossing by Mont-Cenis, as he probably did, he would find at Susa (or, if by the Great St Bernard, still more definitely at Aosta) what Virgil had sung as one of the glories of his native land, the living rivers that flowed under the hoary walls—*fluminaque antiquos subterlabentia muros*. Again, Florence was by that time, what in earlier days Paris and the Île-de-France had been, the great home of modern art. Here, to take only one example, he would see Giotto's Campanile almost as it emerged from the hands of the builders; and at Pavia the palace of the Visconti boasted a specially famous series of Griselda pictures on its walls, which he must have heard of if he did not actually see them. And, lastly, there was the stimulus of song. In the Italian tongue, each word has on an average four times as many possible rhymes as in English; and Italian open-air life lends itself with equal superiority to evening song, when the day's work is done. Chaucer's England was probably more a land of peasant song than any parts nowadays except Wales and the West Riding; but the mass of song in Italy would be as much greater than ours as the mass of picturesque incidents in mountain-country is, by demonstrable calculation, greater than in the lowlands. It was upon this mass of popular *stornelli* and *rispetti* that Boccaccio modelled his own *ottava rima*, which so strongly influenced Chaucer's seven-line stanza, borrowed itself from the French of Machault. The autobiography of Brother Salimbene of Parma, a writer roughly contemporary with Chaucer's grandfather, is crowded with descriptions of this good friar's musical friends; Brother Vita, who sang so sweetly that a nun leapt from her convent window to join him; Brother Henry of Pisa, the great hymn-writer, who borrowed the air of one of his masterpieces from a servant-maid whom he once heard tripping across the cathedral from door to door, and singing as she went "And if thou carest not for me, I will care no more for thee"— *E se tu non cura da me, Io non curarò da te*! If not already before St Francis's time most certainly afterwards, Italy was "a nest of singing-birds" even beyond Elizabethan England. Nor must we look upon Chaucer as merely passive here. Poetry, like life of any kind, is contagious. Salimbene tells us how Brother Vita would amuse himself with provoking the nightingales to alternate song and response. Our own poet, like his then master Boccaccio, would not disdain to sing in direct rivalry with the hundreds of untaught nightingales whom he heard around him. Landor, in one of his best known poems, hailed the young Browning, at that time scarcely known, as the most observant man who had trodden the English lanes since Chaucer; and he went on to prophesy still greater triumphs from Browning's long sojourn in Italy, amid the magic of the South; amid the cliffs and groves of Sorrento and Amalfi, where

The siren waits thee, singing song for song.

That siren, that emulation, Chaucer found from his much briefer, yet not less momentous, Italian journeys.

XXVII. JUST PRICE AND USURY

THIS subject is so characteristic of the difference between medieval and modern life, for good or for evil, that we must dwell upon it at some length.[1]

Until the middle of our period there was very little capitalism in England. There was plenty in Florence and Venice, Cologne and Lübeck, Ghent and Bruges; there we already find merchants of the modern type, risking their own money and other men's lives. In England, for some time after the Conquest, most men risked not only their money but their life. In London, however, and Bristol and a few other towns, there was the beginning of capitalism. It was marked at first mainly among the great foreign merchants who traded with us; Lombards, or men of the Hansa or Flemings; and, with capitalism, came an intensification of the problem of usury, of lending money out at interest. Here, as in so many other ways, the Church did indeed guide, but less definitely and less widely than is often represented: certainly less than her position and her lofty exclusivist pretensions would warrant. The problem of trade morality scarcely existed in the days when the first apostolic Christian community had all things in common; when there were no church buildings and only a fluid hierarchical organization. Even in the succeeding generations, it is natural to find the Christian Fathers either ignoring or reprobating trade, just as they ignored or reprobated the decoration of churches with images. At a far later time, in the Middle Ages proper, Pirenne points out that "the Church, the most powerful landowner of the time", adopted "towards commerce an attitude not merely passive but actively hostile"; "the needs of the bourgeoisie...ran counter to all the interests and ideas of a society dominated materially by the owners of large landed property, and spiritually by the Church, whose aversion to trade was unconquerable" (48–51). For it was inevitable that the conviction of the overwhelming importance of a choice between eternal salvation and eternal damnation should very deeply colour the early Christian theories of industry and commerce.[2] Roman imperial law had treated bargaining as a bald matter of competition: sell as dear and buy as cheaply as you can; all is fair, short of actual cheating. But medieval Church law (and State law as influenced by it) went not so much on the principle "each look after himself", as upon "each look after his neighbour"; "do unto others as ye would they should do unto you". At first, this was taken in a very extreme sense. Sir William Ashley quotes very strong sayings from Tertullian, Jerome and St Augustine: this last even pleads: "Business is in itself an evil, for it turns men from seeking true rest, which is God." Still more interesting, perhaps, is a passage attributed to St John Chrysostom which Sir William does not quote, but which was incorporated in Canon Law by Gratian (*Decretum*, Par. I, dist. 88, cap. II): "Whosoever buyeth a thing, not that he may sell it whole and unchanged, but that it may be a material for fashioning something, he is no merchant. But the man who buyeth it in order that he may gain by selling it again unchanged and as he bought it, that man is of the buyers and sellers who are cast forth from God's temple." In other words, you may buy raw material for your work; but to buy the finished article for trade is sinful, and only one degree better than usury. This, after all, follows logically from St Paul; if no Christian may go to law with his fellow-Christian, then there can be no extensive trade between Christian and Christian. But the Church gradually receded from this impossible position; prohibition gave way to regulation, and there grew up the theory of the Just Price; i.e. a price which enables the seller just to keep up that household which his state of life, whatever it may be, does on the average require. Anything beyond that is sinful superfluity; and any trade which brings a man more than that is unlawful trade. Such was the ideal of the whole later Middle Ages; an ideal, it may be freely confessed, which we did wrong ever to lose sight of altogether. To divorce political economy from ethics is as unscientific as the divorce between any other two sciences.

Thus, in the later Middle Ages, the original crude prohibitions gave way to the notion of the just price as formulated, for instance, by St Thomas Aquinas. With him trade is not sinful in itself, but only dangerous, as tempting to sin. A man has the right of selling things dear enough to keep himself and his family in what may be looked upon as reasonable comfort, or even in the dignity required by his position in life. So far he has a right, but no farther. To sell dearer than this is profiteering. Aquinas's sense of the necessary moral limitations, and therefore of the moral danger, is best expressed in his own words.[3] Learned as he was, he knew that Canon Law had incorporated St John Chrysostom's doctrine. He had to face the fact that this doctrine was reinforced by that Holy Writ which (as we shall see later on) he was bound to accept as final, either in its literal or in its allegorical sense. Christ, he knew, had driven the traders from the Temple. He begins, therefore, by pointing out that there is such a thing as trading for the public good, "to provide a house or a city with the necessities of life", which may be distinguished from trading "not for the necessities of life but for the sake of gain". He continues: "The first kind of exchange is laudable, since it serveth natural necessity; but the second is justly blamed, because, in itself, it serves the greed for gain which knows no limit, but tends to infinity. Therefore trading, considered in itself, has a certain baseness [*turpitudinem*], in that it does not imply, in its nature, an honourable or necessary end. Nevertheless it does not by its nature imply anything vicious or contrary to virtue; wherefore nothing prevents gain from being directed to some necessary or even honourable end, and thus becoming lawful."

This is admirable; but the rock upon which it split was the difficulty of practical application. It supplies a rule for the confessional, but not for business dealings between man and man. We have seen how the Church was willing to go on for four centuries, at least, in reliance upon that word *sanior* as a crucial term of law, yet without ever arriving at a clear conception of this *sanitas*, this "soundness"—how, indeed even on the very verge of the Reformation, the most elaborate practical definition of that crucial word merited the ancient sarcasm *Ignotum per ignotius*. If this was so in the case of a word which, to a resolute legislator, need have offered no more difficulty of practical definition, in view of probable or certain contingencies, than the difficulties which face our framers of rules for cricket and golf clubs, then how much less can we expect a successful practical definition of that word *just*, with all its elusive implications? Therefore medieval practice fell far short of St Thomas's ideal.[4] While the Gild system aimed at enforcing the Just Price, it brought other injustices in its train; Gild morality, at the best, was that of loving your friend within and ignoring, if not hating, your rival outside. Corresponding attempts to regulate wages (as we know from the Statutes of Labourers) were similarly two-edged.

On these principles, the problem of usury necessarily emerged and became the burning question in medieval political economy. In earlier Canon Law we find just the crude repudiation of all usury, as in the Bible. Moreover, this "usury" is originally defined as "any taking of money beyond the capital lent". Indeed, canonists forbid not only the taking but even the expectation of any gain in money; and, further still, even any hope in the lender's mind that he will get favour or any other worldly profit by his loan! As society developed, that doctrine became obviously untenable; but the modifications subsequently made were so piecemeal and, in some of the most important cases, so unofficial, that this remained one of the thorniest subjects for confessors almost into the lifetime of living men—so much so, that about 1830 the difficulty was met by orders from Rome forbidding priests to make enquiries in the confessional as to the penitent's investments.

Two things, it would seem, hampered the medieval Church in solving thoroughly this problem of economic relations. In the first place, we have already seen how the principle of serfdom was ingrained in medieval society, and with it the principle of God-ordained distinctions of classes; not absolutely water-tight, of course, but so strong that it was dangerous to neglect an order which was so evidently providential. "To remain in that state in which he was born and faithfully to fulfil the obligations which it entailed, such was the counsel which the Church gave to every Christian."[5] Therefore, in spite of egalitarian pronouncements here and there (as when, in *Piers Plowman*, we are reminded that a churl's bones in the graveyard are hard to distinguish from those of a knight), no real approach to socialism was possible. We find only sudden and fleeting Bolshevik convulsions, of which the most important was the revolt of the peasants of the Flemish sea-board in the early fourteenth century, and next that of our own John Ball in 1381, with his "When Adam delvéd and Eve span, who was then the gentleman?" That, then, was the first difficulty; and the second was that this insistent problem of usury seldom led the *official* Church to pay serious attention even to the most obvious rules of political economy; for, though St Thomas was a saint and a genius, his work was unofficial. Thus, while the ecclesiastical prohibition of usury rested originally on a narrowly literal interpretation of Old Testament texts, just as the medieval Sabbatarianism did, yet, in so far as the Church abandoned this crude prohibition, the change came less from a general survey of the whole philosophical question than by successive modifications, introduced under pressure of the laws of natural justice and human nature.

The real justification of usury is in that extension of industry and trade which we call the capitalist system. This scarcely existed as yet in the England of 1300. Under capitalism, usury helps in further production. The man who has £10 to spare, instead of keeping it barren in a chest, lends it to some commercial undertaking, either directly, as by taking shares in a railway company, or indirectly through his bank. That money goes to buy more raw material and pay more workmen, and so to increase not only the lender's private funds, but also the world's production and wealth and general comfort. If, on the other hand, £10 is lent to a peasant farmer who is approaching bankruptcy because, for one reason or another, he is unable to keep pace with his competitors—that is, to a man whose only object and whose only possibility is simply to keep himself and his family on the little farm, and drive the wolf from the door, and who will perhaps produce less than a younger or more energetic competitor who would come in when he was turned out—in such a case, from the purely productive point of view, it is probably better that the man and his family should go to the workhouse; so that, although there are far stronger charitable reasons for my lending him money, there is far less reason in political economy than in my entrusting it to the bank. Moreover, if we consider charitable reasons alone, of course I ought to lend to the man gratis or at an almost nominal rate of interest; and yet (still speaking from the purely commercial point of view) I cannot justify my own risk in lending to him except by charging him something even higher than the ordinary rate of interest, in proportion to the feebleness of the security that he can offer me. Therefore the natural tendency in human nature is for those who lend on usury to the poor, in so far as they are business folk at all, to charge high rates and steel their hearts against all compassion. This, then, was a problem far more frequent under medieval economic conditions than even at present. The village population, which is so exceptional with us, was normal between the Conquest and the Reformation. We may almost say that everything then was on a village scale. Moreover, even the town of the Middle Ages was, as we have seen, in one sense more parochial than the modern village, since to a very great extent it aimed at being self-sufficing. Whereas the modern villager shops a good deal in the town, the medieval villager went comparatively seldom to the market or fair unless he lived close by; and, even then, it was often simply for barter and not for money exchange. Moreover, in many cases, even in the towns, craftsmen bought their own materials and sold their own wares: thus the shop-keeping class was only beginning to come into existence. Therefore the law of bargaining was not that which has naturally grown up among enormously greater populations with enormously wider exchange of articles; it was not the old Roman law of *caveat emptor*, bidding each man look after himself, but a system of Gild supervision. The craftsman, again, having chosen his craft and gone through it to the final stage, was thenceforward sealed to it. He must abide by his choice; so that it was natural for those of the same craft to dwell together in the same street; whenever we can trace the street names of medieval towns, about half of them describe the occupations of the in-dwellers. Even of the town merchant, Ashley can write: "His capital was small. He dealt directly with the customer, and between himself and the one or two boys whom he might employ there was no social gulf." That has already been suggested by the inventories of Colchester traders quoted in Chapter xxv. Already, however, the immense trade impulse on the Continent, from the Crusades onwards, began to demand serious revision of the original Christian teaching on usury; and the problem was taken up by the Schoolmen, of whom again we may take St Thomas Aquinas as typical.

It was recognized as a matter of common sense that a loan was a contract, and that a breach of contract might justify the claim for damages. Thus St Thomas grants the legitimacy of interest for *damnum emergens*, e.g. for the actual loss which the lender may suffer if the borrower fails to repay within the stipulated time. He refuses, however, to allow interest for *lucrum cessans*; for the cessation of (potential) gain. The lender may, indeed, plead truly, as a matter of fact: "During the year for which I lent you this £10, I lost what I might have gained by lending it or employing it elsewhere." To that, St Thomas replies: "True;

but why should not your gains cease, in ethics, during this time when you yourself were taking no trouble to work for it?" It will be seen, therefore, that these refinements, though tending in the right direction of philosophic definition, lent themselves to legal fictions, the worst of which was that of a sham contract. In the least objectionable forms of such fictions, the lender would stipulate upon an extremely early date for repayment, beyond which date—so soon as to be practically impossible for the borrower—interest might legally be charged on the admitted principle of *damnum emergens*. In some cases of this kind, the interest under these semi-fraudulent contracts was 5 per cent. per month; that is, 60 per cent. per year, *pro recompensatione damnorum*—and this at a time when the civil law prohibited Jews from charging more than 43 per cent.! Gradually, then, such contracts were softened down into something less grossly unfair, and therefore more customary. In these cases, by the natural working of opposite interests in bargaining, the period of freedom was slightly lengthened and the interest after that free period was considerably reduced. Then, by a similar operation of conflicting interests, a concordat was arrived at by which the excuse of the free period was dropped altogether; interest was now charged from the very first day of the loan, but usually at a far more reasonable rate. This, however, was a definite breach of the theory of Canon Law. Strictly, it was illegal all through the Middle Ages; but in England as elsewhere it was recognized by the civil courts.

Here, as in so many other worldly compromises, the Court of Rome took the lead, not from any essential spirit of injustice, but simply because it was the greatest business organization in Europe, with strongest traditions and widest grasp. Matthew Paris records the complaints of Bishop Grosseteste on his deathbed against Innocent IV (1253).[6] Matthew, it is true, monk though he was, was a severe critic of the Popes; but for the essentials of his picture we have plenty of corroborative evidence. "Though many other popes have afflicted the Church, this one hath oppressed her with a more grievous servitude, and hath multiplied injustices. For the Caursins are manifest usurers; and they have been cast forth from France (for this plague was then unknown in England) by holy fathers and teachers whom we have seen and known personally.... Notwithstanding, this Pope hath raised them up and protected them in their high place; and, if any man speak against them, he is wearied with loss and labour, as we have seen in the case of Bishop Roger of London. The whole world knoweth that usury is held in detestation in the Old and New Testament, and is forbidden by God. Yet now the lord Pope's merchants or money-changers practise their usury publicly in London, to the disgust of the Jews. They plot divers and grievous machinations against men of Holy Church, and especially Religious, compelling men under pressure of penury to lie, and to append their signs-manual to false deeds; which is as it were to commit idolatry and to renounce Truth, which is God.... And if, by chance, thou wilt pay the papal usurer the principal of the money, which thou hast now in thy possession, within a month or less [of the day of borrowing], he will not accept it unless thou pay him the whole hundred pounds. This is worse than a Jew's conditions; for the Jew will receive the principal courteously whensoever thou shalt return it, with only so much interest as is proportionate to the time for which thou hast had it in hand." Elsewhere, Matthew writes in his own name: "From that time forward [1229] the land [of England] has never lacked certain Ultramontanes, who style themselves merchants; most impious usurers, who seek nothing else than to ensnare those men in especial whom the Roman Court is pressing for money."[7] Another Benedictine chronicler, Oxenedes, bitterly resents the fact that "usury, which is forbidden in both Testaments, is now practised almost as a lawful trade by those usurers of the Roman Pontiff who are called 'merchants'". Under the year 1258 he writes again: "The plague of usury..did so ensnare the English religious houses, that there was no conventual house, nor cathedral, nor any so modest foundation but that it was involved in so many debts as made it despair of acquittance at any time."[8] This systematic protection of usurers was imposed upon the Popes by their own rapidly growing practice of selling the richest offices in the Church; for such was the practical effect of demanding from bishops or abbots a whole year's income in advance ("first-fruits", "annates") as a condition of papal institution. One of the greatest of our English archbishops, Pecham, was a Franciscan of those earlier days when St Francis's renunciation of worldly goods was still taken seriously. He accepted the spiritual office, and, in fact, did much for the sadly needed reforms in his diocese and province; but how was he to pay the "Pope's merchants" such a sum of ready money as an earl would not have found it easy to raise? In 1279 he wrote.[9] "To the most holy Father and lord in Christ Nicholas, by divine providence supreme pontiff of the holy Roman Church, his poor little brother John, priest of Canterbury, sendeth greeting, falling down with all reverence and kissing his holy feet.... There hath lately reached me a letter of execution, horrible to see and terrible to hear, whereof the final purpose is this: that unless, within a month from the feast of Michaelmas next coming, I pay fully and completely to the merchants of Lucca, from whom I borrowed at the Court of Rome, the sum of a hundred marks for a hundred pounds [which I am to pay at the end of the term] I shall be forthwith involved in the sentence of excommunication, and shall be denounced as excommunicate in my own and other cathedral churches, with bell, book and candle, on every Sunday and holy-day.... And this although, according to the contract which I signed, I might have secured freedom to myself and my church for an indefinite time, so long as I paid the damages and interest to the aforesaid merchants, in consideration of the losses they would incur by my delay.... Therefore, most holy Father, may it please your most merciful Holiness to reach me the right hand of succour and to revoke this cruel letter... otherwise, I see no other refuge but either to leave this prelacy committed to me, to disperse my household or flock, and to depart as an exile into some distant land, where I may lurk alone in some monastery and bear this anathema with humility until, as God shall give occasion, I shall have succeeded in satisfying the aforesaid merchants from the revenues of my see, in proportion as they can be raised from time to time; or, again, to borrow further from these merchants, and, as a borrower, to fawn upon them and bear with patience their base speech (though, by your Holiness's special mandate, it would be my duty to take strong measures against such lenders), since in these days no other men can be found in England who have money enough, nor, in the face of the present change and clipping of coinage, could I borrow elsewhere [than from these merchants of Lucca]." If great prelates ceased to complain with this freedom of speech, it was not because the abuse ceased, but because it became chronic and hopelessly ineradicable. It became so much a part of the ordinary rich merchant's work that it was finally registered under an apparently innocent name. The word *chevisance* originally meant any kind of bargain or mercantile exchange; but by Chaucer's time it had come to mean "usury", carried on under the current bootlegging system. Here, again, we may detect one of our poet's quiet touches of satire. How should the average modern reader suspect all that underlies that couplet about the merchant?

> So estatly was he of his governaunce
> With his bargaynes and with his chevyssaunce.

But here, as usual, "the moral Gower" bleats out with brutal frankness the things which his friend Chaucer has but hinted without a change of muscle in his countenance. Gower writes, in his *Mirour* (line 7225): "The city usurer keeps on hire his brokers and procurers who search for knights vavasours and squires.... Presently that trick will be played which in modern jargon is called the *chevisance* of money." And we have a royal ordinance of 1365 against usurious contracts which "the more subtly to deceive the people, men call exchange or *chevisance*".[10] A little earlier, Benvenuto da Imola writes in his great commentary on Dante: "He who practiseth usury goeth to hell, and he who practiseth it not, tendeth to destitution."[11] For, by this time, whatever the Church might preach, the merchant's interest coincided so exactly with papal practice that a common-sense *modus vivendi* was found; men did not trouble about their fellows' motives for taking interest, so long as they did not in fact take too extortionately. Mr H. G. Richardson, who has made considerable researches on this subject among the royal archives in Paris, kindly supplies me with the following brief facts. In 1312 20 per cent. was the ordinary rate there; but at the Great Fair of Champagne only 15 per cent.: perhaps because the clients were all well-known and solid merchants. In 1333 the officially legalized rate was 20 per cent. In Vermandois (1350) he finds 40 per cent. permitted, and from 1378 onwards many licences were granted for 50 per cent.

Meanwhile a fresh problem had arisen. As trade expanded, and especially by sea, there came in the question of partnerships in trading companies. Here again St Thomas's solution remained classical throughout the Middle Ages. He decided that, although it was sinful to take any interest which represented neither loss nor labour on the lender's part, yet the risks involved in distant trading might justly count as labour. If, therefore, a ship sails to distant parts freighted with the goods of half a dozen lenders at £100 each, these men must take the full risk of loss which is shared by the owner and captain of the ship. If they are content to accept frankly the chance that, after all, ships and goods may have perished; or again that the goods, though brought safely to the foreign land, were sold at a heavy loss, then they are justified in accepting any percentage of gain which may accrue under more fortunate conditions. If, however, they make a contract securing to them (on whatever terms of interest) the final restitution of their full capital in so far as the borrower's means enable him to restore it, then that contract is usurious. The lender has not earned his money by the "labour" of taking his fair share of the risk.* Yet even this concordat dates from only about 1250; moreover, it is in flat contradiction with a papal decree embodied in Canon Law, Gregory IX's Decretal *Naviganti*!† Moreover, even down to the verge of the Reformation moralists may be found ignorant of St Thomas's refinements; men who condemned all taking of interest as usurious and therefore as contrary to express Divine commands. It is interesting, however, to find in our chancery records a case which reposes on a principle common both to *Naviganti* and to St Thomas's doctrine. In about 1470 we find an "Action brought by Robert Whynbarrogh, clerk of the said sheriffs [of Norwich], who contends that certain money was lent by him to the complainant to be employed to his use in the complainant's business, and that he is therefore entitled to a share of the profits arising out of the transactions in which that money was employed, as well as to the repayment of the principal; 'which is usury'".¹²

The last and perhaps most important modification was the permission to buy rent-charges (*census*), from which comes the ordinary German name for interest, "Zins". *X*, let us say, owns a piece of land from which he derives a yearly rent of £10. *Y* purchases from him for £100 or £150 that rent. In plain words, *Y* invests his £100 or £150 at 10 or 6⅔ per cent. Thus, such purchases might easily be permitted as non-usurious. If *Y* had

---

* It is not that the philosopher here juggles with the term "labour". We shall see, in a later chapter, how Cambridge boys received a groat for their "labour" of submitting to public fustigation.

† For a full account of this almost incredible episode, see my article in *History* for July 1921.

every moral right to buy the land outright, why should he not
buy the yearly produce of that land? At first, however, it was
insisted that the land must actually exist, and that Y must actually
purchase it, though on the condition that X might compel its
redemption by repaying the money. Gradually, however, that
restriction was abandoned in practice. It was too artificial to
maintain itself: men bought and sold rents like any other market-
able commodity, and the *census* became a favourite investment
for religious bodies.

So much has been written lately concerning the medieval *theory*
of Just Price and Usury, with so much neglect of the at least
equally important evidence as to *practice*, that it will be profitable
here to pursue the subject as illustrated by monastic banking.
For, since the monasteries were among the greatest capitalists,
this economic loss touched them as it touched the merchants
outside. A modern scholar, Professor R. Génestal, has made
a detailed study of this movement in twelfth- and thirteenth-
century Normandy, where the social conditions resembled our
own more closely, perhaps, than anywhere else.[13] He points out
that there were two periods: first that of mortgage, and secondly
that of rent-charge. In the first, or mortgage period, the borrowers
from monasteries were almost always nobles or wealthy folk in
temporary need of money. In proof of the thorough business
spirit in which the monks regarded these transactions, we have
the fact that they constantly show themselves unwilling to be
repaid too soon. We therefore find contracts in which the lenders
expressly exclude repayment until 2 or 3 years have elapsed, or 6;
more often 9, or 15, or 18; oftenest of all, 21. Moreover, by
Roman law the mortgager might foreclose after the lapse of 30
years; and, since the monks' usual practice was to lend a sum not
exceeding two-thirds of the real value (sometimes even less), it
was a great advantage to the lender to prolong to this term. So
long as the loan lasted, he received about 15 per cent.; and he had
the security of a pledge which could be sold at a higher price
than the sum lent. Many of the borrowers are men on the point
of starting for the Crusades; no peasant in that position would
have lands to pledge: the land belonged to his lord. Moreover,
the statistics of these mortgages show us that the loan was seldom
below 5 *livres*, and at least half were of 10 *livres* or more. Thus
the conclusion is that the mortgage system served only for the

rich, and only for men who were borrowing for consumption. Therefore it came under papal prohibition, which did in fact practically kill the system so far as monks were concerned. Thenceforward, though the abbeys still invested heavily and profitably, it was under the *census* system. The rate of interest for such rent-charges during the years covered by Génestal (1150–1300), though high for modern ideas, was a good deal lower than that for mortgages in the earlier years. A table which he has drawn up gives forty-two cases at 10 per cent. and sixty-five at a higher rate, the lowest of all being not quite 7 per cent. The average would thus be from 11 to 12 per cent. And—another contrast—the sums invested under the *census* system are much smaller: the large majority are only 1, 2 or 3 *livres*. Moreover, the borrowers, whenever we can trace them, are people living fairly near the abbey, and often actual tenants. Thus he sums up: "During our first period we have seen that credit is rare and unproductive, open only to lords and generally leading them to ruin; at that time the abbeys are of very small importance for the matter [of credit]; they alone, [and not the borrowers], enrich themselves by the mortgage system. The second period, on the contrary, shows us these same abbeys spreading around the benefits of a credit destined to facilitate production, open to the middle classes and especially to rural folk, who, without overburdening themselves, can thus procure what they need for agricultural improvement. The monasteries are real land-banks, thickly spread over the country; they play a most important economic part, and one which they alone could have played." Yet it was as economists that they played it; banking had grown up as naturally in the monasteries as it grew up among the merchants outside. Henry of Ghent in [1280] does indeed take the old strict view of the census-system as usurious. But such rigorists were swept away by the tide: they were hopelessly out of date. The monks of St Martin-des-Champs had been lending money on exactly the same terms as ordinary bankers as early as about 1070. Lamprecht, in a passage which Lord Acton pencil-marked in his own copy of the book, wrote of "the free and easy way in which business was done at Cluny... the bank-business of St André was managed by Jewish financiers in the service of the abbey". It is to these Jews that we must turn in the next chapter.

It is sometimes asserted, though without documentary proof,

that monasteries anticipated the *Mont de Piété* system of gratuitous loans to necessitous folk. Here, for instance, is the plea of Gustav Schnürer, whose voluminous apologetic book, *Kirche und Kultur im Mittelalter*, enjoys a wide circulation in German and French. He writes (II, 188–9): "But especially the monasteries, as the Church had done formerly in the time of decaying Roman [Imperial] money-economy, mitigated much social want by their action as loan-institutions. Since Church teaching forbade the taking of interest, the debtor was protected against usury. They [the monks] lent smaller sums to the peasants, when they came into temporary difficulties through failure of crops; they lent larger sums for pilgrimages, military expeditions, liberation from captivity, and marriages." Schnürer offers no evidence whatever for the one essential point in all this, the *gratuitous* character of such loans; and his assertion is contradicted, on careful inspection, by almost every great monastic chartulary. Génestal, in his monumental study, finds no case of this kind to quote; and readers may find a great deal of evidence to the contrary in the chapter which I have devoted to this subject in the third volume of *Five Centuries of Religion* (ch. XVI). The plea, in fact, is among those which were invented long ago by apologists writing mainly from their imagination, and which have since been repeated from book to book without verification. Anti-clerical legends of that same imaginary class, such as "the Walled-up Nun" and "the Indulgence as an Official Licence for Sin", have long disappeared from the pages of all respectable writers; and it is high time that apologists on the other side should cease to repeat without verification these sweeping assertions of extreme social importance.

Monts de Piété did indeed grow up in the great Continental cities towards the end of our period, and mainly from the impulse given by Churchmen; but they testify especially to the growth of civic activities in social service. As early as 1251 we find in the *Calendar of Papal Letters* (I, 267): "[Papal] confirmation to the Bishops of Bath and Wells and Salisbury of the ordinance by which many burgesses of cities and places in England have set aside a certain sum of money to be lent to the poor without interest, by trustworthy persons, that they may not be oppressed or devoured by usury, with mandate to the same not to allow any interference with the said ordinance." But there is little trace of this system in later generations: nothing resembling the scale on which it was worked in Florence or Siena. English universities, again, adopted the system which was worked at Paris and elsewhere, of "chests" for gratuitous loans. Some benefactor first left a sum of money as foundation; this was kept in a chest under official custody, and loans were made from it without interest. But to the real poor these were useless; for the invariable rule of the "chest" was that the borrower should deposit a pledge of equivalent value. These "chests", therefore, met only the difficulty which we have already seen in a previous chapter, that any one who was away from home in the Middle Ages, like a modern traveller in some distant land, might well be in dire momentary need of money, despite his fundamental solvency or even his great wealth.

THE Jews have grown to embody, if indeed they did not embody from the first, an element very important in society, but, in its crudest form, definitely antagonistic to the cruder forms of other equally important elements. We cannot think of them in the Middle Ages apart from what they were in the Old Testament and what they are to-day.

He was a Jew by birth who said He was come to bring "not peace, but division"; or (to quote from St Matthew) "not peace, but a sword". We ourselves, however unconsciously, are constantly implying the same thing when we say of any man that he is "in deadly earnest": the living flame within this person may have deadly reactions outside. In proportion as one man is determined to follow his own conscience—in proportion as he is wholly possessed by the greatness of any cause which he espouses—in that same proportion must he risk collision with others equally resolute, equally conscientious, yet diverging certainly to some extent (given the endless variety of human character), and possibly diverging in some of the most essential respects. This is nowhere seen more clearly, perhaps, than in the history of Christianity and Judaism in their mutual relations. Here we see exemplified those words of Christ which follow: "The father shall be divided against the son, and the son against the father; the mother against the daughter, and the daughter against the mother." Yet Christ proclaimed emphatically that His mission was not to destroy the Jewish law, but to fulfil it. The whole of the Epistle to the Hebrews is one continuous argument in that sense. Perhaps the most important tenet which Christianity inherited from Judaism was its fundamental doctrine of the Unity of God and the Goodness of God. The first words of the Lord's Prayer are an echo from the Psalmist: "Like as a father pitieth his children, so the Lord pitieth them that fear him." All the earliest Christians were Jews; and, when Gallio treated the contention between them and their unconverted brethren as a mere difference between Tweedledum and Tweedledee, he only anticipated the confusion which seems evident in the mind of so keen an observer as Juvenal, two generations later. Yet in this field, very soon, we find father divided against son, mother against daughter; and the blackest chapter in Christian history is that of the relations between Church and Synagogue.

The key to this mystery, in so far as it can be explained in a few words, lies in two facts: the Jew was exclusive, and the Jew was proselytizing, from the earliest stages of history at which we can see him distinctly. And that history shows very clearly how false it is to suppose that the exclusive spirit and the prose-lytizing spirit are mutually exclusive. To the Jew, Jehovah was the God of Israel; other races, the Gentiles, were outside the Almighty's Covenant: "to Abraham and his seed were the pro-mises made." None of the other religions within the vast compass of the Roman Empire seems to have rested on such an exclusivist foundation. Next, when a succession of cruel conquests broke up and dispersed the Jews—the Babylonian captivity, the fight against Antiochus Epiphanes and those later wars against Rome—then the Hebrew, in his dispersion, became a proselytizer. That is what pagan observers noticed most definitely in him during the first few generations of the Empire. The actual seed of Abraham was dispersed, but the promise made to Abraham might now be claimed by all who could be persuaded to accept circum-cision and the Mosaic Law. Thus in the reception of converts Judaism was far from exclusive; the Pharisees "compassed sea and land to make one proselyte". But, within the fold, there still remained the old exclusivist doctrine of salvation: the uncircum-cized were outside the Covenant. When once we have grasped these two points clearly, we may see why the Jews were unpopular in the Roman Empire, quite apart from their rivalry with Christi-anity. To Horace, the Jew is the boorish unsociable fellow who, if you are not a fellow-Jew, takes a positive pleasure in mis-directing you on your road. To Tacitus, he is an enemy of the human race. For in fact he was intensely clannish; Jew helped fellow-Jew in a way that often put others to shame: but the other side to that picture was his comparative want of fellow-feeling towards the Gentile. We all know by experience what extreme clannishness leads to. He who ignores outsiders is naturally ignored himself; the great world gives him the cold-shoulder. He becomes very sensible of this, and that exaggerates his exclusive-ness; an inferiority-complex comes in to reinforce his pre-existent superiority-complex; and the two grow and grow together. Thus the Jew's injustice to outsiders, and the Gentile's injustice to the Jews, have acted and reacted upon each other for eighteen centuries; and thus the Jew's intense sense of unity, within his own comparatively narrow compass, has been like a particle of grit in the eye of the great world outside.

From the Synagogue, let us now pass to the Church. Christianity, absorbing so much as it did from every strand of thought in the Roman Empire, took over from Judaism not only its trust in One Good and Almighty God but also its combination of exclusiveness and proselytism. What Gibbon calls "the inflexible and intolerant zeal" of early Christianity came into collision with the inflexible and intolerant zeal of ancient Judaism; and the result, when once Christianity had obtained State recognition with State force at the back of it, was a long and terrible conflict. The whole of Western Europe was now dominated by a new creed even more exclusivist and proselytizing than the old Judaism against which it must needs fight. On the first of these points the motto of the orthodox ran *extra ecclesiam nulla salus*. This was taken literally; nobody explained then (as so many explain now) that *extra* in Latin does not mean *outside*, that *ecclesiam* does not mean *Church*, that *nulla* does not mean *no*, nor *salus salvation*. On the second point, even the crudest physical force was too often applied; and men grew accustomed to interpret that Gospel parable, with its "compel them to come in", not only in the tyrannical sense in which St Augustine had expounded it in the heat of that semi-religious, semi-political civil war between Catholic and Donatist, but with even cruder intolerance.

We have no evidence for pre-Conquest Jews settled in England.[1] William of Malmesbury tells us explicitly that the Conqueror brought them in from Rouen. His motive seems plain; he would thus be able to collect his feudal dues, scattered all over the country, not in kind but in coin, and the Jews were the most natural financial agents. For in France they had already been long compelled to specialize in this field. Until the ninth century, they had been comparatively free, though we naturally find a series of ecclesiastical and civil rules which put them at a definite disadvantage against the Christian majority; and there were frequent clashes of the kind that might be expected among those undisciplined populations. Forced baptisms occurred fairly frequently, and Christian-Jewish marriages were forbidden; yet Jews might possess lands, and were prosperous traders. Charlemagne had taken them under his protection; so had his son Louis the Pious. Churchmen of the ninth century complained of their popularity and influence, as physicians and especially as merchants, but not yet as usurers. However, with the decay of royal power and the growth of feudalism, the robber-nobles had been tempted to flay the Jew even more than the peasant. Again, when Christian society began to organize its trade under the Gild system, here also the Jew was an alien and unwelcome element. The eleventh century was marked by massacres, for which excuses were found in an asserted league between the Jews and the Muslim conquerors of Jerusalem. In 1065 Pope Alexander II tried to protect them from massacre; and, to the very end of the Middle Ages, no Pope countenanced such bloodshed. Thus, although the worst cruelties came only with the Crusades and with the later legends of ritual murder, the French Jews were already under severe disabilities when William brought them over: they were practically compelled to specialize in finance. They were not numerous, but they were widely distributed; even in villages a Jew or two might well be found, yet, apart from Paris, it is doubtful whether any town had more than a hundred Jewish households. This state of things was repeated in England: the Jews became widely scattered financiers, especially in the royal service.

For they were the king's men, and, in process of time, became practically the king's chattels. Pollock and Maitland[2] describe one of the two main ideas that our law in later time has about the Jew. "He, with all that he has, belongs to the king. Bracton puts the same thought in these words: 'The Jew can have nothing that is his own, for whatever he acquires, he acquires, not for himself, but for the king; for the Jews live not for themselves but for others.' The other main idea is one which will not seem strange to us after what we have said of villeinage. This servility is a relative servility; in relation to all men save the king the Jew is free. He will require some special treatment, for if he is to be here at all and do any good, he must be allowed to do things that are forbidden to Christians, notably to take interest on money lent; and courts of justice must pay some regard to his religion; for example, must suffer him to swear upon the Pentateuch instead of the Gospels; but in general, if his royal master's interests are not concerned, he is to be dealt with as though he were a Gentile.

A third principle is accepted—the Jews themselves would strongly desire its acceptance—namely that when the interests of neither the king nor any other Gentile are concerned the Jews may arrange their own affairs and settle their own disputes in their own way and by their own Hebrew law." Again: "The Jew's relation to the king is very much like the villein's relation to his lord." Yet, for several generations, this subjection was scarcely more unfavourable in practice, apart from exceptional exercises of tyranny, than that of the villein. Mr Joseph Jacobs sums up judicially the legal (as apart from religious and social) status which Jews had acquired in England at the end of the twelfth century.[3] He writes: "They could not be regarded as aliens any more than could the Norman nobles with whom they had originally come over; besides, alienage could not become hereditary.... They were not heretics, since their right to exist was recognized by the Church. They were usurers for the most part, and their property, like that of all usurers, escheated to the king at their demise. But, on the other hand, their usurious debts could be recovered at law, whereas the Christian usurer could not recover more than his original loan. They were in direct relation to the king and his courts; but this did not imply any arbitrary power of the king to tax them or to take their money without repayment, as is frequently exemplified in the Pipe-Rolls. The aids, reliefs, fines and amercements demanded from them were no other than those asked from the rest of the king's subjects, though the amount contributed by the Jews may have been larger. They were the king's 'men', it is true, but no more than the barons of the time; and they had the special privilege of the baronial rank, and could move from place to place and settle anywhere without restriction. It will be seen how this privilege was afterward taken away from them. Altogether, the status of the English Jews, who partook of the nature of baron, alien, heretic and usurer, was peculiar; but, on the whole, their lot was not an unfavourable one."

Yet, before the end of the century, very unfavourable changes came. The Jews were no longer so useful to kings and great nobles and even popes. As usurers, they had rivals in the southern Frenchmen ("Caursins", i.e. men of Cahors) and, presently, in those Italian merchants who gave their name and character to our Lombard Street. The rise of the English Gilds increased that rivalry; kings and great men could now borrow on usury from

English "merchants". In 1186, the Jews had been assessed, for
personal property, at one-fourth the value of the whole country;
and, about the same time, Aaron of Lincoln alone had left £15,000
worth of debts owing to him from barons throughout the country.⁴
A single Jew of Gloucester, in 1170, had financed Strongbow's
conquest of Ireland. Yet in 1255, when Henry III pawned the
whole "Judaismus" of England to Richard of Cornwall, it was
for only 5000 marks. Not only in usury, but in other ways the
Jews were losing ground heavily through consecutive legal restric-
tions.⁵ For, though trade was permitted to them, yet the Gilds
were already securing a monopoly of skilled labour, and the
Gilds Merchant monopolized the markets. In 1253 Jews were
in a manner bound to the soil, like the serf their legal analogue;
it was enacted that they might dwell only in one of the 25 towns
which possessed an "archa" [chest] for the preservation of their
documents and money contracts. In 1269 they were forbidden
to claim the landed property which might revert to them by the
non-payment of a mortgage; and in 1271, to hold land of any
kind. In 1275, the *Statutum de Judaismo* restrained them still
further, and forbade their lending on usury. In 1278 there was
a great outcry against coin-clipping; 293 Jews were executed in
London, and it is quite possible that all were guilty. For, as
Mr Jacobs truly observes, "by depriving the Jews of a resort to
usury, Edward was practically preventing them from earning
a living at all under the conditions of life then existing in feudal
England; and in principle the 'Statute of Judaism' expelled them
fifteen years before the final expulsion".⁶

For, all this while, the natural and insistent pressure of religious
intolerance was increasing. The ordinary manners of that age
made no allowance for the co-existence, under one and the same
State, of two creeds in deadly earnest. Christian and Muslim and
Jew might enjoy equal rights in Sicily; but that was under the
infidel Frederick II. Elsewhere, the great churches consecrated
intolerance in the statuary of their portals, where the crowned
Church bore on one side her triumphant banner and, on the
other, a corresponding niche showed the Synagogue with head
bent, bandaged eyes, and a staff breaking in her hands.

In Norman times, this difficulty had always existed in the background. William of Malmesbury, in his history of Rufus's reign,
relates how "the Jews gave proofs of their insolence towards

God. At one time, at Rouen, they endeavoured to prevail, by
means of presents, on some converted Jews to return to Judaism;
at another, in London, entering into controversy with our bishops;
because the king (in jest, as I suppose) had said that if they
mastered the Christians in open argument he would become one
of their sect. The question therefore was agitated with much
apprehension on the part of the bishop and clergy, fearful, through
pious anxiety, for the Christian faith. From this contest, however,
the Jews reaped nothing but confusion; though they used repeatedly to boast that they were vanquished not by argument
but by power."7 Again, Mr Jacobs recounts how Henry II "was indeed accused by the contemporary chroniclers of unduly favouring
those 'enemies of Christ'. They lived on excellent terms with
their neighbours, including the clergy; they entered churches
freely, and took refuge in the abbeys in times of commotion.
There is even a record of two Cistercian monks having been
converted to Judaism; and there is evidence that the Jews freely
criticized the more assailable sides of Catholicism, the performing
of miracles and the worship of images. Meanwhile they themselves
lived in ostentatious opulence in houses resembling palaces, and
helped to build a large number of the abbeys and monasteries of the
country. By the end of Henry's reign they had incurred the ill-will
of the upper classes with whom they mostly came in contact."8

Moreover, religious causes became increasingly operative. In
1198, Innocent III commanded Richard of Cornwall, with all
other Christian princes, to compel remission of all usury demanded
by Jews from Christians. In 1205, he laid down the principle
that all Jews were doomed to perpetual servitude because they
had crucified Jesus. Thus St Thomas Aquinas is on unassailable
ground when he decides that, "since the Jews are the slaves of
the Church, she can dispose of their possessions".9 In 1215
Innocent imposed upon their garments a perpetual badge of
infamy; and Archbishop Langton enforced this in England (1218).
In 1222 a deacon was burned at the stake for having apostatized
and married a Jewess; but there is no record of punishment for
the few earlier apostasies to Judaism. Presently came in the
horrible fiction of ritual murder. The legend of St Hugh of Lincoln,
told in Chaucer's Tale of the Prioress, dates from 1256; this fiction
brought death to 18 Jews who refused to plead, and long imprisonment for 73 others. An even earlier story of martyrdom is that

of "St William" of Norwich. Religion was pleaded also in excuse for many odious regulations, as Pollock and Maitland remind us.[10] "They were to fast in Lent; they were to wear distinctive badges upon their garments; they were not to keep Christian servants or have intercourse with Christian women; they were not to enter the churches; they were to acquire no more schools or synagogues than they already possessed." The same authors, in their section on the marriage law, write: "We have to suppose a marriage between two infidels and that one of them is converted to Christianity. In such a case the Christian is not bound to cohabit with the infidel consort, and if the infidel chooses to go off, the marriage can be dissolved and the Christian will be free to marry again.... It is probable that in their dealings with Jews the English courts accorded this privilege to the faithful. In 1234 a Jewish widow was refused her dower on the ground that her husband had been converted and that she had refused to adhere to him and be converted with him."[11] The annals of Cambridge supply a somewhat similar case, except that the operative factor here is not Church law but feudal custom, working upon the principle that the Jew is a sort of serf to the king. In 1169 "La Countesse, the Jewess of Cambridge, and her sons and the Jews of Lincoln, paid the king a fine of 7 marks of gold [i.e. £42, roughly equivalent to £1700 modern] for a Jewess of Lincoln, whom a son of La Countesse had married without the king's licence."[12] Another Cambridgeshire document of 1241 shows royal commissioners appointed for distraining the Jews who had not yet paid their tallage, and to seize the wives and children of recalcitrants.[13]

In 1232 Henry III founded a *Domus Conversorum* in London for converted Jews; yet, until 1280, the kings still followed the example of their forefathers and claimed all the property of such a convert, in virtue of their royal ownership over that "chattel". In 1235 Henry issued a proclamation prohibiting Christian nurses from serving Jews. This prohibition would be natural enough in any case, considering the normal relations of Church and Synagogue; but it derives further significance from a letter of Innocent III, incorporated in Canon Law, which rehearses how Jews would compel Christian nurses, for the three days succeeding their Easter Communion, to spill their milk, lest the nursling should receive contamination from the consecrated Host. This gives us an illustration not only of the usual orthodox custom of communicating only once a year, but also of the materialism to which the doctrine tempted Jewish thought; a materialism no less crude than that to which orthodox writers testify for popular thought within their own camp. In 1282, Archbishop Pecham closed all the synagogues in Canterbury diocese; and the Dominicans obtained a writ from Edward I compelling Jews to listen to conversion-sermons. Nor was the intolerance on one side only. As Mr Jacobs confesses:[14] "The Jews had throughout been careless in showing their contempt for certain aspects of Christianity. One had seized the cross carried in front of a procession at the University of Oxford in 1268, and in 1274 a Jew was burned for blasphemy at Norwich. Edward had accordingly issued a proclamation declaring any Jew found guilty of blasphemy to be liable to the death penalty. At the end of 1286 Pope Honorius IV addressed a special rescript to the archbishops of York and Canterbury, pointing out the evil effects on the religious life of England of free intercourse with the perfidious Jews, who studied the Talmud and its abominations, enticed the faithful to apostasy, caused their Christian servants to work on Sundays and holidays, and generally brought the Christian faith into disrepute. On this account he called upon the English State and Church to do their utmost to prevent such pernicious intercourse." Next year, the Synod of Exeter "repeated the ordinary Church laws against commensality between Jews and Christians, and against Jews holding public office, or having Christian servants, or appearing in public at Easter; forbidding Jewish physicians to practise", and prohibiting the erection of new synagogues. Edward I, as a loyal son of the Church, followed this up logically in action. He immediately expelled the Jews from his duchy of Gascony; and "on his return to England (July 18, 1290) he issued writs to the sheriffs of all the English counties ordering them to enforce a decree to the effect that all Jews should leave England before All Saints' Day of that year. They were allowed to carry their portable property; but their houses escheated to the king, except in the case of a few favoured persons who were allowed to sell theirs before they left. Some of them were robbed by the captains who undertook to transport them to Witsand; others were drowned on their way to France. Of the 16,000 who left, about one-tenth went to Flanders, their passage being paid by the king; and a number are found a short time later in the Paris Jewry. The king's booty was not of great amount, for the total rental of the houses which fell into his hands was not more than £130, and the debts owed to the Jews, of which he could collect only the principal, did not exceed £9000. Parliament was said to have voted one-tenth of the tithes and one-fifteenth of the personal property in gratitude for the expulsion, but this merely represents contemporary prejudice. Edward's act was not an act of grace to the nation; as has been seen, no alternative was left to him. The Church would not allow the Jews to become an integral part of the English nation, and they therefore had to leave the country." On two earlier occasions, in 1254 and 1255, they themselves had pleaded to be allowed to leave the kingdom before the last penny had been forced from them. Pollock and Maitland sum up judicially here: "The system could not work well; it oppressed both Jew and Englishman. Despised and disliked the once chosen people would always have been, in a society of medieval Christians; perhaps they would have been accused of crucifying children and occasionally massacred; but they would not have been so persistently hated as they were, had they not been made the engines of royal indigence. From the middle of the thirteenth century onwards the king was compelled to rob them of their privileges, to forbid them to hold land, to forbid them even to take interest. This last prohibition could not be carried into effect; there was little or nothing that the Jews could profitably do if they were cut off from lending money. Their expulsion in 1290 looks like the only possible solution of a difficult problem."[15] St Louis, in 1254, had already banished nearly all from his own lands; in 1306, Philip IV added plunder to expulsion; in 1321, excuses for a pogrom were found in the accusation that they poisoned fountains in order to infect the population with leprosy. In 1321, Pope John XXII would have expelled them from Rome, but Robert of Anjou intervened in their favour. All these points are rehearsed in a plain-spoken article of *The Catholic Encyclopaedia* (VIII, 394), which adds that in Germany their sufferings were still greater. Their quasi-imprisonment in the Ghettos of Rome and other cities is well known. It is pleaded that this measure had its welcome side of affording them some protection from casual mob-violence; yet that, however true, is a two-edged plea. The Ghetto was in fact something of a precedent for the modern Nazi "protective arrest".

WE must not forget how much of this had sprung originally
from the Jew's own pride in his creed, and the tenacity
with which he had held to the exclusivist principle
"Outside the Covenant, no salvation". We must bear in mind the
offence given by a minority of these pariahs in their wealth and
ostentation, and their sacrilegious holding of Church vessels and
ornaments to pledge. Far-seeing statesmen, also, must have foreseen what Pollock and Maitland point out in their survey: "Many
an ancient tie between men—the tie of kinship, the tie of homage—
is being dissolved or transmuted by the touch of Jewish gold;
land is being brought to market and feudal rights are being
capitalized." The modern historian may welcome that change;
but we cannot blame our ancestors for seeing it with other eyes.
But this influence was only indirect; we must not accept the legend
that the Jew ordinarily exercised secret and immediate political
power in the Middle Ages. As Dr J. W. Parkes has pointed out,
Kipling rests upon a misapprehension of the actual facts in his
story of the Jews who decided that Magna Carta should be
signed. For money (as he points out) means power only when
its owner either can give or withhold it at his own choice; but,
as the Jew had no power to withhold, he could exercise no power
by giving. Nor could he conceal the amount of his money; for
he could not claim payment for any debt that was not registered
in the treasury of that prince whose chattel he was; our own Star
Chamber very likely took its name from such documents (in
Hebrew, *Sh'tars*) of which a good number have survived.

Lastly, the Jewish usurer was often made a scapegoat for the
rest. There is great significance in the petition of the lesser barons
in 1258 against their greater brethren who were swallowing them
up.[1] "*Item*, they beg for a remedy in this matter; *viz*. that Jews
sometimes transfer their debts and lands which they hold in
pledge to barons and to the greater folk of the kingdom, who by
that occasion enter into the estates of the lesser [land-owners]:
and although the debtors are ready to pay the aforesaid debt with
usury, the aforesaid magnates prolong the business, in order that
by some means the said lands and tenements may remain in their

own hands, saying that they cannot dispense, and know not how to dispense, with the Jew to whom the debt was owing; and they constantly delay the repayment of the said money, so that by reason of death or of some other chance there is evident and manifest peril of imminent loss of inheritance for those who had possessed the aforesaid holdings. *Item*, they [the lesser barons] seek remedy in the matter cf Christian usurers, as for instance concerning the Caursins who dwell in London, seeing that it would seem contrary to the Christian religion to maintain or foster any men of that sort, especially from the time that they have adopted the name of Christians. Moreover, through these men's usuries many folk are impoverished and ruined; and also they get and buy many merchandises coming to London, both by water and by land, to the grievous detriment of the merchants and all the folk of the said city, and to the great loss of our Lord King." From this very document it transpires that the worst sinners of all were the Caursins, nominal Christians; and we have seen how Matthew Paris describes the Caursin victory, with papal alliance and papal help, over the Bishop of London's well-meaning attempt to banish usury from his own metropolis.[2]

Moreover, offensive as Jewish pride might have been, there was sometimes excuse for it. By the confession of their most orthodox adversaries, the Christians might well have profited by their example in two most important respects. First, their care for their poor, which Christian moralists cite to shame their own brethren. Certainly those niggardly monastic prescriptions with regard to gleaning, printed on p. 479 of my *Medieval Village*, contrast strongly with the medieval Hebrew law, which runs: "If a man put a basket beneath the vine while he was gathering the grapes, such a one is a robber of the poor. From what time are all men permitted to glean from the field? After the last of the poor have gone. And to take grape-gleanings and defective clusters? After the poor have gone into the vineyard and re-turned....If a man would keep aught back [for his own poor kins-folk] he should take away half and give half [to the poor that come to him]....A poor man that is journeying from place to place should be given not less than one loaf....If he spends the night [in such a place] he should be given what is needful to support him for the night. If he stays over the Sabbath he should be given food enough for three meals. If a man has food enough for two meals he may not take aught from the [Paupers'] Dish; and, if enough for fourteen meals he may not take aught from the [Poor] Fund." Secondly, by the acknowledgment of Christian writers again, the ordinary Jew put the ordinary Churchman to shame by a far better knowledge of his own sacred Scriptures.

The Jews were in those days, as now, patient observers, and unwearied in pursuit of their own lines of thought. As translators, and as theoretical scientists, they did much to bring Greek and Arab culture into the West. The Bishop of Paris might seek out and burn their sacred books; but he could not destroy their influence in his own university. As practising physicians, they were then as now in the front rank. And, finally, they represented, and knew themselves to represent, an older civilization than that of their rivals. They had generations of culture behind them in the days when Tacitus studied Germany as the home of the noble savage, and painted simple German virtues with the object of rebuking his own over-sophisticated society of Rome. The Jew, therefore, felt towards his rivals much as the Muslim did. Prince Ousâma, in his precious autobiography, shows his scorn of these "Frankish" knights and their women, as of half-educated school-boys and schoolgirls. He is disgusted not only at their cruel sport with old women, but with other points betraying imperfect civiliza-tion. And, while the "Frank" was not ashamed to strike his womenkind, and definite prescriptions for wife-beating stood in his Canon Law (as we shall see in a later chapter), Judaism did at least legislate against this. A medieval regulation runs: "The cry of the daughters of our people has been heard concerning the sons of Israel who raise their hands to strike their wives. Yet who has given a husband the authority to beat his wife? Is he not rather forbidden to strike any person in Israel? Nevertheless have we heard of cases where Jewish women complained regarding their treatment before the Communities, and no action was taken on their behalf. We have therefore decreed that any Jew may be compelled, on application of his wife or one of her near relatives, to undertake by a *herem* not to beat his wife in anger or cruelty or so as to disgrace her, for that is against Jewish practice. If anyone will stubbornly refuse to obey our words, the Court of the place to which the wife or her relatives will bring complaint, shall assign her maintenance according to her station and according to the custom of the place where she dwells. They shall fix her alimony as though her husband were away on a distant journey."[3]

This chapter cannot be complete without some contemporary picture of the great massacres. The greatest of all, at York, was engineered by a group of the lesser nobility who were heavily indebted to these usurers, and who in fact battened on their spoil. That of Lynn affords a juster instance, since, even through the natural bias of a Churchman, we have here the story of an unusually honest chronicler who tries to see both sides: William, the Austin canon of Newburgh.[4] King's Lynn (as it has been ever since Henry VIII) was Bishop's Lynn all through the Middle Ages. William has just been relating the outbreak and massacre at Richard's coronation; and he adds that the zeal of the Londoners has "risen in its vehemence to white-heat, not indeed sincerely (that is, merely for faith's sake), but either in envy of the Jews' prosperity or as gaping after their fortunes. Bold and covetous men thought to do God service if they despoiled or destroyed folk who rebelled against Christ; and they wrought with cheerful fury, hindered by little or no scruples of conscience, the business of their own greed; a thing which God's justice was far from approving, though He had aptly ordained it, in order that He might by this means restrain the insolence of that perfidious race, and put a bridle upon blasphemous tongues. In the city called Lynn, illustrious for its trade and commerce, where very many of this race dwelt, and where they were fierce in their multitude and their great wealth and the King's protection, the first movement against them, as hath been reported to me, arose on this occasion. It chanced that one of their superstition was converted to the Christian faith; wherefore they, thirsting for his blood as that of a deserter and transgressor, sought occasion to wreak their malice upon him. One day, as he passed by, they caught up their arms and fell upon him: but he took refuge in the church hard by.*
Yet their madness ceased not there, but they began with pertinacious fury and assault to besiege that very church, in order that they might break the doors and drag the fugitive out to punishment. A vast clamour arose from those who were within the church; with resounding cries they called for Christian help. Their noise and report kindled to clamour the Christian folk who

---

* Jews' Lane at Lynn was at one corner of the greater market-place, and some 200 yards from the church of St Nicholas.

were hard by; and, at that news, those who were far off ran to arms. The Lynn citizens, for fear of the king, acted more remissly; but the young foreigners,* who had come thither in multitude for the sake of trade, rushed bravely upon those proud fighters. These, then, quitted the siege of the church and, unable to sustain the Christian assault, they took to flight. Some were slain as they fled; their houses were stormed and plundered by the Christians and given up to avenging flames; and very many Jews stained the fire or their foemen's sword with their blood. Next day there came a certain distinguished Jewish physician, whom even the Christians had honoured and befriended for the sake of his skill and his modesty. This man lamented the slaughter of his friends in somewhat immoderate terms; and, as though he prophesied vengeance, he awoke the still breathing fury [of the Christians]. They, therefore, seized him forthwith and made him, then and there, the latest victim of Jewish madness. The young foreigners, laden with booty, took to their ships, and sailed thence with all speed, lest perchance they should be submitted to question by the royal servants. The Lynn folk, when they were called to account by the king's officers, cast the blame upon the departed foreigners."

Shortly afterwards (writes William) there was a great Lenten-tide fair at Stamford, thronged now more than ever by young men bound for the Crusade. These men, "being indignant that the enemies of Christ's Cross who dwelt at Stamford should possess so much, while they themselves lacked for the cost of this great journey, thought fit to extort from them, as unjust possessors, that which they might apply to the needs of the pilgrimage which they had undertaken. Therefore, thinking to serve Christ if they assaulted these men whose goods they coveted, they rushed boldly upon them, without opposition to this great adventure either from the Stamford folk or from those who had come for the fair; nay, even with help from some of them. Some of the Jews were slain, the rest were received into the [royal] castle and escaped with difficulty. Their houses were plundered, and a great wealth of money stolen. The robbers went away with the gain of their work, and none was brought to judgment for public discipline on that account. But one most audacious youth, John by name,

---

* *Peregrini juvenes*: the men of Ely and Wisbech and Boston would be "foreigners" in Lynn parlance.

passed on to Northampton, where he left part of his money with
a man who, inflamed himself with greed for the same, slew him
secretly and cast his body forth from the city by night. It was
found and by chance recognized by some, while the greedy
murderer fled secretly. Soon old women began to dream, and
fallacious signs of miracles appeared there, so that simple folk
attributed to him the merit of a martyr, honouring the dead man's
sepulchre with solemn watchings and gifts. Roused by the report,
the foolish herd began to flock thither first from the neighbouring
parts and then, in their devout curiosity, even from divers provinces; and no man came empty-handed to his sepulchre, since
they desired either to see the miracles of this new martyr or to
gain his spiritual help. The prudent did indeed laugh at this;
yet it was grateful to the clergy, for the sake of the profits that
flowed from that superstition. The matter was referred to the
bishop, a man of excellent virtue, who, coming to the place in
the spirit of fortitude, profaned the shrine of this false martyr,
who had been exalted by the zeal of simple and covetous folk, and,
with his pontifical authority, forbade under formal anathema this
superstitious veneration of the dead man. Thus, by the pious and
efficacious work of a good pastor, all that operation of the deceiving
spirit was extinguished and brought to nought."

Our chronicler then goes on to relate the similar illegalities at
Lincoln (where, however, the royal officers brought fairly prompt
protection) and at York, where the tragedy was darkest of all.
There, the Jews "had built in the midst of the city, at most profuse
expense, houses of great size, comparable to royal palaces. . . .
Therefore very many men of that province had conspired against
them, not suffering that these men should be rich while they
themselves were in want; and, without any scruple of Christian
conscience, thirsting for the unbelievers' blood in greed for robbery." The Jews took refuge in the royal castle, where they were
besieged by a furious mob under the leadership of an ex-Premon-
stratensian hermit and some others of the clergy. These men
"thought to render great service to God by ridding the earth
of this people that rebelleth against the Lord, their darkened
minds being blind to that which is written in the person of David
(nay, in that of our Lord, since it is said in our Saviour's person)
*God shall let me see over mine enemies: slay them not, lest at any time
my people forget* (Ps. lviii. *Vulg.*). . . . Thus the Jews ought indeed to

live among Christians for our profit, but, by reason of their iniquity, to be our servants." The defence of the castle seemed at last hopeless, and that which followed must be told, here again, in the very words of this enlightened ecclesiastic. "There was there a certain elder (according to the letter, which killeth), a most famous teacher of law, who, as is said, had come from beyond the sea to teach the English Jews. He was honoured by all, and all obeyed him as one of the prophets. When therefore they asked his counsel at this time, he answered: 'God, to whom we must not say "why doest thou thus?" commandeth us now to die for His law. And lo, death is at our door, as ye see, unless perchance (which God forbid!) by reason of the brief space of this life ye think fit to desert our Holy Law, and choose (which to good and manly souls is harder than any death) to live as apostates, in the utmost disgrace, at the mercy of impious enemies. Since therefore we ought to prefer a glorious death to a life of deepest shame, we must choose the most honourable and easiest kind of death; for, if we fall into their hands, we shall die in mockery at their arbitrary choice. Therefore, since our Creator Himself doth now ask again for that life which He gave us, let us render it willingly and devoutly back with our own hands, nor let us await the ministration of our enemies' cruelty to restore that which God doth demand. For many of our race, in their divers tribulations, are known to have wrought in this praiseworthy fashion, supplying us beforehand with the example of a most decorous choice.' When he had thus spoken, very many embraced his fatal counsel; yet to some this seemed a hard saying.* Then said this elder: 'Let those who accept not so good and pious a counsel sit apart, as cut off from this holy community; for to us this mortal life is already worthless in comparison with our love for our Law.' Then, at the will of this most crazy elder, lest their foes should enrich themselves with the spoils, their precious garments were burned under the eyes of all, while the much-prized vessels, and whatsoever else could not be consumed with fire, were rendered worthless by subtle and shameful defilement. This done, they set fire to the roof; yet this, with its too

---

* Compare Joinville's frank words describing defeat and capture at the battle of Mansourah: "Then spake a cellarer of mine...'My counsel is that we should let ourselves be slain [rather than yield to these infidels]; thus we shall all go to Paradise'. But we believed him not" (c. LXIII, § 319).

solid materials, burned but slowly. While this horrible business was in progress, the elder prepared for sacrifice in rebuke to those also who had separated themselves for love of their own lives. So, when that man, grown old in evil days, directed that those who had more constancy of mind should slay their own wives and children, then that most renowned Joce cut with his keenest knife the throat of his own beloved wife Anna, nor did he spare his own children also. When the other men in turn had done thus, that most unhappy elder slaughtered Joce, as being more honourable than the rest. Soon all were slain, together with their master in error, and the tower began to burn within with that fire which, as we have said, had been set to it." The others climbed to the battlements of the tower, cast down to the besiegers the bodies of their fellows, and pleaded for baptism: "Vexation maketh us to understand [Isaiah xxviii. 19] and we acknowledge the truth of Christianity." The mob promised them their lives: but "no sooner had they come forth than, although they constantly demanded baptism, these butchers most cruelly slew them. I myself would unhesitatingly affirm concerning these whom that beastly cruelty thus sacrificed, that if there was no falsity in their petition for holy baptism, then they were in no wise defrauded thereof; in their own blood were they baptized.* But, whether it were falsely or truly that they sought the sacred font, we cannot excuse that execrable cruelty of their butchers. Beyond all doubt these men's first crime is that, without any orderly power, they presumed to shed men's blood like water. The second was, that their rage was rather in envy and malice than in righteous zeal; their third, that they grudged the Jews the Christian grace which these implored; and the fourth, that with a lie they betrayed these poor wretches to come forth to sacrifice. At that time, the whole city was indeed horrible and foul to behold, with so many miserable bodies that lay unburied all around the castle." The mob broke into the cathedral, compelled the clergy to surrender those Jews' bonds which were stored there for safety, and burned them in the midst of the minster. Yet, concludes William, "even unto this day no man hath been sentenced to death for that slaughter of the Jews". The only orthodox victim, in fact, during this whole uproar and siege, was the hermit who in his white robes was always there with religious encouragement. "It was said that on those siege-

* See later in Chapter xxxii.

Auto-de-Fe of Jews.

days, before he went forth to the bloody work, he offered at
daybreak the Bloodless Sacrifice; for he was a priest, and had so
far persuaded his own blinded mind, as he sought to persuade
others, that this work was a holy business." As he helped to
move the battering-tower up to the walls, a stone from above
crushed him to the earth; and William records this as a just punishment upon a priestly warrior.

A later monastic chronicler, Knighton of Leicester, while he
rejoices over the deed, admits likewise the impurity of the motives.
He writes how "the zeal of the Christians conspired against the
Jews in England, not indeed sincerely, for faith's sake, but either
in envy of their prosperity or as gaping after their fortune, a thing
which God's justice was far from approving but which He aptly
ordained in order that, by this means, He might restrain the insolence of this perfidious race. Beyond those things which the
Jews had suffered in their goods and their persons at Lincoln
and Lynn, at York also, after a long siege and affliction, the Rabbi,
the Master of the Jews, cut the veins of four hundred Jews and
then his own, and cut the throat of his wife." He goes on to
comment, almost in Newburgh's words, on the false miracles at
Northampton.[5]

WE cannot do better than begin here with Professor Petit-Dutaillis,[1] whose labours on English constitutional history have done so much to complement the great work of Stubbs. He writes: "Thanks to Henry II who, we are told, was capable of legal innovation, and to his advisers who understood the principles of Roman Law and knew its technicalities, the English monarchy was the only lay power in Western Europe to establish a common-law by the beginning of the thirteenth century. In France and Germany local custom still prevailed. The characteristic of royal justice in England was that it held local custom as of little account, and that, through its system of assizes and writs, it established a procedure and a jurisprudence of general application which was, on the whole, favourable to a free middle class and hostile to the seignorial spirit. We might well add 'hostile to the clerical spirit'; for Henry II sought to limit ecclesiastical jurisdiction and to make certain that criminous clerks were punished. The constitutions of Clarendon formed an important and significant part of his legislation." It is true that Henry's advisers were nearly all clerics; so that, as Pollock and Maitland note with felicitous irony, "it is by popish clergymen that our Common Law is converted from a rude mass of customs into an articulate system; and when the popish clergymen, yielding at length to the pope's commands, no longer sit as the principal justices of the King's Court, the creative age of our medieval law is over".[2] This, however, must be read in the light of the clerical monopoly over all English schools in those days, from the lowest to the highest; so that any man who could even read was presumed by law to be a clergyman. Even so, there is no certainty as to the clerical status of Glanvill, who was one of the greatest of these lawyers; and in Italy, where the clerical monopoly did not exist, the greatest lawyers were commonly laymen. With us, it was at Henry's command that these bishop-lawyers worked, and against the will of the Popes, who recognized clearly that such royal ministers were but unclerical clerics, and that the Church was losing through their services, however indirectly, as much as the State was gaining. In this particular matter the popish clergymen were loyal servants to our king, and disobedient to their pontiff.

Next to the Common Law, we owe most, perhaps, to the Jury system. Here again, as Petit-Dutaillis points out, Henry II was the great initiator. "It was an institution of Frankish origin; the Frankish kings employed the jury to discover criminals and false officials; William the Conqueror introduced the jury to England and used it in the compilation of Domesday Book; but before the reign of Henry II it had been more frequently used for administrative purposes than judicial. Henry II did not cease to use it for obtaining information, but he must have the credit for making it a smoothly-working judicial institution....In using the elected jury in this way the English kings were sowing seeds of a representative system in their counties."

The administration of this Common Law in England, supported by the Jury, was based upon two territorial divisions; the Shire and its subdivision, the Hundred. The Hundred Court sat monthly, and dealt with minor cases; it was presided over by the deputy of the Sheriff. From the twelfth century onwards it lost much of its importance, in proportion as the King's Court of Westminster centralized at the expense of the local courts. In the Shire, the royal representative was the Sheriff (Shire-reeve) in judicial as in fiscal and military affairs. Twice a year, he held a court also in each Hundred, at which the main business was the maintenance and proper working of the Tithing System. From before the Conquest, justice had been secured partly through the division of each *township* (to use a convenient word which covers both *town* and *village*) into tithings, or groups of ten men. These ten were responsible for each other, and were legally represented by one of the group, who was called *tithing-man* or *capital pledge*, the system itself being termed *frankpledge*. We have already seen a similar principle of mutual responsibility imposed upon the Hundred in cases of murder (Chapter v) and its utility for the maintenance of order in smaller areas is obvious. Like everything else in those days, the system was far less regular in many districts than theory demanded; but its operation at Norwich, where it was perhaps exceptionally efficient, has been worked out by Mr W. Hudson with his usual patience and clearness.* In that city "the total number of tithings was about 160. In modern language,

* *Records of the City of Norwich*, I, cxxxiv.

the city of Norwich in the thirteenth and fourteenth centuries was organized into 12 (or finally 10) police districts, containing 160 police associations." Each capital pledge was bound to report the misdoings of his own group, and was fined for concealment. Here, for instance, is the beginning of the Leet Court Roll for 1288.[3] "The capital pledges, namely [list of 12 names for one subleet, of which there were then 11 in Norwich], present on their oath that Ernald de Castro wounded Hugh de Bromholm and drew blood from him contrary to the peace, Likewise they present that Nicholas le Jay wounded a certain clerk, a stranger, and cut off two fingers of the said clerk and the hue was raised there and the said Nicholas was taken and imprisoned at the suit of Hugh de Bromholm, constable of the aforesaid leet; and Ernald and others escaped....Concerning those who sell and buy corn, they present that Robert Gerveys buys corn before it comes to the market, whereby the Bailiffs, etc. [i.e. lose their custom].... They present that all the alewives sell two gallons at one penny and two gallons at one penny halfpenny [sic]....All [the jurors] are in mercy" [i.e. are amerced for concealment].

The Shire was concerned with major criminal and Crown pleas; but the Sheriff dealt with criminal cases twice a year in the Hundred Courts, that is, in the neighbourhood where the crime had been committed and evidence was most easily obtained. Gradually the Crown took to itself all criminal jurisdiction (whether directly or by delegation) and the manor, on the other hand, took to itself most of the minor jurisdiction. On the manor were held two courts: the Court Leet for police, and the Court Baron for civil cases, such as ownership of land. At Norwich, as we have seen, it was the Court Leet which dealt with the Frankpledge system. The offences presented "were very numerous, and embraced nearly the whole field of local jurisdiction. Even murder, manslaughter, or death by accident might be presented, but they were not decided by the court. The main presentments were for theft (if serious, this was reserved for a higher court), assaults, raising the hue and cry wrongfully, or without due cause, nuisances of all sorts, market and trade offences (forestalling, regrating, etc.)." By far the commonest offence, here and in other towns, was breach of the assize of ale. For bread and for ale, Government had a fixed tariff, varying according to the price of corn. Mr Hudson notes how at Norwich, as elsewhere, "almost every housewife of the leading families brewed ale and sold it to her neighbours, and invariably charged more than the fixed price. The authorities evidently expected and wished this course to be taken; for these ladies were regularly presented and amerced every year for the same offence, paid their amercements and went away to go through the same process in the future as in the past. Much the same course was pursued by other trades and occupations. Fishmongers, tanners, poulterers, cooks, etc., are fined wholesale year after year for breaking every by-law that concerned their business. In short, instead of a trader (as now) taking out a licence to do his business on certain conditions which he is expected to keep, he was bound by conditions which he was expected to break and afterwards fined for the breach. The same financial result was attained or aimed at by a different method."4 For the judicial system in English cities had not emerged very far beyond that rudimentary stage of sanctions which is displayed by the present League of Nations. By law, that is, in theory, repetition of the offence should have increased the severity of the fine in proportion to its frequency; but, in fact, the wholesale offender enjoyed a reduction in virtue of his larger business, if indeed he did not escape altogether. For medieval justice, from the king's or pope's court down to that of the manor, was, by the universal testimony of contemporaries, stained by open venality. The judge who steadily refuses "gifts" is extolled as a marvel; that, in fact, is one of St Thomas More's claims to sanctity. In *Piers Plowman* "Lady Meed" (that is, the Almighty Dollar) rules the king's courts; and, in the cities, mayors wink at the misdoings of wealthy and unscrupulous capitalists. Moreover, this venality infected even the field in which the Church boasted herself as most uncompromising: even that matrimony which she had erected into one of the Seven Sacraments. Here, again, we shall see in a later chapter that Langland is a witness, with unexceptionable colleagues both before and after him, down to Erasmus on the verge of the Reformation. Moreover, the most unimpeachable statistics from our city archives show clearly what went on behind the scenes. At Norwich, the roll of 1289 shows us what fines were adjudged, and what were collected. The former total was £72. 18s. 10d.; moreover, this, by strict law, should have been very much higher. Yet, even of this mild and diminished total, all that the collectors could account for, after considerable delay, was £17. 0s. 2d.

"Some are excused by the Bailiffs without reason assigned; some 'at the instance' of certain great people wishing to do a good turn for a friend. Again, others make a bargain with the collector, thus expressed, as for instance, 'john de Swaffham is not in tithing. Amercement 2s. He paid 6d. the rest is excused. He is quit.' Sometimes an entry is marked 'vad', i.e. *vadiat*, or *vadiatur*, he gives a pledge, or, it is pledged. The Collector had seized a jug, or basin, or chair. But by far the larger number of entries are marked 'd', i.e. *debet*, he owes it."[5] All our civic records tell much the same tale. Here, for instance, is a case quoted by Miss Abram (p. 263): "John Bristowe of Reading was ordered to pay a fine of four thousand tiles, because he had been rebellious to the Mayor, but he was let off three thousand of them on the spot; and sometimes offenders were allowed to go unpunished because they were too poor to pay a fine: the idea of imprisonment as an alternative did not find favour because it entailed a good deal of trouble and expense on the community."

Let us now take a wider survey of "the King's Peace" in England. Every township had one or two constables. At Norwich, one of the greatest cities in the land, there was one constable to every hundred able-bodied men on the muster-rolls, with subordinate officers under him, *vinteners*, or captains of twenty, and *decennars*, captains of ten. What sort of peace those constables were bound to keep may be read in the royal writs of 1252–3 for Watch and Ward. This enacts: "(1) That watches be held in the several townships as hath been wont, and by honest and able men. (2) That the hue and cry be followed according to the ancient use, so that all who neglect and refuse to follow it up shall be taken into custody as abettors of the wrongdoers, and shall be delivered up to the Sheriff. Moreover, in every township, let four or six men be chosen according to its size, to follow the hue and cry hastily and swiftly, and to pursue the wrongdoers, if need be, with bows and arrows and other light arms, which should be provided at the common cost of the township and remain ever for the use thereof. And to this end let two free and lawful men be chosen from the most powerful in each hundred, who shall oversee the work and see that the aforesaid watches and pursuits be rightly carried out. (3) That no stranger abide in the township except by day, and that he depart while it is yet daylight. (4) That no stranger be harboured in county townships beyond one day, or two at most, save only in time of harvest, unless his host be willing to answer for him....(5) That the mayor and bailiffs of all cities and boroughs be bidden that, if any merchant or stranger bearing money do show them the said money and beg for safe conduct, then they must so conduct him through the evil passes and doubtful ways; and if he lose aught for default of such conduct or under their conduct, then let him be indemnified by the inhabitants of the said borough or city." This system was extended and consolidated in 1285, by an ordinance which fixed for the rest of the Middle Ages the form taken by our constabulary and militia; it gave us a nation organized for the double purpose of soldiery and police.

With all this, though England was more orderly than other great states, yet the coroners' rolls show manslaughter in enormous preponderance over death by accident. It is impossible to judge, at this distance, whether most of these cases would pass for wilful murder at the present day; but the statistics seem to point to at least ten times as many definite murders, per head of population, and possibly even twice or thrice that proportion. Certainly the manslayer and the thief—for grave theft was, in law, no less a hanging matter—had in those days far greater chances of escape. The rolls recount, with wearisome iteration, that "he has fled, and has left no chattels" for confiscation; or, again, he has taken sanctuary and abjured the realm.

It is a prehistoric and universal principle that the burden of defence should rest upon all able-bodied males. The decadence of ancient Rome, even in art and literature, synchronized with those generations which accustomed themselves to be defended by hired troops, and even to a great extent fed and amused at the public expense. France in the fourteenth century had let this principle slip; musters were indeed commanded sometimes, but only as an oblique form of taxation; the man was allowed, and even encouraged, to buy himself off; we may say more, royal officials might even compel him to choose redemption instead of personal service. Under St Louis himself, when the inhabitants of three villages in the South maintained (with perfect justice), that they would not pay this time for substitutes but come in person at the royal call for a levy of defence against the Spaniards, then the *viguier* of Béziers settled the dispute with one level volley: "March to the bridge of Vidorle or don't march, just as you please.

I intend to get £12. 10s. from you. You bloody peasants, whether you will or whether you won't, you shall pay all the same!"— *O rustici sanguinolenti, vos dabitis, velitis vel non.*[6] Matters were very different in England, where the Fyrd, the Anglo-Saxon militia system, was reorganized by Henry II and again by Edward I.[7] By the latter's "Statute of Winchester", every able-bodied man was bound not only to possess arms on a scale proportionate to his wealth, but also to learn their use. For Edward was determined to wed practice with theory: he had learned from his Welsh enemies that the longbow, already a well-known weapon among his own subjects, was far superior in battle to the crossbow: therefore he gradually set about training a large force of archers. Falkirk (1298) was the first important battle in which the archery was used in scientific combination with cavalry. Bannockburn (1314) was the last in which the English repeated the old blunder of relying on mounted knights and men-at-arms, and allowing the infantry to act as a more or less disordered mass. Mr Hudson has printed from the Norwich archives lists of armed citizens between 1355 and 1370 which show that the city provided and reviewed a somewhat larger proportion than would be furnished by the modern system of conscription on the Continent. Many of these men, of course, turned out with no more than the minimum requirement of club and knife. The next step was to add a sword or an axe to those primitive weapons; and so on, through the archers, to the numerous "half-armed men", who had in addition to their offensive weapons a plated doublet with visor and iron gauntlets; and finally the "fully-armed", who had in addition a shirt of mail under the doublet, with neck-piece and arm-plates, and who boasted each a total equipment which must have cost some £50 or £60 of modern money.

These archers of Norwich were evidently of the upper class, men accustomed to shoot at game, which, in the advanced Eastern Counties, would be comparatively rare. But, for the army in general, the great majority of archers were recruited from forest districts such as Charnwood or Cheshire and the borderland of Wales; while the "knife-men" came mainly from hilly districts like Wales and Cornwall. Under this system, in 1346, while our armies were winning Crécy in France, and the Scots attempted to take us at a disadvantage in the rear, they received one of the most crushing defeats in their history. Again, a threatened invasion in 1360 called out all men from sixteen to sixty; many clergy fought in person, and others hired substitutes. These facts have far greater importance than has commonly been assigned to them. We may feel that war, even at its best, is thoroughly unworthy of our present civilization; yet, just as it takes two to make a quarrel, so also it takes both sides to maintain peace; and, when the fire is once kindled, it is better to be victor than vanquished. Moreover, when we consider that war, even in the fourteenth century, was by no means a mere matter of brute force but required also much force of character and intellect, it is difficult to escape the conclusion that, on the whole, in the long perspective of history, victory has gone to the side best fitted to survive. In that great struggle between medieval England and France, no doubt both sides were morally in the wrong; but, in the events themselves, certain points are beyond dispute. In the first place, the English waged war with greater national cohesion; in our armies, it was possible for a man to rise from the ranks to the highest commands. In France, on the other hand, the nobles and their feudal levies controlled all; and where the citizen militias were brought in, as at Crécy, these were a disorganized rabble destined merely for slaughter. Though Du Guesclin was the greatest general produced on either side, his first important victory was due to the lucky chance that a prince of the blood had sufficient good sense to hand over his command to him for that day; and it was part of his greatness that he clearly recognized the superiority of the English system. Siméon Luce writes truly: "Such seems to have been the opinion of Bertrand du Guesclin, the most renowned captain of the Middle Ages, who never fought a great pitched battle against a real English army if he could possibly help it. At Cocherel his adversaries were mostly Gascons; and at Pontvallain he crushed Knolles's rear-guard by one of those startling marches of which he had the secret; but he was beaten at Auray and Navarette," i.e. in the two great pitched battles in which he met us.[8] We need pursue this side of our subject no farther here, for unquestionably wars and the diplomatic manœuvres which have led to wars have hitherto bulked too large in history.

But two points may here be noted, for their social importance. In the first place, the comparative orderliness of our Peasants' Revolt in 1381, as compared with all similar revolts on the

Continent. We must recognize not only the general discipline of the peasant rebels, but also the extent to which it was possible for the Government to bargain with them collectively; the treachery by which that bargain was subsequently broken is irrelevant to the present question. Secondly, we must note (and this is by far the more important point) that the same system which gave us the most efficient army in Europe supplied us also with the most orderly police force, and enabled "the King's Peace" to become a greater reality here than elsewhere. While Dante was describing the Italy of his day as "a hostelry of pain", our English liberties were growing on from precedent to precedent; and, behind all those ill effects of the Hundred Years' War which cannot be blinked on either side, English civic liberties and the expansion of our trade stand out in startling contrast with the decay of towns and commerce in France. To this we must return in Chapter xxxix; meanwhile let us look more closely into the working of the medieval militia as a police system.

Let us choose a concrete case for quotation and comment. In 1311 William of Wellington, chaplain of the parish of Yelvertoft, quarrelled with one of his parishioners and killed him with a bludgeon.9 The jury "say on their oath that they know no man guilty of John's death save the said William of Wellington. He therefore came before the aforesaid coroner and confessed that he had slain the said John; wherefore he abjured the realm of England in the presence of the said four townships brought together [for this purpose]. And the port of Dover was assigned to him." What, then, happened to this William when he "abjured the realm"? We will blink for a moment the fact that, as a priest, he should by theory have been immune from ordinary justice; let us face his position as if he had been an ordinary layman. By this abjuration he saved himself from summary execution; and the coroner might be detained several days before he could come and deal with him. Meanwhile the community would keep watch over the church or other sanctuary in which he had taken refuge. Then, on the coroner's arrival, the criminal's confession was registered and he took his oath to quit the realm within 40 days. Coming to the gate of the church or churchyard, he swore solemnly before the assembled crowd: "Oyez, oyez, oyez! Coroner and other good folk: I, William of Wellington, for the crime of manslaughter which I have committed, will quit this land of

England nevermore to return, except by leave of the Kings of England or their heirs: so help me God and His saints!" The coroner then assigned him a port, and a reasonable time for the journey; from Yelvertoft to Dover it would have been about a week. His bearing during this week was minutely prescribed: never to stray from the high-road, or spend two nights in the same place; to make straight for his port, and to embark without delay. If at Dover he found no vessel ready to sail, then he was bound daily to walk into the sea up to his knees—or, according to stricter authorities, up to his neck—and to take his rest only on the shore, in proof that he was ready in spirit to leave this land which by his crimes he had forfeited. His dress meanwhile was that of a felon condemned to death—a long, loose white tunic, bare feet, and a wooden cross in his hand to mark that he was under protection of Holy Church. English law was glad to have thus rid itself of a villain, and troubled no further; but the records leave us sceptical whether any very large proportion of these unwilling pilgrims actually found their way across the sea. No doubt in some cases, in spite of ecclesiastical protection, they would be waylaid and fallen upon by friends of the murdered man. In many more cases, and probably in the majority, this criminal would see no reason why he should take so much trouble to go to France, where he might meet with no better reception than in England. He would therefore take the earliest opportunity of slipping away from the high-road; thence he would march as a vagrant to some district where he was unknown, and join that class of sturdy beggars or malefactors who bulk so largely in *Piers Plowman*. After all, such men were welcome recruits for the army; and there was generally fighting somewhere. When there was not, as *Piers Plowman* will tell us, the countryside swarmed with discharged and workless soldiers. There is one other alternative: what if William had refused to confess guilt and simply clung to the sanctuary? To judge from the records, at least 50 per cent. did thus refuse; and here both theory and practice leave us uncertain. The law gave him 40 days of grace in any case; yet if, on the expiration of that period, the lay authorities came in and tore him from the altar, they might have to reckon with episcopal excommunication. Therefore the lawyers tried to throw the onus of expulsion upon the bishop or arch-deacon through their servants; but we may well excuse the ecclesiastical authorities for shrinking from thus facing a desperate malefactor. Here, therefore, as in so many other cases, the issue was left more or less to chance: *solvitur ambulando*. The village did its best to starve the man out, and meanwhile to watch him night and day. One offender, whose 40 days had expired on August 12th, 1374, held out against this blockade until September 9th, when he fled; then there was a hue and cry of the whole village. Let us suppose that our priest did the same. He might indeed run the gauntlet and make good his escape, leaving his quondam neighbours to prove before the justices that they had done all they could; failing which, they must pay a fine for their negligence. On the other hand, however, a stick or stone might bring him down at close quarters, or an arrow from afar; then in a moment he would be overpowered and beheaded, and that chase would be long remembered for its excitement in Yelvertoft.

So much for the ordinary offender, but in this case of William of Wellington there was a gross irregularity. St Thomas Becket, "the holy blissful martyr", had by his death consecrated the principle that a felonious cleric might be condemned by clerics alone. Thus the routine was that a clerical homicide or thief, though he might be arrested by layfolk and tried by them, must yet be handed over to the bishop to be finally dealt with. The lay judges took care to pronounce their own decision first; they handed the man over to the bishop as a criminal. But beyond that they had no responsibility, and the bishop commonly admitted him to "compurgation". By this system the accused presented himself with as many "compurgators" as the bishop chose to specify in virtue of the man's own character and the gravity of his offence. The accused himself then swore solemnly on the Gospels to his innocence, and each of the compurgators swore that to the best of his knowledge the accused had sworn the truth. The records themselves would have suggested very strongly in any case that, human nature being such as it is, and the tendency of every class of society being to stick by its fellow-members, this system of compurgation would lead to a good deal of perjury and give the criminal unfair chances of escape. However, we are not left to mere inferences of that kind; for contemporaries sometimes speak quite plainly, and condemn the system in the strongest terms. The great Oxford Chancellor Gascoigne [1450] took care to leave on record in his own hand, on the register of his university, that the system was often "an occasion of intolerable iniquity". Chaucer's contemporary, Gower, says equally plainly that the clergy are thus judges in their own cause and each shields the other: "My turn to-day; to-morrow thou shalt do the like for me." The Commons were finally obliged to press the king for fresh and more stringent laws to remedy the notorious fact that "upon trust of the privilege of the Church, divers persons have been the more bold to commit murder, rape, robbery, theft, and other mischievous deeds, because they have been continually admitted to the benefit of the clergy as often as they did offend in any of the [aforesaid]".

To go back, then, to William of Wellington. A few years before the date of his trial we find Edward I sending out a general warning to the Bishop of Worcester, "forbidding him to take the purgation of clerks detained in his prison, whose crimes are notorious; but with regard to others he may take such purgation". Therefore we need not wonder that, since William's crime was notorious to the people of Yelvertoft (for the attack was in fact most brutal and unprovoked), they had taken the law into their own hands and dealt with their priest as though he had not been anointed with oil. Less than a century later, as we have seen, the citizens of London took to this as a regular policy, in spite of Church Law.

However, in spite of the enlistment of the whole population in favour of the King's Peace, even comparatively orderly England showed a proportion of manslaughters which would be considered scandalous in modern times. Impulse played a part so far more important than reflection; and the chances of escape were so great. Attentive readers of Chaucer must have noticed that when Harry Bailey, the Host, confesses himself to be "perilous with knife in hand", and deplores his wife's instigations to fight, he reckons as his possible fate not the gallows, but only outlawry:

> I wot well she will do me slay some day
> Some neighëbour, and thennë go my way....

The fact is that judicial statistics of the Middle Ages show the murderer to have had many more chances of survival than the convicted thief. The Northumberland Roll of 1279 (to choose a typical instance) gives 72 homicides to only 43 accidental deaths. These 72 deaths were brought home to 83 culprits, of whom only

3 are recorded to have been hanged. Of the remainder, 69 escaped altogether, 6 took sanctuary, 2 were never identified, 1 pleaded his clergy, 1 was imprisoned, and 1 was fined.

We cannot altogether omit the Ordeal, although this was formally abrogated by Innocent III and had been waning in popularity from the Conquest onward, except in cases of trial by battle. The ordinary ordeal was one of the many prehistoric customs finally tolerated, and even blessed, by the Church. There was a solemn ritual for the consecration of the fire or the water, as the case might be. In the water ordeal, the accused who sank was safe; if he floated he was condemned. If the ordeal is that of fire, a red hot iron must be carried three paces; the hand is then sealed up for three days, and if at the end a blister as large as half a walnut is found this is fatal; or, again, another ordeal was to plunge the hand and take out an iron from a cauldron of boiling water. Professor Maitland's comment here is suggestive. "We must, however, not forget the psychology of this system. In itself it may seem the height of absurdity sanctioned by the grossest superstition, but there can be little doubt that in fact the ordeal would be a very effective test in a large number of cases. The man who knew himself to be guilty might very well shrink before it came to the actual point, and make a clean breast of it." For the superstition was two-sided; not only did its psychology fortify justice, but it also weakened the criminal proportionately. Among all the marvellous tales circulated in the Middle Ages—and we must always remember that in those tales the supernatural shows itself equally effectively whether coming from God or from the Devil—there is a considerable number dealing with divine justice upon false swearers. A fisherman, for instance, coming away victorious from the ordeal at Cologne in which he had perjured himself, and being asked whether the hot water had not pained him, dipped his hand over the boatside into the water and answered, "I felt it no more than I feel this." Next moment, he withdrew his hand in agony, for the Rhine water had scalded him! So, again, we may still see a statue in the great church of Abbeville which records the miraculous judgment upon the wife of St Gengulfus, parodied in the *Ingoldsby Legends*. Here the saint, suspecting his wife of infidelity, requested her to pick a stone out of a fountain. There also the cold water scalded her, her sin was proclaimed. In an atmosphere of such stories it must often have needed considerable nerve to face the ordeal at all, and in any case the conscious criminal might show his guilt so clearly in his face, even while he performed the necessary acts, that the priest could safely interpret against him those exceedingly elastic tokens which were supposed to show the judgment of God. It must be noted that the ordeal, though it went out of favour in the middle of our period, was revived in the later Middle Ages for the trial of witches.

Trial by battle was imposed upon the unwilling Anglo-Saxons by their Norman conquerors. This was never so definitely condemned by the Church, even in later times, as other ordeals, and indeed it was not blotted from the English Statute Book until the early nineteenth century. The formalities here, civil and ecclesiastical, were more minute than any other cases. When an "appeal of felony" was made, the accuser and accused must originally fight in person, unless youth or maiming introduced an obviously unfair element. The combatants had to swear solemnly to the truth of their cause and to having no trust in witchcraft. When it is not a question of felony, but only a dispute for ownership of land, substitutes are allowed, and in fact many great folk kept hired champions. The ordinary weapons were evidently traditional—a shield, a pick something like a small ice-axe, and a leather jacket were allowed. The funeral brass of Wyville, Bishop of Salisbury (1375) bears the figure of the episcopal champion standing in a fortified gateway, which no doubt represents the bishop's successful contest for the ownership of Sherborne Castle; and we find mention of a similar episcopal champion in the Rolls of Swinfield, a Bishop of Hereford (1320). Such a battle might last all day long "until the stars appear". In a criminal case the conquered combatant was hanged or mutilated off-hand.

Perhaps the greatest superiority of English over Continental justice was the absence of torture from the law-courts. Here one of our most emphatic witnesses is Sir John Fortescue, in his comparison between fifteenth-century England and France on this matter. He writes: "My penne is both wearie and ashamed to rehearse the outragiousness of torments devised in this behalfe.... But who is so hard harted, which, being once released out of so cruell a Racke, though he bee innocent and faultlesse, would not yet rather accuse himselfe of all kindes of offences, then againe to commit himself to the intollerable crueltie of the torment once proved: and had not rather die at once (seeing death is the end of all miseries) then so often to bee killed, and to sustaine so many hellish furies, painfuller than death it selfe."[10] To this freedom from torture (apart from the *peine forte et dure*) there was only one great exception in all our period. When, in 1311, Philip IV of France desired to destroy the Templars, and made Clement V his unwilling accomplice from beginning to end of that bad business, evidence was easily procured against them in France by means of torture. The prisoners were made to confess things so absurd that no modern historian maintains the particular facts, however he may be tempted to believe, for the sake of king or pope, that there must have been some general truth in the accusations. In England, it was found impossible to obtain condemning evidence. Therefore the Pope wrote to Edward: We hear that you forbid torture as contrary to the laws of your land; but no State law can override Canon Law, Our Law; therefore I command you at once to submit those men to torture. He added a threat: You have already imperilled your soul as a favourer of heretics; and with it a bribe: Withdraw your prohibition, and we grant you remission of your sins. Therefore we find Edward replying that "through reverence for the Holy See" he will give the Inquisition a free hand in England. There is no record that anything more was needed, and that torture was actually applied to these poor wretches in our own country. If not, it is evident that the mere threat of torture was enough, as it well might be: in any case the evidence needed was somehow obtained, and they were condemned. Thus, whether in practice or merely in threat, torture found its way into the English law courts for the first and almost only time until the reign of Mary.

It will be seen, therefore, that this combined military and police system, which was perfected by the Statute of Winchester, was responsible for many of the advantages which England enjoyed in comparison with her neighbour and rival, France. It secured us safety from invasion. During the whole Hundred Years' War, even during the time when we lost command of the seas, the French never did more than burn one or two of our ports and occupy the Isle of Wight for six months. It rendered a large mercenary army unnecessary. When Charles V's ambassador urged upon him that England might be easy to invade, he instanced that Henry VIII had no soldiers of his own beyond his bodyguard of a hundred archers at the Tower. And we shall see that, when Charles VII of France created an army which was finally able to drive out the English invader, that was only at the cost of fixing upon the French people, until the Revolution of 1789, a mercenary army at the sole control of the executive, fed by irresponsible taxation. It was the London trainbands—that is, the more efficient part of the militia—which enabled the parliament to assert our liberties against Charles's professional army in 1642, and it was the militia again which made it possible for Wellington to hold out through the Napoleonic Wars. In the spring of 1914, I had the privilege of discussing these matters with Albert Thomas, right-hand man to the great socialist and pacifist leader Jean Jaurès. He assured me of the loyalty of all socialists to the system of conscription, excepting only the tiny handful who dreamed of a nation completely unarmed. Some fifteen years later, he came to Cambridge as Secretary of the International Labour Bureau at Geneva. I asked him whether the War had done anything to change his mind on that subject. He replied that, on the contrary, it had reinforced his conviction, not only from the military but even more from the social standpoint. "For", he added, "no democracy can afford to leave its military forces at the sole command of the Executive."

This fusion of military and police control did much for the unity of the nation. It favoured the growth of that "Common Law" which is at the base not only of British justice, but of American also: it was in virtue of the Common Law inherited from us that Abraham Lincoln was able to introduce compulsory manhood service in answer to the South. This co-operation of all classes in England prevented the feudal distinctions from stiffening, as in France, into a rigid caste-system. If, in our parliaments, the knights of the shire sat with the burgesses and not with the greater barons, and the lower clergy also were content to dis-interest themselves of all parliamentary business except their own taxation, this was due, at least in a great measure, to the natural co-operation of classes in peace and war. Apart from the clergy with their Canon Law, English Common Law became that of all men; the army and the administrators themselves were bound by it, as well as civilians and subjects; the nobles as well as the commonalty. Here, even in the Middle Ages, was equality in the sense of equal legal standing for all freemen. The law crystallized this as part of the same process by which "blue blood" lost the predominance which it kept in some Continental countries. Our kings had been strong enough to enforce primogeniture among their baronage, and to keep to themselves the right of creating new baronages: thus the younger sons became commoners, and the great lords had to work in co-operation with the other elements of society. Hence the growth of a spirit of reasonable compromise, and, as Maitland pointed out, a tradition of local government which has been of the utmost social value in the position which it has assigned to unpaid and unprofessional work for the State, and in the healthy link which it has maintained between local needs and the central government. The king's writ might not run in medieval England quite as it runs to-day. In the fifteenth-century Chancery Petitions we find an Abbot of Westminster complaining that Roger Power of Bletchington "threatened to make the bringer of the king's writ [in the abbot's favour] eat the same"; and, again, Robert Talbot bringing an action against his adversaries for "disworshipping" the king by compelling the servers of one writ to eat it, "both wax and parchment", and treading another underfoot.[11] But Commines points out, even concerning the Wars of the Roses, how far more orderly the English were in their disorders than the people of France.

So much for State law and justice. Papal law (Canon Law), is too wide a subject for treatment in detail without far more space than the present volume can afford. It has already come in incidentally, and will fill the greater part of Chapter XLVI: therefore, at this point, the briefest summary must suffice. In early Christianity we may say that, as in Islam, Church law was the only law. To St Paul, it was preposterous that brother should go to law with brother, and before unbelievers. With Constantine came in the problem of Church and State. Henceforward we find a series of enactments by which the State undertakes to back up by physical force the regulations which had hitherto reposed only on moral force. Imperial statutes gave to the Church the right of holding property, the protection of sanctuary for her buildings, freedom for the clergy from military service, and, finally, the right of condemnation for heresy, with consequent State punishment for any man thus stigmatized (Theodosian Code, A.D. 438). About 450, the Western Emperor, Valentinian III, granted the Pope power to legislate as chief bishop for the whole

Western Church; so that, from thenceforth, papal decretals had the force of law within the religious sphere. At first, Popes made very modest use of this new privilege: the time was not yet ripe. But Justinian's codification of Civil Law (529) supplied the model and impetus for a similar movement in the Church. Thus there gradually grew up collections of decrees—imperial, papal, synodal —affecting the Church as such: a *Jus Canonicum* in imitation of the *Jus Civile*. Such collections claimed both religious and civil sanction: "If you break these laws, you will be damned while I shall be saved; meanwhile the State will empower me to fine you and to appropriate your fine." This inextricable mixture of legalism and theology, especially in the age of the barbarian conversions, has already been noted in Chapter III.

At this point, an epoch-making step was taken by a Roman monk, Dionysius Exiguus. His compilation of conciliar decrees and papal decretals [A.D. 500] was so much completer and more orderly than its predecessors, that it was frequently quoted by Popes, and, thus by Charlemagne's time, had attained to such a semi-official status as publications like *Bradshaw* and *Hansard* enjoy at the present day. Considerable additions were made by different canonists, especially between 1080 and 1120; and then came another epoch-making work, Gratian's *Decretum*. Here, again, the author was an Italian monk, and his work is correctly described in its original title, *The Concordance of Discordant Canons*. The arrangement, with all its defects, was far more orderly than in any of his predecessors; and this book became the first volume of the *Corpus Juris Canonici*: yet it is characteristic of medieval want of method even in the most important matters, that it never was official in the strictest sense. At the same time, it was possible for such a learned friar as the author of *Dives and Pauper* to speak of Gratian's *Decretum* as "the chief book of Law Canon"; and a solemn papal commission of 1582 edited the whole *Corpus* without any distinction between Gratian and the rest, and with a papal brief forbidding any alteration in the Text of Gratian.* The rest of the *Corpus* was formed from later papal decretals, formally enregistered and arranged from 1234 onwards at the command of different Popes, and ending with those of John XXII

* Compare Professor Imbart de la Tour's criticism in other fields: "The façade of the institutions [of the Dark Ages] was ill fitted to hide the internal anarchy which threatened them." (*Rev. Hist.* LXIII, 23.)

[1317]. From that time forward the great States were becoming too powerful, and the Papacy too insecure on its political foundation, for a policy so provocative of conflict. Yet this law. with all its defects, was far completer and clearer and more methodical than that of any of the great States. From the clergy of Europe it exacted full obedience; our local English Canon Law stood to the *Corpus Juris Canonici* only in the relation of by-law to Statute law. From the laity it demanded, as it still does in its revised code of 1917, obedience above that of the law of the land in case of conflict. Such claims, however, were frequently resisted by the English laity, even before the anti-papal legislation of Edward III; and the total collapse of Canon Law under Henry VIII is well known. His visitors at Oxford, in the year before the Suppression of the Monasteries, forbade the study of Canon Law as part of the advanced policy which moved them to establish three Greek lectureships, beyond the one which Bishop Fox had already founded at Corpus College.

XXXI. FROM SCHOOL TO UNIVERSITY

IN this field admirable pioneer work was done by the late A. F. Leach, in his *Schools of Medieval England* and elsewhere; and we have Hastings Rashdall's monumental *Universities of Europe in the Middle Ages*, of which an edition has been published since his death, revised, corrected, and very fully annotated by Professor Powicke and Principal Emden. The reader who cannot find time for this three-volume monograph will find compendious essays, clear and trustworthy, by Rashdall and Professor G. R. Potter in *The Cambridge Medieval History*. "In England, from the first," writes Leach, "education was the creature of religion; the school was an adjunct of the Church, and the schoolmaster was an ecclesiastical officer. For close on eleven hundred years, from 598 to 1670, all educational institutions were under exclusively ecclesiastical control. The law of education was a branch of the Canon Law. The Church courts had exclusive jurisdiction over schools and universities and colleges, and until 1540 all schoolmasters and scholars were clerks, or clerics or clergy, and in Orders, though not necessarily holy Orders." So definitely was this the case, that at an eminent grammar school like Canterbury the master had even the terrible weapon of excommunication at his disposal, as decreed by Canon Law against anyone who should assault a cleric. In 1314, "Thomas of Birchwood, scholar of the said school, being summoned *ex officio* for many delinquencies against the law of the aforesaid school, viz. hindering the vice-monitor and his scholars from their public teaching, and also for a violent assault on Master Walter, the vice-monitor, appeared and was sworn, and confessed that he had violently assaulted the said Walter".[1] Master Walter was doubtless a Master of Grammar, of that degree to which we shall presently come; and the aggressor was therefore cut off from the communion of the faithful until he should have done due penance.

All this is true not only in England but everywhere north of the Alps. In Italy a good many Roman grammar schools probably survived from imperial times, so that at Milan or Siena, for instance, the present school may well be unbrokenly continuous from its ancestor under the Roman Empire. Consequently, education was much more of a lay matter in Italy throughout the Middle Ages. In England, the first Church decree on the subject is that of the Council of Cloveshoe in 747, which aimed at the establishment of an elementary school in every parish. Eugenius II (826) decreed something of the same kind for all Europe. About 994, an English synod prescribed "that priests shall keep schools in the villages and teach small boys without fee: priests ought always to keep schools of schoolmasters in their houses, and if any of the faithful is willing to give his little ones to be educated he ought to receive them willingly and teach them kindly". That decree, however, is only slightly varied from one of Theodulph, Bishop of Orleans, in 797; which itself repeated a decree of 682 at Constantinople— that is, among people of ancient culture, untouched by the barbarian invasions. Leach writes truly, "applied either to France in the days of Charlemagne or England in the days of Etheldred, these can have been little more than a pious aspiration".

Our next evidence comes from one Aelfric, a pupil of Dunstan, who was Abbot of Eynsham in 1005. His *Colloquy*, a dialogue in Latin for the instruction of schoolboys, gives us a very vivid picture of school at that time. To begin with, we find the rough material. The teacher asks: "Who are you here before me?" and one pupil answers for "us boys" (*nos pueri*). The list of pupils includes a professed monk, ploughmen, shepherds, cowherds, fishermen, fowlers, merchants, shoemakers, hunters and bakers. We must not, of course, take this catalogue too literally; the writer's business was to bring in as many occupations as possible, in order to increase the vocabulary of his scholars. Yet it was necessary for the list to have some sort of verisimilitude. The French grammars of our childhood did indeed ask: "Have you the green penholder of my wife's aunt?" but not "Have you the green blouse and skirt of my wife's uncle?" We have no reason to doubt that there was very much the same mixture among early scholars in a village or town school as there was later in the early days of the universities. Next, the book throws light upon discipline. The teacher asks: "Are you ready to be flogged while you learn?" (*Vultis flagellari in discendo?*). The pupils answer: "We would rather be flogged for learning's sake than be ignorant"; but they add ingratiatingly: "We know that thou art a humane man, and wilt not beat us unless our conduct compels thee."[2] This trait is corroborated everywhere in medieval scholastic records. The great philosopher John the Scot is said to have been slain by his pupils at Malmesbury Abbey with their pens. Abbot Guibert of Nogent gives a heartrending description of his own days under a private tutor; and Caesarius of Heisterbach [1250] reckons that if a boy dies at school he may well deserve the palm of martyrdom.

Again, all the records of the period show the miserable quality of texts and reference books. Even Boethius, the great popularizer, in his book on geometry gives little but a selection of enunciations of propositions of Euclid without the demonstrations. In pre-Conquest England there were schools nominally at each episcopal see, where the clergy were centred and, generally, in practice at most of them. But King Alfred complains of the immense ignorance of his time; and, though we must not exaggerate the contrast introduced by the Normans, we have little record of schools until we come to the Conquest. From that time forward we may some-times find elementary schools in parishes, with occasional monastic and episcopal schools. The elementary school, as we have seen, depended on the goodwill of the particular priest. The grammar schools seem, at first, to have been generally offshoots of the episcopal schools, which, at their best, taught a certain amount of philosophy and theology, but in which a large proportion of scholars would get no farther than the grammar. Very seldom do we find a monk teaching in any grammar school, nor were such, as a rule, founded by monks; although the community of the adjacent monastery was very commonly made into governors of the school, and entrusted with its finances. The monks, contrary to a venerable superstition, were not the ordinary schoolmasters of the Middle Ages. This truth has been emphasized as definitely by Professor Mandonnet, late rector of the Roman Catholic University of Fribourg, as by anyone else. It transpires clearly from St Benedict's Rule that he contemplates monastic education only for the "oblates"; that is, children offered to the monastery and destined to take the vows when they grew up and never to leave the precincts until their death. However, under early missionary conditions, the monks did fairly often teach outsiders; just as, for instance, they sometimes built then their own rough buildings. In our period, however, the only "external" schools in the monasteries were the song and almonry schools. The former was mainly a choir school, of comparatively late growth. When, early in the thirteenth century, every great church built its Lady Chapel and had its supplementary services of Our Lady, it was natural that the monks should commit the singing there to hired boys; and, again, that they should not leave those boys entirely without education. But these song schools were very small—from half a dozen to a dozen pupils. The almonry school, again, like the song school, we scarcely find except in the later Middle Ages, and in the larger monasteries. The almoner gradually began to accept it as one of his duties to board and feed a certain number of young clerics who were anxious to pursue their education; and the monks hired a schoolmaster to teach them. We may emphasize that word "hired", for it is extremely rare to find the monks themselves teaching either in the choir or in the almonry school. We can form a rough statistical conception of these monastic schools. I do not think any one who has studied the monastic records would reckon more, at the Dissolution, than 30 almonry and 30 choir schools in the country, with an average attendance of 12 and 6 respectively. This would give 540 scholars. The number of other schools in England, grammar and elementary, would not be put by the most optimistic calculation higher than 500, with an average attendance of 50 pupils.* We should thus get, in all, less than 26,000 pupils for a population of some 5,000,000. The present-day population of England and Wales is 35,000,000 souls; seven times as many as at the Reformation. With that population, at the medieval rate, we should have only 182,000 pupils, spaced among nearly 4000 schools whose average standard inclined rather to the elementary than to the grammar class. Yet we have in fact, according to *Whitaker's Almanac* for 1931, 1300 secondary schools with an aggregate of 200,000 boys and 180,000 girls, to which must be added 20,000 elementary schools with an attendance of 5,000,000; that is, nearly thirty times more scholars in proportion to population. Nobody will attempt to insist upon those bare figures as conclusive in themselves; the newspapers remind us constantly and healthily of the shortcomings of many modern educational methods. But at least they show how much more seriously book-learning is considered by modern Church and State than by our forefathers.

* If it be true that St Paul's School in London was founded for as many as 153 boys in 1510, that is the largest number known at so early a date. Winchester had 86, Eton rather less. (Lupton's *Colet*, p. 64.)

For it was not that our ancestors were held back by physical difficulties alone. True, they were partly unable, but they were also unwilling; and this is so weighty a matter that it must be given the emphasis which it deserves. I wrote in my *Medieval Village*: "That jealousy of primary education, which remains one of the vividest political pictures in the minds of those who remember the struggle of 1870 and the following years, must be multiplied fourfold when we think ourselves back to the Middle Ages." This has aroused so much misunderstanding that I must try to explain myself here, even at the risk of prolixity and repetition.[3]

Medieval theories of State and Society postulated a far sharper division of classes than we have to-day: that truth is sometimes emphasized even more definitely by the champions than by the critics of medieval ideals. The three main classes were the Churchman for prayer, the soldier for fighting, and the peasant or artisan for labour. There was much natural jealousy against trespass from one division into another, especially if the trespasser were of the labouring class. Even the very democratic author of *Piers Plowman* looks upon it as a topsy-turvy world where "bondmen's bairns be made bishops" (though this, indeed, was of extreme rarity) "and soapsellers and their sons for silver have been knights". St Thomas Aquinas, again, in his commentary on Aristotle's *Politics*, reproduces without comment (though in other cases he feels called upon to protest) the Master's ideal of peasantry: men strong of arm, dull of intellect, and so distrustful of each other as to form no menace to the State.[4] Again, we have that petition of the English House of Commons to the king in 1391, that no bondman should be suffered to send his sons to school, "in order to advance them by clergy". Richard II, it is true, rejected that petition; but a similar attitude meets us everywhere in the Middle Ages, even more on the Continent than in England. It was a like spirit which inspired the notorious objections of the medieval clergy to vernacular translations; objections which Chaucer's contemporary Trevisa met so fully and so wittily in the Preface to his own translation of Higden's *Polychronicon*.[5] In that dialogue, the cleric objects flatly: "It needeth not that all such [men as understand no Latin] should know the Chronicles." This jealous exclusiveness on the part of the educated classes was enormously increased, as we shall see in a later chapter, by the appearance of

the Lollard Bible and the claims of unlearned folk to read the
Scriptures in their own tongue.[6] But it had existed from a much
earlier period; and, after all, it only typified a well-known psychological phenomenon, the specialist's scorn for the amateur. If the
Papacy and hierarchy had fought for popular education, religious
and secular, with anything like the same energy and persistence
with which they asserted the principle of clerical celibacy, for
instance, or their own immunity from State taxation, then the
story of medieval schools would have been very different. It is
quite irrelevant to plead the truism that a bookless man may be
better educated, in reality, than the book-learned. For it is an
equally patent truism that, other things being equal, book-learning
is one of the most valuable factors in education; and history is
far from supporting the implication that illiterate populations are
likely to be more moral or religious than the literate.

As our centuries went on, there began to spring up a considerable number of small endowed schools, not merely dependent
upon the temporary goodwill of a parish priest or a parish clerk.
Such foundations became specially common from about 1350
onwards, when benefactions to monasteries were rapidly drying
up, and men preferred to seek purgatorial relief for their souls
not by endowing monks to sing for them, but by endowing each
his separate chantry-priest to celebrate Masses for him to all
eternity. It was naturally found unhealthy for priests to be thus
endowed, with no work but a daily Mass. Therefore it became
more and more common to impose upon them the further duty
of keeping an elementary school. This was sometimes gratuitous;
but, even when the foundation specified this, it would be natural
that fees should creep in sooner or later. At Hull, for instance,
in 1476, Alcock, who afterwards became Bishop of Ely and founded
Jesus College at Cambridge, instituted a school with a priest to
pray for his soul and a clerk to teach song.

Edward VI, who has sometimes been celebrated as Founder of
Schools, was more rightly characterized by Leach as Destroyer.
It is true that he did found a certain small number of grammar
schools, but these were financed by only a small part of the
foundations of the chantry schools, which were disestablished
and disendowed in his reign on the excuse that their main object
was the celebration of superstitious Masses. Meanwhile there had
grown up at Cambridge a sort of normal school for teachers. In

1439 a priest named William Bingham sent a petition to the king that "whereas your poor beseecher hath found in western land, over the east party of the way leading from Hampton to Coventry and so forth no farther north than Ripon, 70 schools void or more that were occupied all at once within 50 years past, because that there is so great scarcity of masters of grammar, whereof as now be almost none, nor none may be had in your Universities over those that needs must be occupied still there", therefore he besought leave to found a college called God's House for "twenty-four scholars for to commence in grammar, and a priest to govern them, for reformation of the same default, for the love of God and in the way of charity".[7] This house itself, however, gradually decayed and was refounded as an ordinary college (Christ's) by the Lady Margaret, mother to Henry VII. Moreover, when the Renaissance began in England, there was a strong sense of crying educational necessities and of emancipation from monopolistic clerical control. When the great Dean of St Paul's, John Colet, founded the grammar school of that cathedral, Erasmus tells us how, "after he had finished all, he left the perpetual care and oversight of the estate and government of it, not to the clergy, not to the bishop, not to the chapter, not to any great minister at court, but amongst married laymen, to the Company of Mercers, men of probity and reputation. And when he was asked the reason of so committing this trust, he answered to this effect: That there is no absolute certainty in human affairs; but for his part, he found less corruption in such a body of citizens than in any other order or degree of mankind."

At the elementary schools the child began naturally with a horn-book, that is a piece of parchment protected by a transparent layer of horn on which were written the alphabet, the Lord's Prayer and one or two most elementary things. Then, as a rule, he was set to learn Latin with the help of the Psalter, so that *psalterium discere* is a common phrase for pupils at an elementary school, and *psalterium docere* for teachers there. Later the so-called "Primer" was invented; and this brings us to Chaucer's Clergeoun. Here Professor Carleton Brown seems clearly right in surmising a typical mixed grammar and song school. Chaucer's little boy of seven is still at his Primer—a book mainly of psalms and ordinary church prayers, but which often contained, before the psalms, the alphabet and other very elementary matter, in order that it might be used as a school textbook. The boys a little above him learned song also; and he used to listen to them when they practised their hymn to the Virgin. But some of these at least (typified by the *clergeoun's* "*felawe*") sang without understanding more of it than, quite vaguely, this was some sort of hymn to the Virgin. The Clergeoun asks him to construe the words in English; he frankly confesses his inability: "I can no more expound in this mateere; I lernë song, I can but small grammere." Thus, the general indications are in favour of this being an ordinary grammar school; and Professor Brown brings clear proof that song was often taught at such schools.

Among the sidelights on grammar school teaching two are specially illuminating, since the first comes so nearly before Chaucer's lifetime and the second actually within it. The monastic chronicler Higden, in 1327, complains that English boys are compelled to construe their Latin into French; and Trevisa, who translated him, adds that since the Black Death John Cornwall, a grammar master who taught at Oxford, inaugurated a new era by making his boys construe into English; "so that now, in the year of Our Lord 1385, in all the grammar schools children leave French and construe and learn in English." The next case, still more illuminating, is from the register of Bishop Grandisson of Exeter (A.D. 1357): a mandate directed to all archdeacons in his diocese.[8] "We ourselves have learned and learn daily, not without frequent wonder and inward compassion of mind, that among masters or teachers of boys and illiterate folk in our diocese, who instruct them in grammar, there prevails a preposterous and unprofitable method and order of teaching, nay, a superstitious fashion, rather heathen than Christian; for these masters (after their scholars have learned to read or repeat, even imperfectly, the Lord's Prayer, the Ave Maria, the Creed, and the Matins and Hours of the Blessed Virgin, and other such things pertaining to faith and their soul's health, without knowing or understanding how to construe anything of the aforesaid, or decline the words or parse them), then, I say, these masters make them pass on prematurely to learn other advanced [*magistrales*] books of poetry or metre. Whence it cometh to pass that, grown to man's estate, they understand not the things which they daily read or say: moreover (what is more damnable) through lack of understanding they discern not the Catholic Faith. We, therefore, willing by all means and methods in our power to eradicate so horrible and foolish an abuse, already too deep-rooted in our diocese, do now commit and depute to each of you the duty of warning and enjoining all masters and instructors whatsoever, who preside over Grammar Schools within the limits of his archdeaconry (as, by these letters present, we ourselves strictly command, enjoin, and warn them), that they should not, as hitherto, teach the boys whom they receive as grammar pupils only to read or learn by heart [*literaliter*, 'learn in Latin']; but rather that, postponing all else, they should make them construe and understand the Lord's Prayer, the Ave Maria, the Creed, the Matins and Hours of the Blessed Virgin, and decline and parse the words therein, before permitting them to pass on to other books. Moreover we proclaim that we purpose to confer clerical orders henceforth on no boys but upon such as may be found to have learnt after this method."

We may now pass upwards to the Episcopal Schools. These, and the Universities which were their indirect product, illustrate the pathetic desire for learning in a society struggling out of barbarous illiteracy. There had already been a strong and self-conscious revival under Charlemagne, which is best illustrated by a tale from his *Life* by the Monk of St Gall. The story, though doubtless incorrect in detail, is fundamentally true and significant in its picture of those early knights-errant of learning, who could only count on meeting a few souls as thirsty as themselves, here and there, within the intellectual deserts created by barbarian invasions. "Now it happened, when he [Charles] had begun to reign alone in the western parts of the world, and the pursuit of learning had been almost forgotten throughout all his realm, and the worship of the true Godhead was faint and weak, that two Scots [i.e. Irishmen] came from Ireland to the coast of Gaul, along with certain traders of Britain. These Scots were unrivalled for their skill in sacred and secular learning: and day by day, when the crowd gathered round them for traffic, they exhibited no wares for sale, but cried out and said, 'Ho, everyone that desires wisdom, let him draw near and take it at our hands; for it is wisdom that we have for sale'."[9] Charlemagne himself was a great patron of learning: he created a sort of Minister of Education in the person of the York scholar Alcuin, and strove, though vainly, to utilize the monasteries as seminaries for the clergy. His successors, after a short while, did little more than mark time; but the ground gained under him was never entirely lost. Then that great revival of civilization about the year 1000 showed itself, among other ways, in a resurrection of learning; here Lanfranc and Anselm were two of the most conspicuous European figures. From that time forward we find a certain number of cathedral schools rapidly developing in the study of classics, philosophy and theology; Paris, Orleans and Chartres were among the most conspicuous here. At Chartres especially, from the time of Bishop Fulbert [1010], these subjects were taught on a sound classical basis; and better Latin was written than anywhere in Europe down to the Renaissance or even beyond. Great representatives of that school are John of Salisbury, Giraldus Cambrensis, Walter Map and Peter of Blois. But the greatest of all these cathedral teachers was Abailard, whose wandering life drove him to teach at several of these episcopal schools. When indeed, after the great tragedies of his life, he retired into a wilderness on the plain of Troyes, pupils still scented him out as the eagle scents his prey; and (to quote the teacher's own words in his *Historia Calamitatum*), "Here, instead of spacious houses, they built themselves little tabernacles; for delicate food they ate nought but herbs of the field and rough country bread; for soft couches they gathered together straw and stubble; nor had they any tables save clods of earth....My scholars, of their own accord, provided me with all necessaries, not only in food and raiment but in tilling of the fields and defraying the cost of the buildings; so that no household care might withdraw me from my studies." He died in 1142, as the John Baptist of the university movement; the last of those of whom it could be said that, wherever they were, a sort of University gathered round them; and, on the other hand, greatest among those who by teaching at Paris raised that cathedral school so high above the rest that it became naturally the first French University.

The word *universitas* has nothing whatever to do with the supposed ideal of universal knowledge. It was one of the ordinary words in classical Latin for a gild or corporation of any kind. Its two synonyms in the Middle Ages were *studium* and *studium generale*. The sudden rise of these great institutions was not due to the initiative of any Pope, nor, again, was any university *directly* formed from any cathedral school, or founded by monks. These facts are brought out no less definitely by the Dominican Father Denifle than by Dr Rashdall at Oxford. The universities rose and attained their great influence by the same natural growth which created trade unions in modern Britain and has made them, in their present power and organization, almost a fourth estate of the realm. It is true that, by about 1300, lawyers had worked out the theory that papal or imperial licence was necessary for the founding of a university, but even these lawyers had to admit that long custom might count also, and that we might have a university "by custom" (*ex consuetudine*), as genuine as if it had been a papal or imperial foundation. At that time, in fact, out of fourteen Universities then existing, only three had been founded by sovereigns and two (or more strictly one-and-a-half) by Popes; and the nine *ex consuetudine* included Paris, Bologna and others of the first rank, together with Oxford and Cambridge here in England.

Bologna and Paris grew up gradually and, so far as can be seen, simultaneously towards the beginning of the last quarter of the twelfth century. Bologna was a gild of students and Paris a gild of masters. The city of Bologna had for some time possessed a great school of Civil Law, founded on the renewed study of Roman Law as collected and codified by Justinian. Such a nucleus of Civil Law naturally attracted an equally important school of Canon Law. These legists were comparatively elderly students, and comparatively wealthy: later University statutes show us that their incomes were expected to be greater than those of the rest, and the very books they used were written and illuminated on a more expensive scale. It was natural, then, that these foreigners, so far from their home, should form themselves into a gild for mutual protection; or rather into a series of gilds, for there were at least seventeen "nations" at Bologna. Later, when the constitution had crystallized, the executive committee of the University consisted of the heads of these seventeen nations: a fact which, like the similar division into nations at Paris and other universities, tells definitely against the idea that nationalism is a post-Reformation product. These students, then, being essentially well-to-do business men, took the whole management of the University into their own hands, making their teachers into their hired servants. Thus the Professor or Doctor or Master at Bologna (those three titles were originally synonymous at all universities; so that, for instance, what is called a Master of Arts in England is the technical equivalent of a Doctor of Philosophy in Germany) was as definitely subject to his pupils as were, for instance, the licensed booksellers (*librarii, stationarii*) or copyists. The professor had no vote in this society, from which he might be expelled at any time. He was obliged to give heavy caution money if he left the city for a time, lest, like a modern football expert, he should be enticed by higher offers to sell his services elsewhere. He had to give caution money for behaviour at lectures; for unpunctuality he was fined, or for not reaching certain stages of the law-text that he expounded by certain dates in the term; or, again, for reaching those statutory dates by illegitimate skipping of any part of the text. Moreover, the ordinary absence of copyright which we find everywhere in medieval literary life was intensified in his case. We shall presently see how he may be said to have been subjected even to the negation of copyright. So far, Bologna and those Italian and other universities which imitated her formed an exception to the ordinary gild regulations of the Middle Ages. It was, perhaps, unique to find a gild of pupils in any calling who were entitled to hold their masters in subjection. Paris, however, with Oxford and Cambridge and many others, followed the regular gild system. There, the undergraduate was the apprentice. Half way through his course, just as the apprentice to a saddler or a tailor became a "journeyman" (that is, thenceforward he received a small wage while still continuing to learn), so also, at the University, a *baccalaureus* was one who had not yet obtained a regular degree; he had only reached the midway stage of pupil-teacher. When, at the end of his seven years, he had become master, and was thenceforward qualified to teach at any other university, he received this mastership by the double ceremony of *traditio* and *inceptio*. He was crowned with a master's cap,* and he then gave a specimen lesson; very much as the tailor and the saddler attained mastership at the end of their seven years by public proof of capacity in a "masterpiece".

This *traditio*, this handing over of the tools of trade, had an interesting exemplification at Cambridge, at least in the case of a Master of Grammar. For this degree it was not necessary to have gone through the whole Arts course (i.e. the grammar, rhetoric and philosophy course) but simply so much of it as was needed for teaching in a grammar school. At the inception of

---

* Medieval master-masons may be seen portrayed with such caps on their tombstones, as we shall see in Chapter XLII.

more than sixty. Some of these Halls or Hostels, in their later development, were practically what we call now a College. Some were already attracting endowments to themselves, and this basis of endowment and corporate government is what constitutes a College. *Collegium* (like *Universitas*) was an ancient Latin word for gilds of any kind; and the term was naturally applied as soon as these associations had crystallized into sufficient consistency

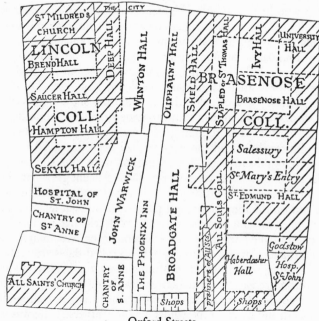

Oxford Streets.

to make collective bargaining possible—that is, as soon as the body was sufficiently definite to sue and be sued in law as a person.

The earliest Colleges were the convents of friars, and later on of monks. The friars especially began settling at universities (especially Bologna and Paris) even in the lifetime of St Francis and St Dominic; and the friaries there constructed set a pattern for future students' associations. The monks came only later and had far less influence upon the universities. Then generous bene-factors began founding what now began to be called definitely Colleges; and these endowed corporations grew so numerous and powerful, and became such an integral part of University life in England, especially after the Reformation, that it is our first task with an intelligent foreigner to explain to him the difference between a College and a University. To put it in its briefest form, we have to say that modern Oxford and Cambridge are each a Federative Republic of Letters in which the Colleges play much the same part as the Cantons in the Swiss Federation.

We may now come to College life. New College at Oxford (1379) was the first at either University to be built on a complete and fully enclosed quadrangle, and to admit undergraduates. It was mainly an educational continuation of Wykeham's grammar school foundation at Winchester. Even to the end, our Colleges were not primarily destined for undergraduates, but for graduates studying for higher degrees in Theology, Law, etc. Dr H. E. Salter writes:[10] "I estimate that in 1360 the six colleges which then existed would contain about 10 undergraduates, 23 bachelors, and 40 masters. The founding of New College nearly doubled these figures, but if all the colleges had been dissolved in 1400 it would not have been a crushing blow to the University." In the fifteenth century the undergraduate element grew considerably stronger, and "pensioners" were admitted, i.e. students who were not on the foundation, but paid for their own maintenance. "It may come as a surprise to many to learn that no medieval college contained what we call commoners or was founded for teaching, and that the college system so called dates from about 1560." Thus, even in the later Middle Ages, the Halls continued to be recognized as the normal academical home of undergraduates. Even then, however, the chamber-deacons were not altogether eliminated, and much of the wilder side of University life was due to these men, living more or less irresponsibly in private lodgings. In the Halls, and sometimes at least in the Colleges, three or four shared a room, and probably sometimes they slept two in a bed. An admirable picture of the life of a poor but orderly student in the golden days of the thirteenth century occurs in the Biography of St Richard Wych, Bishop of Chichester. His father was wealthy and would have married him advantageously: but the youth was already devoted to learning. "Richard therefore hastily left both [his father's] lands and the lady, and all his friends, and betook himself to the University of Oxford and then to that of Paris, where he learned logic. Such was his love of learning, that he cared little or nothing for food or raiment. For, as he was wont to relate, he and two companions who lodged in the same chamber had only their tunics, and one gown between them, and each of them a miserable pallet. When one, therefore, went out with the gown to hear a lecture, the others sat in their room, and so they went forth alternately; and bread with a little wine and pottage sufficed for their food. For their poverty never suffered them to eat flesh or fish, save on the Sunday or on some solemn holy day or in presence of companions or friends; yet he hath oftentimes told me how, in all his days, he had never after led so pleasant and delectable a life."[11]

Richard and his friends were, of course, model private lodgers, in strong contrast with those "chamber-deacons" of whom an Oxford statute complains that "they sleep all day, and at night roam about taverns and houses of ill fame for opportunity of robbery and homicide"—men with whom we may parallel those Irish, Scottish and Welsh scholars of whom the House of Commons twice complained to the king (1422 and 1429) that, "not having whereby they might live, they committed divers manslaughters, murders, rapes and robberies about the country", and finally organized a system of blackmail by keeping the surrounding districts in a state of siege. It is a significant commentary on this that, as we have already seen, habitual night-walking, stalking abroad after curfew, was punished by twice the fine which an undergraduate incurred by shooting an arrow at the proctor with attempt to wound him. Equally characteristic medieval contrasts are brought out by Professor C. H. Haskins, in his *Studies in Medieval Culture*. On the one hand, at Bologna, "an assault with a cutlass in the classroom was charged [to the offender] as a loss of time and money to the assembled scholars". On the other hand, a students' manual at Paris points out that the best models of academical deportment are afforded by the graven images in the churches. J. R. Green, in his *Short History of the English People*, has drawn from life two pictures that cannot be bettered of the model scholar: St Edmund Rich the hero of orthodoxy, and Roger Bacon the hero, and to some extent martyr, of independent research.

The chronic and bitter feuds between Town and Gown, with those even fiercer fights between different nationalities—for North and South of the Trent did so regard each other—prompted

Rashdall to suggest that more than one famous battle-field might perhaps be found upon which less blood has been shed per square yard than upon the Oxford High Street. A specimen may be given here from the Oxford Coroner's Rolls of 1314:[12] The jury "say upon their oath that, on the Saturday aforesaid, after the hour of noon, the Northern clerks on the one part, and the Southern and Western clerks on the other, came to St John's Street and Grope Lane with swords, bucklers, bows, arrows and other arms, and there they fought together; and in that conflict Robert de Bridlington, Adam de Alderbeck, Richard de Louthby and Richard de Holwell stood together in a certain soler [upper chamber] in Gutter Hall, situate in St John's Street, shooting down through a window into Grope Lane: and there the said Robert de Bridlington, with a small arrow, smote the aforesaid Henry of Holy Isle and wounded him hard by the throat, on the left side in front; and the wound was of the breadth of one inch, and in depth even unto the heart; and thus he slew him. Moreover the aforesaid jury say that [the others above-named] incited the said Robert to shoot the same Henry dead, and to slay him, and they were consenting unto his death....And in the same conflict John de Benton came with a falchion into Grope Lane and gave David de Kirkby a blow on the back of the head, six inches in length, and in depth even unto the brain. At which same time came William de la Hyde and smote the aforesaid David with a sword across his right knee and leg: and at the same time came William de Astley and smote the said David under the left arm with a misericorde, and thus slew him. Moreover, concerning the goods of the aforesaid evildoers, or those who have received them, the jury say that they know nothing."

The Oxford Composition of 1252 between the Irish scholars and the rest reads like a treaty of peace between two nations after war. Moreover, the most serious offences were by no means confined to junior men. Out of the 77 gravest offenders recorded in the Oxford Chancellor's Book, 47 are undergraduates and 30 senior men. At Cambridge, in 1418, the Chancellor of the University and the prior of the Augustinian convent egg on the students to riot outside the mayor's house: and next year the aggrieved ex-mayor wants to fight out the quarrel hand-to-hand with the same chancellor, in the church in which they had met to try and patch up the dispute. In 1454 we find a M.A. of

Michaelhouse heading an attack made on King's College "with guns and habiliments of war": in 1533 an attempt is made to force an election by repairing to the Senate house with clubs and swords: and of Dr Crayforde, Master of Clare Hall and twice Vice-Chancellor about this same time, his contemporary Dr Caius says that he was as good a gladiator as Vice-Chancellor: that he cut off one man's hand and threw another by main force out of the Senate house.

Moreover, manslaughter enjoyed even greater chances of impunity at our Universities than elsewhere in medieval society. In the "Great Slaughter" at Oxford between Town and Gown in 1354, out of the 39 man-slayers two were never identified, 22 escaped altogether, four fled to sanctuary, and therefore were only banished, three claimed the privilege of the clergy, and one who would have claimed this had died meanwhile in prison. This leaves only a balance of seven, of whom one or two may have been hanged. Robert of Bridlington, who had shot that fatal arrow from the window of Gutter Hall in 1314, survived for many years, to perish in a later fray with the citizens. Sometimes, in fact, the Oxford scholar was requested to go to prison; and Dr Rashdall, with a touch of friendly malice which even Cantabs must forgive in so great a scholar, suggests that the worst that could happen to a medieval Oxford felon, short of unusually bad luck, would be to go and finish his studies at Cambridge.

The constant use of the word "poor" in foundation statutes has led modern readers very naturally to imagine that benefactors' endowments were originally intended for a class very much worse off than those who enjoy them at present. This, however, rests upon a misunderstanding of medieval legal common-form. By Canon Law it was strictly forbidden to transfer to secular purposes any endowment which had been given to the Church. But nearly all the endowments conferred on our Colleges were of that kind. Peterhouse and Corpus Christi at Cambridge, for instance, were both founded mainly on the income of a parish church, which was served by the Fellows. It was therefore necessary for the foundation deed to emphasize the fact that the new institution was itself one of pious charity. Leach and Rashdall have both shown conclusively that foundation statutes anticipated, not a proletarian standard of scholastic life, but that of the middle, and not even of the lower middle, class. At Winchester College, where the phrase "poor" is very conspicuous, the founder inserts a special clause giving preference to his own kin for entrance to the College, and he was one of the greatest capitalists in England; moreover, Leach traced among the earliest pupils a very large proportion of sons of county families. Yet this "charitable" clause was very naturally appealed to by medieval disciplinarians. Here, for instance, is a paragraph from the statutes of King's College, Cambridge: "Since it befitteth not poor men, and specially such as live by charity, to give the children's bread unto dogs, and we find it written elsewhere *Vae sit eis in peccatum, qui in avibus coeli ludunt,** therefore we command, ordain and will that no scholar, fellow, chaplain, clerk, or servant whatsoever to the said King's College, do keep or possess dogs, hunting or fishing nets, ferrets, falcons, or hawks; nor shall they practise hunting or fishing. Nor shall they in any wise have or hold within our Royal College, singly or in common, any ape, bear, fox, stag, hind, fawn, or badger, or any other such ravening or unaccustomed or strange beast, which neither profit us nor can harm us.† Furthermore, we forbid and expressly interdict the games of dice, hazard, ball and all noxious inordinate unlawful and unhonest sports, and especially all games which afford a cause or occasion for loss of coin, money, goods or chattels of any kind whatsoever, whether within King's College or elsewhere within the University.... And it is our will firmly and expressly to prohibit all of the aforesaid fellows etc. from shooting arrows, or casting or hurling stones, javelins, wood, clods or anything whatsoever, and from making or practising, singly or in common, in person or by deputy, any games or castings whatsoever, within the aforesaid King's College or its enclosed precincts or gardens, whereby, directly or indirectly, the Chapel or Hall or other buildings or edifices of our said College may suffer any sort of harm or loss in the glass windows, walls, roofs, coverings, or any other part thereof, within or without. *Item*, whereas through incautious and inordinate games in the Chapel or Hall of our said King's College, which might perchance be practised therein by the wantonness of some students, the said Chapel and Hall might be harmed and

---

* Baruch iii. 17: "Woe unto those in sin, that take their diversion with the birds of the air."

† I.e. who do not afford the hunter's excuse as expressed in *Piers Plowman*, that he is defending society or property from these wild beasts.

even deformed in its walls, stalls, paintings and glass windows;
we therefore, desiring to provide against such harm, do strictly
command that no casting of stones or balls or of anything else
soever be made in the aforesaid collegiate Chapel, Cloister, Stalls,
or Hall; and we forbid that dancing or wrestling, or other incautious and inordinate sports whatsoever, be practised at any
time within the Chapel, Cloister or Hall aforesaid."[13]

This was in imitation of William of Wykeham, who had found
it necessary for the protection of the carved reredos in the Chapel
of New College to prohibit dancing or jumping either in the
Chapel or in the adjoining Hall. That will remind us of Chaucer's
Clerk:

> In twenty manere koude he trippe and daunce
> (After the scole of Oxenfordë tho),
> And with his leggës casten to and fro.

But a Cambridge man may be permitted to point out that Oxford
had no monopoly here, since the King's College statutes repeated
that prohibition also.

Wykeham specifies chess among the "noxious, inordinate and
unhonest games" forbidden at New College, a prohibition which
has excited astonishment among those who do not realize that
this game was very commonly forbidden to the clergy throughout
the Middle Ages, probably because it was nearly always played
for money. Manslaughter at chess is a not uncommon episode
in medieval romance. Indeed, everywhere in the records of that
time we find natural allusions to quarrels at games, seeing that the
umpire and referee were officials as yet unborn. The tendency of
collegiate and aularian statutes is on the whole distinctly against
games and sports, yet we must not ignore the fact that the aularian
statutes of Oxford [1483] provide that "all members, on being
directed by their principal to go off to the fields or other places
whatsoever on account of proper recreation, and the honour... of
the Hall, shall repair there together and return in like manner;
and none of them shall stay at home, except for some reasonable
cause and with the leave of the principal, on penalty of twopence".
On the other hand, for the member of a Hall to be abroad alone
without excuse entailed a fine of a farthing. The provisions, in
fact, are such as we should expect in a modern Continental
ecclesiastical seminary. For table-manners, we have the same sort
of indication as for those in the monasteries. Professor Haskins

quotes from a manual of advice for students. "Let not a mouthful, once touched with the fingers, be put back into the dish; touch not thine ears or nostrils with naked fingers; cleanse not thy teeth with the steel that is sharpened for those that eat with thee.... He who would drink [at the common cup] must first empty his mouth, and let his lips first be wiped; nor can I avoid this warning: Let him not gnaw the bone with his teeth."[14]

Yet, though colleges were not founded for the very poor, there was much more variety in the medieval university between student and student than in modern times, even when we take account of the immense influx of scholars from elementary schools within this last generation. There were great contrasts in age. If we may take the Exeter registers as typical, there would be at any given time about 600 incumbents distributed between Oxford and Cambridge; and, although a very large number of these might be mere schoolboys, yet some also would be quite elderly men. In wealth, again the contrasts were great. When begging was strictly forbidden by English statute, exception was made for those undergraduates who had official licences to beg; and we know that Luther got through his university course very much on those terms. Again, the length of the summer vacation may possibly point to the need of manual work both in the hay harvest and in the corn harvest. Dr Salter emphasizes the surprising fact that, in those later generations for which we have fairly full records, "undergraduates in Halls remained at Oxford in the long vacation, and that in Halls the year was not divided into three terms of eight or nine weeks, but into four terms each of twelve weeks....The commoners remained in Oxford for the whole year, and their tutors had no holiday in the long vacation. If this was so, we wonder why the University had a long Vacation, inasmuch as neither tutors nor pupils nor servants took a holiday. Perhaps the explanation may be that the Calendar common to our universities had its origin in some early university in the south, where the heat made it difficult to work in July, August, and September." It might perhaps seem more natural to connect it with what we know of the earliest generations of students, namely, that their economic position was very precarious. In those circumstances, nothing would be more natural than that at medieval Oxford and Cambridge, as at modern American Universities, many should be healthily and profitably engaged in bread-winning for some of the summer months. Further, there was a whole class of "servitors" or "sizars"—that is, poor scholars who came up in complete dependence upon a richer companion, or upon menial work to be found at the College. When the Scottish poet, Barbour, an archdeacon and a rich man, procured a safe conduct to Oxford with three "clerks" in his train, those three seem plainly to have held this position with regard to him. The servitor or sizar fed on the remnants of the others' food, and picked up such learning as he could in such time as he could save from his menial duties. We have already seen, also, the peculiarly medieval institution of "charity chests", from which money was lent out without interest to meet the pressing pecuniary necessities of students who could deposit an equivalent pledge.

Let us end with a brief glimpse of this life from the point of view of the student himself. He very often travelled to the University in company. There was a University official, the "carrier" or "fetcher", who would undertake to help him; or, again, he would travel in a mutually protective group: for, as we have seen, the undergraduate had a not negligible chance of making his first acquaintance with fellow-undergraduates in the guise of amateur outlaws and bandits, whose activities claimed the interference of parliament. Arrived at the University, he might be accosted by a touting master—there again, the chances are distinctly implied by statutes which emphatically forbid this abuse. Once settled in a College (if he had that good fortune) he would find himself expected to attend his first lectures in the morning at 6 o'clock; candles cost money, and everyone in those days rose with the lark. He would do his washing at a trough in the Hall or in the open court; even at the comparatively aristocratic and rich King's College, Cambridge, inventories of deceased Fellows do not always show any trace of private washing apparatus. The statutes are interesting on this point: "Moreover, we strictly and expressly ordain that no dweller in the aforesaid upper rooms...whether in washing his head or hands or feet or any other thing, or in any other manner whatsoever, do spill water, wine, beer, or any other liquor whereby those in the lower rooms may be grieved in their persons, goods or chattels, or in any way molested."[15]

Breakfast was a much less regular institution in the Middle

Ages than to-day. The hardy man would go without it, as he went without afternoon tea until this last generation of ours. Dinner was commonly at 10, an hour which survived at Oxford even into the eighteenth century. After this, and a natural interval of rest, work would go on again from 12 or 1 to 5, the hour of supper. When supper was over, to quote King's again as a model, "after grace duly said...for that which hath been received... then, without further delay, when the loving-cup hath been administered to all who wish to drink, and after the potations in Hall at the hour of curfew, let all the seniors, of whatsoever condition or degree, betake themselves to their studies or to other places, nor let them suffer the juniors to tarry longer in Hall, save only on the principal holy-days, or when College Councils are to be held in Hall after the meal, or other arduous business touching the said Royal College; or again when, in honour of God or of His Mother or of some other saint, the fellows are indulged with a fire in Hall at wintertide. Then it shall be lawful for the scholars and fellows, after dinner or supper, to make a decent tarrying in Hall for recreation's sake, with songs and other honest pastimes, and to treat, in no spirit of levity, of poems, chronicles of realms, and wonders of this world, and other things which are consistent with clerical propriety".[16]

There was very commonly an evening repetition of what had been learned in the day's lectures; but the student would be in bed by 8 or 9. If this seems incredibly strenuous, it must be remembered that the holy-days were also holidays, about 50 in the year; so that the average working week was of five days only. Moreover, we have abundant evidence, especially in complaints from disciplinarian writers or other authorities, that it was common enough for the medieval student, like the modern, to treat his university time as one of enjoyment rather than labour.

The principal alone had a separate room to himself, either in a Hall or in a College. At New College and King's the living rooms were subdivided for two or more students by wooden partitions; and it is characteristic of those foundations that students are specially relieved by statute from the necessity of sleeping two in a bed. After all, perhaps the worst disadvantage to a modern man would be the cold. The lecture halls would often be, especially in earlier days, mere sheds; unceiled, unfloored and unglazed. In Paris, the Street of the Schools was called Straw Street—*Rue*

Plate I

Two miniatures from the Trinity College *Apocalypse*

These illustrate the horrors which are to come in the last days of this world before the great battle of Armageddon. The top picture represents Rev. vi. 12, and the lower represents Rev. xi. 11. Readers may be interested to follow this in the old French version of this MS., which dates from about A.D. 1250

Plate II

Painting of Doom, above the chancel arch, St Thomas's Church, Salisbury

Plate III

King and Queen
Wells Cathedral
From Gardner, *English Medieval Sculpture*

Plate IV

Stone Hill Farm, Chiddingly, Sussex

Plate V

The Synagogue
Rochester Cathedral

From Gardner, *English Medieval Sculpture*

Plate VI

Dartmouth Church: the Pulpit

Plate VII

John Fisher   Erasmus
Thomas More   John Colet

Portraits by Holbein

Plate VIII

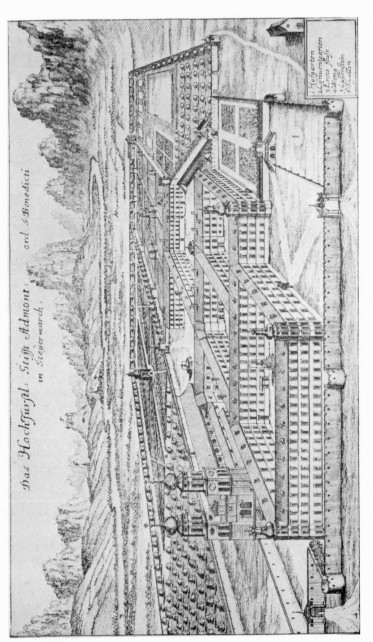

The Abbey of Admont, Styria

du Fouarre—from the straw which covered the floors, and in which grammarians were obliged to sit without chairs or stools. The cold in winter must have been far worse than even that of ordinary medieval indoor life. The question of books, one of the most important of all in this field, deserves as full treatment presently as my space will permit. But what has been said already may go some way to explain why even the medieval student, though inured to physical discomfort in his ordinary life, was commonly unable to hold out to the last against these hardships and the want of ready money. Official records remain in sufficient quantities to prove that only a small minority ever proceeded even to the half-degree of Bachelor, let alone to Master. At Oxford, about 1450, the average number of full degrees of all kinds was 91·5 a year; at Cambridge the number never rose above 50 until Elizabethan times. The total number of students at Oxford at its highest point, in about 1300, was probably not more than 1500; and in 1450 probably 1000 or less. The commonly repeated statement that there were 30,000 before the Black Death will not bear serious examination of the context from which it is quoted; it is a capital example of medieval irresponsibility in thought and word, in the face of numbers too great to be checked off hand by rule of thumb.[17] Of these students, therefore, it is evident that only a minority proceeded even as far as the half-way B.A.[18] At Leipzig the records are full enough to supply statistics from 1427 onwards.[19] Among those who matriculated, the following percentages proceeded to the B.A. and M.A. respectively:

Group of years	Percentage of B.A.	Percentage of M.A.
1429–32	20·4	3·8
1439–42	27·8	6·9
1449–52	33·9	—
1459–62	38·6	5·6
1469–72	36·0	5·4
1479–82	39·4	4·2
1489–92	38·4	3·4
1499–1502	38·5	4·6
1509–12	26·1	3·4

On the Continent, those who proceeded to the full degree were mostly lawyers: "Law", writes Rashdall, "was the leading faculty in by far the greater number of medieval Universities."

There was a current rhyme contrasting the prizes in rank or money to which Medicine and Law might aspire with the poverty of the Arts Scholar with his metaphysical discussions on the Reality of Universals:

> Dat Galenus opes, dat Justinianus honores,
> Sed Genus et Species cogitur ire pedes.

Chaucer's Clerk of Oxenford will be remembered here:

> As leenë was his hors as is a rake,
> And he nas nat right fat, I undertake.

England was an exception in regard to this great preponderance of legists, probably because Roman Law weighed so little with us in comparison with Common and Statute Law. This, again, had its significance for English constitutionalism, as contrasted with the Continental despots whose ministers fed them with autocratic pronouncements from Justinian's Code.

XXXII. SCHOLASTICS AND BIBLE

THE studies of the medieval university were nearly always based upon the "Arts" course. Medieval philosophy followed Aristotle in its division of Arts into the "mechanical" and the "liberal". Mechanical were all that needed manual dexterity, from the cobbler and saddler to the painter and sculptor: indeed, many modern artists, from William Morris to Eric Gill, insist upon this as the only sane definition. Liberal were the arts concerned only with brain-work. These were again divided into sections and subsections by the university authorities. The *Trivium* was the first stage: hence our adjective *trivial* in the sense of "comparatively unimportant". This comprised Grammar, Rhetoric, and Logic. Next came the *Quadrivium*, i.e. Arithmetic, Astronomy, Music and Geometry. This was not so great as it sounds; for the first three were studied only in the most elementary sense for Church purposes, even where they were seriously studied at all; and the last, again, only in its most rudimentary forms. After seven years the student became in England and France a Master of Arts, in Germany a Doctor of Philosophy: different phrases for the same thing. This philosophy was the so-called *scholastic*, a product so definitely medieval that it must be clearly defined before we go farther. It can best be described by noting how far it agrees with or differs from the philosophies of ancient Greece and Rome on the one hand; or on the other, those of modern times. With ancient philosophy it agreed in being based upon dialectics, i.e. upon oral discussion by question and answer; so that even in its most elaborate written forms this dialectic conception is always there, if only in the background. It differed, however, from the ancient in being circumscribed within certain definite theological limits. Modern philosophy, on the other hand, differs from the scholastic on both points. It is not usually dialectic in form; nor again are its foundations circumscribed by authority. This Scholasticism was a natural product of a book-hungry but comparatively bookless age. In the best cathedral schools, teaching had been Socratic. Bishop Fulbert, walking to and fro with his pupils on that cathedral terrace at Chartres where we may still stand and look over the river and the valley, discoursed daily to them upon the deepest questions of life and death; and the two brothers who brought that school to its highest pitch in the first half of the twelfth century, Bernard and Thierry, worked naturally by the same methods.

But the sudden rediscovery of all Aristotle's philosophical writings through translations from the Arabic disturbed the balance of these older schools. The humanists who write towards the close of the twelfth century are full of complaints at the increasing neglect of grammatical and historical training, and the undisciplined rawness of the young philosophers.[1] John of Salisbury and Giraldus Cambrensis complained bitterly on this point; and a century later Roger Bacon spoke out still more plainly, with the exaggeration of personal rivalry. He was a little older than St Thomas Aquinas, of whom and of other conspicuous university philosophers of his time he writes: "These are boys of the two Student Orders...who in many cases enter those Orders at or below the age of twenty years. This is the common course, from the English Sea to the farthest confines of Christendom, and more especially beyond the realm of France; so that in Aquitaine, Provence, Spain, Italy, Germany, Hungary, Denmark, and every-where, boys are promiscuously received into the Orders from their tenth to their twentieth year; boys too young to be able to know anything worth knowing, even though they were not already possessed with the aforesaid causes of human error; wherefore, at their entrance into the Orders, they know nought that profiteth to theology."[2] Elsewhere he enters into greater detail, and criticizes the Scholastics of his age in very much the same terms which might have been used by Hume or Thomas Huxley. Their works, he says, are architecturally most imposing, but they rest upon an insecure foundation; upon a Bible misunderstood, an Aristotle misunderstood, and almost total neglect of the mathematical and physical sciences. With regard to Aristotle, Bacon is exaggerated and unjust. It is true that his authority was looked upon as almost sacrosanct, second only to that of the Bible; yet the translations which St Thomas Aquinas, among others, caused to be made straight from Greek into Latin for his own use are far more correct than Bacon's words would lead us to suppose. With regard to the Bible, however, it is difficult to exaggerate the disadvantage at which Scholasticism stood under the influence of what may fairly be called the bibliolatry of the Middle Ages. This was, in a great measure, inherited from Judaism. To quote from *The Jewish Encyclopaedia*: "The traditional view is that the Pentateuch in its entirety emanated from God, every verse and letter being consequently inspired; hence the tannaitic statement that 'he who says the Torah is not from Heaven is a heretic, a despiser of the Word of God, one who has no share in the world to come'....Moses wrote the whole Pentateuch at God's dictation, even, according to R. Simeon, the last eight verses, relating to his own death."[3] So, again, according to St Thomas, the primary interpretation of Holy Writ must be the historical or literal. In this sense one word may, indeed, have different significations according to different contexts. But the literal sense is that which the Author intends: and the Author of Holy Writ is God. There can be no falsehood anywhere in the literal sense of Holy Scripture. We must, indeed, make allowance for certain obvious limitations to the theory of plenary inspiration: (1) the limitations of human language, especially at a remote period; (2) limitations imposed by the primitive mentality of the writer's contemporaries; and (3) the fact that figurative or allegorical language lends itself to misinterpretation by hasty or ignorant readers. But he insists that, wherever the *literal* sense conveys a *statement of fact*, that fact must not be questioned. For instance: "Those things which are said of [the Earthly] Paradise in Scripture are put before us by the method of historical narration. But, in all things which Scripture thus hands down, we must hold to the truth of the story as our foundation, and fabricate our spiritual expositions upon that foundation." Thus [he continues] although the Tree of Life is also a spiritual idea (Proverbs iii. 18), yet there is also an actual Tree of Life growing to the present day in the Earthly Paradise— which Aquinas, of course, located as Dante did.[4] Again, in another section of the *Summa*, St Thomas exemplifies most significantly his view of what might be the literal statement of a passage. Commenting on Exodus xxxiii. 11, "And the Lord spoke to Moses face to face, as a man is wont to speak to his friend", St Thomas says: "When Scripture states that He [the Lord] spoke to him [Moses], this is to be understood as expressing the opinion of the people who thought that Moses was speaking with God, mouth to mouth."[5] God has not in fact a mouth; that word, taken literally, would be grossly anthropomorphic. But where, for instance, we come across a clear statement of historical fact, that must not be questioned. To deny that Elkanah was Samuel's father would be contrary to the Catholic Faith, "for it follows that the Divine Scripture would be false".[6]

A couple of generations later, William of Ockham dealt with the same point. He had many reasons for differing from St Thomas, not only as a Franciscan (to whom Dominicans were by that time often rivals and almost enemies), but also because he did not share the standpoint of Aquinas on several important questions. Yet on this question of Biblical inspiration he is, if possible, still more emphatic. He recurs to it over and over again in his *Dialogus*. The Pope himself may not contradict any biblical detail; it would be heresy in a Pope "if, for instance, he were to preach that David was not the son of Jesse, or that Jeroboam had not been King of Israel". In other places he gives similar concrete instances; it would be heretical to deny that Solomon was Bathsheba's son. It was this spirit which made it almost inevitable for the seventeenth-century Roman Congregation, with papal approval, to condemn Galileo as a man who was guilty of having pushed his scientific speculations to a point which brought them into flat contradiction with Bible certainties. We may see this especially in St Thomas (for it is better still to take him as the crucial example) if we trace two of his most remarkable conclusions back to their source. In one section, after full discussion, he decides definitely that the joy of the Blessed in Heaven will be increased by the sight of the Damned wallowing beneath, in a Hell which he describes (perhaps in virtue of his more voluminous work) at greater length and in cruder terms than Calvin in his *Institutes*. The Blessed will not, of course, rejoice in all these infernal torments *per se*, but incidentally, "considering in them the order of God's justice, and their own liberation, whereat they will rejoice".[7] How can he thus decide, it may be asked, after he himself has pointed out that to rejoice in another's pains may be ordinarily classed as hatred, and that God does not delight in men's pains? Those apparently invincible natural considerations are brushed aside by one plain Bible text: "The just shall rejoice when he shall see the revenge."* That vindictive verse of a Hebrew poet, to St Thomas, outweighs everything else. So was it with Peter Lombard in his *Sentences*, the first permanently standard book of scholastic philosophy: so is it with Thomas's fellow-Dominican and contem-

* Ps. lvii. 11: Douay version; in the Vulgate, *laetabitur justus cum viderit vindictam*.

porary, the great encyclopaedist Vincent of Beauvais; so is it with St Bonaventura, in spite of Franciscan humanity; so is it even in early Renaissance times with that other great Franciscan Scholastic and saint, Bernardino of Siena. He, indeed, even outdoes

The Type and Figure of Justice.

his predecessors and contemporaries, pointing out that all musical harmony needs not only soft but also deep and stern voices, and that God's harmony of heaven could not be complete without these bellowings of the Damned.[8] Not one of these men was sufficiently shocked by his terrible conclusion to look back critically at his premises, and to realize that the logic which had forced him forward to these horrors reposed upon the first fundamental error of bibliolatry, combined with the blind acceptance of an eschatology which owed perhaps almost as much to pagan barbarism as to the Bible.[9]

The Bible, it is true, contains texts which might be cited in support of this eschatology, when once it was ingrained in men's minds. But such extremist interpretations of the Biblical texts were inherited, in a great measure, from militant Judaism and from the natural indignation of Roman Christians against their pagan tormentors. The Eastern Church was more lenient; and Origen, in many ways the greatest of the Greek Fathers, actually believed in the final salvation, after due expiation, of all human souls; but that was counted as one of his heresies. Tertullian painted the future vengeance of God upon pagan persecutors in language which still enjoys, after all these centuries, a melancholy notoriety. For more than a thousand years before the Reformation, and even beyond, the strictest and most invidious interpretation was placed upon that famous maxim of St Cyprian: *Extra Ecclesiam nulla Salus*.[10] Since baptism was spoken of in Scripture as necessary for salvation, therefore theologians only allowed rare exceptions: e.g. the "baptism of blood", for martyrs who had not yet been baptized in those days when infant baptism was not yet the rule; or the "baptism of desire" which has not yet been fulfilled in act.[11] In contrast with the Greek Church, Latin theologians put a strictly literal interpretation upon Mark xvi. 16. St Augustine even taught that unbaptized infants suffered in hell not only the penalty of losing the Beatific Vision but bodily torture also. St Thomas and the Schoolmen did indeed modify that, and persuaded themselves that there was a sort of natural happiness in this hell of the unbaptized; but Dante expresses the real mind of the cultured medieval man, as apart from the ignorant multitude who were far less favourable to pagans. There, in the first circle of the Inferno, he hears the "sighs, which caused the eternal air to tremble"; and Virgil tells him how these come from those who "sinned not", but "had not baptism", and therefore are here "in sadness, without torment...and of these I am myself. For such defects, and for no other fault, are we lost; and only in so far afflicted that without hope we live in desire." The very exceptional nature of any escape from that limbo is proved not only by the cautious and ambiguous language in which Scholasticism wrapped up its concessions to human feeling on this subject, but, still more plainly, by the nature of the exceptions quoted. The Patriarchs of the Old Testament are indeed allowed to have been freed from hell at Christ's coming, and all who, believing in a God and Providence, had thus an *implicit* (i.e. implied) faith in Christ. But now, after Christ's coming, something more than this is needed; there must be *explicit* faith in the Incarnation and the Trinity; and the most violent suppositions are adopted to prove that just a few non-Christians may have had such explicit faith. Moreover, there is the almost universally received legend that Trajan was prayed back from hell by St Gregory I, which stands in plain token that the salvation of a heathen here and there was regarded as miraculous. Finally, neglect of baptism, and irregularity in its administration, were treated as a crime destructive of human souls. Here and there a mystic of not unimpeachable orthodoxy, like Rulman Merswin or Langland, might express his belief in the salvation of good Jews and heathen; but Merswin apologizes for this as "a strange speech".[11] The best authority that St Thomas More can quote for such a liberal notion, and this only with the hope that it may possibly be correct, is that of the commentator Nicholas Lyranus [1320]. But in him we have a writer of suspected orthodoxy, partly owing to his knowledge of Hebrew, and partly to the general tone of his work; hence, afterwards, it became proverbial that this man's music had played the tune to Luther's dance: *Si Lyranus non lyrasset, Lutherus non saltasset.* Erasmus was naturally on More's more tolerant side; but that might come from his own independence of mind, or from his study of the Greek Fathers. The only Ecumenical Council of the West which dealt with this question was that of Florence, which decreed: "The Holy Roman Church professes and preaches that none who is not within the Catholic Church (not only pagans, but neither Jews nor heretics nor schismatics) can partake of eternal life, but shall go into everlasting fire...unless they have joined her [*eidem fuerint aggregati*] before death."*

Such a mental atmosphere almost inevitably developed a pessimism scarcely credible to the modern reader. A minority of

* Compare what William of Newburgh says of the Jews at York in Chapter XXIX.

human beings were "elect": the majority were not indeed "pre-destined" to hell, but their damnation was "foreknown": God knew that this was their final destination.[12] The difference here between St Thomas Aquinas and Calvin is far smaller than men commonly imagine. There is in the British Museum a rare book by Father F.-X. Godts, a Belgian Redemptorist priest, written to stem that mid-nineteenth-century movement, which is now gaining ground so rapidly, for minimizing the literal significance of Christ's stern pronouncement. Father Godts deplores this leniency as an unjustifiable concession to Protestantism and Latitudinarianism, and insists that it never appeared publicly until 1762, when it was formally condemned at Rome. Meanwhile, at least as far down as St Alfonso Liguori [1750] it had been almost universally taught by writers in the Roman Church that the greater part of mankind would miss salvation.[13] Some even foretold hell for an overwhelming majority; and others, like St Alfonso, held that "the more general opinion is that the greater part even of the Faithful [Roman Catholics] are damned". Aquinas writes: "And in this also doth God's mercy chiefly appear, that He raiseth a few [aliquos] to that salvation wherefrom very many [plurimi] fail, in accordance with the common course and inclination of nature."[14] Medieval preachers sometimes estimated the disproportion as one in a thousand, or ten thousand, or even more. Thus Father Godts is able to say, after an exhaustive study of the question: "It is vain to seek even a single Saint who has taught that the number of the elect forms a majority." He might have added that, among all the points on which Rome differs from other Christian Churches, there is not one which can claim anything like such unanimous patristic authority as can be cited for this doctrine of the *Paucitas Salvandorum*. Indeed, Father Godts shows that it comes very near to a *de fide* doctrine, in virtue of this universal patristic consent until recent times.

When we have realized this, and the further doctrine no less universally taught, that a man's last moments decided for him between an eternity of unimaginable bliss or of unspeakable torment, and that the main decisive factor at those moments was his orthodoxy, and that the last deathbed rites were also of immense importance, we are then in a position to follow another of St Thomas's weightiest arguments: the section in which he proves heresy to be the greatest of all sins, meriting the most pitiless punishment, and calling for vengeance alike from God and from man. Nobody, so far as I know, has ever attempted to break a single link in the logical chain by which the saint thus proves the goodness and the necessity of the Medieval Inquisition. He was a true saint as well as a hero of intellect; he would have endured suffering himself, if need were, rather than inflict useless or undeserved pain upon his fellow-man; but he was chained to his rock of theological tradition. The Bible was the word of Just and Almighty God: the Fathers had interpreted the Bible in that sense; behind those facts it would have been iniquitous to enquire. The late Father Bede Jarrett, an able and candid apologist, wrote in his *Social Theories of the Middle Ages* (p. 36): "Aquinas patiently put away all tradition in philosophy." This is doubtless true if, accepting in its strictest sense the limitation implied in that last word *philosophy*, we understand that he refused to follow blindly even Aristotle, the Prince of Philosophers. If, however, we are to take *philosophy* in its widest sense, as including all the subjects with which Aquinas had to deal in his monumental work, we must see in his attitude towards the Bible a fatal exception to this high praise. In this, however, he was simply the man of his age. Let us take Innocent III, the learned and pious and masterful Pope who set his seal upon the whole thirteenth century. In pressing the claims of the Roman See over its great rival, the Patriarchate of Constantinople, Innocent uses his Bible with the most extravagant licence of allegorical interpretation, on the strength of which he calls upon the Greek Emperor to force the Patriarch into "reverence and obedience to Our Apostolic See".[15] Even more crudely literalistic, perhaps, under its allegorical dress, is Innocent's legal ruling with regard to the translation of bishops from one see to another.[16] The bishop, he argues, is married to his see: therefore "no man may doubt that God Almighty has reserved to His own exclusive judgment the dissolution of that spiritual matrimony.... Those whom God hath joined, man shall not separate." Thus (since the Pope is Vicar of Jesus Christ), "it is not so much by Canon Law as by divine institution that [such a separation] is reserved for the Roman Pontiff alone"— that is, to the man who, for centuries now, had taken to himself supreme control over all matrimonial cases. Again and again, in subsequent sentences, the Pope argues from this wild analogy; and the Church accepted his argument with complete subservience.

Three centuries more were destined to elapse before Colet, the future Dean of St Paul's, attracted unusual attention by the unheard-of innovation of lecturing on St Paul's Epistles from the standpoint of a straightforward searcher into the Apostle's actual meaning when he wrote the words we now read in the Bible.

We see here the fundamental weakness of medieval theology, which communicates itself also to those two great handmaids of Theology, Philosophy and Canon Law. Both of these exaggerated that false perspective by which the Bible had long been treated less as a whole than as a collection of separate texts, to be torn from their context and bandied backwards and forwards as missiles in these verbal combats. The whole fabric of Canon Law is vitiated by this ubiquitous flaw. Even if we ignore the episode of the False Decretals, and even though many of its other sources had been purer, and its execution more logical and scientific than in fact it was, yet the very root-conception of medieval Canon Law seems false in the light of history. To base upon the Bible, or even upon the Fathers, a code of legislation enforceable in the law-courts is contrary to the spirit not only of the Gospels, but even of the Prophets, and of all that is best in the Early Fathers. How capriciously Canon Law dealt even with the Bible is instanced by its deductions from the case of Peter and Malchus's Ear. Here we have an amputation which played as important a part in European politics for at least three centuries before the Reformation, as Jenkins's Ear did for a few months in English politics. A note appended in Gratian's *Decretum* to a text from St Ambrose is there falsely ascribed to St Gregory I, and runs as follows:[17] "Peter cut off Malchus's ear, and Christ restored it unto him. From this we may see that if a man hear not [the Church], his ear must be spiritually smitten off by Peter; for it is Peter who hath the power of binding and loosing." We are far here from Christ's rebuke in the next verse of St Matthew, "Put up again thy sword into his place: for all they that take the sword shall perish with the sword". Yet from this biblical fragment, torn from its context, men argued throughout the rest of the Middle Ages with all the merciless strictness and subtlety of the law-courts. In fourteenth-century England *Piers Plowman* speaks of certain "poor fools" among the friars, who suffered for their loyalty to, or exaggeration of, St Francis's doctrine of poverty. Their uncompromising belief in the complete poverty of Christ and His Apostles had been condemned as heretical by Pope John XXII; many had been imprisoned, and some had even lost their lives in that quarrel. Here, again, bibliolatrous fundamentalism and text-slinging played a prominent part. Men quoted against these extremists of apostolic poverty that word of Christ to Peter, "Put up again *thy* sword into his place". He who had said *I am the Truth*, in that simple monosyllable *thy*, proved beyond all question that at least *one* apostle had possessed at least *one* thing of his own, thus destroying the contention that He and His apostles lived by utter renunciation of private property! It may safely be said that no field-preacher of modern times has ever outdone the greatest of medieval scholars in this licence of interpretation from isolated texts. The fact that Innocent and Aquinas were here following the tradition of their day, in proportion as it excuses them personally, reinforces our judgment upon the tradition itself and the age which implicitly accepted it. The most dangerous of errors are those which have the longest pedigree and attract the noblest souls. Roger Bacon complained that the Bible was being displaced in universities by the Sentences; by that compilation in which Peter Lombard detached a number of texts from Scripture and the Fathers, and strove to weave them into a coherent synthesis. Though Bacon's words here contain a demonstrable exaggeration, yet it is certain that the great Schoolmen such as Aquinas and Bonaventura devoted some of their most laborious work to commenting upon the Sentences; and in medieval college catalogues there are far more copies of that volume than of the Bible. If this was so even amongst the most learned, it was incomparably worse among the multitude who knew no Latin, and to whom (as will be seen in Chapter XLIX) vernacular translations were almost altogether forbidden for their souls' health. The mystic Margery Kempe [1420] tells us how, when she supported her objection to oaths by reference to Christ's own words, the clergy cried out to the Archbishop of Canterbury who sat in judgment upon her: "Ah, sir, here we wot well that she hath a devil within her, for she speaketh of the Gospel!" (p. 189). Medieval theology thus moved in a vicious circle. In all other matters than this, the superior certainty of ink and parchment over oral tradition was almost or quite as notorious as it is to-day. As one monastic cartulary puts it, "man is a forgetful beast"—*homo est obliviosum animal*—

unless things be written down in ink.* Yet here, in theology, while on the one hand any particular Bible text might be insisted upon with the most ferocious literalness, on the other, there was scarcely any limit to the licence of interpretation, or even to the studied oblivion, of any passage which might clash inconveniently with a steadily stiffening dogmatic tradition. This was the natural result of the hierarchical caste-system, sheltered from free outside criticism. When, therefore, Europe began to be educated enough for the layman to interest himself in somewhat more than the barest rudiments of his creed, then violent differences of opinion inevitably grew up between the "specialist" and the "amateur". The specialist was powerful enough to suppress criticism until this rift had widened into a gulf; and then came the great revolt which will be dealt with in my final chapters.

This is a consideration which is too often neglected in the present-day rehabilitation of scholastic thought; viz. the reaction of layfolk from the unjust neglect or misrepresentations of the past. We must face both sides equally frankly. The more we admire the intellectual and moral greatness of those Scholastics, and the greater gratitude we feel for their achievements in many directions, the more deeply we must deplore those now abandoned falsehoods which, dominating their age, naturally fettered their thought. Nor is there anything Pharisaical in this outspoken condemnation, so long as we remember the exhortation "Physician, heal thyself". The specialist in every age (not excepting the scientist of to-day, who here has least excuse of all) is tempted to create, or accept on insufficient evidence, dogmas of his own. In every age, the supreme achievement is a Socratic realization of our precise intellectual limitations. Therefore, if there exists in modern Europe a mind of the calibre of Aquinas, it must be even more deplorable that he should be infected as Aquinas was by the fatal illusions of this, his own century. Stubbs, one of the weightiest and most balanced among all our great English historians, summarizes the Scholastics in words which would probably commend themselves to the majority of impartial historians. "They benefited mankind by exercising and training subtle wits, and they reduced dialectics, almost, we might say, logic itself, to absurdity. I do not undervalue them, because the great men among them were so great

---

* I give a few other examples, out of many, in *Five Centuries of Religion*, vol. III, pp. 45 ff.

that even such a method did not destroy them: in reading St Thomas Aquinas, for instance, one is constantly provoked to say, what could not such a mind have done if it had not been fettered by such a method?"[18] By their application of reason to theology, they carried the West far beyond its earlier semi-barbarian stage of still more uncritical citation of authorities and frankly emotional exposition. In combination with the lawyers, who were pursuing parallel methods in their own sphere, these Schoolmen laid the foundations of modern political science. Thus they added definitely to our social inheritance: the West was thenceforward on a higher plane.

Moreover, within their limitations the Schoolmen often showed amazing industry and acumen. Aquinas, in especial, commands hearty admiration even from modern philosophers who are least disposed to accept many of his most important conclusions. They commend him for the almost incredible volume of work which he completed in a comparatively short life, and for his penetration and philosophical grasp. He, like by far the greater number of distinguished Schoolmen, was a friar. In this field England may boast extraordinary distinction. A Swiss Franciscan scholar writes: "The English nation has given to the Franciscan Order a greater number of eminent scholars than all the rest of the nations put together. Indeed, if we consider the real leaders of the Minorite schools, they all belonged, with the exception of Bonaventura, to England."[19] No other country can produce such a Franciscan trio as Roger Bacon (d. 1294), Duns Scotus (d. 1308) and William of Ockham (d. 1349). Duns, it is true, was born in Lowland Scotland; but he taught at Oxford, and the culture of Lowland Scotland was then as characteristically English as that of modern Belgium is French, or that of Austria German. And Robert Grosseteste, Bishop of Lincoln, though not a friar, set an impress upon the Franciscans at Oxford which brought that University to the front rank in Europe.

We cannot choose a better concrete example of St Thomas's method than the section of his *Summa theologica* in which he justifies the Inquisition system (2ª 2ᵃᵉ Quaest. XI). Article 1 discusses whether heresy is a species of infidelity: conclusion, *Yes*. Art. 2: Is it specially concerned with matters of faith? *Yes* again. Art. 3: Are heretics to be tolerated? *No*. Art. 4: Should those who return from heresy be received by the Church? *Yes*, always received *to penitence*, however often they may have relapsed; but it would be wrong "so to receive them always, that they might keep their lives and their other temporal goods". And, since this Article 3 is the most important, we may take it in detail, in its four formal divisions:

A. *Evidence for toleration.* (1) 2 Tim. ii. 23–4. (2) That which is necessary must be tolerated; and heresy must needs exist (1 Cor. xi. 19: "For there must be also heresies"). (3) The Lord bade His servants wait till after the harvest before dealing with the tares: i.e. to the end of this world (Matt. xiii. 25 ff.).

B. *Contrary evidence.* Titus iii. 10. "A man that is a heretic, after the first and second admonition avoid, knowing that he that is such an one is subverted."*

C. *St Thomas's Conclusion.* Let us distinguish between what is right (*a*) for the heretic, or (*b*) the Church. The heretic, who corrupts men's souls, is far more guilty than the coiner who corrupts money, and thus far more worthy of death. Therefore, if he be found pertinacious, the Church justly "leaves him to the secular judgment to be banished from the world by death".

D. *Removal of Objections rehearsed in* (*A*). (1) This requirement of Timothy is satisfied by the Church in that she does "modestly admonish them that resist the truth", and gives them a chance of recantation. (2) The utility which comes from heretics is not in their intention, which is to corrupt the Faith. Therefore "we must look rather to their essential intention, and so exclude them, than to that which is apart from their intention, and so bear with them". (3) This command of the Lord applies only to cases where the tares cannot be uprooted without uprooting the wheat.†

This illustrates the thoroughness of the method which St Thomas follows throughout all this gigantic work. First, we shall find him always speaking as advocate for what seems the weaker side, alleging all that can be cited for that. Then, he marshals similar evidence on the other side, often in many paragraphs,

---

* The Vulgate here has "haereticum hominem...*devita*". Erasmus, at the end of his *Praise of Folly*, quotes a priest who, at a theological discussion in his own presence, and with approval on the part of some others, defended the burning of heretics by quoting St Paul's command *haereticum hominem devita*, under the impression that *devitare* meant "deprive of life".

† This explanation he has taken from St Augustine, who, having for some time taken the side of toleration, confessed himself finally convinced by the practical success of physical punishment against heretics. (Quaest. x, art. viii.)

but often, as here, in the shape of a single Bible text. Then, leaving advocacy on either side, he puts on the judge's cap, weighs the evidence, and pronounces sentence. But, finally, he will not leave the court until he has done his best to explain away everything that had been pleaded on behalf of the mistaken side. The only weakness of this method, it must be repeated, is one which is inherent in the mentality of that age, and which differentiates Scholasticism clearly from both Graeco-Roman and modern philosophy.* Scholasticism worked only within certain definite traditional limits; often wider than we might imagine, but often, again, barbarously narrow. We may use that word *barbarous* advisedly: because, even where the decisive factor may be (as in this case) a single Bible text, that text must needs be interpreted according to traditions which, though finally dignified by the claim of ecclesiastical inerrancy, can often be traced to their source among the ignorant multitude, during the break-up of Graeco-Roman civilization. Aquinas would have been burned if he had denied certain things which, by now, his Church has outgrown. Moreover, even Aristotle's authority was almost sacrosanct: in the nature of the case, medieval thinkers paid enormous respect to classical authorities. Thus the teaching had nearly always begun in the form of commentary upon some consecrated textbook, of which the teacher alone possessed a copy; and, to the very last, it bore the imprint of these origins.

Yet the lecture gradually evolved into something much more like that of modern times. Finally, we find a definite regulation at Paris that the lecturer must go "as though he were preaching a University sermon", or in other words, "as though no man were writing before him"; yet in 1355 it was found necessary to legislate against the abuse of dictating slowly word by word—in other words, of "cramming". The lecturer who did this was to be suspended for a year; "and all students who impede the execution of this our present statute by shouting stamping, stone-throwing or any other device—whether by themselves or through

---

* It is true that there has often been over-emphasis on authority both in ancient and in modern times, and that Protestant bibliolatry and eschatology have often remained frankly medieval. Again, both pagans and Protestants have forcibly suppressed freedom of thought: but never so systematically and successfully as the medieval Church, in whose doctrines intolerance is implicit. The existence of what may be called pre-medieval and post-medieval medievalism does not destroy the distinctive character of medieval thought as a whole.

the agency of their servants or abettors—are hereby cut off from our fellowship for one whole year."[20]

Perhaps the worst weakness was the imperfect command of Latin, although all teaching was done or was supposed to be done in that language. At Oxford, for instance, 5 of the 65 Halls were devoted to the teaching of grammar; that is, to bringing undergraduates to the stage at which it was possible for them to follow the lectures at all. At Cambridge, similarly, the Master of Grammar (*Magister Glomeriae*, as he was called by a significant corruption) became a definite university institution. At the Colleges it was ruled that all conversations should be held in Latin. Sometimes there was a special scholar appointed (on the Continent his common nickname was *lupus* or "wolf") who earned his emoluments on condition of reporting infractions of this Latin rule on the part of his fellow-scholars. Far too little stress is commonly laid upon the immense gulf between those philosophers whose works have come down to us, and the ordinary scholar who sat under them in the lecture room. Again, we can scarcely exaggerate the cultural importance of the conversations of scholars with one another, on their walks or by the evening fire. Underneath the conventionalities of official university teaching we get constant indications of smouldering volcanoes; masters condemned for pantheistical or atheistical tenets. For instance, one Nicholas de Ultricuria was condemned in mid-fourteenth century for a series of propositions derived from Averroës and anticipating most of the sceptical tenets of Berkeley and Hume; and again we have revolutionary political writers like Pierre Dubois, Marsilius of Padua, William of Ockham, whose anti-papal lucubrations must have been fashioned originally in private converse, probably not exclusively in their own generation, but by a succession of scholars passing the torch on from generation to generation. This lends much of its significance to the startling novelties of More's *Utopia*; a book which, after all attempts to discount its serious purpose, certainly indicates extreme freedom of discussion under the surface in the group with which More was familiar, and probably also in other groups at Oxford, Cambridge, and the Inns of Court. Yet here again, in so far as the students were faithful to the Latin-speaking tradition, this must have hampered them considerably. So long as Latin had been a living language among the people, it had been a great advantage to have the Bible and the Liturgy in that language; but in proportion as it died out among the multitude this original prop became gradually a shackle. We often find that even learned men fell back upon the vernacular for their most intimate prayers and speeches; and it may be doubted whether, at any time in the Middle Ages, half a dozen men ever met together with sufficient mastery over Latin to enable each speaker to express his inmost thought as correctly and coherently, and each hearer to pick it up with the same certainty, as that with which men now express themselves and understand each other in their own vernacular. In medieval philosophy there were no "national" schools of thought, in the sense in which that may be predicated of modern philosophy. Yet this internationalism was gained to a great extent by a lowering of the general level; the steam-roller of Latin reduced a large number of natural inequalities; and that, together with the hampering theological restrictions, goes a long way to account for the comparative unprogressiveness of thought from the thirteenth to the end of the fifteenth century.

There remains one most important point, that of book-production at the Universities. Every good College had a certain number of books chained for general use, and often another set for circulation on loan. Full details on this subject are given in Professor F. M. Powicke's admirable monograph on the medieval library of Merton College, Oxford; and, quite recently, an epoch-making study has been published by Dr Jean Destrez, under the title of *La Pecia*, with a fine illustrative album of facsimiles from medieval university manuscripts. Dr Destrez just alludes to the evolution of the monastic scriptorium; but that is not his primary concern. By the end of the thirteenth century, at even great and specially cultured abbeys like St Albans, the main work in the scriptorium was evidently being done by hired workmen; and monastic libraries grew very slowly even with that assistance and by the gifts of wealthy benefactors. But, almost at the same time as the monks were beginning to content themselves with marking time, these new Universities were in the fervour and energy of youth. They, from the very first, were led forward by necessity to enormous advances in the matter of book-multiplication. The monk, whose rule and custom supposed him ordinarily to read only one volume a year, was satisfied with that very slow rate of increase which we find in fact wherever two successive catalogues from the same abbey give us clear evidence. The university student, on the other hand, might well read more pages in a year than the average Religious read in his whole lifetime. St Benedict had never envisaged his brethren as students in anything like that sense; therefore these new Universities created a revolutionary demand.

Pecia, piece, was probably a trade term with the tanners and parchment-makers; it was a skin, trimmed to the largest parallelogram that it will afford. Thus trimmed, it was folded and counterfolded, and formed eight pages of a size which we should call large quarto. Very exceptionally, the *pecia* consisted of a larger gathering than this; but, on the whole, the term signified a definite standard unit, created by the business needs of the first two great medieval Universities, Bologna and Paris. At Bologna, every year, a committee of *peciarii* was chosen from among the masters. The *stationarii* were bound, under oath, to produce all the *exemplaria* which they possessed. Dr Destrez writes: "If the majority of *peciae* in any *exemplar*, or at least 6 of them, seem insufficiently correct, the committee corrects them at the expense of the *stationarius*, who must pay the cost on the spot. For this purpose every master or student of the University is bound, when required, to lend his own book if it is judged to be good. And if the doctor or student, after it has been judged sufficient, refuse to lend it at least within his own house, let him be definitely mulcted of 5 pounds, to be applied to the good of our University"—a significant contradiction of all modern ideas of copyright. The committee then publishes its official list of *exemplaria*: all others are forbidden as false and useless. Each *exemplar* is marked with the number of *peciae* which it contains, and with the price per *pecia* due to the *stationarius* from the borrower. The *stationarius* is upon oath to lend them at that price to all comers, and to put none into circulation which has not been examined and authorized. He must submit them to inspection at the committee's demand; and he must put up a public and conspicuous list, with prices, of his own *exemplaria*. With equal publicity he must post a list of those copyists or illuminators who have been discommoned by the University as unsatisfactory. Finally, seeing that the borrower ordinarily left a pledge instead of paying beforehand, the lender must keep a list of such pledges, safeguard them, and restore them directly the *pecia* comes back. Elaborate precautions are taken; for these "scholars" are keen business men, at least as mature in age as modern Rhodes scholars or research students; indeed, in many cases they are beneficed clergy, undertaking this elaborate and expensive education in order to qualify for archdeaconries or similar posts of honour and profit. It is they who draw up these statutes for the government of their University. Their professors or doctors—the two terms were synonymous— are the hired servants of the scholars, bound by the same network of oaths and prohibitions as the bedels or the university tradesmen. The *stationarius*, when recognized and licensed, must "give sufficient security for 2000 pounds, at least, that he will keep faithfully and restore unhurt the books and other possessions which the scholars have entrusted to him." For, not only did a scholar leave a pledge if he borrowed a *pecia* to copy, but all public sales of books, as apart from private purchase or exchange between scholar and scholar, went through the hands of these *stationarii*, who were sworn on oath to keep clear-priced catalogues, with name of the owner who is selling the volume. A *stationarius* needed, therefore, to be a capitalist; we know that the sixty-three volumes left by the great Accursius (1261) fetched 500 pounds of that day, though they were sold within the family and probably far below auction price. Scholars were forbidden to speculate; if the bookseller knowingly sold to any man who meant to sell again, he was fined five pounds, one of which went to the informer. Similar restrictions were imposed upon all "merchants" who were rich enough to deal in second-hand books.

It was within this network of minute regulations that the professional copyists, illuminators, correctors, and binders worked. The *stationarius* was bound to keep pure and legible texts: he must lend out the books or the *peciae* at a tariff fixed by the University. As the cost of living went up from generation to generation, there was a temptation to diminish the size of the *pecia*: but this could not long go on undiscovered; for the same committee which had fixed the original tariff recorded also the number of *peciae* in each *exemplar*. One of the most interesting points established by the diligence and *flair* of Dr Destrez is this, that where we find two or more varying exemplars of the same book, that is always the oldest which contains the fewest *peciae*. Thus the question of the standard *pecia* became finally a matter for special legislation. In 1486 the University of Padua decreed that it should contain 16 columns, each of 60 lines and 32 letters to the line. Dr Destrez shows us how we may follow the scribe at work. The copyist, arrived at the end of his *pecia*, finds his pen grown blunt; he recuts it or takes a new quill; and the result is obvious at once. Or, again, his ink has grown too thick, or contrariwise he thinks it too pale, and here again the change leaves its mark. By dint of indefatigable attention, Dr Destrez has found nearly thirty *exemplaria*, i.e. the actual MSS. which Bolognese or Parisian authorities licensed as correct, and which their *stationarii* hired out as copies. In some cases these show natural signs of wear and tear, or even of folding by the copyists who found it convenient to carry them upon their person. His account of the gradual deterioration and replacement of worn *peciae* is of special interest, and must go far to revolutionize the textual study of MSS. from university centres.

This advance of book-production, so far beyond anything attempted during the previous eight centuries of monastic writing, must be put definitely to the credit of the medieval universities. So also must we give them all credit for their sharpening of the tools of thought. Those generations which struggled for a working synthesis of the unerrant Bible and the almost unerrant Aristotle did not only quicken men's curiosity to a very high degree, but fashioned instruments for further thought; many of our commonest abstract terms were either fashioned altogether or first popularized by these Schoolmen. When we hear from the lips of an ordinary labourer such a sentence as "it ain't the *quantity* of the food I object to, but the *quality*", that man is drawing a necessary distinction more easily and familiarly than many educated Romans could have done in Cicero's day. Yet while all this mental exercise taught men much; it ingrained also in their minds many things from which the world, both orthodox and unorthodox, has freed itself very slowly and painfully.

Those modern writers who, in violent reaction against past injustices, bid us return to the keen intellectuality of the School-men, are too apt to forget their statue's feet of clay. Immense labour and intellectual enthusiasm were often spent as vainly as the Royal Society is said to have spent itself in long and intricate discussion of Charles II's malicious question: "Why does a living fish weigh more than a dead one?" The king (we are told) listened with secret amusement, and then enquired whether any one of the disputants had begun by verifying the assumed fact.

Dogmatic assumptions as to heaven and hell, expanded by relentless and impeccable logic, led Peter Lombard, St Thomas, St Bonaventura, and St Bernardino, to their terrible picture of blessed souls looking happily down through all eternity upon the unspeakable torments of the damned. The dogma of Ecclesiastical Infallibility, pursued with that remorseless logic which, on one side, was the Schoolman's strength, led inevitably to the slaughter of thousands who were held to have forfeited human rights by attempting, after their own clumsy fashion, to be more Christian than the Pope and his cardinals. Moreover, the intellectual alertness of the early university age (say, from 1180 to 1280) had degenerated, long before the end of our period, into wearisome logomachy and hair-splitting. Erasmus, in a letter to Cardinal Campeggio, pleaded that Luther, however mistaken, should not be condemned unheard. He pointed out that the most respectable men seemed to favour Luther, and that this rough innovator's success came from the fact that "the world, as sick of this doctrine [of the Schoolmen], which laid too much stress upon petty comments or decrees of man, seemed to thirst for that living and most pure water drawn from Evangelical or Apostolic sources".[21] We may take an illustration on a coarser scale, but to that extent clearer. All reasonable folk are grateful for the patience, enthusiasm, and untiring experiments of the alchemists; yet nobody contends that this imposes upon us any duty of accepting their conclusions. I cannot end better than by quoting Rashdall's sane and balanced summary. After pointing out that medieval education was "at once too dogmatic and too disputatious", he sums up:[22] "The rapid multiplication of Universities during the fourteenth and fifteenth centuries was largely due to a direct demand for highly educated lawyers and administrators. In a sense the academic discipline of the Middle Ages was too practical. It trained pure intellect, encouraged habits of laborious subtlety, heroic industry, and intense application, while it left uncultivated the imagination, the taste, the sense of beauty—in a word, all the amenities and refinements of the civilized intellect. It taught men to think and to work rather than to enjoy. Most of what we understand by 'culture', much of what Aristotle understood by the 'noble use of leisure', was unappreciated by the medieval intellect. On the speculative side the Universities were (as has been said, 'the school of the modern spirit': they taught men to reason and to speculate, to doubt and to inquire, to find a pleasure in the things of the intellect both for their own sake and for the sake of their applications to life. They dispelled for ever the obscurantism of the Dark Ages. From a practical point of view their greatest service to mankind was simply this, that they placed the administration of human affairs—in short, the government of the world—in the hands of educated men. The actual rulers—the Kings or the aristocrats—might often be as uneducated or more uneducated than modern democracies, but they had to rule through the instrumentality of a highly educated class."

This chapter must not end without a repeated warning against exaggeration of the distinctiveness of medieval theologico-philosophic thought. Some of its characteristics can be found in pagan philosophy; and the same, or others, were often prominent for long after the Reformation. Its lurid eschatology, for instance, and the Bible "fundamentalism" on which that eschatology was so largely based, were strong in some religious quarters until yesterday. Yet, on the whole, it did differ clearly from both ancient and modern thought; if only in this, that neither of those other two was able to drill men into that same uniformity, at the risk of their very lives, which can be predicated of all medieval thought in its main outlines, apart from permissible minor variations.

THROUGHOUT this chapter, I am glad to acknowledge a heavy debt to the works of Dr Charles Singer, whose volume on *Religion and Science* in Benn's Sixpenny Library should be read by all who are interested in this subject; they will then probably wish to pass on to his larger works.

The decay of science cannot be directly credited to the rise of Christianity; Greek and Roman science had been in full decay before Constantine's recognition of this as the favoured religion of the Empire.[1] In those days, at any rate, Christianity came as a healthy protest against the pessimistic materialism which coloured so much of ancient thought; it objected not to actual observation and experiment (for those were no longer living forces in the Empire), but to the philosophical generalizations of paganism. For a living science two factors are essential: observation and synthesis. Observation must be patient and open-minded; synthesis must be bold and imaginative; each, sincerely used, stimulates, corrects, and supplements the other. This combination, in the Middle Ages, was nearly always imperfect. There was so little penetrating first-hand observation, in proportion to the collection and preservation of past traditions, that Dr Singer can write, without more injustice than is inherent in a single brief and epigrammatic sentence, "Medieval medicine may be summed up as a corrupted version of Galenism." In other words, medical science stood still—or even, to some extent, went backwards, from A.D. 200 to nearly 1500. Moreover, even when we do find traces of patient original observation, this is scarcely ever turned to its proper account by bold philosophic synthesis. Roger Bacon and Cardinal Nicholas of Cusa are perhaps the only two who can be specified, within a whole thousand years of Western Europe, who combined both the essentials, original observation and bold synthesis. Dr J. J. Walsh, in his *Medieval Medicine*, misses here, as on nearly every page of that book, the real root of the matter. He writes concerning Albert the Great, earliest of the great Dominican philosophers and teacher of St Thomas Aquinas: "In Albert's tenth book of his 'Summa', in which he catalogues and describes all the trees, plants, and herbs known in his time, he declares: 'All that is here set down is the result of our own experience, *or has been borrowed from authors whom we know to have written what their personal experience has confirmed;* for in these matters experience alone can be of certainty.' In his impressive Latin phrase, 'experimentum solum certificat in talibus'."[2] The words which I have here italicized are crucial: Albert frankly confesses to taking much of this "experience" from books, which we know now to be frequently most inaccurate. Even the greatest of medieval Schoolmen constantly based themselves on respectable hearsay, partly from classical writers and partly from popular traditions of hoary antiquity. Thus even St Thomas Aquinas himself, in that *Summa contra Gentiles* which is often regarded as his greatest philosophical (as apart from theological) performance, argues with equal confidence from the occult property of the magnet to draw iron, and the equally mysterious force of a certain *remora*, a mythical fish of a foot or eighteen inches, which has power to retard, or even hold up completely, the greatest ships. In the vast mass of Albert's writings, there are comparatively few original observations, though his was a mind of exceptional curiosity. The most that Dr Singer can say for him is that he "was among the few Medieval writers who were real observers of nature.... As an independent observer he is not altogether contemptible." Indeed, it was one of Roger Bacon's most serious criticisms upon the philosophy of both Albert and Aquinas, that it paid so little attention either to mathematics or to physical science. In contrast with these, Bacon praises a few laborious philological and philosophical students of his own time, whose self-effacing originality kept them from popularity, and whose influence on the general current of medieval thought was almost negligible. As Dr Walsh himself notes, Bacon testifies concerning one of these, Peter by name, a researcher in magnetism, "I know of only one person who deserves praise for his work in experimental philosophy, for he does not care for the discourses of men and their wordy warfare, but quietly and diligently pursues the works of wisdom. Therefore, what others grope after blindly, as bats in the evening twilight, this man contemplates in their brilliancy, *because he is a master of experiment.*" Bacon himself did indeed pay not only lip-homage to experiment, but spent a large fortune upon it and did his best to form a school of experimentalists. As Dr Singer says, he "frequently uses the phrase *experimental science*, which is for him the sole means of obtaining knowledge. 'All sciences except this', he writes, 'either merely employ arguments to prove conclusions, like the purely speculative sciences, or have universal and imperfect conclusions. Experimental science alone can ascertain to perfection what can be effected by Nature, what by art, what by fraud. It alone teaches how to judge all the follies of the magicians, just as logic tests argument.'" Cusa, again, ranks as a real scientific investigator: "for he clearly perceived the nature and some of the possibilities of the experimental method and did not hesitate to draw general laws from his conclusions." But Bacon spent a considerable portion of his life in confinement, and his writings were so far suppressed that nothing of them found its way into print until 1733. Cusanus, again, though a cardinal, was led by his own constructive scientific efforts into speculations which orthodox modern critics find it difficult to separate from pantheism; indeed Giordano Bruno, who was burned for pantheism in 1600, publicly acknowledged his intellectual debt to "il divino Cusano".

Astronomy was one of the few subjects to which the Middle Ages did contribute original observation of detail; but, when at last it had outgrown its chrysalis-stage of astrology, and when genius added synthesis to mere observation of detail and cataloguing, then Europe saw the tragedy which culminated in Galileo's condemnation and imprisonment. Moreover, this hostility to impartial observation may be noted, even to the present day, in the orthodox historiography of the Roman Church. It is implicit in the principle which is so clearly stated by that Pope who wrote classical Latin of real refinement, and who first opened the Vatican Library to the reading public. Leo XIII, in his pastoral letter to the French clergy on the study of history, wrote in 1899: "Those who study it must never lose sight of the fact that it contains a collection [*un ensemble*] of dogmatic facts, which impose themselves upon our faith, and which nobody is ever permitted to call in doubt." With that, Albert the Great would have been in complete sympathy; and he would have found a far more impressive phrase in the time-honoured Latin of "extra Ecclesiam nulla salus". The result has been that, throughout the centuries until the present day, and more especially since the foundation of the Institut Catholique at Paris, we have abundant orthodox monographs, often full and accurate in detail, on separate subjects, but these are seldom frankly synthetic even within their own limits. To correct anticlerical misstatements and exaggerations is sometimes easy; again, it is seldom dangerous to confess facts damaging to orthodoxy in detail here and there; but the real crux comes when a thinker passes onward to draw from such mere details what might seem the natural inferences. There, the adventurous historian may only too easily find himself faced by that ring of dogmatic facts which stands like the wall of flame round Paradise: thus far shalt thou go, and no farther! The clearest example here is that of Monsignor Louis Duchesne, whose knowledge of historical detail was perhaps widest and most exact among all these scholars, and whose earlier monographs are still classical. When, towards the end of his life, he set himself to write no longer mere separate essays, but a complete history which should range over the whole field, and in which none of the time-honoured thorny problems could be quietly ignored, then this *Histoire Ancienne de l'Église*, which bade fair to become classical not only throughout the world but even within his own Church, was put upon the *Index Librorum Prohibitorum*.

Thus, though a few new inventions, or reintroductions of old things, stand to the credit of the Middle Ages, these bore little fruit. Lenses, which had been known to the Arabians, were adapted to spectacles in about 1300; and the mariner's compass had been adopted perhaps two centuries earlier. But these led to no discovery of general laws either in the theory of light or in magnetism. Therefore, as Dr Singer points out, there was as yet no conflict between the medieval scientist and the Inquisition: "experimental methods produced no conclusions dangerous to current theology; and, on the other hand, no officer of the Inquisition ever grasped the nature of the scientific method."

Yet that conflict was only a question of time, since Inquisition and Science were essentially inspired by mutually exclusive principles. Modern attempts to represent the Galileo case as a misunderstanding, or a mere unlucky accident, fly in the face of the plainest documentary evidence. It was not that Galileo blundered by stepping outside his own domain of science and attacking Holy Scripture. On the contrary, it was the Roman Church which, relying upon its own authority to interpret the Bible in a sense defended by nobody nowadays, stepped outside its own domain and would have burned the man of science if he had not allowed himself to be silenced in his own scientific field. For it was the Church itself, officially and solemnly, which pronounced that condemnation; the fact is confessed, and proved against the special pleading of modern apologists, by Abbé Vacandard, one of the ablest of Roman Catholic historians. Indeed one of those same apologists, Abbé Choupin, is constrained to admit that "it was certainly in the name of the Pope, and therefore of the Teaching Church, that the judgments of 1616 and 1633 [against Galileo] were pronounced".[3] The fact is, that the Galileo tragedy was implicit in the whole teaching and practice of the medieval Church, which was still unchanged in the seventeenth century. For a thousand years past, every factor had been there except one. There had been no astronomer of Galileo's genius. With him, at last, came the man great enough in astronomy to dash his head against those narrow and unyielding ecclesiastical limitations. Roger Bacon, for his part, seems never to have come into actual conflict with the Inquisition itself, but (almost as dangerous) with the conservatives of his own Franciscan order. A liberal Pope (Clement IV) heard of this remarkable man, and wrote in 1266 bidding Bacon send him a fair copy of his books secretly and without delay, notwithstanding any constitution of the Franciscan order to the contrary: for friars, like monks, were forbidden to publish their writings without authority. For a brief while he enjoyed that papal favour, and produced the most remarkable of his writings in an extraordinarily short space; but in 1277 the shadow fell again upon him. This time (to quote the words of the medieval Franciscan chronicler), the Minister General, "by the advice of many friars, condemned and reprobated the teaching of Friar Roger Bacon of England, master of sacred theology, as containing some suspected novelties, on account of which the same Roger was condemned to prison". Upon this Dr A. G. Little comments: "The teaching and the novelties are not defined by the chronicler, but we may infer that the causes of Bacon's imprisonment were his contempt for authority, his attacks on the Dominicans and on his own Order, his defence and practice of the 'magical sciences', in magic being included the unknown powers of art and nature." For, on those points of "magic", Bacon insisted upon scientific observation, just as the Society for Psychical Research does in our own day. To quote again from Dr Little: Bacon insisted that "the whole question of the 'magical sciences' should be investigated by competent men specially licensed by the pope....As to the books of necromancy, says the writer, it would be better to keep them than to destroy them. Many of the books condemned contain nothing against the Catholic faith; 'nor is it perhaps just that people who have never touched them should presume to judge them'. It was an open repudiation of ecclesiastical authority." We need not wonder that his writings afford us glimpses of other patient researchers of that day, who for us are mute and inglorious. No doubt he did not always practise what he preached; but Professor A. E. Taylor felicitously summarizes his place in this field: Bacon is the man "to whom we probably owe it that the ideal of a mathematical physics was kept alive to bear fruit in a later age".[4]

Another struggle in which he rose far above all contemporaries—the insistence on scientific revision of the Vulgate Bible text, which by that time swarmed with errors—did indeed involve him in no serious conflict; but only, perhaps, because the whole matter remained fruitless for long after his death. No Pope undertook the task until after the Reformation; and, even then, the text thus produced was inferior to those produced under Bacon's system: it is not until our own day that a formal papal commission has at last grappled with and satisfied that crying need in theological science. For historical science Bacon did nothing: indeed, his belief that the morality of pagan Rome was such as to put that of his own age to shame is in flat contradiction to notorious facts. There was still so much in him of the typical Schoolman that, if he had stepped into that field, he would probably have fallen under Stubbs's criticism, that the thirteenth-century mind suffered from "the attempt to substitute abstract reasonings for minute examination of facts in the study of history". But, at his worst, he would have been incapable of those historical aberrations which constantly meet us in the *Lives of the Saints*, and which aroused the disgust of the most orthodox Bishop Melchior Cano in the sixteenth century.* Nor would he have connived at what was only too common, the deliberate substitution of revelation for historical

---

* "Many on our side are either slaves to partiality, or even deliberately invent so much, that I am not only ashamed but disgusted by them." They "have destroyed men's faith in truth for the sake of this faith in falsehood". "Suetonius alone has kept all [the notes of a true historian], and most of our historians have abandoned them all." (*Loci Theologici*, Bk XI, c. 6, written fifteen years after St Thomas More's death.)

observation and records. Somewhere about A.D. 850 Agnellus, Bishop of Ravenna, undertook to write a complete series of lives of his predecessors in that see. He was, for his own time, a remarkable scholar: yet here is his description of his historical methods. "Where I have not found any history of any of these bishops, and have not been able by conversation with aged men, or inspection of the monuments, or from any other authentic source, to obtain information concerning them, in such a case, in order that there might not be a break in the series, I have composed the life myself, with the help of God and the prayers of the brethren." In another place, again: "On account of your prayer, and that my history [of St Aurelian] may not be too short, I will, with divine help, relate boldly what my human intellect is quite unable to declare." We have a similar instance from Flanders. The whole early history of the cathedral and city of Tournai rests upon revelations made in successive visions by a departed saint to a twelfth-century canon, at whose dictation they were incorporated in the official chronicle of the cathedral. Men learned thus that Tournai had been founded by Tarquinius Priscus, who was contemporary with Nebuchadnezzar and Daniel at Babylon. The saint's visions were communicated to St Bernard at the famous Council of Sens; and the chronicler gives no hint of disapproval on the part of that great soul and great intellect. As against this, there were many medieval chroniclers who took real pains to ascertain their facts, and a few who show true historical sense: in England, William of Newburgh and Matthew Paris may be specially mentioned under that head. But there was nothing like historical science; nothing like the modern care for documents, and bee-like passage from flower to flower with steady persistence of collection. What the monks sometimes did within their own abbeys was much rarer than is commonly supposed; and, even at the greatest abbeys, when a chronicler does at last appear he often has to confess the scarcity of documents bequeathed to him by generations or centuries of predeceased brethren. Even then, again, the medieval stress upon impulse as opposed to patient reflection, and the low estimate of labour which was characteristic of that rudimentary civilization, told against science in history as in other fields.

If there was so little system in the record or study of past events, still less was there in scientific zoology, botany and geography. For these subjects our ancestors were mainly dependent upon such ancient classics as Pliny and Solinus. These authors were accepted almost without criticism with their descriptions of "anthropophagi, whose heads do grow beneath their shoulders", and similar fables which survived to some extent far beyond the Renaissance and Reformation. It is true that the thirteenth, fourteenth and fifteenth centuries did produce real travellers whose stories, however strange, are mainly true and valuable; missionary friars like Piano-Carpini, Odoric, Rubruquis; Marco Polo the merchant; and Boldenseele the German knight. These, and many more, form a *corpus* of extreme value for the modern geographer and ethnographer; but, during the whole Middle Ages, no student attempted to submit them to scientific analysis and synthesis. Vincent of Beauvais, that thirteenth-century encyclopaedist whose three enormous folios, together with a fourth by some other Dominican, formed the standard encyclopaedia for all the remainder of our period, gives simply undigested morsels in this field; just as (to Cano's disgust) he does in history. Moreover, the general stress upon authority and discouragement of independent criticism, with the difficulty of balancing *pros* and *cons* upon any subject in an age which was far more bookless than it has been fashionable to assume during the last few modern generations, gave an enormous encouragement to unconscientiously picturesque, or even deliberately false, compilations. Here the stock example is a probable Englishman, Sir John Maundeville. He describes himself as a Knight of St Albans; and the evidence seems strong for some real connection of some such man with St Albans. Yet no such name can be clearly identified in other records; and it seems pretty certain that the book was first written in French at Liége, then translated into Latin, and last into English. Its popularity was almost unexampled; more than 300 MSS. are known to exist still, and it was translated into most European languages. He professes to have started in 1322 and certainly the book was written before 1371. After 34 years of travel, he came home crippled with rheumatic gout, in spite of having drunk thrice or four times from the Fountain of Youth, "whereof they who drink ever, never have sickness, but appear ever young". The English version, by a gross interpolation, makes him submit his book for the Pope's approval at Rome—in days when the Popes were notoriously at Avignon! Again and again he speaks as an eye-witness; yet there is scarcely a sentence in the book which has not been exposed as borrowed, and sometimes distorted, from real travellers like Odoric. But he certainly was a great literary artist: he knows how to exploit to its utmost the thrill of the Great Unknown. Moreover, like Swift in *Gulliver*, he has that trick of the side-touch which lends an air of verisimilitude to his most astounding stories. For instance, "and let no man think that I am jesting"—"and whosoever will may believe me, if he will; and whosoever will not, may choose"—"of [the Earthly] Paradise I cannot speak properly, for I was not there; it is far beyond, and I repent my not going there, but I was not worthy"— again, there is a valley in which diamonds grow like mushrooms, "but some are true, and some are false"—again, genuine balsam has the most miraculous properties; but let it be frankly confessed that there are spurious sorts current in the market. Whether he was indeed an Englishman or not, he is most valuable for the social history of Chaucer's day; for his very falsehoods (as we now recognize them to be) added to his popularity with contemporaries and with later generations. Moreover, there is often deep significance even in his "asides" and his most casual reflections. We see the Bible-ignorance characteristic even of the most educated classes. Ignorance of the actual text, e.g. "In that town [of Beersheba] Abraham the Patriarch dwelt a long time. It was founded by Beersheba the wife of Sir Uriah the Knight, on whom King David begat King Solomon the Wise." Ignorance, again, of its true spirit, as in "if we be right children of Christ, we ought to claim the heritage that our father left us, and take it out of heathen men's hands". Equally significant is his attitude towards the puzzle of duplicate or multiple relics, with which this wandering story is naturally confronted. He finds four different Crowns of Thorns preserved as relics in four different places, and explains that each was employed in successive stages of torture: one of whitethorn, one of barberry, one of wild rose, and one of sea-rushes. There were also two specimens of the spear-head that had pierced the Lord's side; and, more embarrassing still, one was markedly larger than the other. The climax comes with the head of St John at Samaria; "and some men say that the head of St John is at Amiens in Picardy; and other men say that it is the head of St John the Bishop; I know not which is true; but God knows. But, howsoever men worship it, the blessed St John is satisfied."

Behind all this, there was always that which must never be

forgotten when we try to comprehend medieval life—the Apocalyptic spirit. The scientific devotion of a Spinoza, refusing the offered professorship at Heidelberg and preferring to live by polishing lenses in complete independence of contemplation, or, again, the intense and perpetual preoccupation of a Darwin, an Edison, a Henry Ford, had their medieval counterparts in monks and hermits who needed nothing beyond bare food and drink in a cell, and whose mental vision was focused upon nothing nearer than the Day of Judgment. It is difficult to realize the extent to which medieval minds were influenced by Apocalyptic ideas, and the haunting fear of Antichrist and Last Judgment at any moment. St Thomas More himself was inclined to believe that those must be imminent in his own day.

St Augustine, a man of real learning in his generation, and one of the greatest of all Christian philosophers quite apart from his compelling literary force, could write: "Whatever knowledge man has acquired outside Holy Writ, if it be harmful is there condemned; if it be wholesome it is there contained." There we have almost the words which tradition ascribes, rightly or wrongly, to Caliph Omar, condemning to the flames that Library of Alexandria which had no equal in the world before it, and was destined to have no rival, even at an immense distance, for the rest of the Middle Ages. "If all those volumes" (so his words are reported) "contain that which is written in the Koran, then they are superfluous; if anything contrary, then they are mischievous: burn them all." We need scarcely go farther than those words of St Augustine in the fifth century, and St Gregory's attitude in the sixth, and Omar's unquestionable holocaust in the seventh, to explain why, on the whole, Latin Europe possessed in A.D. 1000 scarcely more than the shadow of a shade of what Alexandria had known in the year 200. The first of hindrances (apart from those common to all reconstructions after great wars) was "the wide acceptance of the Christian doctrine that the body was of little importance in comparison with the soul".[5] Yet there was another doctrine which worked not only negatively but positively; that of Macrocosm and Microcosm. This, though primarily Greek and pagan, and never officially proclaimed by the Church, did in fact pass into Christian teaching with many other such elements, and was accepted by ecclesiastical leaders. It represented the world as a living being; Man and Universe are constructed on the same lines; and, in consequence, we must interpret the human frame by extra-human analogies. It was a natural corollary of this creed that men should believe the ocean to contain the counterpart of all that exists on land; the horse had its double in the sea-horse, the lion in the sea-lion, etc. This is the fancy to which Andrew Marvell alludes in his garden-poem:

> That ocean where each kind
> Doth straight its own resemblance find.

This, no doubt, is what the medieval priest was thinking of when he told his flock that the broiled fish (*piscis assus*) of Luke xxiv. 42 was an "ass fish". The consequence of this strained analogy was, that the stars of heaven were believed to influence the parts of man's body and the course of his life. Thus belief in astrology went far to supersede anatomy and physiology. Many pushed this so far as to arrive at absolute fatalism: Chaucer, as we have seen, shared with his contemporaries a lively interest in that problem. Even the greatest minds were deeply preoccupied. St Thomas Aquinas concludes that the stars do indeed influence human actions, but do not compel them: that, of course, would be a negation of freewill. He writes: "We must say that the majority of men follow their passions, which are impulses of sensual appetite whereunto the heavenly bodies may co-operate, while there are a few wise folk who resist such passions. Therefore astrologers, while they are able in the majority of cases [*in pluribus*] to predict truly, and especially in general, yet cannot do so in special cases, since nothing prevents a man from resisting his passions by means of freewill. Wherefore astrologers themselves say that the wise man ruleth the stars, to wit, in so far as he ruleth his own passions" (*Sum. theol.* 1ª. q. cxv, art. 4, ad. 3).

Thus, on the one hand, we must recognize that the medieval Church did steadily maintain among men the general conception of an Orderly Universe, concordant with man's moral aspirations. But from that merit we must deduct much, when we consider how selfishly she interpreted this idea of Order, and how incapable she was of facing that which later experience has taught, that truth emerges at least as much from men's honest differences as from supine acquiescence in the claims of dominant authority, however imposing and time-honoured.

THIS, after all, is the field in which medieval science can best be studied; for here we have something in which all men are interested, great and small. Why was medieval progress so slow in a matter so vital to every rank of society? It is fairly comprehensible that clerical conservatism should have cared little for Bacon's ideal of a scientifically accurate Bible or accurate translations from the Greek Fathers; and, again, that nobody should have paid attention to his hint of possible aeronautics; or, still further, that his similar surmise of an American Continent should have slumbered until it was picked up by Cardinal Peter d'Ailly in the fifteenth century, and treated more seriously by Columbus a couple of generations later. We are not so very much surprised, again, that Europe should not have taken to printing until more than a century after Marco Polo's description of China might have shown the way. But it is far more strange that, in medicine, Dr Singer can pass on from the death of Galen (A.D. 199) to write, "the Dark Ages [for medicine] have begun. Anatomy in the pagan world descends into darkness more abruptly, but not more surely, than philosophy."[1] Here again we must note what the date proves, that it is not merely a question of Christian influence; decay had already set in before Constantine the Great. But why, when the world settled down again, was there not a more real advance in medicine? After the barbarian invasions, there still lingered some remnants of Greek medical science under Islam; and, in the West, Salerno kept some knowledge of the Greek language and tradition, and even some remnants of the ancient writings: but the main stream came through Arabs and Jews. These Arabs were supreme in this post-classical medicine from the eighth to the thirteenth century. The most important of the Greek writers were translated into Arabic; and, for centuries, the West possessed nothing better than Latin versions of these Arabic translations from Hippocrates, Galen and Celsus. Such Arabic-Jewish translations "provided the staple reading in the medieval Universities throughout the Middle Ages". At the monastery of Monte Cassino, Constantinus "the African" (Chaucer's "cursed monk Dan Constantine") began his series of translations from the Arabic. "An ignorant and dishonest worker", Dr Singer calls him;[2] and Professor Gurlt supplies chapter and verse for this characterization (1, 670). To quote Dr Singer again: "This Arabic-Latin literature is generally characterized by the qualities most often associated with the words *medieval* and *scholastic*. It is extremely verbose and almost wholly devoid of the literary graces. An immense amount of attention is paid to the mere arrangement of the material, which often occupies its author more than the ideas that are to be conveyed. Great stress is laid on argument, especially in the form of the syllogism, while observation of Nature is entirely in the background. Above all, there is a constant appeal to the authority of the ancient masters, especially Aristotle and Galen. Lip-service is often paid to Hippocrates, but his spirit is absent from these windy discussions."[3] It is to this scholastic and disputatious spirit, as apart from real observation, "that we owe the almost complete absence of scientific advance between the thirteenth and sixteenth centuries". On the other hand, "monastic medicine had no thought save for the immediate relief of the patient. All theoretical knowledge was permitted to lapse. Anatomy and Physiology perished."[4]

In this field, far more clearly than in any other department of science, we can trace the direct influence of the Church: here, most of all, Europe suffered from that fatal exaggeration which enthroned Theology not merely as mother, but as Queen, of all the sciences. Medicine was discouraged for the clergy by the Councils of Reims in 1125 and Lateran in 1139. Apart from the general principle of contempt for mere flesh, there was here the special principle that "men vowed to religion should not touch those things which cannot honourably be mentioned in speech"; and in fact Abbot Faricius of Abingdon [1110], who had been a noted physician before he became a monk, was rejected for a bishopric for that definite cause. The Council of Tours (1163) forbade surgery for them, on the principle that *The Church abhorreth bloodshed*. Innocent III dealt with the case of a monk who had operated for scrofula upon a woman who, exposing herself afterwards against his bidding to the wind, caught a chill and died. The man had sinned (wrote Innocent) by usurping another man's office; "if, however, this deed was a fault of compassion and not of cupidity, and he was skilled in the exercise of surgery, then, after condign satisfaction, he may be permitted to celebrate divine service again." The Council of Nîmes (1284) and that of Bayeux (1300) decreed: "Let no subdeacon, deacon, or priest exercise any act of surgery which extendeth to cautery or incision." That of Würzburg (1298) repeated the prohibition in other words.[5]

And while the Church thus discouraged surgery, she actually prohibited anatomy. This story is summed up in Professor Gurlt's classical *Geschichte der Chirurgie* (Berlin, 1898, vol. i, p. 673): "All the universities stood under the jurisdiction of the Church; the teaching there was done under her regulations, and the books to be read there were chosen by her; therefore her education, especially in medicine, was purely theoretical and dogmatic, quite unpractical, consisting merely in the recitation of a Greek or Arabian writer in Latin translation, with the professor's interpretation.... Anatomy was in a very poor state in the old universities except Bologna, where Mondino and Berbuccio taught. The statutes of Montpellier, for instance (A.D. 1340), prescribe that there shall be an 'anatomy' at least every two years. These so-called 'anatomies', which, until late in the following centuries, were held periodically and generally lasted several days, consisted in this, that the interior cavities of a corpse (usually a criminal's) were opened by a surgeon, while the professor, standing by, gave an explanation of the contents. In the earlier centuries of the Middle Ages surgery formed no subject of university teaching; scholars had to fall back upon private teachers and upon the study of the surgical works, which existed only in MS.... Soon after 1300, the medical faculty [of Paris] declared itself as an opponent of surgery, and in 1350 it forbade the practice of manual operations to its bachelors. Thus prospective surgeons were, for a long time, thrown back upon private teachers; for at the College of Surgeons in Paris there was no teaching until far later, and it was not until 1634 that its students could follow a surgical course, which was given in Latin. There was no question of clinical teaching in any of the universities.... Thus the medieval instruction at the universities was insufficient, almost entirely oral, consisting of the reading and commenting on ancient authors." Outside this sacred ring stood the mere practical surgeons, the barber-surgeons, men of whom the great doctor Lanfranc wrote satirically: "our pride in these present days [1280] hath left the office of phlebotomy to barbers, though of old it was the work of doctors, and especially when surgeons exercised that office." Such barber-surgeons needed neither Latin nor books; but many of them acquired great practical dexterity, especially in the surgery of wounds, for which the Crusades and other constant wars gave considerable practice. Yet, even there, we may trace the terrible disadvantages of this prohibition of anatomy. Abbot Guibert de Nogent tells us, in special admiration of King Baldwin's generous and humane character, that, when he was severely wounded, and dangerous internal suppuration supervened under a treacherous film of growing flesh, he refused to save himself at the expense of a fellow-creature's life. His physician had recommended "that he should command one of his Saracen prisoners (for it was criminal to ask it of any Christian), of his own stature, to be wounded in the same place wherein he himself had been smitten, and, after the infliction of this wound, to be slain" for post-mortem study. Baldwin's "extreme piety" was shocked at this suggestion; but he permitted the experiment to be made upon a bear, "a beast that is useless except as food for sport".[6] Other great men were not so scrupulous. Frederick II, "the marvel of the world", had strong scientific interests, with the power of gratifying every whim. On one occasion, the chronicler Salimbene tells us, he fed two men sumptuously at dinner, and then sent one to sleep, the other to take vigorous exercise. After a sufficient interval, he caused both to be opened, in order to judge which had digested best. Another time, he enclosed a man in a hermetically sealed cask; and, since the vessel when opened showed no soul, but only the corpse, this strengthened his disbelief in survival after death. Here again we see the materialism of the unbeliever corresponding to the materialism of the Church, with her visions of souls wafted heavenwards from the body in the shape of a little child or a transparent crystal sphere. The naked child especially, comfortably nursed in the folds of Abraham's bosom, was the time-honoured picture in paintings and sculptures of the Last Judgment.*

But let us return to the professional students, and especially the universities. The belief that monks and friars were the doctors of the Middle Ages is a gigantic delusion. If the chroniclers, here and there, celebrate a monk's skill, the context itself nearly always shows that this was exceptional, and that this particular physician, like Abbot Faricius, had mastered his profession outside, in his

* See, for instance, H. S. Bennett, *Life on the Medieval Manor*, facing p. 10.

"worldly" days. A few early friars may be found, here and there, tending lepers as an exercise of extreme Christian charity; but it would be difficult to find a single case, after the days of Francis and Dominic, of leper-hospitals regularly visited by them. Indeed, quite apart from the writings of distinguished ascetics like St Bernard, who cuts short all valetudinarian complaints with the brutal "thou art a monk, not a physician", formal ecclesiastical legislation ought to have been sufficient to cast the gravest doubts upon this legend. Medical books are often found in monastic libraries; but all other evidence suggests that little was known or practised in the infirmary beyond the traditional leechdoms, or the old wives' remedies, to which we shall come presently. As for medical practice among outsiders, this is often expressly forbidden to monks, as offering too great temptations to private property and covetousness.[7] It is in the universities, therefore, that we must study the evolution of medicine, and especially of surgery; for in those days there was no division between the two branches of the profession, and there are some modern practitioners who regard that division as regrettable.

Nearly a century after Constantine's translations from the Arabic came the far more numerous and better translations of Gerard of Cremona (d. 1185), upon whose 92 volumes the later scholastic medicine was almost entirely based. These in their turn were founded upon Arabic versions of Galen. To these writers "the main mass of medical knowledge [in Europe] before 1500 can be traced". And, even within the narrow limitations, the sources themselves were far from pure. The complacent medieval ignorance of Greek left men dependent upon the errors of translators at first or second or third hand; so that one of the first tasks of fifteenth-century medicine was to discover what it was that Galen had actually said. Only then, at the end of the Middle Ages, were really accurate translations made from this man upon whom Western medicine had practically depended for more than 1000 years.

Still worse were the deficiencies of practical anatomy and dissection. In 1238, the heretical Emperor Frederick II did indeed prescribe that, at Salerno, a corpse should be dissected once every five years in the presence of the physicians and surgeons.[8] But it is not till about 1300 that we find regular dissection, public or semi-public, even at the universities; and it is very significant that this is at Bologna, which, with Padua, was least theological among European universities, and where the dominant faculty was Law. The practice probably grew up under cover of legal requirements, as a development from the practice of post-mortem examinations. "But still dissection did no more, and was asked to do no more, than verify [the Arab] Avicenna, whom nobody doubted. It was, in fact, little but an aid to the memory of students."9 For the practice could not possibly become general in face of Boniface VIII's bull forbidding the mutilation of corpses (1300); a bull really aimed rather at injudicious relic-worshippers and superstitious fastidiousness as to places of burial, but which, as contemporary practitioners complained, did in fact tell against them. When, in 1345, Guido da Vigevano wrote a remarkable book with admirable anatomical miniatures, he explained in his preface that the Church forbade the actual process by which these drawings must have been obtained. Not until Sixtus IV (1471–84) did any Pope permit dissections, on condition of an ecclesiastical permit; but he had studied at Bologna and Padua. "From then onward the supply of corpses for dissection, though limited, was fairly regular." The practice was confirmed by Clement VII (1523–4). As the main beginnings of practical anatomy in the Middle Ages were due to the legists, so its finest performances, beyond all comparison, were due to the Renaissance artists and sculptors, in their struggle for perfect representation of the human body. Not until the epoch-making Vesalius, who comes just outside our period, was any medical work illustrated with figures even remotely comparable in accuracy of detail to the studies of Verrocchio, Dürer, Michael Angelo, Raphael, and, above all, Leonardo da Vinci. The whole story of the relations between theology and medicine affords a commentary on that dry remark of Chaucer concerning the Doctour of Physike: "His study was but little of the Bible." And it was the spirit of the medical faculties in the universities, especially at Padua, which gave rise to that proverb which Sir Thomas Browne took for his text: *Ubi tres medici, duo athei.*

This ignorance of anatomical facts, sometimes even of the simplest and most important, was a terrible drawback. The stomach, for instance, was regarded as a cauldron in which the food is cooked by the heat of the liver, which, like a furnace, keeps it simmering. Bernard de Gourdon, Professor at Montpellier from

1285 onwards, wrote what became a standard book for doctors in 1305. In one case, at least, he had to supply the want of human dissection by an empirical observation which has its own grim humour. It is uncertain how far he could distinguish the oesophagus from the stomach; and, if he dimly suspected the peristaltic action of the former (a step beyond Constantinus, for whom it was a mere passive funnel to the stomach), this was because he had learned "that in the case of certain Jews, hung up by the heels, the food given ascended to the stomach, showing that this organ possessed the power of attracting food to itself".[10]

England produced no medical writer of Continental reputation. "John of Gaddesden, the first English writer on medicine (1316), ... was a dexterous plagiarist", as indeed were many of his predecessors and successors on the Continent, after the fashion or example of "Dan Constantine".[11] Our John Arderne [1380], again, though a skilful and successful surgeon, stole most of his writings from other authors. In the preface to his best known book, on the fistula, he gives rules for professional etiquette and success which have been traced back by modern students through a whole pedigree of plagiarism. The section is taken without acknowledgment from William de Saliceto, who in substance rests upon Archimatthaeus of Salerno [1100], who took it, at several removes, from the school of Hippocrates. To that extent, therefore, we must discount our Englishman's work as *cliché*; yet even *cliché* must have some solid substratum of truth if it is to attract both writer and reader; and in this particular case we may trace human nature not only as it was among the ancient Greeks and our own medieval ancestors, but as it is around us and within us to-day. Arderne writes of the "leech":[12] "First, it behoveth him that will profit in this craft that he set God afore evermore in all his works, and evermore call meekly with heart and mouth His help; and sometime help from his earnings poor men after his might, that they by their prayers may get him grace of the Holy Ghost.* And that he be not found temerarious or boastful in his sayings or in his deeds; and abstain he him from much speech, and most among great men; and answer he slyly to things asked, that he be not y-take [i.e. caught] in his words.... Also, be a leche not much laughing nor much playing. And, as

* Compare the saying of Ambroise Paré (1517–90): "I dressed him, and God cured him."

much as he may without harm, flee he the fellowships of knaves and of dishonest persons. And be he evermore occupied in things that pertain to his craft; either read he, or study he, or write or pray he; for the exercise of books honoureth a leech. For why? he shall both be honoured and he shall be more wise. And above all this it profiteth to him that he be found evermore sober; for drunkenness destroyeth all virtue and bringeth it to nought, as

"Ebrietas frangit quidquid sapientia tangit."

saith a wise man, *Ebrietas frangit quicquid sapiencia tangit*:* 'Drunkenness breaketh what so wisdom toucheth.' Be he content, in strange places, of meat and drink there found, using measure in all things. Scorn he no man.... If there be made speech to him of any leech, neither set he him at nought nor praise him too much or commend him, but thus may he courteously answer: 'I have not exact knowledge of him, but I learned nought nor I have not heard of him but good and honest.' And of this shall honour and thankings of each party increase and multiply to him; after this, honour is in the honourant and not in the honoured. Look he not over openly [at] the lady or the daughters or other fair women in great houses, nor proffer them not to kiss,...that he run not into the indignation of the lord nor of none of his. In as much as he may, grieve he no servant, but get he their love and their good will.... When sick men, forsooth, or any of them beside cometh to the leech to ask help or counsel of him, be he not to them over stern nor over homely, but moderate in bearing after the requirements of the persons; to some reverently, to some commonly. For, according to wise men, overmuch home-liness breedeth dispising. Also it speedeth that he have seeming excusations, [e.g.] that he may not incline to their askings, without harming or without indignation of some great man or friend, or for necessary occupation. Or feign he him hurt, or for to be sick,

* This verse is scratched, in a hand of about Arderne's time, on a pillar in Ashwell Church, Herts.

or some other decent cause by which he may likely be excused. Therefore, if he will favour to any man's asking, make he covenant for his travail, and take it beforehand. But advise the leech himself well that he give no certain answer in any cause, but he see first the sickness and the manner of it; and when he hath seen and assaied it, although him seem that the sick may be healed, nevertheless he shall make pronostication to the patient [of] the perils to come if the cure be deferred. And if he see the patient pursue busily the cure, then, after that the state of the patient requireth, ask he boldly more or less [fee]; but ever be he ware of scanty askings, for over scarce askings set at nought both the market and the thing. Therefore for the cure of fistula...when it is curable, ask he competently of a worthy man and a great an hundred mark or forty pound, with robes and fees of an hundred shilling, term of life, by year. Of less men forty pound or forty mark ask he without fees; and take he not less than an hundred shilling. For never in all my life took I less than an hundred shilling for cure of that sickness.* Nevertheless do another man as him think better and more speedful. And if the patients or their friends or servants ask how much time he hopeth to heal it, evermore let the leech promise the double that he supposeth to speed by half; that is, if the leech hope to heal the patient in twenty weeks—that is the common course of curing—add he so many over. For it is better that the term be lengthened than the cure. For prolongation of the cure giveth cause of despairing to the patients, when trust to the leech is most hope of health. And if the patient consider or wonder or ask why that he put him so long a time of curing, since that he healed him by the half, answer he that it was for that the patient was strong-hearted, and suffered well sharp things, and that he was of good complexion and had able flesh to heal; and feign he other causes pleasable to the patient, for patients of such words are proud and delighted. Also dispose a leech him that in clothes and other apparel be he honest, not likening himself in apparel or bearing to ministers, but in clothing and bearing show he the manner of clerks. For why? it is seemly for any discreet man clad with clerk's clothing for to occupy gentlemen's tables. Have the leech also clean hands and well shapen nails, and cleansed from all blackness and filth. And be he

---

* Roughly equivalent to £200 of to-day. There is probably a good deal of boastful exaggeration here: but we do find occasional record of very high fees.

courteous at lords' tables, and displease he not in words or deeds to the guests sitting by; hear he many things but speak he but few....And when he shall speak, be the words short, and, as much as he may, fair and reasonable and without swearing. Beware that there be never found double word in his mouth, for if he be found true in his words few or none shall doubt in his deeds. Learn also a young leech good proverbs pertaining to his craft in comforting of patients....Also it speedeth that a leech can talk of good tales and of honest that may make the patients to laugh, as well of the Bible as of other tragedies; and any other things which are no trouble, while they make or induce a light heart to the patient or the sick man. Discover never the leech unwarily the counsels of his patients, as well of men as of women, nor set not one to another at nought, although he have cause, that he be not guilty of counsel; for if a man see thee conceal well another man's counsel he will trust better in thee. Many things, forsooth, been to be kept of a leech, without these that are said afore, that may not be noted here for over much occupying.... If the patient insist steadfastly that he be cured, or ask if he may be cured, then say the leech thus: 'I doubt not, if God help us, and thy good patience following, if thou wilt competently make satisfaction to me, as such a cure—not little to be commended—supposing all things to be kept that ought to be kept, and left that ought to be left, as it is said, I shall be able to bring this cure to a loveable end and healthful.' And then accord they of covenant, of which covenant—all excusation put aback—take he the half before hand; and then assign a day to the patient when he will begin."

Side by side with these works which have at least some claim to learning, medieval manuscripts swarm with semi-magical recipes and popular traditions of which the most useful prescribe simple decoctions of herbs or common-sense practical observations. Perhaps the most interesting of these, especially when we consider its legendary origin, is the Welsh *Meddygon Myddfai* ("Physicians of Myddfai"). Under the final cliff of the Caermarthenshire Black Mountains stands a pool suggestively dark and lonely, the Lesser Van Lake. Here a peasant called Gwyn, keeping his cattle by the lake-side, saw a beautiful lady on the surface of the water, combing her hair as reflected there. He held out to her his own barley-bread and cheese; she refused, and disappeared under the water. Next day the same vision and the same refusal. On the third day at last, she accepted his gift and came to land. He declared his love and besought her for wife: after long persuasion, she consented, on condition that, if he permitted himself to strike her thrice without reason, she would leave him for ever. Yet, having thus consented in word, she dived again and left him disconsolate. At last, turning round, he saw an old man of majestic appearance, leading two maidens by the hand, indistinguishable twins. He greeted Gwyn courteously, and expressed himself as willing to ratify his daughter's promise, if thè lover could pick out his own lady. Gwyn, who had fortunately noticed a slight peculiarity in the sandal of his beloved, emerged successfully from this test; and the majestic stranger promised to endow the couple with as many cattle as his daughter could enumerate without pausing for breath. At this point it was she who rose nobly to the challenge; and the father proved as good as his word. Gwyn and Nelferch thus lived happily for several years, and had three sons. Their eldest was seven, when Gwyn and his wife were invited to a marriage. She dawdled under the excuse of fatigue; he struck her with the gloves which hung from his hand. She reminded him: "That is the first." Some years after, they were asked to a christening. She burst into tears in the church, and he clapped her impatiently on the shoulder. "I wept for the trouble this poor child would have on earth: but that is your second." Later, again, this child died, and Nelferch burst out laughing. Gwyn laid his hand impatiently on her and demanded the reason. "I laugh because the baby is now free from all pain and suffering: but this is the third time: farewell!" She went home, called all the cattle, who came at the sound of her voice, crossed the hill and came to her own lake, where she and they vanished under the waters. Gwyn drowned himself in despair. His three sons haunted the lake-side day after day, until at last the mother came back. She offered to the eldest a humanitarian mission: he was to found a great line of physicians. She took him to a meadow hard by, and taught him the virtues of all herbs and their use. He became official physician to Rhys Grig, Lord of Llandovery and Dinevor, who gave him lands and privileges, and his descendants shared his medical talents: some claimed descent from him as late as the mid-seventeenth century. Rhys Grig, at least, is an historical personage: he fought constantly against the English and, after varying fortunes, died of wounds received at the siege of Caermarthen in 1234. The book *Meddygon Myddfai* claims to record the supernatural teaching of this fairy-medicine. It is in fact mainly a collection of traditional recipes. Some repose upon long experience and common sense: e.g. go for your drinking water to the place where women get their washing water. Others, again, are of the type of which a specimen may be quoted here. "*Against Toothache.* Take a candle of mutton-fat, mingled with seed of sea-holly; burn this candle as close as possible to the tooth, holding a basin of cold water beneath it. The worms [which are gnawing the tooth] will fall into the water to escape the heat of the candle."[13]

We must, however, credit the Middle Ages, and the Church especially, with important developments of the hospital system, far beyond anything that had been known under pagan Rome. These were partly for the casual sick or poor, but more often still for the aged and infirm: rather almshouses than hospitals in the modern sense. They frequently fell into debt and decay, in those days of economic and social uncertainties; but they were an important factor in medieval life. Leprosy and "St Antony's Fire" were, next to fevers, the most dreaded of medieval diseases. The latter, due to poisoning from corrupt rye-bread, seems to have been at its worst in the eleventh century, when the peasants had so hard a struggle for life. Leprosy, which is plausibly traced to rotten fish, created a large number of charitable hospitals. A good many of these became extinct in process of time. This was perhaps mainly due to the difficulty of maintaining any public endowment for many generations in those days of more troubled social life and comparatively few business safeguards. Clement V, in the Ecumenical Council of Vienne (1311), expressed his bitter indignation at the negligence or dishonesty of executors or governors of leper-houses, almshouses or hospitals, who let them go to ruin or embezzled the revenues.[14] But the occasional disappearance of these leper-hospitals, or their conversion to other uses, may have been due mainly to improved conditions of living: the mass of our population were perhaps better nourished in the fifteenth century than in any age until the time of our grandparents. There would seem to be no indication that the decline of leprosy (with which medieval doctors often seem to have confused other skin diseases) was brought about by any great advance in medical science. There is considerable significance in an Oxford agreement of 1356. By this, the city formally grants to the Chancellor of the University jurisdiction over the market: "and over all flesh or fish that shall be found to be putrid, unclean, vicious or otherwise unfit...on this condition, that the things forfeited be given to the Hospital of St John." Similarly, a Scottish Act of Parliament (1386) enacted that corrupt pork or salmon should be forfeited and given to "the poor leper-folk". At Berwick, a similar law added "if there be no leper-folk, the rotten pork or salmon shall be utterly destroyed".[15] It was this care for leprosy, in earlier times, which did much to develop what is perhaps the only real invention of importance in our period: the realization of the infectious nature of certain diseases. This realization, again, led to the creation of the quarantine system. Against those benefits we must set the generally defective sanitation of towns and cottages. Monasteries and great castles, on the other hand, especially those of the later medieval centuries, such as Hurstmonceux, had often a drainage system so full and elaborate as to give birth to modern legends of "secret passages".

WITH the Inquisition proper, which some might call the most characteristic of all medieval institutions, I have no space to deal fully here. I shall say nothing, concerning the institution itself, which I have not already said at greater length elsewhere, especially in my recent *Inquisition and Liberty*. Here, it will be best to plunge straight into the heart of the subject, to picture things as they were in the golden thirteenth century, and then to explain how almost inevitably they had grown to what they were.

A distinguished Roman Catholic historian of philosophy has written: "The thirteenth century believed that it had realized a state of stable equilibrium.... Their extraordinary optimism led them to believe they had arrived at a state close to perfection."[1] This, behind its obvious exaggerations, is in many ways only too true; society did to a great extent accept the Church's claims to perfection, and her pitiless repression of all that opposed this claim. But, on the other hand, here is a cry which comes to us from the very days which Professor de Wulf is describing. Berthold of Regensburg is here speaking; that Franciscan whom Roger Bacon singles out as the greatest preacher of his time; the man whose influence and success became legendary; the greatest mission preacher, perhaps, of the whole Middle Ages. He is warning his audience against the heretics, one of his commonest and most absorbing themes; and he says: "Had I a sister in a country wherein were only one heretic, yet that one heretic would keep me in fear for her....I myself, by God's grace, am as fast rooted in the Christian faith as any Christian man should rightly be; yet, rather than dwell knowingly one brief fortnight in the same house with an heretic, I would dwell a whole year with five hundred devils!"[2] So also his younger contemporary, the Dominican Étienne de Bourbon, complains that, while heretics pervert many from the Faith, none is ever reconverted. He explains it ingeniously: "Wine may turn into vinegar, but never vinegar to wine." Here, from the modern Professor of Louvain and the ancient Franciscan toiler among the people, we have two complementary sides of one truth which is fundamental to any full comprehension of medieval society. The Church was ubiquitous, omniscient, theoretically inerrant and omnicompetent: therefore, in her official capacity, this Totalitarian State was almost hysterically self-conscious, self-important, and self-confident. Yet all the while, in the background, there were almost equally hysterical misgivings and fears among those earnest Churchmen upon whom fell the burden and heat of toil among the masses. How had this dualism, this paradox, come about?

It is only loosely that we can call the Middle Ages an age of faith; it would be more strictly true to call this period an age of acquiescence. Every great creed at its beginning can afford to be far more liberal than when it has stiffened into tradition. In the Epistle to the Hebrews faith is essentially a reaching out towards the future. By gradual transference, the Church began to regard this virtue as reposing mainly upon past events; thus narrowing its own creed and provoking criticism. Those who are kindled by the fire of any new and great idea see much more clearly than their successors that it is the broad outline that matters. The general spirit which animates them all is so nearly the same that it obliterates minor differences, or at least throws them into the background. Renan points out how much freedom of thought there was in the early days of Islam; and we sometimes find astoundingly liberal ideas in the early Christian Fathers, in whose days faith still looked so much more forward than backward. Justin Martyr, the first of the apologists whose works have come down to us, claims in so many words that Socrates and Heraclitus were Christians, since they lived by reason; that is, Justin sees an ally and a fellow-Christian in every man who really strives with all his heart for the truth.[3] St Augustine, writing nearly 300 years later, goes far to abandon the historical ground, by emphasizing the fact that these almost incredible claims of Christianity have, in fact, fought their way against the heaviest odds, and reached the first rank among world beliefs. Dante, following him, puts the argument into one single sentence which, by its epigrammatic brevity, exaggerates the boldness of the claim. "If" (he says) "the world actually did turn to Christianity without [the persuasion of] miracles, then that [one miracle, in itself,] is such that the others are not worth the hundredth of it."[4] St Gregory the Great finds himself obliged to contend that, in his own days of less and less frequent physical miracles, the real basis for faith is in the moral miracle of the Church's hold upon mankind, and her good effect upon men's minds. St Odo of Cluny, the practical founder of the great Cluniac order, wrote emphatically to the same effect in about A.D. 940. The logical conclusion of all these sayings would seem to be, that the higher faith is a creed independent of physical miracles, and relying solely upon its obvious moral superiority over its competitors. Yet nobody attempted—at least, no orthodox writer—to follow them up to their logical consequences. Here, as on so many other important subjects, the medieval Church was content to suffer incompatible doctrines, and to live from hand to mouth by expedients. Such, then, being the uncertain and inconsistent attitude of great men in the early Middle Ages, it is natural that the first great original thinker produced by Western Christendom after the barbarian invasions should have had great difficulty in reconciling himself with the orthodox teaching of his day. This John the Scot (Johannes Scotus Eriugena) reconciled theology and philosophy in his own mind only by contending that, however they seemed to conflict, they were various aspects of the same truth; that the light of truth is iridescent, always the same in itself, but showing a bewildering variety of colours to the human eye, according to the angle from which we regard it. This was not the sort of doctrine to commend itself to strict orthodoxy; the current teaching was inspired rather by acquiescence than by living faith. While, therefore, saints were driven here and there, by their own love of truth, to speculations which were hardly consistent with many of the main doctrines of the medieval Church, yet, all the while, multitudes lived on in heathen superstitions just veneered with Christianity.

This evidence, which might be indefinitely reinforced, may suffice to suggest that there has been no time—at any rate since the very earliest days of Christianity—at which the official Church doctrine has been both fully probed and consistently accepted. There was in fact a great deal more enquiry in the Middle Ages than historians have usually realized. Joinville is an admirable witness here, because he gives his evidence so naturally and has no axe to grind; and because his testimony is so entirely borne out by other quite independent witnesses. He tells us of involuntary doubt—of the bishop whose life was a torture because he wished passionately to believe, yet could not exclude disbelief in Transubstantiation. Again, he shows us St Louis, naturally one of the kindest-hearted of men, yet so loth that a Christian should risk his faith by arguing with a Jew, that he will not permit this to any but a very learned cleric, adding: "The layman, when he hears any speak ill of the Christian faith, should defend it not with words but with the sword, which he should thrust into the other's belly as far as it will go." And, lastly, he tells us how a friend of his, a friar, met an old woman in the streets of Acre bearing a chafing-dish of live charcoal in her right hand, and a flask of water in her left, and saying that she meant to burn up paradise with the one and quench hell fire with the other, "so that no man might henceforth do right for the hope of heaven or for the fear of hell, but only for the pure love of God, who is so worthy and can do for us what is best".

This last instance is of extreme significance, for it brings us at once to oriental philosophy, and reminds us how much the Crusades did in this way to stimulate freethought. Saracens and Jews had many virtues which honest Christians could not help recognizing; and many prejudices disappeared when men saw others living so respectably under a religion so different from their own.5 Several writers in the thirteenth century give us, in one form or another, the fable of the Three Rings, which Lessing has immortalized in his play of *Nathan the Wise*. And the old woman's words at Acre recall those of the great Mohammedan philosopher Ibn-Roschid (Averroës) who wrote against the idea of heaven represented in the Koran, saying: "Among dangerous fictions, we must class those which tend to make us look upon virtue as only a means to happiness. If that be so, virtue has no meaning, since we abstain from self-gratification only in the hope of being repaid with interest. The brave man thus faces death only to avoid some worse pain; the just man respects another's possessions only in order to earn double their value", and so on. The direct influence of Arab philosophy on freethought in Christendom, and especially that of this particular man, Averroës, was very great. As Renan pointed out, he has the singular fortune of being better known outside than inside his own country. His life, roughly, fills the twelfth century, 1126–98. He is not the greatest of the Arab philosophers, but the last, summing up the work of his predecessors. This Arab culture, of which his is the last flicker, had lasted about 200 years. The Caliph Al Hakem II, who reigned at Cordova from 961–76, collected a library reckoned (with probable exaggeration) at 400,000 volumes, and encouraged Christian and Jewish as well as Muslim scholars. That library was publicly destroyed by reactionaries after his death; and for several generations the pendulum swung backwards and forwards between philosophy and ecclesiastical tradition; so that Averroës was provoked into writing: "Of all tyrannies the worst is the tyranny of the priest." He himself was deprived, for religious reasons, of his position as judge. Thus Renan can truly write: "When, therefore, the sovereigns were intimidated by fanaticism, philosophy disappeared; the manuscripts were destroyed by royal decree; and Christendom alone remembered that Islam had had scholars and thinkers.... Arab philosophy furnishes an almost unique example of a very lofty culture suppressed almost instantaneously without leaving any trace behind, so that it was almost forgotten by the nation which had begotten it."[6]

At this time, however, learning was making such rapid progress in Christendom, and at Paris especially (teachers and pupils having so far multiplied that the formation of a university was imminent or possibly actual), that the doctrines of this Muslim school, translated by Jews from Arabic into Latin, became welcome food for speculation north of the Pyrenees. From that time forward we find occasional condemnations, pointing to a great deal more that was concealed underground, of scholars who are teaching doctrines definitely derived from Averroës and his predecessors. In the first place the Universe is mechanical; there is no God that directs it. Secondly, the universality of the human intellect is so emphasized as practically to deny the individual soul. Thirdly, matter is eternal; there has been no such thing as creation and there will be no such thing as destruction. There, then, are three categorical denials of Christian thought—no Providence, no Immortality, no Creation. William of Auvergne, Bishop of Paris [1240], devoted most of his voluminous writings to a formal refutation of Averroism. He complains of its popularity at his University, writing: "Many men swallow these conclusions, taking them in without investigation by discussion or criticism; but consenting to them and holding them as proved and certain." A century later, St Thomas Aquinas and others show us that similar doctrines had quite a strong following among the teachers in the University. Such teaching, complains Aquinas, lurked in corners and addressed itself chiefly to the unfledged youth; but an Averroist would have answered that this concealment was natural enough, considering the activity of the Inquisition. In 1277 comes a similar batch of condemned propositions, including three still more offensive. And already these sceptics were trying to defend themselves by a subterfuge which remained popular throughout the rest of the Middle Ages—the plea that a thing, though theologically false, might be philosophically true, or *vice versa*.[7] So that, by this time, we have a state of mind which is as definitely sceptical as the scepticism of the eighteenth century or of our own day. It contends, first, that philosophy has a right to her own conclusions, with which theology has no right whatever to interfere; and, secondly, that Christianity must be judged by just the same standard as other religions, and that the wise man will avoid committing himself to any. Dante fills a whole circle of his hell with those who had died in disbelief of the immortality of the soul: "there lie more than a thousand of them."[8] Petrarch, in the next generation, tells us that "modern philosophers are accustomed to think they have done nothing if they fail to bark against Christ and his supernatural teaching";[9] they call Christ an idiot, and look upon all who undertake to defend Christianity as fools. Such kind of talk, he tells us, was fashionable among the upper classes at Venice; but it was specially popular at the University of Paris. About this time the great University of Padua became a focus of Averroism, especially in the medical school. Then, Paduan Averroism spread farther; it spread over all North Italy; so that, by the beginning of the sixteenth century, it had crept out of the obscurity in which the Middle Ages had compelled it to lurk, and had become "almost the official philosophy of Italy in general". The question of the immortality of the soul was discussed even at the Papal Court—but that Pope was Leo X. By this time, the current of Averroism was merged in the general flood of scepticism which accompanied the Renaissance; and we need pursue it no farther.

All this time, far simpler and perhaps more fatal doubts had begun to undermine orthodoxy. These were based partly on man's natural interest in the problem of the Origin of Evil, partly on the urge to get at the actual teaching of this inerrant Bible. For the Bible had slowly drifted out of sight among multitudes ignorant even of Latin (to say nothing of the original languages); and thus, gradually, had become so confined to a particular class, and even to a minority of that class, that it was jealously guarded from the profane populace.

Peter Waldo [1170], a rich merchant of Lyons, was converted in later life by hearing a minstrel recite the story of St Alexis. He hired a priest to translate for him into French the New Testament and "Sentences" from the Fathers. Then he dowered his wife, portioned his two daughters as nuns, and began an evangelical life. His adherents multiplied and preached; in those days it was only bishops who were accustomed to preach, and that seldom enough. The Archbishop of Lyons excommunicated Waldo for thrusting his sickle into another man's harvest. He appealed to the Pope, who treated him kindly and authorized him to preach when permitted by the priests. This, however, was an impossible concordat; the friction grew, and in 1179 this group submitted their scriptures to Alexander III and his Lateran Council, and begged for definite independent leave to preach. Alexander, who was a great man, treated them with considerable leniency; but in 1184 Lucius III banned them, and this excommunication was repeated still more emphatically by Innocent III, at his great Lateran Council of 1215. In 1229 the Council of Toulouse, confirmed by three archbishops and a papal legate, decreed that no layfolk should possess books of scripture except the Psalter and the Hours; nor might they possess even those except in Latin.[10] This struck directly at the Waldensians, whose whole tenets were founded upon Bible-reading and upon the attempt, more or less successful, to recapture the spirit of the early Church. They had tried hitherto to fit this in with the orthodox scheme, as the Wesleyans did later on; but henceforward they became definitely "dissenters". Yet, more than a generation later, when they were persecuted and outlawed and specially odious to the Inquisition, we have reluctant but brilliant testimony in their favour from the Dominican Étienne de Bourbon, their professional persecutor. He writes: "They know the Apostles' Creed excellently in the vulgar tongue, they learn by heart the Gospels of the New Testament in the vulgar tongue, and repeat them aloud to each other.... I have seen a young cowherd who had dwelt but one year in the house of a Waldensian heretic, yet had attended so diligently and repeated so carefully all that he heard as to have learned by heart within that year forty Sunday Gospels, not counting those for feast-days; all which he had learned word for word in his native tongue, apart from other extracts from sermons and prayers. I have also seen some layfolk who were so steeped in their doctrine that they could even repeat by heart a great part of the Evangelists, as Matthew or Luke, and especially all that is said therein of our Lord's teaching and speeches; so that they could repeat them continuously with scarcely a wrong word here and there. This I say on account of their diligence in evil and the negligence of the Catholics in good: for many of these latter are so negligent of their own and their families' salvation as scarce to know their Pater or their Creed, or to teach the same to their servants."[11] Here, however, as in all great quarrels, we must not see the fault on one side only, and we must remember that, within a generation of this time, St Francis was able to show how it was possible to lead truly evangelical lives without quarrelling with the Church. Yet, on the other hand, we cannot honestly condemn the Waldensians, or even the earlier Albigensians, as men whose social and political heresies would have plunged Europe into barbarism. Nearly all the evidence upon which this judgment has often been based is hopelessly tainted; the words either of orthodox clergy, their professional enemies, or of renegades. Moreover, some of the best among the clergy themselves, such as Bourbon and St Bernard's correspondent Erwin, Provost of Steinfeld, were embarrassed by the apparent honesty and moral integrity of these misguided folk. St Bernard himself, in his violent condemnation, characterizes them as "a vile and rustic crew, unlettered, and altogether unwarlike...ignorant peasant-women...they do indeed abstain, but they abstain heretically".[12] The same awkward facts confronted St Thomas More. He was puzzled by the apparent "knowledge in Scripture" and "virtuous behaviour" of some heretics, which gained them the favour of "simple folk". Such men "live virtuously, giving their goods in alms". Against this he can only answer dogmatically from the words of the New Testament: "Beware of the false prophets that come to you in the clothinge of shepe, and yet withinfurth been ravenous wolves." He continues: "For sith that thei, by false doctrine, labour to devoure and destroy mennes soules, we be sure ynough that wolves they be in dede, howe shepishlye soever they looke. And hypocrites must they nedes be, sith they bee so denounced by God's own mouth."[13]

One of the most abhorred heretical tenets, all through our

period, was the refusal to swear, even in the law-courts. Lea quotes a case from the year 1320, "in which a poor old woman at Pamiers was submitted to the dreadful death sentence for heresy simply because she would not take an oath. She answered all interrogations on points of faith in orthodox fashion; but, though offered her life if she would swear on the Gospels, she refused to burden her soul with the sin, and for this she was condemned as a heretic."[14] Modern apologists have attempted to justify this procedure. One of the most prominent, Professor Jean Guiraud of Besançon, in the recent co-operative history of *European Civilization* (IV, 360) writes: "It would serve no purpose to point out at any length how such a social code of morals undermined a society which, in the Middle Ages especially, was based upon the oath." In that last line there is some truth; oaths indeed were demanded at every turn; Rashdall points out how men were sometimes required to take an oath that they would keep their oath. But pious and orthodox contemporaries bewailed this as an apparent transgression of one of Christ's plainest commands, and as leading to constant breaches of the third Commandment. Waldo's contemporary, Petrus Cantor (i.e. Precentor of Notre-Dame-de-Paris), was among the most distinguished Churchmen in Europe; he had refused the bishopric of Tournai and (it is said) that of Paris also, and his writings were read and respected for centuries after his death. In two passages he expresses his misgivings as to what seems so plain a violation of Matthew v. 34 and James v. 12. How can we excuse (he says) the Canon Law which requires witnesses to swear, and the prelates who compel them to it? He quotes the example of that early disciple recorded by Eusebius, who answered with indignation: "I am a Christian: God forbid that I should swear!" Even though this total abstinence be a counsel of perfection, yet "why not strive after it, as we sometimes do after others?" and "why, when a man keeps that [precept of Christ], do we at once cry him down as a Catharist?" that is, as an Albigensian heretic.[15] Moreover, he goes on to indicate one painful consequence; namely, the execrable blasphemies which this promiscuous swearing encourages in common talk, so that "in some princely courts it hath been forbidden, under pain of five *sols*, that any should swear by the Lord's members". Just at this time, the chronicler Guillaume le Breton was extolling Philip Augustus of France for his severity alike against heretics and against Catholic blasphemers, so many of whom "tore the Lord's body in pieces". It will be remembered that, as soon as Chaucer's Poor Parson rebuked the Host for his blasphemous tongue ("What aileth the man, so sinfully to swear?"), the former at once struck in with "I smell a Loller in the wind!" and the Shipman stoutly supported him. A generation later, we have abundant testimony from the mystic Margery Kempe of Lynn: her objection to oaths brought her more than once to the brink of the stake, especially when it became directly embarrassing to men of high estate. We read, for instance (p. 186), how the Archbishop of York "commanded his retinue to fetch a pair of fetters, and said she should be fettered, for she was a false heretic". "And there came many of the Archbishop's retinue, despising her, calling her 'Lollard' and 'heretic', and swearing many a horrible oath that she should be burnt. And she, through the strength of Jesus, spoke back to them: 'Sirs, I dread ye shall be burnt in hell without end, unless ye amend in your swearing of oaths, for ye keep not the commandments of God. I would not swear as ye do for all the money in the world.' Then they went away, as if they had been shamed." So great was the prejudice thus engendered, and so durable (as in the later case of the Quakers) that we even find St Thomas More among those who raised this essentially un-Christian outcry. In recording the Lollard Hitton's contention "that neither bishop nor pope had authority to compel him to swear", More commented that "this point" was "a false heresy" (*Eng. Works*, p. 345 b).

This method of swearing (whether in the law-court or for amusement, for the two were practically inseparable in those days, as Petrus Cantor and other sources show) affords only one example of the anachronistic arguments which are so often excogitated in defence of the Inquisition. Abailard, who is often quoted for the assertion that these heretics were political rebels, writes in fact only of their theological rebellions. If such religious nonconformity nearly always involved social conflict also in the long run, that was due quite as inevitably to the totalitarian tenets of the Church as to the restlessness of the heretics. Medieval authorities leave us in no doubt that, under the Inquisition, theological differences were in themselves sufficient to bring a man to the stake. As Abbé Vacandard puts it: "the tribunals of the Inquisition condemned not only heresies which were calculated to cause social disturbance or upheaval; they struck at all heresies *en bloc*, and at each heresy as such."[16] There is practically nothing that can be truly urged against the medieval heretics which we cannot parallel among the more extravagant of the early Christians. Moreover their tenets, in most cases, explicitly forbade violence and bloodshed. Many of the crimes falsely laid at their door were due, in fact, to other persons who had no religious belief whatever, and who, in those wild days, plundered orthodox churches as freely as they would have plundered heretical conventicles, if they could have found precious metals there.

Indeed, all this modern emphasis on the political and social dangers would be anachronistic, even if it were wholly true. In the mentality of all the chief medieval persecutors, religious faith completely overbalanced political conservatism. Present-day writers, even while they insist most on the medieval accusations of Bolshevism against Cathari and Waldensians, supply sometimes, quite unconsciously, the counterbalancing and decisive consideration. Mr Hollis, the latest apologist for the Spanish Inquisition, has to deal with those many Muslims or Jews who, without real conversion, conformed outwardly under the remorseless pressure of the penal laws. Some of these men cynically sought advancement in the Church itself; and there are cases, probably authentic, of priests who went through the form of the Sacraments without either belief or intention; perhaps (as we are told in one case) with deliberate mockery in their own hearts. Concerning two such cases, perhaps the only two which stand on record, Mr Hollis writes: "It must be clear enough to any one who has any understanding of the Catholic teaching about the Eucharist that to make mocking use of the Sacrament without belief and simply in order to gain some social advantage must, to a Catholic, seem the vilest crime of which human nature is capable. And, strange as it may seem, the evidence quite certainly proves that some *Moriscos* and *Marranos*, not content with receiving as laymen the Sacrament in which they disbelieved, actually managed to get themselves ordained priests, perhaps even bishops, and consecrators of that which they rejected.... Face to face with such appalling confessions, the petty point whether such men's lives were a menace to organized society sinks into insignificance. Even the awful possibility that numerous souls may have been lost through the confidence of people in the integrity of their administration of the Sacraments is of less importance than the enormous insult to God of such lives, rounded off by such confessions. The ordinary arguments for toleration of those from whom God has—or at any rate, from whom God may have—withheld the gift of faith are here irrelevant. The deed is, as Massinger said of an insult to the elevated Host, 'a deed deserving death with torture'. And few will be so foolishly sentimental as to waste time in sympathy for the fates of such wretches who continued with their blasphemies after due warning of the consequences which they would entail."17 We have here the exact thirteenth-century spirit, which is too often ignored by those who insist most strongly, and most justly, upon our facing the actual mentality of that time. No doubt it is unhistorical to forget, even for one moment, that the really orthodox and earnest contemporaries of St Thomas Aquinas felt as Mr Hollis describes. But it would be no less unhistorical to ignore the other side of this medal. To an equally earnest heretic (and there were many such) that current Eucharistic adoration appeared not as the closest communion of man's soul with Almighty God, but as mistaken idolatry; so that the man who broke an image or desecrated a pyx might possess, and give plausible reasons for, exactly the same conviction of doing God service as the priest had in burning him. We, in this age, may blame both alike, and may regard it as a form of blasphemy to claim a divine commission for destroying either a stone image in a church or God's living image in man: but the facts of history compel us to blink neither of those complementary truths. There were men on both sides who claimed to set up their own beliefs as a standard of coercion for all humanity; and, in so far as experience has shown the social defects of such presumption and such impatience, we live now in a better world. Modern compulsion, however dangerous in one country, does at least meet powerful cross-currents in others; and there seems little danger of a single uniform Reign of Terror throughout the civilized world.

Moreover Catharist asceticism, however misguided and imperfect, was not more inhuman than some of the extreme orthodoxy; and there was no more fear of its infecting the whole world than there had been in the case of the Fathers of the Desert. When we are told nowadays that Catharism deserved fire and sword because it "destroyed family life", we are at once reminded of Christ's words in Matthew x. 35 and Luke xiv. 26, and of pagan prejudice against the early Christians as "enemies of the human race". The secret abominations ascribed to heretics by their enemies were practically identical with what heathenism had attributed to the Christians of the Catacombs. It may be freely granted that neither the Cathari nor any other heretical sect of the Middle Ages bade fair to supplant successfully the Roman Church, at any rate for many generations to come. They had, in certain important respects, the crude inferiority of most revolutionaries; an inferiority which would doubtless have come out painfully, and perhaps even fatally, if they had ever become strong enough to seize the reins of government. Yet the world's experience of the last four centuries seems to show clearly that it would have been fortunate if that inferiority had been allowed to fade out by a process of natural selection, and if the thirteenth century could have had sufficient intellectual patience to tolerate rival organizations. For these would have competed with the Church for influence over the people, and therefore would have been compelled to purge gradually their own errors, while in turn they forced upon the Christian Church that purgation for which pious and learned Churchmen had been clamouring vainly from generation to generation, and were destined to clamour, with growing despair, for centuries longer. Petrus Cantor, writing in those days when Popes were launching the wild Crusaders of the north against the Albigensians, thought of the heretics mainly as sadly misguided people who, if impenitent, might fitly be imprisoned. He protested against the common lynch-law, often encouraged by priestly ceremonies at the so-called "Judgment of God" by ordeal. "How doth the Church presume to examine by [this] foreign judgment the hearts of men? Or how is it that the Cathari are given no legitimate respite for deliberation, but are burned off-hand?" "Indeed, certain honest matrons, refusing to consent to the lust of priests of 'the seed of Canaan'*... were written in the book of death and accused as Cathari, and condemned also by a certain accusing and foolish fellow in his zeal for Christian faith, while certain rich Cathari had their purses squeezed and were let go. One man alone, because he was poor and pale, and confessed the faith of Christ faithfully on all points, and put that forward as his hope, was burned, since he said to the

---

* The quotation is from the Apocrypha, Daniel xiii. 56 (the story of the Chaste Susanna and the Lascivious Elders).

assembled bishops that he would refuse to submit to the ordeal of hot iron unless they could first prove to him that he could do this without tempting the Lord and committing mortal sin."[18] It adds to this tragedy that, within a few years, Innocent forbade this very ordeal for heretics, on the explicit ground "Thou shalt not tempt the Lord thy God", and renewed this prohibition at his Ecumenical Council.[19] Yet even so great and good a man as St Bernard, less than a century earlier, had no disapproval for the judgment and condemnation of heretics by that ordeal of water which was destined to play so prominent a part in witch-hunting not only before but after the Reformation.[20]

Unfortunately, on this general question of justice for heretics Peter's reasonable ideas were not accepted and followed up by his generation. On the contrary, the early thirteenth century gradually built up a machinery of repression which was unprecedented in world history for systematic completeness. Moreover this has never since been outdone, in theory at least, by any later despotism; although the progress of modern physical science has enabled present-day governments to surpass their predecessors in strictness of execution. The Church anticipated in discipline the Soviet-Nazi theory of Totalitarianism, just as in religion she anticipated the theory of post-Reformation Puritanism. In her theories she anticipated them; but her actions were less consistent. For good and for evil, as we shall see again and again, there was more difference between theory and practice in the medieval than in the modern world.

What, then, was this Inquisition, founded in 1230–3 by Gregory IX, the friend and patron of St Francis?

The earlier records are nearly always stories of mere lynch-law. The heretic Priscillian (385) was indeed officially tortured and executed, with six of his followers, by the Emperor Maximus; two great saints, Ambrose and Martin, protested against this, but St Leo, later, definitely justified the act; and Pope Hadrian VI, equally learned and liberal, commended it as recently as 1522.[21] Then, with the revival of intellectual life in Europe from about 1000, heresies naturally grew also; orthodox thought was followed by freethought, and, thenceforward, for the next century and a half, we hear more and more frequently of executions by lynch-law. It is sometimes asserted that these lynchings were discountenanced by the mass of the clergy, but never with adequate documentary proof: and, *prima facie*, it is most improbable. Of the great Churchmen some openly approved, others disapproved. But after 1150 no bishop, I believe, can be found protesting against the ever-increasing severities. Then, in 1184, Pope Lucius III created the "Episcopal Inquisition"; a system of strict official enquiry and punishments, diocese by diocese. Soon after, Innocent III sent special commissioners (*inquisitores*) straight from Rome. Princes and magistrates were now commanded by the Church (under pain of excommunication, confiscation and deposition) to execute the sentences of these episcopal or papal *inquisitores*. Then Gregory IX, by his stricter laws and more elaborate organization, which had its mainspring at Rome, created the "Papal Inquisition". At this point burning now comes in, as the standard punishment for impenitent or relapsed nonconformists. The Count of Toulouse, practically a vassal of the Holy See, seems to have decreed this for his own state earlier than 1194; certainly the King of Aragon decreed it in 1197, "in obedience", he said, "to the decrees of the Holy Roman Church". Frederick II, infidel as he was, found it politic to decree it in 1224; that decree was copied into the papal register, and a batch of heretics were burned at Rome in 1231. There is a quite modern plea that Rome may be exonerated, since the Popes took these steps only in order to check imperial encroachment on ecclesiastical functions. But this, even though it were wholly true in fact, would be null in morality: it would simply mean that Gregory IX had astutely and successfully "dished the Whigs".

The tribunal of this Papal Inquisition had scarcely any real precedent, and has had scarcely any parallel in later history. Here, again, apologists plead that it had no invidious feature which cannot be matched elsewhere. That is not strictly true: Bishop Bernard Gui, one of the greatest and most honest inquisitors, confessed frankly that "multa sunt specialia" in its procedure. As Alphandéry puts it in *The Encyclopaedia Britannica* (14th ed. p. 589): "All the accused were presumed to be guilty, the judge being at the same time the accuser." The standard *Inquisitors' Directory* of the next generation, that of Eymeric, explains that, by the usual rule of law [*regulare est*], if a witness retracted his evidence and testified to the contrary, it is the earlier testimony that must stand. But the Inquisition (he explains) had here the special privilege that "since this crime [of heresy] is an exceptional matter, the judge accepts the second testimony", "wherever the presumption is that the witness testifies in zeal for the orthodox faith"—in other words, whenever the testimony is unfavourable to the accused. Upon this passage his official commentator, Pegna, writes: "In the cause of the Faith it is a speciality that we stand by the second testimony"; "this is a concession in favour of the Faith." He claims the consent of all the orthodox authorities, and adds that, if the judge is not convinced of the probability of the man's evidence, he had better not admit it without the additional security of torture.[22] Nor, even though it were true that every odious detail of Inquisitional procedure can be found in some corner of the lay courts, would this plea serve its apologetic purpose. The man who thus collected so many separate details of injustice from different sources, and combined them into one organized whole, was as true an inventor as that other man who first mingled, in their due proportions, the harmless necessary saltpetre and charcoal and sulphur.

Apart from the fact that burning alive had never before been carried out in anything like this wholesale and official fashion, torture was now applied with equally unprecedented frequency and cold-blooded cruelty, not only for the accused but for witnesses also. For this, we need go no further than the *Inquisitors' Directory* of the Dominican Eymeric [1360], frequently printed at Rome under special papal approval, with commentaries by Francis Pegna, Doctor of Divinity and of Canon Law, the "last edition" dating from 1584. If torture produced nothing, it was not strictly legal to repeat it. "But if" (writes Eymeric) "having been tortured reasonably [*decenter*], he will not confess the truth, set other sorts of torment before him, saying that he must pass through all these unless he will confess the truth. If even this fails, a second or third day may be appointed to him, either *in terrorem* or even in truth, for the continuation (not repetition) of torture; for tortures may not be *repeated* unless fresh evidence emerges against him; then indeed, they may: but against *continuation* there is no prohibition." Pegna adds a warning with regard to pregnant women. Such must not be tortured, either in fact or in threat, for fear of abortion; "therefore, if the truth cannot be elicited otherwise than by torture or terror, we must wait until she is delivered of her child."[23] Children below the age of puberty, or old folk, were to be less severely tortured than robust folk.

Imprisonment itself was used as a regular form of torture—which indeed it might easily be, as everyone will realize who has seen a few medieval dungeons.[24]

We must not, it is true, lay undue stress on these cold-blooded horrors of legal phraseology, or upon the similar concrete cases which stand out from the records. Quite apart from the weight of favouritism or bribery in medieval law-courts, a few cases can be quoted, here and there, where inquisitors do forgo their pound of flesh in consideration of sex or extreme youth or age or poverty; and, in many others, they seem clearly to have done less than they might have done by the strictest application of the law. But, on the other hand, St Joan's case is far from unique in showing how much an unfair inquisitor might sometimes do to go even beyond those enormous legal powers which he wielded. And, here again, we must remember that the whole institution was far less a cause than a symptom of that ingrained intolerance which marked the whole population of Europe. Thus, although the Inquisition, in fullest form, operated in England only for a few months until Mary's accession, yet ordinary Church law, commonly backed up by the civil magistrates, sufficed to destroy the most prominent heretics and to drive the rest underground.

Under the Inquisition, no clear case of a verdict of *not guilty* seems ever to have been recorded. At best, it was *not proven*, unless the judges were able to decide that "he was convicted by false witnesses, or by unjust and malevolent folk and mortal enemies, or conspirators who afterwards repent and confess that they have falsely accused him or borne false witness against him".[25] Accusers were commonly sheltered by anonymity; and unfavourable, as apart from favourable, evidence was accepted even from infamous persons, or was extracted from the man's own small children. Advocates for the defence, though nominally allowed at first, soon found that the court chose to involve them in the guilt and the punishment of their condemned clients; so that the very pretence of advocacy was often dropped. The Church thus created a "justice" of her own, so elaborate in detail and so ingeniously elastic that everything was judged criminal which might seriously impede the totalitarian machine. But, for good and for evil, mankind is never consistent, and fewer were actually burned than is often supposed. Bernard Gui, one of the most active inquisitors, convicted altogether 930 heretics: he committed only 42 to the stake, 307 to prison: the rest were compelled to wear the legally prescribed badge of infamy, not only abroad but in their own homes; with other burdensome penances, and confiscation of property. We must here correct a purely modern plea, which is so boldly repeated that it threatens now to become an established legend. We are told that, out of the 930 accused before Bernard Gui, 139 were acquitted altogether, and that this is a proof of inquisitorial justice. Yet in fact it is now confessed, both tacitly and explicitly, that this assertion has rested upon a misunderstanding so gross as to be almost inexplicable. Its authors appeal to Bernard's *Register*; yet this book displays, on page after page, the plainest contrary of what has been so boldly asserted.[26] Moreover, every one of those 930 culprits fell, automatically, under sentence of total confiscation of property: and nobody who watches events in present-day Europe will ignore what must have been the crushing effect upon a whole population of wholesale pillage, together with imprisonment under the notoriously cruel medieval conditions, and, finally, a $4\frac{1}{2}$ per cent. chance of living combustion.

Few historians of repute in any creed can now be found to plead that the Church herself was guiltless here of men's blood, and that the real responsibility rests upon those civil authorities who sent the poor wretch to the stake. That plea was discreetly, but firmly, exploded by the late Abbé Vacandard, of all modern apologists the most learned and candid, who wrote: "To reassure their consciences [the Inquisitors] tried another expedient. In abandoning heretics to the secular arm, they besought the State officials to act with moderation, and avoid 'all bloodshed and all danger of death'. This was, unfortunately, an empty formula which deceived no one. It was intended to safeguard the principle which the Church had taken for her motto: *Ecclesia abhorret a sanguine*. In strongly asserting this traditional law, the Inquisitors imagined that they thereby freed themselves from all responsibility, and kept from imbruing their hands in bloodshed. We must take this for what it is worth. It has been styled 'cunning' and 'hypocrisy'; let us call it simply a legal fiction."[27]

In another passage, Vacandard frankly repudiates the plea that we must consider the Inquisition rather as a bulwark against social and political unrest than against inconvenient religious beliefs. He says very truly: "It made no distinction between those teachings which entailed injury on the family and on society, and those which merely denied certain revealed truths."[28] The four friars burned at Marseilles in 1318 were condemned to the stake on several different counts, the principal of which was their insistence, in contradiction to Pope John XXII, that Christ and his Apostles had possessed no property of their own. The monstrous injustice of Joan of Arc's condemnation, again, was technically on purely theological grounds, however politicians might have worked behind that orthodox legal mask. St Thomas More, if things had so chanced, might as easily have been burned for maintaining with unshaken fortitude the rights of conscience against the Pope, as he was beheaded for defending those same rights against Henry VIII. Modern tolerance often listens benevolently to many apologetic pleas which will not bear the test either of psychology or of actual documentary evidence. This is especially so in Great Britain and America, where freedom of thought has brought us to an equilibrium, a centre of indifference, far removed from the whirl of Continental anticlericalism. It is natural enough that the advocates of a Church which thought and acted for so many centuries on the principles described above, and which has never yet repudiated them—nay, which can scarcely repudiate them without thereby casting overboard certain even more cherished principles—should push their apologetics to the point of demonstrable, though doubtless unintentional, *suppressio veri* and *suggestio falsi*. It is natural, again, that historians whose struggle for impartiality, and generous natural instincts, incline them towards the under-dog, should accept these pleas with all the less suspicior because they themselves have never found time thorougnly to explore the original sources; *non omnia possumus omnes*. But these considerations throw all the greater burden of plain speech upon any student who, having devoted a good deal of time to this subject, feels that the intelligent reading public is in danger or being seriously misled on points of vital importance. Dr H. C. Lea's *Inquisition of the Middle Ages*, though often attacked in detail, has never been shaken in its main conclusions.[29] It has been welcomed with the highest praise by the scholars whose praise is worth most—Acton, Creighton, F. W. Maitland, Bryce. The careful reader may note with amusement how heavily the writings of Lea's severest critics are sometimes indebted to his colossal labours. Admirable handbooks, owing much to him, are to be found in Abbé Vacandard's *L'Inquisition* from one standpoint, and Professor Turberville's *Medieval Heresy and the Inquisition* from another. The deeper we look into Lea's references, with all their occasional inaccuracies, the better we shall understand why Montalembert deplored this institution as one of the most serious stumbling-blocks for those souls who are attracted to his Church;[30] and why Acton could write to the daughter of his friend W. E. Gladstone: "the principle of the Inquisition is murderous"; and again: "[Liberalism] swept away that appalling edifice of intolerance, tyranny, and cruelty which believers in Christ built up to perpetuate their belief. There is much to deduct from the praise of the Church in protecting marriage, abolishing slavery and human sacrifice, preventing war, and helping the poor. No deduction can be made from her evildoing towards unbelievers, heretics, savages and witches. Here her responsibility is more undivided; her initiative and achievement more complete."[31]

XXXVI. THE PAPAL SCHISM

MICHELET, in his *Histoire de France*, notes a strange irony of fate in the year 1398. We then find the Emperor coming solemnly to hold a series of conferences with the King of France concerning the Papacy. The Emperor, Wenceslas, was a confirmed drunkard, and could do no business but quite early in the morning. The King, Charles VI, was seldom sane, but there was most sense in him later in the day when he had eaten and drunken. The Pope (or anti-Pope), sober and sane enough in other ways, was less sane politically, less able to listen to reason where his own power and dignity were concerned, than either the drunkard or the lunatic. For this was that Benedict XIII who finally guttered out like a spent candle 26 years later, cursing and accursed to the very last, in his little Spanish mountain fortress of Peñiscola. This strange colloquy came half-way through the Great Schism; but the same tragi-comic flavour had hung about it from the first. Indeed, if we look at the surface only, history may sometimes seem rather a comedy than a tragedy. When any change has been brewing sufficiently long, the slightest incident, or even the most ridiculous, may revolutionize the world between one day and the next. Icebergs drift southwards, no man knows how long, in the waters which gradually sap their base; until some day, in the twinkling of an eye, the vast mass turns upside down. The world-effect of the Seraievo murder, from north to south and east to west, is now tragically proverbial. And the Great Schism of the Papacy, which produced comparable results nearly six centuries ago, and did so much to herald the English Reformation, was in many of its details scarcely less comic than tragic.

First, the multitudes surging all night long under the windows of the Vatican palace, while the conclave was held, and bellowing, "A Roman, a Roman we will have!"—no longer these French Popes at Avignon, naturally suspected of even more than their actual subservience to the policies of the Kings of France—"A Roman for Pope or at least an Italian!" Then, a hurried and nervous conclave in the early morning, ending in the definite decision to elect the Archbishop of Bari as a compromise between the irreconcilable rivalries of the two main parties. But, simultaneously, came the still more momentous vote to breakfast first before invoking the Holy Ghost and going through the legal formalities. Meanwhile, the mob breakfasted too; they broke into the papal cellars; and soon, inspired on their side by Bacchus, they clamoured to come and salute that Roman Pope who, by this time, must surely have been elected. The cardinals feared to confess frankly that they were compromising upon this archbishop; that they intended an Italian, indeed, but no Roman; not even a cardinal; only a comparatively obscure monk from the south. The more these cardinals shuffled, the more furiously the mob raged, and burst into the hall. Then one cardinal found a ready lie: "The Cardinal of St Peter's is Pope!" The crowd rushed to this Cardinal of St Peter's, who was a real Roman; and amidst that confusion the liar with his brother-cardinals slipped off. This poor supposititious Pope was aged and infirm, and it was only when they had nearly wrung his gouty hands off that the crowd began at last to accept his protests, and to realize that, if there was any real Pope-elect, he was the Archbishop of Bari. Then it was almost the story of that Djinn of the *Arabian Nights*, after the unsuspecting fisherman had released him from his bottle; the mob rushed from room to room in search of the archbishop, whom they would willingly have lynched. At last the tumult was appeased; and, then, some days later, most of the scattered cardinals were collected to ratify formally their informal choice. The Archbishop of Bari took the name of Urban VI; and there was no reason why all should not have gone well, if only this Urban had been either a better man or a worse. The honour turned his head; he betrayed at once all the proverbial vices of a beggar on horseback. He was, in Creighton's words, "a short, stout man, with a swarthy face, full of Neapolitan fire and savagery. His monkish piety burned to distinguish itself by some striking measures of reform; but he was without knowledge of himself or of the world, and knew nothing of the many steps to be taken between good intentions and their practical execution. He thought that he could enforce his will by self-assertion, and that the Cardinals could be reduced to absolute obedience by mere rudeness."[1] The luxury of the cardinals had long been a byword; indeed, it was their anxiety for their silver plate which had complicated their fear of the mob during this election. Urban tried to reform this offensive luxury, but his only idea of reform was to treat them like schoolboys. We have the fullest information on all these little details from the pen of his intimate secretary, Dietrich von Nieheim. Urban had no sense of dignity: he descended to personal abuse with his cardinals, and even offered to strike one of them. He was no less offensive to the Queen and the heir-apparent of Naples. The Duke of Brunswick himself, who captained the Pope's bodyguard, suggested that he should be called not *Urbanus* but *Turbanus*, the Disturber. So the French cardinals revolted, and elected a French Pope, Clement VII; and, though modern historians are fairly unanimous in favour of Urban's lawful election, Christendom languished for 51 years under what may truly be called Papal Paralysis. Catharine of Siena, the greatest saint of the period, was convinced that Urban was Pope beyond all serious question. But the Spanish St Vincent Ferrer wrote, with all reinforcement of scholastic logic, in the exactly contrary sense. All supporters of Urban (he argued) are in mortal sin, doomed to hell in default of repentance, unless they are so ignorant and unlearned that they have never heard the reasons advanced by the French cardinals. He pitilessly brushes aside the objection "that very many devout persons, clergy and monks and nuns, and many princes and doctors are on Urban's side". This, he argues, is a mere snare of the Devil; if the first Christians had taken notice of the mass of good people who clung to paganism, the world would never have been converted.[2] That which St Vincent demonstrated with all the learning of the schools was reinforced by the feminine enthusiasm of Ste Colette; so that, in those days, there was a preponderance of saints in favour of that Pope whose claim is practically abandoned nowadays by the later and less partial judgment of historians of all schools. Nor can we wonder at the impossibility of arriving at any clear decision, in those days when decision mattered most to the Church. In the face of what is known concerning the haphazard development of papal claims and election methods, the Great Schism must appear less as an accident than as a perfectly natural result. It is absurd to treat it, with certain modern writers, as a stroke of sheer ill-luck falling upon an innocent and unsuspecting Church. Yet this plea is sometimes so stressed that we may say, almost without exaggeration, that we are asked to visualize the Schism as a regrettable miscalculation on the part of Divine Providence.

Saints, then, were irreconcilably divided, and decision came ultimately from the politicians. All through the Schism, the cleavage ran almost entirely on nationalistic lines, as Creighton brings out most clearly in detail. The final settlement came with that Council of Constance which, after the model of the University of Paris, voted by "nations", and which, as Figgis puts it, "first [in all Europe] exhibited the conflict of pure politics on the grand scale".[3] England (since the Hundred Years' War was still raging) was naturally against the French Pope, just as Scotland, at war with us, was naturally on his side. And the first English heresiarch, Wyclif, was earlier distinguished as politician than as reformer, when John of Gaunt brought him forward to repudiate with decisive directness the Pope's claim for tribute (1374). Then, in 1377, he was summoned before a council at St Paul's, to answer the archbishop and assembled prelates upon a charge of teaching the errors of Marsilius of Padua.

Thus this comedy, almost this farce, of the election in Rome and the cardinals' breakfast and the papal beggar-on-horseback developed into one of the great tragedies of European history; and we see here the nemesis of those ever-growing and disproportionate pretensions of the Holy See. In insisting so strongly upon papal autocracy, the Popes had scarcely reckoned with the dangers which this involved for Catholicism itself. By narrowing down the idea of the Church first to the clergy, and then to this single Head of the clergy (for it is hardly an exaggeration to say that Boniface's bull *Unam Sanctam* outdoes even the "L'État, c'est moi" of Louis XIV), they rendered the whole institution singularly vulnerable to the changes and chances of this mortal life. As we have seen, they thus tempted the King of France to try to put the Church in his pocket, by reducing the Pope to a position of political dependence upon the French crown. They exposed the Papacy to all the worst disadvantages of an absolute monarchy: a monarchy more aggressive in principle than solid at its foundation. The Schism now gave consistency, flesh and blood, to many hitherto fluid heretical tendencies.

For it is difficult to accept the plea sometimes put forward, that obstinate heretics, after all, were rare in the Middle Ages. It is quite true that England, as compared with many parts of the Continent, was long orthodox. Just as we hear little of formal heresy in all Europe, until the revival of thought in the eleventh and twelfth centuries, so in our own corner of Europe heresy was almost dormant until we began to catch up our more advanced neighbours. That Latin verse of Boccaccio says no more than the truth: "Hispanus et Gallus, studiis tardusque Britannus". In book-learning, the average Briton was a dunce compared with the Spaniard and Frenchman, still more when we compare him with the Italian of Boccaccio's time. We find learned laymen in France before 1200, and a fourteenth-century king, Charles V, who collected such a library and organized such methodical translations as England never saw till printing came. As we have seen, no English layman equalled Dante in learning until St Thomas More. Even that school of mysticism, which flourished among us in the fourteenth and early fifteenth centuries, was far more pietistic and devotional than learned or philosophical.

Enquiry, therefore, was long dormant except among a few scholars who wrote quite over the heads of the multitude. Even our great Schoolmen, the glory of Oxford, studied and taught more at Paris than at home: there is little evidence for Oxonian freethought under the surface, such as we find in France and Italy. Again, we had not the busy foreign trade which, elsewhere, made men exchange ideas as well as wares; our merchants were stay-at-homes compared with those of many great Continental cities. Finally, it was not until the verge of the Reformation that English capitalism came near to its Continental development. Sedentary operatives, herded together, form proverbially the best soil for the crumbs of revolutionary ideas which drop from the highbrows' tables above them; yet all England put together could probably not have shown so many weavers as the single city of Ypres had, with its roll of more than 3000; moreover, Ypres itself was certainly outdone by Ghent and Florence. Nor, again, had we anything like those traditions of keen discussion which distinguished Florence as early as Dante's day. Even the Londoner of the Middle Ages, with all his sterling qualities, was comparatively slow-witted.

Here, however, we are confronted with a paradox which, thrown out by one brilliant journalist, is sometimes repeated seriously even by historians. Mr G. K. Chesterton once wrote: "Never in the whole history of the world did so many people believe so firmly in so many things, the authority for which they could not test, as do Londoners to-day."[4] Here would seem to lurk three gross fallacies. In the first place, the complexity of modern life compels the Londoner to face a multitude of ideas, right or wrong, out of all proportion to those of the medieval peasant, the narrow simplicity of whose life forms one of its greatest attractions for modern romance. The ideas thus forced upon him are probably at least tenfold as numerous, perhaps even a hundredfold; yet he has not ten times more hours in the day for pause and verification. Since we are dealing with ancient times, it may not be too trivial to quote an ancient quip: Why do white sheep eat so much more than black? The answer, of course, is as incontestably true as the fundamental implication of the question is foolish. White sheep eat more than black because there are so many more of them. The modern Londoner has so many more ideas unverified, because he has more ideas altogether.

Secondly, again, the modern Londoner does in fact verify a larger proportion of his ideas than this cynical observation would imply. Complete verification is possible to none of us, not even to the greatest expert; in the large majority of cases we can but roughly test the authority upon which we accept any statement. This testing the average Londoner performs very imperfectly, perhaps, but at least far more fully than his medieval ancestor. He knows that a great many false assertions and false claims are current; but he knows also (competition being such as it is, and young critics so healthily eager to correct their seniors) that we may generally trust the scientist, the lawyer, and the doctor to be right in the main. Our Londoner has never seen a bacillus; but he could give an incomparably more accurate account of the causes of typhoid than could have been given by the medieval expert, let alone by those patients who, on the strength of that expert's astrological calculations, believed themselves to be smitten from the stars.

And, thirdly, the importance of these things believed without full examination by the modern Londoner would seem incomparably smaller than in the Middle Ages. If the modern man "believes in nothing higher than the roof of his own house", that is no more than St Bernardino tells us, in so many words, concerning citizens in his own fifteenth-century Italy. At least he no longer believes in one thing which he cannot test; namely, the horrible eschatology which hypnotized even the greatest among medieval philosophers and theologians. A whole outlook upon life depends upon the conception of God's justice implied in that medieval doctrine; and the modern world can here give far better reasons for its unbelief in the hell of the Middle Ages than St Thomas Aquinas himself could have given for belief. Ninety per cent. of our medieval population was then agricultural; and we have no evidence that these men—or even their professional teachers, the ordinary parish clergy—set themselves to verify anything whatever except things that lay under their nose. Above these, the very greatest intellects, the very coryphaei of medieval philosophy, were withheld almost inescapably from verifying some of the fundamental traditions upon which their whole scheme of this life and of eternity reposed. They were restrained not only by potential prison and stake in the background but, in the case of the best of them, by Lord Acton's feeling: "My religion is dearer to me than life." We are no more justified in judging medieval heresy superficially, on the statistics of its open manifestations, than we should be in emphasizing the fact that, in modern Totalitarian States, obstinate nonconformists form only an infinitesimal fraction of the total population. One of the ablest of pacifist philosophers, Bertrand Russell, is justly emphatic against the delusion that persecution never pays, or that it pays for no longer than a generation or two. The cold judicial murder of one man, approved or tolerated by the multitude, may well reduce a million more to silence and passivity. Moreover, in countless cases it even changes men's minds; so strongly do the majority always live under the sway of exterior impressions.

On the Continent there had already been heresiarchs of the first water. Arnold of Brescia, in St Bernard's days, had preached against clerical opulence, and clerical power in politics, with an energy and success which at one time threatened revolution in the great cities. With the dawn of the fourteenth century came that Pierre Dubois who, working for the French king, insisted that the Popes were responsible for far more wars than they prevented, since they meddled everywhere yet had not sufficient physical force to decide the conflict anywhere without a network of alliances and diplomatic shifts. Soon after this, Marsilius of Padua applied to the papal problem all the political solvents which had been developed in those highly civilized and restless cities of Northern Italy, together with that current of scepticism which ran so strongly under the surface in his Universities of Padua and

Paris. He was still too much a man of his own age, or just possibly too prudent, to expose the whole fraud of those False Decretals which, though not invented in the papal chancery, had been so fruitfully exploited by the Popes of the last four centuries. Yet, even in that field, his historical sense did expose at least one part of this mass of falsehood, the so-called Clementine Constitutions, with a directness which no modern scholar has ever dared to contest: for, after all, historical sense is merely the application to historical records of the natural qualities and the business methods which make for success in every department of life. And, most important of all, he revolutionized Bible interpretation by applying to it that same historical sense. He showed how little the New Testament supports the medieval Petrine claims; how thoroughly imaginative and artificial are those later glosses upon the sacred text which would construct on those tottering foundations a whole palace of Petrine despotism and of divine authority granted to the clergy over the laity, with its corollary of enormous wealth and privileged protection against ordinary law. He demanded disendowment of all superfluities, with State authority of the Church, and control to be exercised over all the weightiest things and persons, Pope included, by an ecclesiastical assembly which should be a real parliament of Christendom. The Franciscan William of Ockham, who joined in this rebellion and was involved in the same papal anathema, even suggested that women should have votes for such a council, since its one essential function was to further the salvation of souls, and women have souls as well as men. Dubois had already gone some way in that direction: the first, perhaps, to venture so far since the Arab Averroës of 150 years earlier. But, the Church organization itself being so fundamentally political, it was as impossible for these as for other reformers to start a purely spiritual movement, even if that had been their natural character and their whole desire. Both Marsilius and Ockham became strong partisans in the violent quarrel between Pope John XXII and the Emperor Louis the Bavarian, and neither attracted in his own day anything like the political attention which he has since enjoyed. Yet a generation afterwards, in 1377, our own Oxford philosopher John Wyclif was summoned to appear at St Paul's, before the archbishop and assembled bishops, on the charge of teaching the heresies of Marsilius: and that opened a new chapter in our Church history.

THE tardy and crude beginnings of English heresy are clearly traced by Mr H. G. Richardson in *The English Historical Review* (Jan. 1936). He shows how, before Wyclif's trial in 1377, only 16 definite cases of heresy can be counted. Yet, in 1382 parliament complained that unlicensed preachers went about the country disseminating heresies and notorious errors, some of which were calculated to "cause discord and dissensions among the different estates of the realm"; errors for which they contrived to get the support of the populace. Here, as Mr Richardson points out, we have partly "the aftermath of the Peasants' Revolt" of 1381. This parliamentary complaint was met by a statute which gave sheriffs and other sufficient magistrates power to arrest and imprison such preachers and their supporters, if any prelate certified them to the chancellor as guilty. For, by this time, those heretical potentialities which had been fluid (so to speak) in the rapidly awaking England of Chaucer's day, had crystallized round one strong and commanding figure.[1]

John Wyclif had risen to the front rank in Oxford philosophy before he was brought forward as a politician; and, even then, it was only by a further development that he became heretic and reformer. Both in himself and in the development of his teaching he may be called characteristically English. By nature he was severe and ascetic; in later life he confessed himself to have erred on the side of harsh judgment and bitterness in controversy. Yet the root of this was moral; at bottom, he was a typical Puritan. His philosophy was a compromise; his moderate realism was unpopular in an academic world in which Ockham's pronounced nominalism reigned in spite of papal condemnation: hence his small philosophic vogue on the Continent, and the practical extinction of his Latin writings abroad, except among the Hussites of Bohemia. Unlike Dubois and Marsilius and Ockham, he appealed at an early stage to the people. His spirit was that of the dialogue which Carlyle took as a motto for the title page of *Latter-Day Pamphlets*. Says one, with detached resignation, "Well, well, God mend all!" "Nay, by God, Donald, but we must help Him to mend it."

That first trial of 1377, nominally theological, was at root rather political; the bishops were resolved to strike down this priestly ally of John of Gaunt and his anticlerical party. It ended in a brawl between Gaunt and Courtenay, and the council broke up in confusion. Three months later, the Pope issued five bulls condemning certain of Wyclif's doctrines and demanding his imprisonment; but his personal popularity and Gaunt's protection rendered these inoperative. Next year came the Great Schism, which changed Wyclif from a critic of the Papacy to a determined opponent.

And not Wyclif alone: for its effect upon all thinking men was devastating. For centuries, Popes had claimed to judge practically everywhere in European politics and in social, even domestic, life, on the logical plea that their commission descended directly from God, through that disciple to whom Christ had given the Keys of Heaven, with a promise of unshaken victory over the Gates of Hell. In that unbreakable bond (pious souls believed) the world was safe; and even those who felt most strongly that, in practice, the Court of Rome was a nest of abuses, were often willing to accept the excuse that God's treasure is providentially contained in earthen vessels, that even among the twelve was one Judas, and other current pleas of the same sort. Now, however, in which of these two earthen vessels—or in which of the three, for to that it came before the Schism was ended—was God's unerring judgment and indefectible spiritual care contained? Was Urban the true son of Peter, and Clement of Judas (as St Catharine held), or *vice versa* (as St Vincent insisted)? Was half of Christendom really in mortal sin? (for from this there seemed no logical escape) and, if so, which half? It was the old problem of the Three Rings: so long as any dispute remained among the rivals, how could any one be genuine? It was not yet realized, of course, that this paralysis would last for nearly forty years, and (in a milder form) even to the present day, since there has never been any official decision between the Italian and the Franco-Spanish line, and succeeding Popes, Urbans and Clements and Benedicts, have named themselves as if Urban VI, Clement VII, and Benedict XIII had all been rightful pontiffs; which, of course, is impossible. But, even from the first, the dilemma was cruel enough. The uncertainty of papal succession, and therefore of inspiration, was so obviously the only absolute certainty in the whole affair, that orthodox and unorthodox agree in regarding this as one of the gravest events of the Middle Ages.

Wyclif had already argued—and this was the reason for coupling him with Marsilius—for strong measures of clerical disendowment. His famous book *Of Civil Lordship* was mainly founded on the teaching of his Oxford master, the Archbishop of Armagh; but he carried his logic farther than the master ever did in fact, or would have been likely ever to do. The book, like so much of medieval political and even religious theory, rests upon feudal foundations. *Lordship*, to begin with, has the double sense of *authority* and *ownership*: the *dominus* of a manor, for instance, was lord of the serf's person and landlord of his little holding. God is the Universal *Dominus* of the universe; no man holds anything but as a feudal grant, a *beneficium*, from Him. But every *beneficium* implies corresponding service. Therefore, in strict logic, bad men have rightful possession of nothing. They may be in present enjoyment of many things; but that is only by usurpation; even if these things had ever been rightfully theirs, they have forfeited that right by neglecting the corresponding service. Here we have socialism; but Wyclif, it may fairly be said, anticipated the Fabian compromise. In theory, the wicked *dominus* is a usurper; but in practice the designs of Providence are best secured by refusing to dispossess him too hastily, at the cost of a revolution which would do more harm than good. In this sense (said Wyclif) "God must obey the Devil"; an epigram which was naturally exploited against him by his theological enemies. He looked forward to a time when the Church might be compelled to yield up her superfluous wealth to the poor. By a later extension, he would even give some of the money to "poor knights", who should be taxed for poor relief, and would thus give to Church money more liberal circulation than at present. But, at bottom, what most concerns Wyclif is to show the theoretical unsoundness of the far-reaching ecclesiastical claim of immunity. We may well be compelled to leave the Church alone for the present; the prelate, for a while, shall still remain *dominus* in practice; but, when he claims this *dominium* as his right, there he is talking of what does not exist; it would be a just stroke of God's hand if anyone should take from him "even that which he seemeth to have". Again, although Wyclif alone among the Schoolmen had expressed disapproval of serfdom on moral grounds, yet there is no sign of his sympathy with the actual rebels of 1381, nor did they claim his support. On the other hand, we cannot altogether dissociate him from John Ball's teaching. These ideas were now in the air; and, if that hedge-preacher had caught nothing directly from this philosopher, yet the agreement of the rough practitioner with the subtle theorist is none the less significant.

Into a mind like Wyclif's, thus disposed already, the news of the Schism fell like a spark upon gunpowder. Hitherto, his scorn had been mainly poured upon the semi-clerical politician-bishops; for such were the majority in his day. Now he was confronted also with the warrior-bishop, Despenser of Norwich, who wasted English lives and treasure in a "crusade" for Urban's cause in France; a purely nationalistic raid upon our ancient enemies, which failed as miserably as it deserved to fail.

Briefly, Wyclif went on from heresy to heresy. Penance and Confession were good if voluntary, but antichristian if compulsory. Purgatory did indeed exist; but Masses for the dead, and papal Indulgences, were a delusion. Image-worship was not necessarily evil, but its current excesses were. At last, he went on to deny Transubstantiation: more and more he had broken with the Papacy and the Sacraments. He set up no formal system to replace what he destroyed. He preached nothing more systematic than an insistence on the Bible as the foundation of Christianity, and upon the necessity of preaching to the ignorant masses, whether by priests or by "lay readers", and upon instruction by pamphlets in the mother-tongue. Here again we may take a hint from the great historian Michelet, too good a Frenchman in his day to be otherwise than severely critical of the English, yet too clear-sighted and honest to deny us our own virtues here and there. Commenting on the French failures in North America, and the final occupation of Canada by the English, he suggests one significant cause. The Frenchman, abroad, tended far more to mingle with the native population: a race of Creoles sprang up wherever he went. Again, in those days he was normally a practising Catholic, dependent upon his priest and his Sacraments; yet priest and Sacraments were seldom to be found there in the wilds. The Englishman, on the other hand, could carry his own atmosphere with him everywhere; he was self-sufficient "avec sa Bible et son Anglaise"; a truth not the less striking for the delicately contemptuous flavour of those last two words.

In Wyclif's case, as in the contemporary Peasants' Revolt, we may find a testimonial to the comparative order and spirit of compromise in England. It cannot be said that the clergy as a whole were specially vindictive. Archbishop Sudbury was very loth to proceed against Wyclif at all: indeed Sudbury was not only a pacific man but something of a broad-churchman; he had publicly expressed doubts as to the general utility of the Canterbury Pilgrimage; and, when the rebels cut off his head in 1381, some good churchfolk saw therein the work of Providence. Even his successor Courtenay, who was a fighting prelate, did no more in this case than his office demanded from him; Wyclif was never personally molested, but died quietly in his own country parish of Lutterworth (1384). Much of this impunity was certainly due to the sympathy felt for him by a large section of Englishmen. The monastic chronicler of Leicester is doubtless exaggerating when he tells us that "every second man one met upon the way" was a Lollard; but unquestionably a large proportion of the population was more or less sympathetic. Gaunt protected him in 1377: but next year it was Gaunt's personal enemy, the Black Prince's widow, who stood between Wyclif and his condemnation by the bishops. Moreover the London citizens, for whom Gaunt was the most hated enemy, were among the heretic's warmest supporters. At Oxford, the theological Faculty itself backed him up until his denial of Transubstantiation; and, even after this, a hostile chronicler admits that "the flower of the university" stood by him; and the publication of the archbishop's sentence against him caused something like a riot there in 1382. For here was neither, on the one hand, a mere doctrinaire, who had lived in books and expected to be able to make a new world after his own bookish and academical fashion. Nor, on the other, was this the mere common-sense man, doing his own job in life excellently by rule of thumb, and expecting to solve wider problems after the same simple downright fashion. Wyclif was one who united high abstract speculation with practical experience, and could see where theory and rule of thumb agreed; one whose doctrines had grown out of his environment, and who therefore revealed to the Englishmen of his time the hitherto only half-conscious needs of their environment. His weakest point, perhaps, was that asperity which he himself confessed publicly with regret. But the world in which he lived was provocative of asperity. It would be possible to compile a catena of criticisms by the most exceptionally orthodox Churchmen, from St Bernard and St Bonaventura down to the official memorials compiled to help the Popes for the two Councils of Lyons in 1245 and 1274, and that of Vienne in 1311, which would rival, or possibly even outdo, a similar catena from Wyclif's works in their condemnation of existing abuses, and their cry for reform. But this Englishman was the first man of outstanding talents, learning, and moral character who saw straight into the practical solution of the problem. He realized, as some at least of those others would probably have realized if they had lived on into those days when hopes deferred had made the heart sick, that the hierarchy was essentially incapable of reforming itself, and that the pressure must come from without; from the laity, in some form or other.

Lollardy, thus born, had a long life before it. It is beside the point to argue, as even so careful a scholar as the late Dr Gairdner did, that we can trace no direct connection between Wyclif and the final Reformation because Wyclif knew nothing of Luther's pet doctrine of Justification by Faith, nor Luther of Wyclif's Dominion theory. The real kernel of the Reformation, doctrinally, was a conviction of the soul's direct responsibility to God; the comparative irrelevance of human mediators and of traditional forms. That conviction grew from generation to generation. Not only did Dr Gairdner write in ignorance of Lollard trials which have since been published, but he ignored, still more fatally, the fact that such a movement as this is not killed by being driven underground, and that other causes besides early Christianity have had their Church of the Catacombs. The House of Commons more than once showed anticlerical tendencies; there was even one session in which it earned the nickname of the Lollard Parliament. But the alliance with politicians, and the exaggerations which naturally mark every movement such as this, culminated in Sir John Oldcastle's rebellion and ruined Lollardy as an open party. Mr Richardson traces the course of repressive legislation from stage to stage.[2] The Church had long possessed one weapon in the writ *De excommunicato capiendo* (otherwise, *Significavit*), by which the sheriff, on receiving notice from a bishop that X was excommunicated and had remained obdurate for 40 days, was bound to arrest and imprison him "until he had made his peace with Holy Church". But this was a slow process, depending much on the whole-hearted co-operation of the civil courts: and the canonist Bishop Lyndwood shows how obstructive (in his view) the latter were, and how favourable to excommunicates. Therefore the petition of 1382, with its attempt to implicate the Lollards in the Peasants' Revolt, demanded stronger measures against these turbulent preachers who stole the support of the populace. So a statutory commission was devised by which, whenever any bishop reported X to the chancellor as a condemned heretic, every royal minister, and, indeed, every subject, must forthwith obey and arrest the man, whose only chance then lay in an appeal to the King's Council. This, however, did not prevent the spread of heretical opinions; so a fresh step was taken in 1388, again conditioned mainly by a political revolution. Commissioners were appointed in every county to search for heretical books and to suppress heresy: sheriffs and other royal officers were to assist. It will be noted how definitely, by each of these statutes, the final fate of the accused is kept in lay hands. "The government was, perhaps, not entirely disinterested: the heretic's possessions might be forfeit, and this was held out as a threat, though under Richard II such a penalty seems never to have been exacted." All this while, although many Lollards were taken, none was burnt. The State was sometimes held out as a menace, and Despenser, the warrior-bishop, threatened "fire and sword" to heretical preachers in his diocese: but, hitherto, this was known to Englishmen only because it was common enough overseas. Now, however, in answer to a Lollard manifesto of 1395, the clergy formally demanded the institution of the death penalty. The Pope, having received a copy of the manifesto, pressed stronger repressive measures upon Richard and the two archbishops, and, among others, upon the mayor and sheriffs of London. Then, in 1397, all the bishops petitioned for the execution of impenitent heretics "as in other realms subject to the Christian religion". But Richard issued no such statute, and no heretic was yet burned.

Then, in 1401 came Henry IV, owing his throne greatly to Church support and naturally disposed to stand by his allies. Though Sautre, the first Lollard martyr, may have been burned shortly before the passing of Henry's act *De haeretico comburendo*, yet the fatal writ was issued "by the King himself and his Council in Parliament", and Mr Richardson adds truly "the reference in the writ to divine, human and canon law does not alter the fact that these had no currency in England except by assent of King and parliament". For the clergy, Roman Canon Law was a final authority, but the lay lords never accepted that principle. When, in 1405, the clergy granted subsidies to Henry IV on condition of his prosecuting heresy, they made no attempt to secure that principal rôle which their brethren had long played on the Continent. Therefore the Papal Inquisition never operated among us between that slight and momentary concession by Edward II and the reign of Mary Tudor. From one point of view, it tells against Lollardy that the Inquisition was less sorely needed among us, and that, after Oldcastle's rebellion, it had no chance with King and Parliament. But, though this shows how no prominent man could be an open Lollard and live, yet it throws the greater stress upon the fundamental reality of a movement which could run so continuously and increasingly underground among simple common folk. Moreover, it cannot be forgotten that the Bohemian Hussites, who so strongly influenced later Church history, were themselves under the influence of Wyclif. There is, therefore, not only rhetoric but fact in the passage where Thomas Fuller describes the execution of that damnatory decree of the Council of Constance, 41 years after Wyclif's death.[3] "In obedience hereunto, Richard Fleming, bishop of Lincoln...sent his officers...to ungrave him accordingly. To Lutterworth they come; Sumner, Commissary, Official, Chancellor, Proctors, Doctors, and the servants—... take what was left out of the grave, and burn them to ashes, and cast them into Swift, a neighbouring brook running hard by. Thus this brook hath conveyed his ashes into Avon, Avon into Severn, Severn into the narrow seas, they into the main ocean. And thus the ashes of Wickcliffe are the emblem of his doctrine, which now is dispersed all the world over."

XXXVIII. THE BLACK DEATH[1]

T HIS terrible pestilence, which is perhaps the worst visitation in all recorded history, has lent itself in our day to a great deal of exaggeration and special pleading; it is frequently invoked as a *deus ex machina* to explain inconvenient facts away. But, when all exaggerations have been discounted, it still remains one of the most important events of our whole period. In this chapter, I shall deal mainly with its effects upon men's world-outlook in England.

Doctors are now agreed that this was the bubonic plague, coming from the East, and carried by fleas and rats, of which there was no lack in medieval Europe. Medieval medicine was naturally powerless to diagnose anything so dependent upon steady and microscopic observation; the plague was therefore often attributed secondarily to planetary influences, and primarily to God's anger against the special wickedness of the age. The Leicester cloisterer Knighton writes: "In those days [1348] there arose a huge rumour and outcry among the people, because when tournaments were held, almost in every place, a band of women would come as if to share the sport, dressed in divers and marvellous dresses of men—sometimes to the number of 40 or 50 ladies, of the fairest and comeliest (though I say not, of the best) among the whole kingdom. Thither they came in party-coloured tunics, one colour or pattern on the right side and another on the left, with short hoods that had pendants like ropes wound round their necks, and belts thickly studded with gold or silver—nay, they even wore, in pouches slung across their bodies, those knives which are called *daggers* in the vulgar tongue; and thus they rode on choice war-horses or other splendid steeds to the place of tournament. There and thus they spent and lavished their possessions, and wearied their bodies with fooleries and wanton buffoonery, if popular report lie not....But God in this matter, as in all others, brought marvellous remedy; for He harassed the places and times appointed for such vanities by opening the floodgates of heaven with rain and thunder and lurid lightning, and by unwonted blasts of tempestuous winds....That same year and the next came the general mortality throughout the world."[2] So, again, in *Piers*

Plowman, Reason "proved that these pestilences were for pure sin, and the south-west wind on Saturday at even [January 15th, 1362] was for pure pride, and no point else".[3] Knighton records another story which, even if it be pure invention, points clearly to the same mentality. "The King of Tharsis, seeing so sudden and unheard of a mortality among his subjects, set out with a great multitude of nobles towards Avignon to the Pope; for he purposed to be baptized a Christian, believing that God's vengeance had fallen upon his people by reason of their evil lack of faith. But, after twenty days' journey, hearing that the plague wrought as great havoc among Christians as among other nations, he turned and went no farther on that way, but hastened home unto his own country: and the Christians, falling upon the rear of his host, slew some 2000 of them."[4] We have here the natural nemesis of those popular superstitions which so often relied upon charms and spells to propitiate the Deity. Bede had told, long ago, how many folk attributed the Yellow Pest of the seventh century to the anger of the old Teutonic gods, and to the impotence of the Cross as a talisman against suffering. He wrote: "Sighere, and very many of the people and of the earls, loving this life and not seeking another, or even not believing it to exist, began to restore the pagan temples which had been forsaken, and to worship images, as if by means of these they could be shielded from the mortality."[5]

The plague reached Europe in 1347, breaking out at Constantinople. Thence it followed the trade route, by Messina and Genoa, to Normandy. In August 1348 the Bishop of Bath and Wells ordered processions throughout his diocese, every Friday, "to beg God to protect the people from the pestilence which had come from the east into the neighbouring kingdom [of France]". He gave an Indulgence of 40 days to all who should give alms, or fast, or pray to avert God's anger. In January 1349 he is again circularizing his diocese.[6] "The contagion of pestilence of this modern time, spreading everywhere, hath left many parish churches and other cures of Our diocese, and the parishioners thereof, without curate and priest; and, since priests cannot be found who for zeal of devotion or for any stipend are willing to undertake the care of the places aforesaid, and to visit the sick and minister ecclesiastical sacraments to them (perchance by reason of the infection and the horror of contagion), therefore, many, as we have heard, are dying without the Sacrament of Penance, not knowing how they should act at such a point of necessity, and believing that, even in case of need, no other confession of their sins is profitable or meritorious except when made to a priest who beareth the keys of the Church." Therefore the bishop enjoins them, in the last resort, to confess even to layfolk, who however must keep the seal of secrecy inviolate; moreover, if the penitent survive, he must repeat his confession later to a priest. If there be no priest to administer extreme unction, then, "as in other matters, faith in the Sacrament should suffice". Here, then, we already find a temporary revolution in the medieval Church: faith must take the place of the Sacrament, not only here and there, but among the multitude; and the parallel revolution in all social relations is fully described by Boccaccio in his famous prologue to the *Decameron*.

There are six points upon which all the chroniclers agree. (1) The unprecedented mortality: though, as to the actual figures, they are often as random as we are accustomed to expect from medieval computations. Some put the mortality at nearly 90 per cent.; an entry in the Norwich records (written 150 years after the event) gives more than 57,000 deaths among a population which pretty certainly never exceeded 17,000 and was in all likelihood considerably less. But most writers put it at about 50 per cent.; and, as we shall see, this is not very far wrong. (2) The suddenness and the helplessness: no efficient remedy, and no means of escape. (3) The consequent loosening of all social ties, whether of family or of parish. (4) The extremes of faith and unfaith during the pestilence. (5) The root cause, extreme sinfulness in that particular age. (6) Yet, afterwards, a still greater hardness of heart. In those last two we may trace the usual medieval mirage; the usual conviction that mankind was going steadily from bad to worse as time went on.

So much for the literary sources, let us now check these by comparison with official documents and similar records.

Mr J. Lunn obtained the degree of Ph.D. at Cambridge in 1930 with a thesis on the Black Death, full of valuable statistics. There, for the first time, the whole evidence from the episcopal registers is analysed and tabulated; and, with his permission, I am making free use here of his statistics. We may begin with the bishops, whose movements he has traced carefully all through.

He shows that there was little difference between their behaviour during the plague and at ordinary times; there was "little to differentiate"; "business went on as usual". In so far as there was a difference, they spent less time than usual in their cathedral cities or any other town, staying longer at their secluded country manors. They ordained clerics as usual, and instituted priests into the many livings vacated by death: but this needed not to involve much personal contact. The mortality among them was less than 18 per cent., as against more than 40 per cent. among the parish clergy.[7]

Let us pass on to these beneficed clergy. Here again Dr Lunn's statistics are of great value, for they exploit fully for the first time the unrivalled riches of the English ecclesiastical records, which yield us numerical certainties far beyond those of any other country, and which, by analogy, cast welcome light on the incidence of this plague throughout Europe. As might be expected, the differences between one comparatively small area and another are startling. Taking the rural deaneries, deaths vary enormously. Leyland deanery, in Lichfield diocese, had none; the next lowest is Ludlow deanery (Hereford) which had only 12. Thence we rise by degrees to the three extremes at the other end; 75 deaths in Ross and in Irchenfield (Hereford both) and 86 in Kenn (Exeter). Yet, when we pass beyond these narrow limits, and take so large an area as a diocese, those irregularities cancel each other out so nearly that, while the lowest diocese is York with 38·97 deaths per cent., the highest are Exeter, Winchester and Norwich with 48·8 each, and Ely with 48·5. The intervening dioceses are Lichfield (39·6), Lincoln (40·1), Hereford (43·2), Worcester (44·5) and Bath and Wells (47·6). Moreover, these differences seem to some extent explicable. It was natural that York, with so many moorland parishes and so sparse a village population over the whole diocese, should suffer comparatively little; Lichfield, again, included all the hills and moorlands of Derbyshire and most of the Midland forests. Norwich diocese, on the other hand, was far more thickly populated, and had four cities of the first rank; Winchester, again, had Southampton, which we know to have suffered very heavily, and Southwark. Again, the separate study of the different deaneries suggests to Dr Lunn that navigable rivers and estuaries did much to disseminate the plague, which we know to have been ship-borne from the first, and which would certainly flourish among folk so closely herded together in their daily work. But, be that as it may, it is a remarkable testimonial to the truth of these statistics that, in the broader generalization of entire dioceses, the percentages should agree so closely. It seems now quite certain that nearly half of the beneficed clergy died during these plague months.

But, though we may accept Dr Lunn's figures with confidence, it is far more difficult to follow some of his deductions, especially as they are expressed briefly and almost dogmatically: certainly without full argument on both sides. He writes: "In all the wealth of ecclesiastical records there is not one which shows that the parish priests took to shameless flight or complete abandonment of their most sacred duties." Before we accept this brief statement, let us look more closely at contemporary and sub-contemporary evidence, which is fairly voluminous. We have judgments on the parish clergy from two monastic chroniclers, Birchington of Canterbury and Dene of Rochester.[8] The former writes: "In this pestilence scarce one-third of the population remained alive. Then, also, there was so great scarcity and rarity of priests that parish churches remained altogether unserved, and beneficed parsons had turned aside from the care of their benefices for fear of death, not knowing where they might dwell." Dene writes: "In this plague many chaplains and hired parish priests would not serve without excessive pay. The Bishop of Rochester, by a mandate of June 27th, 1349, to the Archdeacon of Rochester, commanded these to serve at the same salaries, under pain of suspension and interdict. Moreover, many [*plures*] beneficed clergy, seeing that the number of their parishioners had been so diminished by the plague that they could not live upon such oblations as were left, deserted their benefices." Against these deserters the bishop decreed measures which were not likely to be very effectual. Other bishops, at the same time, were struggling with the same difficulty. We read in the *Victoria County History* for Hampshire: "In April, 1350, when the scourge had abated, the Bishop issued a general admonition to his clergy as to residence in their parishes. Reports, he says, had reached him of some priests shamefully absenting themselves from their cures to the danger of many souls, so that even the Holy Sacrifice for which the church had been built and adorned had not been celebrated. He complained further that in some cases the churches had been left to birds and beasts and were becoming ruinous, and ordered all absentees to return within a month." Therefore, the Archbishop of Canterbury issued a decree for all the dioceses of his province; a decree which, as usual, is named after its first word, *Effrenata*. "The unbridled cupidity of the human race", he declares, has, since the coming of this plague, perverted the hearts of the clergy, who "neglect to bear the cure of souls and to support the mutual burdens of parish priests; nay, they even abandon these altogether [for chantry-Masses and similar jobs]; so that, under a simple title and with little labour, they claim greater profits than the parish priests". In *Piers Plowman* we get similar evidence. The author, describing the evils of his time, writes:

> Parsons and parish priests pleynëd them to the bishop,
> That their parishes were poor sith the pestilence-time,
> To have a licence and a leave at London for to dwell,
> And singen there for simony; for silver is sweet.[9]

Dr Lunn does indeed deal in a brief footnote with Birchington's evidence; yet he ignores not only the fact that it is borne out by almost every Continental chronicler who touches upon the subject, but by even the side-lights from our own English records. To begin with the very earliest document of the kind in our registers, the Bath and Wells proclamation of January 1349 quoted above in this chapter. Here the bishop takes his stand on the fact, which must have been patent to all his hearers, that the sick are dying wholesale without ecclesiastical ministrations. Secondly, he asserts (and this again is a matter in which both he and his hearers must have had the most definite and direct experience) that this default is due, in part at least, to the unwillingness of priests to face the plague. There is, moreover, further documentary evidence which Dr Lunn's statistics themselves have brought out for the first time. The figures for Lichfield diocese (where, with unusual care, the *cause* of each vacancy is registered) in the whole twelve months before the plague give only four priests who resigned their cures. But in the six plague months (April to October 1349) there were 35 resignations. In the following year there were 42, i.e. 21 per six months. Upon this he comments: "But the motives actuating in the 42 cases were most certainly not cowardice, but rather that impoverishment of living which was one result of the plague." It is very difficult to accept this confident assertion. No doubt impoverishment was an extremely important factor; *Piers Plowman* and other documents show this plainly enough. But if it was most important of all—or indeed, as these words would persuade us, the only one worth considering—how can we possibly account for the fact that the post-plague year, for which we have most definite evidence of impoverishment, produced a markedly lower proportion of resignations than the actual plague months, during which cowardice would be the most probable motive? During that half-year of actual plague, while the bishops were publishing frantic appeals for clerical help, out of the 99 Derbyshire vacancies only 77 were caused by death and 22 by resignation. In Lincoln diocese, during the six worst plague months (May–October) there were 97 resignations as against 76 in the six pre-plague months. The disproportion is even greater if we choose six other plague months (July–December), where we have 136 resignations, or nearly double the pre-plague rate. In York diocese the two pre-plague months record an average of only two resignations, while the two worst plague months have an average of $13\frac{1}{2}$. On the other hand, when we look narrowly into the registers, we find another very remarkable change during the plague: the number of vicarages that change hands increases enormously in proportion to the rectories; and this goes definitely to bear out the general complaint that, naturally enough, it was much harder to fill up the poorer livings than the richer. Thus we must always bear in mind the economic nexus; yet to rule out the element of fear seems not only psychologically paradoxical, but false to the plainest documentary evidence. When Dr Lunn goes on to reject Birchington's categorical statement, on the ground that "there was no real scarcity of priests at all", his words cannot be accepted in the sense which his argument requires. Desperate demand produced numerical supply: the registers show that the vacant rectories and vicarages were in fact filled, though we have no evidence that the "chaplaincies" (in modern English, curacies) were. There were enough applicants for the loaves and fishes; but that is all that the documents can tell us. However ready we ourselves may be to confess that we should probably have played an unheroic part in this tragedy, that does not justify our ignoring the circumstances which made against heroism in those days which we are actually studying.

These English considerations are much strengthened by Continental analogies. The plague-ravages, as described by chroniclers abroad, are so exactly parallel to those in England, that we may argue strongly—though not, of course, conclusively—from one to the other. The testimony of those chroniclers is overwhelming against any distinctive clerical self-sacrifice: a unanimity all the more remarkable because they themselves were nearly all clerics, often monks or friars, and sometimes their criticism touches not a rival order, but their own. I have printed the evidence far more fully in my monograph than space will here permit. Briefly, we have the judgment of 22 chroniclers, English and foreign, upon the behaviour of the clergy during the pestilence. Of the eight least unfavourable, one only is entirely favourable; but he speaks only for his own neighbourhood (Catania). The two next best, while praising the friars or the nurses, contrast these with the negligent behaviour of the parish priests. The remainder are frankly, and sometimes violently, unfavourable. It would be difficult to find any historical question, involving so directly and so deeply the reputation of an enormously numerous and influential body, with exceptional facilities for self-defence and self-advertisement, in which the evidence is so overwhelming against them. Even though all these chroniclers had been mistaken as to the facts (though, as we have seen, the official documents go far to support them), there would still remain the plain consideration that, whatever the priests had actually done, public opinion did judge them to have fallen, as a body, far below the height of their sacred office. That belief, in itself, would go far to explain Lollardy and the Reformation. The monastic chronicler Knighton, who lays such stress upon the ravages of the pestilence and the difficulty of getting suitable priests, is equally emphatic as to the sudden rise of the Lollards. Under the year 1382 he tells us how "they multiplied exceedingly like budding plants, and filled the whole realm everywhere, and became as familiar as though all had come forth upon the same day. For this sect was held in the greatest honour at that time; and it multiplied so greatly that you could scarce meet two men on the road but that one of them was a disciple of Wyclif." And, among their heretical doctrines, he specifies: "*Item*, [they hold] that no rector or vicar or prelate of any kind is excused from residing personally in his own parish by the fact that he is in the service of a bishop or archbishop or pope. *Item*, that rectors and vicars who do not celebrate Mass, nor administer the Church sacraments, should even be removed in favour of others; for they are unworthy, and wasters of the Church's goods." Here is an unmistakable echo of what Dene and Birchington and the bishops' registers have told us concerning men's doings and thoughts during the Great Pestilence. This England in which men met so many Lollards by the way was an England in which every man over fifty had seen with his own eyes how Christ's folk had often died like beasts in holes and in the streets without benefit of clergy; he had heard with his own ears how the priest, like the day-labourer, was refusing the old work except at double pay, and was ready to "down tools" in this very natural economic struggle.

Indeed, the effect of this pestilence upon the Reformation is insisted upon with strongest emphasis by those who most regret that revolution; though they naturally plead a very different causation. Cardinal Gasquet wrote: "It is a well-ascertained fact, strange as it may seem, that men are not, as a rule, made better by great and universal visitations of Divine Providence." Another writes: "The Middle Ages would have declined in any case: they were fatigued and were growing old; but the process was at once accelerated and warped by the Black Death. Change would have come; but that it came so rapidly and with such force, and—if I may use the phrase—with such a 'twist', we must set down to that exceeding plague." But can we really accept any conception of Providence which rests upon the assumption of Divine Miscalculation, and which argues that a blow intended to awaken men to their sins—for this is the universal explanation given by orthodox contemporary chroniclers in face of the plague—did actually result in religious ruin for the world? Again, does not the second plea, under cover of a misleading metaphor, beg the question no less definitely? If we would content ourselves with speaking of a "change of direction", which conveys neither good nor evil implication, we are on safe and agreed lines. After the Black Death, as after the Great War of 1914, scarcely anything went on exactly as before. But the words "warped" and "twist" distinctly assume some falsity of direction; they even imply some direction flatly contrary to the previous course of civilization. Yet, if we take the plain evidence as it stands, and conclude that the Black Death opened the eyes of the average man to that truth which St Bernard and successive saints had proclaimed long since in exaggerated language, "the priests are worse than the people", then its effect upon the Reformation would seem plain enough, and its influence, on the whole, not reactionary but progressive and civilizing.

But let us again remind ourselves of those words, "exaggerated language". It was only that the priesthood were becoming, more and more plainly, unequal to their superhuman pretensions and therefore unworthy of their enormous corporate and personal privileges. Otherwise, man for man, they were, as they always have been in all Christian denominations, better than the laity. Yet, as saints had insisted for centuries past, and as men saw now by plain every-day experience, the priests were not sufficiently superior. This foul disease, as we have seen in a previous chapter, accomplished what popes and councils had vainly attempted; it broke down the bad old system of putting ignorant boys into the best livings, while curates at starvation wages did the actual work. Although, on the eve of the Reformation, men still complained that very many parishes were served by incompetent hirelings in the absence of the rector, yet no later list of institutions shows anything approaching to the scandalous proportion of boy-incumbents which stares us in the face from the pre-plague episcopal registers. To emphasize these facts is the historian's plain duty; and it can be done without self-righteousness.

After all, priests and monks and nuns were men and women, and they fled no more than the doctors and notaries; sometimes even less. Yet the horrible trial did show them as men and women; and the rest of medieval history is deeply coloured by the revelation, so convincing in its completeness and universality, that the priests, the class who had sometimes been quasi-deified—those who could be said in loose language to "make the Body of Christ"—were almost as panic-stricken as the rest of mankind.[10] Here, again, we must emphasize that moderating adverb *almost*; for it is evident that, whatever stress we may lay upon the contemporary complaints which I have quoted, the mortality among resident parish priests must have been above the average. The non-resident cleric was, roughly speaking, as favourably placed as any pope or bishop; it depended only upon his conscience to mingle freely with his fellows or to avoid every risk of contagion by retiring to the safest spot he could find; and the evidence shows that there were areas of comparative safety, though it was doubtless often difficult to distinguish these at the actual crisis. But the resident parson, even the least courageous, must have run far greater risks. At the beginning, if only in routine, he would sing his daily Mass, and come in to shrive the sick. Even, when the risk of infection became obvious, few would be so pusillanimous as to abandon at once the most sacred and important of their professional duties. When war has broken out, even the least enterprising soldier has at once a lower chance of survival than the civilian; and when this plague broke out, the least courageous parish priest ran a similar risk. He lived, it is true, under less insanitary domestic conditions than the average artisan or peasant. There was no overcrowding in his house; normally there could only be a single servant, and even when, as was too frequently the case, the parson had sons and daughters, these seldom lived in the house with him; such cohabitation is always mentioned by ecclesiastical disciplinarians as a special aggravation. To this extent, therefore, his chances of survival were above the average; but they must have been more than counterbalanced by his contact with sick folk; and this may to some extent explain the remarkable frequency of change in the poorer livings as compared with the rich rectories. A vicar could not often pay a substitute; he must do the work and take the risk himself; he could not afford to wander in search of some more secluded and healthier spot; he must either cynically repudiate every responsibility of his sacred profession or face considerable extra chances of infection. We may take it as probable, therefore, that the average lay mortality was rather lower, and perhaps a good deal lower, than that among the incumbents. Though some manor rolls show a far higher death-rate, others show surprisingly little, and it is evident that the incidence of the plague was extremely irregular. Therefore I cannot help feeling that the ordinary computation for the laity is too high, and that we must not assume a higher death-rate than one-third for the population of England, or of Europe in general. It will be noted that Birchington suggests two-thirds; but we must always discount the figures of a chronicler.

So much for the layman's body; and now for his soul. The above-quoted episcopal decree of Bath and Wells, with similar measures by which the authorities attempted to guarantee, in the priest's absence, some sort of emergency sacramental guidance for the laity, must have gone far towards spiritual emancipation.

The people began to learn independence of their Professional Mediator; and that lesson, once learned, was never completely forgotten. We shall see something of the same results from that wave of mysticism which marks the fourteenth century: we may see it also in those wild excesses of the Flagellants, and that Dancing Mania which followed upon the plague years. The Church was affected here, to an even stronger degree, than the manor was.

For the landlord (though, here again, modern research warns us increasingly against exaggeration) was met by a sudden shortage of labour, and compelled in the long run to make terms with it. But this was not without a fierce struggle. Parliament, which of course represented the upper-class interests almost exclusively, passed successive acts after the plague, forbidding rise of wages or of prices, or the migration of labourers in search of better employment. But prices were not thus stabilized: nor could the labourer accept the old wage on such terms. Langland, writing little more than twenty years after the first of these acts, describes the effect of this upon the less settled wage-earner:

> And then would Wastour not work, but wandren about...
> Labourers, that have no land to live on but their hands,
> Deigned not to dine to-day on yesterday's cabbage,
> May no penny-ale please them, nor no piece of bacon,
> But if it be fresh flesh or fish, fried or baked,
> And that hot and hotter still, to keep the chill from their maw
> And, but if he be highly hired, else will he chide
> And wail the time that ever he was workman born.
> And then curseth he the King, and all his Council with him,
> That lay down such laws, the labourers to grieve.[11]

Here the satirist is amply corroborated by an entry in the Lincoln-shire Assize Roll of 1353. "The jury present that William de Caburn, of Lymbergh, ploughman, will not work except as a day-labourer or a monthly labourer. And he will not eat salt meat, but only fresh meat; and for this cause he hath departed from the township; for no man dared to hire him in this fashion contrary to the statute of our lord the King."[12] Thus the friction increased from year to year: for this is but one specimen from many. In 1377, Churchmen and others complained to the King in Parliament that villeins will no longer perform servile duties, but band together and riot, so that, "if due remedy be not provided by Parliament, greater mischief (which may God prohibit!) will ensue". As we all know, remedy was not provided, and God did not prohibit, and in 1381 came the great Peasants' Revolt. Professor Levett, whose researches in this field are among the latest and soundest, writes: "The Black Death did not in any strictly economic sense cause the Peasants' Revolt or the breakdown of villeinage; but it gave birth, in many cases, to a smouldering feeling of discontent, an inarticulate desire for change, which found its outlet in the rising of 1381." Thus two of the most characteristic medieval institutions were shaken in a few months: the Church and the Manor. It was far easier henceforth to question the divine right of the priest and the divine right of the landlord.

To sum up: the Black Death, like the Great War of 1914, shook many things to the very base, and overthrew those whose foundations were faulty, while the sounder survived. Each of these catastrophes has shown the astonishing elasticity of human nature. Institutions founded solidly on deep human needs, and movements inspired by elementary natural impulses, after the first shock, were modified, but not broken. Municipal growth, for instance, was not permanently checked. Norwich appears to have been one of the cities which suffered most heavily; yet we find the citizens, very shortly afterwards, paying contributions at the pre-plague valuation without a murmur. Again, the Black Death seems to have had very little effect on the Hundred Years' War; apparently it was always possible to get soldiers. Indeed, the contemporary Paduan chronicler, Guglielmo Cortusio, a learned judge, and evidently something of a philosopher, notes expressly that "at this time [of plague] Christendom was fighting furiously in five places"—England against France, the King of Hungary against Apulia, the King of Bohemia against Bavaria, the Romans against their own Government, and the Eastern Empire against the Turks. This absence of paralysis even through the plague months, this "business as usual", is emphasized also by Dr Lunn in his thesis.

The plague returned in later years at fairly frequent intervals; in 1361, 1368, 1375, 1382, 1390, [1406], 1438–9, 1464–5, and possibly 1471.[13] Some of these may not have been the true bubonic plague. In 1485 came the terrible "sweating sickness", which recurred in 1487, 1499, and 1504. It is sometimes asserted that these visitations were comparable to the Black Death; but that is not borne out by any documentary evidence that has yet been produced. The plague of 1361, which was probably the worst, carried off scarcely more than half the Black Death proportion of clergy, so far as the registers are available. As Dr Creighton points out, nearly all our evidence for these later visitations comes from the towns: "there is not a word in them about the rural districts", and none has been produced from the manor rolls.

No war is inevitable, yet this may be said to have been as nearly so as any. The reign of Henry II had created an impossible situation. He held large portions of France as a feudal vassal, and vague definitions of feudalism constantly led to wars between great vassals and their over-lords. Any such war in France was in fact civil war, and in this particular case civil war was complicated by foreign invasion from England.

No quarrels in history are more fatal than civil wars with aided invasions. It may almost be said that only one thing could have avoided war in those circumstances. If there had been two men like St Louis reigning at the same moment, then reason and justice might now have prevailed, and the English might have been bought out of France or have retired. Again, one thing alone could have shortened the struggle; namely, if the rapid advance in military power at that time could have been made by France, the country which had the greater population and was the stronger in strategical position. What actually happened was exactly the opposite; and the deceptive English successes greatly encouraged the whole national interest in these wars. On the one side was our national covetousness and ambition, with a sense of ancient wrong; for St Louis had definite qualms as to the justice of his grandfather's conquest of Normandy, and Philip the Fair's conquests had been of far more doubtful justice. On the other side was a France no less covetous than we, if only the occasion had offered, and now fighting for her very existence. We may call this the first great national war in English history, in the modified sense in which the word "national" could be used of that time. The nearest approach to it, perhaps, in medieval history was in the wars of Germany against her eastern neighbours, Saxony, the Slavs, Hungary and Bohemia.

Let us first regard it from the purely military standpoint. Here it is difficult to exaggerate its importance. Guibert de Nogent, one of the greatest chroniclers of the Crusades, called his history "Gesta Dei per Francos"—God's Dealings through the French. The greatest majority of successes in those Crusades had been won by natives of what we now call France. France, again, had won a splendid national victory at Bouvines against a strong European coalition; and her defeat by the Flemings at Courtrai had been avenged at Mons-en-Pévèle and Roosebeke. When, at the beginning of the fourteenth century, Pierre Dubois suggested as a policy for European peace that the King of France should make a tame cat of the Pope and then rule righteously over the whole of Europe, we may say that this proposal was quite natural, since it voiced not merely French vanity but also to some extent full European belief. Petrarch, in one of his letters, describes the stupor of the Western World when John's defeat and captivity at Poitiers was noised abroad. As the French historian Luce puts it: "Crécy had been a grievous defeat: Poitiers was a catastrophe comparable to Waterloo, Jena and Sedan." True, the French king had failed to relieve Calais after Crécy, and the English nearly always got the best of the minor encounters for the next ten years. But these victories were small in themselves; very few of them separately were important; and, in those days of difficult communication, few people outside the invaded areas knew how the canker of war was eating into France, or how far it was directly responsible for the disorganization of government and the overtaxation of the people. Then, at last, John raised a vast host to crush these wasps once for all. The result was that he found himself a prisoner; that his people were further taxed with the greatest ransom, perhaps, of the whole Middle Ages; and that the government of France was reduced to more hopeless anarchy than before. We must not, of course, forget the gross tactical blunders committed by John in the actual battle. In addition to all these, he had ordered the Dauphin and his brother, after they had been beaten in a preliminary skirmish, to retire with their men from the field. Yet, even after all this, the French who stood firm still outnumbered the English: but they were hopelessly defeated.

How was this? The root cause was first pointed out by the greatest of authorities on this period, Siméon Luce. He wrote: "The defeat of the French depended upon a deep-seated and irresistible cause, independent not only of the personal bravery of our soldiers, but of the heroism of a leader [like Du Guesclin], and even to a certain point independent of his generalship."[2] That cause was the English military organization, which was then both national and absolutely businesslike. True, manhood service was the theory everywhere in the Middle Ages; but in no great State was it practised as in England. As Luce puts it, "the phrase 'compulsory military service' is modern, is even up-to-date in contemporary politics. But the thing itself is old, and it is oldest among the very people who know least of it nowadays; and Edward III, especially, practised it on a large scale." For, on the English side, there was compulsory manhood service with constant views of arms; muster-rolls of that period still survive in some of our municipal records. In France, on the other hand, this theoretical principle had been allowed to die out in practice, and the so-called "levies" of men were ordered only in order that they might buy themselves off and thus provide money for the old-fashioned feudal host. Even the civic militias were badly organized. We have already seen how, when the inhabitants of three villages in the South maintained, quite justly, that they would no longer pay for substitutes but come in person, the viguier of Béziers settled the dispute with that one level volley: "You bloody peasants! whether you will or whether you won't, you shall pay all the same!"[3] Even in the later stages of the war, the French nation had never really learned that lesson. True, the Grande Ordonnance of 1357—those 67 articles forced upon the Dauphin, the future Charles V, by Étienne Marcel and the democracy of Paris—did indeed insist that the Government should arm not only the townsfolk, but the far more numerous and hardier class of peasantry also. But the Dauphin hated all these articles thus thrust upon him; the country in general was far less politically advanced than those democrats of the capital; and the whole ordinance remained a dead letter.

Therefore France, throughout the later Middle Ages, never had such a national army as we brought to Neville's Cross, nor even in the sense in which our armies of Crécy, Poitiers and Azincourt were national. The first of those, at least, was in large part won by conscripts: and, where an army is national, it is also business-like. Edward I had been a really national king, so far as any medieval sovereign can so be called; and he was also the creator of the national medieval military tactics. He had learned in his Welsh and Scottish wars one lesson of capital importance; the superiority of the longbow to the crossbow. Therefore he, and Edward III after him, encouraged archery, and behind his bowmen were "knife-men" with long daggers; the whole were supported by divisions of the feudal heavy cavalry which protected the bowmen at their work. Thus, when the arrows had thrown the hostile knights and men-at-arms into confusion, the knights charged into the struggling mass and completed the rout. Falkirk was the first great battle in which Edward I developed these tactics; at Bannockburn we fell back into the old feudal blunders for the first and last time; thenceforward this irresistible combination invented by Edward I was the regular routine of English armies. The French might have learned something of this from their defeat by the Flemings at Courtrai. Certainly Crécy and Poitiers were very plain lessons; but they never learned the true secret of national defence during that whole century and more. As Langlois puts it in Lavisse's great co-operative *History of France*: "Falkirk and Courtrai foretell the great disasters of the Hundred Years' War; fifty years afterwards, the English had forgotten nothing of their lesson, and the French had learned nothing." That is why England developed a superiority which, on its smaller scale, throws even the Napoleonic superiority into the shade. For it, the causes lay in the whole system. England did not always produce the greatest generals; the greatest in the whole war, in most men's opinion, was Du Guesclin. Yet Crécy, Poitiers and Azincourt, coming close enough together to fall within the memory of a single man, were perhaps more startling victories, against greater odds, than any similar group in the history of the world. Again, we may contrast our own marches across France, not once or twice only during this long war, with the fact that the French never did more than burn a few of our ports and occupy the Isle of Wight for a few months, even when she and Spain had destroyed our fleet off La Rochelle in 1372, and thus commanded the seas for eight years. If we thus compare English power on land with French impotence all this time, and remember how far France outnumbered us in population, and how fine are the fighting qualities of the French people in themselves, it is difficult to find another parallel to this in military history.

No doubt military history is in itself a small thing; we have, as a rule, too much of it in historical books. But the effect of wars upon social history is a subject of capital importance; and that is why the ablest socialists in modern France and Germany, long before 1914, were paying such close attention to a subject which as citizens they hated, but which, as scientific students of history or politics, they felt it suicidal to neglect. Britain and America are the only two countries in which socialists not only ignore this truth, but seem to boast their ignorance as a virtue.

If we read any French history of political institutions, or of religious and moral life, from 1350 to 1450, then we find the same cry repeated over and over again: "it was miserable; things went from bad to worse; but the root cause was in those disastrous invasions!" We may perhaps feel that they overdo it a little: the English Invader is as convenient to suggest in solution of any historical problem as the Black Death is; and doubtless both are often over-emphasized. But the thing in the main seems undeniable. Although the wars unquestionably caused great suffering in England, and were partly responsible for two great revolts and other smaller risings, and although most of us would willingly wipe the whole page out of the world's history, so long as no more sordid page were substituted for it, yet it seems as though English trade and commerce did, on the whole, increase or hold its own during most of those years. Town life flourished fairly, at least, though there seems to have been a good deal of stagnation and decay in the first three-quarters of the fifteenth century; and this was one of our greatest centuries for parliamentary liberties. Yet, a few miles away, just over the Channel, the growth of towns was completely arrested, and dozens of them, during this century, actually surrendered their liberties because they were no longer able to accept the responsibilities implied in their charters. Meanwhile their parliamentary liberties, after one hopeless and bloody revolt, steadily decreased. In commerce and industry France had never rivalled Lombardy or the Low Countries. Yet, at the beginning of the fourteenth century, the great fairs of Champagne (especially that of Troyes) were among the most important in Europe. These were the meeting-point of the overland trade from the East with merchants from England, the Low Countries, and the great and populous kingdom of France. Already before the Hundred Years' War the merchants had invented a clearing-house system; they paid all their purchases on the last day of the fair, mainly with bills: moreover, there was elaborate and powerful legislation to ensure probity, and credit was so good that loans were made at lower interest than anywhere else. The Hundred Years' War destroyed all this. The roads became infested with brigands, or sunk in morasses. Sometimes they even disappeared altogether, overgrown with shrubs and trees. Rivers silted up:

lords, and even royal officers, multiplied illegal tolls. Market-halls fell into ruins. The great fair of Paris was first abolished; then even those of Champagne, which "in the twelfth and thirteenth centuries attracted merchants from the whole of Europe".[4] Now, therefore, the trade of Northern France went by the Rhine to the Low Countries: that of Southern France to the fair of Geneva. In a single town, Alais, we happen to have exact statistics of depopulation. The taxable property was £40,000 in 1338, £26,000 in 1405, £19,000 in about 1440. In Paris, there are said to have been 24,000 houses in ruins or deserted: this is probably exaggerated; but certainly the authorities were more than once compelled to sell wholesale these empty houses, which no longer paid rates and were a nuisance to the neighbourhood. The French chronicler Thomas Basin relates the miserable devastation of some of the richest parts of Normandy, over which the ebb and flow of war passed again and again. In some of those districts, nothing could be cultivated that lay beyond easy reach of the nearest fortified town or castle. Even there, the peasant was ready to cut his traces and leave his plough the moment the alarm bell rang from the nearest tower; and (says Basin) the very swine grew so accustomed to this stampede that they would run of their own accord when the bell rang out. It has been calculated that the Hundred Years' War diminished the French population by at least one-third, while it kept that of England stationary. In both cases, of course, we must also count the Black Death and other plagues. All this desolation had a disastrous effect upon the Church also. The bishops were no longer able to visit dioceses. The monks ceased to hold their General Chapters. Of the country parishes, many had now no clergy at all; and the old disorders of non-residence and neglect were far worse than ever before. French society, in the latter half of the fifteenth century, was certainly extremely corrupt. The University of Paris was in full decadence; and by far the most remarkable man of letters is that François Villon, "housebreaker and poet", to whom R. L. Stevenson consecrated one of his most interesting essays. And, at last, when the country found comparative rest, this was under the rule of the despot and the mercenary, as in Italy.

It came about thus. The Estates in 1439 granted to Charles VII, for the sake of military security, enormous freedom of taxation. He was permitted to take the whole *taille* of France, i.e. all the taxes which hitherto the feudal lords had raised from their tenants. This at once brought him in 1,800,000 *livres* a year; and with that sum he hired and organized a regular army. But the Estates had made no definite bargain as to the limitations of this system, either in time or in money. Therefore Charles and his successors not only continued it to perpetuity, but raised at their own will the rate of assessment. Hence a fundamental difference between Britain and France until the Revolution of 1789. The French kings were absolute masters both of the national purse and of the national army: they ruled what was, apart from the totalitarian Papacy, the most totalitarian state in Europe: the price of our expulsion from French soil was the riveting of these chains upon the French people. Upon this transaction of 1439 Professor Lodge comments: "Englishmen may hold that orderly government and national independence were dearly purchased by the sacrifice of all securities for constitutional liberty; but it is at least probable that if they had ever found themselves in such an evil plight they would have concluded the same bargain on the same terms." True; yet, without being pharisaical, we have a right to look farther than this, and to follow the French historian Luce in his attempt to trace the fundamental causes why France found herself in such a miserable state that even despotism and the rule of a hireling soldiery came as a relief. Partly, no doubt, we must remember our fortunate insular position, which, without guaranteeing us altogether, certainly made invasion more difficult. Again, we must not forget the madness of Charles VI at a critical moment: but it is difficult to imagine the English Government so completely paralysed by a king's madness. Even before the war, England was already in advance of France in parliamentary government. For we were a smaller nation, with more coherence; and the great feudal lords, even in the thirteenth century, had much less power among us. Thus far we had always the advantage: but greatest of all was our secure insularity. The social contrast between England, secure from invasion, and France, with one eye always necessarily fixed upon the actual or possible invader, was clearly noted by the penetrating eye of Commines. After marking the comparative decency of civil wars in England, even while they last, he points out their brevity. "In England, if any discord arises, in ten days or less one party or the other has gained the upper hand. But it is not thus with our affairs on this side [of the Channel]; for our king had to wage warfare extended over several portions of his kingdom, and to look out for his neighbours; and specially did he need, among all his other business, to content the King of England...that he should not meddle in our affairs", as he is always on the watch to do.[5] Therefore, when all allowances have been made, it is impossible to deny that French historians are right in the main, and that the Hundred Years' War influenced internal politics in France even more disastrously than the foreign invader influenced French politics during the Revolutionary Wars. Then, it was those Austrian and Prussian and English invaders who made the French glad to accept one military tyranny after another: first that of the Committee of Public Safety, and next that of Napoleon: just as, in 1871, it was the foreign invasion which was mainly responsible for the horrors of the Paris Commune and its repression.

Prudent French statesmen saw this new ordinance of 1439 in its full significance. Presently, we find Bishop Jean-Jouvenel des Ursins pleading, in a memorial to Charles VII: Now that the English are at last driven out of France, need this host of mercenaries be maintained? Is there no danger of the soldiers oppressing the people?—he dares not add, "and of the king ruling tyrannically by their means". But upon the irresponsible taxation he does venture to speak plainly: "Your kingdom is called France, because your subjects ought to be free [francs] indeed. Yet, at present, they are more subject to arbitrary taxation than the very serfs are."

We may trace the English citizen-soldier, bearing the burden of arms and therefore the more conscious of his responsibility for war and peace, in Bishop Latimer's fond recollections of his father the yeoman farmer, whose armour he buckled on for Blackheath Field, and in his praise of the robust sport of archery. The contrast between this and France, again, may be read in the story of their fifteenth-century revolts. In both cases, we have great nobles as revolutionaries; but the rest is far different. In France, these were nearly always jealous princes of royal blood, mustering their retainers and hiring mercenaries against the Crown's comparatively orderly government, backed up by its standing army. Both parties fought thus over the bodies of the helpless peasantry; and Sir John Fortescue described the result in words not too overcharged with patriotic exaggeration.[6] Moreover, just as the war had been made at the peasant's expense, so also was the peace;

king compromised with nobles on terms which allowed both to domineer still more over the common man. Our English rebellions were very different: men rose and fought not against good but against bad or weak government. Thus, in the Wars of the Roses, when great nobles led the movement, they had, on the whole, the support of the towns. Therefore, while ambitious lords and their retainers were slaying each other, the commoners partly stood aside, allowing these their social enemies to commit political suicide; or, in so far as they interfered, they consulted their own best interests, and those of the realm, by throwing their sword into the scale of order. Everywhere our central authority, when strong, was able to call upon the local levies, which sometimes (at Towton, for instance) made serious contributions to the victory. The law-courts sat all through: there was no serious interruption to trade and industry. Here again we turn to Commines, an historian of wide political experience and unprecedented philosophic insight. He noted that in England, despite all the brutalities of civil strife, "there are no buildings destroyed or demolished by war, and there the mischief of it falls on those who make the war". "This England is", he says, "among all the world's lordships of which I have knowledge, that where public weal is best ordered, and where least violence reigns over the people. . . . The king can undertake no enterprise of account without assembling his parliament; which is a thing most wise and holy; and therefore are these kings stronger and better served" than the despotic sovereigns of the Continent.7 There is some real reason for regarding the fifteenth century as the golden age of the English agricultural labourer, who in 1381 had shown so much more political sense, discipline and self-restraint than his French brother.

Nor may we look upon the French purely as innocent victims throughout all these quarrels and wars. The effect of the English invasions upon French life, in every department, is nowhere set out so fully, and with such impartiality (since these are documents written with a single business aim, without the remotest afterthought of appeal to posterity), as in the text and the introduction of Father Denifle's *Désolation des Églises*. In that book we have a collection, not of political documents, but of supplications to the different Popes during those hundred years, setting forth the exact reasons which made it impossible for such and such a bishop to visit his own diocese, for such and such a monastery to keep the rule of St Benedict any longer, and so on. These supplications entirely dispel the notion that the horrible ravages of the Hundred Years' War were due to the greater barbarity of the victors—a cheap conclusion to which people sometimes jump, arguing confusedly that, since war is a relic of barbarism, therefore the victory is likely to go to the more barbarous side. After all, war is at least so far a Judgment of God, that, on the whole, men's finest qualities do tell there as elsewhere: St Thomas More brought that out plainly in his *Utopia*. Denifle shows clearly how the worst barbarities were often inflicted on the French by their own fellow-countrymen; by the mercenaries who were hired to fight for them, and who, no longer receiving their pay, or sometimes striking for higher pay, pillaged their own country. Petit-Dutaillis quotes the case of "letters of remission granted by Charles VII to a mercenary who, from his youth upwards, had served the king without ever receiving 'any pay, wages, or recompense', and who 'had as it were been compelled to pillage'". This, he points out, "justifies the exclamation of [Charles's minister,] Jouvenel des Ursins: 'For God's sake, Sire, pardon me; for in truth I may well say that herein you have committed a great fault'". Again, Father Denifle shows the English discipline as enormously superior to the French; we find the Frenchmen themselves complaining that, whereas a safe-conduct from an English captain would be respected by English soldiers, formal French safe-conducts were broken whenever French soldiers thought they could gain by the treachery. Moreover, the one supreme French glory in the whole war—the heroism of Joan of Arc—the one thing in those hundred years which really redeems human nature—was miserably neglected by many of her own compatriots at the time. Denifle points out how, after the English had succeeded in burning her, the French seemed to have grown really ashamed of the victim, and practically to have forgotten her heroism within twenty years of her death.

Therefore, looking closely into the social life of both countries, whatever faults we may find in the England of those years, we may find worse in France. True, the trial wrought her into a single country and roused a real feeling of nationality, real patriotism. But even in England we may trace much of this; and the suffering and discontent among us; the lowering of political morality which is often traced as one of the causes of the Wars of the Roses; all these were distinctly less noticeable than in France.

One very serious politico-social effect of the Hundred Years' War upon France must here be added. A glance at any historical atlas will show how, twice over, half of France was in possession of the King of England. That in itself was a great evil; but, far worse than this, those two halves at different periods were almost entirely different. They had scarcely anything in common but Guienne in the narrower sense, Ponthieu and Calais. The English obtained by the Treaty of Troyes precisely what they had not been able to get by the Treaty of Brétigny, and *vice versa*. To realize the significance of this, let us think of the Irish question of modern times as impartially as we can, and consider the moral effect of those French changes backwards and forwards, without any pretence of consulting the provinces concerned. Imagine the Ulster question decided by force of arms one year, and a few years afterwards by equal violence on exactly opposite lines— Ulster fighting to keep out of the British Empire, and the South fighting to come in. From that point of view we may gauge the impossibility of settled civilization in such conditions, and the readiness to support any single tyranny in exchange for this double tyranny or this treble tyranny, for in France there was the Burgundian alien also. We may understand the undying hatred of the invader that was left by the war, and the tenfold sense of patriotism, but a patriotism mainly centred in one office—in one man—the king. Here we find much that explains the later dictum of French royalty: "l'État, c'est moi." Even that was better than no state at all; better than a conglomerate of provinces in which a man might say: "to-day I am French, to-morrow I may be English."

These last eighteen years of world-history have exposed the fatal error—however generous, in most minds—of building upon the assumption that physical force is rapidly losing its influence on human affairs. Is it not, to begin with, a gross psychological error to treat physical force as a thing so clearly separable from intellectual and moral that we may pigeon-hole them separately without further thought? Air-bombs and poison-gas (to take force at its most deadly) are highly intellectual products, while dynamite in the mine and arsenic in medicine can serve moral ends in a fashion unknown to our ancestors. War has never been a mere matter of brute force; else why has the mammoth perished, and man come to a world-mastery which is disputable (so some scientists tell us) only by the insects? Physical courage is doubtless inferior to moral courage, but would any moralist venture to deny its superiority, *caeteris paribus*, over physical cowardice? Or, again, will any observer of his fellow-men venture to maintain that, in proportion as a man is physically brave, in that same proportion he is likely to lack moral courage? War is the enemy: but the first step towards conquest of any enemy is to understand him; to measure him not on his weak side alone, but also in his strength. Here, therefore, I see no reason for disguising my settled conviction that true pacifism—instructed and cool-headed pacifism, as apart from those negative books which rely mainly on hysterical denunciations of war and descriptions of the soldier as a hired murderer—has nothing to lose, but very much to gain, from a penetrating study of war in its social effects; and especially, perhaps, in England.

XL. THE MYSTICS

How are we to define this word *Mystic*?

Dr Inge, in his *Christian Mysticism*, devotes an appendix of fourteen pages to quotations and discussions of definitions. The two briefest are by the two greatest, perhaps, of his authors. St Bonaventura writes (in a sentence later adopted by Jean Gerson): "It is the reaching out of the soul to God through the yearning of love." Goethe wrote: "It is the scholastic of the heart, the dialectic of the feelings"; i.e. the attempt to solve the Riddle of the Universe, not by logic, but by sympathetic intuition. Hence it has always a tendency to symbolism: its language is necessarily symbolical. The mystic mind, intent upon God, seeks to find Him everywhere; that is, it seeks to penetrate to Him through the visible objects of this universe. Therefore, in the simplest, most familiar sights and sounds, it finds bodings and shadowings-forth of things unseen, unheard. But, even with the aid of the boldest symbolism of language, the mystic feels himself still more helpless and inarticulate than we all feel when we try to express our exact and inmost meaning. In the ordinary process of thinking, we start from a comparatively simple foundation, upon which we build higher and higher, refinement upon refinement, until we reach the furthest limits of coherent thought. The mystic, on the other hand, starts where coherent thought ends—or at least consciously coherent thought—and tries to face the Riddle of the Universe not by systematic observation and measurement of each detail, but by focusing the entire mental horizon into one single vision in which all detail is lost, and the solitary impression left upon the mental retina is a vague, but overpoweringly real and harmonious, image of the Infinite One and All. Poetry, for instance, usually begins where argument ends; and most great poetry is more or less mystical. Wordsworth was penetrated through and through with the mystic significance of all natural things. Take his Ode on the *Intimations of Immortality*, or his *Tintern Abbey* where he says of wild nature:

> I have felt
> A presence that disturbs me with the joy
> Of elevated thoughts; a sense sublime

> Of something far more deeply interfused,
> Whose dwelling is the light of setting suns,
> And the round ocean and the living air,
> And the blue sky, and in the mind of man:
> A motion and a spirit, that impels
> All thinking things, all objects of all thought,
> And rolls through all things.

But perhaps the most magnificent manifestation of poetic mysticism is the last canto of Dante's *Paradiso*, where God Himself, and all the meaning of God's universe, are seen for one moment in one piercing point of light; and thenceforward this forms the one supreme reality in the seer's mind: so that Dante can conclude in those words of Boethius: "My will and desire were rolled, with the even motion of a wheel, by the Love that moves the sun and the rest of the stars." Thus St Augustine can define virtue as "the setting of love in order": "brevis et vera definitio virtutis, *ordo* est *amoris*": that is, the discovery of some Unity, whether a person or a law, in harmony with which we can regulate and guide our natural instincts. Thus there have been, and are, mystics in all creeds. Indeed, perhaps the clearest and most comprehensive definition is that of a great modern writer who called himself a philosophic atheist. Dr McTaggart wrote in *The New Quarterly* for July 1909 (p. 316): "It seems to me that the essential characteristics of mysticism are two in number. In the first place, it is essential to mysticism that it asserts a greater unity in the universe than is recognized in ordinary experience, or in science.... The second essential characteristic of mysticism is the affirmation that it is possible to be conscious of this unity in some manner which brings the knower into closer and more direct relation with what is known than can be done in ordinary discursive thought."

There was a great revival of mysticism, as of thought in general, during the twelfth century. First came the School of St-Victor at Paris and secondly, above all, St Bernard, in whom all the preponderatingly orthodox mystics of later times were steeped, from St Bonaventura to Thomas à Kempis. Much of the *Imitation* is a mosaic from St Bernard. Then came another great wave of mysticism with the Franciscan revival. In thinkers like St Bonaventura, it took a perfectly orthodox direction, especially in the contemplation of the life of Christ and the manipulation of the details of the Gospel story into every possible refinement of delicate symbolism. From a pupil of St Bonaventura, who wrote

The Hundred Meditations on the Life of Christ, comes much of the art symbolism of the later Middle Ages. But there was a strain among the Franciscan mystics tending to follow the dangerous lines of Joachim of Fiore [1200]. This man had thought out a Theory of Development in the Christian Church; a coming New Age in which the Scriptures should be read with quite other eyes, and in which the Church should revert to something like the unsacerdotal conditions of early monasticism. This theory formed a great refuge for the Spiritual Franciscans; that is, the poor "fools" spoken of compassionately in *Piers Plowman*; the small minority who clung with even exaggerated loyalty to the original gospel of absolute poverty, and finally found themselves in collision not only with the more worldly elements in their own order, but with Pope John XXII himself.[1] To the extremists among these Spirituals, the Sacraments of the Church were mere symbols, destined presently to be superseded, in an age when Love should rule the world. Finally, in the scriptural Abomination of Desolation they saw a simoniacal pope, who towards the end of the world would come to the tiara; that is, John XXII. This last age would begin in 1260; from thenceforward the reign of the Holy Ghost will have begun; the reign of the Everlasting Gospel. The manifesto of this party ("Introduction to the Everlasting Gospel") was suppressed by a papal commission as quietly as possible, in view of the striking and scandalous interest which it aroused at the University of Paris, and even more among the laity. But in England the Spirituals were far less numerous or influential; and that allusion in *Piers Plowman* is almost unique.

Far more important was that Dominican mysticism at the turn of the thirteenth century which has been admirably traced by the late Father Denifle.[2] He shows how this movement arose from an adaptation of the scholastic philosophy to unlearned folk, mostly nuns, and in the vulgar tongue. Between 1228 and 1286 the policy of the Dominican order swung backwards and forwards on the question of the care of nunneries. On the one hand it was far harder for women, even consecrated women, than for men to keep their house in order in face of the unsettled society around them. Yet, on the other hand, the official care of these women threw a great deal of extra work and trouble upon the friars, and even involved some risk of scandal; a point upon which St Bonaventura laid great stress at this very time in connection with the same problem as presented to his own Franciscan order. In 1286, then, the Dominican General Chapter came to its final decision, that the men should undertake the spiritual and to a certain extent the temporal guidance of the women, but that the friars thus sent to the nunneries should be exclusively *docti fratres*, that is, men of mature age who had done their full university course, not only in the arts but also in theology. This had an epoch-making influence on the Upper Rhine, one of the most thickly populated and cultured districts of Europe. At the end of this century the Teutonic province of Dominicans had seventy nunneries, while all the other provinces of Europe together had only ninety. Moreover the Teutonic province had only forty-eight men's houses. The significance of this will appear when we contrast it with England, where there were forty men's Dominican convents to only one (Dartford) nunnery. This, according to Denifle, explains why mysticism, sporadic elsewhere, became endemic in the Dominican order, and especially on the Rhine, where Strassburg alone possessed seven nunneries. These *docti fratres*, from preaching Scholasticism to male audiences, were led more and more into mystic language in their sermons to women, and thence among the laity in general. Thus the cold evidence of statistics and of monastic legislation brings the most striking corroboration to what Goethe had seen with poetic penetration: this movement which stirred all Europe, passing up and down the Rhine and thence by the ordinary trade routes, was truly "the scholastic of the heart".

First and most celebrated is Meister Eckhart [1260]–1327. His mysticism rests on a scholastic method of terminology, which in his many vernacular writings he translated as best he could into the language of the people. Denifle strongly repudiates the idea of opposition between mysticism and scholasticism. On that point, as we shall see, our own Rolle is rather exceptional than normal. Eckhart's system starts from something very like John the Scot's conception of God: so great that, on the one hand, no human attribute can be applied to Him: so overwhelming that we can not even attempt an approximate definition except by a series of negations: and so great also that He is immanent in all things, interpenetrates the whole universe, yet (as Eckhart tries, whether logically or not, to maintain) is always above the universe. He says: "God is neither this nor that." "God's simple nature is formless of form, unchanging of change, beingless of being, thingless of things; and therefore it spreads forth into all things in this changing world, and all finite things find their last end in Him."[3] Confronted with the difficulty of putting his thoughts into the vernacular, he was consciously epigrammatic, writing without subtle qualifications, and therefore easily misunderstood. As De Wulf puts it: "To say the least, he borders perilously on Pantheism." In 1326 he was condemned by the Archbishop of Cologne; he appealed to the Pope, but died in the next year. In 1329, twenty-eight of his propositions were condemned by John XXII; that which was most strongly condemned ran: "The eye with which I see God is the same as the eye with which God sees me." This Godlike Eye is, in effect, the *Scintilla* of Aquinas, which goes back to Augustine and the Neoplatonists and is continued by Juliana of Norwich as "the Godly Will". Eckhart calls it *Seelenfünklein*, "Spark of the Soul". In his system, at the apex of the mind there is a divine spark, which is so closely akin to God that it is one with Him, and not merely united to Him. In his earlier views, this Spark was created; but his later doctrine is that it is uncreated, the immanence of the Being and nature of God Himself. "Dies Fünkelein, das ist Gott", he says once. This view was adopted by Suso, and (with modifications) by Tauler, and became one of their chief tenets.

Heinrich Suso (1300–63) lived in the Dominican friary at Constance, where he made himself a little cell and oratory in what was scarcely more than a cupboard under the stairs. This convent, built out into the lake, is nowadays the celebrated Insel Hôtel. His *Autobiography* and his *Little Book of Eternal Wisdom* can both be bought cheaply in English. He "wrote them in German", he said, "because he had thus received them from God"; but, he adds, "one thing, however, a man should know, that there is as great a difference between hearing himself the sweet accords of a harp and hearing another speak of them as there is between the words received in pure grace and that flow out of a living heart, through a living mouth", and those same words when they come "to be set down on dead parchment, especially in the German tongue; for then are they chilled, and they wither like plucked roses: for the sprightliness of their delivery, which, more than anything, moves the heart of man, is then extinguished, and in the dryness of dry hearts are they received. Never was there a string,

how sweet soever, but it became dumb when stretched on a dry
log. A joyless heart can as little understand a joyful tongue as
a German can an Englishman!" "Especially in the German
tongue!" Even Latin, the language of Church and of philosophers,
is insufficient. How much more so, then, is the vernacular,
hitherto almost unused except for poetry! It is precisely this
vernacular, the simple language of popular poetry, which constitutes both Suso's literary charm and his theological weakness,
from the point of view of strict orthodoxy. This translation of
scholastic ideas into the vernacular forced even the writer himself
out of his traditional groove; and here, from him, the ripple
broadened among the people. So Professor De Wulf, though he
insists that Eckhart *meant* in an orthodox sense, writes: "In this
way [Eckhart's teaching] contributed *indirectly* to that debasement
of religion which culminated in the Reformation"—in other
words, to the breakdown of conservatism in religion. Thus a
mystical movement is always followed by a freethought movement, through the impulse it gives to individualism.

From these Continental examples, which form a necessary introduction, we may pass on to one English life which illustrates,
better perhaps than any exposition of doctrines, the individualism
which is essential to mysticism. The Church had become too
strictly collectivist. Since John XXII (d. 1334), it had become
a heresy and a matter for burning that Franciscans should wear
the kind of garment they might want to wear. Therefore minds
of strong individuality escaped from this into the mystic life,
where they could breathe freely apart from that all-controlling
influence of the official clergy; a life strongly unsacerdotal, though
not as yet antisacerdotal.

For Richard Rolle of Hampole (d. 1349) we possess, fortunately,
a biography written in view of his canonization.[4] He was born
in the diocese of York, and sent to Oxford at the expense of
Thos. Neville, Archdeacon of Durham. His interests there were
mainly theological; but at the age of eighteen he felt the hollow-
ness of the world, and came home. Here began a career of which
we must not measure the eccentricity by modern standards only.
Rolle begged of his sister, to whom he was united by close
affection, her white and grey frocks. "When therefore he had
taken them, he forthwith amputated the sleeves of the grey one,
and cut off the buttons from the white one, and sewed together

as best he could the sleeves of the white tunic, so that they might be to some extent adapted to his purpose. Then he put off his own garments and put on the white frock next his skin; over which he put the grey frock with the amputated sleeves, thrusting his arms through the holes which this amputation had made; then he drew over all this a rain-cloak [with hood]; in order that to some extent, after his own fashion, he might shape himself roughly into the likeness of an hermit, so far as was possible at that moment. When his sister saw this she was filled with amazement, and cried: 'My brother is gone mad, my brother is gone mad!' At which words he drove her from him with threatening gestures, and fled forthwith without delay, lest his friends and acquaintance should lay hands on him." Thence Rolle went into a neighbouring church, and was found absorbed in prayer in Lady de Dalton's pew; this is perhaps our earliest documentary notice of a private pew in an English church. She came in to Vespers; her servants would have turned him out; but she "of her humility" would not suffer this man's prayers to be interrupted. When, after Vespers, she arose from prayer, then her sons, who were Oxford men, cried: "Why, this is the son of William Rolle! we knew him at Oxford." Next day (which was the Assumption of the Blessed Virgin Mary), unauthorized and uninvited, he put on a surplice and helped in the services of Matins and Mass; this he might legally do, having received clerical tonsure as an Oxford undergraduate. But then, at sermon-time, having asked first the priest's blessing, he got up into the pulpit, and preached to the rapture and amazement of the whole congregation. Sir John de Dalton, examining him privately and satisfying himself of his sanity, gave him a proper hermit's dress, and a cell for his abode. Thenceforward we sometimes find him wandering abroad and preaching: but on the whole it may be said that he spent the rest of his life in ascetic exercises and contemplation, with religious talk or writing, in this and other hermitages. His writings are philosophically less original than those of the rest whom I have mentioned, and certainly less scholastic: he constantly sneers at the learning of the schools. What external influence he had was probably derived, through Anglo-Norman religious poems, from the Parisian school of St-Victor. We see in him a lovable, loving man entirely absorbed in religion, but with neither the force of Eckhart nor the poetry and passion of St Catharine of Siena. His mind (must we say?)

was as well meaning, but scarcely more orderly than that hermit's dress made out of the two frocks. Yet his emotional and poetic mysticism, and his commentaries on the Psalter, became popular among monks and recluses, if we may judge from the preponderance of surviving copies from monastic libraries. The Austin Canon Walter Hilton [d. 1395] is more nearly parallel to the great Continental mystics; his *Scale of Perfection* became and remained a devotional classic second only in popularity to the *Imitatio*: he "is perhaps, in his mingled practical and transcendental teaching, the most typical mystic of the English school", which everywhere laid far more stress on devotion than on philosophy.[5] The anchorite Juliana of Norwich [1343–1413] was the first English

Lynn Town Hall.

literary woman known to us. Again, it was for a recluse that an anonymous author of the same time wrote *The Cloud of Unknowing*, whose popularity is attested by numerous surviving MSS., and whose literary and pietistic merit is remarkable. Margery Kempe of Lynn, who was thought to have been a recluse when only a small fragment of her book was known, is now discovered to have been something very different. As a middle-aged and then as an elderly married woman, she was even more unconventional than the youthful Rolle. For years she led the life of a religious tramp, bearding bishops and allowing herself many eccentricities which, in conjunction with her puritan objection to swearing and lying, brought her more than once into serious suspicion of Lollardy. Her autobiography should be read by all who are curious to explore the byways of Chaucer's England.[6] One passage may be quoted for its close concordance with the world-outlook, almost at the same moment, of Langland in his cot on Cornhill and St Bernardino in his mission work throughout Tuscany. Margery, when once she had been converted from a worldly past of which she writes with Bunyan-like repentance, spent all the rest of her life "with great sobbings and sighings after the bliss of heaven...so much, that she could not well restrain herself from speaking thereof; for wherever she was in any company she would say oftentimes: 'It is full merry in heaven!' And they that knew her behaviour beforetime, and now heard her speaking so much of the bliss of heaven, said to her: 'Why speak ye so of the mirth that is in heaven? Ye know it not, and ye have not been there, any more than we.' And were wroth with her; for she would not hear nor speak of worldly things as they did, and as she did aforetime." So also Langland and St Bernardino were troubled by those who believed in nothing higher than the roof of their own house. We must go back beyond the dawn of history if we wish to find an age in which the sensitive soul did not say "man is born to trouble as the sparks fly upward", and the careless did not reply "let us eat and drink, for to-morrow we die".

Almost as interesting from an-other point of view is Rulman Merswin (1307–82), the rich and patrician banker of Strassburg. Converted late in life, he devoted his fortune to founding a religious community, and pleaded strongly (as Nicholas Lyranus had pleaded with more hesitation a generation earlier) that heaven must somehow be opened to good Jews, of whom

St Margaret's, Lynn.

he had doubtless met many in his business career. There is possibly some significance in the facts that two English writers, Langland and Juliana of Norwich, were also specially concerned with the same problem of Jewish or heathen salvation, and that St Thomas More inclined also towards the merciful side. This contrasted strongly with the ordinary orthodox view, as expressed by the Austin Canon Mannyng of Bourne. He complains, in his popular didactic poem of *Handlyng Synne* (E.E.T.S. 1901, p. 298), that not only some "lewd folk" but, what is more to be deplored, some priests say of the Jews "we wot not whether they be saved or no". He writes: "certes they are all in error, and in the faith they are not clear; for shall never Jew that dieth Jew of heaven bliss have part nor proof, but he be christened in the Holy Ghost, and in the sacrament be full steadfast." I have quoted this at far greater length in *Social Life in Britain* (pp. 47 ff.).

We may trace, therefore, two more or less distinct currents of mysticism. First, the older school of St Bernard and the Augustinian Canons of St-Victor outside the walls of Paris. This school found its continuation in the *Deutsch Theologia* (a sort of *Imitatio Christi* which strongly influenced Luther), in the Parisian Chancellor Jean Gerson, and finally in Thomas à Kempis. It is marked by docility, regularity and loyalty to the old ways; but it had much of that broad and unsectarian feeling characteristic of mystics in general, among whom we may often read whole pages without meeting any proof that the author is Christian or Mohammedan, Buddhist or Hindu. Again, there was the younger mysticism of the friars, as shown in the Fraticelli and the Dominicans from Eckhart onwards; men who struck out a line so bold as to promise a conflict with conservatism. Intermediate between those we may put Cardinal Nicholas Cusanus (d. 1464), who combined very wide reading and bold speculation with the most zealously loyal intentions. He was deeply influenced by Eckhart; and, as De Wulf confesses: "We may say of him as of Eckhart, that he preserved his orthodoxy only at the expense of his logic." He was accused of teaching the identity of the Creator and Creation by one of his contemporaries; and a century later Giordano Bruno's bold and outspoken pantheism was avowedly based on the "divino Cusano". The cardinal himself, however, pressed negative arguments only in order to arrive at positive results. And when, in 1453, all Europe was dismayed at the fall of Constantinople, Cusanus took this as his text for toleration in religion (*Dialogus de Pace*). Christianity (he pleaded) is the supreme religion, but in all we may find some rays of the Eternal Truth; let men therefore live at peace one with another. We have here, perhaps, the furthest point at which medieval orthodoxy ever arrived in pursuit of that thesis sentimentally defended by Rulman Merswin and Langland, with some slender and vague support from the Schoolmen, that God must somehow find a way of His own for bringing the good Jew or pagan to heaven.[7]

In these mystical movements we may trace that steady stream of religiosity among layfolk which Professor R. W. Chambers has so admirably brought out, on its literary side, in his *Continuity of English Prose.* Georges de Lagarde, again, has described it with great penetration and sympathy, laying stress upon its pathetic striving in the thirteenth and fourteenth centuries for a true return to the Apostolic Age, and its significance as a presage of religious revolution in the sixteenth.[8]

This is the natural point at which to deal with a subject not directly mystical, yet closely allied: namely, the influence of the friars on popular thought, and especially that of the Franciscans.

It cannot be a mere chance that Innocent III, who in 1209 (or 1210) had authorized St Francis's venture among the poor, not without great searchings of heart, should have taken advantage of the great Lateran Council in 1215 to strive for a higher standard of religious education in the parishes. Other forces were at work simultaneously; but certainly there was a remarkable movement round about the turn of the twelfth century. All through the thirteenth, we find an increasing flood of popular religious works, competing as directly with the ordinary minstrel—the writers' own prefaces sometimes tell us this explicitly—as modern religion has begun to compete with the picture-palace. St Francis had told his disciples to be God's gleemen—*joculatores Dei.* He himself is recorded to have preached one of his most remarkable sermons from the text of a French love-song: and one of his early disciples, Brother Henry of Pisa, resolved that "the Devil should not have all the best tunes", and turned current love-songs into hymns. Again and again, men not only composed manuals to aid the popular preacher with skeletons of subjects and hints of style, but collected also *The Alphabet of Tales*, *The Mirror of the Unlearned*, and scores of similar compilations of anecdotes for pulpit use. To Dante, this system had already become wearisome in its exaggerations; and Chaucer's contemporary, the Dante-commentator Benvenuto da Imola, echoed his master's condemnation of "the fables that are proclaimed yearly from the pulpit on this side and on that".[9] But this, however regrettable in theology, was on the whole advantageous for literature. Whatever style the friars encouraged, it was certainly not, until in their decadence they became wearisome, that one style for which, according to Voltaire, there is nothing to be said—the *genre ennuyeux*. And here, just about the year 1200, we have in English literature perhaps the best example in Europe.

The book *Ormulum* was so named by its author Orm, a priest
and monk. He set himself to remedy the scandal that the laity
scarcely ever understood a single word of the Gospel recited at
Mass: even St Francis, with his native Italian to help him and his
familiarity with the most educated class in one of the most cultured
regions of Europe, understood the Mass-Gospel only "to some
extent". Therefore (writes Orm):

> I here have turnëd into English gospel's holy lore....
> If English folk, for love of Christ, it wouldë gladly leernen...
> This have I into English turnëd for their soulës needë;
> And, if they cast it all away, it turneth them to sin.

His version is in rhymeless lines of invariable accuracy, 8 and 7
syllables to the line and 15 to the couplet; perhaps he counted them
on his fingers, like Milton's friend. He has his own orthography,
denoting a short syllable by a double consonant. He undertook
to translate all the 52 Sunday Gospels, with a brief patristic exposition of each; this would have taken him at least 80,000 lines. But
this unique MS. contains only 10,000; evidently he never lived
to finish it; and there is no trace elsewhere of his peculiar spelling.
I print a specimen textually in the notes; here, it is more convenient
to modernize.

Matthew iv. 1, 2 runs as follows in the late fourteenth-century
version printed by Miss Paues: "Then Jesus was led into the
desert through a spirit, there he should be tempted of the devil;
and, when he had fasted forty days and forty nights, afterwards
he hungred."

In *Ormulum*, this runs to 16 lines, nearly three times as many
syllables:[10]

> Forthright so Jesus baptized was
>   He went him into wastë
> The Gospel saith that he was led
>   Through Ghost into the wastë,
> And that, for that he shouldë there
>   Be tempted through the devil.
> And Christ remained in wastë land
>   For that he wouldë fasten;
> And he took then to fasten there
>   As he was in the wastë.
> And all withouten meat and drink
>   Held Christ his fastë there

For forty dayës all on end,
  By dayës and by nightës;
And when his fastë ended was,
  Then lusted he for foodë.

In comparison with that, let us take St Francis's Sermon to the Birds, or indeed any other chapter at random from the *Little Flowers*, or the *Mirror of Perfection*. There, with but little actual quotation from the Gospel, is the true Gospel spirit: yet here, in *Ormulum*, for all this monk's pains to give us the full Gospel words, the thing is as dead as any good and well-meaning man could make it. It has the chill, the stuffiness of a cell, while the early Franciscan records have all the freshness of the open air. Nor need we to go to Italy for the contrast: we may take the *Luve Ron* of Friar Thomas of Hales, definitely later than Orm, but not so very much later.[11] A girl had asked him to write her a love-poem for Christ, and he started from the reminder of the perishableness of earthly glory:

Where is Paris and Heleyne
  That weren as bright and fair to see?
Amadis, Tristram, and Dideyne,
  Yseult, and allë they?
Hector, with his sharpë mien
  And Caesar, rich of worldës fee?
They be y-gliden out of the reign
  As the sheaf is from the clee.

So we may probably interpret that somewhat obscure last line, remembering how *clee* is a still common word in Shropshire, for instance, for *hill*: "The Reaper Death has gathered all the great folk, and left the hillside bare."

Nor was the impulse given to art less noteworthy than this new spirit in literature. In Italy, the great new friars' churches, preaching-halls with almost unlimited wall-space, invited painting on a hitherto unwonted scale. At the same time, the new and brilliant mass of legends—here, again, especially the Franciscan, definitely more naïve and picturesque than the Dominican—challenged the painter and sculptor, while they left him a free hand; for here were no formal traditions or time-honoured conventions that he was professionally bound to follow. If in England the change was not so great as in Italy—for our own friars' churches were not quite so different in style from their predecessors—yet at least there were a considerable number of new buildings and, especially, a greater profusion of stained glass. The author of *Piers the Ploughman's Crede* notes this in the typical Franciscan church of Chaucer's time:[12]

> With windows well y-wrought, and wallës well high,
> That must be portray'd and painted and polished full clean
> With gay glittering glass, glowing as the sun

in which the generous donor shall see his own figure kneeling before Christ,

> And Saint Francis himself shall folden thee in his cope,
> And present thee to the Trinity, and pray for thy sinnes.

In the Dominican church, again,

> Wide windows y-wrought, y-written full thick,
> Shinen with shapen shields to shewen about,
> With markës of merchants y-mingled between,
> More than twenty and two twice y-numbered,
> There is none herald that hath half such a roll.

While even the refectory has "windows of glass, wrought as a church".

So, again, in *Piers Plowman* itself, the friar pleads with the rich lady:

> We have a window a working, will stand us full high;
> Would ye glaze the gable, and grave there your name,
> In Mass and in Matins for meed we should sing
> Suddenly and soothly, as for a sister of our Order.[13]

Every considerable town, almost, had its friary, and many, like Cambridge and Lynn and Norwich, had all four orders. Nearly all the surviving Dooms, vivid and compelling representations of the Last Judgment at the west end of a cathedral or over the chancel-arch of a parish church, date from after the coming of the friars. And, as already hinted, the *Hundred Meditations* of St Bonaventura's Franciscan disciple inspired not only paintings and carvings but still more, perhaps, the religious stage. There was thus a crescendo of action and interaction. The player caught sparks from the artist and the artist from the player, until both had reached the fullest development that was possible on the traditional medieval lines; and then the Renaissance, with its greater freedom from gild conventions, was welcomed alike by the artists and by their public. What killed Gothic art was not the Reformation, but a gradual change in the whole world-outlook, and the inextinguishable love of novelty in the human mind. All through the Middle Ages, the artist had worked not only in the creative spirit, but also in that competitive and destructive mood which will never be completely separated from the instinct to express one's own individuality. Splendid thirteenth-century work was destroyed to make room for the new fashions of the fifteenth: more than half of the Romanesque windows in our cathedrals have been broken away for the insertion of Perpendicular tracery. At the Renaissance, already before 1500, classical details were becoming fashionable in England; and this invasion was far completer on the Continent. The amount of Gothic architecture destroyed at the Dissolution of our monasteries was less considerable than that which had been destroyed in consistently Roman Catholic countries like France and Austria, even before the French Revolution. Westminster and Canterbury, Durham and Norwich and Ely, show incomparably more of the medieval monastic architecture than those Continental abbeys of which some are still the greatest in the Western World—St-Denis, Cluny, Marmoutier, Fulda, Melk, Farfa or Monte Cassino.

Whence, on the verge of the Reformation, a German sympathizer with the land-toilers quoted Christ's words in John xv. 1: "My Father is [a] husbandman", he had been anticipated in the spirit of that theme, generations earlier, by our English Langland in his *Piers Plowman*.

This poem has come down to us in three versions, labelled by scholars as A, B and C. Each can be dated fairly exactly by its historical allusions. A was written not earlier than 1362 or 1363; B was continued, patched and padded out, not earlier than 1377; and C was patched and padded again, possibly as early as 1393, more probably about 1398 or 1399. The manuscripts give no hint of multiple authorship, and there is a strong similarity of style between all three versions. Thus the natural assumption is that all are by the same author; and this is strengthened by the fact that wherever the author speaks of himself these separate allusions are consistent with each other. Moreover, in one manuscript of the fifteenth century the authorship is definitely ascribed to one William Langland; and this manuscript contains the full, or "C" text. Therefore, although distinguished scholars have lately ascribed the poem, in the state in which we have it, to five different authors, the weight of authority is at present in favour of the conservative view; and, in any case, for the purpose of this present chapter it matters little whether we owe the poem to one single man or to such a like-minded group as, for instance, Carlyle, Emerson and Ruskin.

The poem entitles itself "The Vision of William Concerning Piers the Plowman". Who then was William, and who was Piers Plowman? The second question is the easier to answer. He is, in the first place, the working man who gives that plain answer to the riddle of life which the official Church and State had failed to give; the man who guides Humanity to the shrine of Saint Truth. In brief, we may describe him as Carlyle's Peasant Saint. Thence, by an evolution very similar to that of Beatrice in Dante's poem, this Plowman stands for Humanity at its simplest and truest and highest; that is, for the human nature of Jesus Christ. Thence again, by a transition almost inevitable in the Middle Ages, Piers Plowman stands for Christ's successors, Peter and the

Popes. The identity of William (or, as he calls himself in the poem, "Long Will") seems a good deal clearer now through the researches of Canon Bannister, Mr A. H. Bright and Professor R. W. Chambers. He was the son (as one manuscript tells us) of Eustace de Rokayle, and his home was Ledbury, under the Malvern hills. He may well have taken his name from the farm of Longlands in the neighbouring village of Colwall; and he was probably illegitimate, the son of a peasant girl, and therefore born in bondage. It is significant that in the "C" text we find an alteration which confesses that Holy Church made him a free man, the most natural interpretation of which would be that his clerical orders brought about his legal emancipation. He had influential friends, who died in youth; we know, in fact, that Eustace de Rokayle, tenant of Hugh Despenser, died in 1349, when Langland would have been just emerging from his teens. His relatives refused the help he had expected from them, and it is quite possible that our Long Will may be that William of Colwall who was ordained to the lower clerical orders in 1348. He was unsuited for field-work. He tells us that his long figure makes it difficult for him to stoop. He got some help from a neighbour, very likely Sir James of Brodibury; and, after a year of suffering through famine on the countryside (1354 and 1355 were such years), he drifted off to London. But the poem, naturally enough, contains many allusions, direct or indirect, to his native Malvern.

Thus he would be an older contemporary of Chaucer, and his life would fill roughly the years 1330–1400. The Black Death of 1349 would naturally account for his lack of friends as he grew into manhood; and he looks back regretfully not only to misfortunes in his youth, not only to lost chances, but to wasted opportunities also. His conscience tells him "thou wert lief for to learn, but loth for to study". He had very likely begun as choir-boy or charity-boy at a monastic school: there was one priory at Little Malvern just over the hill from Colwall, and another, much more important, at Great Malvern. We find him writing:[1]

> For if heaven be on this earth, or ease to any soul
> It is in cloister or in school, by many skills I find.
> For in cloister cometh no man to chide nor to fight,
> But all is buxomness there and books, to read and to learn;
> And great love and liking; for each of them loveth other.*

* Throughout this chapter I abridge and modernize freely in order to avoid frequent explanations. Buxom (German *beugsam*) means "pliable", "obedient".

A sentiment which need be none the less sincere for being borrowed from Peter of Blois (Ep. XII, *ad fin.*).

Of course *school*, in this passage, includes university as well as grammar school. The reality of medieval university life, as we have seen, was less idyllic than this: Oxford High Street is, in fact, one of the minor battlefields of history. But this yearning idealism would be natural enough in a man who had lost his own early chances, and who wrote like Charles Lamb, "defrauded in his young years of the sweet food of an academic institution". The monastery, also, was often less idyllic, as Langland shows us in the very same passage from which I have quoted. There he goes on to describe the monks of his later life as habitual breakers of their own Rule, careless of the poor, and even of their own churches, where they allowed the rain to drip through the roof upon the altar; and this leads him to a prophecy which, after the great religious revolution, enthusiastic Protestants seized upon as inspired:

> But there shall come a king, and confess you monks and nuns,
> And beat you, as the Bible telleth, for breaking of your Rule;
> And then shall the Abbot of Abingdon, and all his issue for ever,
> Have a knock of a king, and incurable the wound.[2]

Those, however, were the monks of his later life: those of his youth had been better. He describes their discipline as not unreal.[3] He is far more tender to the monks than to the nuns or friars. We may take it that he had learnt religion in his youth from men who deserved the title of Religious; that he might claim to have seen with his eyes and to have handled with his hands true Christianity, after which mere shallow scepticism was impossible. We see in him a man profoundly disillusioned, yet thoroughly religious; and, in spite of the claim of later enthusiastic reformers, he hated the Lollards of his own day as much as he did the imperfect clergy.

But (he writes) "Fortune failed me at my most need"; and he is now living "in London and on London both", in a cot on Cornhill. It needs much imagination to imagine a thatched hovel on that spot; but there it was that Langland dwelt nearly six centuries ago, with Kitte his wife and Kalote his daughter. He was a cleric in lower orders; "The tools that I work with", he says, "are *Dirige* and *Placebo*." Those were the opening words of the anthems for Matins and Evensong respectively at a funeral service; our modern *dirge* is simply a corruption of *dirige*. Such recitations at funeral services for the souls of departed kinsfolk were open to all clerks in lower orders; and his contemporaries knew perfectly well from this confession that he was one of the multitude who eked out a more or less scanty existence by all kinds of small clerical jobs. He describes himself as a mere educated beggar, rewarded commonly by a meal in the kitchen; "my bag is my belly"; yet he is rich in precious experience of life. Over and over again, some phrase or single word testifies to a past heart-ache. He might have said of his own heart, as George Herbert said of his, how in the cauldron of Christ's blood

> It was dipt and dyed,
> And washed and wrung; the very wringing yet
> Enforceth tears.

Knowledge, he tells us, comes through suffering. The high road to learning runs through the gate of "suffer both well and woe"; and if we would stand like God, above all earthly changes, then we must first learn "to see much and suffer more".

> "Who suffereth more than God?" quoth [Reason]: "No person,
>   I believe"...
> "To see much and suffer more, certes", quoth I, "is Do-Well."[4]

His best successes had come from failures rightly taken. He laments his youth gone, his money lost, his friends dead or estranged, and perhaps some dearer losses still; but he knows that he has gained the pearl of price. For (as he says to Conscience who is examining him)

> ...I confess
> That I have lost time, and time misspended—
> And yet I hope, as he that oftentimes hath traded
> And ever hath lost and lost, till at last, by some good hap,
> He bought such a bargain that he was better for ever—
> For the Kingdom of Heaven is like to a treasure hid in a field—
> So hope I to have some day, of God the Lord Almighty,
> A gobbet of His grace, and so to begin a time
> That all times of my time to profit shall turn.[5]

Thus, his highest note of poetry comes from the struggles and failures of his life. The whole poem testifies to his love of beauty, to his lust of the eye. He is an enthusiastic and a curious observer of trees and flowers, beasts and birds, of the sights and sounds of the forest and the seashore; yet now from day to day he tramps the sordid streets of London. He hints at love in youth, and certainly he had a high ideal of marriage; but he confesses himself ill-mated. He loved learning; he was greedy of all writings and sciences, yet he was too poor to buy books or to pay for study. All this time, however, he goes on like Matthew Arnold's Scholar Gipsy—

> Still nursing the unconquerable hope,
> Still clutching the inviolable shade,

waiting always for "the spark from Heaven to fall", and at heaven-sent moments committing to paper stray scraps of his philosophy concerning this world and the next.[6]

The modern reader can scarcely realize how difficult it is to speak of an "edition" of any medieval book, or even of an "authentic text". After Professor J. M. Manly's exhaustive study of all the existing MSS. of Chaucer's *Canterbury Tales*, it is one of his most definite conclusions that there never was any one standard text, to the exclusion of variants. Authors often lent their writings piecemeal to friends; then patched them and altered, and lent them again to others who again copied them; so that the poet himself, confronted with the parallel texts printed by the Chaucer Society, would probably be unable to choose any one as representing accurately his final choice. If this was so with the comparatively wealthy and leisured Chaucer, how much more difficult was the task of authorship for Langland, a typical specimen of the "learned proletariat"? In his day, it would cost just about as much to get a respectable fair copy of a book made as, in our own, to print an edition of 500 copies. Thus it is natural enough that we should find, in *Piers Plowman*, an incoherence which constitutes the real difficulty of the poem, apart from the fact that the language itself approaches far less closely than Chaucer's to that of the Court and the City, and is therefore far less modern. In so far as we can condense Langland's message into a few words, we must sum it up as a long search for three degrees of excellence in life—Do Well, Do Better, and Do Best. In one passage he sums this up: *Learn* does well, *Teach* does better, *Love* does best of the three: we may express them in Latin as *Disce, Doce, Dilige*.[7] Yet, even after this summing-up, we have page after page of miscellaneous, and often confused, discussion. In short, this Vision of William concerning Piers the

Plowman presents a medley comparable to the six paper bags from which Carlyle professes to have selected his *Sartor Resartus*: scraps "ranging from metaphysical discussions to washing-bills and advertisements".

We may trace, in fact, a close resemblance between Langland and Carlyle, and a remarkable contrast between him and Chaucer. Chaucer was a well-to-do citizen, courtier and great poet; Langland had as violent an inferiority-complex as Carlyle. He tells us how he was reputed a madman for not reverencing "lords and ladies and persons in fur and silver". Chaucer, again, was fastidious; not only with the delicacy of the courtier, but with that of liberal and artistic culture to boot: he disliked crowds, and preferred to study man in the individual. Langland, on the other hand, loved a crowd, especially a London crowd, as heartily as Lamb did. Jusserand notes how his descriptions of multitudes are not only vivid, but characteristic: each of his crowds has an individuality of its own. Those differences of taste are symptoms of deeper mental divergences. Chaucer, with his interest in the individual, generally stops short of the deepest problems of humanity, or just studies them for a moment and dismisses them lightly as insoluble. Langland loved not only the man, but Humanity. "Christ on his Cross", he writes, "made us all blood-brethren"; and what interests him most in humanity is the vastness of the issues which depend on our brief, struggling, uncertain life of probation on earth. Chaucer took life as he found it. To him, the world was Vanity Fair in Thackeray's sense, and his moral was very much like Thackeray's: "Come, children, let us shut up the box and the puppets, for the play is played out." To Langland, it was Vanity Fair in Bunyan's sense—a place of continual struggle and real danger. He saw no possibility of taking the world as we find it. Rather, he nourished the perpetual question: "How can I leave it a better world?" Here, again, we may be reminded of Carlyle's "nay, by God, Donald, but we must help Him to mend it!" In short, Chaucer is so great a poet that he cannot help being a real moralist; and Langland is so intense in his moral convictions that he sometimes rises naturally to a true height of poetry. Even the most beautiful of his descriptions of nature (and he does show the keenest sense of the beauty, as well as the mystery, of this visible universe) leads him to ponder sadly, like Wordsworth, on "that which man hath made of man".

For instance:

> Birdës I beheld that in bushes madë nests,
> Had never wight wit to work the least.
> I had wonder at whom, and where, the pie learned
> To lay the sticks in which she layeth and breedeth;
> There is no wright, as I ween, should work her nest for pay;
> If any mason made a mold thereto, much wonder it were...
> But that most movëd me, and my mood changëd,
> That Reason rewarded and rulëd allë beastës
> Save man and his mate.[8]

He loved sweet sights and sounds as much (if we dare say so) as Chaucer; yet, above all and beyond all, he was haunted by a sense of sweeter harmonies unheard, fairer visions unseen, greater realities unrealized. Even more than Dante he was possessed with the conviction, so widespread among thoughtful men in the thirteenth and fourteenth centuries, that the world was morally and religiously bankrupt, and drawing fast to its end. To him the City of God is already in flames; flames which cast their lurid glare upon every human face he sees—a conflagration which forms the perpetual background of all our life—so that our slightest actions and most insignificant gestures cast shadows which stretch up to the very stars. Here we have no abiding City; this is the City of Destruction. We cannot flee from it altogether, as Bunyan did; yet at least let us flee from the destruction that is in it. We may fairly compare Langland also with the Samuel Butler of our own day: no ascetic, but a born rebel; a man waging irreconcilable warfare with everything that cannot justify itself, either by truth in fact or by truth to social morality; a man who did not care how much he contradicted himself, so long as he could keep his own standpoint in constant contradiction to that which he felt to be false, whether intellectually or morally: wayward, paradoxical, impossible for an absolute guide, but most stimulating in all that he has to tell us.

To have mentioned Langland even for a moment in the same breath as Dante may be felt to require some justification. Superficially, perhaps, it is rather a contrast than a comparison. Dante's great poem has all the characteristics of a cathedral like Amiens or Salisbury, wonderfully complete in conception, harmonious in execution, and elaborate in detail; in a sense he may be said to have put all Scholasticism into his poetry. Langland, on the other hand, worked only by scraps and patches. We could have guessed that, even though he had never confessed it; and his nature is as essentially English as Dante's is Latin. He is far less anxious for the harmony of his whole than for truth of detail. He struggles less to frame a whole working theory of the universe than to drive home those truths of which he does feel absolutely certain, leaving the reader to co-ordinate as best he may. Yet in one essential point the two stand out unsurpassed in medieval poetry. Carlyle said of the *Commedia*, "at bottom, this is the sincerest of poems". Langland, though immensely inferior in learning and art, yet, like Dante, put his whole life into his poem; at every word the pen was dipped in his heart's blood. Thus, all through, he was mainly concerned to hammer in, with almost wearisome repetition, the truths of which he himself was most convinced. Over and over again he recurs to three main points; the dignity of Poverty; the paramount importance of Truth; the everlasting significance of Christ's sacrifice for mankind.

Poverty, because he himself was poor. As Carlyle says of Luther: "I find it altogether suitable to his function in this earth... that he was born poor and brought up poor, one of the poorest of men." Langland has the deepest pity for "prisoners in pits and poor folk in cottages, Charged with children and with chief lord's rent". "The poor", he says, "are God's minstrels";[9] and, again:

> ...Jesus Christ of Heaven
> In a poor man's apparel pursueth us ever...
> For on Calvary of Christ's blood Christendom gan spring
> And brethren we became there in blood, and gentlemen each one.[10]

If sometimes he seems to be praising the poor for mere poverty's sake, he never leaves us long in doubt. He always reminds us that those whom he admires are the good poor, the good maimed and halt: these men "have their purgatory here on earth".[11] He seems out of sympathy with the Peasants' Revolt of his time, and with negative rather than constructive levelling socialisms;[12] yet his hero, his saint, is the perfect peasant.

As to *Truth*, he repeats three times in different places his own motto: "When all treasures are tried, Truth is the best." Truth, indeed, is God Almighty, Lord of Heaven and earth

> For he is father of faith, and formëd you all,
> Both with fell and with face, and gave you fivë wits
> For to worship Him therewith the while that ye be here.

Therefore Truth is the highest shrine and goal of our pilgrimage here on earth. In one of the earliest and most striking
scenes of the poem, he describes men as awakened to sin by the
scourge of plagues and wars, a multitude crying to God *Who shall
show us Truth?* "blustering forth as beasts", and helpless to find
their way. Then suddenly upon the scene comes the professional
religious wanderer, his hat garnished with such pilgrim-tokens
as we may still buy in facsimile at Canterbury, tokens from Rome
and Jerusalem and St James of Compostela. The pilgrims seize
eagerly upon this man: "Where is the shrine of Saint Truth?"
The professional shakes his head; that is a saint he has never heard
of. Suddenly, at this moment, a plowman puts up his head from
behind a hedge; and this is our Peter, our hero, who, first in his
simple peasant form and then as Christ and the Popes, will accompany us throughout the rest of the poem.[13] Piers is ready to guide
men to this shrine; but that simple monosyllable, Truth, the
moment we attempt to realize it, is found to contain the most
complicated ideas. "What is truth? said jesting Pilate." How can
we of the fourteenth century reconcile the facts of life with the
Church's dogma, which itself is so inescapable a fact in our lives?
How can we reconcile the doctrine of Papal Indulgences with the
Gospel doctrine that men will be judged according to their fruits?
How can we reconcile the good lives of many Jews and pagans
with the strictness with which the Church excludes almost all
of them from God's mercies? How (deeper still) can we reconcile
the origin of evil with God's goodness, and predestination with
freewill? It is all these difficulties that bring us to our third point,
the author's emphasis on Christ's Redemption.

For, after all these innumerable disquisitions, he always recurs
to that subject. Confessing the weakness of theology and philosophy, he falls back on plainer and more practical points; above
all, on that wherein he finds the breadth and height of all theory,
with the solidity and stability of all practice; the *Life and Passion
of Jesus Christ*. Over and over again, with growing emphasis as
the poem proceeds, and as his metaphysical discussions bring
him back to the old insoluble problems, he recurs to this plain
point, and on that high note he ends.

We may trace this evolution in a bird's-eye view of the whole
poem. The author first falls asleep on Malvern hills and dreams
of a Field Full of Folk; he contemplates that wide eastward view,

almost unrivalled in England, which stretches to Edgehill. Hard by, he sees a Castle on a Cliff, and a Den in the Dale, answering exactly to Eastnor Castle on the high ground and that other of which nothing but the moat now remains in the swampy flat under the Herefordshire Beacon. There it is that Langland sees these swarming multitudes; high and low, good and bad; a medley ending with a living picture of a London crowd, with its cries of the cooks and the taverners who would stampede us in to eat and drink. What is the meaning of this Castle on the Cliff and this Den in the Dale? A fair and noble lady, clad in white linen, comes down and tells him:

> Son, seest thou this people...?
> The most part of this people that passeth on this earth,
> If they have worship in this world, they want no better;
> Of other heaven than here take they no tale.[14]

The Castle (she says) is the abode of Truth, God's Castle; this Dungeon is the Devil's, wherein he holds the wicked as his prisoners. It is very probable that Bunyan had read Langland, or at least heard tales from him, and that we here have the original of Giant Despair and Doubting Castle. But, to continue:

> Then had I wonder in my wit what woman it was
> That such wise words of holy writ shewed,
> And asked her by the High Name, ere she thence went
> What she were certainly, that taught me so fair?
> "Holy Church I am", quoth she, "thou oughtest me to know,
> I fondled thee first in my arms *and the faith* taught,*
> And thou broughtest me pledges, my bidding to fulfil
> And to love me loyally while thy life endureth."
> Then I bent on my knees, and cried her of grace,
> And prayed her piteously pray for my sins,
> And also lead me truly on Christ to believe,
> That I might work His will, that wrought me to be man,
> "Teach me to no treasure, but tell me this same thing
> How I may save my soul, for sacred are thy words."
> "When all treasures are tried", quoth she, "Truth is the best;
> It is as precious a prize as dear God himself.
> Whoso is true of his tongue, and telleth nought but that,
> And doeth the works therewith, and willeth no man ill,
> He is a god, by the gospel, aground and aloft
> And alike to our Lord, by St Luke's words:
> *My mother and my brethren are they that keep the word of God.*"[15]

* The "C" text here reads: "And free thee made."

Then, if Truth be God, will not Holy Church help the dreamer to distinguish true from false?

> "Look upon thy left side, and to where they stand!
> Falsehood and Flattery, and many more their friends."
> I lookëd there to my left side, as the lady said,
> And there was I ware of a woman in rich and royal weed.
> Crownëd with a coronet, no better hath the King,
> Her fingers rich with rubies, as red as burning coals.
> Her array ravished me; such richness saw I never;
> I wondered what she was, and whose wife she were.[16]

This, says Holy Church, is Lady Meed; that is, Reward, a word constantly used in the evil sense of ill-gotten gains and bribery. Lady Meed, in fact, is the medieval Almighty Dollar; she and her friends rule the world.

Then Langland sleeps and dreams again. In this second dream, things seem a little better. All the Seven Deadly Sins confess and repent—a splendid series of pictures for our satirist. They want to live well for the future—to live according to Truth. But where is Truth? Here it is that the professional pilgrim and Piers Plowman crop up. That man, in the strength of his fifty years of honest work and faith in God, undertakes to guide the multitude to Heaven. All want his guidance, lords and ladies, lawyers and labourers; and presently Piers gets a "pardon", an Indulgence, straight from God, like the Pope's own.[17] A priest here intervenes:

> "Piers," quoth a priest then, "thy pardon must I read,
> For I will construe each clause and teach it thee in English."
> And Piers at his prayer the pardon unfoldeth,
> And I, behind them both, beheld all the bull.
> All in two lines it lay, and naught a leaf more,
> And was written right thus in witness of truth
> *And those who have done good will go into eternal life*
> *But those who have done evil will go into everlasting fire.*
> "Peter!" quoth the priest then, "I can no pardon find
> But 'do well and have well, and God shall have thy soul,
> And do evil and have evil, hope thou none other
> [But] after thy death-day, the devil shall have thy soul!'"
> And Piers for pure pain pullëd it in twain
> And said, *Though I walk through the valley of the shadow of death,*
> *I will fear no evil, for thou art with me. . . .*
> The priest and Perkyn opposed one another,
> And I through their words awoke, and waited about...
> Meatless and moneyless on Malvern hills,
> Musing on this dream of mine; and my way I went.

Many times this dream hath made me to study
Of that I saw sleeping, if it so be might,
And also for Piers the Plowman full pensive in heart,
And which a pardon Piers had, all the people to comfort,
And how the priest impugnëd it with two proper words...
And how the priest proved no pardon to Do-Well.
Yet deemed I that Do-Well Indulgences passeth...
And passeth all the pardon of St Peter's Church.
Now hath the pope power, pardon to grant the people
Withouten any penance to passen into heaven;
This is our belief, as lettered men us teacheth
Whatsoever thou shalt bind on earth shall be bound in heaven, etc.,
And so believe I loyally, (Lord forbid else!)
That pardon and penance and prayers do save
Souls that have sinned sevenfold and deadly.
But to trust to these pardons, truly me thinketh,
Is naught so sure for the soul, certës, as is Do-Well.
Wherefore counsel I you that be rich on this earth,
Upon trust of your treasure pardons to have
Be ye never the bolder to break the Ten Commands.
And specially ye masters, mayors and judges
That have the wealth of this world, and for wise men be holden
To purchase you pardon and the pope's bulls!
At the dreadful doom, when the dead shall arise
And comen all before Christ, their accounts for to yield.
How thou leddest thy life here and His laws keptest,
And how thou didest day by day, the doom will rehearse;
A pocketful of pardons then, nor Provincials' letters,
Though ye be found in the fraternity of all the four Orders [of friars]
And have Indulgences double-fold, but if Do-Well you help
I set your patents and your pardons at one pie's heel.

This was, indeed, as serious a problem in Langland's day as in our own. Henry of Ghent (d. 1293) was one of the greatest philosophers of his age. Just a century before Langland expressed those difficulties, he was saying much the same in his own academic language. In the 15th of his *Quodlibeta*, or General Discussions, he considers the question "Whether Indulgences may be taken at their face value": *Utrum Indulgentiae Praelatorum tantum valeant quantum sonant.* Must we really believe (he asks) that, so long as the recipient is contrite and confessed, an Indulgence of 40 days (for instance) is worth exactly the same to a worse man as to a better? Some men argue that there is a real difference in those two cases; that this pardon means more to the worthier recipient, but that the Church offers the same face value to both. Thus "by a certain pious fraud, she preaches to all men a greater value than [such pardons] have for many men, in order that she may thus attract them to earn at least somewhat of the Indulgences". This, he feels, is a pernicious doctrine. He admits that Indulgences are nowhere explicitly mentioned in the Bible, but feels that, the system having grown up in the Church, "we must firmly believe that Christ conferred general powers on this head, even though [the prelates] have received none in special words". Some doctors, comparing the Pope's power with that absolute authority wielded by the Emperors of Rome, argue for the absolute face value of everything that they grant. Thus, even "if the prelates so inordinately remit the penalties due to sin, or so lavish their Indulgences, that men set such trust in these abundantly and easily earned Indulgences as to be altogether called away from works of penance, satisfaction, and mercy, yet that which they [the prelates] remit is remitted before the face of God, and that which they indulge is in fact indulged, and this without any work being enjoined [upon the penitent]; or if some trifling work be enjoined which tendeth not to the honour of God or the profit of the Church; as, for instance, if the Pope should say to a man: 'Pick up that blade of straw from the earth, and, of the plenitude of Our power, We remit or indulge unto thee all penalties due for thy sins, whereunto thou art bound to God'." To this Henry answers: "Whether that be so, God knoweth: I know not"; and we may well understand how our English scholar-tramp Langland could more easily state than resolve so knotty a problem.[18]

Here, then, is a climax; and at this point comes the great change of scene upon which, together with other reasons, some critics would base a change of authorship. Yet the break here is really no greater than what we have already seen after Lady Meed's marriage; and the remainder of the poem still maintains its earlier character. It tells of the long search after Dowel, Dobet,* Dobest. We now have a series of religious disquisitions, all sorts of problems with very little formal answer. The poem itself, indeed, admirably exemplifies what the author cites as one of the characteristics of his own day:

> I have heard high men eating at table
> Carping, as they clerkës were, of Christ and of His mights
> And lay faults upon the Father that formëd us all....

* *Bet* is the true English comparative of *well*: our modern *better* is a pleonasm, like *worser*.

> "Why would our Saviour suffer such a worm in his bliss,
> That beguilëd the woman, and the man after...?
> Why should we, that now live, for the works of Adam
> Rot or suffer torment? reason would it never."
> Such motives they move, these masters in their glory,
> And maken men to disbelieve that muse much on their words.[19]

That view, however popular, is essentially superficial which treats the Schoolmen and preachers and mystics—or, often enough, the Schoolmen alone—as all-important for the history of medieval thought. Indeed, if we were compelled to neglect one class of witnesses, it might even be less dangerous to turn away from these official teachers than to ignore those numerous, though far more modest, witnesses who give us occasional glimpses into the mind of the multitude. By all means let us study what was hatched in the lecture-room or the cloister or the hermitage; but let us also try to realize what the more ordinary man thought in London streets. And here, as elsewhere, the poem of *Piers Plowman* does very faithfully speak for the man in the street. The ordinary Englishman, in his more serious and enquiring moods, did not visualize himself as living under an omnibeneficent ecclesiastical authority which harmonized all faith and reason for him. If he thought for himself, if he tried to digest all that he heard and to make it into flesh and blood of his own, he was beset by much the same difficulties, under different outward forms, as those which beset the religious thinker of to-day. Moreover, he had learned by bitter experience the danger of trusting too implicitly to the official teacher. For (says Langland)

> It seemeth now soothly to the worldës sight
> That Goddës word worketh not on learned nor on lewëd,
> But in such a manner as Mark meaneth in the Gospel
> *While the blind leadeth the blind, both fall into the ditch.**

Therefore (he proceeds), let these "correctors" (the hierarchy) first correct themselves, and then the lower clergy will cease to call their superiors, as they call them now in Chaucer's England, "dumb dogs". Thus in those days, as now, the ordinary enquiring soul had to work out its own salvation. At every point Langland finds himself brought up against some weighty uncertainty; but at every such check he falls back upon Christ and the Cross.

* B. x. 274. This text, as Langland gives it in Latin, is not in Mark; it is quoted loosely from Matthew or Luke.

This comes out most clearly in the last three cantos of the poem, which deserve a summary to themselves. These show Langland's most continuous height of poetry; we need not characterize them, as we must the earlier cantos, with Horace's description, "scattered fragments of a poet". On that account, therefore, these are the cantos which stand least in need of modernization; the strength of his feeling guides him to such plain and forcible words as were destined to outlive the ravages of time. On the other hand, they give no idea of his strength in comedy.

We must here remind ourselves of the evolution of Piers Plowman from the Peasant Saint to Superman, to Godhead in the Flesh, and finally to Christ's successors. The poem here forms a pageant. To Langland, as to Chaucer, miracle-plays were full of suggestion; and it is characteristic that Chaucer should have been mainly impressed by their comic side, Langland by their tragic. His picture of the descent to hell, for instance, may be seen in many medieval paintings, as at the south-east corner of King's College Chapel, Cambridge, and in the miracle-play of the "Harrowing of Hell".

Here, then, one Palm Sunday, Langland found himself shirtless and wet-shod, like a beggar, again on Malvern hills. There again he fell into a dream mingled with boys' voices, the organ, the cry of *Hosanna!* and *All Glory, Laud and Honour*, that Palm Sunday hymn which is still popular to-day. He saw in this dream how

> One semblable to the Samaritan,* and somedeal to Piers the Plowman
> Barefoot, on an ass's back, bootless came pricking.
> Eagerly he lookëd, as a knight to win his spurs.
> Then lookëd Faith from a window, and cried: "Ha, son of David!"
> As doth a herald of arms, when a knight cometh to joust.
> Then I asked of Faith, what all that fare bemeant;
> "What shall joust with Jesus" (quoth I), "Jewës or Scribes?"
> "Nay" (quoth he), "the foul fiend, and false doom and death."

Then follow the incidents of the Passion, most vivid in general conception, though the details are not always correct; for instance, the vinegar and myrrh which were passed to our Lord upon a sponge are described here as a poison which was offered Him.

> *It is finished,* quoth Christ, and commenced for to swoon.
> Piteously and pale, as a prisoner that dieth,
> The Lord of life and of light laid his eyen together.

* The Good Samaritan was one of the few Gospel parables that were ever portrayed in medieval churches; it was taken to typify Christ the Saviour.

The day for dread withdrew, and dark became the sun;
The wall waggëd and clave, and all the world quakëd.
Dead men for that din came out of deepë gravës,
And told why that tempest so long time endurëd:
"For a bitter battle", these dead bodies said,
"Life wageth with death in this darkness; the one fordoeth the other,
And no wight shall see certainly which shall have the mastery
Ere Sunday about sunrising." Therewith they sank to the earth.

The scene changes now to the Lower Regions. We see a vast
and gloomy cavern, with a dim light in the background, and two
fair maidens, one coming from the east and one from the west.
These are the Mercy and Truth of Psalm lxxxv: "Mercy and Truth
have met together; Righteousness and Peace have kissed each
other." Truth asks: "What means this din, with the darkness
and the dawning light behind?" Mercy answers, but Truth dis-
believes. Then come Righteousness and Peace from the north
and south respectively. The same debate follows between them,
and the same incredulity. Meanwhile the light is broadening,
and Peace quotes: "Heaviness may endure for a night, but joy
cometh in the morning." Righteousness is still incredulous, but
here at last the Voice Itself breaks the silence, coming from that
light and addressing the gates of hell: *Lift up your heads, O ye gates,
and be ye lift up, ye everlasting doors, and the King of Glory shall
come in.* For a while, the infernal parliament hesitates in anxious
debate. Then the Voice sounds again, nearer and louder, till it
compels attention and answer:

"What Lord art thou", quoth Lucifer, "that callest at the gate?"
"Lo, the King of Glory", the light soon said,
"And Lord of might and of main, and all manner virtues.
Dukes of this dim place, anon undo these gates,
That Christ may come in, the King's son of heaven."
And with that breath hell brake, and Belial's bars were loosëd.
Patriarchs and prophets, the people that walked in darkness,
Sang aloud St John's song: *Behold the Lamb of God,*
And those that our Lord lovëd, into His light be caught,
And said, "Lo, my soul to amend for all sinful souls.
Now, Satan, beginneth thy guile against thyself to turn.
Thou that art doctor of death, drink the draught that thou madest;
For I, that am Lord of life, love is my drink.
And for that drink today I diëd upon earth.
I fought so, me thirsteth yet, for man's soul's sake;
Yet may no drink me moisten nor my thirstë slake
Till the vintage shall fall in the vale of Jehoshaphat,

That I must drink full ripe at the rising of the dead.
And then shall I come as a King, crownèd with angels
And have out of hell all human souls.
And for thy lying now, Lucifer, that thou liedst to Eve
Thou shalt abide it bitter"; and bound him then with chains.
Many hundreds of angels then harped aloud and sang.
Then pipèd Peace of poesie a note:
"After sharp showers", quoth Peace, "most sheen in the sun;
Is no weather warmer than after watery clouds;
Nor no Love liever nor friends more firm of heart
Than after war and woe, when Love and Peace be masters.
Let no people then", quoth Peace, "perceive that ever we chid;
For impossible is no thing to him that is almighty."
"Thou sayest sooth", quoth Righteousness, and reverently her kissed,
"Peace and peace here", said she, "world without end!"
Truth trumpèd then, and sang *Te Deum Laudamus*,
And then luted Mercy, in a loud note,
"Behold how sweet and joyful to dwell together in unity!"
Till the day dawned, I saw these damsels dance.
Then rang the Resurrection bells; and right with that I wakèd,
And callèd Kit my wife, and Calote my daughter,
And bade them rise and reverence Goddès resurrection,
And creep to the cross on their knees, and kiss it for a jewel;
For God's blessed body it bare for our boot,
And it afeareth the fiend: for such is its might
There may no grisly ghost glide where it walketh.

The author sleeps again on Easter Day and has a fresh vision, a continuation of the last. Christ appears to him in the armour and blazonry of Piers Plowman (that is, in His human nature), painted all bloody with his victorious fight. Then comes the Day of Pentecost; the Holy Ghost in the likeness of lightning lighting on the Apostles' heads; and thenceforward Piers Plowman is St Peter; the power has passed to a mortal ruler. Grace (for the poem, like Bunyan's story, is full of impersonated virtues and vices) prophesies trouble to come after Christ's death. Piers Plowman (now, that is, the Pope) is appointed by Christ as "my steward and my reeve on earth". He is given the four evangelists to plough with. The seed that he is to sow is the four cardinal virtues, and he has a barn to harbour his grain in, the barn of Truth, built with the timber of the Cross, and entitled "Unity, that is Holy Church". Piers then goes forth to plough. The powers of evil attack him, and colour belief so quaintly with their sophistry that good and evil are hopelessly confused together, both in faith and in practice. Therefore Conscience hastily summons all true Christians into this true barn, this Unity, in defence of Holy Church. This brings about a momentary revival, but men are found readier to bewail their sins than to amend their lives and make restitution. Antichrist now musters his powers of evil for a desperate assault. The monks and friars join in with him, all but a few poor "fools" who choose to suffer for their spiritual folly; an evident allusion, as we have seen, to the persecution of the "Spiritual" friars by their relaxed brethren. Then, at the prayer of Conscience, Nature sends a plague to teach men better lives. There is indeed a brief diversion, but relapse soon follows. The battle is renewed; and now the worst enemies of Holy Church are found to be the clergy themselves. The friars, in especial, offer their help, but they turn out to be mere traitors. Their so-called spiritual remedies are quack drugs, stupefying the sense of sin and personal responsibility. Antichrist, seeing this, attacks all the more fiercely. Cries of despair arise: Where is Contrition? where is real sorrow for sin, through which alone we can get God's grace? where is that Contrition whom we have set to keep the gate of our citadel?

> "He lieth and dreameth", said Peace, "and so do many others;
> The Friar with his physic this folk hath enchanted,
> And plastered them so easily, they dread no sin."

We are now only seven lines from the end of the poem, and there seems no room but for despair. If we ended here, we should say that Langland, like Gerson in the next generation, is ready to cry to the world: "our age has neither faith nor morals"; or, again: "the Church is eaten up with an incurable cancer, and the very remedies do but make her sick."[20] Indeed, an able critic of to-day, Mr Christopher Dawson, has actually made that strange mistake. He writes: "It is characteristic of the Nordic strain in Langland's poetry that his Christian epic should end, like the *Volospa* and the epics of the heathen north, on a note of defeat and despair—with the vision of a final battle for a lost cause against the unloosed hosts of hell." What Langland actually says in those last seven lines is very different from this. For him, no truth can ever become a "lost cause". At an earlier point of the poem, it is true, Mr Dawson could have written those words with more justice. He can there say truly: "In despair Langland

calls on his fellows, the common people, to make a last stand for
the cause of Catholic unity:

> ...Come with me, ye fools
> Into Unity of Holy Church, and hold we us there,
> And cry we to Nature, to come and defend
> Us fools from the fiend, for the love of Piers Plowman,
> And call we to the commons, that they come into Unity
> And there abide and do battle against Belial's children."[21]

But to break off and end there is to mistake the real man and his
whole poem: for at this despairing point we are still thirteen pages
from the end of the book. In those remaining pages the visionary
poet, contrite and confessed, takes refuge in Unity, but only to
find that this fortress is being besieged not only by Antichrist but
also by false clergy, a hundred of them dressed in dissolute lay
attire with long daggers at their belt; these are backed up by sixty
more "cursed priests of the marches of Ireland", who blaspheme
and attack so fiercely that they "hadden almost Unity and Holiness
adown". Conscience therefore welcomes the friars into Unity, as
allies; but he finds these to be mere flatterers, quack-doctors of
souls; they drug into helpless stupor the very porter of the gate,
upon whom all depends! We have here that curse of the Prophet
Micah, "a man's enemies are the men of his own house"—*inimici
hominis domestici ejus*. Up to that point the words *defeat* and
despair may truly be used; for, under the searchlight of bitter
experience, that minority of truly spiritual folk are apparently
now exposed as "fools". All their trust had reposed upon Unity,
and Unity is now exploded. It has shown itself not as true unity
for the love of Piers Plowman (that is, of the Christ-Man), but
as an ideal of unity which is being betrayed by its own most
trusted children. It seems now to be that hollow unity which
Jeremiah lamented in Israel: "A wonderful and horrible thing is
committed in the land; the prophets prophesy falsely, and the
priests bear rule by their means; and my people love to have it so:
and what will ye do in the end thereof?"[22] Here, then, at the
worst need, is where our poet shows his true spiritual greatness.
He is possessed by a living conviction of that truth which lies
at the root of Christianity and which had carried the Cross to
conquest under the pagan persecutions; the truth that victory may
be wrested from what seems the most hopeless defeat. For Langland, as Jusserand has said with perfect truth, is one of those rare

thinkers who are consumed with burning enthusiasm for sober
and moderate ideals. At the core, this hesitating dreamer is
as solid as the most dogmatic extremist. He is sensitive to all
evil, and fearless to face it, yet invulnerable in his faith, since the
breakdown of outer bulwarks drives him only to more direct
communion with the mystic message which speaks straight to his
own heart, and which he can no more disbelieve than he can
disbelieve in his own existence. If indeed true religion seems to
be dying out from the Visible Church, yet the Kingdom of God
is always within us. If, in that which claims to be the One True
Fold, Christ is daily crucified afresh, then let us shake the dust
from our feet, and go forth as pilgrims—if so it must be, as
solitary pilgrims—in search of the Christ that is to be. How far?
Over the wide world, till we have found what we seek, or till
the night comes. That is the burden of these last seven lines, when
once the situation has been recognized, humanly speaking, as
hopeless:

> "By Christ", quoth Conscience then, "I will become a pilgrim,
> And walk on, as wide as the world lasteth,
> To seek Piers the Plowman,* that Pride may be destroyed,
> And that Friars may find their guerdon who flatter for greed of gain,
> And contradict me, Conscience. Come, Nature, avenge my wrongs,
> And send me good hap and health, till I have Piers the Plowman",
> And then he groaned after Grace, till I 'gan awake.

Here endeth the dialogue of Peter the Plowman.

If, therefore, we are to sum up with Mr Dawson, it can only
be in a far wider sense than he himself seems to intend. He writes:
"Here is the Catholic Englishman *par excellence*, at once the most
English of Catholic poets and the most Catholic of English poets:
a man in whom Catholic faith and national feeling are fused in
a single flame. He saw Christ walking in English fields in the
dress of an English labourer, and to understand his work is to
know English religion in its most autochthonous and yet most
Catholic form." The equivoque lies here in that common but
loose habit, often fatal to historical accuracy, of using the simple
word *Catholic* to distinguish the Papal Church in especial; although
(as Cardinal Gasparri has recently told the world in the Pope's
name) this should scientifically be called *Roman Catholic*, since

---

* I.e. Christ in His true relation to struggling humanity.

(argues the cardinal) "the word 'Roman' was precisely the expression which distinguished the Catholic religion from all other Christian confessions".[23] In the widest sense, Piers Plowman is indeed very English and very Catholic. But, if we aim at strict historical accuracy, and insert *Roman* into these sentences, they will not do at all. Langland represents the Englishman whose tie to Rome was fast loosening: the man who was already beginning to feel it equally difficult to do without organized religion or to do with it, and who was (as we shall soon see again) in serious doubt about Indulgences. It is this man's spiritual descendants who, in St Thomas More's day, will make it possible for the Spanish ambassador to write from London "nearly all the people here hate the priests". Langland was a worthy precursor of those Anglicans who not only accept the Creeds, but pray regularly for "the good estate of the Catholick Church", of which they esteem themselves members. Langland is pre-eminently Catholic in the sense that he belongs to that great world-wide type which, in all ages and countries, has stood out from the confused and shifting mass of ordinary humanity. In him we may recognize the pagan Horace's "just and inflexible man", steady and undaunted even among the ruins of a collapsing universe. Again, he is the Anglican George Herbert's model, who "like season'd timber, never gives, but, though the whole world turn to coal, then chiefly lives". And, lastly, he anticipates the agnostic Henley's defiance of Fortune: "I am the master of my fate, I am the captain of my soul!" There is perennial interest in the true story of any man's feelings and beliefs; and this poem, with all its incoherence, under its accumulated rust and dirt of five centuries, is fresh and living even to-day. Indeed, it is now beginning to come to its own, and historians are increasingly ready to realize how direct a light is thrown upon modern religious and social problems by this almost unknown William, who faced honestly the difficulties and doubts of his age, and fought them all down; and who has left us the best of his experience and his reflections in the book we call *Piers Plowman.*

THE medieval artist worked under conditions essentially different from the modern.[1] The modern is individualistic, and sometimes achieves a reputation by pushing caprice to its utmost limits. Medieval art, on the contrary, was strictly collectivist. The men who worked at the great cathedrals were under a discipline comparable to that of an army; indeed they were often actual conscripts. Quite apart from what might be done in the so-called Dark Ages, when the whole neighbourhood was at the mercy of each predatory lord, the kings of the later Middle Ages claimed and exercised the right of impressing masons, carpenters, and other artisans for whatever great work they had in hand. A warlike countess in eleventh-century Normandy brought in a celebrated mason to build her a stronger castle than he had built for any of her rivals, and then killed him to make sure of not being outdone in her turn. Chaucer, again, when Clerk of the King's Works, had to impress masons, just as other officers were impressing soldiers, to serve the king; and even the Chapels of Eton and King's College, Cambridge, were partly built by forced labour. In other ways also these great building schemes were carried on under an approximation to military conditions. The learner passed through an exacting mill in later, if not in earlier, times. Although royal castles like Caernarvon and Beaumauris seem to have been built with less foundation on the apprenticeship system than we should expect from any other gild, and Messrs Knoop and Jones have shown that there was something of the same laxity elsewhere in England, yet the fifteenth-century masons' codes show definitely that strict discipline was aimed at, if not always obtained. In Germany, again, at the end of the Middle Ages, rules seem to have been strictly enforced; and the masters of the masons' and carpenters' gilds gradually reinforced their own position, and made it difficult for the ordinary workman to join their select society, by insisting on ever-increasing expense for his "masterpiece", whether in time or in money. We have a striking example of this gild discipline in the case of Jodocus Tauchen of Breslau, a distinguished carver who was boycotted for using methods of work which his fellows disapproved.[2] Again, as in war, materials were costly and man-power comparatively cheap. Moreover, the privations were shared fairly equally between officers and men; while the ordinary mason received a wage comparable to that of a modern taxi-driver, the master-mason himself was ordinarily paid no higher than a first-rate chauffeur in a wealthy man's establishment. Their fame, again, was rather collective than individual. The number of actual names which have come down to us, though they would make a long list, is very small in comparison with the vast mass of buildings and the multitudes who worked upon them. Even where the stones bear a banker-mark, which was the workman's sign-manual, that signature was seldom or never made in voluntary self-advertise-ment, but was imposed upon the workman by his clerk of the works or other superior who needed to check the quality or quantity of his labour. It was only with the Renaissance that the artist's signature became normal.

Thus the medieval artist's conditions differed very widely from those of the man of letters. In literature, apart from the extent to which the universities adopted the gild system, writers had as much individual freedom as was compatible with the ordinary social conditions of their time. Though there was a Gild of Meistersänger in Germany, and something similar at an earlier date in Flanders, England had not even the rudiments of a Society of Authors, apart from the quite different scriveners' gilds, where the members did not compose, but only transcribed. Thus we find far greater differences of quality in this field. Though medieval art is not so uniformly good as some enthusiasts have told us, yet certainly it never sinks to so low a level as those poems which Chaucer ridiculed in his "Tale of Sir Thopas", or as we find in long passages from Lydgate ("the voluminous, prosaic and drivelling monk" as Ritson called him) or in other rhymesters who wrote below even Lydgate's level. On the other hand, while no medieval artist sinks so low, yet none stands above the rest as Dante stands in literature; we might even add, perhaps, as Petrarch and Boccaccio and Chaucer stand, or Froissart and Matthew Paris.

Yet in some ways we may come closer to the medieval artist than to his brother the poet. Creighton has noted his ubiquity, if only we would look for him. Masses of what was most beautiful in medieval architecture have perished; not in Britain alone but perhaps even more in those countries which were never seriously touched by the Reformation. Montalembert, the greatest of modern monastic panegyrists, reminds us that a Frenchman who wishes to see the medieval abbey in its completeness will find the best approach to this in an English cathedral close. In France, in Spain, in Italy, in Southern Germany and Austria, the destruction of monastic buildings by their own inmates was limited only by want of money. Bavaria is here a very striking example; it may be studied compendiously in Oefele's *Monumenta Boica*, where this eighteenth-century antiquary gives bird's-eye views of the rich abbeys from which he is printing his MSS., and which look more like modern workhouses or asylums than like their medieval prototypes. Throughout Europe, then, while the castle is commonly in ruins and the abbey is often ruined or rebuilt beyond recognition, the majority of parish churches are very nearly what they were in the Middle Ages; more so in England than anywhere else. Except the hills and the streams, there is nothing to rival our churches in durability, even when we take account of those which have been (to borrow Ruskin's happy phrase) "utterly restored". And, quite apart from those rare and welcome inscriptions in which a mason has occasionally recorded his own name with pardonable pride, we find very frequently, wherever the restorer has not worked too thoroughly, these banker-marks which bring us face to face with the man himself. On page 732 will be found a conspectus of marks from St Nicholas at Lynn (1399–1419), which are repeated at other neighbouring churches.

There is also in Western art a greater continuity from imperial times than can be found in popular literature. The Roman gilds (*collegia*) seem never to have died out altogether in Italy; and certainly the Byzantine influence was definite. One of the commonest medieval terms for a mason was *lathomus* or *latomus* (Greek λατόμος). These Byzantine building conditions, following the trade routes, produced the so-called Romanesque architecture, which spread throughout Italy and then over the Alps, either due northward down the Rhine or north-westward through France and across from Normandy to England. There were no barriers in this mason-work comparable to the barriers of speech. Greek literature, for nearly all the Middle Ages, was almost unknown in the West; with Greek art it was very different. The man who at Constantinople had dressed marble or the finer stones could transfer his skill without much loss to the coarser stones of the

West. Byzantine illustrators of the Bible or of Vergil, and those miniaturists who worked upon parchment, as their brethren worked in mosaic, have supplied models not only to medieval draughtsmen and colourists but for most of the Western carvers also. Those "Anglo-Saxon attitudes", with which Lewis Carroll has humorously familiarized us in their vivid mannerism, are directly copied from Byzantine illustrations of the Psalms or the Apocalypse.

Here, as in almost every other field, we must go back again to that European Renaissance of about A.D. 1000. Something of this revival was due to the fact that society had lived in constant expectation of Christ's second coming; an expectation which was frequently renewed by the occurrence of what seemed peculiarly significant events or dates. The Apocalypse, with the emphasis which it laid upon the thousand-year-long Reign of the Saints, focused men's minds naturally upon that year 1000. This is a factor which cannot be ignored, though it has often been exaggerated out of all proportion on the strength of the chronicler Ralph Glaber, who tells us of the feeling of rejuvenescence which came when those fateful years were passed; not only the thousandth from Christ's birth but also the thousandth from His Crucifixion. We have already seen his words: "It was as though the very world had shaken herself and cast off her old age, and were clothing herself everywhere in a white robe of churches."[3] The chronicler was himself a Cluniac monk, writing in the early and great days of his own order, which had set itself 100 years earlier to reform European monachism: a reform which constituted one of the main currents of this Renaissance. Glaber's "white robe of churches" marks roughly the beginning of Romanesque architecture; a style which may be characterized as monastic in the sense that it was always ordered and paid for by the monks and, on very exceptional occasions, part of it was actually wrought with their own hands. But this monastic art was only an occasional by-product of the monastic ideal. St Benedict no more contemplated founding colonies of artists than of scholars. The monk's main business was to save his own soul, and incidentally, by the same process, to help others towards heaven. The so-called *Mirror of Monks*, in about 1100, insists that the cloisterer shall be like Melchizedek "without father, without mother, without kindred". Even the Franciscans, whose ideal was far more widely removed from that "holy boorishness" which St Jerome specifies as the monk's temptation, often slid into it unawares. David of Augsburg [1280] warns his younger brethren that it is their business to take no more notice of their fellow-men, except for purposes of religious edification, than if they were a flock of sheep.[4] St Bernard, more than a century earlier, had condemned much of the monastic art of his time as a waste of money and energy; as a sort of Judaic ceremonialism which was pardonable for the ignorant laity but with which the monk, under his deeper sense of religion, ought to dispense. Nearly every monastic reform showed something of this severe Puritan tendency. On the other hand, there were many monks who felt that their vast endowments could not be better employed than for the glory of God in painting and sculpture and music. That artistic school is admirably represented by the monk who wrote under the name of Theophilus, and whom modern research has identified with Roger of Helmershausen.[5] This man was himself an artist, and wrote a manual for artist pupils, full of interesting details concerning materials and methods. He rises at one point to eloquent enthusiasm: "Cheered by these supporting virtues, my beloved son, thou hast approached God's house in all faith, and adorned it with such abundant comeliness. In illuminating the vaults and the walls with every diversity of handiwork, and all the hues of the rainbow, thou hast in a manner shown forth to every beholder a vision of God's paradise, bright as springtide with flowers of every hue, and with the fresh green of grass and leaves...whereby thou makest men to praise God in His creatures, and to preach His wonders in His works. For the beholder's eye knoweth not where first to rest its gaze: if we look upward to the vaults, they are even as a mantle embroidered with flowers: if, again, we look upon the walls, there also is a kind of paradise; or if we consider the light that streams through the windows, then we cannot but marvel at the priceless beauty of the glass and at the variety of this most precious work.... Labour therefore now, my good pupil, happy in this life before God's face and man's, and happier still in the life to come, through whose labour and zeal so many burnt-offerings are devoted unto God! Kindle thyself now to a still ampler scope of art, and set thyself with all thy might to fulfil that which is yet lacking to the furniture of God's house, without which the Sacraments cannot be celebrated, nor God be served with due ministrations." Still earlier comes the description of Tuotilo of St Gallen by the chronicler of that house. "Tuotilo was supple and sinewy in arm and limb, the very model of an athlete. Ready of speech, clear of voice, a delicate carver and painter. Musical, with especial skill upon the harp and the flute; for he taught the harp to the sons of noble families around. He was a crafty messenger, to run far or near; skilled in building and all the kindred arts. He had a natural gift of ready and forcible expression in German or Latin, in earnest or jest; so that the Emperor Charles once said: 'curses on the fellow who made so gifted a man into a monk.'"

This "monastic" period, then, was conditioned by the patronage of the great abbeys, and sometimes by the artistic sense and direction of the monks themselves. The original workmen, on the other hand, were for the most part comparatively unskilled labourers; and even the master-mason was often too inexperienced to grapple thoroughly with the engineering problems with which his growing ambitions confronted him. Bishop Creighton had his own trenchant way of putting this: Our first question (he said) on being shown over any great Romanesque church should be this: "When was it that the central tower fell?" Among the multitude of miracles recorded in monastic chronicles and Lives of Saints, a considerable proportion deal with building accidents: for instance, a scaffold falls or a building collapses before it is finished, and (through the merits of such-and-such a saint) there is little or no harm done to life or limb. As the abbeys grew richer and their churches greater, the appeal to lay-architects became commoner. It was a vast effort of engineering skill which led from Romanesque to Gothic art, and which turned the heavy monumental building into a machine of marvellous construction in its adjustment of weights and thrusts, and even in its elasticity in face of expansion and contraction under heat and cold and in resistance to tempestuous winds. That evolution was due to lay-artists, and especially to the rivalry of bishops and their cities, determined to outdo the great monastic models. We can trace the transition among the few recorded names of masters. Henry III had as his royal painter a monk of Westminster, and Edward I had one from Bury St Edmund's; these are survivals from the old state of things. When we come to Edward II we find a very different royal painter. A precious fragment of the royal Household Account Rolls has come down to us, recording: "Item, paid to

Jak de Seint Albon, Painter to the King, who danced on a table before the King's majesty and made him laugh beyond measure, 50 shillings in manner of gift through the King's own hands, in aid of Jak himself, his wife, and his children." Similarly Bishop Grosseteste [1240], among the statutes which he published for the orderly government of his diocese, commanded that painters should not be allowed to grind their colours upon the altars of the churches.[6] Pigments in those days were bought only in the rough, and a marble grinding-slab was part of an artist's full equipment. The wandering painter could not easily carry this about, even where he could afford to possess it; hence the over-mastering temptation to utilize the great consecrated altar-slab.

Here then we have the lay-artist fully developed, working upon the church for his living, but sometimes far from ecclesiastically minded. He would lodge in the monastic precincts while the work was proceeding; but many anecdotes show us the friction natural to this period of transition. One of the most significant is that of St Stephen of Obazine, who, as a Cistercian, interpreted so strictly for himself and his own monks the Benedictine pro-hibition of flesh-food, that he would suffer no butcher's meat upon the premises, even for the use of these unfortunate hirelings who were guiltless of Benedictine vows.[7] He evidently reasoned: "Who builds good churches must himself be good"—a sophism which Dr Johnson had not yet arisen to explode. The workmen, loathing the daily round of herbs and pulse, secretly bought a pig and cooked it in the forest, bringing back the unconsumed rem-nants to hide at home. A little bird brought the news to St Stephen, who came round with several of his seniors, and discovered the abomination hidden betwixt two barrels in the masons' lodge. What should be done with this unclean flesh? The seniors coun-selled moderation, but the saint knew no compromise in such a matter; he cast the pork solemnly upon the dunghill, with every attendant circumstance of ignominy. The workmen, learning this, threw down their tools and proclaimed a general strike. St Stephen, after vainly arguing the question on moral grounds, fell back upon the employer's last resource in all ages, and assured them that he could get plenty of better men in their stead. No doubt the capitalist had a distinctly more favourable position in the twelfth century, as against the striking operative, than he has now; but we may also infer from other authentic evidence that St Stephen was one of those men whose real piety and charity are bound up with so plain a resolve to have their own way in the long run, that men find it cheaper to grant it them at once. However this may be, the masons were presently "pricked to the heart", and "resumed the work, to their own profit and that of their souls". Equally significant in its own way is the story of the artist penitent of St Berchaire [1140].[8] This man had been dedicated as a child to monastic life, and the monks taught him art. When he grew up he ran away to neighbouring Châlons, where the bishop was building a new cathedral. Here he was well paid; but, after some time, the bishop incautiously took him in his train to Montier-en-Der, an abbey where St Berchaire lay buried. The monks, finding that they had here an artistic expert, persuaded the bishop to transfer him, and kept him not as a monk but as an indulged guest. They set him to carve a crucifix; but Christ, indignant to be fashioned by these polluted hands, smote him with sore sickness. This was evidently a fever; and what the monastic chronicler describes is plainly an artist's delirium. He besought them to clothe him in a monastic cowl and to pray round him. "Soon, therefore, a vast host of demons burst upon him, led by two more grisly than the rest, who rushed with savage violence into the sick man's chamber and strove with all their power to tear his wretched soul from his body. Yet, by God's merciful protection, there came a pause in their onslaught, wherein one of the demons reproached his fellow for his delay in bearing off this soul which they had come to snatch. The other answered that he was powerless against the protection of the most renowned martyr St Berchaire, whose holy bones were there buried and worshipped; 'Yea', said the first, 'and I can do nothing because I see him fortified with the Last Communion of the Body of Christ, and defended by the prayers of St Berchaire's monks.' Thus their dispute dragged on, while the poor wretch shuddered at the horrible tumult; when, suddenly and marvellously, while the sick man lay as a helpless spectator of all these things, there appeared a single Hand, which in its unspeakable mercy scattered the demons and put them to flight, thus, by God's commanding power, supplying the patient's weakness....For, suddenly, on the label of the crucifix which stood at the foot of the prostrate artist, there burst forth to his sight an ethereal globe surrounded with milk-white circles and adorned at certain marked points with shining stars. Here, by God's grace,

the globe was seen to cleave in twain, and there shone in the midst
of this division a heavenly queen, clad in fine-spun robes of so
ineffable beauty that none could doubt her to be the Mother of
God. Her sacred head shone with glory and bliss, and she moved
downwards along the cross, gliding from top to bottom as on a
track of beaten gold, and taking her seat as Mistress in the throne
of Her Son. Then this most pitiful Virgin deigned to comfort this
monk, broken in body by the grievous torments of his sickness,
and in soul by the devices of these demons. 'Poor wretch!' she
said, 'Lo! my Son hath been moved to mercy by my prayers and
by those of His servant St Berchaire. He hath now granted thee
a respite for repentance, that thou mayest return into the place
wherein thou wast offered to God and to His saints, and mayest
henceforth amend thy life as He would have it.' With these words
she stretched out the hand of mercy in the face of the dismayed
crowd of devils; then raised him from his couch, and left him in
good health, eager to tell the bystanders the lamentable story of all
that he had suffered and seen."

These stories will explain how, as architecture developed, it
came more and more definitely into lay hands. It has been claimed
that masons' gilds existed already in the twelfth century; but they
do not come into full documentary light until 1260. St Louis had
chosen a strong and upright man, Étienne Boileau, as Provost of
the Merchants (i.e. Mayor) at Paris, in order to put an end to
municipal corruption there. Étienne compiled a *Book of Gilds*,
including that of the masons. There is nothing definite to differentiate them here from the corporations of other trades or handi-
works. It is true that secrecy was enforced upon their members;
but so it was in other gilds. Again, we can attach no mystic
importance to the first syllable of the term "freemason". It
seems practically certain that the original freemason was one who
worked in freestone, i.e. the finer stones that lent themselves to
greater freedom of handling. Certainly the word "freestone"
occurs earlier than the word "freemason"; and in documents
where the latter is found it is generally in contradistinction from
"rough-mason", "rough-hewer", "hard-hewer". Gradually,
however, this gild did begin to present exceptional, if not unique,
characteristics. To begin with, it was very specially concerned
with the Church. We must not altogether forget castles and a few
great houses; but the towns were built almost entirely of wood,

and "the stone house" is sometimes a quite distinctive title; therefore the large majority of stone buildings were ecclesiastical, from the cathedral down to the little chapel of a hamlet. The mason, therefore, serving the Church in this way, would naturally enjoy more, if only a little more, of ecclesiastical favour and protection. Again, his was a wandering life. Only a few great towns had their small settled communities of masons; the rest wandered from job to job as they were required. I have shown elsewhere, in *Art and the Reformation*, how the fifteen masons who worked at St Nicholas at Lynn [1399–1419] can be traced at eleven churches round, one of them almost thirty miles distant. This nomadic life rendered them comparatively independent. In the town, if anything were wrong with a single workman, the gild could punish him; again, if the gild itself

A Mason's Signature.

broke law or by-law, then everybody knew where to find it, and its funds could be confiscated in the last resort. It is no mere chance, therefore, that it was men of the building trades who were found most recalcitrant to those Statutes of Labourers by which parliament, after the Black Death, attempted to keep wages down. Wyclif complains of them as great offenders against those statutes; and, under Henry VI, the problem was important enough to call for parliamentary interference. It seems quite evident that the masons' gild of the later Middle Ages, while it was strong in fellowship between member and member, was as slippery as an eel in its relation to the civic authorities or to King and Parliament. Moreover, for these very same reasons it survived the general suppression of gilds at the Reformation. Freemasonry played a great part, therefore, in international thought at least from about 1717 onwards and perhaps still earlier. There were on the one hand strong internationalist sympathies among the highbrows of different nations; we see it from Erasmus onwards; yet no open internationalist League of Highbrows was possible. No government would have allowed men thus to set up such elaborate communities of their own within, and yet apart from, the Great Community of the State. Here, however, in freemasonry, was something which, for some reason or other, attracted a few scholars, if only because they may have hoped to find here an ancient esoteric wisdom dating from Solomon and his Temple. At any rate, the fact is that highbrows gradually found their way into it. It may well be, as suggested in what is by far the best book on this subject, that the earliest non-working Freemasons had entered out of mere antiquarian or social inquisitiveness.9 But, once inside, they can scarcely have failed to discover what chances this gave them for quiet interchange of thought; and thus Freemasonry would gradually become the considerable social force, efficiently organized for charitable and other purposes, which we know it to be in modern Britain. Elias Ashmole, founder of the Ashmolean Museum at Oxford, is the first who is known to have joined in this way (1646). But, before 1700, the practice had become relatively common. It was formally decided that men might be "Freemasons" in the new sense, without ever touching mallet or chisel; and the distinction was thus established between "speculative" and "operative" masons. Freemasonry, thus developed, was introduced into France by the Catholic and Jacobite Lord Derwentwater in 1725. The greater political freedom of Protestant countries has worked for tolerance between speculative Freemasonry and the State. Roman Catholic States, on the other hand, have always been irreconcilably opposed to such a body, as a thing contrary to the very essence of their being. Consequently, it has been condemned in five papal bulls, from 1738 to 1864, with the result that it is now scarcely possible for a Continental Freemason to be a Christian of any kind. In England, on the other hand, it was possible for a Catholic like Lord Petre to be at the same time leader in the struggle for Catholic Emancipation and Grand Master of the English Freemasons.

The medieval craftsman was, according to modern ideas, very poorly paid. We must bear in mind, to begin with, that scholastic philosophers, following Aristotle, drew only one main distinction in art, between the "liberal" and the "mechanical". The former included all the "humanities", the latter included everything manual. There was, therefore, no essential distinction between the cobbler or tailor on the one hand, and Giotto or the Della Robbias on the other; indeed, in more than one place we find that the painters' gild was a mere branch of the saddlers', through the accident that the heavy wooden medieval saddles were often elaborately painted. Aristotle's point of view coincides probably with most men's feeling in our own generation, though it is far from regulating our general practice. The medieval artist, like the Japanese wood-engraver, was paid as an artisan, and generally expected no further reward than praise and the satisfaction in his own craftsmanship. Nor can we say, as has often been contended, that what the artist lacked in money was made up for him in general reverence for his art. Apart from what we have seen of his liability to the press-gang, we have explicit testimony for the attitude of the general public. When Dante put into his *Commedia* the brilliant miniaturists Oderisi and Franco, as types of the fickleness of fame, this attracted the notice of his distinguished commentator in Chaucer's days, the Bolognese professor Benvenuto da Imola. He tells us how "some men" marvelled that the great poet should thus immortalize "men of unknown name and low occupation", *homines ignoti nominis et bassae artis*. But herein, thinks Benvenuto, Dante showed his genius, "for thereby he giveth silently to be understood how the love of glory doth so fasten upon all men indifferently, that even petty

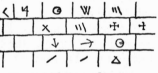

Masons' Marks at Gloucester.

artisans—*parvi artifices*—are anxious to earn it, just as we see that painters append their names to their works".[10]

Moreover we have the witness of formal documents. In 1384, when the master-mason of Troyes Cathedral married, the Chapter gave him a present of eight pints of wine and two loaves of bread, but cut off his wages for that day. Here they were entirely within their rights. He and his fellows were bound to work from sunrise to sunset in the winter half, and from "a little after sunrise to nearly sunset in summer", without leaving their lodge "except to take a competent dinner once a day"; and apparently in case of absence from sickness the man lost his wages. Quicherat, who discovered these documents, writes: "The Chapter of Troyes kept its workmen under its absolute control...employing them as it chose for day-wages or for piece-work, prescribing what was to be done, and accepting the work only if it came up to the specified standard."[11] The account-book of Eton College Chapel tells the same tale. When, in 1448, Robert Goodgroom took a full hour for his dinner, he was fined half a day's pay, "for he would keep his hours, and never go to work till the clock smite". A little later the accounts report the fining of 21 other masons "because they would not go to their work till 2 of the clock; and all maketh Goodgroom!" Similarly, the account-rolls of Renaissance Popes show them sometimes setting first-rate sculptors to the drudgery of cutting cannon-balls, which in those days were more often made of stone than of metal.[12] Again, ecclesiastical hindrances might sometimes be not only negative, but active and positive. The register of Bishop Baldock of London, in 1306, contains a letter addressed to the Prior of Holy Trinity, Aldgate; a monastery which, later on, was Chaucer's next-door neighbour. The letter is headed: "For the matter of the Crucifix wrongfully carved."[13] It rehearses how a certain Tidemann of Germany has made for the Rector of St Mildred in the Poultry "a certain crucifix with a cross-piece quite contrary to the true representation of the cross...to which the indiscreet populace flocks in crowds as to a true crucifix, which it certainly is not: whence, as we foresee, grave peril might arise for their souls". Because the said Tidemann is said to be an alien and unlearned, and therefore naturally ignorant of "the traditional mysteries attaching to the true shape of cross and crucifix", therefore, when he has surrendered the bond for £23 which the rector has given him, he may take away this crucifix now sequestrated and guarded in your monastery—provided that he carry it away secretly and without scandal, before dawn or after dark, into some other diocese. Meanwhile he must take a solemn oath that "henceforth he will neither make nor offer for sale such deformed crucifixes in our city or diocese of London". The explanation of this may probably be found in a book written twenty or thirty years earlier by Luke, Bishop of Tuy in Spain. He writes with horror of the "heretics" who are now attempting to pollute the orthodox faith by "painting or carving ill-shapen images of saints, in order that by gazing on such images the devotion of Christian folk may be turned unto loathing. In derision and scorn of Christ's Cross, they carve images of our Lord with one foot laid over the other, so that both are pierced by a single nail, thus striving either to annul or to render doubtful men's faith in the Holy Cross and the traditions of the sainted Fathers, by superinducing these diversities or novelties." For the earliest crucifixes of all had never been realistic:

the figure was draped to the feet, which were nailed separately. It is only in the thirteenth century that "complete realism is reached by the substitution of one nail in the feet, instead of two as in the old tradition, and the resulting crossing of the legs" (*Catholic Encyclopaedia*, 1908, IV, 529). The unfortunate Tidemann, if he had lived a little longer, would have seen his own fashion completely victorious; for though the old draped crucifixes survive here and there (e.g. at Romsey Abbey or St Étienne-de-Beauvais, where they were built into the wall, and could not be removed without great damage), they are a nine days' wonder to the antiquaries.[14] Moreover, even in the later Middle Ages they had become so unusual that the popular imagination created a new and strange saint out of them, a certain "Liberata" or "Wilgeforte" or "Uncumber", to whose image, as St Thomas More tells us, London wives would pray and offer oats at St Paul's Cathedral, where "in stede of Saint Wilgeforte [they] call her saynt Uncumber, bicause they reken that for a peke of otes she will not faile to uncomber them of their housbondes" (*English Works*, 1557, p. 194 b).

Both Boccaccio and his younger contemporary Sacchetti depict the painter as a man who neither enjoyed special public esteem nor took very special pleasure in his work. These instances, however, must not blind us to the inspiration and the fire which kindled the best of these men, and doubtless the rank and file also in their rarer moments. Legends of artistic rivalry are among the most picturesque in medieval records. In Britain the best known of these is that of the Prentice's Pillar at Rosslyn. In its usual form this tells how the master-mason, wishing to attain perfection, travelled as far as Rome to collect models and inspiration; but only to find that his apprentice, inspired meanwhile by love for a girl of his own age, had outdone the best that he himself could dream of. In his jealous fury he brained the apprentice with his hammer. A similar French story attaches to a tomb at St-Ouen-de-Rouen. Here is a great sepulchral slab which, as the inscription itself tells us, is that of Alexandre de Berneval, the master-mason who built the southern transept and died in 1440. The other figure is that of his son Colin, who succeeded him and built the northern transept, but whose descendants or friends neglected to chisel the inscription on the margin of the figure which he had prepared for himself. Each of these figures stands upon a lion; and from these beasts, facing each other, popular imagination had constructed already in the seventeenth century a legend of artistic jealousy and murder. Alexandre holds in his hand a model of his own beautiful transept window; therefore the story tells how this was the apprentice, and how the master, furious to be outdone, slew him in revenge.

As early as about 1250 we find a French master-mason, Villard de Honnecourt, compiling a book of drawings and hints for his pupils.[15] An English edition of this *Album*
was published by Professor Willis; the drawings are of extraordinary interest. We see sketches from great buildings like Reims which he takes as models; again, designs of his own; again, studies of statuary or painting, wrestlers, warriors, dicers, animals of all sorts, from the grass-hopper and dragon-fly to the lion. He shows interest in and knowledge of en-gineering problems; and, in his lighter moments, love of mechanical toys; for instance, a chafing-dish full of hot charcoal which may be held in the hands yet cannot possibly upset; or trigonometrical mea-surements either of the height of a tower or of the exact point on the ground where an egg may be placed in order that a ripe pear should fall upon it. Especially in-genious is his design for perpetual motion, which he introduces with the words: "Oftentimes do masters dispute" of this

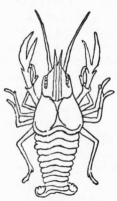

From an Architect's Notebook.

matter. Others of his drawings give us the same lively picture of these artists discussing weighty technical problems or lighter fancies over their evening wine.

As time went on, something like modern capitalism was de-veloped. Henry of Yevele, who was designing and carving in the days when Chaucer was superintending and keeping building accounts, died worth two country manors and several houses in London. Professor D. Knoop and Mr G. P. Jones have worked out an admirable sketch of this man's career, with those of his associates, in the *Journal of the Royal Institute of British Architects*,

1935 (vol. XLII, series 3, no. 14). Again, Thomas Drawsword, the "imager" of York, became sheriff of that city and in 1512 was elected to represent it in parliament. In these later generations the great men not only sold designs but also did a certain amount as contractors. It was this development, and its own over-ripeness, which killed Gothic art. The craftsmen had already run through almost every possible variation, and there was a natural craving for something new, when the Renaissance came in with its revival of Classic art. The real strength of Gothic had been as Morris described it; it was "the people's art". Everybody watched the men at work; everybody was interested in them, as the very children of our own day are interested in the motor-car and all its works. Everywhere there was a call for straightforward effectiveness, which inspired natural and simple treatment in general, while it left further room for the play of high imagination where religion required it, and where the artist or his

A Thirteenth-Century Architect.

prompter was equal to the task. In the case of these carvings and paintings, set there as a "Bible of the poor", and often at a considerable distance from the eye, exaggeration was natural. Where Jacob is represented as confronted with Joseph's blood-stained coat of many colours, the artist is determined that nobody shall fail to realize an aged man in the extremity of grief. When Vasari, writing in the full tide of Renaissance criticism, praises a medieval artist, it is often for his violent expressiveness, e.g. for the pangs of sea-sickness in one picture, or Job's putrid sores in another. We have seen how St Methodius is recorded to have converted King Bogoris of Bulgaria by the lurid pictures of judgment and hell which he painted on the walls of the royal palace. It is natural that, in our own time, artists and art-lovers should look back regretfully at those simpler days when there was not only greater unity of status among the workmen, but more unity of spirit between them and their public. It was something like the literary spirit which travellers describe in the Faröe Islands and Iceland even at the present day; a culture truly living, yet so simple that all classes can share it. It was with true instinct that Morris put this into the foreground of his *Dream of John Ball*.

For satisfaction in his daily work, we have every historical reason to place the medieval artist's career high among workmen of all ages and times. We may see him in imagination tramping, singly or in groups, from town to town or village to village, without more fear of unemployment than that which has always haunted the wage-earner everywhere except in the imagination of a few historians. When great churches or castles were a-building, there was the masons' lodge for work and habitation and fairly congenial company. In the village, or the smaller town which in the Middle Ages was far less populous than very many modern villages, he would lodge at the tavern or with someone of his own class. His work was mainly straightforward, with little temptation to scamp it, since it interested everybody around. All masons had gone through sufficient apprenticeship, whether formal or practical, to please the public and themselves, among generations which had not yet grown tired of seeing things well and simply done, and had not begun to yearn for a change of some kind, were it only for the worse. The majority worked thus, from youth to age, "along the cool sequestered vale of life". A few, on the other hand, had opportunities which gave wide scope to the most brilliant genius, if not so wide as that which the select few have found in later times. Experts are convinced nowadays that in miniature painting, for instance, originality constantly triumphed over convention, and that each of the different groups in which illuminations can be classified owes its existence to one genius, who created a new type for his own generation. Therefore, although Benvenuto and Sacchetti, together with the evidence of cold-blooded documents, compel us to deduct much from those exaggerations which we owe not so much to Ruskin and Morris as to their over-enthusiastic followers, we may still count the medieval artist as one of those who came as near to Arcadian happiness as was possible in a turbulent society. Why should he not be content, when he looked around him? His father or brothers were probably at the plough or the cattle-stall or the smithy. True, these had more chances of a settled family life than he; but his career was incomparably richer than theirs in the interest of travel and of experience among men and cities. In his spare time he drank with his equals at the inn or played with them on the green; his work was upon God's House, which everybody felt to be theirs also; and, if he died at his work, he was laid to rest under its shadow. Masons' tombs, recognizable by the emblematic square and compasses or other tools, could probably be counted by the score among those which still remain in our churches. Moreover, the finer and more self-conscious artists felt themselves champions of a great cause, no less than the modern scientist. This comes out even in the story of their quarrels. It is difficult to separate enthusiasm from rivalry, and rivalry from strife. The *Iliad* recognizes this in the exhortation of Hippolochus to his son.[16] "Strive ever to do thy best, *and to excel all others*"—αἰὲν ἀριστεύειν, καὶ ὑπείροχον ἔμμεναι ἄλλων. Moreover, whole communities were inspired by that same spirit. It is not uncommon for parishioners, in the later Middle Ages, to stipulate with the artist that he must contract to give them a work similar to that of some neighbouring parish, "or better, if may be". Take, for instance, the contract for the rood-loft at Great St Mary's, Cambridge, in 1520. "John Nune of Drynkeston and Roger Bell of Ashfield in the countie of Suffolk, kervers... covenaunte and graunte and also bynden them, ther heyres, and executors by these presents, that they shall make and cause to be made a new Roode lofte....And the briste [*breast, front*] of the sayde new Rodde Loft schal be after and accordyng to the briste of the Roddelofte within the parisshe Chirche of Tripplow [10 miles away] in all maner housyngs, fynyalls, gabeletts, formes, fygures, and rankenesse of Werke, as good or better in every poynte....The bakkesyde of the sayd Roddeloft to be also lyke to the bakkesyde of the Roodelofte of Gasseley or better."[17] Three more times again, in this contract, we have the repetition of that "as good or better". The author of *Dives and Pauper*, probably a friar, took the puritanical view that such rivalry brought base alloy into religion.[18] "I dread me that men do it more for pomp and pride of this world, to have a name and worship thereby in the country, or for envy that one town hath against another, not for devotion but for the worship and the name that they see them have by array and ornaments in Holy Church, or else by sly covetise of men of Holy Church....For the people nowadays...be loth to come in Holy Church when they be bound to come thither, and full loth to hear God's service. Late they come, and soon they go away."

XLIII. LITERARY LIFE

THE conditions of medieval authorship were in one important particular far less radically different from modern conditions than were those of the artist's life. We have seen how those enormous buildings needed strict discipline and co-operation: how the task strained every nerve, and therefore there was something of the same emphasis upon realities as in warfare. Again, the privations were shared by all alike; even the master-mason was only a craftsman with the wages of a modern mechanic; and, lastly, we have seen that the fame was rather collective than individual. When we read in a chronicle that such and such an abbot "made" a magnificent missal or pulpit or altar-piece, that simply means that the abbot ordered and paid, and that the men who actually did the work received little or nothing beyond the common artisan's wages. The whole, therefore, was a great lesson in collectivism. It was William Morris's study of medieval architecture which helped to make a socialist of him.

In literature, on the other hand, there was as much individualism as the theories of Church and State permitted anywhere. It is true that there was then, as there is in every day, a certain tyranny of custom; the troubadours and the minnesänger followed certain conventions, many of which seem artificial to us. But this was only an exaggeration of what we see even in modern times. When the *Saturday Review*, for instance, was at its greatest, under that Venables who had broken Thackeray's nose in a fight at Charterhouse, it was a point of honour for all Saturday Reviewers so to imitate the editor's pungent style that many of their articles could not be distinguished by internal evidence from his. Again, we have seen how the universities and scholastic philosophy imposed a certain discipline. There we find collectivism, and a popularization of knowledge which involved vulgarization in both senses. Thus, to a certain extent, medieval university learning was a people's learning, just as Gothic art was, in Morris's language, "the people's art". When we come, however, to the field of pure literature, we find far more individual freedom, and therefore more inequality of workmanship. In short, for good or for evil, medieval literature was comparatively free from that pressure of gild discipline which plays so great a part in the history of medieval art and craftsmanship. So far as the literature differed in spirit from our own, the medieval moulding forces were not trade union regulations, but the general circumstances of contemporary society.

The beginnings of European vernacular literature on any large scale are in the France of the twelfth century. This movement was roughly contemporaneous with the university movement, and, again, with the great development of sculpture by the cathedral artists. But of these three contemporaries literature was the oldest. These early beginnings, however, were mainly oral. The great period of written French poetry dates roughly from the marriage of Eleanor of Guienne to Henry II in 1152. The patronage of this queen and her sons brought together the two main elements, the troubadour from the south and the trouvère from the north of France. This great movement lasted for about 120 years. During all that time, aristocratic England was practically a colony of France. Moreover, Italy and Germany also were dominated by the French preponderance in the Crusades, especially the Third and Fourth, in which French courts were established at Cyprus and at Constantinople, quite apart from that of Charles of Anjou in Naples and Sicily. During this period the old Epic Cycles, *Charlemagne* and *Arthur*, and the Roman legends, were rewritten by French poets in what proved to be nearly their final form; and all this time Paris University was the great thinking-shop, the main European market of theologico-philosophical ideas. Therefore, when Dante's master Brunetto Latini wrote the little encyclopaedia which he calls *Trésor* [1260], Italian as he was, he wrote it in the language of beyond the Alps, "because the French speech is more delectable and more common to all nations" than his own. Two generations earlier than this, Pietro Bernardone of Assisi had insisted on calling the son born to him his "little Frenchman"— *Francesco*—and thenceforward that name, which is scarcely ever met with at any earlier date, became one of the commonest throughout Europe. St Francis himself showed greater love for French literature than for that of his own country; his intimate companions tell us how constantly he broke forth into French song and speech, and how consciously he modelled himself upon the heroes of French romance. Dante's style, again, was mainly due (next to his one great model Vergil, to whom he ascribes his *bel stilo*) to the troubadours. Petrarch owed them even a greater debt, and Chaucer's first period as a writer was almost entirely French. With this lead from France, and this infiltration of Vergil and the Latin classics through Italy, medieval poetry rose occasionally almost to the highest possibilities of technique. There are lines in Walther v. d. Vogelweide that are quite perfect. Take, again, Chaucer's epilogue to *Troilus and Criseyde*, beginning:

> O youngë freshë folkës, he or she,
> In which aye love upgroweth with your age.

Those lines are technically as perfect as Spenser's.

In the Middle Ages, just as wealth was more evenly distributed, so was culture. The sum-total was less, and therefore enormous superiorities were less possible. It was not that men did not then strive to get as far ahead of their fellows in both fields as they strive at present, but that the circumstances rendered it impossible. The conditions in medieval England resembled those which obtained until quite recent times in Iceland, in the Faröe Islands, and even to some extent in Welsh-speaking Wales; nearly all that the cleric knew (apart from his Liturgy) was known also to the farmer. Hence the preponderance of the oral factor in the early literature of all countries. Goethe, after all, says rightly that writing is a misuse of speech: "Schreiben ist ein Missbrauch der Sprache." It does indeed preserve and spread it, but that which it preserves is "potted" speech. It is not often realized how generally, long after the rise of a vernacular written literature, men were accustomed to read aloud even by themselves. In our own modern times a scholar like H. W. Fowler might plead with much truth that everything worth reading at all, beyond the most ephemeral "literature of information", deserves to be read aloud. Beyond this we must remember that the scarcity of parchment drove medieval writers to a multitude of abbreviations; so that we may doubt whether there were many men so well read and so learned, at any time of the Middle Ages, that they could read an unseen manuscript with anything like the rapidity to which a few professional palaeographers have attained nowadays by intense technical study. The ordinary bishop, indeed, was probably slightly more helpless in this respect than the ordinary university medievalist of to-day, just as the greatest philosopher of to-day may be more helpless in face of a modern written letter than an ordinary clerk. Reading, therefore, was to an enormous extent oral. St Philip heard the Eunuch reading aloud in his chariot as he went down from Jerusalem; and St Augustine devoted a whole chapter of his autobiography to suggestions why his master, St Ambrose, might be found at his leisure moments reading silently to himself (*Confess*. Bk. VI, ch. 3). He was driven to this (thinks St Augustine) by the extreme pressure of other business, and the fear that bystanders might interrupt him to ask the explanation of any difficult passage. If reading had been a silent occupation for the Wife of Bath's clerkly husband, she would never have been provoked to tear those three leaves from his book, and "take him on the cheek" with her fist. Chaucer himself, it is true, after he had spent his working day at the Custom House over paper or parchment, would go home, and there, "as dumb as any stone", would pore over his own favourite books; but in him we have an exceptionally cultured man of this later period, dealing mostly with familiar texts and probably with expensive well-written copies. A hundred years ago it was necessary for S. R. Maitland to spend a good deal of ink in explaining to the public that the Middle Ages were not so utterly destitute of books as historians like Robertson had imagined. But Maitland's impulse drove the pendulum too far the other way; and the modern tendency is certainly to minimize the booklessness of Chaucer's time. His model scholar of Oxford, who had spent on books and lectures his own patrimony and all that he could get from his friends, possessed only 20 volumes at his bed's head. Two centuries earlier, Bernard of Chartres, perhaps the greatest classical teacher north of the Alps during the Middle Ages, left all his own to the cathedral library: they numbered 24. The greatest law teacher of Bologna, Accursius, left a library of 63 volumes. We must remember that these were sometimes bulky, containing two or three good-sized volumes of modern print; yet, even so, this great man's collection, which sold for the sum of £500 of Bologna currency, would number less than 200 in all. Those few, it is true, were comparatively wide in their circulation. Anything recognized as a university textbook, or as a patristic classic, had incomparably greater chances of survival than even the most brilliant book which dealt with less trite subjects or was marked by a rarer individuality; and since, even when writing had reached its fullest medieval stage, poems were commonly written mainly for oral recitation, we may see how the servant in the hall would hear almost as much as his master, while they all gathered round the minstrel at the hearth. This, of course, would tend to maintain the general evenness of the level of culture. Although, from about 1150 onwards, the great epics were written down, yet to the very last the public were enormously dependent upon oral recitation.

So far we may say that this even level of culture was to the good; but on the other side we must remember its necessary restrictions. "A people's art" or "a people's literature" does to a certain extent discourage the highest flights of originality. Medieval literature, then, was restricted, in the first place, by what could be easily committed to memory. The minstrel could seldom afford to buy a book, and still less to carry many about; he must depend upon what he could remember. Secondly, it was restricted to that which could survive the hubbub of the hall; for we must remember that in the Middle Ages silence was not so strict a convention among congregations as it is even during a performance in a modern drawing room. Medieval preachers leave us in no doubt that they anticipated interjections and questions from their audience, and were prepared to answer them. This may explain to some extent the medieval convention of the Prologue, and what so often seems to us its unnecessary length. Such a Prologue, however unexciting in itself, had the advantage of advertising, for five or ten minutes at least, the facts that a recitation was beginning and that, if it was to be heard, the majority of listeners must hold their tongues. Again, it may to some extent explain the similarity of medieval scaffolding; the Month of May, the Dream, and so on. Listeners in those days, like children, loved repetition and reminders of famous things; and much that the modern reader finds so tedious is really analogous to the endless "says I" and "says he" of the conversations we hear in railway-carriages.

Chronologically we may make two main divisions of our subject, marking the break roughly at the year 1350. Again, we may roughly characterize them as the pre-Petrarch and the post-Petrarch eras. Before that date it may be said that nearly all writers were either capitalists or mendicants; but from Petrarch onwards we may date the beginning of the modern man of letters. At the earlier time we had, first, that phenomenon which meets us in every age—the royal or noble author. When Heine, in his *Buch*

Le Grand, tells us how as a boy he used to gloat in the Museum of Düsseldorf over the wood-carvings of the Sovereign Elector Jan Wilhelm, he passes on to explain this ruler's artistic activity. Jan Wilhelm (he says) carved these trifles in his leisure hours, "whereof he had twenty-four per diem". This goes some little way to explain the activities of the royal and noble poets of the Middle Ages. There were men like the Emperor Frederick II and his son Manfred, of whose songs Dante speaks with respect; and, again, there was James I of Scotland with his "King's Quhair". The majority of the troubadours were men of more or less noble birth; but, in the earlier period, by far the most frequent writers were the higher clergy. We have only to run through the titles of any volume in Migne's *Patrologia Latina*, which runs roughly down to A.D. 1200, in order to see that among this mass of theological, philosophical and historical writings there is scarcely one by a cleric of less rank than a dean or an archdeacon. The lower clergy, even when they had the education, had very little opportunity to make themselves heard by the reading public. Dividing the clergy, again, into Regulars and Seculars, we find that, although the Seculars in England produce a larger proportion of chronicles than in any other country, yet those of the Regulars, the cloistered clergy, form the great majority. In theory, it is true, the monk was confined within the precincts of his own abbey or priory; but in practice the cloisterer was seldom able to follow his ideal so strictly as to render himself a passive receptacle of the Holy Ghost. Monks found wide opportunities—in some cases almost unlimited—for hearing and transmitting news through the multitudes of pilgrims and travellers who spent a night or two in the monastery and passed on. Therefore the monastic chronicler at his best is a delicious gossip, with all the freshness of a child. He has a childlike closeness of observation, and very often just that piquant touch of innocent malice in his narration which renders the child's story of its elders so interesting. We have in England one of the greatest of these—Jocelin of Brakelond—whose story of Bury St Edmunds was seized upon by Carlyle for one of his most stirring sermons in *Past and Present*. On the Continent, the greatest in this style is the Franciscan Salimbene of Parma [1280]. Moreover, we sometimes find literary men retiring to a monastery for the leisure that it afforded. Henryson's poem of *The Abbey Walk* begins:

> Alone as I went up and down
> In an abbay was fair to see.

Again, the fifteenth-century carol writer, John Audelay, writes from his lodging among the monks of Haughmond:

> As I lay sick in my languour
> In an Abbey here by west
> This book I made with great dolour
> When I might not sleep, nor have no rest.

Chaucer himself crept into the precincts of Westminster Abbey to die. His house, which he occupied for a few weeks, stood on part of the site of the present Henry VII's Chapel. His friend and contemporary, Gower, not only lived many years within the Priory of Southwark (the present church of St Saviour's by London Bridge), but actually married there, and was tended there by his wife in his blindness. Finally, we have seen how the author of *Piers Plowman* writes:

> If heaven be on this earth, and ease to any soul
> It is in cloister or in school.

Yet, though the monastery or the university was an oasis of the literary man, his quiet was far from complete as compared with the most fortunate of modern students. As to the university, we have seen how commonly the streets were stained with students' blood. As to the monastery, one of our earliest intimate chronicles —that of St Gallen—describes how the envious Sindolf took his penknife and cut a fellow-monk's beautifully written book to pieces; and from Wessobrünn in Bavaria comes the complaint that, in the cloister itself, the monk's fingers might be too cold for writing in the winter months: *dum scripsit, friguit.*[1]

Authors among the secular clergy, it must be repeated, were nearly always men of high position: bishops, abbots, monastic officials or archdeacons at least. These, again, were often of noble birth, and courtiers to boot: men who, like Walter Map and Giraldus Cambrensis and Peter of Blois, had earned promotion partly at least by royal favour, and could not afford to let it go. Yet not only were these men subject to the slavery of court etiquette, but even Giraldus, sprung from the Kings of Wales, had a struggle to reach that public attention which he felt to be his due. The fact is that advertisement in the modern sense was impossible to the medieval author. Nowadays the aspirant's first novel is heralded by a publisher's advertisement which announces that this is destined to be read when Dickens and Thackeray are forgotten; and these publishers' romances, more imaginative even than the authors', are sometimes rewarded by a proportionately preponderant share of the profits. In the Middle Ages a man had to blow his trumpet not vicariously but with his own lips. Giraldus tells us how he "published" his *Topography of Ireland*, written in 1184. He read it at Oxford, "where the clergy of England chiefly flourished in clerkship". He consecrated one day to each of the three divisions of this great book. On the first he read aloud in his own hostel to all the poor scholars of the town; on the second to the Doctors of the different Faculties and pupils of greater note; on the third to the rest of the scholars, with many knights and citizens. For all these readings he supplied meat and drink on the most liberal scale; so that he is able to add, with pardonable pride, "it was a costly and a noble act", to which he knew no parallel in England for his own or any other age.[2] Not, of course, that the proceeding itself was unparalleled; but Giraldus knows of no one who has dared and afforded to practise it on such a scale. If the author was under heavy disadvantages here, he was under still heavier in the matter of livelihood. There was as yet no systematization of literature, and no very perfect organization even at the universities. Men taught here and there at grammar schools or cathedral schools, as best they could. Samson, Abbot of Bury St Edmunds, told Jocelin frankly that, if he could have made bread and cheese by teaching outside, he would never have become a monk. Therefore the man of letters, even after the rise of the universities, was often a hanger-on about the households of great folk. There came, however, a gradual evolution towards modern conditions. Even before the invention of printing, the great universities organized a book trade on something approaching modern lines, and created a whole class of copyists, translators and booksellers. Let us take the prologue to a book which has survived from Paris: "Here is the Code [of Justinian] in Romance [i.e. in French], and all the laws of the Code. Herneis the Romancer sells it; and anyone wishing to have such a book should come to him. His residence is in Paris, in front of Notre-Dame."[3]

Since, then, there was in our period not only no such copyright as we know nowadays, but even what we may call the antipodes of copyright, therefore the plagiarist was a public benefactor. No

"public" in the modern sense was possible as yet; even down to
the end of the Middle Ages it must be mainly a public of private
benefactors. He who has not a patrimony must get a patron.
There was, it is true, as there has been in every day, the Grub
Street author, both before 1350 and after; the joculator, jongleur,
half-minstrel, half-buffoon, who earned what he could from house
to house, from market-place to market-place, from village green
to village green. In this sort of
life, even more than in our own
day, most of these men lost self-
respect. The clergy, to begin
with, formally denied it to them.
The religious encyclopaedia
which was written by Honorius,
commonly called of Autun,
but probably of Augsburg,
asks, "Can a minstrel [i.e. this
half-singer, half-buffoon, the
joculator] be saved?" The answer
is, there is no hope. "They are
ministers of Satan; they laugh
in this world; God shall laugh
at them in the last day."[4] "He
who gives money to a joculator", writes another Churchman, "is feeing the Devil." This
medieval condemnation of the
comedian prevailed in France,
on the official side, even down
to the Revolution. The case
of Molière is notorious.

The Tumbler.

Again, we must not forget the medieval contrasts. Though the
minstrel, like the village dance, was generally condemned by the
Church, yet in fact these tares did manage at all times to flourish
amidst the orthodox wheat; and, as time goes on and monastic
account-rolls become more frequent, we find how much of an
abbey's revenues might be diverted from the actual poor to those
wandering gleemen who enlivened the routine of its daily life.

The struggle out of Grub Street was immensely hindered by
the public opinion which welcomed, rather than reprobated,

literary piracy. The author of *Winnour and Wastour*, a contemporary of Chaucer who was evidently growing old when he wrote, complains bitterly of these beardless boys who learn his poems by rote and go about earning money and reputation by repeating them as their own. Doomsday (he feels) must be near; for the world is going fast downhill:

> Whilom were lordës in land, that loved in their hearts
> To hear makers of mirth that matters could find,...
> But now a child upon chair, withouten chin-weeds,
> That never wrought through wit three words together,
> For he can jangle as a jay and japës tell,   [jests
> He shall be believëd and lovëd and let of a while   [made much of
> Well more than the man that made it himselven.

Yet the lure of the *Vie de Bohême* was irresistible, then as at all times; and there were many who struggled on until they collapsed. Brunetto Latini writes: "What is the wandering minstrel's life? Laughter, and play, and vanity: he mocks at himself, at his wife, at his children, at everybody." But, if the joculator laughed so wildly, this was often to avoid tears. The greatest perhaps of these wandering minstrels, a man who has attained to real literary fame, is the French jongleur, Rutebeuf. His poems are full of autobiographic touches. "By the Lord God in Heaven, when I married my wife I was a poor man indeed; and she was poorer still. I cannot work with my hands; no man shall ever know where my lodging is: I am too poor for that....My bed is of straw—and anyone who has tried knows that a bed of straw is no bed....I don't leave my door open; my house is too desert and poor and naked for that; oftentimes there is neither bread in my chest nor dough in my kneading-trough. Don't blame me if I'm not in a hurry to get back to my home! for I don't get a pleasant reception there unless I can bring back something with me. That's my bitterest burden in life; for I daren't go inside mine own doors when I am empty-handed. Now you know what my life is. What enjoyment do I get out of it?—nothing, but the vague hope of something better tomorrow!"[5] His only hopes are in the bright spots that come every now and then. He haunts a wedding-feast, and may eat in a corner with the dogs. He attends a funeral; and that brings him a little luck. The Count of Poitiers, having won heavily at the gaming-table, throws him a handful of coin; but he knows only too well the door where they cry "welcome" to you in the evening and kick you out next morning. He forestalls the question, "Why, with all your talent, do you never write on love?" "Love", he says, "is only for the rich." It is in fact remarkable how few love-lyrics there are of even tolerable literary merit among the Latin poems of the wandering scholars, the so-called Goliards, when we have discounted three or four of remarkable power.

After 1350, something like modern conditions began to come in. Patrons multiplied; yet until the invention of printing and even for some time afterwards there could be nothing like modern copyright. Now, the authors were often drawn from the lower clergy or the citizen class. Dante is too exceptional in every way to quote as a type; but Petrarch, Boccaccio, and the Villanis, with both authors of the *Roman de la Rose*, Chaucer and Froissart were all of citizen extraction. We may take Froissart as typical, because he has left abundant autobiographical material, which throws as much light on the sort of life that his contemporary Chaucer led, as we should have upon Shakespeare if Marlowe had left an auto-biography. He was probably very slightly older than Chaucer, and outlived him by three or four years.[6] Like Chaucer, he was familiar with the courts of the great, as canon of the collegiate church of Chimay. We may imagine his death-bed like that in Browning:

> What is he buzzing in my ears? Now that I come to die,
> Do I view this world as a vale of tears? Ah, reverend sir, not I!

His most definitely autobiographical work is the *Buisson de Jeunesse*. From that and from other sources we know that he was born at Valenciennes, and therefore a compatriot of our Queen Philippa. His childhood, he tells us, was fed on romances and dances. At school he beat and was beaten; and again, coming home torn and dirty, was punished for having fought. What interested him most in the classroom was not the lessons but the little girls who sat on the benches by his side; for elementary schools, at any rate, were often coeducational in the Middle Ages. He exchanged with them presents of apples and pears and glass rings, and confesses: "I thought more in those days of a chaplet of violets than nowadays of 20 marks from a count." This was all very well; but he began to wonder when he should fall seriously in love. Apparently he was not yet fourteen when the great event came. It was in the month of May, of course, at the hour of prime, under the fresh rising sun. It was at what we might call a garden-party of the Middle Ages; she was sitting under a tree, reading the well-known romance of *Cléomades*. They read on together, and she finally asked him whether he could lend her any other romances. He possessed one—"The Bailiff of Love"—*Le Bailli d'Amour*—not a very romantic-sounding title. When he lent her this he slipped in a little ballade of his own, by way of recommendation. The book came back in due time with his ballade between the exact two pages into which he had slipped it. "Ha," said he, "here is a strange matter!" He was destined to see stranger matters before his own romance was ended. On another occasion he offered her a rose "par amour"; she answered: "The flower is in good hands. Leave it where it is." On a third, he suggested sitting out a dance: "All my delight in life is from you, if we had a little longer alone." She looked a moment at him and then said: "Let's go on dancing; I like dancing best." And so it lingered on. He never got further than to acquire her mirror by a bribe to her waiting maid; and in this he was able for months and years to contemplate his own woe-begotten countenance. She married, but that was not the end. The real quietus was given at another garden-party: "As she passed me she pulled my toupet" (the long ornamental front lock) with such purposeful violence that he understood it as a final and deliberate breach. But later on, at more than fifty, bald and disillusioned, he practically forestalls the last words of Mr Shaw's *You Never Can Tell*—"I'd do it again, sir, I'd do it again!"

We next find him at the court of his compatriot, Queen Philippa, acting the part of Boswell, picking up every possible anecdote of war and politics, and recording them in his *Chronicle*. On one occasion we see him riding with the Black Douglas, that formidable soldier who had cut off the right hand of every English archer whom he could capture, in revenge for the ravage that they worked among his own soldiers. Froissart, on his own grey horse, and with a white greyhound, entertained him while they rode. At another time we find him travelling with Earl Despenser, grandson of the great rebel who lost his head under Edward II. "Well forty times", says Froissart, "he would turn to me and say, 'Do you see that fair city? that was once ours, but it was taken from us by a wicked woman'", that is, by Gray's "She-Wolf of France". But

Philippa died, and with her died Froissart's best hopes at the English court. We see him again dimly at his own Valenciennes in the position of a *couletier*, about which word scholars are still disputing whether it means a bank-clerk or a breeches-maker. In any case Froissart evidently felt himself under a cloud; for here is a great gap in his autobiographical details. Presently, however, he emerges again with a princely patron, and enjoys a succession of these for the rest of his life. At Lestinnes, the last fat living that was given to him, he confesses that he has spent fabulous sums in wine during the last ten years. His *Chronicles* were always in steady demand, as well they might be; for, untrustworthy as he is on minor details, he gives an unrivalled picture of his time. But, with all his pains, he gradually became conscious of a gap in these stories of war and adventure. Nearly all that he had told was of Northern and Central France, while the South had been almost as picturesque a theatre. At last, therefore, he made up his mind to visit the court of Gaston de Foix, at Orthez in the Pyrenees. On the way, at Pamiers, he fell in by good fortune with Sir Espaing de Lyon, a great actor himself in those military dramas. Over and over again, on the way, this knight was able to point out the scene of some noteworthy deed of arms: how the town of Artigat had been taken by a company of Gascons and English disguised as merchants, who drank first with the gate-keepers and then "slew them so privily that none knew thereof...and so took all the men of the town, sitting drinking or else in their beds"; how, again, the Bastard of Lourdes, with three companions dressed like monks, "for well they had the habit and countenance of monks", caught a rich merchant on the highway, who paid a ransom of 500 francs; and how, at last, this same Bastard of Lourdes at the head of five hundred, and Ernaulton Bisette at the head of an equal company, veteran warriors on each side, met in clash upon a sudden foray and fought until both captains were slain, and each party was so weary that they ceased by agreement. "Behold, yonder is the [memorial] cross....And with those words, we came to the cross; and there we said for their souls a *Pater Noster* and an *Ave Maria*."

At Orthez, again, Froissart found no lack of material. He had not even to search; for it was thrown upon him. Men would ask him, "Have you heard of this? or of that?" and then some new story would be recorded forthwith upon his tablets. He had brought thither his own romance of *Méliador*, a poem which, by one of the most wonderful coincidences and pieces of detective work in all literary history, has suddenly turned up again in our generation after apparent loss for all these centuries. This, then, he would read to his princely patron, as Gaston sat up during the watches of the night. For the great count's life had been clouded by a sad misadventure. In a fit of wrath, he had taken his young son by the throat with an open penknife in his hand, and had thus lost the only heir to his title. Thenceforward, he lived the life of an eccentric, turning night into day. Froissart, however, was well paid for his labour; the earl gave him "80 crowns, and my own book again". So, with this fresh prospect of another patron, and a rich collection of stories from the battlefield and from the realm of ghosts, he drifted off again towards the papal court at Avignon. We need follow him no farther; he died a few years afterwards in his comfortable house at Lestinnes, having left to posterity a priceless record of all one side of fourteenth-century society: the aristocratic side, and the lower classes from the aristocratic point of view. If Chaucer had written chronicles and left us an autobiography they would probably have been much the same.

There, then, we have the two extremes: Rutebeuf, the man of Grub Street, as against Froissart at his succession of princely courts. In between these we may put an English poet, who in his own turn has told us a good deal about himself—Thomas Hoccleve (1368-1446).[7] We find this man, at the age of nineteen, as clerk in the Office of the Privy Seal. Twelve years later (1399) he is granted a pension of £10 until he shall obtain a benefice without cure of souls of double that value; we may roughly multiply these sums by 30 to get an idea of their significance in modern times. This was, of course, the ordinary way of rewarding civil servants at that day. Just as there were no university professorships in the modern sense, and the professor had to support himself as non-resident rector of some living, so again the king commonly rewarded all his servants, from the minister down to the scrivener, with an absentee rectory or something of the kind. When Hoccleve finally got a benefice, after about 25 years of waiting, it was in the form of a corrody at a monastery—that is, food, drink, lodging and dress for life. Long before those 25 years were up he had grown impatient of bachelorhood and cut off his main chance for a rich benefice by marrying and thus separating himself from all possibility of priesthood.

> I gasyd longĕ firste, and waytid faste
> After some benefice; and whan non cam,
> By proces I me weddid attë laste.
> And, God it wot, it sore me aghaste
>   To byndë me where I was at my large;
>   But done it was: I toke on me that charge.

The literary value of his poems is not great; their main interest is autobiographical. They give us an early example of the civil servant who nourishes literary ambitions; and, again, pictures of bachelor or semi-bachelor life in Chaucer's London, separated by rural paths and miry roads from the royal palace and offices at Westminster. Hoccleve's confessions of personal weakness are not only frank, but even grovelling, as Rousseau is sometimes: we see in him something of the man who has so long been a hanger-on that he has lost self-respect. Brunetto's joculator "mocks at himself, at his wife, at his children, at everybody"; but Hoccleve stops short at this *everybody*: he confesses himself too cowardly to touch those who might strike back.

> My freendës seiden vn-to me ful oftë,
> My misreulë me causë wolde a fit;
> And redden me, in esy wyse and softë,
> A lyte and lytë to withdrawen it;
> But that nat mightë synke in-to my wit,
> So was the lust y-rootid in myn hertë.
> And now I am so rype vn-to my pit....   [grave.
> Excesse at borde hath leyd his knyf with me....*
> The outward signe of Bachus and his lure,
> That at his dorë hangith day by day
> Excitith [us] to taaste of his moisture
> So often that man can nat wel seyn nay.
> For me, I seye I was enclyned ay
> With-outen daunger thidir for to hye me,
> But if swich charge vpon my bakë lay
> That I moot it forbere as for a tymë....†

Upon which Hoccleve proceeds to moralize as unctuously as the repentant Falstaff. Tavern-haunting (he says) bears two inevitable

---

* It was usual to eat in couples, two to a dish. Each brought his own knife; forks were superfluous; spoons were carefully watched over by the steward.

† In Hoccleve, as in Chaucer, the so-called *e* mute is still a real syllable: compare Chaucer's rhyme of *Romë* with *Come hither, lovë, to me.*

fruits: it wastes his purse and tempts him to slander; "for in the cuppë seelden founden is that any wight his neighëburgh commendeth"; thus we harm ourselves, our friends, and God. Only one personal advantage he confesses here; his cowardice keeps him cautious of his tongue. For the rest, he is as wax in the hands of the tempter. His work is at Westminster, his tavern is in the city—probably in Eastcheap. In summer, "heat and unlust and superfluity" move him to take a boat,

> And in the wyntir, for the way was deep,
> Unto the brigge I dressid me also,
> And ther the bootmen took up-on me keep,
> For they my riot kneewen fern ago:
> With them was I y-tuggëd to and fro,
> So wel was him that I with woldë fare;
> For riot paieth largely everemo;
> He styntith nevere til his purs be bare.

He was perfectly conscious of this folly, but unable to resist. The boatmen caught him with flattery; for they never called him less than "master", and "so tikelid me that nycë reverence, that it me madë larger of despense". At night, again, potations were too free: "with repleet spirit wente I to my bed, and bathid there in superfluitee." No man was less willing than he to rise in the morning, unless it be his fellow-clerks Prentys and Arondel, for "often they their bed loven so wel, that of the day it draweth to bee prymë or they ryse up". He makes no pretence of love for his job. A scrivener cannot talk or sing at his work.

> Thise artificers, see I day be day,
>   In the hotteste of all ther bysnysse,
> Talken and synge, and makë game and play
>   And forth thir labour passith with gladnesse;
>   But we laboure in traveillous stilnesse;
>   We stowpe and stare vpon the shepës skyn,
>   And keepë muste our song and wordës in.
>
> What man that thre and twenti yere and more
>   In wryting hath continued, as have I,
> I dar wel sayn it smerteth hym ful sore
>   In every veyne and place of his body;
>   And eyën most it greeveth trewëly
>   Of any crafte that man can ymagyne:
>   Fadir, in feith, it spilt hath wel-ny myne.

We may complement this with the far more comfortable picture of the schoolmaster Henryson at Dunfermline, describing how he came to begin his *Testament of Criseyde*, the best of all poems in the post-Chaucerian school. It was a cold day of early spring; colder still in those northern latitudes. There had been showers of hail; the sun was now set, and Venus rose as the evening star. Henryson watched her rising through the windows of his little oratory.

> Throughout the glass her beames burst so fair
> That I might see on every side me by.
> The northern wind had purified the air
> And shed the misty cloudës from the sky.
> The frost freezëd, the blastës bitterly
> From Pole Arctic came whistling loud and shrill,
> And caused me to remove against my will.
>
> I mend the fire and warmëd me about:
> Then took a drink, my spirits to comfort
> And armëd me well for the cold thereout.
> To cut the winter night, and make it short,
> I took a book, and left all other sport,
> Written by worthy Chaucer glorious,
> Of fair Cresseid and worthy Troilus.

PRACTICALLY all our modern sports were known in a simple form in the Middle Ages. We can see this by running down the index of Strutt's *Sports and Pastimes of the English People*, where we pick out at once, for instance, the following titles: Archery, Blind-man's-buff, Bowling, Chess, Dice, Draughts, Fives, Football, Hammer-throwing, Hockey, Morris-dancing, Quarter-staff, Quoits, Shuttlecock, Skittles, Tennis, Wrestling. Men played, it is true, under what we should consider great disadvantages, such as the roughness of the ground and other obvious hindrances. But these, after all, were comparatively superficial. It was more serious that the organization of these games was extremely rudimentary, quite apart from rivalries between neighbouring villages in football, wrestling, archery, and so on; rivalries which, like those of present international athletics, were apt sometimes to produce as much friction as friendliness. There was for no game any written rule, nor was there any regular arrangement for umpiring. The romance of Fulk Fitzwarine tells how Prince John, the future king, losing his temper at chess, tried to brain the hero with the board, which was doubtless of solid oak with good square corners.[1] Scott, again, in his Preface to *Ivanhoe*, records how one of John Hampden's ancestors lost three manors for striking the Black Prince with his racket at tennis:

> Tring, Wing, and Ivingho
> Hampden must forgo
> For striking of a blow,
> And glad he could escape so.

The Church, therefore, looked rather askance at these sports: we have seen how some college statutes explicitly forbade chess. To begin with, we must constantly remind ourselves how puritanical, in the modern sense, a great deal of Church doctrine was throughout the Middle Ages. Even in the remotest corners of social life we find occasional influences of these theological ideas: e.g. the stress laid upon the fall of man; the idea of the body as evil in contrast with the divine soul; the low opinion of women, as we shall see more fully in a later chapter. University regulations, in so far as they took note at all of sport, did so almost always in a negative sense. Even so great a man and so free an intellect as Abailard was able to persuade himself that sickness of the body was good for mental progress. The great early Scholastics, such as Albert the Great and St Thomas Aquinas, give moderate approval to Aristotle's praise of bodily exercise as beneficial to man's development on the whole. Bishop Grosseteste, it is true, puts this more plainly; but Grosseteste was one of the very few great men of the Latin Middle Ages who knew something of Greek and had caught something of the Greek spirit at first hand.

It is better to approach a subject like this in the concrete than in the abstract; and a very good idea of the ordinary sports of a great town may be gathered from the description of London written by Fitzstephen, St Thomas Becket's chaplain. We may take it in the racy translation of the sixteenth-century antiquary, John Stow:

"Let us now come to the sports and pastimes, seeing it is fit that a Citie should not only be commodious and serious, but also merrie and sportful....London, for the shews upon Theaters, and Comicall pastimes, hath holy playes—representations of myracles which holy Confessours have wrought, or representations of torments wherein the constancie of Martyrs appeared. Every yeare also at Shrovetuesday, (that we may begin with childrens sports, seeing we al have beene children,) the schoole boyes do bring Cockes of the game to their Master, and all the forenoone delight themselves in Cockfighting: after dinner all the youthes go into the fields to play at the bal. The schollers of every schoole have their ball, or [staff], in their hands: the auncient and wealthy men of the Citie come foorth on horsebacke to see the sport of the yong men, and to take part of the pleasure in beholding their agilitie. Every Fryday in Lent a fresh company of young men comes into the field on horsebacke, and the best horsm[a]n conducteth the rest. Then march forth the citizens sons, and other yong men with disarmed launces and shields, and there they practise feates of warre. Many Courtiers likewise, when the king lieth nere, and attendants of noblemen doe repaire to these exercises; and, while the hope of victorie doth inflame their minds, do shew good proofe how serviceable they would be in martiall affayres. In Easter holydayes they fight battailes on the water. A shield is hanged upon a pole, fixed in the midst of the stream; a boat is prepared without oares to bee caried by violence of the water, and in the fore part thereof standeth a young man readie to give charge upon the shield with his launce; if so be hee breaketh his launce against the shield, and doth not fall, he is thought to have performed a worthy deed. If so be without breaking his launce he runneth strongly against the shield, downe he falleth into the water, for the boat is violently forced with the tide; but on each side of the shield ride two boates, furnished with yong men, which recover him that falleth as soone as they may. Upon the bridge, wharfes, and houses, by the rivers side stand great numbers to see, and laugh therat. In the holy dayes all the Somer the youths are exercised in leaping, dancing, shooting, wrastling, casting the stone, and practising their shields: the Maidens trip in their Timbrels, and daunce as long as they can well see. In Winter, every holy day before dinner, the Boares prepared for brawne are set to fight, or else Buls and Beares are bayted.

"When the great fenne or Moore, which watreth the wals of the Citie on the Northside, is frozen, many yong men play upon the yce; some, striding as wide as they may, do slide swiftly: others make themselves seates of ice, as great as Milstones: one sits downe, many hand in hand doe draw him, and, one slipping on a sudden, all fall togither: some tie bones to their feete, and under their heeles, and shoving themselves by a little picked staffe, doe slide as swiftly as a bird flieth in the ayre, or an arrow out of a Crossebow. Sometime two runne togither with Poles, and, hitting one the other, eyther one or both doe fall, not without hurt: some breake their armes, some their legges, but youth desirus of glorie in this sort exerciseth it selfe agaynst the time of warre. Many of the Citizens doe delight themselves in Hawkes, and houndes, for they have libertie of hunting in Middlesex, Hartfordshire, all Chiltron, and in Kent to the water of Cray."

We find sometimes definite matches arranged; as when, in 1222, "the citizens kept games of defence and wrestlings near unto the Hospital of St Giles in the Field, where they challenged and had the mastery of the men in the suburbs and other commoners"; again in 1453 we hear of a tumult made against the Prior of the Hospitallers "at the wrestling beside Clerkenwell". In 1253 again, when the Londoners had a great display of tilting at the quintain, the king's servants "came as it were in spite of the citizens to that game, and [gave] reproachful names to the Londoners.... The said Londoners, not able to bear so to be misused, fell upon the king's servants and beat them shrewdly; so that upon complaint to the king he fined the citizens to pay a thousand marks." It was on account of disorders of this kind at tournaments, and especially for the bloodshed they occasioned—since there was not only the chance of sudden death, "unhouseled and unaneled", in the field itself, but also of vendettas and treacherous murder afterwards—that Popes repeatedly forbade tournaments altogether: a prohibition to which kings listened or not as they chose. Léon Gautier writes truly: "From [1143 to 1314], we find a long series of anathemas and papal thunderbolts.... Philippe-Auguste once made his children swear to take no part in any tourney....But popes and kings were impotent here, and men laughed at their prohibitions."[2]

It is indeed from Coroners' Rolls and similar documents that we learn most in many ways about our medieval sports. With regard to football, for instance, we find a papal dispensation given in 1321 "to William de Spalding, canon of Sculdham, of the order of Semp[r]ingham. During a game of ball [ad pilam], as he kicked the ball [cum pede], a lay friend of his, also called William, ran against him and wounded himself on a sheathed knife carried by the canon, so severely that he died within six days. Dispensation is granted, as no blame is attached to William de Spalding, who, feeling deeply the death of his friend, and, fearing what might be said by his enemies, has applied to the Pope."[3] Similar mischances are frequently recorded at wrestlings. Over and over again we get from the Coroners' Rolls that story of the old ballad:

> They warstled up, they warstled down, till John fell on the ground;
> A dirk fell out of Willie's pouch, and gave him a deadly wound.

Poaching was naturally then, as always, the villager's most exciting sport; but hunting on any larger scale was far more dangerous for him then than now. Trained hawks were especially prized by the upper classes, and a whole statute of 1360 deals with the question of the lost or stray falcon. The bird must be carefully kept by whoever finds it; and if, within four months, the owner does not claim it, the sheriff may take it and give a reward to the finder. If on the other hand the finder "conceal it from the lord whose it was, or from his falconers, and thereof be attainted, he shall have imprisonment for two years and yield to the lord the price of the hawk if he have whereof; and if not he shall the longer be in prison." It is interesting, and all the more so in view of the Hunting Monk in Chaucer's Prologue, to read two items from the account-rolls of Nicholas de Litlington, Abbot of Westminster, with which we may compare Margaret Paston's offering of an image of wax of the weight of her sick husband to Our Lady of Walsingham:

"1368 *Item*, for a waxen image of a falcon bought to offer [at the altar] for a sick falcon, *6d*.

"1368/9 *Item*, for a collar bought at the lord Abbot's bidding for his greyhound Sturdy, *3d*."⁴

The contemporary *Ménagier de Paris*, that priceless book in which a Parisian citizen instructs his young wife in her social and religious duties, and which represents the usages of good society in England also, writes, "At this stage of training your hawk, you must keep him on your fist more than ever before, taking him to law-courts and among folk assembled in church or elsewhere, and into the streets. Keep him thus as long as you can, by day or night; and sometimes perch him in the streets, that he may see and accustom himself to men, horses, carts, hounds, and all other things." When Sir Philip Neville's precious falcon was stolen, his friend the Bishop of Durham issued a general mandate to all archdeacons and clergy of his diocese to proclaim at Mass the sentence of excommunication against the offenders unless it were returned within ten days (1376). Two years later, the bishop, on his own account, issued an equally solemn excommunication against those "sons of iniquity, name unknown", who "to the grievous peril of their souls" "have abstracted stealthily and secretly from our forest of Weardale certain birds called Merlin-hawks in the vulgar tongue."⁵ Indeed, no chapter on sport would be even approximately complete without a few words consecrated directly to the village poacher. He is a prominent person in the Durham manorial rolls; everywhere the court-records breathe suspicion of him and his dog. The Forest Laws condemned the latter, if caught, to lose one foot, thus spoiling him for life. Again, this poacher comes so prominently into one of the less known alliterative poems of Chaucer's age, *The Parlement of the Thre*

Ages, that a few lines may be quoted here in more modern form. The author writes how:

> In the moneth of May, when mirthës be many,
> And the season of summer, when soft be the weathers,
> As I went to the wood, my weirdës to dree,
> Into the shaws, myself a shot me to get
> At an hart or an hind, happen as it might,

he waited on a bank at sunrise where "the grass was green, growen with flowers":

> The primrose, the periwinkle and penny-royal the rich;
> The dew upon daisies drenched full fine,
> Burgeons and blossoms and branches full sweet,
> And the merry mists full mildly gan fall,
> The cuckoo, the cushat, keen were they both,—
> And each fowl in that frith fainer than other,
> That the dark was done and the day lightened.

Here, after wearisome waiting, a herd of deer at last comes by. Our man crouches there in the bushes, scarce daring even to breathe. One great hart scents him, and pauses a moment to snuff the air and look around: "but gnattës greatly me grievëd, and gnawëd mine eyen." His fortitude had its reward: at one favourable moment he let fly, and "Dead as a door-nail down was he fallen." Hastily our poacher guts the body, and buries or hides the refuse:

> And heavëd all into an hole, and hid it with fern,
> With heath and with moss concealed it about,
> That no forester of the fee should find it thereafter;
> Hid the horns and the head in a hollow oak,
> That no hunter should get it nor have it in sight.

A modern poacher's autobiography (for much of which I can vouch personally, being of the same Norfolk village) has revealed with frank simplicity that dualism of soul which can be found even in the most primitive minds: on the one hand wild adventure, breach of laws with positive pride and pleasure in rebellion, side by side with underlying respect for those laws, and for the folk who habitually keep them.[6] The medieval angler, again, was as modern as the medieval poacher. That fifteenth-century manual of sport which is commonly ascribed to the Lady Juliana Berners reminds us how, even though he return with an empty creel, he is not without good consolation; for "atte the leest he hath his holsom walke and mery at his ease, a swete ayre of the swete savoure of the meede[we] floures, that makyth hym hungry.... And yf the angler take fysshe, surely thenne is there noo man merier than he is in his spyryte."7

Archery, of course, was a favourite English sport. In 1337 Edward III, in view of his war with France, strictly forbade all other plays or pastimes on pain of death; a sanction which, like many others in the Middle Ages, must be taken with a liberal pinch of salt. But in 1477 we find the Commons petitioning to the king that he should strictly enforce "the laws of this land", to the effect that "no person should use any unlawful plays [such] as dice, quoits, football and such like plays, but that every person mighty and able in body should use his bow, because that the defence of this land standeth much by archers". Latimer's sermon before Edward VI is worth repeating here. "In my time, my poore father was as diligent to teach me to shoote, as to learne me any other thing, and so I thinke other men did their children. He taught me how to draw, how to lay my body in my bowe, and not to draw with strength of armes as other nations doe, but with strength of the body. I had my bowes bought me, according to my age and strength: as I increased in them, so my bowes were made bigger and bigger: for men shall never shoote well, except they be brought up in it. It is a goodly Arte, a wholesome kinde of exercise, and much commended in Phisicke. Marcilius Phicinus in hys booke *de triplici vita* (it is a great whyle since I read him now) but I remember he commendeth this kynde of exercise, and sayth, that it wrestleth agaynst many kindes of diseases. In the reverence of God let it be continued. Let a proclamation goe forth, charging the Justices of Peace, that they see such Actes and Statutes kept, as were made for this purpose."

From this we may now turn to the medieval stage, and first of all to the religious drama. It is true that here, as elsewhere, there is much difficulty in distinguishing clearly between the religious and the secular. In music, for instance, and poetry, there was continual interpenetration. I have already quoted what Friar Salimbene tells us of his friend Henry of Pisa, who caught up an air from a maidservant's love-song, and used it for his own hymn of "Christe Deus, Christe meus, Christe Rex et Domine".8 Again, one of our oldest English lyrics, *Sumer is icumen in*, has come down to us by the fortunate chance that on the manuscript it has religious words set to the same musical notation. We may, however, distinguish roughly, and confine ourselves for the present to the miracle-play, mystery or pageant, terms between which there is no constant and definite distinction. The Roman Mass itself is highly mimetic and dramatic in character. At the very beginning, when the priest says, "Thou shalt sprinkle me with hyssop and I shall be clean", there comes the symbolical aspersion with holy water. Then again there are constant dialogues; e.g. "Lift up your hearts"; "We lift them up unto the Lord". Again, the priest just before entering upon the Canon of the Mass, as he recites to himself "I will wash my hands in innocency", goes through a symbolical friction of hands. In the Canon itself, he spreads out his hands to bless the elements. At the Consecration of the Host he elevates the Host and Chalice for the adoration of the faithful; and then as he says "Remember, O Lord...us sinners" he strikes himself on the breast; and strikes again at "O Lamb of God that takest away the sins of the world, have mercy upon us"; and for the third time before communicating. Or take again the service for the consecration or reconsecration of a church. In many of our churches the consecration-crosses may still be seen here and there; at Exeter Cathedral and at the great collegiate church of St Mary Ottery very carefully carved or moulded in bronze; but ordinarily simply painted on the plaster of the wall inside. One, for instance, has survived within a few hundred yards of where I write now, on the north wall of Holy Trinity, Cambridge, Those crosses were anointed, each in its turn, with holy oil by the bishop as the last act of his consecration of the church. The ceremonial is most impressive. The bishop approaches from the churchyard, followed by all his clergy but one. That cleric is posted within the church "in ambush" (*quasi latens*). The bishop smites three blows upon the door with his staff: and then the anthem is struck up: "Lift up your heads, O ye gates, and be ye lift up, ye everlasting doors, and the King of Glory shall come in." Then comes from within the question, "Who is the King of Glory?" and the reply follows: "The Lord of Hosts, he is the King of Glory." With those words the "ambushed" cleric opens the doors and slips out, *quasi fugiens*, as an expelled power of evil, to join the rest of the procession. From this liturgical drama was evolved later on a whole set of miracle-plays, the so-called "Harrowing of Hell", which is faithfully reproduced in the last Passus but two of *Piers Plowman*.*

Most important of all, however, was the Easter ceremonial. That may be traced definitely, in germ, as far back as the ninth century. It forms, again, one of the most striking episodes in the so-called *Revelation to the Monk of Evesham* (really, *Eynsham*). According to this ceremonial, in memory of Christ's burial, the great cross of the church was taken down and hidden all Friday and Saturday behind the altar. Then, before Matins on Easter Day, came an anthem in dialogue form, paraphrased from the Gospels; the so-called *Quem Quaeritis?* The angel sings: "Whom seek ye in the tomb, O servants of Christ?" to which the Maries reply: "We seek Christ that was crucified, O Host of Heaven." *Angels*: "He is not here; He is risen as He foretold; go, bear tidings that He is risen from the tomb." And then all in chorus: "I am Risen." Gradually this ceremony was much elaborated; and we find in some churches the so-called Easter Sepulchre in connection with it. This was a carved shrine of wood or stone, or even in some cases of metal—iron or silver—and, here and there, an actual small chapel within the church, as may still be seen at Luton in Bedfordshire. This Easter Sepulchre, then, was hung, with a canopy, and the Host in its pyx was generally laid there with the Cross. Watchers, in the guise of Pilate's soldiers, lay all night by it singing psalms, and sometimes even, to keep up the symbolism, in actual or sham armour. Here, as in so many other instances in history, the fullest description we get is not from contemporaries, who were too familiar with the scene to take the trouble of describing it, but from one who was impressed by it when it was already passing away. At Louvain, in 1569, "they make the grave in a high place in the church, where men must go up many steps, which are decked with black cloth from above to beneath, and upon every step stands a silver candlestick, with a wax candle burning in it; and there do walk soldiers in harness, as bright as Saint George, which keep the grave, till the priests come and take

---

* I cannot resist here repeating the story of the Devonshire parish clerk, which was such a favourite with our Devon-born historian, J. A. Froude. This was in the days when the ordinary parish church had no organ, but a fiddle, with perhaps a bass and a few other instruments in the gallery. One Sunday, when this anthem was announced, the parish clerk, who also played the bass fiddle, said audibly across to his neighbour, "Give us the rosin, Jim, and us'll soon show 'em who be the King of Glory!"

him up; and then comes suddenly a flash of fire, wherewith they are all afraid and fall down; and then up starts the man, and they begin to sing *Alleluia*, on all hands, and the clock strikes eleven." Sometimes the ceremony was even more elaborate than this, as may be read in Sir E. K. Chambers's *Medieval Stage* (1, 32), which is the classical book on this subject, and to which everyone who approaches it must now be indebted.

The "Crèche" again, though it may have been sometimes used earlier, owed its immense popularity to St Francis, of whom his biographers tell us that he enacted the scene in an actual stable, with living animals, as part of his constant imitation of the life of Christ. Again, there was often a far more elaborate Epiphany Liturgy (Twelfth-Night) with all the three Kings from the East, which in some versions was so long that it ran to six separate scenes. At the Cathedral of Laon, even the Massacre of the Innocents was symbolically and liturgically performed in the church. At St Paul's in London on Whit Sunday, during the hymn *Veni Creator*, a dove was let down through a hole in the vault, with burning tow, to represent the tongues of fire alighting upon the Apostles. Thus we may say that, by the time we come to the thirteenth century, these and other liturgical dramas were as far advanced as they could be within strictly religious limits. Up to this point we may treat them as "services", *officia*; in their further development they have become "amusements"— *spectacula*.

The earliest, perhaps, of these "Miracles" was that St Nicholas play which may be traced at least as early as the eleventh century, and has recently been excellently analysed by Professor G. R. Coffman.* With great probability he connects the rise of this, primarily, with those new impulses in popular literature, as everywhere else, which we may trace roughly from the fateful year 1000. Secondly, he emphasizes the multiplication of Saints' Lives which naturally accompanied this growth. Thirdly, he urges the probability that those writers, who were lashing their flanks to describe their saintly hero in the most picturesque and striking terms, caught at every possibility of rendering their story semi-

---

* Professor Coffman seems right in distinguishing, at the earliest stage, between "miracle" and "mystery". He produces evidence for the theory that the term miracle was generally confined to plays from saints' lives, and mystery to biblical plays. In the later fourteenth century, however, the names had certainly become to some extent interchangeable.

dramatic; and, finally, the decisive impulse seems to have come from the cult of St Nicholas, very ancient in his own city of Myra in Asia Minor, and again at Bari in Southern Italy, but a fresh importation into Western Europe during these later eleventh-century days. The story probably came through those ubiquitous Norman pilgrims who returned to their homes after visiting sacred places in Rome, in Southern Italy, or beyond the seas. Its spread can be traced especially on the trade route in the Loire valley and in Normandy, and from the Loire valley we have a very illuminating anecdote somewhere about 1080; at the Priory of La Croix, subject to La Charité, which in turn was subject to Cluny. Some monks asked leave to sing on St Nicholas's day "a new and popular history of that saint's life", but were denied by the prior because it was not the traditional Cluniac ecclesiastical chant (as he put it), but the playful (*jocularia*) composition of secular clerks. Twice the prior refused them; on the third time he had them beaten with a brush of twigs (*cum scopa*). Therefore St Nicholas appeared to the prior at night and forced him to sing an antiphon in honour of himself (St Nicholas). The prior was long unwilling, but the saint steadily smote him "after the accustomed fashion of a master to a boy who will not learn his letters". The prior, still reluctant and with tears, sang to the end, St Nicholas laying on every now and then, with the words: "This is what you did to your monks!" The monks themselves were awakened at this noise and flocked in with lights; "and, seeing him rubbing his back lustily and singing this anthem at the same time, they were amazed beyond measure." He greeted them with a "God forgive you, brethren, for making St Nicholas beat me like this!" But the lesson was effectual. He adopted the fashion; and so did the mother house of La Charité, not only for itself but also for all its dependent cells.

The actors in these plays were at first mostly, if not always, schoolboys or young clerics. St Nicholas was the patron saint of such folk, owing to the fact that, by a strange misunderstanding of the symbolism in paintings and carvings of his miracles, he was celebrated in later legend as having raised from the dead three young scholars who had put up at an inn, had been murdered by the landlord and his wife, and salted down and furnished in the guise of pickled pork to travellers. At Cambridge, for instance, King's College has as its official title The College of St Mary and

St Nicholas. The belief that the plays were mainly acted by monks is a time-honoured superstition. The theory is built upon a single instance in England about A.D. 1100; yet it is flatly contradicted by the actual text of the chronicle, which shows clearly that the schoolmaster who played this "miracle" with his boys was not a monk at that time; he took the vows only later, in a fit of penitence for mischief which he had inadvertently caused. Again, the idea that friars played a principal part in the composition or the performance of miracle-plays is due to a misunderstanding perhaps even grosser. It is founded on the doings of a certain Friar Melton at York, who is recorded as *professor sacrae paginae*. This title is interpreted (even, it must be confessed, in such a standard work as *The Cambridge History of English Literature*) as "professor of sacred pageantry", whereas of course it was only the common medieval synonym for "Doctor of Divinity". Moreover, the action of this particular Friar Melton at York was not in foundation of any miracle-play, but in regulation and restriction of those which already existed. On the other hand these plays, though not in any sense predominantly monastic, had naturally a clerical origin, in those days when every scholar was a cleric of some sort. We have seen how Fitzstephen, as early as 1170, speaks of the theatrical performances of these young clerks at Skinner's Well and Clerkenwell, just outside the walls of London. In the thirteenth century we find episcopal prohibition of miracle-plays in churches or churchyards; yet this was frequently broken; and the *Book of Miracles* of St John at Beverley shows incidentally that one was regularly played at the end of the century in the churchyard there.[9]

The significance of Corpus Christi Day must not be missed here, since nothing else can show more plainly the extent to which not only medieval art, but medieval religion also, however taken in hand by the hierarchy at its later stages, grew up essentially from below. The dogma of Transubstantiation was first officially proclaimed by Innocent III in 1215, and this naturally had very great effect not only on the stories of miracles (especially in adding frequency to the much older story of onlookers to whom an actual child appears in the priest's hands immediately after the consecration of the holy wafer) but also on popular devotions of all kinds. About ten years after this decree, a visionary girl in Belgium felt that the Church ought to institute a solemn feast in honour of this dogma. She inspired a young priest with equal enthusiasm; and he composed a church service for the day.[10] That service spread among the common people, and was accepted by the Bishop of Liége in 1246. The struggle was lively, and sometimes even violent, between these innovators and the more conservative clergy in the diocese of Liége; but, after much debate and quarrel, the feast was accepted also by Pope Urban IV (1264) who, however, died before formally promulgating his decree. The final official seal was set to it at the Council of Vienne in 1311. This celebration was always marked by a great procession, with the Host borne at its head; and rich Indulgences were decreed from Rome for those who followed the church services on that day. From thence it was a natural step in a great town like York that each trade gild, with its own separate banner, should form a separate limb of the procession. These banners represented some emblem or some group of figures; and, by a further evolution, they were sometimes so arranged as to form a consecutive picture of Bible history or some part of it. Thence it was a natural step that each of these bodies should have its own play, and thus we get the town cycles. The first recorded of this kind in England is the Chester cycle of 1328, which was indeed written by a monk, Higden. Those original plays, however, have been lost; and the surviving Chester cycle, though it may have been founded upon them, is very much later. Before 1400 there were such cycles at York, Beverley, Coventry, London and Cambridge. Before the Reformation these had spread so far that even little towns and large villages had their own mystery-play. Apparently the movement had decayed to some extent even before the Reformation; and certainly its decadence was then hastened not only by the change of religion, but sometimes by very regrettable violence on the Reformers' part. It was revived under Mary; but under Elizabeth we find only a few rare survivals. Yet, here again, it is from that later time that we find the fullest account of the ancient institution. By this time, in addition to the former names of "miracle" or "mystery", we must add that of "pageant"—that is, a wooden stage (Latin, *pagina*) which was generally, but not always, set on wheels for locomotion. Each gild or group at a great city was responsible for one separate pageant, including not only the scenery, properties and so on, which were kept from year to year, but also competent actors. There was indeed liberal prompting; but at Beverley, at any rate, we find documentary record of a gild which is fined for the incompetence of its actors. For these, then, we may take the description of Archdeacon Rogers at Chester in 1594. "Every company had his pageant, or part, which pageants were a high scaffold with two rooms, a higher and a lower, upon four wheels. In the lower they apparelled themselves; and in the higher room they played, being all open on the top, that all beholders might hear and see them. The places where they played them was in every street. They began first at the Abbey gates, and when the first pageant was played it was wheeled to the high cross before the mayor, and so to every street; and so every street had a pageant playing before them at one time, till all the pageants for the day appointed were played: and when one pageant was near ended, word was brought from street to street, that so they might come in place thereof exceeding orderly, and all the streets have their pageants upon them all at one time playing together; to see which plays was great resort, and also scaffolds and stages made in the streets in those places where they determined to play their pageants." At York, the citizens before whose house the pageants stood were compelled to pay for the honour; or possibly for the pecuniary profit of this arrangement.

So much for the origin of these religious dramas. Let us now take two specimens of the plays themselves; definitely above the average; one of tragedy and one of comedy. The first is from the sacrifice of Isaac in the Chester cycle:

> Father, we must no more meet
> By aught that I may see;
> But do with me then as you will,
> I must obey, and that is skill,
> God's commandment to fulfil
>   For need's so must it be.
> Upon the purpose that you have set you,
> For sooth, father, I will not let you,
> But ever more to you bow,
>   While that ever I may—
> Father, greet well my brethren yinge   [young
> And pray my Mother for her blessing,
> I come no more under her wing,
>   Fare well for ever and aye;
> But Father! I cry you mercy,
> For all that ever I have trespassed to thee,
> Forgiven, Father, that it may be
>   Until Doomësday.

For comedy, on the other hand, perhaps the highest level is in the Shepherd's Play at Wakefield; but this is too long to quote. For the present purpose we can only find room for the scene of Noah and his wife from the Chester Deluge Play. This is a specially English scene: it occurs, I believe, in no other country, and it will be remembered how Chaucer alludes to it: as the

> sorrow of Noah and all his fellowship
> That he had, ere he got his wife to ship.

From this, and from his allusion to Absalom, we may see that what impressed Chaucer most was the comic side of the miracle-play, as Langland was most impressed by the tragic.

N.	Wife, in this castle we shall be kept
	I would thy children and thou in leapt.
NW.	I faith Noah, I had as lief thou slept,
		For all thy frankish fare,
	For I will not do after thy rede.
N.	Good wife, do as thou art bid.
NW.	By Christ, no! ere I see more need,
	Though thou stand all day and rave.
N.	Lord, how crabbëd are women alway!
	They never are meek, that dare I say
	And that is well seen by me today
	In witness of you each one.
	Good wife, let be all this trouble and stir
	That thou makest in this place here,
	For all men think thou art my master
		(And so thou art, by St John!)

[At this point God commands Noah to put the animals into the Ark, and his sons count them in two by two, as in the nursery rhyme.]

N.	Wife come in, why standest thou there?
	Thou art ever froward, that dare I swear;
	Come for God's sake, time it were,
	For fear lest that we drown.
NW.	Yea, sir, set up your sail,
	And now forth with evil heal,
	For, without any fail,
	I will not out of this town!
		But if I have my gossips each one,
		One foot further I will not go on
		They shall not drown, by St John,
		If I may save their life.
	They loved me full well, by Christ!

If thou wilt not have them in thy chest
Why then row forth, Noah, whither thou list,
And get thee a new wife!

N.   Shem, son, thy mother is wrawe
Forsooth, such another I do not know,

SHEM.   Father, I shall set her in, I trow
Withouten any fail.
Mother, my father doth thee send
And bids thee into yonder ship wend:
Look up and see the wind,
    For we be ready to sail.

NW.   Son, go to him and say
I will not come therein today!

N.   Come in, wife, in twenty devils' way
Or else stand without!

H.   Shall we all fetch her in?

N.   Yea, sons, with Christ's blessing and mine,
I would you hasten you betime,
For of this flood I am in doubt.

Gossips' song

The flood comes fleeting in full fast,
On every side it spreadeth full far,
For fear of drowning I am aghast;
Good gossips, let us draw near,
And let us drink, ere we depart,
For oftentimes we have done so;
For at a time thou drinks a quart,
And so will I, ere that I go.
Here is a bottle full of Malmsey, good and strong,
It will rejoice both heart and tongue;
Though Noah think us never so long
Here will we drink alike!

JAPHET.   Mother, we pray you all together
For we are here, your own childer,
Come into the ship for fear of the weather,
For His love that you bought.

NW.   That will not I, for all your call,
But I have my gossips all.

S.   In faith, mother, yet you shall,
Whether you will or not,
    [They hustle Noah's wife in.]

N.   Welcome, wife, into this boat!

NW.   And have thou that for thy not!   [nut, head
Aha! Mary, this is hot!

This brings us to another point. What is the fountain-head of
this comic element in the miracle-play? Why, for instance, is that

Wakefield *Shepherd's Play* a farce almost from beginning to end? We may answer, I think, that this is not only almost inevitable in human nature, but it had its definite precedent in what we may call the liturgical farces of the Feast of Fools, the Boy Bishop, and so on. The Church was compelled to tolerate a large number of heathen customs, only doing her best to baptize them to her own purposes. These heathen customs had, as we shall see, mainly gathered round the different turning-points of the year, and had been designed to propitiate the gods and secure fertility for the fields. The Winter Feast, especially, was prehistoric; and in ancient Rome it took the form of the Saturnalia, beginning on December 17th. The essence of that feast was that the relation between master and man, owner and slave, should for a moment be turned topsy-turvy. That, again, was the essence of the liturgical farces which went by the name of *Deposuit*. In the middle of the service, at that point of the Magnificat when we come to the words *deposuit potentes*—"He hath put down the mighty from their seat"—then the precentor of a great church would transfer his official staff to the Lord of the Feast (the *dominus festi*), who had been chosen beforehand from among the subdeacons. Then followed a riot all the more boisterous because the lower clergy, of whom this subdeacon was the representative, were habitually ill-paid and over-worked, and beneath them was the still lower class of choirboys, often beaten and bullied all the year round. We may say, therefore, that this ceremony of *Deposuit* was the revolt of the clerk and the choirboy; and it thoroughly earned its other name of "Feast of Fools". Similar to this was the "Abbot of Misrule", celebrated by Scott in his novel of *The Abbot*; and again the "Boy Bishop": a boy elected as bishop for a moment by his fellows, and at some great churches furnished with a set of costly robes and ornaments. The Feast of Fools was formally forbidden by the Ecumenical Council of Basel in 1445; and the Pragmatic Sanction between the Pope and the king practically made those prohibitory decrees part of French civil law. The character which the feast had assumed may be judged by the formal letter from the University of Paris to the King of France:

"Priests and clerks may be seen wearing masks and monstrous visages at the hours of office. They dance in the choir dressed as women, or disreputable men, or minstrels. They sing wanton songs. They eat black-puddings at the altar itself, while the celebrant is saying Mass. They play at dice on the altar. They cense with stinking smoke from the soles of old shoes. They run and leap throughout the church, without a blush at their own shame. Finally they drive about the town and its theatres in shabby carriages and carts; and rouse the laughter of their fellows and the bystanders in infamous performances, with indecent gestures and with scurrilous and unchaste words."

Here, then, was a liturgical play of immemorial ancestry, from which the miracles drew much of their rough humour. Moreover, the miracle-plays themselves were not absolutely free from this reproach of an irreverence deeper than the mere admission of comic scenes. Yet these, it must be repeated, had grown up naturally, perhaps almost inevitably, from the compromise which Gregory the Great had wisely recommended to his missionaries in England. "Do not, after all", wrote Gregory, "pull down the temples. Destroy the idols; purify the buildings with holy water; set relics there; and let them become temples of the true God. Thus the people will have no need to change their places of concourse; and where of old they were wont to sacrifice cattle to demons, thither let them continue to resort on the day of the saint to whom the church is dedicated, and slay their beasts no longer as a sacrifice, but for a social meal in honour of Him whom they now worship."

Just as these heathens' feasts became the medieval "Church Ale", so did their other religious ceremonies often survive as popular sports. We find these ceremonies vaguely touched upon by Bede in his *Ecclesiastical History*. They had originally been grouped mainly round the three culminating points of agricultural life, in those ages, when the most civilized life was almost entirely agricultural. At a still earlier stage the main foci had been two, i.e. the beginning and the end of winter: in mid-November, when the first serious snows fall, and again in spring when the first violets show their face and the first swallows arrive. These account for the peculiar sacredness of Martinmas (November 11th) all through the Middle Ages, and again for the fact that the Resurrection Feast coincided with the pagan *Eostre*, and borrowed its name. The feasts gathered themselves more definitely round the first ploughing ("Plough Monday" was the first Monday after Twelfth Day), the first sowing, and the harvest. The author of *Dives and Pauper* condemns, among other popular superstitions, that of "ledyng of the plough aboute the fire as for gode begynnyng of the yere, that they schudde fare the better alle the yere followyng".[11]

These heathen festivals were often concerned, as is common in the primitive mentality, with some compulsion exercised upon the god. The dipping of some image or symbol in water was often part of it; and this, again, was perpetuated in the medieval custom, by no means extinct to the present day, of plunging the saint's statue into a neighbouring river in order to compel rain in times of drought. At Villeneuve-St-George, for instance, one of the first villages on the Seine that we pass on our journey southwards, where the church was appropriated to the monks of St-Germain-des-Prés, the thirteenth-century villagers were accustomed to exercise this spell of a water-bath over their negligent or recalcitrant patron saint.[12] One of the most interesting medieval sports of the kind took place at Hocktide; that is, the Monday and Tuesday following the second Sunday after Easter. Those days so conspicuous in popular memory that they are often used in formal legal documents. On Hock-Monday the women "hocked" the men; they went about the streets and roads with ropes, with which they caught and bound any man they came across, and demanded a forfeit for his release. On Hock-Tuesday the men retaliated upon the women. We find the Bishop of Worcester forbidding this practice in 1450; but in spite of such disfavour in higher quarters it was a regular source of parochial revenue, and we constantly find recorded in churchwardens' accounts the sums collected on Hockdays.

Even more popular and long-lived was the dance round the Maypole, which was a definite survival of the pagan spring festivals; and upon which, again, the clergy often frowned. Bishop Grosseteste, for instance, specifically forbade it for his whole great diocese in the early thirteenth century. This May Dance gradually crystallized into a king-and-queen play, to which were added in later days the characters of Robin Hood and Maid Marion; moreover it was frequently associated with the Morris Dance. This May-day play was so complicated that it was often composed and carried out by professional minstrels. The Sword Dance, again, is probably a survival of the ancient superstition, so brilliantly expounded by Sir James Frazer, of the Martyr-King; of the idea that, in order to ensure prosperity, a human sacrifice must be made, and the greater the personage the more efficacious the sacrifice. This, again, is bound up with the equally frequent prehistoric idea of enacting the death and resurrection of summer. That kind of ceremonial would also appeal to all martial instincts; and it is natural that we should find it noticed by Tacitus in his description of the ancient Germans. In proportion as this Sword Dance was elaborated, comic accompaniments were also brought in; so that at this point what we may call the pagan liturgy goes through the same natural evolution as we have seen in the Christian liturgy. The Morris Dance itself became more and more elaborate, often with the accompaniment of a hobby-horse and a clown and a comic woman, Bet or Marion.

The Plough Monday plays, with their infinite variations, nearly always follow a certain type which may be divided into three acts. There is first the presentation, a prologue, as for instance in *Midsummer Night's Dream*. Then comes the drama itself, ending in a fight, a death and the doctor called in, who restores the dead to life; this we see in our puppet-play of Punch and Judy. Then comes the collection; either one of the characters goes round begging for money, or this is done by an appointed official. These dramas gradually shaded off into the more elaborate form of the St George play, the popularity of which may be gauged by a significant passage in the *Paston Letters* (1473). Here Sir John complains of "W. Woode, whyche promysed...he wold never goo ffro me; and ther uppon I have kepyd hym thys iij yer to pleye Seynt Jorge and Robyn Hod and the Shryff off Nottyng-ham; and now, when I wolde have good horse, he is goon into Bernysdale, and I withowt a keeper". The great Earl of Northum-berland also made regular provision for "liveries for Robin Hood" in his household.

It is evident that, by this time, the popularity of these sports was leading to the creation, side by side with the professional minstrel, of a class of semi-professional players. All popular sports had a growing tendency to crystallize round Christmas. When Christianity first began to claim the allegiance of the Roman world, the rulers of the Church were confronted by a series of immemorial winter-feasts which together made the latter half of December and the beginning of January into one continuous carnival. The exact origin of December 25th as the traditional date of the birth of Christ is wrapped in obscurity. The most we can say is that, by A.D. 336 at least, that feast fell between December

8th and December 27th. Its final definite fixture for the 25th was probably due to an attempt to harmonize it with the pre-Christian Roman calendar. From Rome it gradually spread over East and West, not reaching Jerusalem until after A.D. 500, and never adopted at all by the distant Church of Armenia. It was established at Antioch about A.D. 375 and at Alexandria about 430. But, before this feast had been fixed to an exact day, it had naturally attracted to itself a great deal of pre-Christian merry-making. The early Fathers protested against these Christmas sports, as they did against nearly all other pagan enjoyments; but it ended at Rome, as it ended later on at Canterbury, with their acceptance and the transference of prohibition into attempts at regulation. In Bede we find Christmas, Epiphany (Twelfth Night) and Easter as integral feasts in English Christianity. Therefore it was specially about Christmastide that what we may call the liturgical farces gathered; and that of the Boy Bishop, which was the least extravagant, was not only definitely fixed at many cathedrals, but also regularly patronized by monasteries.

Meanwhile the layfolk were inventing for themselves other similar dramatic representations, which were naturally still more frowned upon by the Church authorities. We have interesting testimony to this in two documents from the Register of Bishop Grandisson of Exeter. The first describes how "a certain sect of malignant men", calling themselves the Order of Brothelyngham, dressed as monks and chose "a certain lunatic and mad fellow" as their abbot; and how, having set him up in the "theatre", they go round about the streets and squares of the city with great noise of horns, capturing layfolk and clergy and extorting "certain sums of money in place of sacrifice, nay, rather of sacrilege" (1348). The term *Brothelyngham* is doubtless a parody on the actual monastic order of Sempringham, which was often called Simplingham; *brothel*, again, was a common name for any foul fellow. In the other case (1352) the bishop finds himself compelled to fulminate against a play composed "in contumely and approbrium" of the leather-dressers (*allutarii*) of Exeter; a play which, as he says, is only too likely to lead to breaches of the peace at the Devil's instigation. He therefore forbids the performance on pain of excommunication; but at the same time he admonishes these leather-dressers that they have brought it upon themselves "by selling their goods at more than the just price in

these modern times" (*modernis temporibus*), in which the King
and the Council have fixed prices; in other words, they have
contravened the Statute of Labourers.[13] We must not, however,
jump from the fact that the bishop mentions *theatrum* at Exeter to
the conclusion, which is sometimes drawn, that the city already
possessed a theatre in the modern sense. *Theatrum* in medieval
Latin need mean no more than its original sense of "a gazing
place" of any kind. It may be found, for instance, applied to the
village green; and the Exeter *theatrum* may perfectly well have
been any of the open spaces. However, there is no doubt that by
this time the drama was growing in England; and already in the
fourteenth century we find "moralities" (a sort of mystery-play
in which the motive is moral rather than definitely religious) and,
again, a great multitude of lay pageants. London naturally set the
lead here. Stow, telling us that he will enumerate a few of them,
begins with that with which the citizens greeted Edward I on his
return from the victory over Wallace at Falkirk in 1298. Others,
equally magnificent, greeted Henry V after Azincourt in 1415,
and again in 1421 when he brought his French bride home. Other
towns tried to follow the same example in their own fashion, e.g.
Coventry, Worcester and York.

Then grew up something much more like the modern drama,
the so-called Interlude. Sir E. K. Chambers is probably right in
explaining this word not as a play in the interval between two
other plays, or between two courses at a banquet, "but *ludus*
carried on between (*inter*) two or more performers"; in short, a
ludus in dialogue. This, as he points out, might apply to any kind
of dramatic performance whatever; and as a matter of fact we find
it applied at early dates to miracle-plays, but thence gradually
restricting itself to something different. Thus, "while Interlude
was only the subordinate name for plays of the Miracle-type, it
was the normal name, varied chiefly by *Play* and *Disguising*, for
plays given in the banqueting halls of the great". From the early
fifteenth century onward we find travelling troupes of Interlude
players; these may be the *lusores* who are so frequently mentioned
in account-rolls as having been entertained and paid in monasteries.
This growth naturally kindled gradual rivalry with the pre-
existing professional minstrels. Thus the latter petitioned for and
received the grant of a Royal Minstrels' Gild in 1469. The players,
like the minstrels, "put themselves under the protection of nobles

and persons of honour". The earliest upon record are those of Henry Bourchier, Earl of Essex, and those of Richard, Duke of Gloucester, afterwards Richard III. Henry VII had four "King's Players, alias, in the vulgar tongue, *les pleyars of the Kyngs enterluds*", each receiving five marks a year, with a special bonus when he played before the king. At vacation times they toured the provinces. Once they accompanied the Princess Margaret to her wedding with James IV of Scotland. Henry VIII increased their number to eight. These new conditions naturally reacted upon the plays. The performance now must be brief and pithy; Interludes seldom run beyond a thousand lines. "Again, economy in travelling and the inconvenience of crowding the hall both went to put a limit on the number of actors: four men and a boy, probably in apprenticeship to one of them, for the women's parts, may be taken as a normal troupe.... The simplest of scenic apparatus, and a few boards on trestles for a stage, had of course to suffice." It will be remembered how one of St Thomas More's earliest distinctions was that, whilst still a page under Cardinal Morton, he came suddenly upon the stage of an Interlude and improvised a scene of his own. From the halls of great folk they spread to those of the gentlemen of the Inns of Court, and again to the universities. The earliest Sir E. K. Chambers has noted are at Magdalen College, Oxford, from 1486 onward, overlapping in point of time the performances of *Quem Quaeritis?* in the chapel. In 1512 Oxford granted a degree in Grammar to Edward Watson on condition of his composing a comedy. St John's was the first at Cambridge, with the *Plutus* of Aristophanes in 1536; and it is very probable that *Gammer Gurton's Needle* was first performed at Christ's. The Eton plays can be traced back to 1526, and it is quite possible that the Westminster boys' play is equally early.

It will be seen that the medieval hierarchy was not without excuse for frowning so often upon the popular drama, and giving so little encouragement to popular sports. For we must take into consideration not only the ultra-puritanism of St John Chrysostom with his "Christ was crucified, and dost thou laugh?" but the solid fact that nearly all these sports were prehistoric and therefore pre-Christian, and that they often gave the plainest testimony to that ancestry. For this I have given much fuller evidence in my *Medieval Village*, pp. 272 ff. Exaggerated stress is often laid nowadays upon the attitude of our early Reformers towards sport. "Every schoolboy", to use Macaulay's classical phrase, knows Macaulay's epigram that the Puritans objected to bear-baiting not because it gave pain to the bear but because it gave pleasure to the spectators. This is not true even as a direct statement: many Puritans were excellent sportsmen both in theory and in practice. But the wider implications which are often given to the statement are still less reconcilable with fact. When we come across sixteenth- or seventeenth-century clerics dealing with popular sports, it would be very difficult to decide on internal evidence whether the writer was on the Roman or the non-Roman side. Here are the words of the great Roman Catholic canonist Van Espen [1710]: "If we consider those dances, leapings and skippings which are performed nowadays, especially in the country among persons of both sexes, it will be evident that they exactly fit that which the Fathers have said about the spectacles and dances of their own day, and that, as St Charles Borromeo said, 'such meetings are scarcely ever brought about without many and most grievous offences against God'." Here Van Espen gives a whole list of sequelae, ranging from "foul thoughts" to "fornication and adultery".[14]

If this shocks us at first sight, we shall understand it when we consider the age and the circumstances. Here is an earnest man, bent upon great and serious truths, but somewhat warped by his professional separation from, even while he mingles with, average humanity. Meanwhile, however, the average man goes very much upon his own average way. Whether in those distant days or in our own, the toiler needs (as Fénelon reminded his well-meaning *curé*) to forget, if only for one day in the week, the burden of his toil. Normally, the mere feeling of being alive is a pleasure, intense in proportion as it can consciously express itself: this human instinct is not denied even by those who may sneer at it as unreasonable. And if, in any age, that conscious expression of vitality is wild and ill regulated, some part of the fault must be charged to those who knew, and might have taught, better.

THIS is an enormous field, of which I can here touch only the fringe, in anticipation of the exhaustive study with which Professor Eileen Power has long been engaged. Meanwhile, however, those who wish to pursue the subject further should consult her article in *The Legacy of the Middle Ages* and her *Medieval English Nunneries*, together with Miss A. Abram's *English Life and Manners in the later Middle Ages*, and Thomas Wright's *Womankind in Western Europe*. For Renaissance women see P. S. Allen's *Age of Erasmus*, pp. 197–8.

There is, perhaps, no subject in which it would be more dangerous to judge from legislation alone. In law, medieval woman had certainly great disadvantages, of which the most startling was her crude subjection to physical violence. We find here a significant contrast between the much older Jewish civilization and that of these comparatively recent feudal lords whose Germanic fathers, not so many generations earlier, had broken in upon the Roman Empire. We must here recall that decision of Rabbi Perez, who died shortly before 1300. It is not an authoritative conciliar decision; but it represents fairly what an influential Rabbi attempted to enforce in his congregation. "The cry of the daughters of our people has been heard concerning the sons of Israel who raise their hands to strike their wives. Yet who has given a husband the authority to beat his wife? Is he not rather forbidden to strike any person in Israel?...Nevertheless have we heard of cases where Jewish women complained regarding their treatment before the Communities, and no action was taken on their behalf. We have therefore decreed that any Jew may be compelled, on application of his wife or one of her near relatives, to undertake by a *herem* [written document] not to beat his wife in anger or cruelty or so as to disgrace her, for that is against Jewish practice. If anyone will stubbornly refuse to obey our words, the Court of the place, to which the wife or her relatives will bring complaint, shall assign her maintenance according to her station and according to the custom of the place where she dwells. They shall fix her alimony as though her husband were away on a distant journey."[1] With this we may compare the pronouncement of a theological encyclopaedia of exactly this same period, by the Dominican Nicolas Byard. "A man may chastise his wife and beat her [*verberare*] for her correction; for she is of his household, and therefore the lord may chastise his own, as it is written in Gratian's *Decretum*, under the gloss *judicari*." The writer goes on to compare their relation in this respect to that of schoolmaster and schoolboy.[2] Turning to the text of Gratian referred to, we find: "A husband may judge his wife by correcting her, but not by beating her [*verberando*]...but he may chastise her [*castigare*] temperately, since she is of his household"; and this is followed by a reference to the *Code of Civil Law*, where *verberando* is forbidden. But the context seems to show clearly that our encyclopaedist applied this prohibition of "verberation" only to such systematic stripes as were permitted to a master in the case of a slave, and that the "temperate castigation" included an occasional hasty buffet. In two other passages of Gratian's *Decretum* this principle is more plainly laid down. A decree of the Council of Toledo (A.D. 400) prescribes that "if the wives of any clergy have sinned", the husbands may "keep them bound in their house, compelling them to salutary fasting, yet not unto death"; or, as the annotator puts it "macerating them with stripes [*verberibus*] and hunger". A third passage, again, runs: "The husband is bound to chastise his wife moderately, unless he be a cleric, in which case he may chastise her the harder" [*durius*], with a reference back to that earlier Toledo decree. Moreover, in the *Corpus Juris Canonici* these are quite in keeping with other passages concerning the relations of husband and wife. "It is a natural human order that the women should serve their husbands and the children their parents; for there is no justice where the greater serves the less." "Woman was not made in God's image." "It is plain enough from this that wives should be subject to their husbands, and should almost be servants"—*famulas*, a word often used for slaves. Again: "Since the husband is the head of the wife, while the man's head is Christ, every wife who is not subject to her husband, that is to her head, is guilty of the same offence as the man is when he is not subject unto Christ his head."[3] St Thomas More's treatment of this subject goes some way to bear out Professor Chambers's remark that there are even more medieval than modern features in his *Utopia*. For in that model community, "the eldest (as I said) ruleth the family. The wives be

ministers to their husbands, the children to their parents, and, to
be short, the younger to their elders." "The husbands chastise
their wives, and the parents their children." "In the holy days
that be the last days of the months and years, before they come to
the church, the wives fall down prostrate before their husband's
feet at home and the children before the feet of their parents,

The Wife-Beater.

confessing and acknowledging themselves offenders either by
some actual deed, or by omission of their duty, and desire pardon
of their offence. Thus, if any cloud of privy displeasure was risen
at home, by this satisfaction it is overblown, that they may be
present at the sacrifices with pure and charitable minds."[4]

When we turn from Canon Law to Customary Law and practice, the case is still plainer. Léon Gautier, the great panegyrist
of chivalry, confesses that "examples [of woman-beating] are
plentiful in the best romances of adventure". He continues:

"There are even two cases specified by the legislator, in which the husband's palm may lawfully fall upon his wife's back or nose: first, if she ever falls into the shame of adultery, and, secondly, if she permits herself to give her lord the lie. True, legislation tends to soften this; and good Beaumanoir of the thirteenth century, in his *Customs of Beauvoisis*, declares that the husband may beat his wife only 'reasonably'."[5] I have read that, in one of the new towns which were founded in Gascony about this time, one clause of the statutes ran: "Tout habitant de Villefranche a le droit de battre sa femme, pourvu que la mort ne s'ensuive pas." We have conclusive evidence, again, from that *Book of the Knight of La Tour-Landry* which sets forth the duties and usages of upper-class society, and which became the most popular manual of its kind not only in fourteenth-century France but in England and all the great European countries. There were eight printed editions before 1538 in French, English and German. In that book, the Knight tells his daughters how one wife had been rash enough to scold her husband most outrageously in public.[6] He continues: "And he, that was angry of her governance, smote her with his fist down to the earth; and then with his foot he struck her in the visage and brake her nose, and all her life after she had her nose crooked, the which shent and disfigured her visage after, that she might not for shame show her visage, it was so foul blemished. And this she had for her evil and great language, that she was wont to say to her husband." "For the nose is the fairest member that man or woman hath, and sitteth in the middle of the visage."

Let us pass on to other disabilities, of a kind which lasted on into more modern times, or which even exist sometimes to-day.

Women could inherit estates and titles; they could become baronesses, but not sit in parliament. The myth of a great abbess sitting among the lords, in virtue of her baronial dignity, has often been exploded. Stubbs wrote truly, "no lady of any rank whatever was ever summoned either in person or by proxy to a full and proper Parliament. There are instances of countesses, baronesses, and abbesses being summoned to send proxies or to furnish their military service, but not to attend Parliament as peeresses. The nearest approach to such a summons is that of 4 abbesses who, in 1306, were cited to the Great Council held to grant an aid on the knighting of the Prince of Wales."[7] Nor, again, had women real testamentary freedom. The Commons in

Parliament complained (1344) how "prelates...allow serfs and women to make wills, which is against reason...may it please the king and his council to find remedy, so that his people may remain in the same estate as they were wont to have in the time of all his progenitors". The answer ran: "The King wills that law and reason be kept in the matter."[8] In the struggle which ensued, the more liberal spirit of the Church was worsted, "and slowly the spiritual tribunals were brought to a reluctant admission that the wife has only such testamentary power as her husband is pleased to allow her, and that his consent can be revoked at any time before he has suffered the will to be proved". But, on the other hand, "the ecclesiastical lawyers themselves had not been able to formulate a clear theory about the matter".[9] Yet it is only fair to quote Vinogradoff's judgment that the Church was the most powerful opponent of the system which excluded women from the right of succession to land; and it was not Canon but Common Law which ruled that the word of women cannot be admitted in proof by the law-courts, "because of their frailty".[10]

Far more invidious was the law of "petty treason", though its incidence was naturally far less frequent. Under this head came originally any plot against the life, but in later times only the actual killing, of one's "lord": and the husband was the wife's lord, just as he was the servant's.[11] Thus, in 1386, "one Nigel Hakeneye was slain by his wife and servant-maid and the aforesaid Tydman; for which felony the said wife and servant-maid were burned, and the said Tydman fled away". In France and Germany, the penalty was sometimes burial alive. This scandal of death for petty treason survived the Reformation.

Again, women could not become licensed physicians. A petition to parliament sets forth how all kinds of unlearned men intermeddle with the practice of physic: let none but bachelors or doctors of medicine do thus, under pain of imprisonment and a fine of £2; the same penalty is pronounced upon any woman who practises.[12] On the other hand, women were the natural herbalists and charm-doctors among the common folk. They were often forbidden to trade; for instance, in 1355, the London gild of brace-makers decreed "that no one of the said trade shall be so daring as to set any woman to work in his trade, other than his wedded wife or his daughter".[13] "Many craft regulations exclude female labour, some because the work was considered too heavy, but

most for the reason, with which we are familiar, that the competition of women undercut the men. Then, as now, women's
wages were lower than those of men, even for the same work."[14]
In many towns the statutes were indulgent to the widows of
gildsmen, who might keep on the family business. At fifteenth-
century Coventry, all single women of able body, and under the
age of fifty, were compelled to "go to [domestic] service till they
be married."[15] Women, of course, did a great deal of field-work;
and the builders' account-rolls often show them working at the
rougher jobs side by side with men. Miss A. Abram, who has
published a study of *Women Traders in Medieval London*, concludes: "If we sum up the evidence gathered from the various
sources which have passed under our review, we are led to the
conclusion that the women traders of Medieval London were
persons of strong character and undeniable business ability, and
that they played a not inconsiderable and very useful part in the
industrial life of the city."[16]

For in fact, where the capacity and the will exist, statutory
restrictions are constantly swept away. So noted the Cambridge
canonist John of Ayton, in the early fourteenth century. He is
commenting on the statutes of Cardinal Ottobon (papal legate in
England and afterwards Pope Hadrian V), which in their last
clause prescribe that the official nunnery-visitors "shall cause the
statutes here decreed to be exactly obeyed". At this point Ayton
exclaims: "Cause to be obeyed! but certainly this almost passeth
the wit of mortal man; therefore we must here insert the proviso
'so far as in them lieth'.... For the nuns answer roundly to these
statutes, as to others which have been decreed to check their
wantonness; 'The men who made these statutes sat well at their
ease when they decreed these things against us, imposing such
hard and intolerable restrictions!' Therefore we see plainly that
these statutes are kept either ill or not at all. Wherefore then did
the Holy Fathers thus labour to beat the air?"[17] Lina Duff-
Gordon's *Home Life in Italy* shows us how in that country,
although assertive and militant feminism would stand no chance
of success, yet the mother has in fact enormous power in her own
household, making or unmaking the marriage of a grown-up son,
and playing the domestic dictator within her own province, which
is a region far wider than in other countries where women's
liberties are more definitely asserted. The late Dr C. M. Doughty

assured me that there was much of this also among the Bedouin Arabs, in spite of what might seem the utter legal subjection of the women.* Guizot, again, points out the extent to which the medieval wife sometimes received and shouldered the whole burden of the family. In a baronial household, the eldest son was from childhood upwards a sort of Prince of Wales, beginning very early to share his father's power and responsibilities, yet in fact enormously under the influence of a strong-willed or able mother. We must not forget, also, that the medieval lady who might receive those blows was the true-blooded female of the lord who dealt them: a sister-spirit, it might be, to that countess who killed the architect of her castle lest he should go off and build one equally strong for someone else. Women's disabilities in medieval society were not of that steady and calculated quality, and had none of that leaden pressure which weighed upon the Turkish wife and daughter. We must rather think of them in terms of Thomas Carlyle's aristocratic patroness Lady Ashburton, who replied to a friend's "I should die if I were married to that man!" with "No, I should kill!" Let us remember Chaucer's Wife of Bath capable of reinforcing "the arrows of her crabbed eloquence" with her fist; and Harry Bailey's wife; and, in history, that Countess of Montfort whose defence of her husband's castle inspires some of Froissart's finest pages; or again, the heroine of Perelada; or Jeanne Hachette (who, as her nickname implies, cracked many skulls among the Burgundian besiegers of Beauvais) and Joan of Arc. Finally, we may count Agnes Paston, who faced even worse physical violence than her husband in defence of the family interests, and who was no less redoubtable to her children than to her enemies. For we find a lady-cousin writing to stress the necessity of getting one of Agnes's daughters married as soon as possible, seeing that the old lady is commonly at war with the girl, who "hath since Easter the most part been beaten once in the week or twice, and sometimes twice on one day, and her head broken [i.e. *blood drawn*] in two or three places."[18]

Have we not here one of the commonest of medieval phenomena, that custom counted more than written law? Our popula-

---

* Compare P. S. Allen's judgment on the society of A.D. 1500 (*Age of Erasmus*, p. 201): "The inference is probable that though the sphere of women was in many ways restricted, they were within their own dominion, the household, supreme—more so perhaps than they are to-day."

tion, in the pre-Christian stage, had paid considerable respect to women, though this may have been not inconsistent with personal violence in a society where impulse often outweighed self-control. This is fully brought out in G. F. Browne's *Importance of Women in Anglo-Saxon Times* (S.P.C.K. 1919, p. 11). He writes: "In many of the tribes the chief deity was a goddess, worshipped with very reverential care. In time of peace the men in some of the tribes left to the women the management and the work of the farms which provided their means of support. It seems clear, too, that while the tribes worshipped a goddess, the men of the tribes ascribed to their women some mysterious force of insight and foresight. 'They conceive', Tacitus says, 'that in woman is a certain uncanny and prophetic sense: they neither scorn to consult them nor slight their answers.'" This must be one of the reasons for the fact, which was noted as definitely by contemporaries as by modern scholars, that witches were numerous out of all proportion to the wizards. Again, Browne writes: "Plutarch tells us of the Celtae that they were, from very early times indeed, firm believers in the wisdom of their women.... When Hannibal made a league with the Celtae...this was the article which the Celts put into the conditions: 'If the Celtae have complaints against the Carthaginians, the Carthaginian commander in Spain shall judge it. But if the Carthaginians have anything to lay to the charge of the Celtae, it shall be brought before the

The Wife of Bath.

Celtic women.'"[19] The Roman Church took, on the whole, a different view, laying disproportionate stress upon St Paul's dictum that the woman must not speak in Church. The Wife of Bath had only too much reason to complain:

> For, trusteth wel, it is an impossible
> That any clerk wol spekë good of wyvës—
> But if it be of hooly Seintës lyvës—
> Ne of noon oother womman never the mo.

Chaucer's friend Gower emphasizes the inferiority of the sex

from Creation onwards: otherwise the Almighty would have fashioned Eve not from Adam's rib but from his head.* A few years later, St Bernardino of Siena exercised his almost unrivalled pulpit eloquence against female fashions. Addressing the typical over-dressed woman in his congregation, he cries, "Oh, if it were my business, if I were your husband, I would give you such a drubbing with feet and fists, that I would make you remember for a while!"[20] More than a century later, in 1530, the year of the so-called "Reformation Parliament", a *Commentary on the Rule of St Augustine* was addressed to Abbot Mylne of Cambuskenneth, from the convent at Paris, by one of his special pupils. This Robert Richardson, coming to that passage where St Augustine warns his devotees against the fair sex, outdoes even that which, in Chaucer, men sometimes imagine to be a mere caricature. Woman, he writes, "has always been the most conspicuous mischief of the human race. For she is an animal prouder than the lion, that fiercest and proudest of the brute creation; more wanton than the ape; more venomous than the asp; more false and deceitful than the syren. Nor can any of the fiercest beasts be worthily compared with the feminine monster. The lions feared Daniel in their den, and so did the dragon; yet mad Jezebel slew the righteous Naboth. Jonas escaped safe from the whale's belly; yet Samson, stoutest of mankind, escaped not the hands of his own wife. John Baptist lived many years unhurt among dragons and asps; yet Herodias no sooner knew him than she slew him. Why should I pursue this matter further?" yet further our Robert pursues it, like his namesake Robert Montgomery, for half a page more; and he reverts to it twice or thrice later.[21] It would be difficult to find any parallel to the far more favourable comparison which Professor Power quotes from a Cambridge MS., except, of course, in poetry. There the troubadour stood a whole horizon apart from the preacher; "so that women found themselves perpetually oscillating between a pit and a pedestal."[22]

Moreover whereas papal legislation accepted resignedly the

* Herein he exaggerates from the far more moderate judgment of Peter Lombard, in those *Sentences* which were the great textbook of medieval theology. Peter writes (bk. II, dist. xviii c.): "She was formed from the man's side, to show that she was created for his consort, lest perchance, if she had been made from his head, she should seem to be preferred above him in domination; or, if from his feet, then to be subject to him in slavery." From the side therefore, "in order that he should learn to place her beside himself whom he had learned to have been taken from his rib".

habitual breach of St Benedict's rule of claustration by his male devotees, Boniface VIII insisted upon the strictest and most harem-like seclusion for the nuns; so strict that it was scarcely ever maintained in its completeness. For, here again, Canon Law drew a clear line between the sexes; the nun is a Spouse of Christ; therefore unchastity on her part involves three crimes, incest, sacrilege, and adultery.[23] It is from Canon Law also that the Anglican Church has drawn that sentence of the marriage service which lends itself most to modern criticism. "Of two evils", writes Gratian, "the least should be chosen; and this is proved by the example of St Paul, who conceded the less evil, that is, marriage and conjugal intercourse, by reason of incontinence, in order that the greater and more grievous alternative of fornication should be avoided."[24] Marriage, he writes elsewhere, is like a sea-voyage; for "even as he who goeth by ship subjecteth himself to divers perils, nor is he ruled by his own impulses but by the winds, so is it with him that hath a wife". It is often asserted, off-hand, that the Mary-cult did much to raise women's status in the Middle Ages. No doubt it had some effect; but there seems no evidence for any far-reaching influence in that direction. The Virgin-Mother stood, in common idea, too far above ordinary humanity to suggest any immediate connection, except as a semi-divine intercessor; as a being who could not be thought of as a Jewess without something of a religious shock; such is the story that St Thomas More tells us à propos of a lady of his own day.[25]

On the other hand, time does seem to have done something solid for women's emancipation. It is strange to find the first philosophical plea in this direction from the Mohammedan Averroës, in the late twelfth century. He argued that women differ from men not in quality but in degree; they are apt to all men's occupations, though to a less degree. Sometimes they even surpass them. The example of certain African states shows their aptitude for war; and there would be nothing extraordinary in their reaching the government of the state. Among sheep-dogs, does not the female guard the flock just as well as the male?[26] The late thirteenth and the fourteenth century seem to show an unusual proportion of conspicuous women-mystics, spending much of their lives in a state of half-trance, receiving divine revelations as to the wickedness of the world, and threatening clergy and people with sudden vengeance in default of speedy

repentance and conversion. Again, Dubois the Frenchman and
the Englishman Ockham had, on this subject, ideas which must
have seemed revolutionary in their age. Dubois would have a
specially educated class of women-missionaries.[27] The girls should
be taught theology and medicine, and sent out either to the clergy
of the Greek Church—where, since there had never been any rule
of priestly celibacy, the priests might be specially impressionable
to the proselytism of such advocates—or to the Muslim and other
infidels. Such peaceful matrimonial penetration, he feels very
reasonably, might go far to atone for the military failures of the
Crusades. Ockham, for his part, demanded ecclesiastical constitutionalism as a substitute for the prevailing papal despotism.[28]
Christendom was to be ruled no longer autocratically, but by a
systematic series of world-councils; and, since women also have
souls to save, why should not they likewise have votes? This
feminism culminates in the Bible-translator Tyndale, who, in his
controversy with St Thomas More, argued for some degree of
ecclesiastical equality not only in an imaginary Utopia but in
ordinary workaday England. He wrote: "Women be no meet
vessels to rule or to preach, for both are forbidden them; yet hath
God endowed them with his Spirit at sundry times, and shewed
his power and goodness upon them, and wrought wonderful
things by them, because he would not have them despised. We
read that women have judged all Israel, and have been great
prophetesses, and have done mighty deeds. Yea, and if stories be
true, women have preached since the opening of the New Testament. Do not our women now christen and minister the sacrament of baptism in time of need? Might they not, by as good
reason, preach also, if necessity required? If a woman were driven
into some island, where Christ was never preached, might she
there not preach him, if she had the gift thereto? Might she not
also baptize? And why might she not, by the same reason,
minister the sacrament of the body and blood of Christ, and teach
them how to choose officers and ministers?"[29]

Throughout the later Middle Ages we find, for what they are
worth, fairly frequent complaints of growing feminine licence.
We must discount these as we do all medieval complaints of a
wicked present contrasted with a golden age in the past; but they
have some reality at the back of them. Abbot Guibert de Nogent,
the friend of St Bernard, concludes the picture of his own

admirable mother with bitter reflections on his own time.[30] "Lord, thou knowest how hardly—nay, almost how impossibly—that virtue [of chastity] is kept by women of our time: whereas of old there was such modesty that scarce any marriage was branded even by common gossip! Alas, how miserably, between those days and ours, maidenly modesty and honour have fallen off, and the mother's guardianship has decayed both in appearance and in fact; so that in all their behaviour nothing can be noted but unseemly mirth, wherein are no sounds but of jest, with winking eyes and babbling tongues, and wanton gait. . . . By these modern fashions, and others like them, this age of ours is corrupted and spreads further corruption." The Knight of La Tour-Landry, again, would place the age of real modesty about the time of his own and Chaucer's father, a date by which, according to Guibert's calculations, the growing shamelessness of the world ought long ago to have worn God's patience threadbare. Each was so far right that he lived (as we all do) in a time of transition, and that he saw (as we too see) much that might certainly be changed for the better. One cause that made for the increase of woman's freedom was the growth of the towns. "In some respects the Bourgeoisie showed a greater sense of the normal personality of women than did either the Aristocracy or the Church, borough law had to take account of the woman trader, and in many towns there existed 'customs' for the treatment of a married woman carrying on a trade of her own as a *femme sole*. These are in striking contrast with the laws regulating the position of the married woman under the common law; and, although they were intended for the protection of the husband, they were also an effective improvement in the status of the wife."[31]

Social freedom was greater then, as it naturally is everywhere, within the highest class and the lowest, the nobles and the peasants. Then, as now, Mrs Grundy was a bourgeoise. The books of deportment which have come down to us were naturally rather for the middle classes, and they are painful in their primness. The *Good Wife* warns her daughter—

> And when thou goest in the way, go thou not too fast,
> Brandish not with thy head, nor with thy shoulders cast.

The *Ménagier de Paris* writes to his young wife: "If you are walking out, go with your head turned straight forward, your eyelids low and fixed, and your look straight before you down to the ground at twelve yards, without turning your eyes on man or woman, to the right or to the left, or staring upwards, or moving your eyes about from one place to another, or laughing, or stopping to talk to anyone in the streets."[32] The maiden, when seated, was expected to keep her hands crossed on her lap: this is alluded to as customary even as late as the end of the sixteenth century in France. In England, side by side with a good many formalities now forgotten, there was one custom in Erasmus's day

Maidenly Deportment.

which delighted him. Writing back to a friend at Paris University, he celebrates in classical hyperboles the attractiveness of our girls, and adds: "The English also have a custom which can never be enough extolled. Whithersoever you go, you are received with kisses by all present; at your departure they send you off with kisses. You come back: kisses again. They come to you, kisses are handed round; they quit you with a fresh distribution of kisses. We meet in the streets with copious kisses; in short, whithersoever we turn, it is a whole world of osculation. If you, dear friend, ever tasted how soft and sweet these are, you would desire to leave your home not for ten years, as Solon did, but as a sojourner in England unto death."[33]

When the English girl came to possess children of her own, her turn of legal domination arrived at least over that portion of the family. The *Good Wife* advises her daughter:

> And if thy children be rebèl, and will not them low,
> If any of them misdoeth, neither ban them nor blow   [curse nor cuff
> But take a smart rod, and beat them on a row
> Till they cry for mercy, and be of their guilt acknow.[34]   [acknowledge

Small girls sometimes went to the elementary schools with boys; and a few outside girls, and even boys, were occasionally taught by the nuns in their convents. These pupils, however, were very commonly discouraged, and sometimes actually forbidden, by the visiting bishop or other authority, since such teaching of outsiders found no place in the Benedictine Rule, and disciplinarians feared more disturbance of conventual discipline than benefit to the pupils. Nor was higher education often encouraged. The Knight of La Tour-Landry probably voices the average opinion when he writes: "Howbeit there be suche men that have opynion that thei wolde not that [t]her wyves nor [t]her doughtres shulde knowe no thinge of the scripture. As touchinge unto the holy scripture, it is no force [it matters not] thoughe women medille not nor knowe but litelle therof but forto rede [for] every woman it is the better that [she] canne rede and have knowinge of the lawe of God."[35] Most men of our period would have agreed heartily with what Diderot puts into the mouth of Rameau's nephew. The interlocutor has expressed his desire of teaching his daughter "à raisonner juste, si je puis; chose si peu commune parmi les hommes, et plus rare encore parmi les femmes". To which the nephew answers: "Eh! laissez-la déraisonner autant qu'elle voudra, pourvu qu'elle soit jolie, amusante et coquette."

Ladies hawking.

Yet, though very few women arrived at anything like the university stage in education, it seems probable that more of them could read and write than the men, especially in the upper classes at the period of the romances of adventure. Doubtless they were more flexible, as in our own day they are far better linguists, having less of that masculine dignity which forbids our stooping to conquer so vulgar a thing as the common speech of foreign people. Then, as now, the women were the main readers of romances and the main church-goers.[36] In the higher classes, they were often devoted to sport. John of Salisbury, in his polemic against contemporary devotion to hunting and neglect of philosophy or literature, argues that we may condemn the former "from the bare fact that the worser [*deterior*] sex is the more skilful at hawking; a fact which might give room for complaint against Nature, unless we noted that the worser elements are always more prone to rapine".[37]

It may be just worth while to note that Erasmus, who knew so many countries, seems to bracket English women with their Italian sisters as specially devoted to finery of dress. (Comment on I Tim. ii. 9, printed by Jortin, vol. ii, p. 223.)

XLVI. MARRIAGE AND DIVORCE

W E come now to one of the most important questions of all; that of the marriage contract. One fair rough criterion of any civilization is the clearness and sanctity of its contracts. And, in this particular matter, the woman has far more interest than the man; for, as the physically weaker party, and the less able to stand up by herself against economic competition, she suffers far more through the break-up of a household and the care of the derelict children; nor can we imagine any state of society—unless, perhaps, we ever arrived at mechanical incubation, as with poultry—in which she would not be the party more interested in stability of marriage than her mate.

From Adam and Eve onwards, the woman's duty had always been to spin; thus *spinster* became a natural designation for an unmarried girl. In early European civilization (e.g. under Charlemagne) there were great spinning-chambers, *gynaecea*, for the girls. "The great emperor was so anxious that womankind should be employed in productive labour, that he made his own daughters work in the domestic gynaeceum as diligently as the other females."[1] Though these seem to have died out gradually, until economic progress revived the system again in fifteenth-century England, and much earlier in Italy and the Low Countries, yet there was always a tendency, natural in medieval circumstances, to deal with the younger female population in the mass. In 1285, a French lord manumitted by will, "for the health of my soul, one hundred girls from my two estates".[2] No less than sixty-five of these were named Jeanne; not a single Mary or her mother Anne; those names were too sacred for ordinary girls.

There were necessarily a good many single women, even outside the nunneries. For those, after all, absorbed only a very small fraction of the total spinster population: the nuns did not number one-twentieth of the men who, as clerics in major orders or cloisterers, were similarly withdrawn from the marriage-market. Miss Abram notes how that Coventry regulation testifies to an appreciable number of single women among the working classes. Yet, among the upper classes, this was different; it was so natural for the unmarried daughters to be dowered to a convent, in default of sufficient dowry for a husband, that the "old maid" was as unusual a phenomenon in the Middle Ages as in modern upper-class French society. Pollock and Maitland write: "It is hardly too much to say that the early Medieval law never seems to have contemplated the existence of an unmarried woman of full age.... Her position is never the subject of statute law, as is that of widows; hence it seems probable that among the higher classes the independent 'femme sole' was, outside the convent, a negligible quantity."[3]

Thus the *mariage de convenance* was the normal arrangement in every class, from the noble to the peasant. "They were often dictated solely by the interests of the land. 'Let me not to the marriage of true fiefs admit impediments' may be said to have been the dominating motive of a great lord with a son or daughter or ward to marry."[4] Pollock and Maitland, from the purely legal point of view, sum up: "In Henry III's day a marriage between a boy of four or five years and a girl who was no older seems capable of ratification, and as a matter of fact parents and guardians often betrothed, or attempted to betroth, children who were less than seven years old. Even the Church could say no more than that babies in the cradle were not to be given in marriage, except under the pressure of some urgent need, such as the desire for peace."[5] Léon Gautier, on the other hand, studying the great chivalric romances of adventure, where he finds the *mariage de convenance* painfully prominent, confesses: "Whatever may be said, those are not the conditions for truly free marriage, or, to speak plainly, for a truly Christian one." Erasmus felt much the same: he wrote: "In Britain, the sons of noblemen come into the power of guardians if their father dies; this right is bought or obtained from the king. Whenever such a guardianship falls out of the family, then the ward's possessions are sometimes so dealt with that he can hope for little fruit from his lands unless he marries the wife prescribed by his guardian....And this they call matrimony, although the Roman Civil Law took care that the guardian or tutor should not marry the girl committed to his charge, nor even his children should so marry: yet Church Law forbiddeth it not."[6]

Let us take three concrete instances of matrimonial suits. Pollock and Maitland quote a case from about A.D. 1200.[7] Grace, though probably a supposititious child, passed as daughter to Sir

Thomas of Saleby, and was therefore a great heiress. The king gave her in ward, on Thomas's death, "to Adam Neville, the chief forester's brother. When she was but four years old, Adam proposed to marry her. The bishop forbad the marriage; but, whilst the bishop was in Normandy, the marriage was solemnized by a priest....King John sold Grace to his chamberlain Norman for two hundred marks; and, when Norman died, the king sold the poor girl once more for three hundred marks to the third and worst of all her husbands, Brian de Lisle. In the end she died childless." Here, again, are two from the Lichfield episcopal registers.[8]

"*Report of the process of dissolution of marriage between John, son of John de Arde[r]ne, Kt., and Cecilia, daughter of Nicholas de Eton, Kt.** The libel, supported by the evidence of witnesses who had known the parties from their infancy, was that they were married in the face of the Church when under marriageable age, John being about 11; that John always said he would not consent, and moved the question of dissolution directly he came of age; that these facts are well known in the Parishes of Aldeford, Stopport, and Prestbury, and the neighbourhood. The witnesses called were William de Wevere, aged 40 and upwards, freeman, Henry de Ravencroft, aged 38 and upwards, freeman, and John Buchard (or Bruchard) aged 40 and upwards, freeman....Judgment was given on the Monday after Palm Sunday, and the marriage declared null and void."[9] Shortly afterwards, in 1378, "before the Bishop sitting as a tribunal in the chapel of his manor of Heywood at the hour of prime in the presence of a notary and witnesses, William Thiknes, of noble birth [*domicellus*], aged 70 and upwards, appeared and declared that when he was 12 he married of his own free will Elizabeth Cune [Coyney], aged 8, and they regarded each other as husband and wife. When he was 20, moved by what spirit he knew not, he was secretly married—without saying anything about his former marriage—to Katherine Smynnerton; the ceremony was performed in the oratory of his manor of Thiknes by the Chaplain who was then ministering there. Banns were not published and the required solemnities of law were omitted. By Katherine he had offspring, William and Eve, still surviving, and

---

* This marriage was no doubt arranged by John's stepmother, who was also Cecilia's mother. Joan de Stokport married first Sir Nich. de Eton, and afterwards Sir John de Arderne. See Ormerod's *Cheshire.*

seven other sons and daughters now dead. All this time Elizabeth was alive and not divorced, being at once a maid and a wife, as she affirmed to her confessor at the time of her death. When Katherine died, he married publicly, after banns, Margery de Audeley, who is still surviving, and by her had offspring, who are now regarded as his right heirs. He said that he made this statement not from hate or love of any of his sons or daughters, but that all might have justice, and he prayed that a record should be made of the facts, which the Bishop ordered to be done."[9]

Among quite ordinary townsfolk, there was often not enough money at stake to make expensive litigation profitable: but we commonly get dry indications such as this, from the fifteenth-century Chancery records. "William Durham and Margaret his wife, daughter of John Walker, complainants. William Smyth, of Olcotys, Co. York defendant. Action brought concerning the dower of the said Margaret, paid to the said William Smyth on agreement that one of his sons should wed her."[10] Among village-folk, again, it was in medieval England as in Molière's France: "Les pères et les mères ont la maudite coutume de demander toujours *Qu'a-t-il?* et *Qu'a-t-elle?* et le compère Pierre a marié sa fille Simonette au gros Thomas pour un quartier de vigne qu'il avait davantage que le jeune Robin où elle avait toute son amitié."*[11] Those who have intimate knowledge of French society warn us against too hasty judgments on the results, and point out that there is often a very healthy *camaraderie* between such a husband and wife. But that difference does exist, and cannot be left out of account, between the ordinary English marriage in Chaucer's day and in ours. We may perhaps find a curious inverted romanticism in the pity which moved St Thomas More to choose the elder sister while his personal preference pointed to the younger; but nothing of that kind marked his second marriage.[12] As described by Erasmus, that union was Utopian on one of those points where Utopian manners were rather medieval than modern. "A few months after the death of the first he chose a widow, rather for the care of his family than for delight, 'neither a beauty nor a maid', as himself was wont to say in jest, but a keen

---

* "Fathers and mothers have the accursed custom of always asking *How much has he?* and *How much has she?* and old Peter has married his daughter Simonette to fat Thomas, for a little bit of vineyard that he had beyond young Robin, upon whom she had set her heart."

and vigilant materfamilias; yet he lived as gently and smoothly with her as though she had been the fairest of maidens. Scarce doth any husband get so much obedience by command and severity as this man doth by blandishments and jests. What could he not obtain, seeing that this woman, already aging, and far from soft in disposition, finally gave the strictest attention and learned to play on the cithern, the harp and the clavichord, and that, at her husband's request, she daily performs the prescribed task at these instruments?"

Again, there was an even greater difference in the legal contrast itself. On the one hand, marriage was definitely claimed as a Sacrament, from Peter Lombard onwards. It is true that, even thus, one of the greatest Schoolmen, Guillaume Durand, explicitly admitted that it cannot be called a Sacrament in the strict sense,[13] and the present orthodox doctrine was not made a question of faith until the Council of Trent; yet the whole later Middle Ages were sufficiently unanimous in favour of this sacramental claim to justify the Church's insistence that she herself should be the sole judge in matrimonial cases. But, on the other hand, what with the inherent difficulties of the subject, and the historical difficulties, and the Church's own hesitations and lack of clear thought, the matrimonial litigation of the Middle Ages was not only among the most frequent but also among the most hopelessly perplexed.

We must never for a moment forget that the Church had here a very difficult task. She had to do her best to avoid a clash with old Roman Law on the one hand, and, on the other, the unwritten immemorial customs of the semi-barbarian tribes which she had converted. Yet, in spite of the late Master of Balliol's protest, it is difficult to avoid the conclusions of Pollock and Maitland in their *History of English Law*: "Reckless of mundane consequences, the Church, while she treated marriage as a formless contract, multiplied impediments which made the formation of a valid marriage a matter of chance.... When we weigh the merits of the medieval Church and have remembered all her good deeds, we have to put into the other scale as a weighty counterpoise the incalculable harm done by a marriage law which was a maze of flighty fancies and misapplied logic." And, giving a concrete case in full, from the year 1302, they add: "After reading this judgment it is difficult to believe that the ecclesiastical courts were pre-eminently fit to administer the law of marriage and divorce."

For, although marriage was extolled as a Sacrament of the Church, the Church was not indispensable: the parties themselves were the only necessary celebrants. The mere exchange of a verbal pledge, "I take thee to my wife" (or "husband"), followed by

The Tree of Consanguinity.

cohabitation, without priest or Church ceremony of any kind, and even without witnesses of any kind, constituted a marriage as valid before God as if the Pope himself had been the celebrant. Such a marriage was indeed "irregular"; the parties were liable to severe punishment if the Church courts chose to proceed against them; but of its validity there could be no question, though of course this would be impossible to prove unless both parties testified on oath to facts which they alone knew. Moreover, mere children were perfectly competent to bind themselves thus: the boy need only be fourteen and the girl twelve, a difference which our canonist Ayton ungallantly explains by the proverb "ill weeds grow apace".

On the other hand, the most carefully arranged marriage, celebrated with every precaution in the face of the Church, might be invalidated by the discovery of certain fairly numerous impediments, of which the most important lay in consanguinity or affinity. If the parties were related within the fourth degree—that is, if they had a common great-great-grandparent—then their union was null and void, unless a papal dispensation could be procured. In the average village, where there were only about seventy families, the arithmetical chances of finding a mate outside those prohibited degrees must have been small. In the days when the prohibition extended to seven degrees—that is, until the Lateran Council of 1215—they must have been almost negligible. But we hear of little matrimonial legislation between villagers, because there it was seldom sufficiently to anyone's interest to upset a marriage and transfer an inheritance. Among the nobility, on the other hand, litigation was constant. For not only blood-relationship was reckoned, but affinity through marriage; and, as a last straw, affinity at the baptismal font. This was a strong social bond, as the term *gossip* denotes; God-sibs were folk related as godmother or godfather at the baptism of the same child. The Church made this into a matrimonial impediment; and here was a great resource in unjust or collusive divorces. If one party, or both, could not swear to some too-late discovered consanguinity, they could at least swear to "gossipy", in days when baptismal registers were unknown.

Again, even in the weddings conducted with scrupulous conformity to the Church ritual, there were many survivals from less refined times which disgusted a fastidious scholar like Erasmus.[14] He complains that the marriage preliminaries themselves are almost more indecent than among the heathen. Thence, after the Church ceremony, the pair are brought home to "a public and tumultuous feast. They rise from table to join in wanton dances until supper, where the tender girl cannot refuse any man, but the house is open to the whole city. Then the unhappy maiden is compelled to join hands with the drunken, the scabby, and sometimes with criminals who are come more intent upon theft than upon dancing: in Britain she must even kiss with them. After an uproarious supper, dancing again, then fresh drinking: scarce can the wearied pair go to bed even after midnight. After a scanty interval, all revel with mad tumult at the chamber door, burst into the room, with obscene words, and return to the madness of yestreen. For, in some regions, this Corybantic fury is prolonged for three days....Is this the way to enter into a Sacrament?" Not only were monks forbidden to attend weddings, for propriety's sake, but the Rule of the Third Order of St Francis extended the prohibition to pious layfolk also.[15]

In theory, divorce did not exist for the medieval Church; the marriage was marriage for ever. Though the word *divortium* was commonly used in chronicles and official documents, perhaps as commonly as any other, yet the most that the Church ever decreed in the strictest sense was nullity; she decided that, owing to some fatal impediment, there never had been true marriage, and the parties were therefore now as free as though they had never lived together. Again, she might recognize incompatibilities, or other reasons for a *separation from bed and board*; they were indeed married, but need no longer live together; yet this separation gave them no power of contracting any other lawful union. But the frequency with which the word *divortium* was used, even by lawyers, might in itself suggest the partial survival of something very like the real thing *divorce*; and we have in fact abundant evidence to this effect. As Léon Gautier again confesses, "after a few years of marriage, a husband who wearied of his wife [in the upper classes] could suddenly discover that they were related... and here was a revival, under canonical and pious forms, of the ancient practice of divorce."[16] "Nor was even this subterfuge necessary in the Dark Ages. Pope Gregory II (726) decided that, if a wife is incurably sick, the husband may marry another, so long as he does not neglect to support the first. Two early Church Councils ruled to the same effect."[17] Bishop Jonas of Orleans [840] complains that men cast off their wives if they find them to be of servile condition; others, having dissipated their wives' dowries or changed their own humour, "shamelessly desert them, delighting in prudent and handsomer and wealthier mates".[18]

St Peter Damian (d. 1072) lived under the eyes of many Popes at Rome, and was a bosom-friend of the great Gregory VII. He stigmatized the society of his day, in plain terms, as less obedient to the laws of religion, in many cases, than the very pagans. Gregory VII, he says, held in this very year a great council in which he condemned and excommunicated all irregular unions between man and woman; "yet, among so many thousands of these [offending] folk, who has seen a single one torn away from the abomination of this unhallowed contract?" Where a separation does take place, it is often because the man, repenting a bargain that is now wearisome, "weaves a false line of consanguinity; he accumulates proofs to fabricate unheard of names of ancestors, and appeals for evidence in support of this allegation to old folk whom he well knows to have long ended their life in this world....Indeed, the laws are put up for sale, and money justifies the delinquents....Money sets the laws in motion, and the false interpreter bends its obscure sentences to his own meaning. Money softens the judge's heart with the oil of unrighteousness towards the rich, while it impels him to exercise the rigour of rigid punishment upon the poor."[19] St Anselm, Archbishop of Canterbury 1093–1109, echoing the words of his predecessor Lanfranc, writes to the King of Ireland: "We hear that marriages, in your kingdom, are dissolved and changed without any reason....It is said that men exchange their wives for those of other men as freely and publicly as any one changes one horse for another." Petrus Cantor, one of the greatest and most pious writers of about 1200, condemned on this point the Church in general. He writes of the extent to which Church law is stultified by "dispensations" which flatly contradict the original legislation, and continues: "See also how that most holy Sacrament of the Church, viz. Matrimony, by reason of traditions concerning the third degree of affinity, and certain other traditions, becomes at one moment invalid, at another sound and firm, through the chatterings of advocates, who rely upon the nets of tradition in order thus to fill their own purses and empty those of other people, so that the Sacrament of Matrimony is turned to derision among the layfolk."* Peter tells us also that

---

* Migne, *P.L.* vol. 203, 235. But Migne has here omitted the words which follow in the best MS. (Trin. Coll. Camb. 372). After *layfolk* this runs on: "for they say, 'I will marry this woman and grow rich [with her money], for I will leave her whenever I wish and let her be in the third degree of affinity to me'."

Ivo Bishop of Chartres, the greatest Church lawyer of the century, was so outraged by the absurd complexity of papal regulations on this subject that "in his indignation, he cast to the ground the volume of [papal] decretals, as a worthless and useless book".[20] A satire of the time of Edward II tells the same tale:[21]

If a man have a wyf,
And he love her nowt,
Bryng hyr to the constery   [consistory court,
Ther trewth schuld be wrowt.
Bring twei fals wytnes with hym,
And hymself the thrydde,
And he schal be deperted   [separated
As fair as he wold bydde,
     From his wyf;
He shal be mayntend fulle wel   [backed up
     To lede a sory lyf.   [disreputable

When he is deperted
From his trew spowse,
Take his neyghëborës wyf
And bryng her to house.
Gif he have selver
Among the clerkes to sende,
He may have hir to hys wyf
To hys lifës ende
          With onskylle   [unreason
Thei that so fair with falsenes dele,
Goddes corse on [t]her bille!   [charter, writ

The Dominican Bromyard, in Chaucer's day, describes the abuses in detail, and sums up, "nowadays, when a wife displeases, or another woman is coveted, then a divorce is procured"—*divortium procuratur*.[22] The contemporary poem of *Piers Plowman* tells the same tale; a man may get rid of his wife by giving the judge a fur cloak; Church lawyers "make and unmake matrimony for money".[23] Chaucer's friend John Gower complained, in his turn, of the complexity of papal decrees as to marriage, and of the ease with which one could evade them by bribery at the fountain-head. He asks: "How can it really be a mortal sin to violate these prohibitions, when one may always buy a dispensation? This is simply to manufacture fresh sins for the sake of filthy lucre."[24] Finally, Erasmus criticized the whole system cautiously, but severely, in his treatise *On the Institution of Christian Marriage*, addressed to Queen Katharine of Aragon. He exposed, in plainest language, both the difficulty of knowing for certain whether two persons were within the forbidden degrees of relationship, and the fatal folly of allowing a boy of fourteen and a girl of twelve to contract a valid marriage without priest or witnesses by the mere exchange of verbal promise followed by cohabitation. Why (he asks) cannot Popes make the marriage contract as secure as Civil Law makes contracts of far less importance? Then, "the world will not see so many unhappy and perplexed marriages, nor so many divorces." "The Emperor's law, and national decrees, are vigilant lest any quarrel arise from men's contracts with each other: yet such is human perversity that no contract gives rise to more trouble than that of matrimony. The cause seems to lie partly in the nature of the subject, but partly in the collision between State Law and Church Law.... Church Law itself is sometimes self-contradictory." As things now are, "it is no uncommon case, especially in France, for a girl of scarce ten years to be married and a mother next year....It seems portentous, and yet we sometimes see it, especially in Britain and in Italy, that a tender child is married to a septuagenarian....Yet Church laws do not rescind such nuptials, although they are satirized by public jests and epigrams."[25] This was written in 1526; and, in 1530, Pope Clement VII was willing to negotiate with Henry VIII on the basis that he should be allowed two wives simultaneously. It was asserted publicly, with great probability, that his predecessor Eugenius IV, in 1437, had given a similar permission to Henry IV of Castile.[26] Therefore, although St Thomas More was ready to die rather than commit the lie of the soul by admitting Henry VIII's superiority over the Pope in matters of marriage law and Church authority, yet we cannot legitimately argue from that to his Utopians' attitude towards divorce. It by no means follows that this most remarkable of all More's writings was a mere *jeu d'esprit*; that it was no mirror of the writer's serious hopes for world-betterment. Nor can we even press the divorce question into support of the more moderate view that *Utopia* is at best a picture of bare worldly prosperity, apart from the all-important theological virtues. In *Utopia*, More tells us, "matrimony is never broken, but by death; except adultery break the bond, or else the intolerable wayward manners of either party. For if either of them find themself for any such cause grieved, they may by the licence of the council change and take another. But the other party liveth ever after in infamy and out of wedlock. Howbeit the husband to put away his wife for no other fault, but for that some mishap is fallen to her body, this by no means they will suffer. For they judge it a great point of cruelty, that anybody in their most need of help and comfort should be cast off and forsaken, and that old age, which both bringeth sickness with it, and is a sickness itself, should unkindly and unfaithfully be dealt withal. But now and then it chanceth, where as the man and the woman cannot well agree between themselves, both of them finding [some] other with whom they hope to live more quietly and merrily, that they, by the full consent of them both, be divorced asunder and married again to other. But that not without the authority of the council, which agreeth to no divorces before they and their wives have diligently tried and examined the matter. Yea, and then also they be loath to consent to it, because they know this to be the next way to break love between man and wife, to be in easy hope of a new marriage. Breakers of wedlock be punished with most grievous bondage. And if both the offenders were married, then the parties which in that behalf have suffered wrong, being divorced from the adulterers, be married together, if they will, or else to whom they lust."[27] When we compare this with what his friend Erasmus wrote some ten years later, it is difficult to believe that the suggestions here put forward in *Utopia* were not sober and serious.[28] For it is agreed on all sides that the book is a direct criticism of contemporary society, and especially of England at that date. Erasmus says in so many words in his letter to Hutten: "His *Utopia* was written to indicate the points on which states are least well managed, and he had Britain especially in his eye, since that was what he saw most clearly and knew best." Wherever the Utopians are described as doing anything remarkable, we must look for a blamable, or at least questionable, lack of such doings in Henry VIII's England; and, conversely, the Utopians are remarkable for avoiding just those things for which English society could be most seriously criticized. When, therefore, the absence of cruel desertion is extolled in this imaginary prosperous republic, it can scarcely be that the author wrote without mental reference to what, as a lawyer, he must have known as a frequent occurrence in England, under cover of those hypocritical formalities which only increased the essential barbarity of the deed.

The subject is so important for the history of civilization, and

a child had been born] twelve fustigations round the church with a candle [in his hand] weighing half a pound." Then, in 1453, we have "Richard Wilson and Agnes his wife. The man demands divorce, for he saith that she wished to have killed himself, William [*sic*]. The woman demanded that he should be compelled to cleave unto her and live with her, and that he should put forward whatsoever he may have against her in due form of law at the next session." This, apparently, was not done. Finally, in 1455, "Thomas Kyrkeham and Isabella his wife. The woman sought a divorce and separation from bed and board by reason of the man's cruelty [*saeviciam*]. The man denied; and afterwards, by the labour of the judge, she bent her knees and humbly begged forgiveness of her husband, and the man pardoned her whatever offence she had formerly committed; and furthermore the man sware upon the book that he will not inflict the fear of death and mutilation of limb upon the woman"—*quod non inferet mulieri metum mortis ac mutilacionem membrorum.*

We find plenty of corroborative evidence elsewhere. In 1256, a similar case came before the Archbishop of York at his manor of Cawood.[30] Alice Sterling "demanded one Hamon, a cobbler of Caveringham, as her husband." He had given her the effectual promise three times at least before witnesses, and they had then lived together. "The man confessed to have contracted with her at Burton *per verba de praesenti* [i.e. in the present tense, which made it binding; not merely 'I will take thee', but 'I take thee']; expressing their mutual matrimonial consent, but only on condition that the woman would pay him three marks and a half, that he might go with her to Rome." The mystery of this condition is at once solved by the succeeding sentences, in which the man pleads pre-contract on his own part with another woman near Spalding, "in face of the Church, at All Saints Hungate, Lincoln, twenty years ago". They now hoped to patch up this matter at the Papal Court. The case was adjourned for further evidence; and, here again, the register tells us no more.

Modern society cannot afford to adopt an attitude of contempt for all these medieval difficulties. Erasmus, with ancient classical authors to back him up, pointed out that marriage, under whatever conditions, is of all contracts the most problematical and speculative. Medieval sovereigns, however, had the advantage of minimizing the ordinary human risks in this field: through their envoys they could make the most detailed and business-like enquiries. Edward II sent his trusted minister, Bishop Stapeldon, the founder of Exeter College, Oxford, to inspect Philippa of Hainault as prospective wife to the future Edward III. The report survives in that bishop's register, headed: "*Inspection and Description of the Daughter of the Count of Hainault, Philippa by name.*" The document runs as follows: "The lady whom we saw has not uncomely hair, betwixt blue-black and brown. Her head is clean-shaped; her forehead high and broad, and standing somewhat forward. Her face narrows between the eyes, and the lower part of her face is still more narrow and slender than the forehead. Her eyes are blackish-brown and deep. Her nose is fairly smooth and even, save that it is somewhat broad at the tip and also flattened, yet it is no snub-nose. Her nostrils are also broad, her mouth fairly wide. Her lips somewhat full, and especially the lower lip. Her teeth which have fallen and grown again are white enough, but the rest are not so white. The lower teeth project a little beyond the upper; yet this is but little seen. Her ears and chin are comely enough. Her neck, shoulders, and all her body and lower limbs are reasonably well shapen; all her limbs are well set and unmaimed; and nought is amiss so far as a man may see. Moreover, she is brown of skin all over, and much like her father; and in all things she is pleasant enough, as it seems to us. And the damsel will be of the age of nine years on St John's day next to come, as her mother saith. She is neither too tall nor too short for such an age; she is of fair carriage, and well taught in all that becometh her rank, and highly esteemed and well beloved of her father and mother and of all her meinie, in so far as we could inquire and learn the truth."[31]

Henry VII, in accordance with his well-known character, was even more cautious and business-like. His queen had died in February 1503. He thought of marrying again, and "his first thoughts were directed to the young queen of Naples, widow of Ferdinand the Second. To ascertain how far she was likely to prove a suitable match for him, he sent three gentlemen into Spain on a very confidential mission."[32] Their terms of reference were to pursue closely and privately a host of articles of enquiry, of which a few may be given here as specimens. "(6) *Item*, specially to mark the favour of her visage, whether she be painted or not, and whether it be fat or lean, sharp or round, and whether her countenance be cheerful and amiable, frowning or melancholy, stedfast or light, or blushing in communication. (7) *Item*, to note the clearness of her skin....(9) *Item*, to note well her eyes, brows, teeth and lips. (10) *Item*, to mark well the fashion of her nose and the height and breadth of her forehead....(12) *Item*, to mark her arms, whether they be great or small, long or short. (13) *Item*, to see her hands bare, and to note the fashion of them, whether the palm of her hand be thick or thin, and whether her hands be fat or lean, long or short....(16) *Item*, to mark her breasts and paps, whether they be big or small. (17) *Item*, to mark whether there appear any hair about her lips or not. (18) *Item*, that they endeavour them to speak with the said young queen fasting, and that she may tell unto them some matter at length, and to approach as near to her mouth as they honestly may, to the intent that they may feel the condition of her breath, whether it be sweet or not, and to mark at every time when they speak with her if they feel any savour of spices, rosewater, or musk by the breath of her mouth or not. (19) *Item*, to note the height of her stature and to inquire whether she wear any slippers, and of what height her slippers be, to the intent that they be not deceived in the very height and stature of her; and if they may come to the sight of her slippers, then to note the fashion of her foot. (20) *Item*, to inquire whether she have any sickness of her nativity, deformity or blemish in her body, and what that should be, or whether she hath been commonly in health or sometimes sick and sometimes whole, and to know the specialities of such diseases and sickness.*...(22) *Item*, to enquire of the manner of her diet and whether she be a great feeder or drinker, and whether she useth often to eat or drink, and whether she drinketh wine or water or both....(24) *Item*, the said King's servants, by the wisest ways that they can use, shall make inquisition and ensearch what land or livelihood the said young queen hath or shall have after the decease of her mother, either by the title of jointure or otherwise, in the realm of Naples, or in any other place or country; what is the yearly value thereof, and whether she shall have the same to her and heirs for ever or else during her life only, and to know the specialities of the title and value thereof in every behalf as near as they can." Henry's ambassadors made many secret enquiries, but could get no

---

* On this point they secretly pumped her apothecary, and received satisfactory answers.

satisfactory answer to this last all-important question. As the editor puts it (p. xlix): "The young queen appears to have had but one disqualification. She was healthy, beautiful, and well formed, but moneyless." Henry VII remained a widower. Froissart records how "it is the usage in France that any lady, daughter to any great lord, if the king should marry her, first she should be seen and viewed all naked by certain ladies thereto admitted, to know if she were proper and meet to bring forth children".[33]

IN a previous chapter, describing the genesis of the Dominican school of mysticism, I did not lay sufficient stress on the extent to which it met a crying general need. This popularized religious philosophy, this "scholastic of the heart", would have shown little vitality in the convents, and certainly would not have spread as it did among the people at large, if there had not been a deep and wide craving for something more living than the current theology. Moreover, the same craving was strong among the learned classes also. Nominalism was triumphant in the schools of the later Middle Ages. The moderate realism of the Dominican Aquinas [1250] was attacked on both sides by his Franciscan successors. Duns Scotus [1280] fell into extreme realism, and William of Ockham [1320] into decided nominalism. Ockham's nominalism, in spite of repeated condemnation by Popes, was triumphant in his lifetime and for the rest of the Middle Ages: on the whole, it is more in the tenor of modern philosophy. But any decidedly nominalistic philosophy has always a materialistic tendency. "From the point of view of the modern non-metaphysical man of Science Ockham represents perfection of common-sense: 'Ockham's Philosophy is that of centuries later.' On nearly every purely logical or psychological question Ockham gives an answer which, right or wrong, might still be maintained in almost the same terms by a modern philosopher."[1] This, then, was the philosophy which reigned specially in England, and among the English and Teutonic students at Paris, and at all the Teutonic universities. Ockham was Luther's "dear master", and the more idealistic Scholasticism of Aquinas and Bonaventura, though finally destined to triumph again in the Church, and to become the official philosophy of Roman Catholicism, certainly held only the second place during the last two centuries before the Reformation. Wyclif's writings (as Rashdall points out) would probably have been treated far more seriously on the Continent, but that he and his Oxford masters belonged to the then losing party in philosophy, the realists; for by that time there was a moderate realist reaction at Oxford. Therefore, since a nominalistic atmosphere is less favourable to religious fervour than a realistic; there was a growing gulf between the philosophy and the religious feeling of the later Middle Ages. We have seen how, the farther philosophy was pursued in the schools, the stronger grew the tendency to exclude the chief Christian mysteries from its domain. St Thomas first, and then still more emphatically the reactionary Ockham, had withdrawn one dogma after another from the domain of pure reason. All the main distinctive tenets of Christianity, according to the now reigning schools of thought, lay beyond the sphere of rational proof; and Duns Scotus insisted that even the immortality of the soul rested upon faith alone, or at least mainly upon faith. It will be evident how inevitably this tendency favoured the state of mind which Renan describes as "water-tight compartments in the soul". The extreme of scepticism on the one hand, with an extreme credulity on the other, can thus flourish side by side in the same mind, which finds some reason of its own for not bringing them face to face with each other. We have seen how, from the thirteenth century onwards, it had been common (though of course never really orthodox) to draw a distinction between theological and philosophical truth: a doctrine, it was said, might be philosophically true, though theologically false. When one of Wyclif's Oxford disciples supported Wyclif's attack on Transubstantiation, and said to the masters in congregation, quite publicly, that there was no idolatry like the worship of the consecrated Host, the chancellor contented himself with saying "now you are speaking as a philosopher", and passed no further censure on him.[2] Those, of course, were the shifts of men who seriously doubted parts of the orthodox creed, yet may not have felt justified in absolutely denying them; and who certainly had no wish to push their denial to the extreme of probable martyrdom. But some of the most orthodox minds also made distinctions which tended almost as definitely to the separation of the philosophical and religious spheres. The more persistently men follow their ideas to the extremest logical conclusions, the more convinced do many of them become that the things which really interest us most are not to be learned from logic alone: that while, on the one hand, we must never shrink from logic, yet, on the other, some of our most inevitable and instinctive sentiments (and, what is more, our most civilized sentiments) cannot be brought directly under logical laws, at any rate in our present state of knowledge. We live even more by intuition than by logic. Therefore, in all ages, the most strictly scientific men have often consciously kept a corner of their minds free from the strict rule of logic. Roger Bacon, in his insistence upon the study of physical science and actual observation as a corner-stone of philosophy, adds that, to know God truly, we must retire more and more into our own souls. And that is the direction in which not only learned but unlearned men tended increasingly during the fourteenth and fifteenth centuries. As in Langland's mind, so also in the minds of many other pious and thoughtful folk, every fresh shock drove living religion farther and farther inwards upon itself. Let us enumerate these shocks. First, there was the abandonment of the Crusading ideal: then the unmistakable decadence of the Papacy between Innocent III and John XXII, with the Great Pestilence of 1348–9 and its many terrible successors; and the Great Schism; and the Hundred Years' War in France; and the still more barbarous civil wars in Italy. All these contributed to prepare a great revulsion of religious feeling. It was not that the world was growing really worse; in many ways it was demonstrably better in the fourteenth and fifteenth centuries than in the glorious thirteenth. But everywhere the multitude was growing in power and knowledge; and therefore, though the institutions and rulers may not have been worse, the fabric of society was more intolerable to the moral sense of thinking people. Thus, then, we get those beginnings of Dominican mysticism, when philosophers, dragged against their will from the universities to teach these unlearned but spiritually minded people, found that the simplification of their own language forced upon their own minds a simpler and more direct mode of thought. Thus, again, in turn, these simpler thoughts, brought into contact with the hitherto inarticulate souls which had been yearning passionately for some living word to raise them out of themselves, flamed up into an intenser conviction than the debates of the schools could ever have kindled; for almost everyone of these spiritual teachers had some Egeria; some one or two disciples among the nuns from whom he learned almost more than he brought. When, therefore, school philosophy, thus simplified and inspired, began to teach that the one thing needful was for each soul to creep as closely as it could, and as directly as it could, into the bosom of Eternal Love—in other words, when the logician had given place to the mystic—then this was felt to be a word of authority, very different from the words of the Scribes and

Pharisees. We must not forget, however, how much of this new message was itself due to the reigning Church. Quite apart from the fact that all the leaders of this movement were loyal Churchmen, the Church itself was always there—Church organization as well as the actual fabric of parish church or cathedral—as a refuge for any soul that longed to take refuge from the turmoil of the world. And when the clergy themselves were unsympathetic, as they very often were unsympathetic to this mysticism, no less than the Anglican Establishment has been to Methodism and so many other -*isms*, then the mystic retired to a little corner of his own, a little sanctuary of his own, within the Church. We see this in St Catharine of Siena's case. Her family, resenting her mystical preoccupations, laid upon her the worst drudgery of the household, but were surprised to find that she kept unbroken serenity of soul. Her explanation was simple: "I make a little corner apart in my heart for the Lord Jesus." So it was with many other mystics, with the result that many of them attained an unthought-of spiritual independence; they found gradually that the Church militant itself was no longer essential to them. Thus mysticism, by emphasizing the necessity of the soul's direct intercourse with God, makes naturally for the toleration of religious differences. He that earnestly seeks peace on one side will not willingly pick quarrels in other directions; the more a man was convinced that he himself had found God in his own way, the less was he tempted to quarrel with others who claimed to have arrived at the same goal by different paths. Dr Inge writes very truly: "Augustine and Pelagius would alike have agreed with Eckhart's commonsense declaration, *Besser ein Lebemeister als tausend Lesemeister*: 'better is one master of life than a thousand lecturers'."

On the one hand, then, mysticism made a natural outlet for aspirations which the official Church no longer satisfied, *ex officio* at any rate. And, on the other hand, it tended to sap the foundations of officialism. No doubt its origin in England is partly independent, due to the working of the same spirit everywhere; but much of the influence seems to have come to us, and especially to London and the Eastern Counties, by the ordinary trade routes, together with Rhenish wines and cloth and metal-work. On the other hand, the commercial intercourse with Germany and the Netherlands encouraged much freer speculation than we see in any of those mystics. London, the Eastern Counties and the

Midlands were also the great foci of Lollardy. What thinking men with a strong religious bent, but unpledged to official religion, were saying in Chaucer's England, may be read in *Piers Plowman*. Here we have the superior "man in the street" in London, with whom even the king had to reckon ("for where the men of London are at accord and fully agreed, no man dares gainsay them"), and where the citizens, if they found black sheep among the clergy, punished them out of hand, without leaving the job to the bishop. The whole poem is penetrated with religion, and mystical religion. He does not go out of his way to quarrel with orthodoxy; but, as we have seen, he is quite sure of certain things which could scarcely be reconciled with the ordinary orthodoxy of his day.

Moreover, we have also seen how he tells us of much freer speech than he himself used—the fashionable freethought among great folk in his day:

> At meat in their mirthës, when minstrels be still,
> Then tell they of the Trinity a tale or twain,
> And bring forth a bold reason, and take Bernard to witness;
> Thus they drivel at their dais, the deity to know,
> And gnaw on God with the gorge, when their gut is full.
> Such motives they move, these masters in their glory,
> And maken men to misbelieve that muse much on their words.[3]

We get extraordinarily similar evidence from Sacchetti at the same time in Florence. Equally plain-spoken is the poem on political and social questions. Piers says to the Knight:

> Misuse not thy bondman, the better mayst thou speed;
> Though he be thine underling here, well may hap in heaven
> That he will be worthier set, and with more bliss
> Than thou, but thou do better, and live as thou shouldst.[4]

Again, he calls down vengeance on "brewsters and baxters, butchers and cooks"; "for these are men on this mold that most harm worken to the poor people, that piecemeal buyen: for they poison the people privily and oft". This they do with the connivance of the mayor and his serjeants: thus they bribe and grow rich by dishonest trade, and buy town property, and build great houses for themselves.[5] His creed inspired him with a sense of the true brotherhood of rich and poor, though he had no sympathy with the idle or unreasonable poor. He preached what in our days would be called Christian socialism:

For all we are Christ's creatures, and of his coffers rich,
And brethren as of one blood, beggars as well as earls.
For on Calvary of Christ's blood Christendom gan spring
And blood-brethren we became there, and gentlemen each one.[6]

He feels that Christianity is in its essence a levelling creed; that Christ fought against social as well as religious prejudices; and this he expresses in his naïve way:

The Jews, that were gentlemen, Jesus they despised,
Both his love and his law; now are they lowë churls...
And those that became Christians through counsel of the Baptist
Are franklins, free men, and gentlemen with Jesus.[7]

This is only what hundreds of people talked about daily in London and other busy towns. Few men wrote it down— for the best of reasons—but from all parts of Europe we get similar anticipations of theories which are not realized until modern times; or, indeed, which we are still striving to realize now. "John of Paris (d. 1306), deduces the right of taxation from the fact that private property needs the protection of the state and its tribunals, and therefore should contribute; but it may be taxed only 'in casu necessitatis' and proportionately." Philippe de Maizières, in 1376, argued that unjust taxation is a sin; the Church has a right to refuse absolution in the confessional unless the offender does penance and makes restitution; the people have a right to refuse payment and even to depose the ruler.[8] That, of course, is what we first enforced three centuries later, and the French not until 1789. Moreover, there are medieval or early Renaissance pronouncements on the social question which have an even more modern ring. The Florentine Doni writes, at about the time when the Reformation was beginning in England, but under a definitely Roman Catholic government: "The rich man says 'I pay for all the services done to me'—Yes, but what do you pay with? with your own labour? No sir, [even when you pay] it is with other men's labour that you pay." The fact is, that the capitalist system is far older than it has often been represented. Already in the fifteenth century there was a great deal of sweating, and very bad sweating. Again, that agricultural crisis which was doubtless rendered more acute by the Suppression of the Monasteries had begun long before, and partly as a result of the frequent enclosures of open land which the monasteries themselves had been making for centuries before the

Reformation. The citizen, who had begun by wresting his own liberties from feudal lords, soon became himself an oppressor; and (especially in Germany) there were at the end of the Middle Ages thousands of artisans who were compelled, not only by circumstances but by customary law, to remain journeymen all their lives. In Italy the great cities oppressed the peasants more than the barons did. The poor suffered; they talked, and sometimes they mutinied, but all was of little avail. We have seen how, as early as the thirteenth century, Berthold of Regensburg pointed out that poor folk were as helpless as fish in the water, since they could not trust each other and show a united front: "None are so false as peasants are to each other."9 But, if the wage-earners could not yet join to make solid collective bargains, the middle classes at least could combine; they, on their smaller scale, could hold together, and the whole story of the transition from medieval to modern times is a story of smaller corporations growing up within, and bursting by their growth, that great corporation which had inherited the hierarchical tradition of the Roman Empire and a great deal of its universality—the Church.

Here, as so often, we find that the disruptive forces had been started or fostered by the very body which they finally burst asunder. Gregory VII had called the democracy to his help against the feudalization of the Church, more especially the lower classes of Milan, who, when they had formed a definitely papal party, became known by the name of *Patarini*. Hating as they did the growing feudalism of the clergy, they therefore became his willing and devoted allies in the fight against a married priesthood which was fast becoming hereditary. Yet, a century later, these same Patarini were not only anti-clerical but anti-papal heretics, making common cause with, if not identical with, the Cathari or Albigenses of France. Again, it was the Popes who stirred all Europe to the Crusades: but all the enduring effects of the Crusades worked adversely to the Papacy. They created a spirit of world commerce which might otherwise have taken centuries to develop. The great maritime cities of Italy, from being mere ports of passage for these thousands of armed men, became emporia of Eastern wares; men found it was more profitable to trade with Saracens—even to smuggle arms to Saracens—than to fight with them. This, again, did much to break up the stagnation of populations who had until now been almost altogether agricultural, fast bound in feudalism and iron. Not only did towns grow up rapidly, but the circulation of money increased enormously. Hitherto lords had been able to live in barbaric magnificence by travelling from manor to manor on their own estates, they and their train eating up the whole produce of the year in a few days, and then passing on to eat up the next manor. But these same lords could do nothing on a Crusade without turning their land or its produce into ready money. Thus, from about 1150 onwards, there suddenly grows up a very numerous and important class of money-changers, who presently develop into bankers. They were most numerous on the great Eastern trade routes, the South of France and Italy. Of course a banker cannot live—let alone grow rich—without taking interest. Dante shows us the usurers writhing naked on a burning soil under a rain of fire; but his sub-contemporary Benvenuto da Imola comments on this passage: "He who taketh usury goeth to hell, and he who taketh none is on the brink of bankruptcy", *vergit ad inopiam*.[10] A Franciscan of Dante's time complains how sadly the practice had grown even since the coming of the friars: "Those who once would not have given such men the kiss of peace [in church] are ready now to kiss their feet...and [the usurer] who would once have been buried with the burial of a dog, is now entombed before the High Altar."[11] Equally clear is the undesigned coincidence of facts; in the thirteenth century, while usury was still a despised and dangerous trade, the average rate of interest was at least 10 per cent.; in the fourteenth century it had often fallen to 7, or even 5 per cent.; and the foreign bankers had given their name to a street in London—Lombard Street. Thus, while the knight often ruined himself on the Crusades, the citizens grew fat on them; new towns sprang up, and old towns bought for themselves, or manœuvred themselves into, a position of independence. This new civil growth was a far more serious rival to the Church than the old feudal powers had been. The baron had often robbed the Church or maltreated the Churchman, but he had done this with an evil conscience, and priest or monk might win back from the lord's deathbed even more than the Church had lost during his life. On the other hand the difference between citizens and clergy was more often one of ideal, and the clergy were not always or altogether in the right. In this matter of usury, for instance, while strict clerical theory reprobated it, vast numbers of clergy borrowed at interest, and not a few even lent at interest. We have seen how new bishops could not pay their first-fruits to the Pope without the help of bankers. In fact, the Papal Court of the later Middle Ages was the great resort of usurers; and, though it is true that medieval Popes were comparatively merciful to the Jews, yet contemporary Churchmen sometimes tell us plainly that they did this for business reasons, to the general scandal of Christendom.

Again, the clergy had too often set their faces against the growth of civic liberties. To the distinguished Churchman Guibert of Nogent, in 1120, the name of free borough, "communio", was "new and abominable"—*novum ac pessimum nomen*—it seemed positively irreligious for citizens to combine for securing control of their own money-matters, and holding their own courts of justice. Yet gradually these village communities had gained urban rights; steadily, again, they forced their way onwards; until, long before the end of the Middle Ages, they had become a real power not only in State but in Church.

This civic development deserves a place side by side with the revival of letters and the development of popular religion in any picture of the transition from medieval to modern times. Let me quote, if only to discount them heavily, the words of Mrs J. R. Green concerning the fifteenth century. "All this heritage of squalor and rough disorder, however, was no longer accepted without protest. Old abuses were brought to light and denounced. Towns were swept and garnished, stately market crosses set up, and new Guild-halls everywhere built with shops and stalls and storage rooms for the traders. A new interest was awakened in the state of streets and lanes and central squares when waggons and pack horses began to struggle through the mire with their loads on market day...."[12] And, again: "In Canterbury and Worcester and Nottingham and Bristol and a host of other towns we may still admire the new houses that were being raised for the traders, with their picturesque outlines and fine carved work. Waste places in the boroughs were covered with buildings and formed into new wards. On every side corporations, instinct with municipal pride, built Common Halls, set up stately crosses in the market-place such as we still see at Winchester or Marlborough, paved the streets, or provided a new water-supply for the growing population. If we count up the new gates, and quays, and bridges, and wharves, and harbours, and sluices, and aqueducts, and markets of which the town records furnish accounts, we are filled with amazement at an activity which was really stupendous."[13]

This, as I have said, must be heavily discounted in the light of more recent research. Mr M. M. Postan, studying microscopically the statistics of trade and industry, is convinced that there was depression and decay from the first decade of the fifteenth century, at latest, until about 1480. Dr H. E. Salter's *Medieval Oxford* corroborates this strongly.[14] Yet, even in days when imports and exports are going ill, there may be compensations in home trade or industries; and, again, when these are torpid, there may still be life elsewhere. The laity certainly took interest in their churches and their civic buildings; it is difficult to trace any relaxation of building activity in any generation of the fifteenth century. At Oxford and Cambridge the earliest university buildings date from this time—apart, of course, from churches and colleges. Whether the edifice were raised by public subscription, or through the munificence of some soldier fattened on the plunder of France, or of a capitalist wool-merchant, it testifies to the growing influence of the laity. Even Bishop Wykeham, one of the greatest of these builders, had made his colossal fortune as a minister of state, enriched by royal influence with a multitude of pluralities in contravention of strict Church law. Thus there was a steady, if not uniform, growth of the lay spirit as time went on. Whatever the economic set-back may have been, it did not avail to quench the natural consciousness of increasing civic importance, sometimes marked by equally natural exaggerations. It was almost inevitable that this should have shown itself first in Italy, where there was so much more continuity with ancient Roman civilization, and where commerce and manufacture had risen more nearly to modern development. Here, then, we must go back to Marsilius, whose political theories for Church and State owed so much to the every-day experiences of civic life in his native Padua. This man's thought, as Lagarde points out, "developed upwards from physics to social philosophy", whereas "the theologians who follow St Thomas, on the contrary, start from theology and metaphysics and develop downwards to sociology". Thus we get theories so revolutionary that "they remind us irresistibly of the great reformers of succeeding ages: Luther, Hobbes, Descartes or Rousseau".[15] Marsilius boldly seizes his opponent's sword and turns it against himself. "The laity are mistaken in discussing with the clergy to argue for their own place side by side with the spirituality. The 'spirituality' is non-existent apart from the lay-folk; it is in the name of spirituality that the laity should put these usurpers to flight." The people are the true rulers of the ecclesiastical as of the civil State; the Christian population inherits, for the management of its own affairs, that *majestas* which was the heritage of the Roman republic, and which the people had lent, rather than given, to the Emperors. The Pope had no divine primacy: he was, it is true, a functionary useful in many ways and sometimes almost (though nowhere absolutely) indispensable. He had, in justice, no right of inflicting pecuniary or corporal punishments, and his sentences of excommunication were by no means always ratified in heaven. From all this there followed the most pronounced Erastianism. It was most natural that Gregory XI should condemn Wyclif as a follower of the heresies of Marsilius; but it is surprising that the learned and pious Gerson, a generation later, should apparently give a testimonial to the *Defensor Pacis*, which he does not show signs of having really read. This, however, as Lagarde points out, is a testimony to the revived interest in a man who, in his own generation, had seemed too paradoxical to attract the serious attention he merited. Now, from about 1375 onwards, "we see everywhere a revival of Marsilius's work which, thrust less brutally forward [than in 1324], seduces the most different minds and is destined to dominate the preoccupations of many 'consultants' at the Council of Constance".

According to Marsilius's theory, the State's duty was not only to tax the clergy, but to assume control of ecclesiastical endowments and of all educational establishments, and to relieve the poor out of the surplus of clerical revenues. For, beyond this, it should even fix the number of churches and priests, appoint and pay the clergy, superintend their work, and remove them if necessary. Some of these proposals were really carried out to some extent in the great cities of the fifteenth and early sixteenth centuries. Even in Chaucer's time, the citizens of London invented far more effective disciplinary methods against criminous clergy than the bishop had ever been able to enforce. At Venice, as Sacchetti tells us, the townsfolk took clerical morals even more definitely into their own hands. When Henry VII came to the throne, one of his first statutes was to recognize popular pressure for the tightening of ecclesiastical discipline and the protection of bishops against trickery exercised by such sinners as were rich and shameless enough to threaten retaliation in the law-courts.[16] It runs: "For the more sure and likely Reformation of Priests, Clerks, and Religious Men, culpable, or by their Demerits openly reported for incontinent living in their Bodies, contrary to their Order; It is enacted, ordained and established, by the Advice and Assent of the Lords Spiritual and Temporal, and the Commons in the said Parliament assembled, and by Authority of the same, that it be lawful to all Archbishops and Bishops, and other Ordinaries, having Episcopal Jurisdiction, to punish and chastise Priests, Clerks and Religious Men, being within the Bounds of their Jurisdiction, as shall be convicted afore them by Examination, and other lawful Proof, requisite by the Law of the Church, of Adultery, Fornication, Incest, or any other fleshly Incontinency, by committing them to Ward and Prison, there to abide for such time as shall be thought to their Discretions convenient for the Quality and Quantity of their Trespass; and that none of the said Archbishops, Bishops or other Ordinaries aforesaid, be thereof chargeable of, to, or upon Action of false or wrongful Imprisonment, but that they be utterly thereof discharged, in any of the cases aforesaid, by virtue of this Act." Moreover, while layfolk were glad everywhere to give liberally for the fabric and maintenance of their own parish church, if only as a matter of local pride, yet they asserted rights of their own over these churches, and over the parish finance, which sometimes surprise modern historians, and scandalize some of their readers.[17] This was so not only in the town, but in the villages also, during the last generations of the Middle Ages. At the same time there were frequent quarrels about tithes; and citizens grew more and more unwilling to pay the very oppressive church-dues which, from being purely voluntary, had long since assumed the binding force of immemorial custom. The power of the purse figures largely in the revolt against the Roman Court, as in the revolt against Charles I. At York, for instance, the mayor and burgesses had the appointment of nearly all the chantry-priests: in Germany this was even more general; and many German cities taxed their clergy as though they had been layfolk, in spite of papal and imperial decrees to the contrary. The great preacher Johann Geiler, in 1500, declared that the whole town council of Strassburg were in a state of mortal sin on this account; but, in spite of the respect inspired by his character and intellect, the town council stuck to their system of taxation.

Again, the fifteenth-century towns took many matters into their own hands which had hitherto been left to, or monopolized by, the clergy. In Italy, there had been town hospitals, managed by citizens and not by clergy, as early as the twelfth century; in the fifteenth century this was the rule in Italy and not uncommon everywhere in Europe. So also with the schools; they were more and more frequently founded by laymen and managed by laymen, though of course the Church still asserted, and generally made good, her prescriptive right to control the teaching. Already in 1432, the founder of Sevenoaks Grammar School laid down the rule that the master should *not* be in Holy Orders (though he was doubtless in lower).[18] In 1443 a London citizen put the school he founded into the hands of the Mercers' Company, to the exclusion of clerical control. When Dean Colet founded St Paul's School (1510) he made a similar arrangement, of which Erasmus has twice recorded the significance.[19] "Over the revenues, and the entire management, he set neither priests, nor the bishop, nor the [cathedral] chapter, as they call it, nor noblemen; but some married citizens of established reputation. And, when asked the reason, he said that, though there was nothing certain in human affairs, he yet found the least corruption in them." "Nothing gave Colet so much anxiety as the question to whom he should entrust the management of his school....And so he appointed as master of his school a married man with a large family. The government of it he entrusted to a number of his lay fellow-citizens, of whose integrity he thought he had proof, and to their successors in order. And though this provision did not by any means free him from anxiety, he said that, as human affairs then were, this course appeared to him the least hazardous." Here, again, the trustees and governors were the Mercers' Company. The founder of a charity at Nürnberg (1388) similarly insisted that it should be governed by layfolk; and the Strassburg town council in 1500 refused to admit the clergy into the town hospital as patients, or the Béguines (Sisters of Charity) as nurses.[20] Again, the right of asylum which churches and churchyards had enjoyed was often curtailed about this time both in Germany and in England. The monastic reforms decreed by the Council of Bâle were carried out both in France and in Northern Germany with the help of secular princes and their servants, in the teeth not only of the unwilling monks but often of their diocesan bishops also. As we have seen, the mystic was finding the priest far less necessary than he had been. And now the Bible begins to show him, in many people's eyes, no longer as a merely negative factor, but as a positive obstacle to pure Christianity. That, however, belongs to a later chapter.

Meanwhile, the revived study of Antiquity was beginning to tell also. This came late in England; but its effects, though slow, were far reaching. The phrase "New Learning" became a shibboleth, much as "Catholic" had long been, and as "Reformation" and "Freethought" were to become later on. On one side it was a somewhat self-righteous appellation, the implications of which were strongly resented by the other side. Thus it became a party-cry, accepted conventionally by friends and foes alike, but in very different senses; on the one side a battle-slogan, on the other a term of blame or contempt.

Yet there this new learning was, a fresh thing that must be reckoned with, and that old men could ignore only at their own peril. Greece had taught John the Scot [850], one of the most original of all medieval thinkers.[21] But it had also brought him into suspicion with the orthodox; William of Malmesbury described John as one who, "holding his eyes fast upon the Greeks, has deflected from the path of the Latins". Four centuries later, Bishop Grosseteste of Lincoln had studied Greek; and it was his teaching which had lent to Oxford thought much of its early originality and distinction. His pupil, Roger Bacon, had cried in the wilderness for a revival of Greek studies, for lack of which the Bible itself was sometimes misunderstood, and no man knew the original texts of the New Testament or the early Fathers.[22] "Therefore the Church sleepeth, seeing that she doth nothing in this field, nor hath done anything for 70 years past", except Grosseteste's translations. "The negligence of the Church is marvellous; for, since the time of Pope Damasus [A.D. 384] there hath been no pope, nor any inferior pontiff, who hath been solicitous for the furtherance of the Church through translations, except the aforesaid glorious bishop." Yet Grosseteste, one of our truest saints, ended his life in vain protests against the corruption of the Roman Court, and Bacon spent most of his later life in prison. Though the Council of Vienne (1311) decreed that Greek should be studied at the principal universities, this decree remained practically a dead letter. On the other hand, it was a pious and orthodox Prior of Canterbury Cathedral, Selling, who finally broke this spell, and became the pioneer of Greek studies on the verge of the Reformation. In 1464 he went with Hadley, a fellow-monk, to Padua, Bologna and Rome. At Bologna he studied Greek, and returned in 1467. After another very brief visit to Italy, he was made prior in 1472 and ruled with universal applause till his death in 1495. On a later journey as ambassador to Rome, he took with him his pupil Linacre, who, with his companion Grocyn, studied Greek at the Italian universities and came back to teach it at Oxford. Here, however, the mere passive neglect of so many past generations turned into active antagonism in the face of this unwelcome novelty. There were, of course, a few enlightened scholars among the clergy; and Bishop Fox of Winchester, founding Corpus Christi College at Oxford in 1517, not only discouraged Scholasticism in his statutes, but established a lectureship in Greek. Yet "in Oxford itself there was considerable opposition to the new revival of Greek scholarship....Some members of the University were of opinion that Greek literature was thoroughly infected with heresy; others, who had acquired a reputation in the schools, were unwilling to apply themselves to a branch of study in which their dialectical skill would prove useless; others again regarded all innovations as dangerous. In opposition to the Grecians who pursued their studies at Corpus Christi College, a number of clerks banded themselves together under the name of Trojans....The adherents of the new learning were assailed with every sort of ridicule, and openly derided in the streets. So far indeed was opposition carried that, in the spring of 1518, a priest who should have preached a Lenten sermon in one of the churches of Oxford, delivered in its stead a vehement denunciation of Greek and other polite literature, seasoned with jeers and personal allusions."[23] These were the men whom Tyndale, some twelve years later, described in his highly coloured style as "the old barking curs, Duns's disciples and the draff called Scotists, the children of darkness", who "raged in every pulpit against Greek, Latin and Hebrew". St Thomas More, at the news of these discreditable quarrels, wrote a long public epistle to the Oxford authorities. He had to remind them that Scholasticism was often devoted to comparatively unimportant *quaestiones* "in a barbarous idiom"; that the New Testament had been written in Greek, and that the Council of Vienne had attempted, however vainly, to remedy the ignorance of the Latin Church in this field. "Lastly, after contrasting the conduct of the Oxonians with that of their contemporaries at Cambridge, who were contributing towards the support of a Greek teacher, he warned them that any further opposition to sound learning would alienate the favour of their Chancellor Warham, their great patron Wolsey, and their king. Erasmus states that Henry VIII himself took up the matter at the instigation of More and Pace, and that thus the noisy advocates of ignorance were put to silence."[24] So effectually, in fact, that in 1523 Oxford invited, and received with enthusiasm, the personal teaching of the great Spanish scholar Vives, the open and declared enemy of Scholasticism.

Yet, in this very year, More received a despairing letter from Oxford. "The University lamented that abbots had almost ceased to send their monks to the schools, nobles their sons, and beneficed clergy their relations and parishioners. The halls were falling into ruin, and the endowed colleges alone maintained a semblance of prosperity. So again, three years later, Dr London of New College mentions that sixteen halls had lately been abandoned, and that the total number of scholars residing in the different halls did not exceed one hundred and forty."[25] This may well be exaggerated; and certainly it was partly due to severe visitations of the Sweating Sickness; but we must read the words also in the light of similar evidence from Cambridge. St John Fisher, preaching there as chancellor before Henry VII, had said: "Somehow, I know not how, whether it were the continual strifes with the townsmen...or the long abiding of the fever, that...carried off many of our learned men—or that there were few or no helpers and patrons of letters—whatever were the true causes, doubtless there had stolen over wellnigh all of us a weariness of learning and of study, so that not a few did take counsel in their own minds how they might [get away from the University]."[26] Yet Cambridge was not outwardly unprosperous; she had her new colleges, and, in spite of her great numerical inferiority to Oxford, she owned nine out of the twenty bishops in the country in 1500. Within the next few years, Fisher himself became the practical founder of two new colleges, Christ's and St John's, where, by statute, neither Civil nor Canon Law might be studied, popular as those studies had been in the Middle Ages. But this innovation was not enough; and Cambridge, like Oxford, needed a new spirit still. We may apply to England the summary with which Professor Huizinga ends his *Waning of the Middle Ages* (p. 308). "The fifteenth century in France and the Netherlands is still medieval at heart. The diapason of life had not yet changed. Scholastic thought, with symbolism and strong formalism, the thoroughly dualistic conception of life and the world still dominated. The two poles of the mind continued to be Chivalry and Hierarchy. Profound pessimism spread a general gloom over life. The Gothic principle prevailed in art. But all these forms and modes were on the wane. A high and strong culture is declining, but at the same time and in the same sphere new things are being born. The tide is turning, the tone of life is about to change."

FISHER was a noble man, laborious and learned, but greater still in character. Holbein's portraits go far to reveal both him and his fellow-martyr More. Fisher is the rugged north-countryman: his great cheekbones and the strong framework of his face proclaim a vigorous physique, while the hollow cheeks, with severe lines of mouth and chin, bespeak hard work and spare diet and self-control: there are patience and suffering in his eyebrows. He was a great man, and progressive; but the new spirit came too late into his life, and he remained thoroughly medieval to the last. The real Renaissance came first to London and Oxford with Colet and More; London counts here, perhaps, as definitely as Oxford itself. It passed on to Cambridge, not long after, with Erasmus and Croke. Though Linacre, and then Grocyn, had brought Greek to Oxford from 1484 onwards, yet their influence was limited, and might well have died out with them. But presently another Oxford man, John Colet, caught their enthusiasm, went himself to Italy, and came back with the resolution of putting his new learning to a deeper purpose. In 1496 he began lecturing publicly on St Paul's epistles. Here was a double innovation. First, it was irregular for a mere Master of Arts to lecture upon theology: such a trespass, indeed, had been the adventure which had brought Abailard into one of his worst troubles. Secondly, it was quite new for anyone to lecture on the Bible from the critical and historical point of view. In the Middle Ages, it had gradually become the accepted convention that every verse of the Scriptures had four senses, of which the allegorical was the highest, and the literal the lowest. Yet here was a Master of Arts undertaking to treat the sacred text historically, and to explain, as best he could, exactly what St Paul himself had been thinking of when he said this or that. But our Master of Arts, here, was a man of uncompromising earnestness and straightforwardness. Erasmus, who knew many scholars, and measured them all with a very sure eye, wrote of Colet that he was one who said what he meant, and meant what he said.

This man, then, was the only surviving son of a rich London merchant who had been Lord Mayor; and, having learned what

Oxford and Italy could teach him, he now determined to devote his life and energies to the Church. His lectures combined a high measure of scientific accuracy with unusual warmth of conviction; in any case they would have marked an epoch in Oxford history. But Colet's appearance on the university stage gained double force from the action and reaction between himself and another Londoner, twelve years his junior, Thomas More. More's father had been a London judge when Colet's father was Lord Mayor, and the two men must have known each other from early days. More was a precocious student; he went up to Oxford at fifteen, and gradually found such an absorbing interest in Greek scholarship that his father's stern orthodoxy and strict sense of business were shocked; he took this brilliant scholar away from the University and sent him to pursue purely legal studies at Lincoln's Inn. Thus, More just missed Colet's lectures at Oxford; but two years later (1498) we find a strong intimacy already between him and Erasmus and Colet; Erasmus, a man of Colet's age, having come to England to seek his fortune, and to Oxford for the sake of learning Greek.

Next year we find Erasmus writing enthusiastically of the Oxford group: "When I listen to my friend Colet it seems to me like listening to Plato himself. In Grocyn, who does not admire the wide range of his knowledge? What could be more deep, searching and refined than the judgment of Linacre? When ever did Nature mould a character more gentle, endearing, and happy than Thomas More's?" But Erasmus, though well enough paid for a mere scholar of that century, was delicate in health, with the fastidious taste natural to such a mind and body. Finding neither in Oxford nor in London the pecuniary independence that he sought, after less than two years he moved to Paris (January 1500). Five years later, he came back to England for a few months; this time not to Oxford, but to London, where Colet and Grocyn and More were. By this time (1505) Colet had become Dean of St Paul's. About four years later again, Erasmus returned, and wrote his *Praise of Folly* in More's house in Bucklersbury. Henry VIII had just come to the throne; scholars welcomed him as a youth of real learning and love for learned men. Erasmus, meanwhile, had acquired a good deal more Greek by his own exertions; in October 1511 he came to Cambridge to teach the language, and was soon made Lady Margaret Professor of

Divinity. He had chosen Cambridge rather than Oxford, partly because all his old Oxford friends had now gone down or were dead, but mainly because of the bitter opposition there to the new Greek. Clement V, at the Council of Vienne (1311) had decreed the foundation of a Greek professorship at four of the main European universities: yet even the fundamental intention here was in the interests not of theologico-philosophic science but of missionary work in the East; and the slight traces of such professorships had disappeared before the Renaissance, so that Greek was still regarded with suspicion by the orthodox. At Cambridge the conservative opposition never went so far as at Oxford; as we have seen, even those who did not learn Greek themselves, contributed to the salary of Erasmus who taught it. Yet Erasmus's Greek class disappointed his expectations; the lectures of Richard Croke, a few years later, were far more immediately productive than his. But it was mostly at Cambridge that Erasmus wrote two of his greatest works—his edition of St Jerome's collected writings and his New Testament. Moreover, we must remember that his influence in conversation must have been enormous; quite apart from anything he published. He was the great stylist of his day; the great satirist, side by side with the great humorists of that age, Rabelais and St Thomas More. Rabelais, however, deliberately disguised his deeper purpose under scurrility and buffoonery. Erasmus, on the other hand, was a reformer rather after Voltaire's pattern; keen to dissect, biting in his criticism, but with little constructive power. His treatise on War is a splendid piece of rhetoric; but it shows no recognition of the deeper causes underlying war, or the real root of the evil. The constructive power was shown by More, this hard-working lawyer, judge, and statesman, who wrote, not as a man of letters, but because his heart was full, and because he seemed to see some chance of mending the world, if only by a few degrees. By far the highest product of all those free and familiar talks among that English group of reformers was not Erasmus's *Colloquies* or his *Praise of Folly*, brilliant as they are, but More's *Utopia*.[1]

In considering this book, we may begin with two subjects of greatest actuality at the present moment—*War* and *Tolerance*. More, like Colet and Erasmus and the large majority of scholars of every generation, was far more of a pacifist than a militarist. But he was very far from a non-resister. While the Utopians can do without money, their neighbours cannot; therefore, though this model republic has little temptation to create wars of aggression, the commonest prudence dictates that it should be prepared to defend itself against the aggression of others. Its ideal is that which Pascal has put into a single pregnant sentence: a world in which force is just, and justice has force at its disposal. More, therefore, devotes a whole chapter to the Utopian military system.² Their wars are never aggressive, with one exception to be noted later. "They never go to battle, but either in the defence of their own country, or to drive out of their friends' land the enemies that have invaded it, or by their power to deliver from the yoke and bondage of tyranny some people that be herewith oppressed." Yet they carefully avoid the extreme of supposing that we can defend ourselves against foreign aggression by merely sitting down and thinking of war as an impossible thing; or merely denouncing it as an anachronistic barbarism. The Utopians, then, do everything they can to avoid it on the one hand; but, on the other, they take great pains to ensure that, if war be forced upon them, they themselves shall emerge not as conquered people, but as conquerors. Most of their fighting they do through hired soldiers, mainly from a tribe of barbarous mountaineers who are always ready to hire themselves to the highest bidder; there More obviously alludes to the Swiss of his day. Next, as far as possible, they cast the burden upon their allies, as an equitable return for the protection and other benefits which the Utopians confer upon them. When, at last, they must throw their own citizens into the field, they take care that this shall be done in the most businesslike way possible. All able-bodied Utopian citizens are trained to arms. This is as the law provided in More's own England; for instance, only two years before *Utopia* was written, the sheriffs of Somerset and Dorset had proclaimed a levy of all men from sixteen to sixty to defend our South Coast against a threatened French invasion. In Utopia, then, as in medieval and even Elizabethan England, all men were liable for immediate service at any national emergency; and the Utopians went one step beyond England. "They do daily practise and exercise themselves in the discipline of war; and not only the men, but also the women upon certain appointed days, lest they should be found deficient in the feat of arms, if need should require." "Women that be willing to accompany their husbands in time of war be not prohibited or letted: yea, they provoke and exhort them to it with praises; and in the field the wives do stand every one by their own husband's side....It is a great reproach and dishonesty for the husband to come home without his wife, or the wife without her husband." Though all must thus be trained for war, and in case of invasion all are called out to defend their homes, yet, so far as foreign expeditions are concerned, "they thrust no man forth into war against his will". Like the modern Swiss, they have conscription and training for home defence only, and trust that this will carry them through all emergencies. Since they are a businesslike people, their national ingenuity spends itself partly on the invention of new warlike engines or new combinations in strategy and tactics. Again, they recognize as men of business that the main object of war is to end it as soon and cheaply as possible; therefore they consider it a far greater triumph to win by cunning than by bloodshed. More's emphasis upon this side of warfare is, as Dr Hans Baron has pointed out, truly Machiavellian; these two exact contemporaries argue with equal force that there are certain circumstances in which the end is so great that it justifies almost any means.[3] Again, More makes one exception to their rule of merely defensive warfare. When the increase of population drives the Utopians to colonize, they send out a colony to the nearest territory they can find which is still uncultivated: here they settle down. In this new land, they admit the aboriginal inhabitants to an equality with themselves if these will consent to co-operate with them: but "if they resist and rebel, then they make war against them. For they count this the most just cause of war, when any people holdeth a piece of ground void and vacant to no good nor justifiable use, keeping others from the use and possession of it, which notwithstanding by the law of nature ought thereof to be nourished and relieved." It is interesting to note that this last thesis has the qualified support of as distinguished a modern pacifist as Bertrand (now Earl) Russell[4] and that the gist of the Utopian military system is in harmony with the teaching of modern socialists in all Continental countries.[5] Moreover, the Utopians are modern enough to realize the value of non-military sanctions, when efficiently applied. If their friends are injured by any other nation, "they wreak their vengeance by abstaining from intercourse with that nation till they have made satisfaction"[6]— *ejus commercio gentis abstinent.*

From war let us now pass to the less ungrateful question of Tolerance. The book takes here a bold and, for its time, even an extreme, line. All religions are tolerated in Utopia, and almost all religious discussion, so long as the speaker does not urge his arguments in an offensive manner. Those who deny the existence of any other life but the present are, indeed, looked upon as less likely to be sober and dutiful citizens, and are therefore subjected to certain disabilities. "He that is thus minded is deprived of all honours, excluded from all offices, and rejected from all common administrations in the republic. And thus he is of all sorts despised, as of an unprofitable and of a base and vile nature. Howbeit they put him to no punishment, because they be persuaded that it is in no man's power to believe what he list.... But they suffer him not to dispute in his opinion; but that prohibition is only against dispute among the common people; for else, apart, among the priests and men of gravity, they do not only suffer but also exhort him to dispute and argue, hoping that, at the last, his madness will give place to reason." Again, as to objectionable manners of disputation, he instances the case of a Utopian whom the Christian travellers had converted and baptized, and who at once began disputing hotly and intolerantly against the non-Christians, "calling them wicked and devilish and the children of everlasting damnation. When he had thus long reasoned the matter, they laid hold on him, accused him, and condemned him into exile, not as a despiser of religion, but as a seditious person and a raiser up of discussion among the people." Otherwise, then, all differences are tolerated, by a law which the Utopians found to be not only charitable, but congruent with political experience.[7] For King Utopus, the great conqueror who had subdued this island and drawn up its model constitution, "hearing that the inhabitants of the land were, before his coming thither, at continual dissension and strife among themselves for their religions; perceiving also that this common dissension (whiles every several sect took several parts in fighting for their country) was the only occasion of his conquest over them all; as soon as he had gotten the victory, first of all he made a decree, that it should be lawful for every man to favour and follow what religion he would, and that he might do the best he could to bring other to his opinion, so that he did it peaceably, gently, quietly and soberly, without hasty and contentious rebuking and inveighing against other.... This law did King Utopus make not only for the maintenance of peace, which he saw through continual contention and mortal hatred utterly extinguished; but also because he thought this decree should make for the furtherance of religion. Whereof he durst define and determine nothing unadvisedly, as doubting whether God, desiring manifold and diverse sorts of honour, would inspire sundry men with sundry kinds of religion. And this surely he thought a very unmeet and foolish thing, and a point of arrogant presumption, to compel all other by violence and threatenings to agree to the same that thou believest to be true. Furthermore though there be one religion which alone is true, and all other vain and superstitious, yet did he well foresee (so that the matter were handled with reason, and sober modesty) that the truth, of [its] own power, would at the last issue out and come to light. But if contention and debate in that behalf should continually be used, as the worst men be most obstinate and stubborn, and in their evil opinion most constant; he perceived that then the best and holiest religion would be trodden underfoot and destroyed by most vain superstitions, even as good corn is by thorns and weeds overgrown and choked. Therefore all this matter he left undiscussed, and gave to every man free liberty and choice to believe what he would."

It was in consonance with this that public worship should have a vague and general character:[8] "Nothing is heard or seen in the churches, but that which seemeth to agree indifferently with all [religious creeds]. If there be a distinct kind of sacrifice peculiar to any several sect, that they execute at home in their own houses. The public sacrifices be so ordered, that they be no derogation nor prejudice to any of the private sacrifices and religions. Therefore no image of any god is seen in the church, to the intent that it may be free for every man to conceive God, by his own religion, after what likeness and similitude he will." This diversity, however, turns no more to the detriment of dignified ceremonial or artistic beauty than it does to true personal religion. "Their churches be very gorgeous, and not only of fine and curious workmanship, but also (which in the fewness of them was necessary) very wide and large, and able to receive a great company of people. But they be all somewhat dark. Howbeit that was not done through ignorance in building, but, as they say, by the counsel of the priests. Because they thought that overmuch light doth disperse men's cogitations, whereas in dim and doubtful light they be gathered together, and more earnestly fixed upon religion and devotion.... They burn frankincense and other sweet savours, and light also a great number of wax candles and tapers, not supposing this gear to be anything available to the divine nature, as neither the prayers of men. But this unhurtful and harmless kind of worship pleaseth them. And by these sweet savours and lights, and other such ceremonies, men feel themselves secretly lifted up and encouraged to devotion with more willing and fervent hearts.... When [the last] prayer is said they fall down to the ground again, and a little after they rise up and go to dinner. And the residue of the day they pass over in plays and exercise of chivalry." Again, the priests have immense power; their excommunication is dreaded as a most formidable weapon, and in his own person even a criminal priest is immune. This is because "they have priests of exceeding holiness, and therefore very few": thus Hythlodaye explains it to More, and thus More publishes it to an England where, as he himself admitted in the hottest of his orthodox controversial writings, one of the worst sores of society was the excessive numbers of clergy, the want of proper care in their selection and ordination, and the mean worldly shifts to which many clerics were driven, if they were to escape sheer starvation. Not only here, but throughout this great book, we may see how More had one foot in the medieval past, and the other not only in this modern world of ours, but in the world that is to be. "The remarkable thing about *Utopia*" (writes Professor Chambers, p. 125) "is the extent to which it adumbrates social and political reforms which have either been actually carried into practice, or which have come to be regarded as very practical politics. Utopia is depicted as a sternly righteous and puritanical State, where few of us would feel quite happy; yet we go on using the word 'Utopia' to signify an easy-going paradise, whose only fault is that it is too happy and ideal to be realized."

The next point of interest in the Utopian is one which we have already touched upon by anticipation—his attitude towards women. In war, he recognizes scarcely any difference between the sexes, but that of physical strength. In religion, he is equally broad-minded. The Utopians choose their priests with the utmost care: "there be but thirteen in every city." These are treated with the greatest respect, both by law and by custom; yet "women are not excluded from the priesthood, howbeit few be chosen, and none but widows and old women". Here, again, no reader who is not familiar with medieval and Reformation-period religious literature can realize how far More is beyond his time. Occasionally, however, we find him definitely of his own time; and this lends, perhaps, all the more force to his liberality of mind in the wider fields. It is not only that he frankly recognizes the necessity of man being, in general, senior partner in marriage. This would seem a physical necessity from which it is difficult in any case to escape. For, looking only to the general rule, and apart from exceptional cases, we must treat marriage either as a strict or as a loose contract; there is no other alternative. If it be a loose contract, to be determined at will by either of the contracting parties, this gives an enormously unfair advantage to the man, who can earn his living separately far more easily than the woman. If, on the other hand, the contract be, as a general rule, indissoluble, even thus there must be a distinct understanding as to the representative and more responsible partner, in the few cases in which agreement can be obtained in no other way; and, here again, other things being equal, it is the physically stronger and more independent who will necessarily be accepted by outsiders as the representative partner, even if there be no law in the matter. More, therefore, in general assumes masculine supremacy in the family; and that in a far more definite form than thoughtful people would admit nowadays. He, who in pure literature did so much to anticipate Shakespearian drama, might well have written *The Taming of the Shrew*. For we need go no further than the great playwrights to see that More's downright "masculinism", however repugnant to modern manners, was entirely in harmony with those of medieval and Tudor and even later times. Yet, here again, it is only fair to take him at his highest level; and we may be proud that the medieval Ockham and the Renaissance writer in Europe who most definitely advocated the claims of women were both Englishmen. While Ockham went no further than to suggest the vote for them, More would associate them equally with men, in the highest privileges of citizenship and in the citizen's heaviest burdens of citizenship, so far as this is physically possible.

We must deal more briefly with the rest of the book. Let us note, first, More's sovereign common sense all through. We must, of course, make allowance here and there for some touches which are obviously playful, added as a mere seasoning to tickle the reader's palate. We must make a little allowance, too, for passages where his main object is to satirize modern conditions: for instance, what he writes about international treaties, and again on sanitation, where numberless documentary details might be quoted to show that More's purpose is to shame the Londoners of his day out of the disorderly and insanitary conditions which too often prevailed in their city. But, if we make these allowances, and take the serious part of his book seriously, it is astonishing how well it stands the test of 400 years' experience since his day: "rich in saving common sense and (as the greatest only are) in its simplicity sublime". He insists everywhere upon the value of steady method, and the necessity of enlisting the total forces of the nation in every truly national enterprise. The Utopians are not men of genius; their secret is the secret of greatness in all ages—hard work, and an open mind. "I think verily, though it might be that we did surpass them in wit, yet in study, in travail, and in laboursome endeavour they far pass us.... Whereas they quickly, and almost at the first moment of meeting with it, made their own whatsoever among us hath been prudently devised, yet I suppose it would be long before we would receive anything that among these Utopians is better instituted than among us." When a work is recognized as necessary, the whole able-bodied population is at once set to it: we have "conscription of labour". "Thus, the work being divided into so great a number of workmen, was with exceeding marvellous speed dispatched": "therefore by the labour of so many [the work] is made in less time than any man [here] would believe."

Everything is methodically planned, as far as possible. More's description of the division of the whole land into cities and administrative districts practically anticipates, by nearly three centuries, the methods by which the French Revolutionary Government brought order into the hopeless chaos of French administration under the Ancien Régime. The theme of the whole book is the terrible waste in human affairs which is created simply by muddle and want of method; and, above all, the labour that runs to waste because so many live in idleness while others drudge from dawn to dark like brute beasts: whereas, by patient application and good-will, the work might so be apportioned that none had so disgracefully little to do, and none was so inhumanly overburdened. His ideal is a six hours' work-day, and six hours of honourable leisure for the very poorest: a contented land, a land of temperate, cheerful mirth, and of natural song: a real "Merry England", not in an imaginary past, but in a predominantly new future. For More cherishes no vague sentimentality; he that will not work, neither shall he eat. He sees clearly that it is absurd to talk of a living wage for every man, unless every man is compelled to accept his duties to the State as clearly as he claims his privileges from the State. The criminal classes become bondmen in Utopia, and are set to the worst drudgery; yet not without hope of release on good behaviour: here, again, there are some modern Swiss cantons which come very nearly up to More's ideal.

The Utopians have a kind of monastic order—or rather, two sorts of men voluntarily devoting themselves to religion. The first sort live a life of celibacy and abstain from butcher's meat, according to the ideal of the strict monk of the Middle Ages. The second sort marry, and have families, and eat butcher's meat, because they think they can work better on such diet. The Utopians "count the former sect the holier" (writes More with delicate irony) "but the latter the wiser". In short, his ideal is Christian, but it is also utilitarian. Pleasure, rational pleasure, is the main aim of human life—pleasure which takes account not only of to-day but also of to-morrow, not only of ourselves but also of our neighbours. More cannot understand a whole society framed upon the exclusively puritan ideal. For (he says) "if it be a point of humanity for man to bring health and comfort to man, and especially to mitigate and assuage the grief of others, and by taking from them the sorrow and heaviness of life, to restore them to joy, that is to say, to pleasure; why may it not then be said that nature doth provoke every man to do the same to himself? For a joyful life, that is to say, a pleasant life, is either evil (and if it be so, then thou shouldst not only help no man thereto, but rather, as much as in thee lieth, withdraw all men from it, as noisome and hurtful) or else, if thou not only mayest, but also of duty art bound to procure it to others, why not chiefly to thyself, to whom thou art bound to shew as much favour and gentleness as to others? For when nature biddeth thee to be good and gentle to others, she commandeth thee not to be cruel and ungentle to thyself. Therefore even very nature (say they) prescribeth to us a joyful life, that is to say, pleasure as the end of all our operations."9 On this particular point, then, More is utilitarian, with the utilitarianism of a reasonable disciple of J. S. Mill. The reader may find for himself (for the little book is accessible in many editions) many other points in which More has anticipated the trend of the modern world. And as he shows his common sense in postulating so little for his ideal republic, demanding only what seems in theory a very moderate amount of order and regularity and self-control in human society, so also he shows equal sense in indicating clearly that even this moderate aim can be attained, if at all, only after long years and many struggles. His concluding words run: "I must needs confess and grant that many things be in the Utopian republic which, in our cities, I may rather wish for than hope after." This sentence is thoroughly characteristic of his genial and ironical satire. He had learned much in style, as well as in matter, from Plato; much of his subtle irony. In this Utopia, more than in any but the merest fragments of his hastily written English works, you see the real More—the real scholar and thinker, looking away from present-day controversies into the far future of the human race.

In all university history, this is the moment we may love most to dwell on. We prize our universities for the constant public teaching they keep up, and also for their constant production of such books as few men can compose who do not enjoy academic leisure and opportunities. But more important, perhaps, than either of these is the quiet ferment of thought under the surface: the groups of familiar friends who from age to age, by the fireside or in the gardens, discuss freely the eternal problems of life and death, and thus bring each fresh generation one degree nearer—if only one hair's breadth nearer—to the solution of those problems. And in such free thought and discussion we always find the two distinct elements personified here by Erasmus and More. First, the negative element of mere indignation at the abuses which still exist in society, an element which finds vent in the easiest of all kinds of literature, satire, wherein we

> Compound for sins we are inclined to
> By damning those we have no mind to.

And, secondly, the far harder task of keeping hold on realities and preserving the sense of proportion all through our discontent: the mind of Sophocles, who "saw life steadily and saw it whole".

The mind of More, too, who tried to form a clear idea in his own head of some social machinery which would really work among ordinary men such as we know them, if all that is out of date in the existing machinery could be scrapped.

In spite of very weighty modern arguments to the contrary, I cannot believe that More raises any serious question in *Utopia* which he had not seriously considered himself, at one time or another, during those first thirty-eight years of his life; nor, again, that he would not gladly have listened, at any time, to a free and fundamental discussion on any one of them, between competent and self-controlled disputants. His was no cloistered and fugitive faith; and, definitely as he may have decided in later years against one or other of the ideas or practices which seemed commendable in Utopia, we cannot conclude even from those convictions that he would not have admitted the matter to be fairly arguable on the opposite side. No contemporary, it seems, can be quoted who took *Utopia* for a mere *jeu d'esprit*, or even as a preponderantly irresponsible paradox. Nor can we justly ignore More's share in that *Praise of Folly*, of the same period as *Utopia*, which contains some of Erasmus's most outspoken criticisms on Church life. We must remember, again, that against orthodox critics he defended Erasmus as his peculiarly dear friend. Nowadays, his treatment of the divorce question in *Utopia* is sometimes cited as a case where he could not possibly have been serious: yet that is because modern historians do not always realize how much more embryonic and fluid Roman doctrine was in those ages than at the present day. It was in More's lifetime that Clement VII was willing to treat with Henry VIII on the basis of legalized bigamy.

We must certainly bear in mind, what Professor Chambers insists upon with just emphasis, that the Middle Ages drew a clear distinction between the "cardinal" (or "natural") virtues and the "theological". The former were Prudence, Justice, Temperance and Fortitude; the latter, far higher, were Faith, Hope and Charity (the last word in that wider sense which included Love of God). *Utopia*, then, was written to show how far a society could advance upon the basis of the four lower virtues alone. Yet, even if we accept this distinction to the full, must not the book raise in every thoughtful mind the inevitable question: If the mere natural virtues can blossom into a State so far superior to actual Christendom in peacefulness and the ordinary decencies of life, can we then really maintain the immense superiority of the theological virtues? And, especially, was Henry VIII's England justified in treating Faith as so all-important that the blackest of all crimes is that of repudiating ecclesiastical tradition?[10] Professor Chambers rightly reminds us that even the State of Utopia falls definitely short of the modern ideal of toleration; so much so that, in conceivable extreme circumstances, a man might there be judicially executed for his faith. But More gives no hint that this has ever actually happened or was likely to happen; and in general religious peace Utopia contrasts as strongly with More's Europe as it does in international peace. The narrator, Hythlodaye, had five other Christians with him. Two, it is true, died during the sojourn. But even the four did not take their missionary opportunities very seriously. In the spirit of the much-abused modern Cowper-Temple clause for teaching in schools, they preached not the distinctive doctrines of the Roman Church, but Christ's "name, teaching, morals and miracles", together with that constancy of the Christian martyrs which "has brought such populous nations into their sect"—*in suam sectam*. This teaching impressed the Utopians, and partly because it "seemed nearest to that particular opinion [*haeresis*] which is most powerful" among this people, where everybody may choose what religion he will. Therefore "no small number" were baptized. But among these travellers there was no Christian priest, and no bishop to ordain any such. Yet the Utopians (without any hint of dissent from Hythlodaye and his three fellow-Catholics) contemplated (and perhaps actually consummated) "the choice, without any bishop sent unto them, of somebody from their own number to exert the character of the priesthood", i.e. to institute a Mass-less, Transubstantiation-less Christianity! Moreover, the typical religious brawler in Utopia is the orthodox who has *trop de zèle*, and who, among this "naturally" virtuous folk, behaves as the orthodox commonly behaved in More's "theologically" virtuous England.[11] In the face of this, can we safely deny that More, in his earliest maturity, nourished germs, at least, of those new ideas which are incalculably more powerful than dynamite?

For, two or three years before More wrote this book (i.e. in 1513 or 1514), Machiavelli in his *Discourses on Livy* was emphasizing the immense advantage that ancient Rome had possessed in her single tolerant State religion, side by side with the disastrous political results of papal claims in Europe during the past few centuries. He, like Dubois and Marsilius, laid all the heaviest responsibility for this perpetual bloodshed on the Holy See; and More knew enough of history to realize that this was fairly common talk among the laity. Therefore, without venturing to decide how far these Utopian ideas are his own, and how far they are imputable only to the imaginary narrator Ralph Hythlodaye, we must certainly face the fact that More's mere suggestion from behind such a mask was extraordinarily bold. Moreover, it is difficult to believe that a man of More's powerful imagination and knowledge of mankind can have failed to realize that *Utopia* would have considerable explosive effect. Modern Roman Catholic writers have much justification for treating the Renaissance as a more formidable enemy in the sixteenth century than the Reformation: and the younger More displays something, at least, of that spirit which Lagarde feels to have constituted the main force of Marsilius. "The true enemy [of ecclesiastical dominion] is that insidious, ardent and conquering work which sows suspicion and doubt in men's minds, and which, by means of a new, direct, and vigorous dialectic, scientifically saps the most firmly-established truths".[12] Everybody admits *Utopia* to be a definite satire upon Tudor England; what right, therefore, have we to suppose that More's eye was turned all this while upon State conditions alone, to the exclusion of the Church, of which he tells us so much?

But in one way More's life and death, with that of St John Fisher, is quite as significant for our social history as his writings. The execution of those two great men brought out, with a clearness which no man could then ignore, the unstable equilibrium between Church and State. Men had lived for generations in a Totalitarian Church, and now the Totalitarian State was coming into England. Rome insisted then, as she does still, that her laws, in case of conflict, must prevail over those of any State to which the faithful Churchman may happen to belong. Popes had often waged wars in virtue of these claims: Machiavelli pointed out as emphatically in More's day as Dubois and Marsilius had done a couple of centuries earlier, that the Popes had created in Europe more wars than they had prevented. Therefore, first under a sovereign like Philip the Fair in France, and then under Henry VIII in England, honest men lived always in a potentially impossible position, and might at any moment, by ill fortune, find themselves actually and irremediably fixed between the upper and the nether millstone. So it was with More and Fisher. There was, however, this difference between them, that Fisher twice, at least, invited a foreign invasion of England, in terms which in any country and any age of history would have rendered him liable to the death-penalty as a political offender.[13] The full significance of such an invitation can be realized only by those who know that, when Paul III declared open war against Henry VIII, he decreed slavery as the punishment for every royalist prisoner whom the papalist invaders might capture.[14] More, on the other hand, seems to have abstained with marvellous tact and constancy from anything of that kind, and probably died as a pure martyr for conscience' sake, though there would be greater historical certainty if the messenger had not burned the Fisher-More correspondence, saying that "there was no better keeper than the fire".[15] Yet, if the wheel of fortune had happened to turn the other way, this man who was incapable of any lie of the soul might have escaped Henry's axe only to fall into papal fire. John XXII, as we have seen in Chapter xxxv, condemned as heresy the doctrine that Christ and his apostles had lived without property of any kind, of which the natural corollary was that the most perfect religion would be Christian communism. Four devoted Franciscans were burned at Marseilles in 1318, mainly on that count. To those four men the Pope had one simple answer: It is my function to interpret the Bible; I interpret it in a sense contrary to yours; therefore, recant or burn.[16] Let us imagine More thus confronted with John XXII. He is the most respected and in many ways most distinguished layman in the whole land; and he is immovably convinced that Christ and His apostles had been Utopian in their communism. Threats and cajolery are in vain; he will not descend to the lie of the soul. By holding out thus alone, amid an obsequious world, would he not have made John feel exactly as Henry felt, that this single conspicuous and incorruptible dissentient was the one fatal obstacle to his totalitarian policy? The denial of the poverty of Christ was almost as necessary to John XXII's political position in 1318 as the denial of papal supremacy was to Henry's in 1534. More, who warned Henry in 1513, "the Pope is a prince as you are", would have found, in 1318, that a pope might be a politician no less unscrupulous and pitiless than an English king. Admitting, as we must, the occasional truth of Caiaphas's words, "it is expedient that one man should die for the people", must we not recognize that from More's blood there sprang one precious fruit: namely, clearness of thought upon that century-old confusion between Church and State? From 1580 onwards, Roman Catholic suspects were submitted to what they nicknamed "the bloody question". This was: "In the event of a Catholic invasion, which side would the accused take, the Queen's or the Pope's?" Upon this we have the comment of Professor Meyer, in a book published with the orthodox *imprimatur*: "A faithful son of the Catholic Church could only answer: 'If the invasion was for no worldly object, but solely for the restoration of the Catholic religion, then I should take part with the invaders'—a reply which would certainly send him to the gallows.... When a man frankly admits, at a moment when war is imminent, that he would side with his country's foes, he cannot expect mercy."[17]

Yet this is an anticipation, however logical, of my last chapter.

XLIX. THE FIGHT FOR THE BIBLE

IT is sometimes urged, with considerable justice, that modern historians take too little notice of the religious factor in social life. Distinguished writers may even be found protesting that the differences among Christian sects interest them no more than the quarrel between Tweedledum and Tweedledee: yet these same men would never dream of ignoring racial or climatic differences. The attitude of Europe in general towards Life after Death was almost as universal in its main outlines, and almost as different from that of a great part of modern Europe, as are the heat of Africa, and the skin of an Ethiopian, in contrast with what we feel and see around us everywhere in Britain. It is irrelevant whether our own personal preference is for a tropical or temperate climate, for white skins or black; the point is that, in thinking or writing of African society, we must remember that our common human motives are at work there under, for us, most uncommon and peculiar conditions. So was it also in the Middle Ages. Within a spiritual climate very different from our own, among men hedged round by certain limitations over which modern thought bears us as easily as the aeroplane crosses the sea, the same elementary social forces were at work as to-day; and the main conflicts of thought were essentially the same. The struggle was always, at bottom, between the conservative and the progressive mind, each with those same qualities and defects which each shows at the present day. That, from beginning to end, is the main point of interest; that is eternal, under the most various manifestations of detail. That is what matters more to us than the things which our forefathers believed, or professed to believe, that they were fighting for at the moment. From that higher point of view, therefore, the Bible in history should interest the agnostic scarcely less than the most fervent believer. The fifteenth-century fight for a free Bible was more epoch-making than the fight for free tea in Boston harbour. The forces there arrayed were those which have stood up against each other in almost every European revolution or civil war; and in the majority, perhaps, of international wars. They were the very forces which now divide one-half of Europe against the other, and which make a gulf wider and deeper than the Pacific between Japan on one side, North America and Australia on the other. In this chapter, therefore, we must try to deal with the quarrel over the Christian Scriptures from that point of view which links it with the long vista of world-history.

Miss M. Deanesly's *Lollard Bible* has cast such clear light upon the story of English vernacular versions that no considerable scholar on either side ventures nowadays to support St Thomas More's claim to have seen orthodox pre-Wycliffite translations, licensed by bishops. There had been fragmentary versions of the Gospels and the Psalms into Anglo-Saxon, and the mystic Rolle had translated and commented the Psalter in the early fourteenth century: but, if indeed the whole Bible was ever translated, it can never have circulated beyond a few copies, so utterly do we lack any sure trace of the book. In England, as on the Continent, the first attempt to familiarize ordinary readers with the Scriptures was by people whom the Church condemned as heretics.

In the Greek Church, no serious difficulty of this kind has ever occurred. St John Chrysostom [370] repeatedly bids his hearers read the Bible for themselves: "Hear, I adjure you, all secular folk, get yourselves Bibles, which are medicine for the soul; or at least, if ye will do no more, get yourselves the New Testament." Elsewhere, he emphasizes Christ's command: "Christ, referring the Jews to the Scriptures, sent them not to a mere reading but to accurate examination. For He did not say [merely] *Read the Scriptures*, but *Search the Scriptures*....He commands them to dig with exactitude, in order that they may find those things that lie deep." And, finally, he even insists upon the Bible as the ultimate touchstone of truth: "For, even as a safe door, so doth it shut out heretics from entrance, setting us in safety concerning all the things which we desire, and not permitting us to go astray."[1] Here we have, as early as the late fourth century, what goes far to explain the different fortunes of the Eastern and Western Church in the Middle Ages. Greek never became a completely dead language in the East; thus there was no excuse for shutting up the Bible from the laity, even if that had been possible. Though New Testament Greek gradually became mainly unintelligible to the multitude when read in the liturgy, yet educated men could always get at least the rough sense of it. In the West, meanwhile, a very different social problem was created by the barbarian invasions. The two original languages, Hebrew and Greek, were almost altogether unknown; and even the Latin translations gradually became unintelligible to the laity. Moreover, during the general illiteracy of the Dark Ages, they were unintelligible to the majority of the priesthood, even if they had been actually procurable, since men were so little concerned in overcoming the difficulties of book-multiplication, that there was not one copy for each monk in the very richest and most efficient monasteries. For something like a thousand years, the average price of a Bible was at least equal to the whole yearly income of a well-to-do priest, and often much greater. Even if he had had the ability and enterprise to write out a copy for himself, the bare materials would have cost him a considerable sum. We ourselves are so accustomed to see it in a handy form that few people realize what a large book it really is. In the earlier Middle Ages it often ran to two or more folio volumes; and the common name for it was not "the Book" but "the Library": *Bibliotheca*, a term which has entrapped more than one unwary antiquary in the past. It was not till the midthirteenth century, after the Franciscan-Dominican revival, and in the full current of the new university book-trade, that the Paris booksellers produced those little portable Bibles, in minute writing upon delicate vellum, which became possibly almost as numerous as the copies of Peter Lombard's *Sentences*, but which seldom or never show any sign of wear. It would be hard to find any copy answering even remotely to Luther's well-thumbed Psalter, which he refused to exchange for a fine new one lest he should lose his local memory, so valuable to a working student. Many well-worn medieval volumes of other kinds have come down to us; but, in the surviving Bibles, it is hard to find any trace of wear even where we might most confidently expect it; e.g. in the Psalms or the Gospels. Moreover, there was not sufficient demand to call with compelling urgency for supply: even at Oxford, in the midfourteenth century, Archbishop Fitzralph complains of the difficulty of procuring "useful" Bibles.[2] The greatest men of the Middle Ages sometimes knew their Bible as well as modern theologians; but among the parish priests, as we have seen, scarcely one could ever have pored over the whole book as ancient cottagers might sometimes be found doing in Victorian England. Thus a natural gulf opened between the Bible and the people, deepened first by carelessness and finally by a natural, yet fatal, jealousy. In the East, Ulphilas, a Gothic bishop, hastened to provide his fellow-countrymen with nearly all the Scriptures in their own tongue; and his contemporary St Chrysostom set up a Gothic church in Constantinople, where lessons from this version were read as part of the liturgy.[3] But Ulphilas was an Arian; and in the West no orthodox prelate or missionary did the like for the converted barbarians. As *The Catholic Encyclopaedia* puts it: "What prevented the earliest English missionaries from translating the Scriptures into the vernacular, or what caused the loss of such immediate translations, if any were made, is hard to determine at this late date" (xv, 374). Charlemagne tried here, as elsewhere, to remedy ecclesiastical remissness; he demanded that, wherever necessary, there should be an interpreter for the portion of Scripture read in church. But here, as elsewhere, he could not do for the hierarchy what they would not do for themselves; and "thus a custom which arose only through tenacity of ecclesiastical practice and clerical remissness was afterwards justified by the theory that a holy speech was seemly for the Holy Scripture. The abandonment of intelligibility was connected with the development of the Catholic service to a business of the priests, before and for the passively interested congregation."

Thus, though the Waldensians struggled to return here to the custom of primitive Christianity, this very attempt, like the attempt to follow literally Christ's prohibition of swearing, became a proof presumptive of heresy. As a natural consequence, heretics and freethinkers were increasingly convinced that papal claims were incompatible with Scripture knowledge. Marsilius and Ockham appealed constantly and emphatically to the written word against the current traditions. Marsilius studied the sacred text "in full independence", instead of following the university routine of his day.[4] Tradition (he feels) has killed all familiarity with "the true and simple beginnings" of our faith: he is scandalized by those who, with the plain Gospel words before them, "believe rather in the tradition of men, whether holy or not holy, than in Christ's own plainest words".[5] It was equally natural, again, that Wyclif should have insisted upon the Bible as the touchstone of faith, and should have set his disciples to make that translation for which the time was now evidently ripe and over-ripe. In the next century, we find two German theologians, Goch and Wessel, treating the Bible as the main standard of Christian faith to the individual man, in much the same terms as modern Protestantism; yet Wessel, in his youth, had been a friend of Thomas à Kempis, and Goch, at least, remained essentially orthodox to the end of his life.[6] St Thomas More himself, in the very heat of his bitter controversy with Tyndale, admitted that the Church was here far behind the times. He acknowledged that, though Archbishop Arundel's decree of 1408 had threatened burning alive, in the last resort, for any man who should read or promulgate any translation made since Wyclif's day, yet the Church had done nothing since that date to provide a pure translation for the people. Heretics would club together to get their Tyndale's translation published, but no Catholic printer would risk his capital on a well-meaning "orthodox" edition which, after all, the bishop might condemn. He adds: "and surely how it hath happened that in all this while [since 1408] God hath either not suffered, or not provided that any good and virtuous man hath had the mind in faithful wise to translate it, and thereupon either the clergy, or at the least wise, some one Bishop to approve it, this can I nothing tell." Yet More would not allow even such an approved translation to be used by all men, but "all the copies should come whole into the Bishop's hand; which he may after his discretion and wisdom deliver unto such as he perceiveth honest, sad and virtuous", under condition that, after the recipient's death, this copy should be returned to the bishop. Moreover, he feels that the bishop might justly allow a man to read Matthew or Mark or Luke, but forbid John; permit the Acts or Ephesians, and refuse Romans or Revelation.[7] It is astounding that a few modern writers, on the strength of a few scrappy quotations carefully chosen to exclude this evidence, should claim this as a policy of "the open Bible".

The facts are clearly and accurately given by Miss Deanesly. From 1080 onwards, we frequently find popes, councils, and bishops forbidding vernacular versions; nobody has yet produced a decree freely permitting them. The laity were not allowed to read even Mass-books in their own language, until shortly before the Reformation. The first orthodox Catholic who can be found explicitly recommending the faithful laity to read the Bible in their own tongue is the friar Otto of Passau in 1386. But Germany was here beyond the general European standard. In England, the numerous pre-Wycliffite manuals of devotion, while they prescribe reading for the layfolk, never suggest English Bible reading;

and only one of the writers, the celebrated Walter Hilton, recom-
mends those who can read Latin to study the Gospels as a preliminary to meditation. Another goes out of his way to explain
that the layman will get good from hearing the Latin gospel at
Mass, "though thou understand it nought", just as an adder is
affected by the charm pronounced over her, though she does not
understand the words. About A.D. 1400, the lawfulness of an
English Bible began to be seriously debated; yet there is no
orthodox pre-Reformation writer who explicitly approves of it.
Quite characteristic is the *Chastising of God's Children*, possibly
written for a nun, which says "many men reproveth to have the
psalter or mattins, or the gospel in English, or the Bible, because
they may not be translated into no vulgar word by the word as it
standeth, without great circumlocution after the feeling of the first
writers, which translated that into Latin by the Holy Ghost". In
other words, not only was the Bible itself so inspired that (as we
have seen in Chapter XXXII), whenever its words cannot otherwise be explained away, it must be taken as absolutely binding even
on questions of history and geography and botany, but this
Vulgate translation was also a separately inspired work which it
would be profane, if not heretical, to touch. Indeed, that is a
spirit still living at the present day; not only do we sometimes find
the Vulgate quoted as an "original" authority, but there is not,
even now, any English version of the Scriptures "authorized", in
any strict sense, for the Roman Catholic reader.

Such an exclusive spirit, however, can scarcely have commended
itself for a moment to More in his earlier uncontroversial years,
and to More's friend Erasmus it was utterly repugnant: his learning,
with his genius for textual criticism, led him from that side to the
exact conclusion at which ordinary religious folk were beginning
to aim from the opposite standpoint. We must dwell a little longer
on this, since there can be few better proofs of the depth of any
movement than the fact that it is supported by honest men from
very different directions.

Ordinary folk (it is often pleaded nowadays) were fully satisfied
in the Middle Ages with the pictures on church walls and in church
windows—"The Bible of the Poor"; or, at any rate, with these
pictures as supplemented by religious plays, which were occasional
in the villages and periodical in the towns. This is not true: and,
if it were, it would cut the ground from beneath the apologist's

own feet. A man thus contented would be at a very low stage of religious development; he would correspond to the slum-dweller who finds no great quarrel with his debased surroundings. No historian will seriously dispute the reminder that "it is absurd to talk as though the stock from which the people of modern Europe have sprung was not essentially healthy in mind and body".[8] Men were ready for more religion than they actually got. It became increasingly common to accompany the religious images with long descriptive inscriptions in the vulgar tongue, such as we still see at the back of the splendid choir-stalls at Amiens, and as John Trevisa describes in the castle chapel of Berkeley. So, again, with the miracle-plays and the liturgical dramas from which they had sprung. The *Concordia Regularis* (often attributed to St Dunstan [980] but really by St Ethelwold of Winchester [970]) speaks of the drama of *Quem Quaeritis?* as composed "for the strengthening of faith in the unlearned vulgar". In [1150] the Abbess Herrad of Landsberg says the same: this Resurrection play, and the crèche, and similar inventions were instituted "in order to strengthen the belief of the faithful and to attract the unbeliever": but now (she adds bitterly) they are mingled with "buffoonery, unbecoming jokes...and all sorts of disorder". Her contemporary Gerhoh of Reichersberg echoes this lament: these plays in the churches, so far from furthering the cause of Christ, degenerate into "vanities and false insanities", and make rather for the cause of Antichrist. In 1244 Bishop Grosseteste wrote "the clergy [of our diocese], as I hear, makes plays which they call Miracles", and directed his archdeacons to "exterminate these altogether, in so far as it is in your power".[9] Robert Manning of Bourn [1300], like Ethelwold and Herrad, regarded these plays as essentially instructive:

> To make men be in belief of God,
> That He rose in flesh and blood...
> To make men to believe steadfastly
> That God was born of Virgin Marie,

so long as the performing clergy do not bedizen themselves in masks, or play in the churchyards.[10] But, from about 1370, a sermon has survived which condemns miracle-plays altogether.[11] "Sithen it is against the behests of God, that biddeth that thou shalt not take God's name in vain, it is against our belief; and so it may not give occasion of turning men to the belief but of perverting; and therefore many men weenen that there is no Hell of everlasting pains, but that God doth but threaten us and not do it indeed, as by playing of miracles in sign and not in deed." And a little later (1431) we have documentary evidence from the York archives which is above all suspicion of partisanship. The masons' gild appealed to the city council for a change. "They murmured among themselves concerning their own pageant on Corpus Christi Day, when Fergus was scourged, seeing that the matter of that pageant is not contained in Holy Scripture, and it caused rather laughter and clamour than devotion, and sometimes quarrels, contentions and fights proceeded therefrom among the people."[12] The council therefore granted them the play of Herod instead: but later (apparently about 1470) the apocryphal play was taken up by the linen-weavers. All this evidence is quite apart from the frequent official condemnation of the Feast of Fools, and similar plays which had ceased to wear even the pretence of an edifying religious garb.

Beneath and behind these popular dramas, however, there was a true and deep current of religious literature, partly in verse but far more considerable in prose. The full significance of this was never realized until Professor R. W. Chambers's recent essay on *The Continuity of English Prose*. No sketch of the later medieval generations, however brief, can afford to neglect this, and no reader can rise from Professor Chambers's book without feeling the better and wiser for it. We see there how neither the priest nor the prophet were lacking in any generation: we find parish clergy and cloistered clergy side by side with definitely unsacerdotal mystics like Rolle and women like Juliana of Norwich. One addition only we may be prompted to make for ourselves. The essayist not only omits full consideration of the extent to which these orthodox writers must have been stimulated to compete for popular favour against those Lollard tracts which persecution and censorship have destroyed, but he hardly does full justice to the minority of such tracts which have come down to us. In especial, that long apologia of William Thorpe in 1407 may bear comparison with the best of orthodox writers, even with More himself, for both matter and style.[13] Thus, both the orthodox and the heretic, each in his own fashion, testify indirectly to a great yearning among the multitude; religious folk in the fifteenth century were a Bible-hungry public.

In the opposite hemisphere, so to speak, learned men were already realizing that it was impossible to sit indefinitely upon the safety-valve. A distinguished Oxford scholar, Reginald Pecock, became bishop first of St Asaph and then of Chichester. Realizing that there was at least a show of serious reason in the Lollard objections, he undertook to meet them by rational argument. He had little difficulty in exposing one exaggeration to which they had been driven by these embargoes laid upon the Bible; he showed that, even if they could get freely at the sacred text, they would not find the royal road to truth that many hoped for through all their spiritual difficulties. But the bishop's mere appeal to reason, together with a certain tactless vanity, proved his ruin. A council at Lambeth (1457) condemned him as a heretic; nothing but public recantation at St Paul's Cross saved his body from the fire to which his books were committed. Gascoigne, the famous Oxford chancellor, wrote of Pecock with greater loathing, if possible, than of the Lollards: the Abbot of St Albans cursed him as an "impious poisoner", striving to infect the people in their faith; and commissioners reported to the king that "the damnable doctrine and pestiferous sect of Reginald Pecock exceedeth in malice all other heresies to us known by hearsay or in writing". The unhappy rationalist was condemned to solitary imprisonment in Thorney Abbey amid the fens, where he died after about three years [1460].[14]

Meanwhile the art of printing began to work a great change, and vernacular Bibles appeared on the Continent. They were discountenanced, if not even directly forbidden, by bishops and Church synods. Not one of them contains a censor's *imprimatur*, nor was any printed at a monastic press; nor did the printer himself dare to give his name to the first four and to some of the succeeding editions.[15] But, long before 1500, the press had reached a development which made Church control almost impossible; so that, before Luther's New Testament of 1522, fourteen Bibles had been printed in German and four in Dutch.

Since all these editions of that costly book were undertaken by private speculators, it is evident that the popular demand was very great: and this was presently reinforced by a man who had equal interest in scholarship and in human nature. In 1516, the year in which More published *Utopia* and a year before Luther came forward, Erasmus laid the foundation of modern New Testament scholarship in his critical edition of the Greek text, dedicated to Leo X: so great was its success among scholars that he lived to correct five more editions. In his Latin *Paraphrases* on the New Testament, dedicated to Charles V (1522), he expressed a very outspoken desire to see the Bible freed from the agelong frost in which it was still locked up from the general public.

This is a matter of such importance for our social and literary history that we must mark, before proceeding further, how far St Thomas More came towards agreement with Erasmus on this particular point; a matter too little emphasized in any book I have met with. We may read it especially in More's letter of rebuke to that young (unnamed) monk who cried *Heretic!* against Erasmus for his *New Testament* and his *Praise of Folly*.[16] Why (asks the monk) should this upstart presume to amend the Vulgate version, already so perfectly done by St Jerome? To this More answers that, in fact, what Jerome did was not what Jerome himself wanted, but just what he could. "His labours were ruined by those same plagues which now infest those of Erasmus, the ignorance and envy of the very men whom he had striven to benefit. It is certain that, in the edition which is now used in our churches, scarcely any vestiges of St Jerome's labours are left.... Do not bawl at me that the Church has for so many ages approved this translation. She reads it either because it is the best she possesses or, as I think, more truly, the earliest; one which, when once it had been received and had soaked in, could not easily be exchanged even for a better one. *Approve* she never did: nor does her bare use amount to [official] approval. On the contrary, it is notorious that there has never been any Bible-student who has learned even a little of both languages [Greek and Hebrew] and who has not found much to amend in that translator."* More goes on to defend earnestly—we may almost say, passionately— Erasmus's right, as a scholar, to vary from the Vulgate in his

---

* More here exaggerates the extent to which the Vulgate depraves St Jerome's actual text; but he does not exaggerate the extent to which Jerome was hampered by the deficiencies of pre-existing translations, already dear to the conservatives of his day. The Vulgate, of course, was first "approved" in the strictest official sense by the Council of Trent: "We decree and declare that this ancient and Vulgate edition, which hath been tried by long use for so many centuries in the Church herself, is to be held as authentic in public readings, disputations and sermons and expositions, and that no man dare or presume to reject it on any pretext whatsoever." The Vatican edition, issued by Pope Clement VIII, made it unlawful to use any other in Church, or to print any other text of the Vulgate, or even to insert various readings in the margin.

translation of even a word like λόγος, with its immense theological importance; and he reminds his monk that nobody is competent to judge in such cases but those who have at least some serious tincture of Greek scholarship. We must not forget these words when we consider the violence with which, in 1533, More himself attacked Tyndale for departing from the Vulgate in six crucial cases, in one of which, at least, no modern Greek scholar would undertake to defend the orthodox text.* He was, it is true, less inconsistent than he has often been taken to be: yet it seems highly paradoxical to represent More the chancellor or ex-chancellor as a person identical in feeling with the younger More in the days of his intimacy with Erasmus.

Let us return, then, to those Erasmian prefaces.[17] He can see no valid excuse for this Bible secretiveness. He notes how "none [of the Jews] was more pertinacious in their opposition to Christ, than those who had in their special possession the works in which His coming had been promised and foreshadowed....Let [the accredited custodians of the Bible] have the first place as teachers; but I do not see why the unlearned should be warned off, especially from the Gospels, as profane persons are warned away from sacred things; for they were published to the unlearned as to the learned, to Greeks as to Scythians, to slaves as to freemen, to women as to men, to common folk no less than to kings.... Christ rebuked His disciples who forbade the access of children; for of such (He said) is the Kingdom of Heaven: let us not, therefore, drive the little ones away from the reading of the Gospels....Let us consider who were the hearers of Christ himself. Were not these a promiscuous multitude, among whom were the blind and lame, beggars and publicans, centurions, artisans, women and children? Is Christ offended that such should read Him as He chose for his hearers? In my opinion the husbandman should read Him, with

* The Greek has μετανοεῖτε—"change your minds", "repent". The Vulgate gives *poenitentiam agite*, "do penance", a distortion which has the most obvious theological significance (Matt. iii. 2). In the remaining five cases, no worse can be said of Tyndale than that he gave a comparatively non-committal word in place of one which, by long use, had acquired a sense favourable to papal pretensions. For *church* he printed *congregation*; for *priest*, *elder*; for *charity*, *love*; for *confess*, [*ac*]*knowledge*; for *grace*, *favour*. Erasmus himself renders *ecclesia* in seven places by the word *congregatio*, and in two others by the similar *concio*. (Tyndale's *Answer to More*, Parker Soc., 1850, pp. 13 ff.) Professor Taft's preface to More's *Apology* (*E.E.T.S.* vol. 180, 1930) is extremely unfair to Tyndale; and he is evidently ill equipped as an historian of this period, at any rate so far as religion and social life are concerned.

the smith and the mason, and even prostitutes and bawds and Turks. If Christ refused not His voice to these, neither do I refuse His books.... Nor should we hasten to warn the unlearned away, if it befall that one such arise who falleth into error by this occasion; for that is not the fault of reading: it is the man's fault.... Christ, even to-day, has His Jews, impatient that their own Moses should be cast into the shade by His light. He has His Scribes and Pharisees to lie in wait for Him.... Some men look upon it as impious to turn the Holy Scriptures into French or English"; yet the Evangelists turned Christ's Aramaic speech into Greek, and St Jerome gave the Church this Latin version which she treats as sacrosanct. "Why should it seem improper that each should hear the Gospel in his native and intelligible tongue, the Frenchman in French, the English in English, the German in German, and the Indian in Indian? To me it seems more indecent—nay, rather ridiculous—that our unlearned and our women, parrot-wise, mutter their Psalms and Paternoster in Latin, not understanding their own words. I feel with St Jerome that we can more justly celebrate the glory of the Cross, and with more magnificent triumph, if it be proclaimed in every tongue by the whole human race. Let the ploughman at his plough sing from the Psalms in his own tongue. Let the weaver at his loom while away his labour with chant from the Gospels; let the steersman chant beside the tiller to which he is chained. Nay, as the housewife sits at her spinning-wheel, let her gossip or her kinswoman recite to her from the Scriptures.... In my judgement, it lies in great part at the priests' door when we find so many Christians so untaught that they know little more of their religion than those folk who have least pretence of Christian profession.... There are many of fifty years or more who know not what they vowed at baptism, who do not even dream of the meaning of the Creed or the Lord's Prayer or the Church Sacraments. This we have oftentimes discovered either from familiar speech or from secret confessions. Nay, more lamentable still, many [*plerique*] of us priests have never seriously considered within ourselves what it is to be a true Christian.... Who ever saw either more atrocious or more long-drawn wars between heathen folk than we have seen now for some years past among Christian nations?... How can we marvel that tumults should arise in the Church while Jesus is away?" (Matt. xiv. 24). Erasmus prefixed a similar plea to the later editions of his Greek Testament. Those words were addressed, if only by implication, to the Pope and the Emperor; and More in his private letters shows strong general sympathy with Erasmus's Bible labours. He could not afford, in later public controversy, to speak so plainly: yet even behind his detestation of Tyndale's theology we may read his uneasy sense that this heretic's main contentions were justified. In the third book of his *Dialogue* (ch. 16) where the adversary pleads that Bible translations are more strictly forbidden here than on the Continent, and that "the English Bible is in so few men's hands, when so many would fain have it", he answers: "That is very truth." The innovators, he confesses, circulate their translation at great expense in money and risk of death, while no orthodox printer dares to venture his money on a counter-edition. Then, after enjoining those great precautions against misuse, of a kind that no Church whatever attempts to enforce in modern times, he confesses quite clearly that abuse is no conclusive excuse for forbidding use; that would be like cutting off one's head for fear of toothache (p. 244). After all "it might be with diligence well and truly translated by some good Catholic and well learned man, or by divers dividing the labour among them...and after that might the work be allowed and approved by the [bishops]".

We have a most significant sidelight here from a most unexpected source, while Erasmus and More were still alive. Alfonso de Castro, a learned Spanish friar, was made confessor to Philip and Mary, and died as bishop-elect of Compostela. In 1555, he had the courage to preach before the English court against the burning of heretics. But in 1534 he had already printed, and dedicated to Charles V, his book *Against All Heresies*, which went through many Latin editions and was translated into French. In that volume he points out the difficulty of proving to the heretic that his own interpretation of the Bible is false. "I ask, by whom is [such a man] to be taught? Not by another man; for in the case of any man he will plead that he is mistaken, and will therefore refuse to embrace his interpretation. For any man may err in faith, even though he be a pope. For it is certain that Pope Liberius was an Arian, and that Anastasius favoured the Nestorians cannot be doubted by any reader of history....I do not think that there is any man so impudent in his flattery of the Pope as to attribute to him the impossibility of erring or being deceived in his interpretation of Holy Scripture. For, since it is well known that many [*plures*] of the Popes have been so illiterate as to be utterly ignorant of grammar [i.e. of ordinary Latin], how should they be able to interpret Holy Scripture?" Two years after those words were printed, William Tyndale was burned for having given to his fellow-countrymen that which Erasmus recommended. He accompanied it, no doubt, with aggressive phrases and comments which were highly displeasing to the orthodox of his day, yet which in some cases, at least, are definitely more consonant with modern scholarship; and it is one of the tragedies of history that St Thomas More was consenting unto his death. We must not lay exaggerated stress upon the violence of Tyndale's language; for that was the habit of those times; More himself is equally violent, especially against Luther. In Utopia, the land where a man was condemned to exile for "calling his religious opponents profane, and the followers of them wicked and devilish and the children of everlasting damnation", our saintly chancellor would scarce have scaped whipping. But the very violence displayed on both sides showed that the time was over-ripe: we may remember here what the Strassburg Cathedral preacher, Johann Geiler, said in his sermon before the Emperor in More's generation: "The crash must come!"—*Es muss brechen!*

MUCH of what has been written in the preceding chapter is absolutely irrelevant to the intrinsic value of that book for which men fought and were willing to give their lives. To repeat my simile of that chapter, I have tried to lay as little emphasis on the spiritual value of these Bibles as on the market value of the Boston tea-chests: to stress social politics rather than religion.

But now we must go further, in so far as this can be done without involving ourselves directly in religious controversy. The literary value of the Bible has been acknowledged by so many thinkers who would reject much of its dogmatic teaching, that no social history of England can be complete without some serious estimate of what the book has brought into English life. Let us see, then, what this *Bibliotheca* brought to the English mind; what stimulus for thought and what models of style. And let us exclude for the while, in so far as this is possible, all purely theological considerations; let us try to regard these Scriptures as though they were Mohammedan or Buddhist in their origin.

We need not speak of the four Gospels, though that would strengthen the case. Let us allow the violent supposition that the majority of seriously minded medieval folk knew, roughly at least, the main life-history and sayings of Christ as recorded by the Evangelists. Nor, again, need we consider the many simple, but striking, legends of Genesis, such as Adam and Eve, Cain and Abel, Noah's Ark and the Tower of Babel: let us again suppose that these had been fairly well known through the church walls and the miracle-play. Let us leave these, and consider only that to which the printed translations of Tyndale and Coverdale unquestionably introduced the mass of Englishmen for the first time. It is an enumeration which may make us understand why medieval scholars called this body of scripture *Bibliotheca*, the Library; for the book is indeed a whole library in itself.

First, in the domain of historical literature. We may compare it with the greatest of all chroniclers in England, who would probably be generally admitted as greatest of all Europe, Matthew Paris. Let us take any page at random from Bohn's translation of this book, and another from Samuel, Kings, or Chronicles. As to matter, the Bible is far richer in its compression and depth of human interest, and in style the superiority is still more marked. When the learned Professor Emil Michael, S.J., published his monograph on the Italian chronicler Salimbene, one of the most remarkable of medieval stylists, he unsuspectingly selected three special illustrations of his author's striking power of expression, two of which are among the most familiar to English Bible readers: the "bear robbed of her whelps" (II Sam. xvii. 8) and "the eagle that hasteth to the prey" (Job ix. 26). Here we have an undesigned, but very remarkable testimonial to the literary force of the Hebrew Scriptures.[2] There could be no better lesson in style than to read at one sitting through those historical books of the Bible; from the story of Hannah, uncomforted by that, *am I not more to thee than ten sons?* and her face working as she prayed, and Eli's suspicion that she was drunken; thence, through all the vicissitudes of judges and kings and the seventy years of captivity, down to Nehemiah and the rebuilding of the Temple with sword in one hand and trowel in the other. There we have the Epic of the Race, the *Légende des Siècles* of Judaism; a story as remarkable in literature as the Jew is remarkable in history, both for his friends and for his enemies. First, the mere family: Abraham down to Joseph and his brethren. Thence the family becomes a tribe, and the tribe a nation, with its national hero in Moses. In the life of this leader the Epistle to the Hebrews traces the power of faith—forward-looking faith, as apart from mere belief in tradition—faith in the man's own future and in the destiny of his people. By faith his mother hid him; by faith he chose to cast in his lot with his own oppressed fellow-Hebrews; by faith he forsook Egypt and faced the perils of the wilderness; and faith sustained him for the Pisgah-sight and beyond—"I have caused thee to see it with thine eyes, but thou shalt not go in thither"—down to his lonely death, "no man knoweth his sepulchre unto this day", and that epitaph written on men's hearts: "his eye was not dim, nor his natural force abated...and there arose not since in Israel a prophet like unto Moses, whom the Lord knew face to face." Thence, again, we pass through the succession of judges—Jephthah and Samson and Gideon; then the kings with their flashes of glory and gloom; Elijah and Elisha and their struggle against idolatry, literally to the death: then the striking legend of Esther, and the heroism of the Maccabees in their resistance to the foreign invader. We can scarcely say even of Greece or Rome that they have so dramatic a story as this, compressed into so few pages.

As those Greek and Roman historians embroidered their narrative with oratory, so also does the Bible. Stephen's speech of defence before the accusing Jews, and Paul's before Agrippa, will bear comparison with the best of their kind in antiquity. So again with elegiac poetry: for instance, Psalms xix, xx, xxiii, cxxi, cxxvi. In idylls, the Bible is equally rich. That of David and Jonathan, crowned by David's lament, is imperishable; and Ruth is one of the world's greatest stories. First, that vow of fidelity to Naomi which is cherished traditionally even in a society which has half forgotten its origin: "The Lord do so to me, and more also, if aught but death part thee and me!" Thence to the gleaning in the field of Boaz, "in tears amid the alien corn"; and the threshing-floor by night; and that scene of suspense at the city gate; and, at the happy end, Naomi with her newborn grandchild, better (say the women) than her own flesh and blood: "for thy daughter-in-law, which loveth thee, which is better to thee than seven sons, hath borne him."

Again, we have here an oriental love-poem, the Song of Songs, sheltered under the name of Solomon. To realize its full literary excellence, we must read it as it stands, apart from the allegorical mysticism which medieval commentators read into each verse. We have the most charming touches of nature:

> For, lo, the winter is past,
>   The rain is over and gone;
> The flowers appear on the earth,
>   The time of the singing-birds is come,
>   And the voice of the turtle is heard in our land....
> Come, my beloved, let us go forth into the field,
>   Let us lodge in the villages,
> Let us get up early to the vineyards;
>   Let us see if the vine flourish,
> Whether the tender grape appear
>   And the pomegranates bud forth.

And accents of immortal passion:

> Set me as a seal upon thine heart,
>   As a seal upon thine arm;
> For love is strong as death;
>   Jealousy is cruel as the grave....
> My beloved is mine, and I am his...until the day break,
>   and the shadows flee away.

The book of Proverbs was deservedly popular in the sixteenth and seventeenth centuries, when society was at a stage most suitable for education through pithy adages; it has been claimed as one of the main formative forces in the old-world Scottish character. We have, again, a whole literature of essays in Ecclesiastes, Ecclesiasticus and Wisdom; essays not after the modern type in which Macaulay was supreme, but after that of Bacon and Montaigne. Indeed, we have one author no less sceptical than Montaigne; he who wrote the earlier part—and possibly, with a change of mind, the whole—of Ecclesiastes. "Vanity of vanities, all is vanity!" "A man hath no pre-eminence above a beast, for all is vanity: all go unto one place; all are of the dust, and all turn to dust again." However, so long as we desire to live, action is necessary: "il faut planter ses choux." "In the morning sow thy seed, and in the evening withhold not thine hand; for thou knowest not whether shall prosper, either this or that, or whether they both shall be alike good." Finally, "let us hear the conclusion of the whole matter: Fear God, and keep His commandments, for this is the whole duty of man." Whether we conclude that one author wrote all this book, or that we have here a pessimist edited by a moderate optimist, there we have it to ponder over, like Montaigne or Amiel, and far beyond either of those in the eloquence of its last two chapters.

Let us come back to that: no other book—not even Shakespeare—has had half this book's influence upon English prose and verse style. Even in satire, it is supreme; for satire can never be at its best unless it is both heartfelt and just in the main. Take, for instance, Elijah's comments on the priests of Baal, while they leapt upon the altar and cut themselves with knives (I Kings xviii. 26). Or, even better, Isaiah's words on the image-maker and image-worshipper (xliv. 14). "He taketh the cypress and the oak...he burneth part thereof in the fire; with part thereof he eateth flesh; he roasteth roast and is satisfied; yea, he warmeth himself, and saith 'aha, I am warm, I have seen the fire!' And the residue thereof he maketh a god, even his graven image; he falleth down unto it, and worshippeth it, and prayeth to it, and saith 'Deliver me, for thou art my god!'" Or, again, Isaiah's vision of the Babylonian despot, the persecutor, sent down at last to dree his weird in the underworld (xiv. 9). "Hell from beneath is moved for thee to meet thee at thy coming; it stirreth up the dead for thee, even all the chief ones of the earth; it hath raised up from their thrones all the kings of nations. All they shall speak and say unto thee, 'Art thou also become weak as we? art thou become like unto us? Thy pomp is brought down to the grave, and the noise of thy viols: the worm is spread under thee, and the worms cover thee. How art thou fallen from heaven, O Lucifer, son of the morning!'"

There are many passages in which the simplest words attain to the height of consummate art, as in the Psalmist's "though I walk through the valley of the shadow of death", or "no man may deliver his brother, or make agreement unto God for him", or David's "would God I had died for thee, O Absalom, my son, my son!" But Hebrew poetry is a model also for calculated and rhetorical balance of phrases, deep answering to deep. So in Isaiah (lv. 1): "Ho, every one that thirsteth, come ye to the waters, and he that hath no money; come ye, buy and eat, yea, come, buy wine and milk without money and without price. Wherefore do ye spend money for that which is not bread? and your labour for that which satisfieth not?" Of rhetoric in this good and original sense, as the art of conveying our thoughts in the most striking manner, there is much in the Old Testament; as, for instance, throughout the thirty-second chapter of Deuteronomy. Perhaps the most continuously high level is maintained in the Epistle to the Hebrews, and especially where the author urges his fellows to face these startling new developments, not in the spirit of regret for a changing past but in that of faith for the future (xi–xii). "And what shall I say more? for the time would fail me to tell of Gideon and of Barak and of Samson and of Jephtha; and of David also, and Samuel and of the prophets: who through faith subdued kingdoms, wrought righteousness, obtained promises, stopped the mouths of lions, quenched the violence of fire, escaped the edge of the sword, out of weakness were made strong, waxed valiant in fight, turned to flight the armies of the aliens. . . . And others had trial of cruel mockings and scourgings; yea, moreover, of bonds and imprisonments. They were stoned, they were sawn asunder, were tempted, were slain with sword: they wandered about in sheep-skins and goatskins, being destitute, afflicted, tormented (of whom the world was not worthy); they wandered in deserts and in mountains and in dens and caves of the earth. Wherefore, seeing we also are compassed about with so great a cloud of witnesses, let us lay aside every weight, and the sin which doth so easily beset us, and let us run with patience the race that is set before us, looking unto Jesus, the author and finisher of our faith; who for the joy that was set before him endured the cross, despising the shame, and is set down at the right hand of the throne of God." That writer had studied in the Greek schools of rhetoric; and so had St Paul, whose highest flights are loftier still. "Who shall separate us from the love of Christ? shall tribulation, or distress, or persecution, or famine, or nakedness, or peril or sword? (as it is written, *for thy sake we are killed all the day long; we are accounted as sheep for the slaughter.*) Nay, in all these things we are more than conquerors through Him that loved us. For I am persuaded that neither death, nor life, nor angels, nor principalities, nor powers, nor things present nor things to come, nor height, nor depth, nor any other creature, shall be able to separate us from the love of God, which is in Christ Jesus our Lord." (Romans viii. 35.) Yet separate quotations, even of this length, give but little idea of the cumulative force of such chapters, consecutively read.

Even more necessary, again, is the reading of the whole Bible if we would fully realize its dramatic power. Here, it is impossible not to think of that flood of drama, unexampled in any modern country for richness and suddenness, which came in with the Elizabethans. In the Middle Ages, it was not necessary even for a Doctor of Divinity to be familiar with the whole Bible. The most living time was probably the first century of the Franciscan-Dominican revival, when the earliest Concordance was compiled, and when we find friars like Salimbene who were proud to fit every thought or word with a Scripture text. Yet even the friars drifted into conventionalism as time went on, and Chaucer's Franciscan boasts of preaching rather according to the gloss than by the simple text. As a rule, it is only outstanding men like St Bernard or Thomas à Kempis who show the text-omniscience of later Anglican and Nonconformist divines. Even to the Divinity Professor, this book was rather a collection of texts for disputation or for separate meditation: it was a nine days' wonder when Colet lectured on the whole Paul as a living author. There was only too much truth underlying Roger Bacon's exaggerated complaint that Peter Lombard's *Sentences* had displaced the actual Bible in the universities. Then, with a sudden flood, came in this great spiritual drama: that of the human soul and its Creator: one which has no exact parallel anywhere, at least in Western literature, and to which there is no pretence of a parallel, apart from Dante's great work, between Euripides and *Hamlet*. The book is full of smaller dramas on the smallest scale, as in that psalm whose influence we have seen upon the miracle-play: "Lift up your heads, O ye gates" (xxiv. 7). Or again in three sentences of Ezekiel (xxiv. 15): "The word came unto me saying, Son of man, behold I take from thee the desire of thine eyes with a stroke; yet neither shalt thou mourn nor weep, neither shall thy tears run down....So I spake unto the people in the morning, and at even my wife died; and I did in the morning as I was commanded." On a far fuller scale, we have the whole book of Job, and the last twenty-five chapters of Isaiah, from "comfort ye, comfort ye my people!" to "they shall not hurt or destroy in all my holy mountain, saith the Lord". But, above all, the whole succession of books forms one great tragedy: the human soul struggling for, and on the whole maintaining with complete success, its mystical conviction "that there is a greater unity in the universe than is recognized in ordinary experience or in science, and that the knower can be brought closer to that which is known than can be done in ordinary discursive thought". In so far as a single instance will illustrate this, we may take Habakkuk iii. 17–18; probably the very verses which inspired the most untheological poet La Fontaine with his proverbial enthusiasm for Habakkuk as a stylist. "Although the fig tree shall not blossom, neither shall fruit be in the vines; the labour of the olive shall fail, and the fields shall yield no meat; the flock shall be cut off from the fold, and there shall be no herd in the stalls: yet will I rejoice in the Lord; I will joy in the God of my salvation!" The literary value of those verses is necessarily coloured to some extent by our personal beliefs, yet it need not depend upon them; and the same may be said of the whole sequence from Adam and Eve down to the last chapters of the Apocalypse: "And I John saw the holy city, new Jerusalem, coming down from God out of heaven, prepared as a bride adorned for her husband....And there shall be no night there...and they shall reign for ever and ever....And let him that is athirst come; and whosoever will, let him take the water of life freely."

This, then, is the *Bibliotheca* which, practically inaccessible to the English public before 1526, came in at that moment with a force all the more irresistible because Tyndale sealed it ten years later with his blood. We may form a faint idea of this revelation by imagining an England in which scarcely one man in ten thousand had ever read the full text of Shakespeare, from end to end, while the man who knew Lamb's *Tales* was exceptionally educated. Into such a world (we imagine) comes suddenly that whole mass of drama; and the great Shakespeare folio is set up for public reading in every parish; and the whole is now multiplied by the printing-press beyond any book before or since. For the Bible has had no rival, even the most distant, as a "best seller". Before Tyndale's martyrdom in 1536 six editions of his New Testament had been printed; partly, it is true, because the orthodox bought them up for the flames: from the aggregate of all those six editions there remain now less than a dozen perfect copies, with a few fragments. But between 1536 and 1550 at least twenty-one more editions were printed. The first complete English Bible was printed by Coverdale in 1535, and was so successful commercially that two other translations followed in 1537 and 1539. In the latter year a new edition of Coverdale's (the so-called "Great Bible") was printed and ordered to be set up in every church: six other editions followed before 1541. Nearly all of this printing was a private venture of the booksellers. It may safely be asserted that, during the half-century after Tyndale's first version, more capital was risked and greater profits were made from the Bible than from all the rest of English printed books put together. Then, at last, Erasmus's aspirations were realized, and the poorest was able to get something of this New Learning—the oldest in Christendom, and yet here, in 1538, the newest. Westcott quotes from an Anglican apologia in the year when the Great Bible was set up in our churches.[3] "Englishmen have now in hand, every Church and place and almost every man, the Holy Bible and the New Testament in their mother tongue, instead of the old fabulous and fantastic books of the Table Round, Launcelot du Lac and such other, whose impure filth and vain fabulosity the light of God has abolished utterly." And he gives a concrete instance. One William Maldon told how, as soon as Henry VIII "had allowed the Bible to be set forth to be read in all churches, immediately several poor men in the town of Chelmsford in Essex, where his father lived and he was born, bought the New Testament and on Sundays sat reading it in the lower end of the Church. Many would flock about them to hear them reading, and he among the rest, being then but fifteen years old, came every Sunday to hear the glad and sweet tidings of the Gospel. But his father, observing it once, angrily fetched him away and would have him say the Latin Matins with him; which grieved him much. And, as he returned at other times to hear the Scripture read, his father still would fetch him away. This put him upon the thoughts of learning to read English that so he might read the New Testament himself. Which when he had by diligence effected, he and his father's apprentice bought the New Testament, joining their stocks together, and to conceal it laid it under the bed-straw and read it at convenient times." Such a body of literature as this, appealing to every class, could scarcely fail to revolutionize the literature of the nation. We need only go back to those two episodes which are at the high-water mark of pre-Reformation miracle-play tragedy —Isaac's speech to Abraham, and the Crucifixion scene—or, again, to the Passion as treated by a real poet in the last cantos of *Piers Plowman*. In sheer poetic force, none of these comes anywhere near to what is wrung from the half-atheist Marlowe by the last agony of Faustus:

> Oh, Faustus!
> Now hast thou but one bare hour to live,
> And then thou must be damn'd perpetually.
> Stand still, you ever-moving spheres of heav'n,
> That time may cease, and midnight never come;
>
> . . . .
>
> The stars move still, time runs, the clock will strike,
> The devil will come, and Faustus must be damn'd.
> Oh, I'll leap up to heav'n!—Who pulls me down?
> See where Christ's blood streams in the firmament:
> One drop of blood will save me: Oh, my Christ!—
> Rend not my heart for naming of my Christ;
> Yet will I call on him.—Oh, spare me, Lucifer!
> Where is it now?—'tis gone!
> And see, a threatening arm, an angry brow—
> Mountains and hills, come, come, and fall on me,
> And hide me from the heavy wrath of heav'n
> No? Then will I headlong run into the earth:
> Gape, earth!—Oh no, it will not harbour me.

There, the Bible has inspired both thought and diction. There is nothing quite like it in all medieval literature: not even in Dante: nor has it been surpassed in its own way since Marlowe's time. Walter Scott held that Goethe had chosen the wiser course in avoiding, at that point, any direct comparison with his predecessor of eight generations earlier. For there not only the poet, but his hearers also, were in a brave new world, provocative of individual thought. Both he and the least orthodox of them had enough belief to tremble, if no more; his "rend not my heart for naming of my Christ" was as topical in 1588 as Faust's Easter-Day confession in the Age of Enlightenment: "Die Botschaft hör' ich wohl, allein mir fehlt der Glaube."* And, for expression, Marlowe and his hearers had now the whole religious and psychological vocabulary of the Jewish and Christian ages: the Open Bible. No finer testimonial has ever been given than that which we have from the courageous agnostic Thomas Huxley. "Consider the great historical fact that, for three centuries, this book has been woven into the life of all that is best and noblest in English history; that it has become the national epic of Britain, and is as familiar to noble and simple, from John-o'-Groat's House to Land's End, as Dante and Tasso once were to the Italians; that it is written in the noblest and purest English, and abounds in exquisite beauties of pure literary form; and finally, that it forbids the veriest hind who never left his village to be ignorant of the existence of other countries and other civilizations, and of a great past stretching back to the furthest limits of the oldest civilizations of the world."[4]

* "I do indeed hear the [Resurrection] message, but I lack the faith."

LI. PEASANT AND HIGHBROW

To understand either the Middle Ages or the Reformation, we must beware of exaggerating the fundamental unity of medieval thought and practice. The extreme violence with which Unity was proclaimed, and often enforced, did indeed achieve long and considerable success. The gospel of the uselessness of persecution is true only if we look forward to a far longer time than the vast majority of men take into their calculations. We have seen how this was as true in Piers Plowman's day as it is in ours:

> The most partie of this poeple that passeth on this erthe,
> Have thei worschip in this worlde, thei wilne no better, [consideration
> Of other hevene than here, hold thei no tale.[1]

The Totalitarian Church had, originally, corresponded very nearly to healthy and growing aspirations; it had done much to free the soul from an inferiority-complex and to help the body by bringing order into anarchy. This Roman Church had played, in her turn, the rôle which St Augustine ascribes to the Roman Empire; she had been the παιδαγωγός—half-nurse, half-tutor— to a new-born era. The orthodox ecclesiastical historian has a comparatively easy task for the first thousand years of history. Mr Christopher Dawson's excellent *Making of Europe* affords an admirable example of this; up to that point, even the modern agnostic is willing to go a long way with him. But it is with the revival of learning and active thought, before the eleventh century has run out, that the apologist's task becomes really difficult. From that time forward, we have increasing evidence both for learned scepticism and for popular scepticism; and, presently, for a far more serious phenomenon; namely, popular attempts to out-bid the Church with the multitude, and to face her constructively with a rival body of doctrines and a rival organization. It is idle to argue from the comparatively small public signs of Lollardy after the suppression of Oldcastle's rebellion. Even though the documentary evidence had been more scanty than it actually is, why should there have been a keener competition for public martyrdom, by the peculiarly painful death of fire, in the England of

1500, than there is for more straightforward execution in present-day Russia, Italy, or Germany?

Every revolution, in detail, is apt to become a wearisome and painful story; and critics of the Reformation have always, though not always consciously, ignored some of the most significant facts. This it is which has lent colourable plausibility to the recent fashion of explaining it away as a series of unlucky chances. This theory, stated in its most forcible and uncompromising form, seems scarcely distinguishable from naked fatalism. Whereas, from St Augustine down to Bossuet, that hammer of Protestants, the orthodox always traced the finger of God in every corner of human history, we are now told that the gravest issues for true religion may well hang, since they have erewhile hung, upon the hazard of the dice. Bossuet, encouraged by the power of Louis XIV to expect the recatholicizing of Europe through French armies, wrote in that strain to the royal pupil for whom he composed his *Discours sur l'Histoire Universelle.* "Remember, your Highness, that this long chain of particular causes, which make and unmake empires, depends upon the secret orders of God's Providence.... It is thus that God reigns over all the nations. Let us cease to speak of Chance or Fortune; or let us speak of them only as a name to cover our ignorance....It is because we do not understand the whole, that we find chance or irregularity in particular events....God alone knows how to reduce all [human powers] to His own will; therefore everything is surprising if we only look at separate events; yet all advances in regular succession." Elsewhere Bossuet could write: "The whole state is in [the Prince]; the will of the whole people is contained in his will." Therefore, so long as Louis was successful, Providence evidently reigned over all human affairs. As *The Catholic Encyclopaedia* puts it in the article on Bossuet, if it were not for this witness to God in history, then "fortune, or rather chance, would be the mistress of human affairs; the existence of humanity would be only a bad dream". Yet it is precisely this evil dream which we of to-day are invited to share. It is sufficient to quote from the most popular—and, so far as vigour of style is concerned, deservedly popular—of these modern pleas.[2] "The breakdown of our civilization in the sixteenth century, with its difficult saving of all that could be saved, and the loss of all the rest, was an *accident.*" "The ground was prepared [for the Reformation] by a number of successive political and other accidents." "I call this the most important division of my subject, the English *Accident*. I have chosen the word with care." Covetous men, under Henry VIII, got "a sudden accidental opportunity", and the Church was wrecked. Twice, it will be seen, the author's own italics lend force to this neo-Christian worship of the Goddess Chance, which Horace had relegated to "the swine of Epicurus's sty". And it is in correction of this theory, which seems as difficult to reconcile with our actual records as with any sane conception of Divine Providence, that so much evidence must here be produced as can be compressed into two brief chapters. There is perhaps no event in history, not even the French Revolution, which more plainly displays an age-long accumulation of forces before the final bursting of the dykes—*Es muss brechen!*

The causes of this sixteenth-century Revolution may be divided roughly into four classes—moral, doctrinal, economic and political. We may begin with the moral causes, since these are most strongly emphasized by friends of the movement, and most flatly denied by its enemies. And here it will be best to start from a concrete case, sufficiently typical.[3]

In 1428, the Bishop of Norwich sat in solemn judgment upon Margery Backster, wife of a carpenter in the Norfolk village of Martham, where a fine perpendicular nave and tower still testify to the zeal of parishioners in that century. She was accused of having warned her neighbour to abstain from all swearing, either by God or by any saint: "and if ye do the contrary, the bee will sting your tongue and venom your soul."[*] She had invited the neighbour and her maid to "come secretly, in the night, to her chamber, and there she should hear her husband read the law of Christ unto them, which law was written in a book that her husband was wont to read to her by night, and that her husband is well learned in the Christian verity". This neighbour testified also: "The said Margery said to this deponent, that every faithful man or woman is not bound to fast in Lent, or on other days appointed for fasting by the Church; and that every man may

---

* Here, as we saw in Chapter xxxv, she would have had the hearty support of great and orthodox theologians in the past. Yet Christ's prohibition had, by this time, been so forgotten or explained away that St Thomas More could condemn it off-hand as "a false heresy"—that is, as cause for burning even though the person could be found in no other fault. (*English Works*, p. 344: case of Thomas Hitton.)

lawfully eat flesh and all other meats upon the said days and times; and that it were better to eat the fragments left upon Thursday at night on the fasting days, than to go to the market to bring themselves in debt to buy fish." Moreover, "that Agnes Berthem, her servant, being sent to the house of the said Margery the Saturday after Ash-Wednesday, the said Margery not being within, found a brass pot standing over the fire, with a piece of bacon and oatmeal seething in it; as the said Agnes reported to this deponent". Other accusations were that she said: "You do evil to kneel or to pray to such images in the churches" since they were made by common carpenters: that she repudiated Transubstantiation, spoke of Becket as "a false traitor, and damned in hell", and cursed "pope, cardinals, archbishops and bishops, and especially the Bishop of Norwich" who had lately burned three Lollards in his diocese. These great clerics, she said, have deceived the people while they live in luxury themselves, and they have granted Indulgences which "brought the simple people to cursed idolatry". She reprobated pilgrimages, "neither to Our Lady of Walsingham, nor to any other saint or place": and holy-water and church bells. "Moreover [she said], that she should not be burned, although she were convicted of Lollardy, for that she had a charter of salvation in her body." As to William White, the priest whom the Bishop of Norwich had burned in that same year, Margery herself had followed with the crowd to see his martyrdom, "where she saw that when he would have opened his mouth to speak unto the people to instruct them, a devil (one of Bishop Caiaphas's servants) struck him on the lips and struck his mouth, that he could in no case declare the will of God".

Margery's ultimate fate is not recorded. Probably she was not burned, or we should have heard more of her; very likely, also, she owed her life to such a recantation as we ourselves might have stooped to, with the pitiless fire in sight. But the petty details of this story are no less pathetic and instructive than the tragic side of it: they show Lollardy among common folk as a very living force in human nature; one which persecution could no more stamp out, in the long run, than it was able in post-Reformation days to extinguish the embers of the Roman creed, or prevent their bursting into flame. Margery was in the current of a strong movement in her Norfolk of that day. "In the valley of the Waveney, just on the borders of the two counties [Norfolk and

Suffolk], a remarkable religious movement had been going on for some time. The leaders were a small band of unbeneficed clergy, who were what we should now call the curates-in-charge of the parishes where they were living. At least nine of these parish priests were implicated.*. . . The whole district was in a ferment of religious excitement, and priests and people seemed to be of one mind. White, driven out of Kent, found safety and welcome here [in East Anglia]."⁴ Grasping these facts clearly, let us now see how far these obscure parish priests and these working men and women can be justified by comparison with Colet and Erasmus and More.

Margery's manners, it is true, had not that repose which stamps the class of Vere de Vere in More's *Utopia*: but neither had More's own, when he "saw red" against Tyndale and the Lutherans, nor had those of Erasmus in his argument with Luther. Sympathy with either side in this eternal conflict (for eternal it is, under different forms) must not blind us to men's equal earnestness on the other part. More, in the face of iconoclasm, felt the burning indignation of the Psalmist: "But now they break down all the carved work thereof with axes and hammers." Yet Margery, for her part, had read in her husband's book what the prophets had said about graven images: her contemptuous words about carpenter-made saints are evidently founded upon Isaiah xliv. 16; and she doubtless knew also how Josiah had earned undying glory among the kings of the True God by breaking in pieces the images, and polluting the altars and the sacred places with dead men's bones, and burning all the vessels that were made for the service of Baal, and "putting down" the idolatrous priests (II Kings xxiii. 4 ff.). We have no reason whatever to suppose that she was less sincere in her faith than the Bishop of Norwich in his; and this our later age, if it had to choose between the two beliefs, would incline rather to hers. This equality of conviction between orthodox and heretic is too often ignored by those very writers who insist most strongly on the necessity of thinking ourselves into the actual mental atmosphere of a distant age. It was ignored, with fatal results, by the More of later years in his controversies; and he was compelled to admit some real truth in Tyndale's complaint: "if our shepherds had been as well willing

* "Out of 25 heretics of whose trials we have record during these 10 years [1414–24], 11 were in Holy Orders." G. M. Trevelyan, *England in the Age of Wycliffe* (1900), p. 340.

to feed as to shear, we had needed no such [ignorance], nor they to have burnt so many as they have." But he answers: "as for many such as have been burned, all the preaching in the world would not have holpen their obstinacy." Yet (he adds) there is another point beside preaching upon which the prelates have been negligent: if they had burned men more strictly in the past, they would have saved society from many more autos-de-fe in the future. "There should have been more burned, by a great many, than there have been within this seven year last passed; the lack whereof, I fear me, will make more burned within this seven years next coming than else should have needed to have been burned in seven score."[5] Yet the earlier More, we must in reason believe, had been far more tolerant in mind. His "undenominational religion" of Utopia gave no excuse or opportunity for the iconoclast to break images. But neither (on the other hand) could it breed sacramentalists so bigoted as to believe that they did God service by burning anyone for deliberately rejecting or defiling that outward and visible sign in which they themselves saw an inward spiritual grace. Each Utopian lived by "his own sect", and let others live. Erasmus, again, was not far removed from Margery in this matter of image-worship: in one place he points out how it was unknown to the early Christians, and, in another, how it was so exaggerated as to border on idolatry. True, these protests were "veiled in the obscurity of a learned language", and Erasmus would never have had the least sympathy with Lollard vandalism. But, rude and iconoclastic as these folk may sometimes have been, we have no excuse whatever for regarding them as mere anarchists. In an anti-Lollard poem written about Margery's time, which exults in Oldcastle's failure and ridicules his followers, "there is no mention of any design against society or property, which would certainly have been mentioned in this long satire if there had been the least ground for it".* Later, it is true, Lollardy developed under persecution to something more political and more violent. But that is a constant phenomenon in history; it is conspicuous (among other places) in that great religious and social revolution which we call Christianity. It is a weak point of all revolutions that they tempt the violent element; just as, on the other side, pacifism can never quite get rid of those who foster inertia or cowardice under the cloak of peace.

* Trevelyan, *l.c.* p. 370: see also the next note on that page.

Apart, then, from that un-Utopian intolerance and bitterness, which was common to both sides, how far did the best minds agree with Margery in those days?[6]

As to the bishops, the anti-Lollard Gascoigne bears more damning testimony to their worldliness and tyranny than she. So, again, does Erasmus in many places. Commenting in his *New Testament* on I Peter v. 3, he writes: "*Feed* your flock, not *oppress* and *despoil* it." The early Christian bishops were fathers indeed: but "now the ruck of the bishops [*episcoporum vulgus*] hears of nothing from its learned flatterers but 'lordships', 'dominions', 'swords', 'keys', 'powers'; hence comes the more than royal pomp of some, and their more than tyrannical ferocity".[7] Elsewhere, he writes even more fully and unfavourably. The pitilessness of the religious rebels is explained, though not excused, by centuries of ill-employed authority.

As to pilgrimages, we have seen in Chapter III how St Boniface spoke of their moral abuses as strongly as any Lollard, or more. So, again, one of Erasmus's wittiest and best known *Colloquies* is that in which he mocked at Walsingham, and went on to record how plainly Colet showed his disgust at being asked to worship Becket's shoe at Canterbury: "they pick out the filthiest things they can find and ask us to kiss them!"[8]

As to the Bible, Professor Trevelyan (pp. 342, 370) gives plain evidence "not only that the Bishop of Norwich persecuted for Bible-reading, but that the Lollards had further difficulties to contend with in searching the Scriptures". Yet on this point we have seen Erasmus's impassioned plea, and even More's regretful admissions, in Chapter XLIX.

Finally, on this question of Church fasts, which even by itself might have brought Margery Backster to the stake, Erasmus is still more trenchant and outspoken. His words are worth quoting at some length, since they cast light on English thought in general, with that insularity and that preference of compromise to strict logic which marked us already in those days. It is an exaggeration, at the very least, to suppose that our isolation from the Continent began with the Reformation. Insular was our immemorial refusal to allow torture in our law-courts, even in support of professedly religious aims, except for that momentary lapse under Edward II. On that point we stood far apart from those countries where the Inquisition reigned unchecked for three centuries; and Fortescue's *Praises of the Laws of England*, written almost in Margery Backster's time, marks such a contrast between us and France as that which is brought out between us and Italy, to a considerable extent, by the *Italian Relation of England* in Henry VII's reign.*

To return to Erasmus on fasting. He comes twice at least to this subject, at considerable length. It is the main theme of his *Colloquy* between *The Butcher and the Fishmonger* ('Ιχθυοφαγία) and it fills the nine folio pages of his letter to the Bishop of Basel *Concerning the Prohibition of Flesh-eating*. In the first (*Opera*, 1703, vol. 1), the Fishmonger (who is a natural defender of the fasting laws) pleads that the Pope's laws bind all churchfolk, under pain of hell:† and that the decrees of a General Council are "an oracle from heaven, with a weight equal to the Gospels, or at least nearly so".⁹ The Butcher reminds him that Annas and Caiaphas claimed much the same for their own laws concerning the washing of hands before meals: while, on the other hand,

Hell-Pains.

St Paul was careful to avoid such dogmatism, lest he should thus lay a snare for the weaker brethren. Do we really (he continues) need all these ecclesiastical by-laws? We turn the world upside down if Church privileges seem to be attacked. Yet we are blind to the far worse danger of attributing so much to human authority that we attribute too little to that of God. "If a priest lets his hair grow, or adopts lay dress, he is cast into prison and severely

---

* More himself implies that England is peculiar in two ways: its extreme severity against the vernacular Bible (*English Works*, p. 224 c) and certain relaxations of fasts among the clergy (*ibid.* p. 895).

† We must bear in mind here that, in proportion as the age-long customary threats of hell grew blunt with over-repetition, fresh efforts were made (as in this edifying popular book of about Margery Backster's time) to ring fresh changes on the old tune.

punished: if he drinks in a brothel or frequents a harlot, or plays at dice, or defiles other men's wives, or never touches a religious book, yet he is a pillar of the Church. I do not excuse his change of dress, but I do blame this preposterous judgment." Again: "In these days some men have been cast into prison for daring to bake on Sunday, when perchance there was lack of bread." "Soon afterwards" (he proceeds) "on a Palm Sunday, I had to go to a village hard by: the road was encumbered by a drunken procession, worthy of the heathen Bacchus; I enquired the cause, and found that it was because wine was somewhat cheaper in that village than in town. If these [drunken] men had tasted an egg, they would have been haled off to prison like parricides; yet none punished them, none expressed his detestation for their shirking the sermon, shirking vespers, and displaying this public intemperance on so holy a day." So speaks the Butcher: and the Fishmonger answers: "You need not be so surprised at that. In the midst of cities, at cookshops hard by the church, on every holy day men drink and sing and dance and fight with such noise and tumult that neither Mass can be said nor the sermon heard. If one of those men at that time had stitched at a shoe, or if he had tasted pork on a Friday, he would risk his life." The Butcher again takes up his tale. "In England, the common folk in Lententide prepare their ordinary supper on alternate days, and no man marvels; yet if a man under dangerous fever ventured to touch chicken-broth, the thing is held worse than sacrilege. In that [English] country, in Lent, at which season the fast is as ancient and as sacred as any in Christendom, you may sup with impunity, as I have said: but, if you ventured to do the same on any Friday outside Lent, no man would suffer it. If you ask, why? then they plead the custom of their country. They abominate [*execrantur*] the man who neglects the custom of the realm; yet they pardon themselves for neglecting the custom of the whole Church." Here, and again in his later treatise, Erasmus praises the custom of Italy, where, even in Lent, veal and kid and lamb are publicly exposed in the market, "nor doth any man reprobate the buyer or eater, even though he show no sign of illness". In one respect, indeed, Erasmus would not have altogether defended Margery: "Those who eat contumaciously and seditiously are rightly punished by the civil magistrates." "But" (he adds) "whatever anyone eats in his own house for his bodily health is a matter for physicians to care for, not magistrates. If a tumult is excited, even for that cause, by the unrighteousness of some folk, let them be arraigned for sedition; but not the man who has ministered to his own health without violating either God's law or man's." This, says Erasmus, is only one example of the extent to which human observances are put above the essentials of religion and morality. How many priests there are who would be more horrified to celebrate with an unconsecrated chalice and paten, or in ordinary daily dress, than to approach the altar reeking from last night's debauch! Again: "Man's decree forbids the reception of the bastard, the lame, the one-eyed to Holy Orders. How squeamish are we here! Yet meanwhile we receive indifferently [for ordination] the unlearned, dicers, drunkards, fighters and man-slayers. Men plead in excuse: 'Diseases of the soul are hidden from us.' I speak not of hidden things; I speak of things which are more openly evident than bodily defects." Indeed, the gist of this whole dialogue is summed up in two sentences from the Butcher: "Where, all this while, is that liberty of the spirit which the apostles promise from the Gospel? the liberty so often inculcated by St Paul, who cries: *The kingdom of God is not meat and drink?*" Again: "After all, the world is full of pharisaical folk who cannot claim holiness for themselves except by such petty observances."

Still more plain-spoken on this subject of fasting, if possible, is Erasmus's letter to the Bishop of Basel.[10] In this he complains: "We Christians are burdened with far more frequent fasts than even the Jews were." The result of this rule is that, while the hard-working artisan must "eat meagre" on Fridays and in Lent, the rich man may feed luxuriously on expensive fish,* or get liberty even for meat by purchasing dispensation at Rome. If dispensation is needed, why should it not be given, without fee, by the parish priest, who knows the man's circumstances far better than the Pope can? Yet we have zealots who preach hell-fire against those who violate these artificial fasts.

Anyone who follows Dr Jortin through his collection of passages from Erasmus's most serious writings—for instance, from his notes to the New Testament and his paraphrases of the Gospels and Epistles—must be struck to find him speaking even more plainly there than in his more popular satirical books. *The Catholic Encyclopaedia* summarizes his teaching very truly (p. 512):

* We have seen how Margery Backster emphasized this economic argument.

"He rejected the divine origin of...the indissolubility of marriage....Fasts, pilgrimages, veneration of saints and their relics, the prayers of the Breviary, celibacy and religious orders in general, he classed among the perversities of a formalistic scholasticism....In his edition of the Greek New Testament and in his Paraphrases of the same he forestalled the Protestant view of the Scriptures." Yet this Greek Testament was dedicated to Leo X; it and the Paraphrases sold by the tens of thousands, and earned the admiration of scholars from end to end of Europe. Clement VII patronized him in those later days; Adrian VI offered him a deanery and Paul III would have made him a cardinal. He wrote of kings and nobles with equal freedom; yet Charles V and George of Saxony were his steady patrons. St Thomas More, again, may almost be claimed as partner in *The Praise of Folly*; for it was written in his house, dedicated to him, and defended by him against Dorpius, Erasmus's most serious critic.[11] Again, More seldom showed warmer indignation or more bitter sarcasm than against the unnamed English monk who attacked the character of "Erasmus, my darling", the intimate (says More) of St John Fisher, Archbishop Warham, Colet, and the best scholars of our land; a man whose Greek Testament has been twice approved by the Pope.[12] Indeed, the St Thomas More of later life showed in this matter, as in others of equal controversial difficulty, an "economy of truth" which detracts very seriously from the value of his defence of the Church. He has no reprobation for the substance of what Erasmus writes, but he is outraged by Tyndale's brutal insistence upon those same subjects, no longer merely in polite Latin but in English meant for the common people. So, again, when the lawyer Christopher St Germain quoted Gerson's terrible condemnation of ecclesiastical corruptions, More could not contradict this great Chancellor of Paris University; he only deprecated the translation of these things into English for general reading.[13] Everything tends to corroborate the judgment of Erasmus's greatest editor, Dr P. S. Allen: "he gave utterance to what all felt, but none dared to whisper but he."[14] More was passionately attached to the Church; but what he felt in his heart about Church reform can generally be caught only in the "whisper" of his private letters. Therefore, we must again remind ourselves of Erasmus's most significant agreement with Margery Backster on those points of capital importance upon which she, in her poverty and her lack of powerful patrons, stood face to face with an agonizing death. The scholar, from his lofty European standpoint, saw essentially the same on these points as this obscure Norfolk villager: and, when such agreement of criticism is reached in any society, then we must lift up our heads, for revolution draweth nigh.

Other and more invidious moral questions need less elaboration in this chapter. They have often been rehearsed, but never, to my knowledge, really met in detail. Clerical morals in the England of 1500 were, on the whole, such as would be tolerated in no civilized country of to-day. A distinguished bishop, Guillaume Durand, at the Pope's request, had drawn up for the Ecumenical Council of Vienne, in 1311, a list of matters that most urgently needed reform.[15] He had insisted that Europe "might be reformed, if the Church of Rome would begin by removing evil examples, [first] from itself and then gradually from evil prelates and the rest; for by such evil examples men are scandalized, and the whole people are as it were infected, and (as Isaiah saith) they that rule over them suffer God's name to be blasphemed for this". In some cases, the mere titles of the good bishop's chapters speak volumes; here are two of them. "Concerning the avoidance of the cohabitation of clergy and women; and against the keeping of brothels near churches, or hard by the lord Pope's palace in Rome; and that the lord Pope's marshal and other like persons should not take money from the harlots or brothel-keepers."[16] Again: "Concerning the incontinence of clerical persons, and whether we should ordain in the Western Church as the Eastern doth, taking no vow of chastity from those who minister at the altar, especially considering that the Eastern custom held good in the Apostles' time." In equally plain language this learned and pious bishop condemned the abuse of Indulgences, the irreverence with which the clergy habitually walked about or conversed with their friends during divine service, and their frequent ignorance even of the very language of their service books. This, be it noted, was before the Black Death, which is so often quoted with ludicrous exaggeration in palliation of Church abuses in the sixteenth century. Yet that Council of Vienne did next to nothing in this field of reform; nor did any of the great councils which followed. We have seen what was the state of an English diocese in 1397 (Chapter XIII) and how our poets then spoke of clerical morals. Constance was the council that most seriously struggled for reform; yet nothing was there done even in the most urgent matter, that of the monasteries, comparable in historical importance to the burning of John Hus who had striven to purify the Church. A generation later than this, the great Oxford Chancellor Gascoigne agreed with the Lollards, whom he otherwise loathed, that parsons bought licences for concubinage from the hierarchy; and St Thomas More could not really deny this even in face of the hated Tyndale's accusations. Erasmus, in his treatise addressed to the Bishop of Basel, argues from this licence for sin as an incontrovertible and notorious fact.[17] "What swarms of priests are nourished in the monasteries! and, beyond these, the multitude of priests is innumerable; yet, among all these, how rare are those who live chastely! I speak of those who publicly keep concubines in their houses instead of wives; yet, even so, I touch not upon the mysteries of their more secret lusts: I speak only of those things which are notorious [notissima] even to the multitude....A great proportion [magna pars] of the priests live in ill fame, and it is with a conscience far from serene that they handle the sacred mysteries. Hence their fruit is in great part ruined, since their disreputable life renders their doctrine contemptible [dedecorosa] to the people." He pleads for making celibacy optional, and adds: "I doubt not that there are many [plerique] bishops who see clearly that things are as I describe them; but I fear that, here again, money is the real obstacle to our following the course we see to be best. If the bishops try to change, perhaps their officials [i.e. archdeacons and deans] will cry out against it; for these men smell more gain from the priests' concubines than they would get from their wives. It is not just that money should have such power among us that, in a matter of such moment, we should follow any but a straightforward policy." To what has been already said in an earlier chapter I must here add three unexceptionable witnesses who exactly fill in the century from Margery Backster to Erasmus.

Gascoigne, in his *Liber Veritatum*, repeats to weariness that the clergy are ruining the Church.[18] "Alas," he writes, "the man who nowadays undertakes the cure of souls either is very evil, or is good and perfect to no purpose. For, if he do according to the works of many of his fellows, he will be very wicked; and if he do not according to their works he will be reviled by many and despised by still more." He shows us how hard it was even for a determined bishop like Praty of Chichester to eject a notorious black sheep from his living, and how little the majority of prelates were inclined to undertake such invidious duties: "for by one bishop the love of sin has of late been fostered, since the parishioners of one rectory have said: 'Now we believe adultery and fornication to be no sin; for if it were a sin our bishop would have deprived our rector of his cure; for our bishop knows that our rector has been publicly taken in adultery with his own parishioner, the wife of another man; yet the bishop has not expelled him from his cure.'[19] Moreover, even at Oxford, where he had committed several rapes, this man was afterwards admitted to the degree of Doctor of Canon Law." Some forty years later Dean Colet wrote: "O priests! O priesthood! O the detestable boldness of wicked men in this our generation! O the abominable impiety of those miserable priests, of whom this age of ours contains a great multitude, who fear not to rush from the bosom of some foul harlot into the temple of the Church, to the altar of Christ, to the mysteries of God!"[20] Again, only a few years before Luther's public appearance, the same cry of despair was raised by the great prelate who was so soon to suffer death for his loyalty to the Pope: "An we take heed and call to mind" (wrote St John Fisher to the Mother of King Henry VII) "how many vices reign nowadays in Christ's Church, as well in the clergy as in the common people; how many also be unlike in their living unto such in times past, perchance we shall think that Almighty God slumbereth not only, but also that He hath slept soundly a great season."

One of More's defensive arguments ran thus, that the clergy, after all, are drawn from the laity: such as our layfolk are, such will be our clerics. A true plea, doubtless, in the main; but fatally double-edged. Lay morality, by the evidence of all our witnesses, was as low in the Middle Ages as it has ever been in post-Reformation England: here the Hereford visitation and similar official records agree with the literary sources. It was as St Bernard (with many learned and pious men after him) quoted from Isaiah: like priests, like people, *sicut sacerdos, sic populus*. Wales, Scotland and Ireland were in this respect even behind England; indeed, the Calendars of Papal Registers show an irregularity of life among the Irish clergy which would not be tolerated nowadays in any Christian land, except perhaps in Southern Italy or pre-revolutionary Spain, or the South American republics. Moreover, these things which modern apologists attempt to palliate were so notorious in their own day that more than one orthodox writer can be found uttering the clear prophecy: This cannot last: the real strength of heresy lies in the ignorance and immorality of our clergy: we must get reform or revolution.* Yet the rapid growth of the Indulgence abuse only made things worse. Gascoigne, the Lollard-hater, wrote in words which from Luther's pen would have been accused of gross exaggeration: "Sinners say nowadays 'I care not how many or what evils I do in God's sight; for I can easily and quickly get plenary remission of all guilt and penalty whatsoever [*cujusdam culpae et poenae*] by an absolution and Indulgence granted to me by the Pope, whose written grant I have bought for 4*d.* or 6*d.*, or have won as a stake for a game of tennis."[21]

Modern historical research is rendering it more and more difficult to believe that "the hold of the [medieval] Church was due to the fact that it could satisfy the best cravings of the whole man; his love of beauty, his desire for goodness, his endeavour after truth".[22] If there is any generation of the Middle Ages to which we may truly apply this praise, it is frankly inapplicable to the fifteenth century in England. The idea would seem to rest upon that equivoque which has often been pointed out in Augustine's *City of God.* Inadvertently or semi-consciously, the saint sometimes applies to the actual Church, the organized institution, the Church militant, words which are strictly true only of the Ideal Church. There were many, no doubt, who did find their ideal in the institutional Church; but there were others, not less zealous for righteousness and truth, who found it increasingly difficult to reconcile their conscience with what they saw and heard within the walls of those impressive buildings upon whose structure and furniture so much was spent in the later Middle Ages. *Dives and Pauper,* as we have seen, gave clear voice to what many men must have thought who had little sympathy with actual militant Lollardy. These men did not lack the love of beauty; some, like Milton, had a deeper sense of art than the average conservative; but such beauty could not satisfy them fully unless they saw it happily married to truth.

* See *Camb. Mod. Hist.* I, 678. Another contemporary of Erasmus who insisted upon this was Gianfrancesco Pico, nephew to St Thomas More's admired hero, in a memorial addressed to Leo X.

LII. THE BURSTING OF THE DYKES

So much for the Moral basis of the Reformation; we must pass on now to the Doctrinal. Erasmus has told us, what a dozen great Churchmen had said before him and what human nature herself tells us, that institutions, like individuals, will in the long run find their teaching judged by their behaviour. It was the essential sanity of the English public which bred closer and closer criticism of the cleric, first in his person and then in his teaching. Christ's words do but reinforce what common sense will always suggest: "By their fruits ye shall know them."

We have seen (Chapter XXXII) how Scholasticism had always lacked one element essential to a perfect philosophy: it never applied thoroughly scientific enquiry to its own fundamental assumptions. It rested upon belief in a barbarian's hell, and in the inerrancy of a written book, and in the infallibility of the Church: and these three elements, in combination, had the devastating force of mingled sulphur, saltpetre, and charcoal. For upon these theological assumptions the Schoolmen built a strictly—one may say ferociously—logical system, which coloured the whole thought of those ages, and from which the mystic alone, by treating this logic as irrelevant and seeking his own direct way to God through other paths, could escape without necessarily losing his orthodoxy. For, within that stately scholastic framework, there were innumerable quiet corners for the meditations and the adoration of a simple soul; and few men would have quarrelled with these immemorial ecclesiastical traditions if only the teachers had, with any consistency, shown forth their faith by their works. Here, again, we may find Erasmus speaking to the Bishop of Basel with the voice, essentially, of Margery Backster.[1] A bishop, he argues, can secure far better obedience by persuasion than by force or threats, or by constantly writing *We ordain; We decree; We determine; We bid; We will; We command*. A respected and paternal bishop has more power than even a king, with all his threats, can exert. "Do we not see, as soon as one arises who is commended by any opinion of sanctity, and who shows any appearance of a

Gospel-preacher,* with what enthusiasm the people hang from his lips, and what heartfelt favour they grant him?...If the people sees a man to be a true priest and bishop, his exhortation will not be without fruit. But if his publicly irreligious [*impia*] life, his impure morals, his gross ignorance, his insatiable greed, and his barbarous savageness have utterly alienated people's minds, how shall they profit by his precepts?" We must remember, what nobody in Margery's Norfolk could have forgotten, that Bishop Despenser had been appointed by the Pope to the see of Norwich rather for military than for theological service; that he had fought against the peasants in their great revolt of 1381, and had led a "Crusade" in 1383 against the French as supporters of the anti-pope; moreover, that the scandal had been increased for pious souls by such profusion of Indulgences granted to these "Crusaders" as had given double force to the criticisms of Wyclif and his followers. Therefore what Erasmus wrote, in those measured words, to a personal friend whose integrity he could trust, and what he gave to the world under that double guarantee of his own reputation and the bishop's, is what thousands were saying under their breath, while those few who cried aloud, like Tyndale, fell inevitably into the hysterical scream of a throat that was grappled by murderous fingers. Even scholastic philosophy, before 1500, had lost most of its salt; and Margery herself could not have spoken more contemptuously of the reigning theologians than Erasmus constantly did; nor could she have found cruder contrasts between their teaching and what she found in her Bible. The fact that some revival was taking place in the Church on the eve of the Reformation tells in no way against the force of this doctrinal revolt. Revolution notoriously comes most often at the point when there has been just enough improvement to make the multitude hope for more, while it provokes the die-hards to sit all the tighter upon the safety-valve. On this point, again, Erasmus is only the most conspicuous among a great cloud of witnesses; and More backs him up in his famous *Letter to the Unnamed Monk*. For the saint, while doing justice to the piety of those monks who sit in their cloister "like an oyster or a sponge,

---

* It was one of Bishop Pecock's *faux pas* that, meeting the too undeniable Lollard accusation against our bishops as "dumb dogs", he argued that bishops are not bound to be preachers. The anti-Lollard Gascoigne cannot contain his indignation at this apology for spiritual incompetence on the part of the episcopacy.

always fixed to its rock", adds "if we look to labour, this man [Erasmus] sometimes works harder in one day than you [monks] in many months. Or, if we reckon the usefulness of the labour, he has sometimes brought more profit to the Church in a single month, than ye have in many years, unless ye think that some man's fasts or rosaries [*preculas*] carry us as far and wide as so many excellent volumes [of his], whereby the whole world is instructed in righteousness".[2]

We may say of most medieval thinkers, no doubt, what Mr Bernard Shaw has said concerning the communist in modern Moscow; he feels himself in an atmosphere of perfect freedom despite the penal laws; for he never has the slightest temptation to transgress them. But we shall never know how many others are now living in Moscow, and how many there were in Chaucer's London, who thought not with the multitude but for themselves, and would gladly have seen the whole thing swept away. We only know for certain that some such there were; and that, for everyone whom we can trace in written record, there must have been hundreds who, for the most obvious reasons, have left no record behind them. We know also that the medieval clergy, while they discouraged Bible reading among ordinary folk, were themselves in many cases almost incredibly ignorant of the sacred text; indeed, unable even to construe a single sentence of the most important parts of their own daily Mass. And, in process of time, the machinery of coercion, as embodied in the papal or the episcopal Inquisition abroad and in the statute *De Haeretico Comburendo* at home, began to defeat its own objects. As early as the twelfth century it had driven the scientific mind into the subterfuge of what has been called "the double truth"; the plea that a thing might be theologically true, but philosophically false, or *vice versa*.[3] Ordinary folk, on the other hand, saw more and more clearly that this storm of persecution was, to some extent at least, the violence of panic terror; a truth which became more and more evident in proportion as the persecutors, having struck down the leaders of heresy, descended from their lofty pedestal to treat the humble weaver and cobbler as enemies whose existence constituted an unpardonable danger to the great Roman Church. It is one of the best known inquisitors, Nicholas Eymeric, writing in about 1375, who complains that few rich heretics are left now; consequently prosecutions are ceasing to be pecuniarily profitable, and therefore the princes of Europe are no longer willing to pay the Inquisitors' expenses.[4] This brings me to the third cause, the Economic.

It is often falsely asserted that the Reformation was a plunder of the poor; that it dispossessed them of their heritage in favour of a squirearchy. The fact is that the medieval Church, on its financial side, was a squirearchy richer and more jealous of its possessions than any which has existed since the Reformation. What that revolution did was to transfer enormous wealth from one squirearchy to another; from a squirearchy which, in its very nature, was intensely conservative and seldom let go anything of its possessions, to another which lived far more among the people, and whose very extravagances often led to the division of land; so that there grew up in Elizabethan and Jacobean times a whole class of small yeoman farmers.

The medieval Church was, no doubt, more friendly to the poor than any State institution of those days would have been. But it was far from that Christian fraternity and generous beneficence which is often claimed for it, and which the earliest Christianity had actually displayed. It was deeply feudalized; it was no longer a really democratic institution, in any strict sense of that word. Popes were the most absolute sovereigns of their day, and sometimes the most luxurious and most directly responsible for those wars which were chronic in Christendom. Marsilius of Padua and Pierre Dubois noted that last fact already in the early fourteenth century; and Machiavelli repeated it still more emphatically about the time when More was writing his *Utopia*. Bishops and abbots had enormous wealth, and lived too often in ostentation and luxury. Archdeacons and rural deans were notorious takers of bribes. Among the parish clergy, even those who wanted to give generous doles had often little power. The monasteries, which drew two-thirds of the income from nearly one-third of the English parishes, were, it is true, the main distributors of such charities as could be counted upon by the medieval poor: but we have irrefragable evidence that they thus gave back far less than they took.[5] The great Oxford Chancellor Gascoigne described the seven Rivers of Babylon, the seven floods of iniquity; one of these was this absorption of parochial funds by the monasteries.[6] In the north of England, where parishes were fewer, the loss of monastic doles at the Dissolution was much more severely felt than elsewhere; but, during the centuries succeeding that event, the English poor have suffered less, on the whole, than those of France and Austria and Italy and Spain. We of this generation have not too much cause for complacency on this score; but at least we have got beyond the Middle Ages, and can stand without shame in comparison with Continental society.

The friction over tithes, great under any conditions, was much increased by the fact that, in so many cases, those hard-won sheaves of corn went to monks who were necessarily absentees— perhaps even Frenchmen or Italians—or to a parson who was absentee by mere abuse and lack of hierarchical discipline, or to churchwardens whose honesty was not above suspicion. Parochial embezzlement, either by clergy or by laity, bulks large in the episcopal visitation records. Christopher St Germain, the distinguished lawyer who (as More complained) played "the candid friend" to his Church by setting forth the grievances of laity against clergy, found one of the chief sources of clerical unpopularity in "the extreme and covetous demeanour of some curates with their parishes...and, though many spiritual men be not fellows with them in the extremities, yet none of them that have been best and most indifferent have not done anything to reform them that use such extremities, nor to make them think that any default is in them in that doing, but rather as it were with a deaf ear have dissembled it and suffered it to pass over, and have endeavoured themselves more to oppress all the lay people that would speak against it, than reform them that do it".[7] For the offerings which had at first been voluntary became gradually so regular that they were even enforceable by law; they were practically treated in most cases as personal perquisites of the clergy; and they were often extorted with the most cynical disregard of religious proprieties. From at least 1217 onwards, different Church councils attempted to check priests who began their examination in the confessional with enquiries as to non-payment of tithes, and who refused to administer the Holy Sacrament to parishioners who were in arrear with their (originally free-will) Easter offerings.[8] Towards the end of the same century, this prohibition had to be renewed in stronger language, "lest by this taking of money with one hand while Christ's body is offered with the other, the mystery of our Redemption be bought and sold". But the acts of succeeding councils show the same continual struggle against trading in holy things, especially against in-junctions of pecuniary fines in the confessional, whether nakedly or under the thin disguise of Masses to be said in the parish church, and therefore to the profit of the priest who imposed them. Wyclif's complaints on this head are borne out by unexception-able documents; and, more than ten years after Luther had raised the standard of revolt, such refusals to administer the communion to defaulting parishioners were perhaps more frequent in England than they had ever been before; so at least St Germain asserts.

However great a part mere cupidity may have played in the Dissolution of the Monasteries, and however shameful the injustices and the vandalism of its methods, these were at least a few degrees less disgraceful than the suppression of the Templars by the French king in collusion with Clement V. No torture was applied to the English monks as had been done by king and Pope in France; and Henry's worst cruelty, his political execution of the Carthusians, pales before the burning of those Templars for crimes which historians of all schools know to have been imaginary, though confession had been wrung from the victims on the rack. Our dispossessed monks and nuns, as Mr G. Baskerville has shown at last by exhaustive study of the actual documents, were pensioned with such an approach to general regularity and decency as gives the lie direct to what he calls "the indefatigable inaccuracy of sentimental writers" who have been asserting the contrary for the last forty years.[9] Moreover, there is scarcely a country in the world in which it has not been found necessary, since the Refor-mation, to dissolve the monastic orders and permit them to start again under such State control as that to which all other associa-tions are subjected. As to their moral and material decay in the sixteenth century, the evidence is overwhelming. Anyone who is surprised at Erasmus's bitter comments in his Bible commen-taries may turn to those of that most voluminous and orthodox of commentators, Cardinal Hugues de St-Cher, nearly three cen-turies earlier. This cardinal's strictures, by themselves, would suffice to explain how Henry was able to overturn so easily an institution so venerable and powerful.[10]

Fourthly, and last, let us come to the Political causes. Boniface VIII, in his bull Unam Sanctam, formulated explicitly the claims which had been more or less distinctly implied by Gregory VII and Innocent III. That bull is of immense importance, since it is one of the very few papal pronouncements, during all these nine-teen centuries of Christian history, which are admitted to be *ex cathedra* by even the most minimizing authorities: by those who admit only a half dozen or less of infallible decrees since Pentecost. In that bull Boniface claims authority over all sovereigns, even in the temporal sphere.* This led to an immediate revolt on the part of the strongest king in Europe, Philippe-le-Bel of France; yet it was duly embodied in Canon Law, where it stood until 1917. Therefore from 1302 onwards, in every land, Church and State were necessarily in such an unstable equilibrium as that which we were all deploring in Europe on the eve of the Great War. There was a mass of explosives which any chance spark might ignite. In all countries, from at least the thirteenth century onwards, there was a growing tendency to look upon the Pope as a foreign potentate drawing immense sums out of the realm. Then, when the Great Schism came, and when even saints could not tell the world whether the true Pope was the man in Rome or the man in Avignon, some began naturally to wonder what truth there was in the Papacy at all. As doubts increased, repressive measures became more violent; we have seen how Archbishop Arundel, in 1407/8, even proclaimed as heretics, in the same breath, the man who denies or misinterprets the Bible, and him who denies or misinterprets a papal decretal. Yet among those decretals he and his contemporaries included a mass of now acknowledged for-geries, together with such genuine documents, almost equally embarrassing to the modern apologist, as the bull *Unam Sanctam*. This schism was healed only by methods which went some way to encourage the idea of national churches, and only after the ventila-tion of such erastian arguments as had already been used by Marsilius and Ockham in their support of the civil power against the Papacy. Again, when certain serious monastic reforms were initiated by the councils which opposed the Popes, these were carried out, in so far as they ever came to practical success, only under constant threat of physical force by the State, and by the frequent employment of such force. Meanwhile the Papacy, as soon as it could shake itself clear of conciliar control, developed

---

* This claim is withdrawn by modern theologians from the "infallible" sphere, because it is not repeated in the final, "defining", clause. But it is plainly made in the earlier part of the bull, and so also in Boniface's other official pronounce-ments at this time.

more and more frankly into a petty Italian principate, with petty ambitions and petty wars of its own. Any country of Europe, at any moment, might suddenly find itself involved in one of these politico-religious wars.

One of these risks lay in the constant chances of friction with the Pope's army, the clergy. At almost every popular revolt, from the fourteenth century onwards, the mob had attacked monasteries, as now in Spain. From an earlier date still, there had been a steady popular superstition that it was unlucky to meet a priest on the road. We have seen how, when the Black Death came, most priests neglected or fled from the sick. In 1514, the Bishop of London complained that the growth of heresy had made it idle to expect justice for any cleric in the City courts; and in 1529 the Spanish envoy reported to his royal master: "Nearly all the people here [in London] hate the priests."[11] No doubt there were mixed feelings here. No doubt sinners hated the good priests for reproving them, just as good men despised the ignorance and worldliness of bad priests. But even St Thomas More, in the heat of his arguments against Tyndale, was forced to admit that there were far too many clergy, and too little care taken in ordaining them. Those who lived truly up to their profession were too few to counterbalance the contempt felt for those whom Erasmus so often holds up to scorn. It needed very little more to make Englishmen regard these men as an alien body, and their sovereign the Pope as an alien potentate or even as a direct enemy.

That little, it is well known, came through Henry's wish for a divorce. But it was not so much Henry's lusts which kindled the conflagration, as his desire for at least outward decency. His contemporary Francis I was a more notorious libertine, whose name was connected with far more women than Henry's; but such peccadilloes never caused any coolness between him and Rome. Henry, however, needed an heir for his throne; and his quarrel with the Pope was not over lust but over matrimony. We are sometimes told that Anne Boleyn forced his hand by standing out for marriage; but at the court of Francis any such insistence on the part of a coveted woman would have been futile and ridiculous. Again, even in strict morality, Henry had a slight advantage over the Pope. True, he did ask for a licence of bigamy; but, equally certainly, the Pope was quite ready to negotiate with him about such a licence.[12] When it is pleaded that this negotiation was only a pretence, only a subtle move in that political chess-match by which the pontiff hoped to play for final victory, then this excuse reinforces the point that, in so far as the Reformation was due to political causes, it reflects slightly less discredit on Henry than on Rome.

There is no escaping, at any point in our period, from the significance of the Pope's claim to a Totalitarian State. His Church trumpeted itself as a *Societas Perfecta*, with all the political implications of earthly states, including military force in the last resort; indeed, that claim is so fundamental that it survives to the present day.[13] Pius IX reminded Bismarck that all baptized Germans, whether Catholic or Protestant, were by Church Law papal subjects; and even in this twentieth century Roman theologians have republished, with papal approbation, the claim that their master could in justice (as apart from mere expediency) employ force to bring back all baptized Christians to his fold. Thus, in Tudor times, the change of religion in England was necessarily inseparable from politics. We see this most plainly in Elizabeth's reign. The interrogatory which Roman Catholics then dreaded most, that which was regularly imposed after the Armada, and which they called *The Bloody Question*, ran thus: In the event of a Catholic invasion of England, which side would you take, the Queen's, or the Pope's? Upon the man's answer to this question depended his classification as religious nonconformist or political enemy, and therefore his life or death. But how could any government, in those days at least, do less than this? To us, the maxim *Touch not Mine Anointed* may seem an old wives' tale divorced from all present-day political significance; but in Tudor days these papal claims were a political reality more formidable than the policy of any other European State. Henry and the Reformers, for different reasons, had to face (as Boniface VIII had put it) the Two Swords. They knew that Christ had proclaimed Himself as coming to bring not peace but a sword, and that the New Testament describes the word of God as sharper than any two-edged sword, piercing even to the dividing asunder of soul and spirit. Of this spiritual sword, rightly or wrongly, the Reformers were convinced that they need harbour no fear. But they had to deal also with that weapon of which Christ had said to Peter: "Put up again thy sword into his place; for all they that take the sword shall perish with the sword." In Henry's day the full and free exchange of reasons was still so impossible, through the fixed policy of one party and the passions of both, that no state could arrive at a decision without an appeal to arms. And, after all, was it not more honourable thus to break openly with the Pope, than to go on for centuries, like the sovereigns of France and Austria and Spain and the Italian States, in nominal religious submission and loyalty, but with selfish disloyalty always in the background whenever the question touched the sovereign's pocket or his pride?

The Reformation did at least clear the air. An agnostic outsider, to whom modern Protestantism may be as alien in thought as modern Roman Catholicism, may yet recognize clearly the superiority of a world in which those two rival creeds can now exist side by side, as compared with an earlier world in which one party felt bound in conscience to say: "Be my brother in religion, or I shall burn you here and God will burn you to all eternity." Though Protestants have too often disgraced their own tenets by intolerance, yet this division into two parties, each unable to exterminate the other by force, and therefore each driven to vie with the other in religious enthusiasm and reasonable argument and good works, has done more for tolerance and for civilization than was ever done by the ideal of absolute uniformity in belief, whether through argument or through force. Society as a whole did move forward during the Middle Ages; but there was one important field of morality in which it went backward for at least four centuries before the Reformation: and that field was, the maintenance of religious belief by actual or potential violence. But for the Reformation, it is difficult to see how the world could ever have learned what it has now gathered from the experience of generations; viz. that agreement to differ is more really religious than forced agreement, whether that compulsion be the force of the rack and the stake before men's eyes, or the force of immemorial custom in a society which has been reduced to uniformity by the weeding out and the breeding out of all those men whose thoughts run naturally outside the general groove. For centuries the Church had attempted vainly, and not always even sincerely, to reform herself. It is generally held, even by her stoutest apologists, that she was in 1530 less pure than in 1230; and, though future students may very likely treat this as a somewhat superficial judgment, still it is agreed on all hands that the

300 years preceding the Reformation had brought no material change for the better. Yet nowadays, 400 years after the Reformation, the difference is so enormous that men are often tempted to reject the most definite medieval evidence on no other ground than that it shocks their present ideas of right and wrong: they cannot believe that men so like ourselves essentially, men whom we are so loath to condemn in themselves, should have behaved as they are definitely recorded to have done: there must (it is dimly felt) be some mistake somewhere!

It is not necessary to believe that the Reformers were better men than their opponents; we need only to face the apparent fact that a world in which both parties can live side by side is a better world. Selfish and material causes played too great a part in that change, as in all similar upheavals; but to ascribe the Reformation to such causes alone is to imitate Gibbon's cynicism without Gibbon's extenuating circumstances. Purely political motives have played at least as great a part in the retention of medieval faith in some countries, as in its abandonment elsewhere. It is as easy to find personal defects in the Reformers as to sneer with Gibbon at the gross falsehoods and unedifying truths with which the early Christian traditions are alloyed; but, when arguments of this kind are unduly pressed, the simplest and truest reply is such a *tu quoque* as Newman constantly used, as the Fathers used, and as Christ used Himself. Half of St Augustine's great *City of God* is devoted to showing that Christianity, with all its faults, is better than the paganism it has replaced. The Reformers, it is true, were only men; but of what sort were those others who for centuries had held the key of knowledge, and who would not suffer others to enter in? Moreover, even in doctrine, the change has been so great that superficial observers get an entirely false perspective; they judge the majoritarian Latin Church of the Middle Ages, which lived by the steady and relentless "liquidation" of its minorities, by what they see and hear around them in that Roman Church which commands less than 6 per cent. in the England of to-day, and thus (to use Cardinal Vaughan's simile) has one hand tied behind its back. Few men or women in modern Britain could sustain successfully that searching cross-examination upon matters of faith which was an essential factor in the proceedings of the medieval Inquisition. Indeed, it might perfectly well be found that, even among the most loyal modern subjects of the Roman

Church, there is not one who does not think in his inmost heart, on one or two important points at least, in terms which would have given to the highest medieval authorities excellent reasons for sending him to the stake.

In any case, for good or evil, the Reformation begins the modern world in England. "It is the gigantic figure of Luther, not the comparatively commonplace figure of the victorious Henry VII at Bosworth field, that begins a new age, after which nothing can be the same."[4] Or again, in the words of the late Dr Barry, writing as an orthodox Roman Catholic in *The Cambridge Modern History*: "In truth, it was not the Revival of Learning that shook Europe to its base, but the assault on a complicated and decaying system in which politics, finance and privileges were blended with religion."[5]

Two architects of St-Ouen at Rouen (see p. 569).

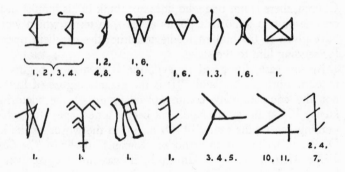

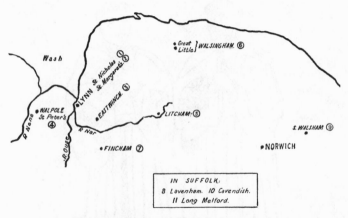

Wandering masons in Norfolk (see p. 557).

The numbers show the churches at which each particular mark may be found repeated. At East Winch and Litcham there are also definite similarities in tracery and mouldings. See details in my *Art and the Reformation*, pp. 154–6.

NOTES

These references are in many cases repeated from my own statements in other books, where fuller vouchers and details are given. Unless otherwise stated, they are published by the Cambridge University Press.

> *Five Cent[uries of Religion]*, vols. I–III.
> *[The] Med[ieval] Vill[age]*.
> *Ten Medieval Studies.*
> *Social Life [in Britain from the Conquest to the Reformation]*.
> *Life in [the] M[iddle] A[ges]*, vols. I–IV.
> *Art and [the] Ref[ormation]* (Blackwell, Oxford).
> *Chaucer and his England* (Methuen).
> *[From] St F[rancis] to D[ante]* (Duckworth).
> *Rom[anism] and Truth*, 2 vols. (Faith Press, Leighton Buzzard).

The following abbreviations are used:

C.P.L.	Calendar of Papal Letters.
E.E.T.S.	Early English Text Society.
P.L.	Migne, *Patrologia Latina*.
R.S.	Rolls Series.
S.S.	Surtees Society.

CHAPTER I (pp. 8–19)

(1) M. Rostovzef, *Storia Economica e Sociale del Imperio Romano* (1933), 588. (2) *P.L.* LXXVI. 1009 (Bk II, hom. vi). (3) Rostovzef, 591. (4) *Hist. Eccl.* Bk IV, c. 13.

CHAPTER II (pp. 20–33)

(1) See M. P. Charlesworth, *The Virtues of a Roman Emperor* (Clarendon Press, 1937). (2) *P.L.* LIX. 42 (1). (3) *Register* of Greg. I, Bk III, letter 61. (4) *Liber de Antiquis Legibus* (1863), 34. (5) Stubbs, *Const. Hist.* I. 135. (6) *Decret. Greg.* Lib. I, tit. vi, c. 22. (7) *Sext. Decret.* Lib. I, tit. vi, c. 9.

CHAPTER III (pp. 34–44)

(1) Bede, *Hist. Eccl.* Bk III, c. 25. (2) Readers interested in this subject should consult Bishop G. F. Browne's *Importance of Women in Anglo-Saxon England*, 60 ff., and F. H. Thurston's *No Popery*, 147 ff., where Browne is corrected on several important points, though others are left unanswered. (3) Lavisse and Rambaud, *Hist. Générale*, I. 296. (4) *P.L.* LXXXIX. 702 (Ep. XII). (5) *Ibid.* 811, 813. Here, for instance, are extracts from Boniface's letter to Pope Zacharias in 742 (Migne, *P.L.* LXXXIX. 746): "Carloman, chief of the Franks, has summoned me and asked me to convoke a synod in that part of the Frankish realm which is in his power.... For the Franks, as the elders say, have held no synod for more than 80 years, nor had any archbishop, nor have founded or renewed canonical laws for the Church. Nowadays, among the majority of the cities, the episcopal sees have been given over to the possession of greedy layfolk or adulterine clerks,

CHAPTER III (pp. 34–44) *continued*

fornicators and publicans, who enjoy them in secular fashion....If, among these, I find deacons, as they are called, who from their boyhood onward have been always in fornication and adultery, leading their lives continually in all uncleanness, who have come to the diaconate by that token and who now, within the diaconate, keep in their bed four or five concubines or more, yet neither blush nor fear to call themselves deacons and to read the Gospel [at Mass], and who, coming thus in such unchastity to the order of priesthood, persisting in the same sins and adding sin to sin, perform the priestly office and claim the power of interceding for the people, and offering the holy oblations; and in these latest days (what is worse) by the same token they rise from step to step and are ordained and created bishops—if (I say) I find such men among them, I beseech [your Holiness] that I may have your precept and your written authority in judgment upon such things, that the sinners may be convinced and rebuked by your Apostolic answer. Moreover, bishops are found among them who, though they say that they are no fornicators or adulterers, are yet drunken and quarrelsome, or hunters, and men who fight under arms in battle, and shed men's blood with their own hands, whether of heathens or of Christians." (6) See Addis and Arnold, *Catholic Dictionary* (10th ed. revised), 554, and Hefele, *Beiträge*. I have summed up the discussion on this subject on pp. 25 ff. of the 20th of my *Medieval Studies (6d.)*. (7) *P.L.* LXXXIX. 526. (8) *Ibid.* 751. (9) *Ibid.* 951. (10) *Ibid.* 946. (11) *Ibid.* 768. (12) *Register*, Bk II, letter 51; this country was probably Dalmatia.

CHAPTER IV (pp. 45–56)

(1) Pollock and Maitland, *Hist. Eng. Law* (2nd ed.), I. 67. (2) *Camb. Med. Hist.* II. 647. (3) Lavisse and Rambaud, *Hist. Générale*, II. 48. (4) H. Pirenne, *Econom. and Soc. Hist. of Med. Europe*, 202.

CHAPTER V (pp. 57–67)

(1) *De Gestis Regum* (R.S.), II. 304. (2) Stubbs, *Select Charters* (1890), 201 (Bk x, ch. 10). (3) Ed. Lumby (R.S.), II. 165.

CHAPTER VI (pp. 68–79)

(1) *Documents* (ed. H. Philpott, 1861), 2. (2) *Norfolk Archaeology*, XX. 179; *History Teachers' Miscellany*, I. 165. (3) Wilkins, *Concilia*, I. 287.

CHAPTER VII (pp. 80–91)

(1) Froissart (Globe ed.), 251. (2) *Babees Book* (E.E.T.S.), introd. xlvi. (3) W. J. Ashley, *Economic History*, vol. I, pt ii, 333. (4) *Miracles of K. Hen. VI* (ed. R. A. Knox and Shane Leslie, 1923), 131. (5) *Eynsham Cartulary* (Oxford Hist. Soc.), II. introd. xx. (6) *Piers Plowman*, B, Prol. 103; II. 93, 95; VI. 107; C, VI. 9. (7) *First Sermon before Ed. VI.* (8) This has been conclusively proved by Mr Geoffrey Baskerville, in his *English Monks and the Suppression of the Monasteries* (Cape, 1937), which for the first time utilizes the vast mass of material among the public records. (9) *Predigten* (ed. F. Pfeiffer), I. 478.

CHAPTER VIII (pp. 92–102)

(1) F. Curschmann, *Hungersnöte im Mittelalter* (Leipzig, 1900), 9, 20, 25–6, 49, 52.
(2) *Social Life,* 472. (3) *Five Cent.* I. Appendix XXIII. (4) *Lanercost Chronicle,* 109. (5) *Exempla* (ed. Crane, 1878), 131. (6) *Life in M.A.* I. 90. (7) G. L. Kittredge, in the preface to F. J. Child and H. C. Sargent, *English and Scottish Popular Ballads* (Boston, 1904), p. xviii. There is an interesting article on notices of sport in the Kingston parish accounts in the *Journal of British Master Glass-Painters* for Oct. 1935.

CHAPTER IX (pp. 103–118)

(1) *Modern Language Review,* Jan. 1907. (2) *P.L.* CIV. 158. (3) *P.L.* CIV. 214; CV. 161; R. L. Poole, *Illust. Hist. Med. Thoughts* (1920), 29. Cardinal Gasquet (*Eve of Ref.* (1900), 303) quotes liberally from *Dives and Pauper* to prove the falsity of the Reformers' belief that "the Church had given occasion to wrong ideas of worship in the minds of the common people, and that the reverence shown to the symbol of our redemption [i.e. the *Cross*] on that occasion [Good Friday] amounted practically to idolatry". He takes the liberty of omitting a passage, *from the same pages of the book from which he quotes,* which gives the lie direct to his apologetics. For the author of *Dives and Pauper* writes, concerning the statutory Church ceremonies relating to the Cross: "And this blyndeth moche people in their redynge [*interpretation*] For they meane [*think*] that al the prayers that holy church maketh to the crosse, that she maketh them to the tre [*wood*] that Christ died on, or els to the crosse in the church, as in that anteme *O crux splendidior*. And so for leudnes [*ignorance*] they ben deceyued, and worshypp creatures as god himself" (Com. I, c. 4 (ed. Berthelet), f. 15 v°). The Cardinal's quotations from *Dives and Pauper* in his *Parish Life in England* are also very inaccurate. (4) *P.L.* CXLII. 675. (5) *Lives of the Brethren* (translated by Fr J. P. Conway, O.P. 1896), 290. From the recollections of Blessed Cecilia, a Roman nun who had been clothed by St Dominic himself. The saint came one night to her convent in Rome, and preached to the sisters from behind the grille. He warned them against the different shapes taken by devils to deceive the elect. "The venerable father had scarcely said the word ere the enemy of mankind came on the scene in the shape of a sparrow, and began to fly through the air, and hopping even on the Sisters' heads, so that they could have handled him had they been so minded, and all this to hinder the preaching. S. Dominic, observing this, called Sister Maximilla, and said: 'Get up and catch him, and fetch him here to me.' She got up and, putting out her hand, had no difficulty in seizing hold of him, and handed him out through the window to S. Dominic. S. Dominic held him fast in one hand and commenced plucking off the feathers with the other, saying the while: 'You wretch, you rogue!' When he had plucked him clean of all his feathers amid much laughter from the Brothers and Sisters, and awful shrieks of the sparrow, he pitched him out, saying: 'Fly now if you can, enemy of mankind.' 'You can cry out and trouble us, but you can't hurt us!'...And so it came about that he employed for God's glory what the enemy of mankind had from envy done for their hurt and hindrance. The sparrow which flew in that night disappeared, and no one saw whither he went." (6) *L'Église et la Pitié envers les Animaux,* par la Marquise de Rambures (Paris, Lecoffre; London, Burns and Oates, 1903). (7) *Alphabet of Tales* (E.E.T.S.), 71. (8) See *Five Cent.* I. 107ff. and Appendix XI. (9) *Ibid.* 112ff. (10) *Depositions of Durham* (S.S. 1845), 27. (11) *Calendar of Chancery Petitions,* I. 103, 111, 112, 173. (12) Surtees Society, 1890, 343. (13) See especially pp. 416, 464–5, 506, 540, 549.

CHAPTER X (pp. 119–136)

(1) *Élections Épiscopales*, 135. (2) *Hist. Dunelm. Scriptores Tres* (S.S.), 118. (3) A. L. Smith, *Church and State in the M.A.* 18–19. (4) Eadmer, *Vita Anselmi*, Lib. I, c. v, 37. (5) R. W. Church, *St Anselm*, 92–3. (6) Grandisson, *Register*, 586. (7) *Ibid.* 1027. (8) *Piers Plowman*, B, xv. 537; C, xviii. 260. (9) *Register*, 979. (10) *Gemma Ecclesiastica* (R.S.), ii. 325. (11) *Mat. Hist. Thos Becket* (R.S.), vii. 20, 59; cf. iii. 44. (12) Ep. 166 (*P.L.* cxcix. 156).

CHAPTER XI (pp. 137–141)

(1) The vouchers for all statements in this chapter may be found in the second volume of my *Five Centuries of Religion*, and in Dr R. A. R. Hartridge's *History of Vicarages in the Middle Ages* (C.U. Press, 1930). (2) *Reg. Wykeham*, I. 361 ff.

CHAPTER XII (pp. 142–153)

(1) Rashdall's *Universities* (1st ed.), 701, 704. (2) *Opera* (R.S.), iii. 234, 368. (3) Wilkins, *Concilia* (1st ed.), ii. 150. (4) E.g. C.P.L. v. 179, 258, 528; vi, *passim*. (5) More's *English Works* (1557), 328; cf. *Reg. Rad. de Salopia* (Somerset Record Soc.), 131; *Reg. Stapeldon*, 179. (6) *Opera* (1703), v. 808; P. S. Allen, *Selections from Erasmus*, 17. (7) *Prologue* to *Vox Clamantis*, Bk I, l. 11; *Mirour de l'Omme*, l. 18,445. (8) *Mirour*, ll. 18,752 ff. (9) *Ibid.* l. 20,545. (10) *Ibid.* l. 20,137. (11) *Ibid.* l. 20,861. (12) *Ibid.* ll. 21,113 ff. (13) *Vox Clamantis*, Bk iv, ll. 551 ff. (14) *Piers Plowman*, B, xix. 439; xx. 278 ff. (15) G. Mollat, *Les Papes d'Avignon* (1912), 234.

CHAPTER XIII (pp. 154–170)

(1) *Decret. Greg.* Lib. iii, tit. v, c. 15; cf. c. 5. (2) A. L. Smith, *Church and State in the M.A.* 8. (3) *Reg. Romeyn* (S.S.), I. 91. (4) *Cal. Chancery Proceedings*, I. 149, 166. (5) Wilkins, *Concilia* (1st ed.), I. 586, 589, 669 ff., 693, 704. (6) *Ep. ad Ecgbertum*, § 3. (7) Tyndale's *Answer to More* (Parker Soc. 1850), 75. (8) *Opera* (R.S.), I. 90; II. 341–6. (9) *St Osmund's Register* (R.S.), I. 304 ff. (10) More's *English Works* (1557), 561. (11) *Instructions for Parish Priests* (E.E.T.S.), 10. (12) *Rev. Hist.* lxiii (1897), 22–3; lxvii. 12; lxviii. 23–47. (13) *Times Lit. Sup.* (Dec. 28, 1935), 892. (14) Gasquet, *Parish Life in Med. Eng.* 20; Crump and Jacob, *Legacy of the M.A.* 33. (15) *Instructions for Parish Priests* (E.E.T.S.), 24. (16) *Reg. Romeyn* (S.S.), I. 106. (17) *York Fabric Rolls* (S.S.), 263. (18) Wilkins, *Concilia* (1st ed.), ii. 160. (19) Pollock and Maitland, *Hist. Eng. Law*, I. 356; Holdsworth, iii. 535. (20) *Hist. Ag. Prices*, I. 683. (21) *Trans. Royal Hist. Soc.* (3rd series), vi. 115. (22) Wilkins, *Concilia* (1st ed.), ii. 697. (23) Hartridge, *Vicarages*, 159–61. (24) C. R. Haines, *Dover Priory*, 421, 443, 451. (25) *Oxford Archaeol. Soc. Report*, 1925. (26) *Dives and Pauper*, Com. v, c. 8.

CHAPTER XIV (pp. 171–178)

(1) A certain school of journalist-historians is adopting nowadays the policy of attempting to laugh Lea out of court as an inaccurate and bigoted compiler. This gains some plausibility from the multiplicity and startling nature of his facts, which lend colour to the charge of exaggeration, and from the unfavourable light they cast upon the Roman Church of the Middle Ages, thus suggesting the suspicion of religious prejudice. Yet Lord Acton, the most learned of modern British historians, who claimed that his Roman Catholic faith was dearer to him than his life, testified to Lea's accuracy and general impartiality, with a warmth

and expansiveness which he seldom showed to any book, in *The English Historical Review*. The misrepresentation has lately taken such proportions (especially in the third and fourth volumes of the co-operative *History of European Civilization* edited by Mr E. Eyre and sold, though not controlled, by the Oxford University Press) that I have dealt with it in a separate monograph, under the title of *Sectarian History* (72 Kimberley Road, Cambridge, 2s. 6d. post-free). It is evident that two of the contributors to that history, undertaking to correct Lea on a crucial point of religious history, had not even read the first page of the document to which they professedly appeal. The fact is that Lea's bulky work has never been corrected except on an almost negligible minority of details; and, if he had lived twice as long and been able to read twice as much, he could have doubled the mass of his already overwhelming evidence.   (2) A. L. Smith, *Church and State in M.A.* 13.   (3) *Ten Medieval Studies*, 141–6.   (4) *E.H.R.* XLIV. 444–5, 451, 453; XLV. 93–4, 100, 447, 458.   (5) The greatest evidential force of these visitations lies in their cumulative effect, so long as we do not forget to discount them as we discount all evidence from police reports. I therefore add here a selection of details omitted from my text lest they should be wearisome, yet necessary for any full comprehension of parish life in a rather wild district. (A) The visitors report as follows upon *Clunbury*. The parishioners say that Sir Edward, chaplain [in modern parlance, *curate*] of the parish, doth not serve the parishioners duly, as he should; nay, rather, he stirreth quarrels and contentions among the parishioners, and doth other detestable things, to the scandal of the church. *Item*, that the said Sir Edward was called upon to administer extreme unction to Richard Crowe on his deathbed; yet he expressly refused to do this, and thus the said Richard died without that sacrament by default of the said chaplain. *Item*, that the said Sir Edward absented himself from the church on the feast of Corpus Christi, so that the parishioners had no divine service, by default of the said Sir Edward. *Item*, that William, son of John Phyppes, lately deceased, was buried without Mass and burial service, by default of the said chaplain. *Item*, William Webbe's son was buried without Mass and service, as above. *Item*, that Sir Edward refused to receive to her purification Maiota, wife to John Crowe [*corner of leaf torn off*] unless she would offer [a fee] at his will. *Item* the said Sir Edward is incontinent with Alice, daughter of Thomas Eynones, and even baptized his own son begotten on her, and afterwards knew her carnally and begat on her another child [*corner torn off*]. Byllyng obtained letters from the lord archbishop of Canterbury and the lord bishop of Hereford containing an indulgence for benefactors of the bridge of Parsloe, in virtue whereof he collected in [these] parts 20s., which he spendeth to his own uses, paying nought for the repair of the said bridge [*torn corner*] common usurer. [*Torn corner*] is a common usurer. *Item*, that the prior of Wenlock refuseth to have the cure of souls here, saying that this pertaineth to the vicar, wherefore he saith he himself hath no cure of souls there. *Item*, that the vicar is bound to find a deacon to serve in the Church, which he doth not. *Item*, that the rector [i.e. the prior and convent of Wenlock] is bound to find a set of vestments for ordinary days. *Item*, that the rector is bound to find an ordinal-book, and doth not. *Item*, that Richard Davys of Churton is a common worker on Sundays and holy-days [*added in another hand:* "He was dismissed."]. (B) *Selections from other parishes*. At Kilpeck (p. 287) "Sir John, their chaplain of the place, haunteth the taverns and chattereth indecently there, to the great scandal etc. [*sic*]. *Item*, he is incontinent with one Margaret, surname unknown." At the next village of Garwy "the sidesmen say that Sir Thomas Folyot haunteth taverns inordinately and excessively, to the great scandal of the clergy, and that he revealed publicly the confessions of Robert Scheppert his parishioner....Richard, the chaplain, is unfit for cure of souls there, for he knoweth not the Welsh tongue, and many parishioners there know no English". In another village, the priest had celebrated a clandestine marriage for 12*d.* (444) and the parishioners report two other clandestine marriages. The servant of another kept a tavern in the rectory (445). Of another it is reported "he merchandizeth, to wit, buyeth and selleth divers goods to get gain thereby" (446). Another "refused burial to Jane, daughter of Davy Godemon, without just cause, and left her body unburied" (447). At another parish "the rector resideth not, and they know not where he dwelleth; otherwise all is well there" (447). At another (448) the outgoing curate "carried off with him from the church two silk chasubles, one red and one white, with a new surplice, to the grievous damage of the parishioners". Another had forged a will (449). Another "came, vested in his surplice, as is customary, with bell and lantern, to visit a certain Alice Clerke at the point of death, with an empty pyx, without the Body of Christ, to the great scandal [of the parish], causing the people to adore the Sacrament where it was not" (449). In that same parish "R. R. smote one J. S. violently with his fist in church, before the high altar.... Moreover noon was sometimes past before Mass was finished on Sundays and holy-days"; one priest had refused to purify a parishioner and the vicar "absenteth himself from his post, notwithstanding his oath" (449–50). Another (450) "is drunken and continually frequenteth the taverns, against clerical decency, nor doth he duly perform divine service". At Dymock, "The rector is bound by ancient custom to distribute weekly to the poor two bushels of mixed rye and wheat, which hath now been withdrawn for 20 years and more....Richard Stokke, lately promoted to Holy Orders, keepeth a certain Isabel Llarau, with whom he hath contracted (as he asserts) before such ordination, but the marriage was not yet celebrated between them" (453). Another priest extorted money from his parishioners for giving them Holy Communion (99). At Leominster, one priest is (99) "a common trader in beasts and sheep, buying and selling for profit, and partner in the gain accruing in the parish from baggers"; so also is another; a third is incontinent and a fourth haunts taverns "and other indecent [*inhonesta*] places". Another "threatens those parishioners who are in the bishop's service for the reporting of the transgressions and defaults of delinquents [i.e. the sidesmen] because they reported his transgressions". Another (445) receives 7 marks a year as chantry chaplain for the late vicar's soul, and breaks the oath which binds him to celebrate duly. At Staunton Lacy (432) the priest is "a common trader".   (6) *Reg. Stapeldon,* 107, 133; *Reg. Grandisson,* 570.

CHAPTER XV (pp. 179–186)

(1) Wadding, *Annales Minorum,* an. 1242, § 17.   (2) *Catholic Dictionary* (Addis and Arnold, 1885), 782 a.   (3) The story has been told by the Bollandist Fr H. Delehaye with his usual exhaustive learning (Acad. Royale de Bruxelles, *Bulletin, Classe des Lettres* (1899), 171). A summary by Fr H. Thurston, S.J., with useful further information as to English conditions, may be found in *The Nineteenth Century* for July 1899. Fr Thurston writes concerning Innocent III's patronage of this epistle: "There is not the least foundation for such a statement, and as a matter of fact the fabrication was one of very ancient date, which may be traced back to the time of Licinianus, Bishop of Carthagena at the end of the sixth century." But Fr Delehaye, who has traced the letter in all its ramifications, permits himself no such scepticism: and, after all, Eustache's mission happened in the lifetime of both Wendover and Matthew Paris. The fact that nobody now believes Christ to have written this letter is no proof that Innocent did not believe it, as these two first-rate chroniclers apparently did. The astounding vogue of this almost incredible forgery for a thousand years, in spite of papal and conciliar

CHAPTER XV (pp. 179–186) *continued*

repudiation in its earlier stages, is traced very fully by Fr Delehaye, but not sufficiently in *The Nineteenth Century*. (4) Blomefield's *Norfolk*, IX. 276. (5) *Provinciale*, 56–7. (6) *Depositions etc. of Durham* (S.S. 1845), 26 ff. (7) *Dives and Pauper*, Com. IV, c. 11. (8) D. Hay Fleming, *Influence of the Reformation*, 28.

CHAPTER XVI (pp. 187–196)

(1) *The Knight of La Tour Landry* (E.E.T.S.), 41–2. (2) *Dives and Pauper*, Com. I, c. 11 *ad fin.* (3) *Lay Folks' Mass-Book* (E.E.T.S. 1879), introd. xxvii. Compare p. 158, where the editor prints a conversation recorded from 1527 between the future Queen Mary of Scotland, then thirteen years old, and her chaplain (*aumônier*), Giles de Guez, who taught her French.

"M. I have good memory, maistre Amnere, how ye sayd one day that we ought not to pray at Masse, but rather onely to here and harken...
G. Ye, verely, madame...
M. In my God, I can not se what we shall do at the Masse, if we pray not.
G. Ye shall thynke to the mystery of the Masse and shall herken the wordes that the preest say.
M. Yee, and what shall do they which understande it not?
G. They shall beholde, and shall here, and thynke, and by that they shall understande."

Similarly we find, in the unusually enlightened and broad-minded *Dives and Pauper*: "every prayer that is made to the worship of God by way of charity and for a good end with purpose to please God, that prayer is made with devotion, though he that prayeth be distracte and thinketh not on his words, and peradventure understandeth them not, ne hath but little liking therein." *Charity* has here its frequent sense of "love towards God", which, in the later Middle Ages, practically became "Church orthodoxy". (4) In the new edition of Rashdall's *Universities of Europe*, the editor of vol. III has added a note which ignores essential qualifications in that great scholar's judgment on this point, and which throws doubt upon it without adequate rebutting evidence. (5) *Dives and Pauper*, Com. V, c. 10. (6) *Prediche Volgari*, I. 66. (7) De la Bigne, *Max. Bib. Patrum*, XXV, Lib. II, cc. 83 and 86. (8) *Preaching in Med. Eng.* 169, 173. (9) *Summa Major*, pars III, tit. 2, c. 4, § 13. (10) *Opera* (1745), I. 83; *Five Cent.* II. 595. (11) *Dives and Pauper*, Com. I, ch. 46. (12) *Exempla* (ed. Crane), 112. (13) Froissart (Globe ed.), 60, 209, 392 ff., 439, 460.

CHAPTER XVII (pp. 197–206)

(1) Brit Mus. MS. Arundel 285, f. 165 b. (2) I quote here from my translation into modern English (Methuen). (3) G. de Lagarde, *Naissance de l'esprit laïque*, II. 240, note. (4) *Med. Vill.* 262. (5) *Speculum* (July 1936).

CHAPTER XVIII (pp. 207–222)

(1) On the whole, the best English essay on this subject is probably that of R. W. Church, which has been reprinted in more than one cheap edition. Very valuable also is Professor E. G. Gardner's little primer, *Dante* (Dent, 1900).

CHAPTER XIX (pp. 223–234)

(1) Radulfus Niger (ed. Anstruther), 169. (2) *Ep.* XIV (*Life in M.A.* III. 2).

CHAPTER XX (pp. 235–247)

(1) This is printed in *Chivalry*. A series of studies to illustrate its historical significance and civilizing influence. By members of King's College, London. Edited by Professor Edgar Prestage (Kegan Paul, Trench, Trubner and Co. 1928). The most elaborate book from the conservative and sympathetic side is Léon Gautier, *La Chevalerie* (Nouvelle Édition, Dentu; 850 pp. n.d.). (2) Ed. 1846, pp. 31, 105. (3) A. Abram, *Eng. Life and Manners in the Later M.A.* 99. (4) Froissart (Globe ed.), 198. (5) *Blonde of Oxford* (Camden Soc.), 14. (6) *English Association Tract*, no. 51 (1892). (7) A. Abram, *l.c.* 1; cf. 162, 188, 204, 231–2, 284. (8) *Sir Gawayne and the Green Knight* (E.E.T.S.), ll. 915 ff. (9) *English Association Tract*, no. 51, p. 14. (10) *Petri Blesensis Epistolae*, no. xciv. (11) A. Abram, *l.c.* 140. (12) A. S. Green, *Town Life in the Fifteenth Century*, I. 261. (13) Froissart (Globe ed.), 349; cf. 104, 126, 198, 380.

CHAPTER XXI (pp. 248–257)

(1) *Times Lit. Supp.* (Aug. 19th, 1926). (2) Froissart (Globe ed.), 201. (3) M. Arnold, *Discourses in America*, 141; J. H. Newman, *Par. and Plain Sermons*, VI. 25. (4) The best studies on Malory are those of E. Vinaver, *Malory*, and E. Hicks, *Sir Thomas Malory*.

CHAPTER XXII (pp. 258–268)

(1) Cf. A. Harnack, *Das Mönchtum* (Giessen, 1903). (2) L. Duchesne, *Hist. ancienne de l'Église*, II. 491. (3) *Ibid.* 493. Cf. Martène, *Comment. in Regulam S.B.* (1690), 816; *Hist. Lausiaca*, c. 7; More's *English Works*, 227. (4) *P.L.* XVI. 1168 (*Ep.* XLI, § 27); Duchesne, *Hist. ancienne de l'Église*, II. 521. (5) A. Savine, *English Monasteries on the Eve of the Dissolution*, 87. (6) *Ibid.* 266.

CHAPTER XXIII (pp. 269–281)

(1) *Piers Plowman*, B, XX. 60; *Ten Medieval Studies*, 172, corrected by 179–80. (2) *Dives and Pauper*, Com. VII, c. 12. (3) *P.L.* CLXXVI. 949 ff.; *St F. to D.* (2nd ed.), 65 ff., 367–8.

CHAPTER XXIV (pp. 282–298)

(1) In this connection we may note that the Lord Mayor of London was elected or sworn in on the Feast of Saints Simon and Jude, October 28th, and that the same feast was of similar significance at Paris. In 1262 St Louis ordained that all the "communes" of the Île de France and Normandy should present their accounts on November 16th, but that the mayors should be sworn in on October 29th.

CHAPTER XXV (pp. 299–316)

(1) *Social Life*, 373. (2) E. L. Cutts, *Scenes and Characters of the M.A.* 508 ff. (from *Rotuli Parliamentorum*, I. 228). (3) *Social Life*, 324. (4) *Epistolae* (ed. Allen), V. 613; *Letters and Papers*, IV, ii, 1090; compare P. S. Allen, *Age of Erasmus*, chap. XXV. (5) *Babees Book* (E.E.T.S.), introd. lxv. (6) *Ibid.* introd. lxiii. (7) *Social Life*, 314. (8) *Ibid.* 329. (9) *Babees Book*, introd. (10) E. L. Cutts, *Scenes etc.* 509. (11) *Art and Ref.* 116. (12) *Œuvres de Montaigne* (ed. Buchon), 646. (13) *Book of Husbandry* (ed. Skeat), 101. (14) *Social Life*, 383. (15) *Cal. Early Chancery Proc.* II (1903), 163. (16) A. Abram, *Engl. Life and Manners in the Later M.A.* 130 ff. (17) *Ibid.* 132.

CHAPTER XXVI (pp. 317–330)

(1) *Life of St Godric* (S.S. 1847).   (2) R. Beazley, *Dawn of Med. Geography*, II. 460.   (3) Eileen Power and M. M. Postan, *English Trade in the Fifteenth Century* (1933).   (4) *Social Life*, 427.   (5) *Ibid.* 420.   (6) *Ibid.* 422. (7) Froissart (Globe ed.), 83.   (8) For full text see *Social Life*, 427 ff.

CHAPTER XXVII (pp. 331–345)

(1) Much of this chapter is transcribed from a paper which I read before the Historical Association at Cambridge in 1921, and which evoked no contradiction of fact. It was printed in *History* for July of that year.   (2) *History* (July 1921), 63.   (3) *Summa Theol.* 2ª, 2ᵃᵉ, LXXVII. 4.   (4) On this point there is an extraordinary misstatement in Dr G. O'Brien's essay on *Medieval Economic Teaching* (p. 122). He writes: "In the fourteenth and fifteenth centuries there is little to be found [in the theorists] bearing on the subject [of the Fair Price].... The reason for this paucity of authority upon a subject of so much importance is that...the proper remuneration of labour was so universally recognised as a duty, and so satisfactorily enforced, that it seems to have been taken for granted, and therefore passed over, by the writers of the period." It would be difficult to find a plainer instance of the danger of studying *theory* alone (for Dr O'Brien frankly confesses that limitation in his preface) and of deducing from such one-sided evidence all sorts of wider inferences as to actual *practice*.   (5) Crump and Jacob, *Legacy of the M.A.* 343 (by Prof. Gabriel le Bras, Strasbourg). (6) *Chron. Major* (R.S.), v. 465 (A.D. 1253).   (7) *Ibid.* III. 188–9.   (8) Oxenedes, *Chron.* (R.S.), 168, 197.   (9) *Social Life*, 345.   (10) *Chaucer and his England*, 194.   (11) *Comentum* (ed. Lacaita), I. 579; *Social Life*, 342. (12) *Cal. Early Chancery Proc.* II (1903), 109.   (13) *Rôle des monastères comme établissements de crédit* (1901), 56–69.

CHAPTER XXVIII (pp. 346–355)

(1) *Jewish Encyclopaedia*, v. 161 ff.   (2) *Hist. Eng. Law* (1895), I. 451. (3) *Jew. Encyc.* v. 164.   (4) *Ibid.* 162.   (5) *Ibid.* 166.   (6) *Ibid.* 166. (7) Will. Malmesbury, *Chronicle*, Bk IV, c. 1.   (8) *Jew. Encyc.* v. 162. (9) *Summa Theol.* 2ª, 2ᵃᵉ, q. x, art. x, conclusion.   (10) *Hist. Eng. Law*, I. 456.   (11) *Ibid.* II. 391.   (12) Cooper, *Annals of Cambridge*, I. 27. (13) *Ibid.* I. 44.   (14) *Jew. Encyc.* v. 165–6.   (15) *Hist. Eng. Law*, I. 453.

CHAPTER XXIX (pp. 356–365)

(1) Stubbs, *Select Charters*, 385.   (2) *Chron. Major* (R.S.), III. 332. (3) L. F. A. Berliner, *Jewish Self-Government in the M.A.* 217.   (4) *Chronicon* (ed. Hearne), II. 367.   (5) Knighton (R.S.), I. 157. For the whole subject of chapters XXVIII and XXIX see a recent paper by Dr Cecil Roth, *The Challenge to Jewish History* (The Jewish Hist. Soc. of England, Univ. Coll. London, 1936–7).

CHAPTER XXX (pp. 366–384)

(1) *Feudal Monarchy in France and England*, 137.   (2) *Hist. Eng. Law* (1895), I. 112. Since these words have been pressed into the theory that we owe our Common Law rather to the Church than to our kings, it is well to note how entirely Bishop Stubbs agrees with Petit-Dutaillis (and it may be added, with medieval chroniclers themselves) in regarding Henry II as the main initiator, and giving similar credit to other sovereigns. Stubbs writes (*Lectures on Medieval and Modern History* (1886), 210): "We all know how enormous is the debt which

CHAPTER XXX (pp. 366–384) *continued*

English law owes to the great legislators of the twelfth, thirteenth, and fourteenth centuries; Henry II and Edward I are, both of them, conspicuous examples of both the tendencies which I have coupled under the term; in their better actions defenders of the law, in their worse actions captious defenders of their right. The same is approximately true in other countries; Lewis IX is not only the great legislator of France, but almost the single example of the period, in which the more powerful sovereign grants to his competitor, even in the hour of his utmost weakness, the full extent of his legal right; the treatment of Henry III by S. Lewis is a very striking example of the respect for rights that do not happen to be your own. As to generalities, I need only remark that the names of Frederick II and Alfonso the Wise stand by those of Edward and Lewis as the founders of the non-Roman jurisprudence of Europe; and that in Germany in the fourteenth century the two great legislators are the two champions of the rival houses, Lewis of Bavaria on the one side, and Charles the IV on the other; the codification of Bavarian law and the issue of the Golden Bull were at all events attempts in the direction of civilisation in accordance with the highest existing ideal." (3) Hudson-Tingey, *Records of the City of Norwich*, I. 357. (4) *Ibid.* introd. cxxxviii. (5) *Ibid.* introd. cxxxix. (6) *Med. Vill.* 342. (7) *Chaucer and his England*, 235. (8) *Jeunesse de B. du Guesclin* (1882), 158. (9) *Chaucer and his England*, 284. (10) J. Fortescue, *De Laudibus* (1616), 46; *Social Life*, 518. (11) *Cal. Early Chancery Petitions*, I. 261; cf. 197.

CHAPTER XXXI (pp. 385–410)

(1) A. F. Leach, *Educational Charters and Documents*, xxix and 259. (2) *Social Life*, 54. (3) *Med. Vill.* 254; cf. F. M. Powicke, *Christian Life in the M.A.* (1935), 82. (4) *Comment.* Bk VII, lect. 8. (5) *Social Life*, 179. (6) M. Deanesly, *The Lollard Bible*, 131 ff., 150. (7) A. F. Leach, *l.c.* 402. (8) *Reg. Grandisson*, 1192; *Life in M.A.* II. 113. Grammar-school methods in the later Middle Ages are admirably described in P. S. Allen's *Age of Erasmus*, chap. II. (9) Trans. A. J. Grant (King's Classics), 59. (10) *Medieval Oxford* (Oxf. Hist. Soc. 1936), 97–8. (11) *Social Life*, 61. (12) J. E. T. Rogers, *Oxford City Documents*, 150 ff.; *Life in M.A.* II. 76. (13) *Social Life*, 73. (14) *Stud. in Med. Culture*, 79. (15) *Social Life*, 75. (16) *Ibid.* 71. (17) This story of the 30,000 Oxford students is an admirable instance of what has been called "plundering and blundering". It is still repeated, now and then, by writers who have evidently never handled the book upon which it is based. Archbishop FitzRalph of Armagh, commonly called Armachanus, wrote his *Defensorium Curatorum* in 1357 (E. Browne, *Fasciculus*, II. 473). He there asserts that, in his earlier days, there had been 30,000 students at Oxford, whereas there were not 6000 at this moment. First, we must note the wild extravagance of medieval writers and even statesmen, wherever large numbers are concerned. The Commons, in 1371, voted a tax on the supposition that there were 50,000 parishes in England. In fact there were less than 9000 as parliament could easily have discovered on reference to the bishops. But in volumes of monastic chronicles and similar records it is not infrequently noted that there are 40,000 or 50,000 parishes; and upon this false basis the budget of 1371 was calculated, with a deficit of over 75 per cent. in actual receipts. Secondly, those who quote FitzRalph as attributing this decrease to the Black Death have evidently not read the book itself. FitzRalph, *in this very sentence*, attributes the depopulation of his University to the crooked manœuvres of the Friars, his inveterate enemies, and the consequent unpopularity of an Oxford in which Friars were the main wire-pullers. This same feud with the Friars impels him to assert that his own diocese produced yearly a crop of 2000

CHAPTER XXXI (pp. 385–410) *continued*

felons of the blackest description—man-slayers, incendiaries, robbers, etc.—whom the Friars regularly absolve from their crimes (p. 468). No careful reader of this treatise can doubt that the archbishop is carried away everywhere by passion and rhetoric. For the most trustworthy arguments on this subject see H. E. Salter, *Medieval Oxford* (1936), 108 ff.   (18) Salter, *l.c.* 106.   (19) J. B. Mullinger in *Encyc. Brit.* (14th ed.), XXVII. 761.

CHAPTER XXXII (pp. 411–432)

(1) Rashdall, *Universities* (1st ed.), I. 68.   (2) R. Bacon, *Opp. Ined.* (R.S.), 426.
(3) Vol. VI. 607 b; compare III. 149 b.   (4) *Summa Theol.* I ᵃ, q. CII, art. 1.
(5) *Ibid.* I ᵃ, II ᵃ ᵉ, q. XCVIII, art. 3.   (6) *Ibid.* I ᵃ, q. XXXII, art. 4. Compare *Catholic Encyclopaedia* (art. 'Bible', 605 b): "The Church adheres to the literal sense of Holy Writ as long as either the context or the nature of the case does not suggest a metaphorical interpretation." Compare Renan's judgment in his *Souvenirs d'Enfance et de Jeunesse* (1883), 280. He points out how the methods of St Thomas were final for Scholasticism: they are repeated from generation to generation down to the orthodox theological summaries of the present day. "Everywhere we get the same texts, cut into pieces and separated from the explanatory context, the same triumphant syllogisms founded upon the void, the same default of historical criticism produced by the confusion of dates and of attendant circumstances."   (7) *Ibid.* Supp. q. XCIV.   (8) *Opera* (1745), II. 78; cf. *Rom. and Truth*, I. 51.   (9) St Bernardino writes (*l.c.* 77): "Verissime aeternas poenas per Sanctas Scripturas novi."   (10) The subject was debated at length in *The Church Times* for March 8th, 15th and 22nd (1935) and *The Listener*, March 20th, August 7th. The earliest orthodox Latin theologian who was quoted by defenders of the modern view as deciding explicitly on their side was Cardinal de Lugo, who wrote in about 1640, when it had already become evident that orthodoxy must abate some of its claims in deference to Protestantism and Freethought.   (11) *Buch v. d. Neun Felsen*, p. 54.   (12) *Summa Theol.* I ᵃ, q. XXIII, art. 7.   (13) F. X. Godts, *De Paucitate Salvandorum* (Roulers, 1899); see especially pp. 25, 30.   (14) *Summa Theol.* I ᵃ, q. XXIII, art. 7.   (15) See Innocent's own *Register*, Bk II, ep. 209 (*P.L.* CCXIV. 758). Innocent is pressing the Roman claims upon the Patriarch of Constantinople. First, of course, he quotes *Upon This Rock*, etc. and interprets it in that most literal sense which had been rejected by a majority of the early Fathers. Then, the *Feed My Sheep* of John xxi. 16. Christ (he here argues) draws no distinction between one kind of sheep and another: He simply commands *feed my* sheep, thrice over, in order to express clearly that *all* men, without distinction, are committed to Peter's care. Hence it follows indisputably that Greeks, no less than Romans, are subject to the See of Peter. Moreover, on that same occasion, Peter alone of the apostles leapt into the sea. "Now the word *sea* stands for the *world*." This he proceeds to prove by the traditional gloss on Ps. ciii. 25, which rests on a patent misinterpretation of the word *hoc* in the Vulgate translation: an interpretation, therefore, which is unintelligible even in the modern Roman Catholic (Douay) version, which has here corrected the Vulgate. Innocent then proceeds: "Therefore, in that Peter plunged into the sea, he thereby expressed that singular privilege of the Pontificate whereby he had undertaken the government of the whole world." Moreover, when the Psalmist says "He saved me from many waters", *many waters* means allegorically *many people*; therefore Peter, by walking miraculously on the sea, which is the vastest existing aggregate of waters, "proved that he had received power over all the nations". No interpretation is suggested for the fiasco which terminated that particular Petrine promenade. Lastly (to

CHAPTER XXXII (pp. 411–432) *continued*

omit others almost as far-fetched) it was Peter who saw that vision of the great linen sheet wherein were all manner of four-footed beasts and creeping things, which seemed to him unclean, but of which God said to him *Arise, Peter, slay and eat.* "Whereby", continues Innocent, "is plainly intended the fact that Peter was set over all the nations of the world; since that linen sheet signifieth the world; and the universal character of its contents signifieth all peoples, both Jew and Gentile." Fortified by these Biblical arguments, he requires the Patriarch's attendance at a Church Council, "to render reverence and obedience to Our Apostolic See according to thy canonical rank: lest, if thou disobey (which we do not believe) we be compelled to proceed both against thy Emperor himself (who, if he will, can enforce that which we command) and also against thine own person and the Greek Church". On the strength of interpretations of this kind, the Pope was ready to treat all Greeks as schismatics and, in the event of obstinate resistance, to employ the sword against them. (16) *Decret. Greg.* Lib. I, tit. vii, c. 2. (17) Pars II, c. XXIV, q. I, c. 17. (18) *Seventeen Lectures* (1886), 90. (19) Fr Hilarin Felder, *Gesch. d. wissenschaftlichen Studien im Franziskaner-Orden,* 316. Cf. A. G. Little, *Studies in English Franciscan History,* 193. (20) Rashdall, *Universities* (1st ed.), 438. (21) Ep. 547 (*Opera,* III. 596 c). (22) Rashdall, *l.c.* 707–8.

CHAPTER XXXIII (pp. 433–443)

(1) C. Singer, *Short History of Medicine* (1928), 61. (2) J. J. Walsh, *Medical History Manuals* (1920), 15. (3) L. Choupin, *Valeur des décisions etc.* 141. (4) E. Eyre (ed.), *European Civilization,* III. 832. (5) C. Singer, *Evolution of Anatomy,* 65.

CHAPTER XXXIV (pp. 444–456)

(1) C. Singer, *Evolution of Anatomy,* 63. To this, and to Dr Singer's *Short History of Medicine,* this chapter is very deeply indebted; some matters I have verified also in Gurlt's encyclopaedic *Geschichte der Chirurgie.* (2) C. Singer, *Short Hist. Med.* 68. (3) *Ibid.* 69. (4) *Ibid.* 72. (5) The above statements may be verified from Gurlt, *l.c.* I. 672 and L. Thomassinus, *Vet. et Nov. Eccl. Disc.* (1706), II. 227–8. (6) *P.L.* CLVI. 798; *Life in M.A.* II. 7. (7) The voluminous evidence for ecclesiastical prohibitions or restrictions of medicine is briefly and clearly summarized by the editors of *Johannes de Mirfeld,* 129, 159. They give fresh evidence also in support of Sir Thomas Browne's proverb, *Ubi tres medici, duo athei* (p. 132). Fr Hilarin Felder (*l.c.* 392) quotes the text of two of the most important official prohibitions, and comments: "It is plainly signified by these that the study of medicine, since it was not directly connected with theology, was not adapted, as a worldly occupation, to Religious. The Dominicans, in fact, expounded the relevant decisions in that sense, and considered the study of physic, in the sense of medicine, as forbidden by the Church." (8) T. Puschmann, *Gesch. d. medizinischen Unterrichts,* 205 (Eng. trans. 244). (9) C. Singer, *Short Hist. Med.* 71; cf. *Ev. Anat.* 85. (10) P. H. S. Hartley and H. R. Aldridge, *Johannes de Mirfeld,* 151, note: see also p. 129 of the same book for a contemporary summary of ecclesiastical hindrances to scientific medicine. For the "cauldron", see *Ten Medieval Studies,* 41. (11) See Traill's *Social England* (illustrated ed.), II. 122. (12) Arderne, *Treatise on the Fistula* (E.E.T.S.), 1 ff.; *Social Life,* 497. (13) *Meddygon Myddfai* (ed. Diverres) (*Le plus ancien texte etc.* 1913), 51; (ed. Pughe), 51. (14) *Clement,* Lib. III, tit. xi, c. 2. (15) To the evidence for lepers and rotten food printed on p. 508 of *Social Life in Britain,* add Bromyard, *Summa Predicantium,* E. iii, 26.

CHAPTER XXXV (pp. 457–476)

(1) *Philosophy and Civilization in the M.A.* 268.   (2) *Ten Medieval Studies,*
37.   (3) That which I write in the next few pages is developed more fully,
with references, in the second chapter of my *Inquisition and Liberty* (Heinemann,
1937), and more fully still in my *Christ, St Francis, and To-day* (C.U.
Press), 26–38.   (4) Dante, *Paradiso,* XXIV. 106.   (5) See the story of
Saladin and the Crusaders in Caesarius of Heisterbach, *Dialogus Miraculorum,*
dist. IV, c. 15 (ed. Strange, I. 188; trans. Scott and Bland, I. 212).   (6) E. Renan,
L'Averroïsme, introd. iii.   (7) Renan, *l.c.* 273; Rashdall, *Universities* (1st ed.),
362, n. 2.   (8) *Inferno,* cantos IX and X.   (9) Renan, *l.c.* 333, 336.
(10) M. Deanesly, *Lollard Bible,* 36.   (11) Étienne de Bourbon, *Anecd.
historiques* (1877), 308; cf. 291. I deal fully with this subject in *Ten Medieval
Studies,* ch. VII.   (12) *P.L.* CLXXXIII. 1088–102; cf. 82, 676.   (13) *English
Works,* 262, 280, 282; cf. 355.   (14) H. C. Lea, *History of the Inquisition
of the Middle Ages* (1887), I. 87.   (15) *P.L.* CCV. 241, 322.   (16) *L'Inquisition,* 284.   (17) Eyre, *European Civilization,* III. 699.   (18) *P.L.*
CCV. 230.   (19) *Register,* Lib. XII, ep. 138.   (20) *Serm. 66 in Cant.* § 12.
His ablest Roman Catholic biographer, Vacandard, confessed: "I am inclined to
think that Bernard believed in its efficacity, or at least in its juridical value."
Then, after quoting the saint textually, he asks: "If Bernard had not believed in
the validity of this ordeal, how could he say that the accused were convicted,
irrefragably convicted?" And he refers to an article which gives full proof of
the belief in this ordeal of water among great Churchmen of the twelfth century.
(21) Lea's treatment of this episode is one of the few cases in which Vacandard
meets him directly hand to hand and sums up: "it will be seen how the author, *who
is nevertheless trying to be impartial,* distorts the facts" (*L'Inquisition* [1907], 36).
Any reader who follows the difference of opinion between these two honest men
(for Vacandard quotes St Leo's exact words, p. 32) will probably judge that,
though the author exaggerates on one side, his critic exaggerates still more on the
other. When Lea writes that St Leo declared the heretics ought to be killed
Vacandard insists that he has here put into the Pope's mouth words which were
actually spoken by the Emperor. Strictly, this is true; but, considering that Leo
writes "our fathers acted rightly...for they saw that [here follow the Emperor's
words justifying the execution]", it is difficult to deny Lea's main point that the
Pope, by repeating these words with approval, and with the plain word *saw* where,
if he wanted not to commit himself, he would have written *thought,* may be said
to have uttered them himself. Incidentally, one critic of Lea, perhaps the bitterest
of all, has recently permitted himself to quote this criticism from Vacandard,
with the silent omission of those crucial words which I have here italicized (see my
Sectarian History, 68).   (22) Eymeric, *Directorium Inquisitorum* (ed. Pegna,
Rome, 1585, with approval of Pope Gregory XIII), 654–6; pars III, quaest. LXV.
This is one of the main points upon which Baumgarten charges Lea with guilty
misrepresentation, yet without a shadow of proof for his accusation beyond the
vague unvouched assertions of the Jesuit periodical *Civiltà Cattolica.* Alphandéry
(*Encyc. Brit.* 596) supports Lea: and any reader who has access to the British
Museum may judge for himself.   (23) Eymeric, *l.c.* 517–19.   (24) Douais,
Documents etc. (1900), I. 67.   (25) Eymeric, *l.c.* 510.   (26) This *Register*
is printed in the second part of Limborch's *Hist. Inquisitionis.* The very first page
records as follows: "(1) Peter of St Laurent-de-Garrigues✠.* Visitations of
Toulouse twice a year: in the octaves of Easter to the Church of St-Sernin; on
the Invention of St Stephen in August [i.e. Aug. 2] at the Church of St Stephen.

* This abbreviation signifies "condemned to wear the cross of infamy"; for
which see the case of Raymonde just below.

CHAPTER XXXV (pp. 457–476) continued

And the pilgrimages [enjoined] were remitted him by reason of his debility and old age. (2) Tholosana, wife of Bernard Hugues of Roche-Vidal ✠. The minor pilgrimages contained in the Inquisitor's letters, and visitations of Toulouse as above. The Inquisitors reserve the power of increasing, diminishing and augmenting the aforesaid penance, and of bringing back the aforesaid persons to prison, without fresh cause [*sine nova causa*] if they judge it expedient." This is the regular form: the last batch of all (pp. 337–8) differs only in being slightly more explicit. We may trace some of these accused from stage to stage. In March one Raymonde, wife of Jacques Géraud, was condemned, on a confession extorted from her in prison and retracted afterwards (p. 119). In Sept. 1319 she was let out of prison on oath, to wear "two crosses of felt, of saffron colour, on all her garments except her shift; and let one arm be of the length of two palms, and the other cross-piece one palm and a half, and each arm of three fingers' breadth; one on the breast in front and the other between her shoulders at the back; let her never go, whether within or without her house, without displaying these; let her repair or renew them if they are torn or worn out with age". She must also perform a series of penances and pilgrimages and compulsory attendance at Church, and take an oath "to prosecute [*persequantur*] heretics, by whatever name they may be called, and those who believe or abet or harbour or defend them, and all who have fled for heresy's sake". There is the usual reservation for return to prison at the Inquisitor's pleasure *sine nova causa* (p. 214). Either Raymonde gave just cause or the Inquisitor was pleased to exercise his powers afresh; for in Sept. 1322 she was let out again, with a batch which had been "many years in prison" under the same grievous penalties and on the same cat-and-mouse conditions as before (p. 338). This, then, is a specimen of the 137 cases which Professor Guiraud and Mr Hollis describe as complete acquittals, evidently never having even glanced at this document on the strength of which they flatly contradict such learned and accurate writers as Lea and Tanon! (27) Vacandard, *l.c.* 241 ff. (28) *Ibid.* 159. (29) Lea's monumental work has been so unscrupulously handled by popular controversialists on the Roman Catholic side, that I seize this opportunity of rectifying one of the most important misstatements. Far fuller evidence will be found in my booklet on *Sectarian History* (post-free for 2s. 6d. from 72 Kimberley Road, Cambridge), but the following episode deserves to be far more widely known. Professor E. P. Cheyney, in 1911, read a paper on Lea and his writings. He there described how Lord Acton, originator of *The Cambridge Modern History*, invited Lea "to write a chapter in the first volume to be called 'The Eve of the Reformation'. In his letter Lord Acton uses the following expressions: 'This is the most important and most critical and cardinal chapter, which I am anxious to be allowed to place in your hands. It is clear that you are the one indicated and predestined writer, there is no one else....I know of none whom I could go to, if you refuse....After some other intervening letters, the correspondence was resumed in March and April, 1898, when Mr Lea sent the manuscript of the chapter, which was acknowledged by Lord Acton with renewed thanks, and eventually printed exactly as written. Eight years later, after Lord Acton's death, during a controversy that arose concerning his Catholic orthodoxy, a correspondent in the *Tablet*, a London Catholic journal, denied that Lord Acton had asked Mr Lea to write this famous chapter. In answer to this Mr Lea prepared a communication to the same paper giving an outline of the correspondence which I have just described. Before sending this letter, however, he saw an article in the London *Times* of Oct. 30, 1906, by the present Lord Acton, upholding his father's orthodoxy. In a spirit of kindliness, and fearing to make this filial task more difficult, Mr Lea decided not to send the correction he had prepared, laid it away among his papers, and the facts are now made public for the first time" (*Proceedings of the American*

CHAPTER XXXV (pp. 457–476) continued

Philosophical Society, vol. 1, No. 198 (Jan. 1911), pp. xviii, xxvi, repeated in Professor E. C. Bradley's *Henry Charles Lea* (Philadelphia, 1931)). Even his severest Catholic critics have restricted their condemnation to a few parts of his work. Lord Bryce, who followed on as next speaker at this meeting, lent his exceptionally weighty authority, saying: "Few recent writers have had their statements so seldom questioned, and rarely indeed was he proved to have been in error.…In accompanying him one feels one's self always on firm ground.… Mr Lea was a Protestant by birth and conviction, but he was, as a scholar ought to be, perfectly fair in his treatment of ecclesiastical and religious questions." (30) Montalembert in *Contemp. Review* for Jan. 1875 (p. 200): "I grant indeed that the Inquisition in Spain destroyed Protestantism in its germ; but I defy anyone to prove that it has not given it throughout Europe the support of public opinion and the sympathies of outraged humanity." (31) *Letters to Mary Gladstone*, 185.

CHAPTER XXXVI (pp. 477–484)

(1) *Hist. of the Papacy* (1907), I. 67. (2) *De Moderno Ecclesiae Schismate* (ed. Sorbelli), 180. (3) *Trans. R. Hist. Soc.* (1899), 103. (4) Crump and Jacob, *Legacy of the M.A.* 25.

CHAPTER XXXVII (pp. 485–492)

(1) Among many excellent books on this subject, readers should refer specially to Dr H. B. Workman, *John Wyclif* (Oxford, 1926, 2 vols.); Dr R. L. Poole, *Wyclif and Movements for Reformation* (1889) and B. L. Manning in *Camb. Med. Hist.* VII, ch. XVI. (2) *E.H.R.* (Jan. 1936). (3) *Church History*, Bk IV, cent. XV (I. 53).

CHAPTER XXXVIII (pp. 493–506)

(1) Much more on this subject will be found in my monograph on *The Black Death* in Benn's sixpenny series. (2) Knighton's *Chronicle* (R.S.), II. 57. (3) B, passus V. 13. (4) Knighton, *l.c.* 59. (5) *Eccl. Hist.* III. 30; cf. IV. 27; W. Bright, *Early English Ch. Hist.* (3rd ed.), 238. (6) Wilkins, *Concilia* (1st ed.), II. 745. (7) This question is of such immense importance for social and religious history that I add here, for the benefit of readers who would wish to follow it more fully, a great deal of evidence for which there was no space in my text. Dr Lunn begins his 6th chapter by noting how the great plagues of more modern times called forth (for instance) the heroism of St Charles Borromeo at Milan in the sixteenth century, and of Bishop Belzunce at Marseilles in the eighteenth; but, in our fourteenth-century England, "the name of this great pestilence is bare of any association with acts of sacrifice". Our bishops did what they could to warn their flocks of its coming, and to make it easier for the sick to get confession and absolution. "So far they proceeded, and then they stopped. Not one went further, and no record has survived which testifies to any outstanding act of charity which one bishop performed during the period of the plague." Mr Lunn then deprecates too hasty conclusions from this silence, and deals with the bishops' movements *seriatim*. *Ely* was absent from his diocese at the time. *Norwich* was William Bateman, founder of Trinity Hall at Cambridge. He also was absent for a short while, during the first deaths in February, but he was at Norwich on the 29th. Before March 7 he was in London, and was absent all April and May. June was by far the worst month in this diocese; on May 30 he was at his manor of Terling in Essex: June 5, at Ipswich: thence he crossed his diocese to Dereham (8th) and backwards to Yarmouth (11th). Thence inland to Beccles (13th), and thence to Terling (18th) and London (19th). We cannot

CHAPTER XXXVIII (pp. 493–506) continued

trace him in his diocese again until July 10, at his manor of Hoxne, 15 miles away from Norwich, the city in which mortality was certainly very heavy, even when exaggerations have been cleared away. At the beginning of August he was at South Elmham, 15 miles from Norwich. The scanty further records do not once locate him at Norwich. The last places him at Poringland, 5 miles off. From all this Mr Lunn infers that "the plague does not seem to have provoked anything exceptional from Bateman", either in the form of self-sacrifice or of running away from his city and diocese. Yet for myself, I cannot help feeling that the record is less colourless than this estimate would imply. Norwich, his capital, was one of the greatest cities in the kingdom: Yarmouth and Ipswich also were high in the scale, and Lynn not far behind. At Norwich he spent a week or less during the whole period, and not at the worst time: at Yarmouth two days, at Ipswich three; Lynn he apparently never visited at all. Yet Norwich and Yarmouth certainly suffered very heavily indeed, and at Lynn the bishop had his convenient country palace of Gaywood, three miles from the town gate. The records show Bateman to have spent certainly more than 15 weeks, and probably a great deal more, in London or at village manors during those 9 months of unprecedented mortality in his diocese. Again, the bishop of *Bath and Wells* "during his long episcopate of 34 years, is recorded as having been in Wells only 9 times, and he never once visited Bath". He was accustomed normally to spend about half the year, from November or December to May, in his favourite manor at Wiveliscombe, a remote village in the very corner of his diocese. On August 17, 1348, the bishop had warned his flock that a dire pestilence had invaded the land and was creeping upon them: let them repent and return to Almighty God. The actual ravages certainly began in his diocese before January 10, 1349; and yet meanwhile the bishop lay at his wonted Wiveliscombe until May 13 at least. Thenceforward he visited different towns and villages in his diocese until November 25, when he was again at Wiveliscombe until May 14. "His itinerary during the period June–November 1349 contains nothing to differentiate it from his earlier and later summer tours. It was varied neither more nor less. His retreat to Wiveliscombe was not prolonged by reason of the plague. Everything went on as usual." That is, if we take the 12 months from January 10, 1349 to January 10, 1350, we shall find that nearly half (24½ weeks out of 52) were spent in that remote corner of his diocese. *Lincoln* was in the hands of Gynewell, a prelate of at least average character and energy. Mr Lunn here sums up: "Once more there is the same inevitable and identical conclusion—the Black Death made precious little difference to Gynewell." He went about, visiting his diocese, with the regularity natural to a newly appointed bishop. Grandisson, of *Exeter*, was very distinctly above the average of contemporary bishops. He also was nearly always accustomed to stay at his favourite village manor of Chudleigh for Christmas and the spring. This year, 1348–9, he extended his stay there for 4 months longer than usual, and was scarcely ever at Exeter during the plague. On the other hand, Chudleigh was fairly central for the whole diocese, and it lay in "one of the worst plague spots, not only in Exeter but in England". The bishop of *Lichfield* moved about a good deal, and, so far as can be traced, mainly in the least affected areas: certainly not in the greater towns of his diocese. The archbishop of *York* spent the whole of the plague period at three manors of his diocese, two of which were in villages and one in the small town of Ripon. *Rochester* was aged and decrepit; he does not seem to have visited any of his towns, but many of his attendants died, which "at least indicates that the bishop did not entirely escape risks of personal infection". *Canterbury* records are very defective, but two archbishops died during this period, very probably of the plague. *Worcester* administered his diocese from his village manor of Hartlebury, and died August 6, 1349: he had no successor until the plague was over. The prior visited widely; but we have no

CHAPTER XXXVIII (pp. 493–506) *continued*

evidence that this was more than the usual *sede vacante* formality, which cost little trouble and brought in rich fees. For *Salisbury* "the Black Death did not influence Wyville's movements in the slightest". For *Winchester* "here, again is the same conclusion. Edyngdon's whereabouts were little affected by the Black Death". For *Hereford*, "meagre as are the details of Trillek's itinerary which have survived, they betray nothing unusual". After this exhaustive survey from all the episcopal registers available, Dr Lunn sums up. "But the strangest feature of all is that Trillek himself never caught the disease.... Trillek admitted to sacred orders no less than 1231 clerks. Add to these the numbers of those instituted to benefices in 1349 (i.e. 159) and something approaching 1400 represents the total of those with whom the bishop must have come into close personal contact during the Plague Year. From this angle, one can easily visualize the great risks of contagious infection which the majority of these bishops daily incurred. The increased mortality among the royal coroners is evidence of this risk. But one of the great perplexities of this bewildering Plague in England lies in the remarkable escape of the bench of bishops from the fatal effects of the Black Death; for two sees only were vacant out of seventeen. And what is applicable in Trillek's case, is true, in a greater or lesser degree, in the case of the others." I must confess myself unable to follow this conclusion, even though we had no more evidence before us than these bare itineraries. Indeed, Dr Lunn himself seems to take away from the bishops, with one hand, that which he grants with the other. We may not unfairly compare a calamity of this magnitude to the sudden outburst of a great war, and these bishops to the superior officers of an army. Surely something more is demanded, in both cases, than this testimonial of "nothing to differentiate", and "everything went on as usual". Sometimes we find, indeed, definitely less than usual, when such a prelate as Grandisson stayed away four months longer than usual from his own city of Exeter, and lay in a great moorland manor where, even though the mortality were worst in the villages around, he and his household would avoid all the worst risks, except in so far as a bishop's ordinary routine work was dangerous. But is it not easy to exaggerate that danger? The business of institution could well have been carried on in a great hall, with bishop and clerks at one end and candidate at the other, except for a very brief space of personal contact. Indeed, it might have been arranged in even more distant fashion than this. So, again, with the 1231 clerks whom Trillek ordained. The ceremony would take place in a cathedral or some other spacious church, attended by scarcely any miscellaneous congregation, and with only a moment or two of personal contact in each case with a candidate who was not specially likely to spread infection. It cannot be compared with the coroner's work, faced with a corpse and a miscellaneous gathering in a far smaller and more probably infected building; still less with that of a devoted priest beside one deathbed after another. Dr Lunn's own conscientious statistics would seem to suggest very plain reasons why, when more than 40 per cent. of the beneficed clergy were dying, only 12 per cent. died from the episcopal bench. For a great deal of fuller evidence, see my *Black Death*, 51–60. There are 22 chroniclers, English and foreign, who mention the behaviour of the priests at all, for good or evil: I do not reckon here those who might be taken to condemn them by implication, as when a Pisan chronicler writes "all men fled from death". The only really definite favourable testimonial is from Catania, where it is said "the priests did not in any way fear to go to the sick men's houses through *excessive fear of death*". No other among the eight most favourable witnesses goes so far as this; and two of them contrast the real self-sacrifice of friars with the flight or timid negligence of the parish priests. Of the remaining frankly unfavourable chroniclers, most give the same sort of evidence as Birchington: e.g. "even the priests and doctors fled in fear from the sick and dead": "the

CHAPTER XXXVIII (pp. 493–506) *continued*

pope, shut up in his own chamber, wherein great fires were constantly burning, gave access to no man." For all these witnesses we must of course make the same allowance for medieval exaggeration which we have made repeatedly on other subjects. But, looking carefully at each, we must see that such a discount would render their testimony almost unanimous. If for the "all" of these unfavourable witnesses we substitute "the majority", that statement will be contradicted by only one, or perhaps two, of the more favourable testimonies. We must remember, again, that nearly all the 22 witnesses are themselves clerics testifying to the behaviour of their own order, and that (as St Thomas More frankly acknowledged) the temptation of clannishness was very strong among the clergy. True, there were often strong jealousies also: but we cannot suppose that (to take a few instances) the Carmelite of Paris, and the Canon of Bruges, and the Bishop of Strassburg's chaplain, and the Lombard cardinal's nephew, and the Dominican of Pisa slandered the parish clergy with wholesale and gratuitous falsehoods; and that only one or two writers could be found to oppose these slanders plainly: indeed, such an excuse would only cast a darker shade upon medieval society. Dr Lunn, in a later communication, has convinced me that, with regard to the refusal or resignation of benefices, I have not drawn a sufficiently clear distinction between the days when the plague was actually raging and those later weeks or months during which the deaths seem to have ceased. But, however clearly we may try to draw this line, it seems impossible to rule out the influence of fear for some considerable time after men were no longer dying all around. Moreover, my main point is unaffected; viz. that the clergy lost seriously in public respect. For we can scarcely suppose that those priests who suffered parishioners to die without the Sacraments were less criticized when they had mercenary motives than if they had been driven away by fear. With regard to the Bishops, he points out that it would be difficult to find any on the Continent who did more than his English brethren for visitation or relief of the sick. That is quite true; the Pope took the most elaborate precautions to cut himself off from the whole of his flock. But here, again, the fact rather strengthens my main thesis, that the clergy lost so much ground in the Black Death as to explain a great deal of the anticlericalism which confessedly influenced the later Middle Ages. (8) H. Wharton, *Anglia Sacra*, I. 42 and 375–6. Each of these authors writes of his own diocese. Birchington was a Canterbury monk almost or quite contemporary with the plague: the first "edition" of his chronicle breaks off at 1367 (Wharton, xx). Dene was a notary in the service of a distinguished bishop, Hamo of Hythe (*ibid.* xxxiii), who ruled from 1319 to 1352. His chronicle extends in its present form from 1314 to 1350 (the last 8 years seem to be lost); he is therefore in the strictest sense contemporary with what he records. It should be noted how seriously Cardinal Gasquet minimizes these two men's plain evidence (*Gt Pestilence*, 105; *Black Death*, 93). (9) B, *Prologue*, 83. (10) For the loose sense in which the phrases *facere* or *conficere Corpus Christi* were used, even by theologians, see correspondence in *The Times* from Dec. 12, 1924 to Jan. 3, 1925. Abbot Ford, by far the most learned of the correspondents, appealed not very successfully to pagan classical usage; for his authorities, Cicero and Virgil, writing of altar-sacrifices, used *facere* quite differently, not with the accusative but with the ablative. Moreover, we sometimes find, in this matter of priestly privilege, the most startling language from great writers. St Norbert, Archbishop of Magdeburg and founder of the Great Premonstratensian Order, says in one of his sermons "O priest, thou art not thyself, for thou art a god"—O Sacerdos, tu non es tu, quia deus es (Ch. Taiée, *Prémontré*, I. 155). In the fourteenth century, Peter of Palermo (Petrus Hieremiae), in his *Lententide Sermons*, put the priest even above the Virgin Mary, since she cannot absolve sinners as he does after confession (*Quadragesimale*, Sermon xx). (11) *Piers Plowman*, B, VI. 336. (12) B. H. Putnam, *Statute of Labourers*, 169. (13) Traill, *Social*

CHAPTER XXXVIII (pp. 493–506) *continued*

England (illustrated ed.), II. 322, 532, 570, 753. Mr H. E. Bell of the Public Record Office has worked out the statistics of parochial institutions apart from exchanges and resignations—a pretty safe index of mortality—in two dioceses, for (A) 1348–50 and (B) 1361–2 respectively. Exeter A 435; B 253. Hereford A 190; B 65 [record slightly incomplete]. Compare Prof. A. Hamilton Thompson on "Pestilences of the Fourteenth Cent. in Dioc. York" (*Archaeol. Journal*, vol. LXXV).

CHAPTER XXXIX (pp. 507–518)

(1) For this subject the most valuable monograph is that of S. Luce, *La Jeunesse de Bertrand du Guesclin*. The Globe Froissart gives the atmosphere vividly, in spite of Froissart's frequent inaccuracies of detail. (2) Luce, *l.c.* 125 ff. (3) *Med. Vill.* 342. (4) H. Pirenne, *Econom. and Soc. Hist. of Med. Europe*, 98, 100. (5) *Mémoires* (ed. Buchon), 139 a. (6) *Social Life*, 33, 510. (7) *Mémoires* (ed. Buchon), 136 a.

CHAPTER XL (pp. 519–533)

(1) *Piers Plowman*, B, XX. 60 (cf. *Five Centuries of Religion*, II. 282). Friars and monks joined in with Antichrist for the sake of filthy lucre,

> "And all the convent forth cam to welcome that tyraunt,
> And alle hise, as wel as hym, saue onlich folis;
> Which folis were well leuer to deye than to lyue loyalty
> Lenger, sith leuté was so rebuked,
> And a fals fende antecriste ouer alle folke regned."

(2) *Archiv f. Litt.- und Kirchengesch.* II. 641 ff. (3) W. R. Inge, *Christian Mysticism*, ch. IV. (4) E.E.T.S. vol. 20. (5) Evelyn Underhill in *Camb. Med. Hist.* VII. 804–7. (6) An admirable edition of this remarkable autobiography, reasonably modernized in spelling, etc. for the ordinary reader, has just been published by the owner of the unique MS., Col. Bowden-Butler. (7) See L. Capéran, *Le Problème du salut des infidèles* (1934), especially pp. 184 ff. (8) *Naissance de l'esprit laïque*, II. 223. (9) *Comentum* (ed. Lacaita), V. 39. (10) Here is the original in Orm's own spelling. Throughout the poem, he makes a *short* syllable by doubling the consonant:

> "Forrþrihht se Jesuss fullhtnedd wass,
> He wennde himm inntill wesste.
> Þe Goddspell sezzþ þatt he wass ledd
> Þurrh Gast inntill þe wesste,
> Annd þatt forr þatt he shollde þaer
> Beon fandedd þurrh þe deofell.
> Crist bilae i wessteland,
> Forr þatt he wollde fasstenn,
> He toc þa to fasstenn þaer
> Þaer he wass i þe wesste.
> All wiþþutenn mete & drinnch
> Heold Crist hiss fasste þaere
> Fowwerrtiz dazhess azz onnan
> Bi dazhess, & bi nahhtess.
> Whanne hiss fasste forþedd wass
> Þa lisste himm affterr fode."

(*Ormulum* (ed. R. Holt, 1878), II. 39.)

(11) E.E.T.S. vol. 49, p. 95. (12) E.E.T.S. (1867), 5, 7. (13) *Piers Plowman*, C, IV. 51; cf. A, III. 49, B, III. 48.

CHAPTER XLI (pp. 534–554)

(1) B, x. 300.   (2) B, x. 317.   (3) B, v. 172, 460.   (4) B, xi. 371.
(5) C, vi. 92.   (6) B, ix. 158; xi. 16, 45; xv. 3 ff., 48; xvi. 3; cf. A, xii. 6.
(7) B, xiii. 135.   (8) B, xi. 336. This illustration of the magpie had already
been used by two distinguished Parisian philosophers in the early thirteenth
century: Bishop Guillaume d'Auvergne (*Opp.* 1674, i. 1058) and Guillaume
d'Auxerre (*In Sent.* Regnault [1505], 758): "artificium picae, quo compingit
nidum suum, quem nemo carpentariorum vel architectorum effigiare potest."
(9) B, xiii. 440.   (10) B, xi. 180.   (11) B, vii. 105.   (12) B, vi. 25, 117.
(13) B, v. 517.   (14) B, i. 5.   (15) B, i. 71.   (16) B, ii. 5.   (17) B, vii.
106; but see the whole of this passus.   (18) Hen. a Gandavo, *Quodlibeta*
(Venice, 1613), ii. 388 a, 390 c, 391 a (*Quod.* xv, quaest. xiv).   (19) B, x. 101;
cf. 52.   (20) Gerson, *Opera* (1606), ii. 556 a, 649 b.   (21) B, xx. 212.
(22) Jeremiah v. 30.   (23) *Blue Book on Malta* (1930), 48.

CHAPTER XLII (pp. 555–572)

(1) For this subject the reader should consult W. R. Lethaby, *Westminster and
the King's Craftsmen*; D. Knoop and G. P. Jones, *The Medieval Mason* (the first
full exploitation of the rich documentary evidence by two writers whose artistic
interest is reinforced by special competence in economic history). The present
chapter is mainly a summary from my own *Art and the Reformation*.   (2) *Art
and Ref.* 133.   (3) *P.L.* cxlii. 651.   (4) *St F. to D.* (2nd ed.), 65, 366.
(5) *Art and Ref.* ch. v, esp. 95 ff.   (6) *Ibid.* 73–4.   (7) *Ibid.* 65 ff.   (8) *Ibid.*
59 ff.   (9) *An Introduction to Freemasonry*, by Prof. D. Knoop and Mr G. P.
Jones, teachers of Economics and Econ. Hist. at Sheffield University (Manch.
Univ. Press, 1937). See especially pp. 62 ff.   (10) *Comentum* (ed. Lacaita), iii.
309.   (11) *Art and Ref.* 88.   (12) *Ibid.* 93.   (13) *Ibid.* 132.   (14) *Ibid.*
287.   (15) *Ibid.* 99 ff.   (16) *Iliad*, vi. 208.   (17) *Camb. Ant. Soc. Trans.*
(1869), 64 ff.   (18) *Dives and Pauper*, Com. i, c. 51 *ad fin.*

CHAPTER XLIII (pp. 573–589)

(1) For Sindolf see *Life in M.A.* iv. 52–7. The other writer, Brother Ludwig of
Wessobrunn in Bavaria, ended his copyist's work with three pathetic verses:
"The book which you now see was written in the outer seats [of the cloister];
while I wrote I froze; and, what I could not write by the beams of day, I finished
by candle-light." (Wattenbach, *Schriftwesen des Mittelalters* (1896), 287; cf. 518.)
(2) *Opera* (R.S.), i. 72; cf. Rashdall, *Universities* (1st ed.), ii. 341.   (3) T. G.
Law, *Collected Essays* (1904), 7.   (4) *P.L.* clxxii. 1148; Bromyard, *Sum.
Pred.* E, iii. 24; E. K. Chambers, *Med. Stage*, i. 28 ff.   (5) See *Rutebeuf*, by
Prof. L. Cledat; a study of a typical *jongleur*.   (6) Mary Darmesteter's
Froissart (Hachette, 1894) is an admirable biography of this poet-chronicler.
(7) His works are published by the E.E.T.S. (vols. 72–3).

CHAPTER XLIV (pp. 590–613)

(1) *Fulk Fitzwarine* (King's Classics), 42.   (2) *La Chevalerie*, 681–3.   (3)
Social Life, 400.   (4) *Ibid.* 396; so also for *Mén. de Paris*.   (5) *Depos.
Durham* (S.S. 1845), 20–1.   (6) *I walked by Night*, edited by Miss Haggard.
(7) T. Wright, *Womankind in Western Europe*, 245.   (8) *St F. to D.* (2nd ed.),
98 ff.   (9) *Social Life*, 497.   (10) Abbé Fleury, *Hist. Écclésiastique*, an. 1264.
(11) J. Brand, *Popular Antiquities* (ed. Bohn), i. 506.   (12) *Med. Vill.* 267.
(13) *Reg. Grandisson*, ii. 1055, 1120.   (14) *Jus Eccles.* pars ii. tit. xvii. c. 5.

CHAPTER XLV (pp. 614–628)

(1) L. Finkelstein, *Jewish Self-Government in the M.A.* (1924), 217. (2) MS. Royal 6 E. VI, f. 214a; *Life in M.A.* III. 119. (3) Gratian, *Decretum*, pars II, causa XXXIII, q. 5, cc. 11 to 19. (4) *Utopia* (ed. Lumby, 1879), 87, 124, 156. (5) Gautier, *La Chevalerie*, 350; Alwyn Schultz, *Höfisches Leben*, I. 163. (6) E.E.T.S. (1868), 25. (7) W. Stubbs, *Const. Hist.* III. 438 (chap. xx). (8) *Rotuli Parliamentorum*, II. 239a and III. 218a. (9) Pollock and Maitland, *Hist. Eng. Law* (1st ed.), II. 429. (10) *Ibid.* I. 467; Crump and Jacob, *Legacy of the M.A.* 349. (11) Pollock and Maitland, *l.c.* II. 504. (12) *Rot. Parl.* IV. 158a. (13) H. T. Riley, *Memorials*, 277; *Social Life*, 455; *Legacy of the M.A.* 412. (14) *Legacy of the M.A.* 412. (15) *Social Life*, 455. (16) *Rot. Parl.* v. 112b; *Economic Journal* (June 1916), 285. (17) Lyndwood, *Provinciale* (1679), append. 155; *Social Life*, 455. (18) *Paston Letters* (1900), I. 89. (19) G. F. Browne, *Importance of Women in Anglo-Saxon Times*, 19. (20) *Prediche Volgari*, III. 176; *Chaucer and his England*, 215. (21) *Robertus Richardinus* (Scot. Hist. Soc. 1936), 112, 114–15. (22) Crump and Jacob, *Legacy of the M.A.* 401–2. (23) Gratian, *Decretum*, pars II, causa XXVII, q. I, c. 14. Therefore French law, until the Revolution, made it a capital offence: see C. L. Richard, *Analysis Conciliorum* (1778), IV. 135. (24) Gratian, *Decretum*, pars I, dist. XIII, c. 2. (25) More, *English Works* (1557), 136: "Ye be wiser I wote well, than the gentlewoman was, which in talking once with my father whan she harde saye that our Lady was a Jew, first could not beleve it, but saide, what ye mock I wis, I pray you tel trouth. And whan it was so fully affermed that she at last bileved it, was she a Jewe quod she, so help me God and halidom I shall love her the worse while I live." (26) Renan, *Averroës*, 161. (27) Pierre Dubois, *De Recuperatione*, 79 ff. (28) *Social Life*, 456. (29) Tyndale's *Answer to Sir T. More's Dialogue* (Parker Soc.), 18. (30) *Chaucer and his England*, 220. (31) *Legacy of the M.A.* 407. (32) T. Wright, *Womankind in Western Europe*, 158–9. (33) Erasmus, Ep. 65 (*Opera*, III. i. 56). (34) *Social Life*, 450. (35) *Ibid.* 434. (36) T. Wright, *l.c.* 223, 230. (37) *P.L.* CXCIX. 393.

CHAPTER XLVI (pp. 629–646)

(1) T. Wright, *Womankind in Western Europe*, 47. (2) S. Baluze, *Miscellanea*, IV. 383. (3) Pollock and Maitland, *Hist. Eng. Law*, II. 437; cf. I. 482–5. (4) *Legacy of the M.A.* 414. (5) Pollock and Maitland, *l.c.* II. 391. (6) *Opera* (1704), v. 650. (7) Pollock and Maitland, *l.c.* II. 392. (8) *Salt Collections*, VIII. 134. (9) *Ibid.* 135. (10) *Cal. Early Chancery Cases*, I. 82. (11) *Médecin Malgré lui*, II. 2. (12) R. W. Chambers, *Sir Thomas More* (1935), 95; cf. Erasmus, Ep. 447 (*Opera*, VI. 475). (13) *In IV Sent.* dist. 26, q. 3. (14) *Opera* (1704), v. 677. (15) *Chaucer and his England*, 109. (16) *Ibid.* 205; L. Gautier, *La Chevalerie*, 352; compare T. Wright, *l.c.* 176. (17) Addis and Arnold, *Catholic Dictionary* (10th ed. by Dr Scannell), 554. (18) *P.L.* CVI. 189. (19) *P.L.* CXLIV. 283–5. (20) *Ibid.* 164; cf. 93. (21) T. Wright, *l.c.* 166. (22) *Summa Predicantium*, A, XVII, § 3. (23) B, II. 60; XV. 236; XX. 135. (24) *Mirour de l'Omme*, ll. 18,461 ff. (25) *Opera* (1704), v. 627, 641, 666, 670. (26) Pollard, *Henry VIII* (1905), 207. I give the evidence more fully in *Jesuits and the Middle Ages*, 27–8 (Wessex Press, Taunton, 6d. post-free). (27) *Utopia* (ed. Lumby), 123. (28) *Opera* (1704), VI. 476 (letter 447). (29) *Depos. Durham* (S.S. 1845), 26 ff. (30) *Reg. Romeyn*, I. 70. (31) *Reg. Stapeldon*, 169 (A.D. 1319); *Chaucer and his England*, 181. (32) *Memorials of K. Hen. VII* (R.S.), 223 ff. (33) Froissart (tr. Berners, 1812), II. 11.

CHAPTER XLVII (pp. 647–663)

(1) Rashdall, *Universities* (1st ed.), II. 538. As he points out, Nominalism was the less idealistic of the two rival currents in medieval philosophy. The pure Realist followed Plato, and interpreted him in the extremest sense: everything here on earth has its prototype in idea, that is, in the mind of God. A jest founded upon this extreme realism may be found in my *St Francis to Dante* (2nd ed. 90). To the Realist, therefore, the general was more real than the particular; the colour *white* or *black* was more real than a white or black horse. To the extreme Nominalist, on the other hand, the particular thing is the reality, and genera, species, or qualities are mere words which we coin to describe them. The tide of controversy in the schools oscillated between these two extremes throughout the Middle Ages, following in general, as might be expected, a middle course. But William of Ockham was a strong Nominalist; and his tenets, though condemned by Rome, were on the whole the dominant tenets of later Scholasticism. (2nd ed. I. 40; II. 263.)   (2) *Fasc. Zizaniorum* (R.S.), 307; Rashdall in *Dict. Nat. Biog., Wyclif*, 226.   (3) B, X. 52, 100.   (4) B, VI. 46.   (5) B, III. 76.   (6) B, XI. 192.   (7) B, XIX. 34.   (8) Gierke, *Polit. Theories* (trans. Maitland), 323. (9) *Life in M.A.* III. 62.   (10) *Comentum* (ed. Lacaita, I. 579) on *Inf.* XVII. 52. (11) Nicole Bozon (ed. Toulmin Smith), 35; *St F. to D.* (2nd ed.), 340. (12) *Town Life in Fifteenth Century*, II. 32.   (13) *Ibid.* I. 18.   (14) Especially 87 ff., 127–8. This valuable volume comes most opportunely as the 100th publication of the Oxford Historical Society.   (15) G. de Lagarde, *Naissance de l'esprit laïque*, II. 91. My other quotations from this author are from the same volume, pp. 189, 193, 328.   (16) Statute of 1 Hen. VII, c. 4.   (17) Gasquet, *The Eve of the Reformation* (1900), 339: "it was popular government in a true sense that then regulated all parochial matters. Every adult of both sexes had a voice in this system of government." Compare the same author's Catholic Truth Society pamphlet, *The Layman in the Pre-Reformation Parish*, 71: "The entire management of these parish funds was in the hands of the people." The Rt Hon. J. F. Hope, as a Roman Catholic layman, recently ventured to suggest some sort of reversion to this state of things; but he was at once put into his place by the Rt Rev. Mgr Provost Moriarty (*Catholic Herald*, March 2nd, 1929; *Catholic Times*, March 15th; *Universe*, March 20th). The result was a pamphlet by Mr W. Woollen, *The Layman in the Parish* (Sands and Co. 6*d.*), in which the evidence is fairly stated. Similar evidence is given by Miss A. Abram (*English Life and Manners in the later M.A.* 102): "In the 15th century municipal authorities took a prominent part in the provision and administration of poor relief. At Sandwich, the burgesses controlled two hospitals, and at Rye and other towns money for charitable purposes was supplied by municipal funds. In Lydd corn was distributed at Easter and Christmas. The 'almys' of the town of Southampton 'were settled on a plan', and lists were kept of the weekly payments: in 1441 they amounted each week to £4. 2*s.* 1*d.*, a sum which was then large enough to relieve about a hundred and fifty people. The Corporation of Reading expended payments made for the use of the town weights and scales upon the poor and infirm. The arrangements managed by the civic officials were of a more practical and business-like character than the picturesque but indiscriminate charity of wealthy nobles and monasteries, and when it became necessary for the State to organize poor-relief, it took many hints from them." Strong evidence in the same direction has lately been published by Dr W. J. Marx, of Mount St Joseph College, *The Development of Charity in Medieval Louvain* (1936). His last chapter describes in full the "Passing of Control from Church to Town" in the century and a half before the Reformation.   (18) A. F. Leach, *Educational Charters and Documents* (introd. xxxviii).   (19) J. H. Lupton, *John Colet*, 166–7.   (20) L. Dacheux, *Jean*

CHAPTER XLVII (pp. 647–663) *continued*

Geiler, 55, 90.   (21) R. L. Poole, *Illustrations of Medieval Thought* (S.P.C.K.), 68.   (22) *Opera Inedita* (R.S.), 92, 351, 424, 434–5, 464–6, 474.   (23) H. Maxwell-Lyte, *Hist. Univ. Oxford*, 434 ff.   (24) *Ibid.* 437.   (25) *Ibid.* 433. (26) Fisher's *English Works* (E.E.T.S. 1876).

CHAPTER XLVIII (pp. 664–680)

(1) While fully sensible of the extraordinary value of Prof. R. W. Chambers's *Sir Thomas More*, which is likely long to remain the standard work on this subject, I am bound to express dissent from his tendency to minimize the critical value of *Utopia*, and to find therein more orthodox Roman Catholicism than the book really shows. Considering More's personal experiences, and the circumstances of his time, it would be little short of a miracle if this man, however great, should have retained in his later years the freedom of a young man's outlook, or that More the chancellor and religious polemist should have been wholly consistent with More the intimate friend of Erasmus and the admired Oxford or London wit. As to More's responsibility for Erasmus's *Praise of Folly*, Froude seems to describe it with little or no exaggeration in his *Erasmus*, pp. 196, 202. (2) *Utopia* (ed. Lumby), 131 ff.   (3) "Machiavelli und Morus", in *Menschen die Geschichte machten*, 217.   (4) *Internat. Journ. Ethics* (Jan. 1915), 134. He writes: "if we are to judge by results, we cannot regret that such wars have taken place." Again, in *Which Way to Peace?* (1936, p. 51), he writes: "There have been wars that have done good—for example, the American War of Independence, and, to take a case where no legal pretext existed, Caesar's conquest of Gaul."   (5) For instance Jean Jaurès, *L'Armée Nouvelle*, translated and summarized in *Democracy and Military Service* (72 Kimberley Road, Cambridge, 1s.).   (6) *Utopia* (ed. Lumby), 132.   (7) *Ibid.* 146.   (8) *Ibid.* 155–9.   (9) *Ibid.* 106.   (10) Aquinas writes (*Summa Theol.* 2ᵃ, 2ᵃᵉ, q. xi, art. 3): "for it is far worse to corrupt the faith, through which cometh the soul's life, than to coin false money, whereby our earthly life is sustained. Wherefore, if forgers of money or other malefactors are justly handed over to immediate death by worldly princes, much more may heretics, from the moment they are convicted of heresy, be not only excommunicated but also justly slain.... Arius was but a single spark in Alexandria; but, since he was not forthwith extinguished, the flame of him ravaged the whole world." More, in his later life, not only equated heresy with murder but even, once at least, judged it as definitely worse (*English Works* (1557), 901; cf. 209, 210, 995). His attitude towards married priests, in those later days, is even less consonant with his *Utopia*; e.g. *English Works*, 485: "For sith the marriage is no marriage, it is but whoredom itself. And I am sure also that it defileth the priest more than double and treble whoredom, sith that his marriage being, as it is, unlawful, and thereby none other but whoredom, doth openly rebuke and shame the sacraments." A priest, by public marriage in church, "cometh there to bind himself to shameless perpetual whoredom".   (11) *Utopia*, *l.c.* 144.   (12) G. de Lagarde, *Naissance de l'esprit laïque*, II. 16.   (13) *Letters and Papers of Henry VIII*, IV. 6199; VI. 1164, 1249; A. F. Pollard, *Henry VIII*, 332: "He told Chapuys that if Charles invaded England he would be doing 'a work as agreeable to God as going against the Turk', and suggested that the Emperor should make use of Reginald Pole 'to whom, according to many, the kingdom would belong'" (Chapuys to Charles, 27th September, 1533). Again, says Chapuys, 'the holy Bishop of Rochester would like you to take active measures immediately, as I wrote in my last; which advice he has sent to me again lately to repeat' (10th October)."   (14) The

CHAPTER XLVIII (pp. 664–680) *continued*

bull is printed in Bp Burnet's *Reformation* (Records, part I, Bk III, § 9; ed. 1841, II. lxxiii).   (15) R. W. Chambers, *Sir Thomas More*, 330.   (16) I deal more fully with this episode in *Inquisition and Freedom* (1937).   (17) O. Meyer, *England and the Catholic Church under Elizabeth*, 157–62.

CHAPTER XLIX (pp. 681–694)

(1) Migne, *Patrologia Graeca*, LIX. 324 (serm. XL in Joh.); cf. 235, 346. (2) E. Brown, *Fasciculus*, II. 474.   (3) Neander, *Church History* (Bohn), III. 181. (4) G. de Lagarde, *Naissance de l'esprit laïque*, II. 70–5.   (5) Marsilius (ed. Previté-Orton), 112, 281.   (6) Ullmann, *Reformers before the Reformation* (Eng. ed.), II. 349.   (7) More's *Dialogue*, Bk III, chs. 14–16. Again, in his *Confutation of Tyndale's Answer*, he condemns all the translations lately made of the Psalter, Primer, and New Testament into English. He adds "which books, albeit that they neither can be there printed without great cost, nor here sold without great adventure and peril, yet cease they not with money sent from hence, to print them there [abroad] and send them hither by the whole vats full at once, and in some places, looking for no lucre, cast them abroad by night, so great a pestilent pleasure have some devilish people caught, with the labour, travail, cost, charge, peril, harm, and hurt of themselves, to seek the destruction of others. As the devil hath a deadly delight to beguile good people, and bring their souls into everlasting torment, without any manner winning, and not without final increase of his eternal pain; so do these heretics, the devil's disciples, set their whole pleasure and study to their own final damnation, in the training of simple souls to hell by their devilish heresies" (*English Works*, 344). More's attitude is fully and excellently discussed by Miss M. Deanesly in different places of her *Lollard Bible* (see index).   (8) F. M. Powicke, *Christian Life in the M.A.* 83.   (9) Grosse-teste's *Letters* (R.S.), 317; E. K. Chambers, *Med. Stage*, II. 98; Creizenach in *Camb. Hist. Eng. Lit.* IV. 37.   (10) *Handlyng Synne* (E.E.T.S.), l. 1303. (11) T. Wright and J. O. Halliwell, *Reliquiae Antiquae*, II. 45.   (12) *York Mem. Book* (S.S.), II. cxxv; cf. XLIX. 124, 245. For this absurd legend of Fergus see L. Toulmin Smith, *York Mystery Plays*, xxviii ff. I give fuller evidence, with a woodcut from a panel at Notre-Dame-de-Paris, in my *Life in the Middle Ages*, II. 139–41. Fergus, or Belzeray, was a wicked Jew who laid hands upon the Virgin Mary's bier when she was carried to her tomb, and whose hands miraculously clave to the wood and broke off from his own arms. The full story is in *The Golden Legend* (Temple Classics, IV. 239).   (13) A. W. Pollard, *Fifteenth Century Prose and Verse*, 99 ff.   (14) W. W. Capes, *English Church in Fourteenth and Fifteenth Centuries*, 209.   (15) M. Deanesly, *Lollard Bible*, 117, 122 ff. It is necessary here to expose the inexplicable misstatement in the Preface to the current Roman *Index of Prohibited Books*, published by Cardinal Merry del Val in the name of a Pope who has filled one of the greatest librarian's posts in Europe (1929, p. xi). This Preface stigmatizes as a mere calumny the idea that "the Church put obstacles in the way of printing and using the Bible in the vulgar tongue". In disproof of this "calumny", it is asserted that "during the 70 years which elapsed between the invention of printing and the publication of Luther's German version, more than 200 editions of the Scriptures [*della Scrittura*] in various vernacular [*correnti*] languages, duly approved by the Church, were spread among the people." This total is evidently arrived at by reckoning as "la Scrittura" such piecemeal publications as a Psalter or a "Plenary" (i.e. the Epistles and Gospels used at Mass). The assertion "approved by the Church" is still more inconsistent with the actual facts.   (16) Printed in full by J. Jortin, *Erasmus*, II. 678.   (17) *Opp.* (1706), VII (Prefatory matter to vols. VI and VII).

CHAPTER L (pp. 695–704)

(1) The best book on this subject is still that of R. G. Moulton, *The Literary Study of the Bible* (1906).   (2) E. Michael, *Salimbene und seine Chronik* (Innsbruck, 1889), 123.   (3) B. F. Westcott, *Hist. Eng. Bible* (2nd ed.), 82. (4) Quoted in *Camb. Hist. Eng. Lit.* IV. 42.

CHAPTER LI (pp. 705–719)

(1) B, I. 7.   (2) See my *Medieval Study*, XIX, "Mr Belloc as Historian" (72 Kimberley Road, Cambridge, 6d. post-free), 4.   (3) Foxe's *Martyrs* (Parker Soc. 1844), III. 594; *Social Life*, 462.   (4) A. Jessopp, *Diocesan Hist. Norwich* (S.P.C.K.), 148.   (5) Tyndale's *Answer to More* (Parker Soc. 1850), 97. (6) Some readers may be glad to have further details of Erasmus's agreement on many points with Margery Backster, with references. *Pilgrimages, or Becket,* Ep. 592 (Jortin, *Erasmus*, II. 194, 207). *Bishops* (Jortin, II. 226). *Bible*-reading by the unlearned he constantly advocated, and reprobated its prohibition. As to *Images and Saints,* he points out in "The Praise of Folly" that the first Christians "prayed to God: they did not know that to pray to a figure drawn with charcoal on a wall would be equally efficacious". Compare Ep. 1072 (c. 1227): "while our churches are filled everywhere with unseemly [*indecoris*] paintings, we are falling almost into idolatry of these superstitions"; cf. Jortin, II. 198: "These things are remnants of ancient paganism" and Ep. 974 (c. 1104). *Fasting,* Ep. 974 (c. 1100, A.D. 1528): "In France, as men write [to me], two men are in danger [of death? *periclitantur*] for no other cause than that, compelled by sickness, they have eaten flesh on two days in Lent"; cf. Jortin, II. 210. *Clerical morals and impurity*; he speaks of "those who by artifice or by fear are thrust into celibacy, so that they have licence to fornicate [*scortari liceat*] but not to marry: thus, if they profess concubinage, they are Catholic priests, but, if they prefer to take wives, they are cast into the fire" (Jortin, II. 206; cf. 214: "nowadays the number of incontinent priests is so enormous [*ingens*] as contrasted with such rarity of those who live chastely"). *Monastic morals* are attacked with equal force. (7) Jortin, *Erasmus*, II. 226. Compare the quotations from Sir John Fortescue printed in my *Social Life*, 31.   (8) Cf. his *Paraphrase on St Matthew xxiii.* 27 and F. Seebohm, *Oxford Reformers* (Everyman), 179 ff.   (9) *Opp.* (1703), I. 787 ff.; cf. 800–2, X. 502.   (10) *Opera*, X. 1202 ff. The reference to Jews in my text is reinforced by a passage elsewhere (note on Matt. xi. 30, *Opera*, VI) where Erasmus points out a text from St Augustine, who complained that the Church, even in his day, had so many petty observances "that it is more intolerable than the condition of the Jews, who, though they have not recognized the days of [Christian] liberty, are yet subjected to burdens of [God's] law, not to human presumptions". In this letter to the Bishop of Basel he points out how such superfluous traditions defeat their own purpose. "On no day are the kitchens more busy than on a fish-day, nor is the elaboration ever greater or the expense heavier. The upshot is, that poor folk hunger, and the rich live even more delicately. Who would not rather eat a silurus (which the common folk call *sturgeon*) or a trout or lamprey, than smoked swine-flesh or mutton?... To forbid flesh in regions where fish are rare is in effect to decree famine.... Nowadays St Paul's saying is everywhere fulfilled: *One is hungry and another is drunken.* To the rich, change of food is a pleasure and a relief from monotony: nor do they ever lead a more delightful life than when they abstain from flesh food. Meanwhile, however, the indigent husbandman, gnawing a raw root or a leek, adds this as a seasoning to his black bran-bread; and, instead of the rich man's wine, he drinks buttermilk, or pond-water, while with unceasing sweat of his brow he scarce maintains his wife and little children and the rest of his household.... It

CHAPTER LI (pp. 705-719) *continued*

may be pleaded: 'If any man be aggrieved by these things, he hath a remedy: let him buy permission to eat from the pope at Rome.' Very true: but not all men have the opportunity or the money to buy an indulgence of this kind: and here, again, the upshot is the same; the rich man, who most needed a flesh-prohibition, who most needed to fast, commonly enjoys relaxation of this decree, while the grievous yoke presses only upon the humble poor man." If relaxation is just at all, let the parish priest have that power, for he knows his man; and let it be granted without fee. The parson has rights of absolution from far worse offences than this: "if he be unfit to grant dispensation in these slight cases, then the fault lies with the bishop who has committed Christ's flock to such a man." The tyrant Dionysius of Syracuse imposed a network of laws, with the set purpose of reaping rich revenues from the multitude who would certainly break them; therefore "for the purity of Church discipline, it would be most advantageous that no just relaxation should be sold for money, and that the power were committed to those who know the man". Moreover, priests and bishops sometimes preach that violation is actually a mortal sin; that the fast-breaker will go to hell. To this Erasmus recurs over and over again in this treatise. "God", he pleads, "is not so severe or irritable as that he should, for any fault, cast those into hell whom He hath redeemed with His own blood." Yet "the bishops, whose office it is to defend men with the sword of God's word, claim for the sake of food and drink, which Christ hath put into our own power, that whosoever breaketh their decree goeth utterly to hell.... Paul is indignant that any man should judge his brother in the matter of meat and drink; and shall I for the sake of these things thrust my brother into hell?... The flesh-eater we execrate as though he had ceased to be a Christian, though the Gospel forbiddeth us to judge any man in things not évil in themselves.... Certainly he who condemneth his brother, who revileth him and bringeth railing accusation against him, sinneth against both Gospel teaching and the Pauline precept; and, in my opinion, his is a more grievous trespass than if he ate flesh for ten years on end. Men call flesh-eaters *Lutherans* and *heretics*: but to speak thus is to gnaw the flesh not of calves but of our own brother. Which is the greater crime? Yet no man is troubled in spirit by that which the Gospels and St Paul forbid, while we are as horrified in these matters which human custom hath brought in, above and beyond the Gospel teaching, as if the whole Christian religion were about to fall at one stroke!" (11) *Opp.* x. 512. (12) Jortin, *Erasmus*, II. 170, 668. (13) *Ibid.* 670-3, 686. (14) *English Works* (1557), 873, 937. (15) *Encyc. Brit.* IX. 731. (16) G. Durandus, *De Modo Generalis Concilii habendi* (Paris, 1671), II. 10, 46. (17) It was under Clement VII, the Pope who negotiated with Henry VIII, that the earliest surviving census of the city of Rome was made (1527). The total population was a little over 55,000. The document is specially valuable as giving the households one by one, with the number of souls in each, and usually the occupier's profession and place of origin. The editor notes how the clergy and papal courtiers were mainly congregated in the three districts of Borgo, Ponte, and Parione, where twenty of the cardinals had their palaces, the remaining five being scattered over eleven other districts. Concerning these three specially clerical districts he writes: "In these, which were populated mainly by celibates, it was natural that there should be a greater number of courtesans, who however abounded in the other districts also. In most cases they are not distinguished here, as in [another census], by their professional title; but all these single women may be easily recognized by their plain *noms de guerre*—Imperia, Lucrezia, Giulia, Alessandra, Pipa, Nanna—with the country of their origin." In the first half-column of Borgo, for instance, we find that Baldassena has indeed a trade, of spice-seller; but there are three others registered simply as "Lucia of Bologna,

CHAPTER LI (pp. 705–719) continued

Isabel of Rome, Gabriela of Cremona", side by side with "Raphael the Jew". In this, which was the quarter of the Vatican Palace, 155 out of the 563 houses are thus kept by single women. For the whole city, with its 9285 houses, 1455 are similarly occupied. In many cases the census records their origin: 816 from different parts of Italy and 272 from abroad. These last range from 116 Spaniards, 56 French, 52 German, to 1 Englishwoman. See *Archivio della soc. rom. di storia patria*, XVII (1894), 375 ff.; and G. de Manteyer, *Le Livre-Journal tenu par Fazy de Rame* (Gap. 1932), I. 353.   (18) *Opp.* X. 1201.   (19) *Loci e Libro Veritatum* (ed. J. E. T. Rogers), 24, 32, 63.   (20) J. H. Lupton, *Life of Colet*, 71.   (21) *Loci e Libro Veritatum*, 123. Gascoigne held the Chancellorship of Oxford University for many years; and his book, apart from its pessimistic bitterness, is essentially true to its title. Compare this testimony with the bold denial of Cardinal Gasquet (*Eve of Ref.* 437): "In the literature of the period [preceding the Reformation], there is nothing to show that the true nature of a 'pardon' or Indulgence was not fully and commonly understood. There is no evidence that it was in any way interpreted as a remission of sin, still less that any one was foolish enough to regard it as permission to commit this or that offence against God." It is characteristic that the pontifical confidence of this assertion has led two other prominent Roman Catholic scholars into the same ditch of error; Bishop Hedley in his article on Indulgences in *The Nineteenth Century* for Jan. 1901 (p. 170) and Fr H. Thurston, S.J., in his attack upon Dr H. C. Lea (*Dublin Review*, Jan. 1900, art. no. 1). In Belgium, Charles V himself complained in 1515 of the Indulgence system as working "to the great burden, damage and loss of my subjects and of this country, which would end by involving their complete ruin". And on Aug. 18, 1517, more than two months before Luther's appearance on the scene, a Dutch monk wrote in the same sense: "Great sums are taken out of the country: it is difficult to say or write how much.... Inconsiderate layfolk chatter unwisely about this.... Contributions [are raised] for fighting the Turks or for Indulgences, but, alas! without ever reaching the effect and the holy object in the name of which they send us these pardons.... I maintain that the Netherlands famed beyond all other countries for the independence and pride of their inhabitants, were never shorn and burdened yearly by such heavy tributes under the tyranny of the pagan Emperors of Rome, as they have been for the last 200 years, thanks to these ruses and intrigues." Moreover, in 1516 a book was printed at Deventer, under the rule of the Prince-bishop of Utrecht, by the Benedictine Abbess of Mariendaal. Writing in Flemish, for popular reading, she tells how a monk came back after death to his friend in the cloister, and told how he had been turned back by St Peter because his Letter of Indulgence, though perfectly *en règle* so far as the papal chancery was concerned, lacked the seal of Jesus Christ. Again, how another was cast, Indulgence and all, into the bottomless pit by a devil of Teutonic speech, who knew no Latin. Upon which the abbess comments "Alas! how often must this German-speaking devil have dragged down to hell these folk who believe not in what the Bible teaches, but who trust to the bulls of pardon which they have gotten!" P. Frédericq, *Bull. Classe Lettres de l'Acad. royale de Belgique* (1899), 42, 6.   (22) Crump and Jacob, *Legacy of the M.A.* 39.

CHAPTER LII (pp. 720–731)

(1) Erasmus, *Opp.* X. 1208–9.   (2) Jortin, *Erasmus*, II. 695–6.   (3) Rashdall, *Universities*, I. 362, note.   (4) *Direct. Inquis.* pars III, q. cviii, § 3 (ed. 1585, p. 708); cf. Lea, *Inquis. M. Ages*, I. 530: "But nowadays, since heretical pravity hath been so far extirpated that pertinacious heretics are rare, and rarer still those who relapse, and rarest of all are rich heretics, but [such as we have] are poor (to

CHAPTER LII (pp. 720–731) *continued*

wit Fraticelli or Béguines or Waldensians), therefore the temporal lords do not get such frequent confiscations of goods as of old, and therefore they are unwilling to pay the Inquisitors so that inquisitions may be made at their [the lords'] expense"—or possibly "the inquisitions are [now] made at the Inquisitors' expense". (5) More himself does not hesitate to jest upon this. In *Utopia* (p. 43) he makes Cardinal Morton's jester allude to the beggars' feeling towards a stingy man: they expect no more help from him "than if [he] were a priest or a monk". The Dissolution cannot be fully understood without such documentary evidence as Mr G. Baskerville has just published in his *English Monks and the Suppression of the Monasteries* (1937). See note 9 here below. (6) *Loci e Libro Veritatum*, 70. (7) *A Treatise concernynge the division betwene the spiritualtie and the temporaltie*, f. 26 a. (8) Wilkins, *Concilia* (1st ed.), I. 549. (9) *R. L. Poole Essays*, 443. Mr Baskerville has now printed in a single volume the scattered evidence which his researches of years have collected. He shows conclusively, from manuscript and printed documents which he has been the first to study exhaustively, that the dispossessed Religious under Henry VIII were incomparably better treated than those who were cast adrift not only by the French Revolution and the Spanish Revolution of 1836, but even by the most orthodox Charles III of Spain (see esp. p. 285). See note 5 here above. (10) See my *Five Centuries of Religion* (II. 527–31), where I have printed half-a-dozen of his plainest utterances. In that volume (pp. 505 ff.) 140 pages are filled with contemporary generalizations by orthodox Churchmen about the monasteries from the twelfth to the sixteenth century; the overwhelming majority are unfavourable, and often in language which would be thought bigoted in a modern historian. This remains true even in face of the two favourable judgments, unknown to me, supplied by Dr A. G. Little in *History* for January 1929. Gascoigne (p. 68) quoted St-Cher as witness for the fact " that all men whom he had known, possessing such plurality of Church livings [as was lamentably frequent everywhere], before their death, had been compelled by their conscience to confess that they had lived damnably by holding two benefices, whereas one sufficed for their needs". (11) *Cal. State Papers (Spain)*, IV. i. 367. (12) Pollard, *Henry VIII*, 206; *Jesuits and the Middle Ages*, 9. (13) See my pamphlet on *Malta and Beyond*, where I give facts which nobody has ventured to contradict. (This and the preceding pamphlet are published at 6d. each post-free from 72 Kimberley Road, Cambridge.) (14) R. W. Chambers, *Sir Thomas More*, 369 (cf. 367). (15) Dr Barry in *Camb. Mod. Hist.* I. 646.

INDEX